Financial Institution Management:
Text and Cases

Financial Institution Management:
Text and Cases
Second Edition

Fred C. Yeager and Neil E. Seitz
Saint Louis University

Reston Publishing Company, Inc.
A Prentice-Hall Company
Reston, Virginia 22090

Library of Congress Cataloging in Publication Data

Yeager, Fred C.
   Financial institution management.

   Includes bibliographies.
    1. Financial institutions—Management.
I. Seitz, Neil II. Title.
HG174.Y4 1985   332.1′068′1   84-15901
ISBN 0–8359–2024–0

© 1985 by Reston Publishing Company, Inc.
   A Prentice-Hall Company
   Reston, Virginia

To Helen, Mary Colleen, Tim, Tom, and Margie
To Bente, Laura, and Kirsten

Contents

Preface

This book differs from most other financial institutions texts in that it focuses on the management, rather than the description, of financial institutions. The concentration is primarily on policy questions, such as the appropriate loan portfolio mix, rather than operating questions such as credit evaluation for a specific loan. The focus was chosen for several reasons:

1. Many students taking financial institution courses will eventually seek employment with financial institutions. Thus, a knowledge of the principles guiding their management will help the students to understand the management policies and decisions, and eventually participate in them.

2. Deregulation of the financial sector has proceeded in the 1980s with roller-coaster speed, producing new challenges and new opportunities for financial institution managers. Legislative and financial market developments in the 1980s have resulted in heightened needs for financial skills. Technological developments, together with an increased tendency on the part of the financial sector to test the limit of profitable activities permitted by regulators, has resulted in large scale interstate and interindustry competition. Manage-

rial tools and techniques such as *gap management, financial futures hedging,* and *option pricing models* have suddenly come of age. Never has the need for financial management skills within our nations financial institutions been greater.

A book which describes without a theme leaves its reader with many facts, but with no conceptual framework within which the facts may be analyzed. Thus this book has a theme—management. Because this book focuses on policy level management decisions, it should help to provide readers with a framework for understanding the material presented. Even the non-management reader will better understand why particular institutions choose to do what they do and, therefore, why the financial system behaves as it does.

This book differs from other financial institution texts in that it includes both text and cases. The cases serve a number of purposes. First, they reinforce learning by illustrating that techniques discussed in the text have application to real-life problems. Second, they have proved useful in helping the student transfer learning from sterile problems to complex real-life situations. Finally, the cases contain substantial information about the financial institutions involved, thereby helping the students to further understand their operations. The cases were contributed by professors and practitioners around the country who took the time to describe actual decision problems being faced by specific financial institutions.

This second edition of our book has benefited immensely from reviews and by the input of college and university professors from across the nation who took the time to respond to user survey requests. As a result of this input and our own experiences and observations of a financial sector in evolution, this current edition contains a number of improvements:

1.   The number of new cases has increased by about 50 percent, with the new cases dealing with interindustry acquisitions, financial futures hedging, gap analysis, restrictive state usury laws, and other issues of the 1980s. These issues and concepts are first introduced within the text.

2.   Two new chapters have been added: a chapter dealing with regulation of the financial sector and the analysis of major legislative developments over time and another new chapter dealing with the United States financial system and money creation.

3.   Certain chapters have been expanded in recognition of new developments. Developments within the rapidly expanding market for consumer financial services are noted, for example, within the Finance Company Management chapter.

In addition to our college and university colleagues throughout the nation, who took the time to offer helpful suggestions, we are grateful to financial institution practitioners who assisted in the development of materials which are published or otherwise reflected within the pages of this book. We are particularly grateful to our academic reviewers; Elliott L. Attamian, Northeastern University; Thomas A. Bankston, Angelo State University; Mona J. Gardner, Illinois State University; B. E. Lee, New Mexico State University; Edward D. Marting, Indiana State University at Evansville; Patricia Matthews, Mount Union College; Walter D. Rogers, Georgetown University; Mark Bayless, University of Detroit; and to a number of our business colleagues, including Robert Schmitz, Craig Chandler, Tom Harvey, John Ream, John Nelke, Charles Papp, and George Poland; all of Citicorp Person to Person, Inc., St. Louis; and to Harry Gallagher and Tom Robinson of the Missouri Financial Services Association. Considerable assistance was also provided by many members of the staff of the Federal Reserve Bank of St. Louis. We recognize, of course, the contributions of colleages who have written most of the cases contained within this book. Each of these contributors is identified on the first page of the respective cases.

This book is designed for a one-semester course at the graduate or advanced undergraduate level. Prior coursework in elementary economics and statistics would be helpful in understanding the material; the student who has not had these courses, however, should still be able to understand the text and analyze the cases (with a little more work).

Our debts start with our parents and end with our students whose candid comments on earlier drafts and on the first edition helped to improve the final product.

We, and the users of this book, owe a particular debt of gratitude to the case writers who took the time to research real business problems and share their information with us. We stand ready to receive and to consider for publication additional cases that users of this book might wish to offer as well as to share new cases and other materials that we at Saint Louis University have developed. Finally, we thank our colleagues at Saint Louis University for their support during this task. Bouquets will be shared with those who have helped in the development of this book. Brickbats should be aimed only at us.

Fred C. Yeager
Neil E. Seitz

Chapter 1

Functions and Goals of Financial Institutions

In a primitive economy each household produces what it needs and fulfillment of personal economic needs does not depend on communication between households. A complex modern economy, with its specialized producers and diverse products, requires a vast amount of communication between units. The great depression of the 1930s bears stark witness to what happens when this communication system fails or is inadequate. The smooth functioning of a modern economy is dependent on intermediaries who act as go-betweens, matching the needs of one unit with the output of another. Financial institutions are among the vital intermediaries contributing to economic health.

Financial intermediation is the process of acquiring surplus funds from economic units—business firms, governmental agencies, and individuals—for the purpose of making available such funds to other economic units. Financial institutions exist for the primary purpose of facilitating the intermediation process. Examples of financial intermediaries in the United States include:

Commercial Banks

Savings and Loan Associations

Mutual Savings Banks

Commercial and Consumer Finance Companies

Leasing Companies

Insurance Companies

Credit Unions

Pension Funds

Certain Governmental Units

Trust Companies

Securities Dealers

Investment Trusts

Financial intermediaries play an important role in society. They issue *securities*[1] to those from whom funds have been entrusted and accept securities from those to whom funds have been loaned or invested. Thus, intermediaries act as a buffer between suppliers and users of funds, gathering funds in quantities and on terms that are acceptable to savers, and supplying funds in quantities and on terms agreeable to the

---

[1]Any form of evidence representing debt or equity is a security.

users. Intermediaries assist society in innumerable ways. Savers and investors benefit in that funds may be left in relative safety, and to the extent securities issued by intermediaries bear interest or dividends, the value of entrusted funds is enhanced. Ultimate users of funds benefit by the availability of capital to purchase homes, acquire durable consumer goods and finance business operations. In performing these functions, financial intermediaries contribute to a high standard of living for those countries with well-developed financial systems.

THE CIRCULAR FLOW OF INCOME AND MONEY

The Circular Flow of Income

Consider a society without financial intermediaries and with no medium of exchange—a barter economy. Income earned in a barter economy is paid in the form of goods and services. Income may be earned by the recipient for any of three basic reasons. First, income may be received in return for the provision of labor. Second, income may be received if the recipient allows others to use his physical property—land, tools, or other goods. Third, income may accumulate if the recipient has provided services of an entrepreneurial nature. The circular flow of income for a barter economy is described in figure 1-1.

Those who are willing and able to do so provide physical property, labor and entrepreneurial ability for production purposes (figure 1-1). Note that either products or services may be produced. In return for contributions of property, labor, and entrepreneurial skills, providers of these resource inputs are entitled to receive production outputs, i.e., income. Thus for each round of resource provision, production output is generated.

It should be pointed out that with the barter economy of figure 1-1, all transactions are "real": for each unit of resource input, a certain amount of production output is immediately ac-

quired. Thus, "financial assets" such as cash, demand deposits, savings accounts, accounts receivable, and other securities are non-existent. It should also be noted that the barter economy will not function smoothly unless there is a complete willingness on the part of providers of resources to accept production outputs regardless of the nature of such outputs. For the circular flow to continue, resource providers must continue to happily swap their services for the output that streams forth.

A complex economy simply could not operate smoothly based on barter. First, the model assumes a comprehensive and complete *coincidence of wants*. In other words, it assumes that producers of products and services will require the precise quantities of physical property, labor, and entrepreneurial ability offered, and these resources will be utilized without delay. The model further assumes that production of goods and services is instantaneous and that suppliers of resources will happily accept all production generated, without regard to the nature of such production, as compensation for the use of their resources. In practice, the automobile worker may be reluctant to accept a transmission as compensation for his week's labor. A complex industrial society could not function in this way.

The barter model does, however, illustrate the important point that resources must be supplied if production is to occur. In addition, the model illustrates the fact that in one way or another, those who provide the resources are compensated, ultimately at least, in terms of goods and services.

We will now begin to expand the model with the introduction of money into the circular flow.

The Circular Flow and Money

An important distinction exists between figure 1-2 and figure 1-1. The providers of resources are now receiving money as compensation. Note that money so received may now be used to acquire goods and services that are produced as a result of resource provision.

Introduction of money into the circular flow

Figure 1–1: Circular flow of income for a barter economy.

means that "real" transactions (the direct exchange of resource inputs for production outputs) are not the only type of transactions that may occur. Since money exists, resource inputs, products, and services may now be exchanged for money. Thus money is functioning as a *standard of value* and a *store of value*.[2] The value of resource inputs or production outputs is defined in terms of money and is stored in money. Since money is accepted in exchange for resources or production, the transactions may be defined as "monetary" transactions.

The introduction of money permits certain other changes to occur (figure 1-2). It is no longer necessary to have a comprehensive and complete coincidence of wants. Since money may now be received in exchange for resources or products, the seller has converted these resources or products into "generalized purchasing power." No longer must the seller accept only those goods or services which the buyer can offer. The introduction of money has made transactions easier and more realistic, thereby making the circular flow function more conviently. Money can be exchanged for goods and services instead of goods and services being exchanged for other goods and services.

Discussion of the circular flow, to this point, implicitly assumed that all who were willing and able to provide resources would do so. In exchange for resources provided, production outputs in the form of products and services would be provided. As we shall see, a major advantage of money is that it provides a means of accommodating providers of resources who may wish to defer their spending of at least some income derived from their provision of land, labor, and physical property.

To the extent that income recipients defer spending, producers of products and services will find that demand for their production declines and that lower levels of production are thus appropriate. Fewer resources are required to produce the smaller levels of production, and resource unemployment will logically develop; national income will decline. On the other hand, certain of those who defer from spending may find a coincidence of wants with producers or other resource providers who wish to engage in current spending in excess of current income. Should such a coincidence of wants develop, those with excess spending power will find others with whom such spending power may be invested. It is reasonable, of course, that lenders or investors should expect to be compensated for providing such spending power. To the extent that comprehensive and complete coincidence of wants exists between those with excess spending power and those to whom such spending power is transferred, a happy situation prevails. All who are able and wish to refrain from current spending may do so, and receive compensation to boot. Production and national income may continue at high levels.

But once again our model must be reevaluated. The assumption of comprehensive and complete coincidence of wants on the part of those with surplus funds and those who wish to acquire such spending power is unrealistic. For example, the borrower may need funds for a long

---

[2]Anything that functions as money *is* money and money functions as a medium of exchange, a standard of value, and a store of value.

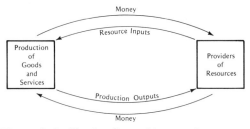

Figure 1–2: Circular flow of income for a money economy.

time to build a factory while the lender is willing to commit funds for only a short time. The need is evident for financial intermediaries whose purpose is to gather funds in quantities and on terms acceptable to savers and investors, as well as to supply funds in quantities and on terms agreeable to users.

THE ROLE OF FINANCIAL INTERMEDIARIES

In order to analyze the full benefits of intermediation, it is useful to identify those services that are performed as a result of the intermediation process. These services may be summarized in terms of the following four categories:

Asset Transmutation

Liquidity

Income Reallocation Over Time

Transactions Aid

Asset Transmutation[3]

Financial institutions hold assets in the form of promises to pay, with terms set to meet the needs of the borrowers. They finance these assets by accepting funds from savers on terms set to meet savers' needs. Thus they convert the borrower's obligation to an asset with a maturity to meet the needs of the saver. This process is known as asset transmutation.

Economic units in need of funds issue *primary securities*. Primary securities include all securities issued by nonfinancial economic units for the purpose of acquiring funds. Examples of primary securities are mortgages executed by individuals or businesses, stocks and bonds sold by corporations, and United States Treasury bills. In each case, primary securities were issued for the purpose of acquiring funds. They may be either debt or equity (part ownership). The

form and maturity of the security is selected to satisfy the needs of the unit acquiring funds.

The securities issued by those acquiring funds may differ in size, maturity, and form from the needs of those with funds. Financial intermediaries solve this problem by acquiring primary securities with funds they have raised through the issuance of *secondary securities*. Secondary securities include all securities issued by financial intermediaries. Examples of secondary securities include demand and time deposits, credit union shares, and cash value of life insurance policies. For selected examples of primary and secondary securities held by economic units as a result of the intermediation process, see table 1-1. Households are net suppliers of funds and nonfinancial businesses are net users; yet some individual households are net users and some individual businesses are net suppliers.

By issuing secondary securities in exchange for financial resources of surplus units and in turn exchanging these resources for primary securities issued by deficit units, intermediaries transmute or convert the securities of business units to obligations desired by households. Through this transmutation process, intermediaries both facilitate the production of real wealth and provide households with the financial rewards associated with such production. In the process, intermediaries generate economies of scale by combining funds received at times and in quantities suitable for producer units. Intermediaries also provide economies of scale by generating knowledge of various alternative investments in producer units, thereby reducing or eliminating the need for individual surplus units to generate independent knowledge of such alternatives. And because intermediaries acquire funds from large numbers of surplus units and provide funds to large numbers of deficit units, substantial diversity is effected and the risk of financial loss is reduced.

Liquidity

Liquidity refers to the ability to generate cash quickly. Some secondary securities are acquired

---

[3]The term is that of Basil J. Moore, *An Introduction to the Theory of Finance.* (New York: The Free Press, 1968).

Table 1-1:

Selected Primary and Secondary Securities

NET DEFICIT ECONOMIC UNITS (Nonfinancial Business Units)		FINANCIAL INTERMEDIARIES		NET SURPLUS ECONOMIC UNITS (Households)	
Assets	Liabilities	Assets	Liabilities	Assets	Liabilities
(Secondary Securities)	(Primary Securities)	(Primary Securities) Loans Leases Investments Stocks Bonds Mortgages	(Secondary Securities) Demand deposits Time deposits Life ins. reserves Pension fund reserves Investment co. shares	(Secondary Securities)	(Primary Securities)

by businesses and households primarily for purposes of liquidity. Secondary securities such as savings and time deposits provide a high degree of liquidity, safety, and income as well. Such instruments are essential to the normal conduct of financial affairs. To the extent economic units acquire secondary securities for purposes of liquidity, intermediaries perform an important financial service.

Income Reallocation Over Time

Many individuals earn satisfactory incomes today, but realize they will eventually face retirement and curtailment of income. They wish to reallocate some of their present income to that future time. They could do this by storing goods, but the acquisition of secondary securities such as savings accounts, pension fund reserves, or investment company shares is more convenient and provides the opportunity to earn a return on these savings. On the other hand, many young individuals and households issue primary securities, thereby allocating future income to the present or making it possible to pay for assets as they are being used. Primary examples of this latter activity are loans for home or automobile purchases.

Business units are also influenced to acquire or issue securities for purposes of income reallocation over time. However, net income reallocation effects on the part of business units differ from those of households in terms of the direction in which income is shifted. Households consist of individuals, many of whom are engaged in the systematic acquisition of secondary securities for no other reason than the expectation of reduced earnings beyond retirement. Business units as a group have no automatic expectation of reduced future earnings. Life expectancy of the typical business corporation is perpetual, and future income under normal economic circumstances is not expected to decline.

Business units also differ from the household sector in terms of the purpose for which primary securities are issued. Households normally issue primary securities so as to acquire goods or services for consumption, and not for the purpose of generating future income. Business units normally issue primary securities for the purpose of investment in assets which are expected to increase future income. Secondary securities acquired by business units are obtained primarily to facilitate transactions and to provide liquidity. In contrast to households, business units seek to issue large quantities of primary securities relative to secondary securities acquired, thereby shifting future income to the present.

Transactions

Certain secondary securities issued by financial intermediaries represent *money* and constitute a part of the payments system. Traditional demand deposits and certain other deposit accounts function as money and are acquired by households and business units to facilitate the exchange of goods and services. To the extent that economic units acquire secondary securities in order to accommodate day-to-day settlement of financial claims, intermediaries serve a major purpose in facilitating monetary transactions.

AN OVERVIEW OF THE SAVINGS MARKET

The supply and use of savings in the economy of the United States is summarized in figure 1-3. As shown in the figure, households are net surplus units with holdings of financial assets exceeding their financial liabilities. The financial institutions, as intermediaries, have financial assets approximately equal to their financial liabilities. Business and government are the primary users of these funds.

It is evident that households hold substantial quantities of both primary and secondary securities. The proportion of each type varies over time due to a complex variety of economic and social conditions. Fluctuations in the market value of corporate stock, for example, have a heavy impact on year-to-year changes in household wealth.

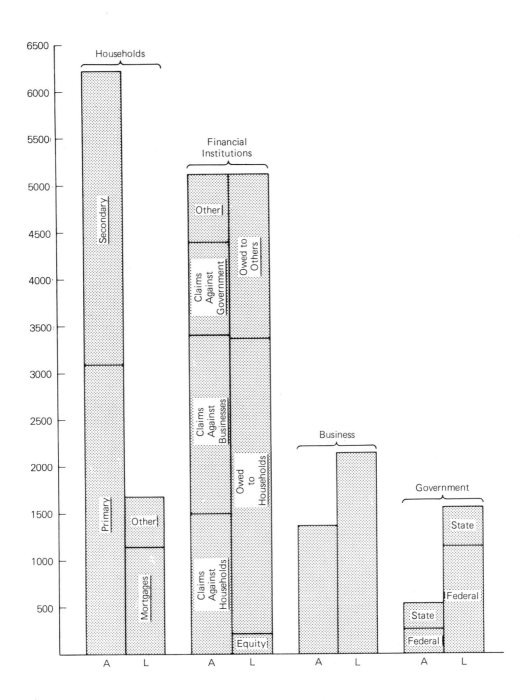

Figure 1–3: Financial assets, liabilities, and equity by sector, in $ billions. (From *Federal Reserve Bulletin,* Federal Reserve *Flow of Funds Accounts, Treasury Bulletin,* and other estimates.)

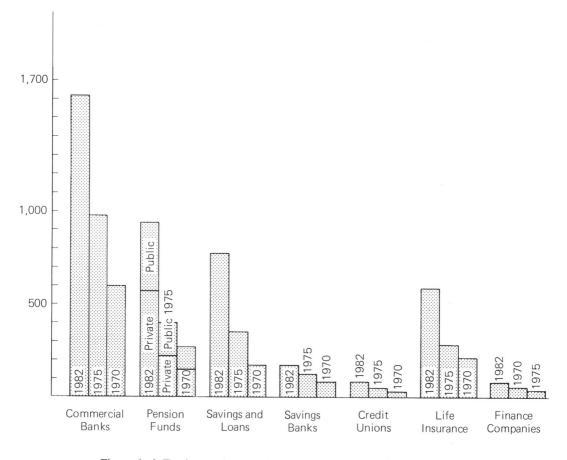

Figure 1–4: Total assets by type of financial institution, in $ billions.

Another major factor influencing household decisions in their acquisition of debt securities is the relative interest rates prevailing for different classes of securities. For example, generally high market interest rates prevailed for many securities in 1980 and 1981. However, maximum rates for most secondary securities were fixed by law,[4] and such maximums or ceilings were less than rates generally available on primary securities. Many households switched from secondary to primary securities during these years.[5]

An overview of the savings market can be completed with a brief look at the relative roles of the various financial institutions. Commercial banks continue to be the most important

---

[4]These regulations will be phased out over a number of years due to the Financial Institution Deregulation and Monetary Control Act of 1980.

[5]This process of shifting from secondary securities issued by financial intermediaries to primary securities is known as *disintermediation*.

financial institutions (figure 1-4). However, banks can be considered a mature industry with a growth rate limited by the growth rate of the economy. Credit unions and pension funds in particular have shown rapid growth in the last decade. This growth is a result of a favorable cost structure for the credit unions and new laws requiring a higher level of funding of pension fund liabilities. Each of these institutions is examined in depth in later chapters.

GOALS OF FINANCIAL INSTITUTIONS

Students and the general public are sometimes confused as to the objectives that guide financial institution managers in their decision making. Because they hold other people's money, financial institutions are probably more closely regulated than any other industry. Furthermore, statements by many critics of the industry seem to reflect the view that financial institutions are quasi-government agencies that should be guided primarily by social objectives. Interviews with executives of financial institutions yield an entirely different viewpoint. For the most part, financial institutions are owned by shareholders who invest their own funds as equity in the institution. They make these investments for the purpose of earning a profit. The management is selected by the board of directors elected by these shareholders. Because they answer to a board of directors elected by shareholders interested in making a profit, financial institution managers view making a profit as their first obligation.

The conflict between the profit objective and the desire to provide services may not be as great as first appears. Like any business, a financial institution can only earn a profit by providing a desired service to some group capable of paying for that service. Thus serving the needs of some sector of society is a prerequisite to profitability. In addition, there are many things that managers, as good citizens, can do to help the community without hurting profits. The conflict arises when a critic feels financial institutions should take actions that would decrease profitability but would contribute to some objective deemed desirable by that particular critic. Legislation has occasionally been passed leading institutions to take actions that would not be taken in simple pursuit of profit. However, general government policy suggests that, within the limits of the law, financial institutions should behave like other businesses in pursuing their profit objective.

The primary focus of this book is on the management of financial institutions as opposed to a pure description of what they do. A primary interest in profitability and efficient usage of funds is assumed. The book begins with a discussion of the environment in which institutions operate and some general principles used in managerial decision making in financial institutions. Attention is then turned to the principles followed in the management of each major type of financial institution. Because of the growing importance of international finance, the final chapter deals with a discussion and analysis of a number of important issues associated with financial institution management on an international scale.

SUMMARY

Financial intermediation is the process of acquiring surplus funds from economic units and of making such funds available to other economic units. In a complex industrial society, a great deal of financial communication and funds transfer is necessary if the economy is to function efficiently. Although surplus units invest directly in securities issued by deficit units, financial institutions accommodate the majority of funds transfers by acting as a buffer between suppliers and users of funds, issuing secondary securities to funds suppliers and accepting primary securities from funds users. In their role as financial middlemen, intermediaries facilitate the circular flow of income. Services relating to transactions, liquidity, income reallocation, and asset transmutation are among the most important of those performed by intermediaries in facilitating this flow.

Growth and development of any society and the well being of its citizens is clearly influenced by the efficiency and capability of its financial institutions.

QUESTIONS

1. How does financial intermediation facilitate the circular flow of income?

2. Distinguish between primary and secondary securities.

3. In what way or ways does the motivation of households differ from that of business firms in their desire to hold secondary securities?

4. What might be the possible economic consequences of disintermediation? Comment on possible means by which the problem of disintermediation may be resolved.

5. Comment on benefits of financial intermediation in terms of the income reallocation and asset transmutation effects.

SELECTED REFERENCES

Campbell, Tim S., and Kracaw, William A. "Information Production, Market Signalling, and the Theory of Financial Intermediation." *Journal of Finance* 35 (September 1980): 863–882.

Fraser, Donald R. and Rose, Peter S. *Financial Institutions and Markets in a Changing World.* Plano, Texas: Business Publications, Inc., 1984.

Kronn, Herman E., and Blyn, Morten R. *A History of Financial Intermediaries.* New York: Random House, 1971.

Murphy, Neil B., and Mandell, Lewis. "Consumer Response to Restructured Financial Institutions: The Case of Maine." *Journal of Money, Credit and Banking* 11 (February 1979): 91–98.

Sametz, Arnold W., and Wachtel, Paul eds. *The Financial Environment and the Flow of Funds in the Next Decade.* Boston: Lexington Books, 1977.

Sealey, C. W. Jr. "Deposit Rate-Setting, Risk Aversion and the Theory of Depository Financial Intermediaries." *Journal of Finance* 35 (December 1980): 1139–1154.

Chapter 2

Financial Systems, the Federal Reserve, and Money Creation

A financial system can be described as a mechanism or framework in which economic exchange is accomodated. The college student who pays tuition with funds earned through a summer job is engaging in economic exchange. The householder who completes the weekly shopping trip after depositing the family paycheck is engaged in economic exchange, as is the office worker who systematically buys shares in a mutual fund in anticipation of a retirement nest egg.

Financial systems can be simple or complex. They can be free of regulation or heavily regulated. They can be technologically efficient or inefficient. In a modern society, the financial system plays a particularly important role in influencing the level of economic activity.

TYPES OF FINANCIAL SYSTEMS

Several basic types of financial systems can be identified. These include:

Direct Barter

Indirect Barter

Warehouse Receipt Systems

Reserve Banking Systems

Fiat Systems

Electronic Systems

Direct Barter

Direct barter was discussed in chapter 1 and is the most fundamental financial system. In a direct barter system, money does not exist, and economic resources (goods or services) are directly traded for other economic resources. Direct barter is an inefficient system because, in the absence of money, there must be a *coincidence of wants* for an exchange of goods or services to occur; e.g., the plumber must find a barber whose pipes need to be fixed. A complex economy could not function with a direct barter system.

Indirect Barter (Commodity Money)

A logical extension and improvement over a direct barter system is the use of one or more commodities as money. Throughout history, gold and silver have been the most widely used commodities for indirect barter; however, almost any commodity can be used. During the colonial period in American history, tobacco leaves were a commonly accepted medium of exchange and for a time served as the cornerstone of the domestic financial system. During World War II, cigarettes were widely used as the medium of exchange (money) by American soldiers held in prisoner of war camps. The major advantage of such indirect barter over direct barter is that a coincidence of wants is not a condition for trade. The value of goods and services are expressed instead in terms of the commodity. For example, one candy bar (contained in POW Red Cross rations) may have been worth two cigarettes while one can of peaches may have "sold" for one cigarette.

Warehouse Receipt System

Although indirect barter—the use of commodity money—is an improvement over direct barter, storage and transportation of the commodity can be a problem. Efficiency of the system can be improved by simply storing the commodity in a warehouse provided for that purpose. Receipts issued by the warehouse owner or operator can then be exchanged for goods or services. For example, gold receipts from goldsmiths were widely used as a medium of exchange.

Fractional Reserve Banking System

In the warehouse-receipt system discussed above, the warehouse owner or operator, if not restricted from doing so, might decide to function as a lender: by lending the commodity under his care, or more likely, by simply issuing warehouse receipts to borrowers who are expected to repay the loan with interest. In making such loans, the warehouse owner would be operating as a fractional reserve banker because the amount of warehouse receipts would exceed the amount of the commodity. Fractional reserve

banking systems have been widely used, but they require careful regulation to avoid abuses such as excessive and risky lending. Typically, the government will specify the maximum ratio of reserves (commodity) to receipts (money).

Fiat Systems

Fiat systems exist when government issues nonconvertible paper notes and defines these notes as money. Typically, the notes are issued initially as payment for goods or services, e.g., payment to members of the military service. Acceptance of these notes within the state or community is typically enhanced by government declaration that the notes are *legal tender*: they *must* be accepted in payment of all debts, public and private. A fractional reserve banking system with fiat money requires financial intermediaries to hold fiat money (or its equivalent) equal to some specified portion of the outstanding deposit receipts it has issued. The United States financial system has evolved from direct and indirect barter, to warehouse receipts, and finally to fractional reserve banking combined with a fiat system. The receipts issued by banks are in the form of checking account and savings account deposit balances.

Electronic Systems

A financial system is useful because it facilitates resource transfer by functioning as the payment mechanism. The financial system is also useful in that it provides the framework within which individuals and institutions keep track of financial assets and liabilities. On payday, an employee might receive either cash or a paycheck for services rendered. Alternatively, computerized electronic impulses could simply reduce the employer's account and increase the employee's account at the local bank. In either case, payment is made and assets are transferred. In the first case, the transfer was accommodated through use of cash or check (a paper based financial system). In the second case, the same result was achieved electronically. The financial system is evolving toward increased use of electronic funds transfers.

Full Faith and Credit

Figure 2-1 provides an overview of selected financial assets held within the financial system. The public held $1.45 trillion in savings and time deposits and $375 billion in demand and checkable deposits by 1984 (figure 2-1). Interestingly, most of these deposits are merely bookkeeping entries. Since only a small fraction of these accounts are backed up by currency in the financial system, banks and thrift institutions could not begin to repay depositors should large numbers of persons demand cash repayment at any given time. An indispensible ingredient in the financial system then, is the widespread belief on the part of the public that the financial system is sound. As long as this confidence in the system is maintained, the system will, in fact, *be* sound. The Federal Reserve System plays a key role in the maintenance of public confidence.

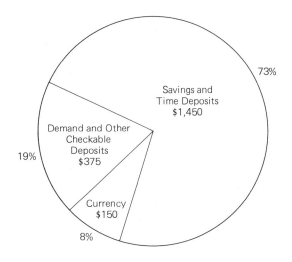

Figure 2–1: Currency, checking-type deposits, and savings held by the nonbank public in banks and thrift institutions. Data are approximate for early, 1984, $ billions. (From the *Federal Reserve Bulletin.*)

THE FEDERAL RESERVE SYSTEM

The Federal Reserve System was created by Congress in 1913 to address four major needs faced by the country:

1. *Payments system.* The Federal Reserve Banks act as banks for bankers. Payments between banks can be handled by additions and subtractions to their account balances with the Federal Reserve Banks.

2. *Unexpected withdrawal demand.* As banks for banks, the Federal Reserve Banks are expected to curtail bank runs arising from loss of confidence by loaning banks money to meet unexpected deposit withdrawal demand.

3. *Supervision and Examination.* To assure sound banking practices, to increase public confidence, and to curtail bank runs, the Federal Reserve Banks play a major role in bank supervision and examination.

4. *Control of the money supply.* It is well recognized that too much money can cause inflation and too little money can cause unemployment. A major role of the Federal Reserve System is to regulate the flow of money and credit to promote economic stability and growth.

Over the years, the role of the Federal Reserve System has been expanded and today includes the direct provision of certain financial services to nonbank financial institutions.

STRUCTURE OF THE FEDERAL RESERVE SYSTEM

Board of Governors

The Federal Reserve System is under the control of a seven-member board of governors appointed by the President and confirmed by the Senate. Their staggered fourteen-year terms are designed to insulate them from political pressure. The chairman and vice chairman are

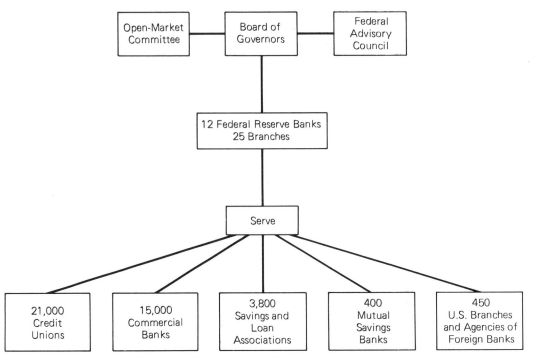

Figure 2–2: Structure of the Federal Reserve System.

selected from this seven-person board by the President of the United States for four-year terms and may be redesignated. The operating structure of the system is summarized in figure 2-2.

Federal Open-Market Committee

Day-to-day actions to control the money supply fall under the jurisdiction of the open market committee. Under the supervision of the open market committee is the buying and selling of securities for the Federal Reserve System's account, effectively paying for securities by creating money. This activity, carried out by the trading desk of the Federal Reserve Bank of New York, is quite important to the economy. Its importance is discussed at length later in this chapter.

Federal Advisory Council

The Federal Advisory Council is composed of bankers and consists of twelve members, one

from each of the Federal Reserve districts. Each of the twelve representatives is elected by directors of the Federal Reserve Bank of the district which he represents. A major purpose of the advisory council is to advise the board of governors concerning current developments.

Federal Reserve Banks

When the Federal Reserve System was created in 1913, the United States was (in a financial sense) a group of economic sections rather than a cohesive union of states. There also existed in 1913, a fear of excessive concentration of the nation's financial resources in one geographic locale. Consequently, the Federal Reserve Act of 1913 divided the nation into twelve financial districts and provided that a Federal Reserve Bank be located in the principal banking city of each district (figure 2-3).

Each of the twelve Federal Reserve Banks is a distinct corporation with its own board of

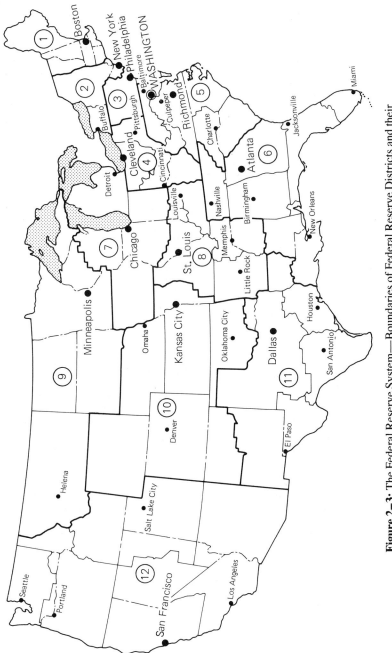

Figure 2–3: The Federal Reserve System—Boundaries of Federal Reserve Districts and their branch territories. Note: Alaska and Hawaii are included in Federal Reserve District 12.

directors. The District Banks are viewed as *quasi*-private institutions in that each is owned by the member banks which purchase stock in the District Federal Reserve Bank. Each Federal Reserve Bank has nine directors, six of which are elected by member banks. The remaining three directors—one of whom is designated as chairman and another as deputy chairman—are appointed by the board of governors. Although overall system policy is the responsibility of the board of governors, the individual Federal Reserve Banks provide input into the policy setting process. In particular, the Federal Reserve Banks perform a number of functions designed to maintain day-to-day operations of the financial system.

FUNCTIONS OF THE FEDERAL RESERVE SYSTEM

The major current purposes and functions of the Federal Reserve System can be summarized as follows:

Maintenance of an Effective Monetary Policy

Supervision and Examination

Financial System Services

Fiscal Agent for the Government

Maintenance of an Effective Monetary Policy

Monetary conditions favorable to high levels of employment, economic growth, price stability, and a sound international balance of payments are objectives shared by all modern economies. Although elusive, such goals are none the less pursued by governments through appropriate fiscal and monetary policies. In general, *monetary policy* refers to the extent to which the volume of money is allowed to grow within the economy over some designated time period.

Supervision and Examination

Financial Institutions—particularly depository institutions such as commercial banks and thrifts—are closely regulated and supervised so as to maintain a high degree of public trust and confidence in the financial system. A major responsibility of the Federal Reserve System is to examine the books and operations of certain banks and other institutions on an ongoing basis. In this regard, the Federal Reserve System examines all bank holding companies,[1] Edge Act corporations,[2] and certain commercial banks.

The body examining a particular bank depends on certain choices made by that bank. First, the bank faces a choice of whether to be chartered by the state or federal government. If the bank is chartered by the federal government, it must be a member bank of the Federal Reserve System[3] and its deposits must be insured by the Federal Deposit Insurance Corporation (FDIC). If the bank has a state charter, it may choose to become a member of the Federal Reserve System, in which case it must also have its deposits insured by the FDIC. If a state bank does not choose to join the Federal Reserve System, it still has the option of having its deposits insured by the FDIC.[4] The assignment of examining duties in light of these choices is spelled out in table 2-1.

Financial System Services[5]

The Federal Reserve System provides a variety of services to the financial community. Prior to passage of the *Monetary Control Act of 1980*,[6]

---

[1] A bank holding company is simply a corporation which owns one or more banks, and possibly other subsidiary (non banking) corporations.

[2] An Edge Act Corporation is a subsidiary of a bank and is engaged in foreign activities (e.g., loans to foreign governments).

[3] A member bank is a bank that owns stock of the Federal Reserve Bank in its particular district. A member bank is *not* one of the twelve district banks of the system.

[4] As a practical matter, as a condition for awarding a bank charter, the various states require that FDIC insurance be obtained by the proposed bank.

[5] Discussion in this section relies heavily on materials provided by the Federal Reserve Bank of St. Louis. The authors are grateful to the Federal Reserve Bank of St. Louis for permission to summarize and/or reproduce these materials.

[6] For a detailed discussion of the Monetary Control Act of 1980, see chapter 3.

Table 2-1:

**Examination Responsibility for Commercial Banks,
Bank Holding Companies, and Edge Act Corporations**

Financial Institution	*Examination Responsibility*
State chartered commercial bank, Federal Reserve System member	Federal Reserve System or state*
State chartered commercial bank, Federal Reserve System nonmember	FDIC
Nationally chartered bank	Comptroller of the currency
Edge Act Corporation	Federal Reserve System
Bank holding companies	Federal Reserve System

*Frequently on a rotating basis, with the state examining one year and the Federal Reserve System examining the next.

these services were provided only to member banks. With passage of the Monetary Control Act, these same services were made more widely available and are now offered to all depository institutions represented in figure 2-2. Services may be categorized as follows:

Coin and Currency

Check Clearing and Funds Transfer

Loans

Fiscal Agent for the Government

Coin and Currency   One responsibility of the Federal Reserve System is to meet the cash requirements of our Nation's economy. On behalf of the U.S. Treasury, the Federal Reserve System circulates coin and currency using depository institutions as a channel of distribution. The cash flows through these institutions for use by the public.

Federal Reserve Banks send out new and reusable coin and Federal Reserve Notes (currency) to depository institutions and accept for credit, redemption, exchange, or replacement currency and coin that is unfit for further circulation. The volume of currency held by the public is subject to seasonal influences. The volume tends to increase, for example, over the Christmas holidays. The amount of currency held by the public has increased over the years and stood at $150 billion by 1984 (figure 2-1).

Check Clearing and Funds Transfer   A ma-

jor function of the Federal Reserve System involves check clearing and funds transfer. While the mechanics of this process will be discussed in the next section, noted here is the fact that the U.S. payments system is largely a paper-based system with more than thirty-five billion checks processed each year. Checks are simply negotiable orders directing that funds be taken from the account of the drawer (payor) and be given to the drawee (payee).

The paper checks are cleared through the financial system when the payor's account is reduced and the payee's account is increased by the amount of the check. If the drawer and drawee maintain accounts at the same bank and the check is originally presented to that bank, the transaction may be handled by the bank itself, and there is no need for the Federal Reserve System to participate in the transfer. Similarly, if the drawer's bank and the drawee's bank are located in the same town (or trading region), the checks could be cleared through a local clearing house established by community financial institutions for that purpose. Yet, many of these are cleared through the Federal Reserve System.[7] Large numbers of checks, however, are

---

[7]Traditionally, checks were processed by the Federal Reserve System without charge. As a consequence of the Monetary Control Act of 1980, service charges were imposed on various services provided by the Federal Reserve System including check processing. Consequently, the volume of checks processed by the Federal Reserve System declined

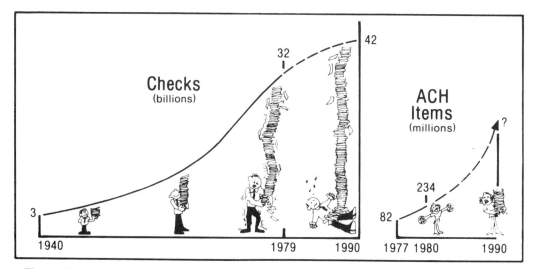

Figure 2–4: National volume trends, 1940–1990. (Source: Federal Reserve Bank of St. Louis.)

drawn on financial institutions which are geographically remote from the institution into which the check is first deposited. Through its nationwide system of Federal Reserve Banks, the Federal Reserve System has the capability to provide for nationwide check clearing.

By the early 1970s, it was believed that funds transfer could be accomodated more efficiently through electronic debit and credit entries between financial institutions for customer accounts. Thus, the financial community established *Automated Clearing Houses* (ACHs) in the early 1970s to clear items locally. By the mid 1980s, thirty-two ACHs were in operation in the United States, with all but one operated by Federal Reserve Banks. These systems were eventually interconnected and were capable of transferring funds electronically, thus replacing large numbers of paper checks. Currently, the ACH services accomodate a large number of transactions, including payroll deposits, recurring government payments such as social security and veterans' payments, and other routine

types of expenditures not only of government but of the private sector as well. The historical and expected growth in check volume and in the number of ACH items processed is illustrated in figure 2-4.

Loans Traditionally, the Federal Reserve System has been a source of liquidity to member banks through its *Discount Window*. As a consequence of the Monetary Control Act of 1980, the Discount Window is now accessible by any depository institution, regardless of Federal Reserve membership, so long as the institution holds *transaction accounts* or *nonpersonal time deposits*.[8]

The principal purpose of the Federal Reserve Discount Window is to make loans to depository institutions so as to provide help for short–term liquidity needs. For example, an institution may experience an unexpected loss of deposits or the need to satisfy an unexpected loan demand in its trading area.

---

from an annual rate of about sixteen billion in early 1981 to about twelve billion by early 1982. ''Fed Irritates Big Banks by Fighting to Regain Share of Check Clearing,'' *Wall Street Journal*, 26 October 1982.

[8]Transaction accounts include demand deposits, negotiable order of withdrawal (NOW) accounts, automatic transfer service (ATS) accounts, share draft accounts, and accounts permitting telephone or similar transfers for payments to third parties. Nonpersonal time deposits are defined as time deposits which are transferable *or* as time deposits held by corporations or by other institutions.

On the other hand, the Discount Window is not intended as a source of funds to assist financial institutions in maximizing profit. For example, it would be inappropriate for a depository financial institution to borrow from the Federal Reserve System and purchase securities for the purpose of investing in securities paying a higher interest rate than the discount rate.

Although the major purpose of the Federal Reserve Discount Window is to accomodate short–term liquidity needs (typically from one to a few days) extended credit may be provided for specific credit needs. For example, smaller institutions serving communities dependent upon farming or resort businesses may qualify for longer term credit under seasonal, or other extended–credit programs.

Fiscal Agent for the Government   The Federal Reserve System performs a large number of financial services on behalf of the United States Government. The process of collecting large sums in taxes and spending equally large sums requires substantial banking services. Each year, the U.S. Treasury sells new and retires old securities valued in the billions of dollars. These sales and redemptions are administered by the Federal Reserve. The Federal Reserve, therefore, functions as a bank for financial institutions and as a bank for the United States Government.

Monetary Operations of the Federal Reserve System

As previously noted, the Federal Reserve System issues currency, buys and sells U.S. government securities, and serves depository financial institutions by making loans and clearing payments between institutions. These activities are illustrated below with sample balance sheets. As the first sample balance sheet shows, the primary assets are loans to financial institutions and U.S. government securities. The primary liabilities are currency that has been issued and deposits received from financial institutions.

SIMPLIFIED COMPOSITE FEDERAL RESERVE BANK BALANCE SHEET
(in $ billions)

Loans to fin. inst.	$ 10	Currency	$100
U.S. government securities	140	Deposits from fin. inst.	50
Other assets	3	Equity	3
Total assets	$153	Total liabilities and net worth	$153

Suppose the Federal Reserve System wishes to expand the volume of loanable funds within the financial system. Such an expansion may be commenced through the purchase of government securities. The securities would likely be purchased directly from a financial institution; but if securities were purchased from an individual, the individual would deposit the check used for payment with a financial institution achieving the same results. In this example, the federal reserve banks purchase $10 billion worth of U.S.

government securities directly from commercial banks. The balance sheet below reflects the changes that occurred. The arrows highlight accounts that have changed. As can be seen, the Federal Reserve pays for these securities by crediting the selling commercial bank's deposit account. Notice that the Federal Reserve Banks do not need money to purchase securities. The transaction merely involves a series of accounting entries.

FEDERAL RESERVE BANK BALANCE SHEET

Loans to fin. inst.	$ 10	Currency	$100
U.S. government securities	150←	Deposits from fin. inst.	60←
Other assets	3	Equity	3
Total assets	$163	Total liabilities and net worth	$163

The selling commercial bank has now replaced U.S. government securities with liquid funds in the form of a deposit with a Federal Reserve Bank. Because financial institutions can settle accounts with each other by transferring ownership of deposits with the Federal Reserve, the commercial bank can view these Federal Reserve deposits as loanable funds. The commercial bank can take advantage of these new funds by making a loan, which is normally accomplished by increasing the borrower's transaction deposit balance. If the borrower then writes a check that is deposited elsewhere and is later presented by another bank for payment, the lending bank can use its federal reserve bank deposit to make payment. Thus, an increase in its Federal Reserve Bank Deposits represents funds that a bank can loan. The Federal Reserve System can increase or decrease the amount of loanable funds by purchasing or selling U.S. government securities.

Continuing with this example, we can observe the process of currency creation. Suppose commercial banks do decide to loan more money and some borrower requests cash. Suppose that the $10 billion Federal Reserve System's purchase of U.S. government securities eventually results in a demand for an additional $2 billion of currency. Since the cash is being withdrawn from commercial banks, these banks will request $2 billion in currency. The Federal Reserve Banks forward the $2 billion in currency to the individual commercial banks, deducting the amounts from the commercial banks' deposit accounts. Thus, deposits from banks decrease by $2 billion and currency liability increases by $2 billion.

FEDERAL RESERVE BANK BALANCE SHEET
(in $ billions)

Loans to fin. inst.	$ 10	Currency	$102←
U.S. government securities	150	Deposits from fin. inst.	58←
Other assets	3	Equity	3
Total assets	$163	Total liabilities and net worth	$163

From the perspective of the Federal Reserve Banks' accounts, currency in circulation and deposits from financial institutions are similar, interchangeable liabilities. Currency is simply physical evidence of a Federal Reserve Bank liability. From the public's point of view, there is little difference between currency and a transactions account deposit since either can be used for payment and one can be readily exchanged for the other. The form in which money is held is based mainly on convenience factors.

A loan to a financial institution is also a matter of offsetting transactions. If commercial banks were to borrow $5 billion from the Federal Reserve Banks, the "loans to financial institutions" account would be increased by $5 billion and the deposits from financial institutions would be increased by $5 billion. Thus, the Federal Reserve Banks do not need a source of funds in order to make loans.

The final type of transaction involves clearing accounts between financial institutions. Financial institutions may pay each other by transferring ownership of part of their Federal Reserve Bank deposit balances. A member bank receives a check written on another bank. The member bank deposits the check with the Federal Reserve Bank, receiving credit to its deposit account for the amount of the check. This amount is then deducted from the balance sheet of the bank on which it was drawn. Of course, each commercial bank may deposit thousands of checks per day, with its deposit balance with the Federal Reserve Bank reflecting the net effect of all checks.

The following example shows the accounts of a Federal Reserve Bank and two member banks before and after a series of checks are cleared. In this example, Bank A deposits checks worth a total of $2 less than checks that are deposited by other banks and written against it. Bank B deposits checks worth $2 more than checks that are deposited against it.

The individual commercial banks show changes in deposit liabilities owed to their customers which offset changes in their accounts with the Federal Reserve Bank. However, total deposit liabilities of commercial banks and Federal Reserve Banks have not changed.

Most of the functions of the Federal Reserve System could be easily handled by other institutions. In many countries, currency is issued as an obligation of the Treasury Department of the government rather than by the central bank.

Checks can be cleared through clearing house associations. In fact, private clearing houses are used for stock and commodity trading as well as for a good deal of check processing. Deposit insurance, not Federal Reserve credit, brought an end to banking panics. There is, however, one function the Federal Reserve System is uniquely qualified to provide: the Federal Reserve System is the primary agency responsible for controlling the money supply.

Federal Reserve Bank	*Before checks are cleared*	*After checks are cleared*
Total assets	$163	$163
Liabilities and equity		
Currency	$100	$100
Deposits from financial institutions		
Bank A	6	4←
Bank B	5	7←
All other financial institutions	49	49
Equity	3	3
	$163	$163
Bank A		
Currency	$ 3	$ 3
Deposits with Fed	6	4←
U.S. gov. securities	70	70
Other assets	1	1
Total assets	$ 80	$ 78
Deposits	$ 70	$ 68←
Equity	10	10
	$ 80	$ 78
Bank B		
Currency	$ 2	$ 2
Deposits with Fed	5	7←
U.S. gov. securities	60	60
Other assets	1	1
Total assets	$ 68	$ 70
Deposits	$ 60	$ 62←
Equity	8	8
Total liabilities	$ 68	$ 70

CREATING AND CONTROLLING THE MONEY SUPPLY

Recall that a major purpose of the Federal Reserve System is to regulate the flow of money and credit in order to promote economic stability and growth. In the United States, as in many other countries, history has aptly demonstrated the severe economic consequences of overly restrictive or overly expansive rates of growth in the money supply.

Table 2-2:

Major Components of Money Stock Measures

M-1 Private demand deposits at commercial banks plus balances in NOW accounts, share draft accounts, and other transaction accounts at financial institutions plus currency held by the nonbank public.

M-2 M-1 plus savings and small denomination time deposit accounts, plus money market mutual fund shares.

M-3 M-2 plus large denomination time deposits.

L M-3 plus other liquid assets such as commercial paper, Treasury bills, etc.

In the United States we learned that loss of faith in the value of money[9] can lead to a collapse of the economic system, with depression following. In other countries, we have seen that failure to control the supply of money can lead to revolution. If money were still primarily in the form of currency, the supply could be controlled by controlling the printing press. With most money being in the form of deposits in financial institutions, controlling the supply is a more complex problem. Various money stock measures are defined in table 2-2.

Our discussion will now center on the way money is created and controlled, and more specifically on ways in which the Federal Reserve and the financial system influence the narrow money supply, specifically M1. Recall that M1 is defined as currency and transaction accounts held by the nonbank public (table 2-2). We begin with some rather elementary accounting transactions.

Step 1: $100 in Currency Is Deposited in Centerre Bank

CHANGES IN CENTERRE BANK'S
BALANCE SHEET

Currency	+$100	Demand Deposits	+$100

---

[9]Checking account money in the 1930s and currency in some earlier crises.

In Step one above, $100 in currency, formerly owned by the nonbank public is now owned by Centerre Bank.[10] In return for the currency, the customer's demand deposit account was credited, and the customer now owns a $100 deposit. Note that the money supply did not change. Only the *composition* of the money supply changed in that the currency component of M1 declined and the demand deposit component of M1 increased by exactly the same amount. It is useful to note at this point that while the Step 1 transaction involved a bank, the financial institution could just as easily have been a credit union, savings and loan, mutual savings bank, i.e., any institution offering transaction (check-type) accounts.

To continue our discussion of creating and controlling the money supply, it is useful at this point to note the importance of *reserve requirements*. All depository financial institutions are required to hold reserves in the form of cash or deposits with the Federal Reserve Bank equal to some percentage of its deposit liabilities (table 2-3.[11]) To simplify the calculations, the *required reserve ratio* in our example is assumed to be 10 percent. Thus, $10 ($100 × 0.10) must be held by Centerre Bank either as currency in the vault or as a deposit with the Federal Reserve. The remaining $90 ($100 − $10) are *excess* reserves and may be loaned or otherwise invested. We note here that any single bank can loan *dollar for dollar of excess reserves*.

Step 2: Excess Reserves Are Loaned

IMPACT ON CENTERRE BANK'S
BALANCE SHEET (CASH LOAN)

Currency	$10		
Loans	90	Demand Deposits	$100

In Step 2, Centerre Bank has loaned its excess reserves and in the process has created $90 in

---

[10]It is important to recall that only currency *outside* depository financial institutions counts as a part of the money supply.

[11]Prior to passage of the Monetary Control Act of 1980, only member banks held reserves with the Federal Reserve. Today, all depository financial institutions must hold reserves with the Federal Reserve.

Table 2-3:

**Reserve Requirements
for Financial Institutions 1984**

Net Transaction Account Balances
$0–$28.9 Million	3%
Over $28.9 Million	12%

Nonpersonal Time Deposits
By original maturity
Less than 1½ years	3%
1½ years or more	0

Eurocurrency Liabilities
All types	3%

Notes: Certain of the above requirements are being phased in over an eight-year period which began in November 1980.

The amount of transaction accounts against which the 3 percent reserve requirement applies is increased annually in accordance with an index established by the Monetary Control Act of 1980.

Nonpersonal time deposits are time deposits which are transferable *or* as time deposits held by corporations or by other institutions.

new money. To simplify our illustration, we will initially assume that loan customers borrowed $90 in cash. Since M1 is defined as currency and transaction accounts held by the nonbank public, and since no change occurred in Demand Deposits held by the public, it is clear that the money supply increased by $90 as a result of the bank loan. Suppose though that Centerre Bank had loaned the $90 by increasing the borrower's demand account (a common means of dispersing loan proceeds), rather than by dispersing cash. In that case, Centerre's balance sheet immediately after making the loan would have changed as follows:

IMPACT ON CENTERRE BANK'S
BALANCE SHEET
(DEMAND DEPOSIT CREDIT)

Currency	$100	Demand Deposits	$190
Loans	90		

It is recognized, however, that in a short time the borrower would likely spend the loan proceeds by drawing checks against his demand deposit. If we assume that these $90 in loan proceeds are spent and that the recipients of these spent funds deposit them in some second bank (or second generation of banks), the result for Centerre Bank is the same as our original Step 2 balance sheet where a cash loan transaction was assumed.

Step 3: $90 in Step 2 Loan Proceeds Are Deposited

IMPACT ON BALANCE SHEET
FOR SECOND GENERATION BANKS

Cash (Reserves)	$90	Demand Deposits	$90

In Step 3, the $90 loan proceeds have been deposited in a second set (generation) of banks. Note that the Step 3 transaction does not change the money supply since the public gave up $90 in money to acquire $90 in deposits (which are also money).

Step 4: Excess Reserves Are Loaned

CHANGE IN BALANCE SHEETS
FOR SECOND GENERATION BANKS

Reserves	$9	Demand Deposits	$90
Loans	81		

In Step 4, loans of $81 ($90−9) have been made; if this *expansion of depository institution credit* is continued to the maximum possible, the $81 will be deposited in some third set of banks. Once again, we note that these additional loans are now part of the money supply and that the money supply has been increased by an additional $81 by virtue of the Step 4 transactions. The initial deposit of $100 in currency can expand the money supply by $900, given a 10 percent reserve requirement, the assumption of no *leakage*,[12] and maximum expansion (table 2-4).

The expansion potential can be formalized in the formula:

$$P = E/r$$

[12]"Leakage" would occur if some borrowers chose to hold loan proceeds in cash.

Table 2-4:

Maximum Expansion of Depository Institution Credit

Depository Financial Institution	Acquired Reserves and Deposits	Required Reserves (10%)	Excess Reserves	Amount Which Can Be Loaned
A	$100	$10.00	$90.00	$90.00
B	90	9.00	81.00	81.00
C	81	8.10	72.90	72.90
.	.	.	.	.
.	.	.	.	.
.	.	.	.	.
Other Institutions	629	72.90		656.10
		Total amount loaned		$900.00

where: P = Potential expansion in the money supply (or expansion of credit)

E = Excess reserves

r = Percentage reserve requirement.

In our example, the original deposit of $100 with Centerre Bank resulted in excess reserves of $90 ($100-10). Thus, total new money created was $900 ($90/0.10).

The actual expansion of credit is likely to be less than this potential figure because of "leakage" to cash. If the first borrower of $90 chose to hold the cash, expansion would be stopped with the first $90. In practice, the creation of $1 of excess reserves appears to increase the money supply by only $2 to $3.

The money supply is controlled by the Federal Reserve System through activities that influence the volume of reserves within the financial system. One way for the Federal Reserve System to influence reserves is to change the legal reserve requirement. An increase in reserve requirements leads to a curtailment of lending activity and, therefore, diminishes the creation of money. Likewise, a decrease in reserve requirements gives banks the authority to make additional loans and create more money.

Reserve requirements are actually changed infrequently because a small change in reserve requirements leads to a large change in the money supply. On the other hand, the money supply is adjusted on a day–to–day basis using *open market operations*—the buying and selling of U.S. government securities by the Federal Reserve Banks.

A situation whereby the Federal Reserve is seeking to increase the money supply through open-market operations is illustrated in figure 2-5. The Federal Reserve Bank of New York, by offering a price acceptable to Citibank, a large New York bank, has acquired $10 million in U.S. Treasury securities (figure 2-5). The Federal Reserve System pays for these by increasing Citibank's reserves by $10 million. Note that the

FEDERAL RESERVE BANK OF NEW YORK	
U.S. Government Securities +$10	Demand Deposits (Citibank) +$10

CITIBANK	
Reserves +$10	
U.S. Government Securities −$10	

Figure 2–5: Federal open-market operations resulting in increased reserves in $ millions.

open-market transaction has caused no change in deposit liabilities on Citibank's balance sheet. Thus, the entire $10 million is now excess reserves. If all of the $10 million is loaned by Citibank, and assuming reserve requirements of 10 percent, new money equal to $100 million ($10/0.10) can potentially be created through the expansion process.

By selling U.S. government securities, the Federal Reserve Banks can reverse the process and decrease the money supply.

The *discount rate* is another method used in controlling the money supply. The discount rate is the rate charged by the Federal Reserve Banks on loans to member banks. The importance of the discount rate is limited by the fact that commercial banks are discouraged from regular borrowing from the Federal Reserve Banks. However, the discount rate is frequently used as a signalling device. An increase in the discount rate would lead banks to begin curtailing their lending activity in anticipation of monetary restriction.

In addition to control of the money supply, the Federal Reserve System has available several other tools for use in attempting to control economic activity. *Regulation Q* sets the interest rates that can be paid on many deposits. However, this tool is being phased out, with present legislation calling for an end to deposit interest rate regulation by 1986. *Margin requirements* determine the percentage of value that purchasers of stocks and bonds are allowed to borrow. If there is evidence of excessive speculative pressure in the securities markets, effective demand can be decreased through an increase in margin requirements. The present 50 percent requirement was set in 1974. Finally, the Federal Reserve System operates in the *foreign exchange markets,* buying and selling dollars to smooth out movements in exchange rates.

An important objective of federal reserve policy is economic growth. The Federal Reserve System shares with the U.S. government a statutory obligation to work toward healthy economic conditions. The Federal Reserve System attempts to draw a reasonable balance between the objectives of encouraging economic growth through the provision of adequate credit and of avoiding inflation brought on by excessive money growth.

As noted earlier, the governing body of the Federal Reserve System is the Federal Reserve Board. Each member is appointed by the President of the United States with the consent of the Senate for a period of fourteen years. This structure was designed to create an "independent" Federal Reserve that would pursue appropriate policy objectives without undue short–term political pressure. However, the chairman only serves a four–year term and is appointed by the President from among the members. Thus, the President generally has an opportunity to appoint someone of his choosing to the board and then appoint that person chairman sometime during his term. The record of the Federal Reserve System with regard to following the economic leadership of the President or striking its own course is mixed, as is opinion on the degree of independence it should have.

SUMMARY

Financial systems change over time in response to changing technology and the needs of society. In the United States, the financial system is a combination of reserve banking, fiat, and electronic systems. Since money is no longer backed directly by anything of value, its supply must be controlled by some agency enjoying a high level of public confidence. In the United States, the Federal Reserve System was structured as an agency free from day–to–day pressures of election politics for this purpose. The Federal Reserve System, which acts as the central bank, controls the supply of money primarily through reserve requirements and open market operations. Its control of the money supply is carried out with the dual (and frequently conflicting) objectives of stable prices and full employment.

The rate of growth in the money supply is a function of excess reserves generated by depository financial institutions which in turn is dependent upon federal reserve policy. The volume of reserves so held influences the amount of new lending and thus the volume of new money created.

QUESTIONS

1. Identify several different types of financial systems. Of the several types, which would best describe the United States financial system?

2. If there exists in the United States only $150 billion in currency, how is it possible for deposits in U.S. financial institutions to exceed $1.8 trillion?

3. Describe the structure and operating characteristics of the Federal Reserve System.

4. To whom does the chairman of the Federal Reserve System report? To what extent does the structure of the system insure independence?

5. What determines the value of money? Is it important to have money backed by precious metals such as gold and silver or by other commodities?

6. Identify and define the various money supply measures.

7. Why are depository financial institutions required to hold reserves?

8. Distinguish between required reserves and excess reserves.

9. Whenever currency is deposited in a commercial bank, the money supply decreases. Do you agree?

10. Discuss how the tools of monetary policy may be used by the Federal Reserve to influence the money supply.

PROBLEMS

1. Suppose $1000 in currency is deposited in a transaction account at Home Federal Savings and Loan Association.

    a. Has the money supply changed?

    b. If the required reserve ratio is 10 percent, how much could Home Federal lend as a result of the $1000 deposit?

    c. Assuming maximum expansion and no leakage, how much new money could the financial system create as a result of the initial deposit?

    d. Answer parts b and c, given a reserve requirement of 12 percent.

2. The following is a hypothetical balance sheet for the Boatmen's National Bank. The reserve ratio is 15 percent.

ASSETS		LIABILITIES	
Reserves	60	Transaction	
Investments	140	Accounts	$400
Loans	200		

    a. How much excess reserves does the bank now have?

    b. If customers deposit $10 in currency in transaction accounts, would the money supply change?

    c. As a result of the $10 deposit, can Boatmen's Bank create money? If so, how and by how much?

    d. Assuming maximum expansion and no leakage, how much new money could be created as the result of the initial $10 deposit?

3. Below are T-accounts for the Federal Reserve Banks and for a commercial bank. Show how a $10 million sale of U.S. government securities to that commercial bank would change the accounts.

Federal Reserve Bank Balance Sheet
(in $ mil.)

Loans to banks	10,000	Currency	$100,000
U.S. government securities	150,000	Deposits from banks	60,000
Other assets	3,000	Equity	3,000
Total assets	163,000		$163,000

First National Bank of Johnstown
(in $ mil.)

Currency	3	Deposits	70
Deposits with Fed	16	Equity	10
U.S. Government Sec	10		$80
Other assets	51		
	$80		

4. Banks are fully loaned up and face 10 percent reserve requirements. The Federal Reserve System purchases $10 million of U.S. government bonds from a commercial bank. Assume any loans by that bank will be made by increasing the borrowers' transaction accounts and will result in the borrowers immediately writing checks against their accounts.

    a. By how much can that bank increase loans?

    b. Ignoring leakage to cash, by how much can all banks in the system increase loans?

SELECTED REFERENCES

Bowden, Elbert V. *Revolution in Banking.* Reston Va.: Reston Publishing Co., 1980.

Brown, Donald M. "The Effect of State Banking Laws on Holding Company Banks" *Federal Reserve Bank of St. Louis Review* 65 (August/September 1983): 26–35.

Dunham, Constance and Guerin-Calvert, Margaret.

"How Quickly Can Thrifts Move Into Commercial Lending?" *Federal Reserve Bank of Boston New England Economic Review* (November/December 1983): 42–54.

Gagnon, Joseph, and Yokas, Steve. "Recent Developments in Federal and New England Banking Laws" *Federal Reserve Bank of Boston New England Economic Review* (January/February 1983): 18–27.

Garcia, Gillian, et al. "The Garn—St. Germain Depository Institutions Act of 1982) *Federal Reserve Bank of Chicago Economic Perspectives* (March/April 1983): 3–31.

Gart, Alan. *The Insider's Guide to the Financial Services Revolution.* New York: McGraw-Hill Book Co., 1984.

Kaufman, George C., Mote, Larry, and Rosenblum, Harvey. "Deregulation of the Financial Sector." *Federal Reserve Bank of Chicago* Economic Perspectives (Fall 1982): 26–36.

Vrabac, Daniel J. "Recent Developments at Banks and Nonbank Depository Institutions" *Federal Reserve Bank of Kansas City Economic Review* (July/August 1983): 33–45.

Wood, John H. "Familiar Developments in Bank Loan Markets" *Federal Reserve Bank of Dallas Economic Review* (November 1983): 1–13.

Chapter 3

Regulation of Financial Institutions

INAUGURATION DAY 1933

The White House, midnight, Friday, March 3, 1933. Across the country the banks of the nation had gradually shuttered their windows and locked their doors. The very machinery of the American economy seemed to be coming to a stop. The rich and fertile nation, overflowing with natural wealth in its fields and forests and mines, equipped with unsurpassed technology, endowed with boundless resources in its men and women, lay stricken. "We are at the end of our rope," a weary President Hoover at last said, as the striking clock announced the day of his retirement. "There is nothing more we can do." [1]

The United States financial system is built on trust and confidence. Central to its well-being is the belief that funds placed on deposit with banks (or other depository institutions) will be available on demand or when due and will be payable to the depositor. Currency represents only a small fraction of the money supply and most

---

[1] Arthur J. Schlesinger, Jr., "The Valley of Darkness," *The Crisis of the Old Order, 1919–1933* (Boston: Houghton-Mifflin Company, 1957), summarized in *Economic Issues* (McGraw-Hill Book Company, 1963): 35–36.

"money" on deposit with financial institutions is represented simply by accounting entries (chapter 2). Clearly, our financial system is backed only by the confidence of the public. As Schlesinger so elequently describes, the nation was in a state of despair in 1933; financial markets had collapsed; the banking system was on the verge of disintegration; unemployment was rampant; and calls for financial reform were heard throughout the nation. On 4 March, 1933, President Franklin D. Roosevelt was installed as President. On 5 March, Congress was called into special session and the President declared a banking holiday. Over the next 100 days, Congress passed sweeping legislative measures and from the financial anguish of the 1930s evolved a strengthened American financial system.

THE AMERICAN FINANCIAL SYSTEM

To develop insight into the American Financial System, it is useful to examine its evolution; and to understand where we are today, it is useful to analyze financial and regulatory developments within four major historical periods of American history: pre 1913, 1913–1933, 1933–1980, and 1980 and beyond.

Regulatory Environment Pre 1913

In contrast with many European economies, characterized by large central banks, controlled—if not owned—by the central government, the American banking system functioned as a decentralized, privately owned and largely privately controlled banking system before 1913. As late as the 1890s, a South Dakota court held banking a strictly private business in which the proprietor had an absolute right to own and operate his bank without supervision or control by any government authority.[2]

As far back as the eighteenth century, the federal government had sought to exert at least some control over banking. The first bank to receive a federal charter was The First Bank of the United States. This first federally chartered bank was given a twenty-year charter (1791–1811). In some ways, the First Bank performed a role similar to that of a Federal Reserve Bank today. In addition to its role as a regular commercial bank, it functioned as a "banker's bank," receiving deposits from and transferring funds on behalf of state chartered banks. It also functioned as a fiscal agent for the federal government by receiving government deposits and transferring these around the country and by lending to the government. This first federally chartered bank served as a regulator of the state banks. It did so by collecting the notes issued by individual state banks and then presenting these to the issuing bank. It asked for immediate redemption in specie (precious metal which backed the notes), thus encouraging state banks to refrain from excessive issue of bank notes. At the end of the twenty-year period however, the bank's charter was not renewed. Some argued that the issuance of a federal bank charter violated the constitution, although the constitution did give government the right to "coin money

and regulate the value thereof." Others objected to the bank's practice of issuing paper notes, arguing that the only "good" money was "hard" money (gold or silver). Also, a number of state chartered banks objected to its regulatory role. Finally, the issue of "states' rights" and the resentment caused by central government interferance into private business insured the demise of the First Bank of the United States.

Following the charter expiration of the First Bank, the nation entered into a period of *State Banking* for the next five years (1811–1816). During this period, the number of state banks approximately tripled; the number increased from 88 in 1811 to 246 in 1816 (figure 3-1). Poor bank management, the lack of a central fiscal agent for the government, rapid expansion of the volume of bank notes, and other abuses resulted in efforts to again charter a national bank. Five years following the demise of the first federally chartered bank, the Second Bank of the United States was given a twenty-year charter (1816–1836). The second bank performed in ways that were similar to that of the first bank; thus it too succumbed to political bickering and its charter was not renewed.

The period 1836–1863 witnessed a return to state banking in the United States. While some states sought to effectively regulate and control banking, others were lax. Banking abuses, overissue of bank notes, counterfeiting, and other such practices were rampant. By 1863, it was widely believed that something must be done to "clean up" American banking. The National Bank Act of 1864 (which superseded legislation passed the previous year) provided for the chartering of banks by the federal government. Unlike the First and Second Banks of the United States which were partially owned by the federal government and which functioned with nationwide branches, the banks provided for in the 1864 Act were privately owned banks with powers similar to those enjoyed by *state chartered* banks. The National Banking System was established to provide a national uniform paper currency, to counteract chaotic local banking, and to help finance the Union war effort.

A major objective of the National Bank Act of

---

[2]Susan Estabrook Kennedy, *The Banking Crisis of 1933* (University Press of Kentucky, 1973): 6.

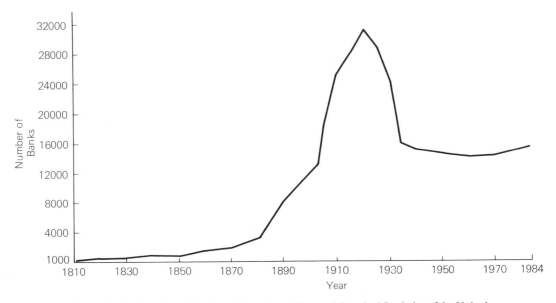

Figure 3–1: Number of Banks in Operation. (From: Historical Statistics of the United States, United States Deparment of Commerce.)

1864 was to encourage *state chartered* banks to join the national bank system. To provide that encouragement, Congress imposed a tax on bank notes issued by banks outside the system. Most state banks joined the system since it would not be profitable to make loans through note issue when the 10 percent tax frequently exceeded interest charged on the loan. Unfortunately, deficiencies still remained in the nation's banking system. Banks joining the National Bank System were required to purchase United States bonds, against which bank notes could be issued. The dependence upon government bonds for note issuance caused bank note shortages. Also, capital requirements for members of the National Bank System were high ($50,000 for population areas of less than 6,000). Thus rural areas were not well served by the system.[3] Finally, a banking panic in 1907 confirmed the inadequacy of the

National Banking System and a National Monetary Commission was formed by Congress in 1908. The commission was charged with the responsibility of studying banking systems at home and abroad and of recommending a new system to the United States Congress. Finally, in 1913, the Federal Reserve System was established.

Regulatory Environment 1913–1933

While the National Monetary Commission recommended the establishment of a strong central bank, the Wilson administration was determined that in correcting weaknesses of the National Bank Act, it would not add to centralized financial power. Rather than one central bank, the Federal Reserve Act of 1913 provided for a system of regional federal reserve banks.

In the early years of the Federal Reserve System, the authority and effectiveness of the Federal Reserve System was limited. Only national banks were required to join and the system did not act as a powerful force to promote

---

[3]Some banks began to make loans by increasing checking account balances rather than note issue, thus avoiding the tax and avoiding the necessity of joining the National Banking System.

monetary stability. While the Federal Reserve System could influence bank reserves through the discount window and through open-market operations, these activities were uncoordinated in that each of the twelve banks set its own discount rate, and open-market operations were effectively controlled by the New York reserve bank rather than by the system. Rather than stabilize the economy through the explosive growth of the 1920s, for example, the Federal Reserve System contributed to the expansion in the late 1920s by lowering the discount rate and by engaging in open-market purchases, thereby inflating credit. Much of this credit was used for real estate and stock market speculation which contributed to inflated markets and their collapse in October 1929. Critics charged that the New York Reserve Bank was effectively ''under the control of Wall Street.'' Indeed in February 1929, the Federal Reserve System asked the Federal Reserve Banks to provide ''direct pressure'' and ask member banks not to make speculative loans. But the New York Federal Reserve Bank opposed this move and did not comply. From a practical point of view, the Federal Reserve System was powerless. If financial institutions met membership and reserve requirements of the Federal Reserve Act of 1913, they needed pay no further deference to the system.[4]

The Hoover Administration tried to deal with the deteriorating situation in the early 1930s. In 1932, it created the Reconstruction Finance Corporation which provided loans to financial and other institutions. In that same year, it also created the Federal Home Loan Bank System which was modeled after the Federal Reserve System and designed to provide a central credit facility for home financing institutions—principally savings and loan associations.

Unfortunately these actions were too few and too late. From the end of 1929 to the beginning of 1933, over five thousand banks—20 percent of the banks in the United States—failed. The situation continued to deteriorate through the spring of 1933, until Hoover's term as President ended in early March (figure 3-2).

Regulatory Environment 1933–1980

On 5 March, 1983, one day after taking office, President Roosevelt declared a four-day bank holiday, which was later extended indefinitely. Within days of this bank holiday announcement, Congress enacted emergency banking legislation, approving the President's authority to proclaim a national banking holiday and providing a framework for reopening closed banks. In effect, the re-opening procedure signaled a more active regulatory role for the Federal Reserve System. The procedure called for the secretary of the treasury to license (and thus authorize the reopening) of any member bank whose financial condition was judged to be sound by the district Federal Reserve Bank.[5] State banking authorities could reopen sound nonmember banks at their discretion.

While much financial legislation was enacted during the Roosevelt administration, perhaps the most significant in terms of its affect on the financial system and particularly depository financial institutions, was the Banking Act of 1933.

The Banking Act of 1933, also known as the *Glass Steagall Act,* introduced broad reform into the United States financial system. The important provisions of the Glass Steagall Act were that it:

1. *Created the Federal Open-Market Committee* and brought open-market operations under formal control of the statutory body of the Federal Reserve System for the first time.

2. *Created the Federal Deposit Insurance Corporation (FDIC)* and provided for a temporary deposit insurance fund, initially insuring deposits to $2500.

---

[4]For an excellent historical analysis of this period, see Susan Estabrook Kennedy, *The Banking Crisis of 1933,* (University Press of Kentucky).

[5]In his first ''fire-side chat'' with the American public (Sunday evening, 12 March 1933), President Roosevelt stated that those banks ''found to be all right'' by treasury examination would be reopened; the remaining banks would resume business eventually. Many of the remaining banks never reopened.

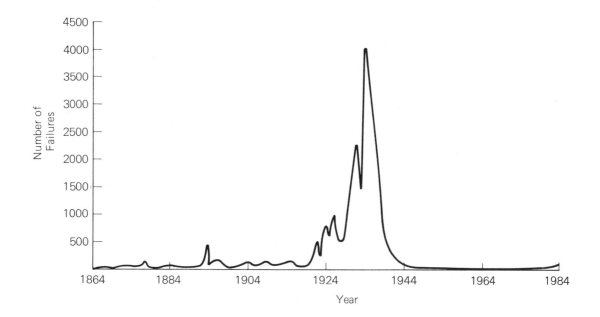

Figure 3–2: Bank Suspensions: 1864–1983. (From *Historical Statistics of the United States,* United States Department of Commerce and FDIC Annual Reports.)

3. *Prohibited the payment of interest on demand deposits and authorized the Federal Reserve Board to regulate interest rates payable on savings and time deposits.*

4. *Prohibited member banks and the affiliates of member banks to engage in investment banking activities.*

5. *Provided for greater regulation of the operations of member banks.*

Thus the Banking Act of 1933 restricted bank operations, centralized banking control, and introduced federal deposit insurance, setting the stage for a tightly controlled regulatory environment which would continue for the next several decades.

Banks were not treated differently from other business in being subjected to these rules. It was felt that recovery would be encouraged if businesses could be protected from competition. Industries as diverse as interstate trucking and stock brokerage were brought under regulatory control. An important aspect of such control was the elimination of price competition.

A fundamental result of legislation enacted in the 1930s was the division of permissable activities among the various financial institutions and the division into compartments of the financial sector. Neither banks nor affiliates of banks could engage in brokerage and other security market activities. Of course, securities firms could not engage in banking. Savings and loan associations could not offer demand deposits, nor could they make commercial or most other types of loans. They were restricted almost totally to the making of home mortgage loans in their local market. Credit unions, established in 1934, could not accept demand deposits and were largely limited to the provision of credit to people ''of small means'' (according to the 1934 Federal Credit Union Act). In later years, the owners of some banks sought to engage in activities prohibited to commercial banks by forming holding companies to which the bank could be sold. The holding company might acquire other nonbank subsidiaries; and since the holding company managers controlled both the bank and nonbank subsidiaries, there existed the possibility that bank resources could be used to favor such nonbank subsidiaries or that other conflict-of-interest situations might arise.

To close the possible loophole in banking regulation that the holding company structure posed, Congress passed the Bank Holding Company Act of 1956 which required holding companies owning one fourth or more of the voting stock of *two or more* banks to register with the Federal Reserve Board. In subsequent amendments (1966 and 1970), Congress revised and extended the Bank Holding Company Act to cover holding companies owning just one bank. These revisions further provided that nonbank companies owned by bank holding companies must be engaged in activities "closely related to banking." Such "closely related" activities were to be decided and defined by the Federal Reserve System (table 3-1).

Since 1956, the number of bank holding companies and the volume of deposits held by them has increased dramatically (table 3-2).

By the 1970s, depression era conditions had faded from the minds of the American public. Federal Deposit Insurance and financial

Table 3-1:

Permissible Nonbank Activities for Bank Holding Companies That Require Prior Approval

1. Making and servicing loans—consumer finance, credit card, mortgage, commercial, factoring
2. Industrial banking
3. Trust company functions
4. Investment or financial advice
5. Leasing personal or real property
6. Community development
7. Data processing
8. Insurance sales
9. Underwriting credit life, accident and health insurance
10. Courier services
11. Management consulting to depository institutions
12. Money orders, savings bonds, and travelers checks
13. Real estate appraising
14. Arranging commercial real estate financing
15. Securities brokerage
16. Underwriting and dealing in government obligations and money market instruments
17. Foreign exchange advisory and transactional services
18. Futures commission merchant

Source: *Federal Reserve Bulletin,* February, 1984, pp. 134–137.

Table 3-2:

Offices and Deposits of Banks Affiliated with Bank Holding Companies by Years

	1956	1970	1971	1975	1980	1981	1982*
Number of companies	53	121	1,567	1,821	3,056	3,702	4,510
Banks	428	895	2,420	3,674	4,954	5,689	6,900
Branches	783	3,260	10,382	18,382	24,970	28,044	32,650
Total offices	1,211	4,155	13,252	22,056	29,924	33,733	39,550
Offices as a percentage of all bank offices	5.7	11.8	36.1	49.4	56.2	61.0	66.0
Domestic deposits (in $ billions)	14.8	78.0	297.0	527.5	840.6	938.6	1,036.0
Domestic deposits as a percentage of all bank deposits	7.5	16.2	55.1	67.1	71.0	74.1	76.0

*Estimated

Source: Bank Holding Company Facts, Spring 1983; Assoc. of Bank Holding Companies.

regulation had accomplished the objective of restoring confidence and of reducing bank and other depository institution failures to a fraction of their former numbers.[6] Indeed, the regulatory authorities followed the practice of merging failed institutions with stronger ones so that deposit and other creditor losses were virtually eliminated. While safety was the primary focus of earlier legislation, quality and price of financial services became the principal issue by the 1970s. The division into compartments of the financial sector was questioned, and a number of government mandated studies were released.

WINDS OF CHANGE

Recent decades have witnessed the completion of several studies of the structure and regulation of financial institutions by special government commissions. Many of the recommendations of these commissions have become law and represent an imporant departure from the limited competition philosophy developed in the 1930s. While safety was the primary focus of earlier legislation, quality and price of services has been the focus of this recent legislation.

Hunt Commission

In 1971, the Hunt Commission (formally, the President's Commission on Financial Structure and Regulation) completed a sweeping study of financial institutions and the supply and demand for credit. The commission concluded that attempts to regulate the flow of funds had led to market inefficiency and had generally failed to achieve stated objectives. In general, the commission recommended that competition be increased. The major specific recommendations of the commission were as follows:

1. *Elimination of interest rate ceilings on deposits.* Deposit rate ceilings were supposed to protect the savings of individuals by pro-

tecting financial institutions from expensive competition for savings. In addition, they were supposed to assure the availability of funds to the housing industry.[7] This latter objective was pursued by allowing thrift institutions to pay a higher rate (first unrestricted, then 0.25 percent) than banks for deposits. This advantage to thrift institutions had been negated in recent years by disintermediation—investors took their money out of financial institutions and invested directly. Rather than securing a stable, low-cost supply of funds, the interest rate ceilings may have contributed to the lack of stability in the supply of funds.

2. *Allow all depository financial institutions to offer a full range of time deposits.* This is consistent with the first recommendation. With the ability to bid at prevailing rates for funds of any maturity, institutions should be in a position to manage the maturity structure of their liabilities. By bidding for longer term deposits, they would also gain in ability to develop more stable sources of funds.

3. *Allow all depository institutions to offer checking account services.* This recommendation followed the general philosophy that the best way to assure low cost services was to allow as many competitors as possible to offer the service.

4. *Broaden lending powers of all institutions.* The commission felt that the public would be better served if more competitors existed for each type of loan. It was also believed that institutions would gain from greater diversity if they were not forced to concentrate on one segment of the market.

Institutional Investor Study

The Institutional Investor Study, sponsored by the Securities and Exchange Commission, was also completed in 1971. The study was

---

[6]In 1934, the number of bank failures declined to sixty one. Beginning in 1943 and for the next three decades, the number of bank failures was less than ten per year.

[7]An unspoken ''advantage'' of regulating interest rates on small savings deposits was that it allowed the federal government to finance part of its debt by selling savings bonds to small investors at an interest rate well below that paid on large denomination U.S. government bonds.

undertaken against a background of complaints that certain institutions, particularly insurance companies, mutual funds, pension funds, and bank trust departments, were distorting the equity capital markets through a tendency to trade large quantities of securities and to buy or sell the same security at the same time. The commission did not find evidence of sheeplike behavior by financial institutions, but it did find that the trading of large blocks of stock caused some distortions in reported prices, primarily because market structure did not lead to an efficient reporting of these prices. Commissions on stock traded on an exchange were fixed at levels that discouraged institutions from using the exchanges. Thus a great deal of trading occurred between institutions not using an exchange. The elimination of fixed commissions and reliance on the market to set commissions was recommended.

National Commission on Consumer Finance

The National Commission on Consumer Finance was created by Congress and completed its work in 1972. An important part of this commission's work was a study of the impact of state usury laws. The commission concluded that attempts to regulate interest rates charged to individuals had failed to achieve the desired results. Usury laws had led to problems such as circuitous methods of charging higher interest rates. For example, if restrictive state usury ceilings result in reduced credit availability, consumers may go to a so-called credit retailer who sells virtually all of his merchandise on credit and in effect builds interest costs into the price of the product. The effect of the usury ceiling in this case is to restrict the consumer's opportunity to shop for the best interest rate and the best price for the product.

As with other studies, this commission concluded that problems could best be dealt with through encouraging competition. This required consumer lending authority to be extended to as many lenders as possible and interest charges to be fully disclosed so that now people can effectively shop for the best interest cost.

The general thrust of the recommendations from all of these studies was that competition should be relied on to allocate funds to their best use, and to provide the best prices to both consumers and institutions. These recommendations stood in sharp contrast to the regulatory philosophy developed in the 1930s. Then it was felt that elimination of competition was the most effective approach to achieving national goals.[8]

What accounted for the change in attitude about the way in which financial institutions should set prices and allocate resources? In a broad sense, this change was part of a general shift in public attitude in recent years. Reliance on competition relative to government control had grown in popularity as a means of achieving the goals of individuals and society. Suggestions for financial institution deregulation paralleled movement toward deregulation in airlines, trucking, and other fields.

Some legislation of the 1970s generally followed the thrust of the recommendations for greater reliance on the marketplace. Brokerage commission regulations were repealed and the result has been the development of a wider variety of services and costs available to individual investors. The brokerage houses previously charged identical commissions and competed by offering other services such as security analysis. Today, conventional brokerage houses compete with discount houses that offer no services other than purchase and sale of securities at the lowest commission possible. The result of freedom from rate regulation has been lower commission rates for many investors and a wider range of available services. However, the advent of the 1980s witnessed a dramatic change in the regulatory environment as Congress moved to further deregulate the financial sector.

---

[8]A continued resistance to the competition-based philosophy is represented by a dissenting statement from Lane Kirkland, then Secretary/Treasurer of the AFL-CIO: "I cannot believe that a financial institution should be encouraged to lend money for only the most profitable purposes." *Report of the President's Commission on Financial Structure and Regulation.* U.S. Government Printing Office, 1972. Stock # 4000-0272.

REGULATORY ENVIRONMENT 1980 AND BEYOND

Although the Hunt Commission and other studies had called for deregulation and greater reliance on market forces, history has shown that significant and substantial financial legislation, particularly legislation that signals shifts in the direction of regulation, is likely to occur when major disruptions have occurred in financial markets. The 1970s and particularly the late 1970s witnessed severe inflation, interest rate increases, and financial market chaos that threatened the solvency of sizable components of the financial sector. Substantial disintermediation occurred as depositors transferred funds from savings and time deposits in financial institutions to newly created *money market funds.* Money market funds merely combined sums received from savers and invested those funds into money market instruments[9] which were not subject to regulatory imposed interest rate ceilings. Fund managers deducted fees from the funds' assets in return for services and were able to pass along high market returns to investors in the fund. Subject to interest-rate restrictions on their deposits, depository financial institutions were unable to compete on a price basis with interest rates generated by the money market funds. Additionally, market interest rates for mortgages and other loans made by depository institutions had exceeded legal usury ceilings in many states. Depository institutions and particularly the thrifts, were thus faced with regulatory restrictions detrimentally affecting both sides of the balance sheet. By 1980, the impact on thrift institutions, particularly savings and loans and mutual savings banks was severe. Saddled with long-term, fixed-rate, low-yielding mortgages made in former years and with the partial deregulation of the liability side of their balance sheet[10], profitability of the industry diminished.

By 1981 the industry was generating negative returns (table 3-3 and figure 3-3) and by some definitions was insolvent. The market value of savings and loan assets (though not the book value) had fallen below the market value of the industry's liabilities.

The Financial Institution Deregulation and Monetary Control Act of 1980

The 1980 Deregulation and Monetary Control Act, commonly referred to as *The Monetary Control Act,* was undoubtedly the most sweeping piece of financial legislation since the Banking Act of 1933 and was signed into law on 30 March 1980. The act contained nine titles, each of which addressed major financial issues. Important provisions contained within this 1980 Act included:

1. *Reserve requirements were imposed on all depository financial institutions.*

2. *Interest rate ceilings on savings and time deposits were to be phased out over a six-year period ending March 1986.*

3. *Federal Deposit Insurance Limit* (FDIC, FSLIC, and NCUA Share Insurance Fund) *was immediately increased from $40,000 to $100,000.*

4. *State Usury ceilings were overridden for home mortgage and mobile home loans.* The override was to be permanent unless reimposed by individual states within three years. Rate ceilings on business and agricultural loans were temporarily suspended for three years, unless reimposed earlier by the individual state. Federal usury ceilings were scaled by a certain number of percentage points above the discount rate. Usury ceilings for federal credit unions were raised from 12 percent to 15 percent, and the national credit union administration was authorized to raise the ceiling even further.

---

[9]Money market instruments are covered in detail in chapter 4.

[10]Beginning in mid 1978, in response to deposit drains attributed largely to the money market funds, depository institutions were permitted to offer money market certificates

on $10,000 minimum deposits. Interest rates were tied to the six-month Treasury bill rate.

Table 3-3:

Net Income for Thrift Institutions 1970 through Early 1982
($ billions; percentages at annual rates)

Year	FSLIC-Insured Savings and Loan Associations		All Operating Mutual Savings Banks	
	Amount	As a Percentage of Average Assets	Amount	As a Percentage of Average Assets
1970...	0.9	0.57	0.2	0.27
1971...	1.3	0.71	0.4	0.48
1972...	1.7	0.77	0.6	0.60
1973...	1.9	0.76	0.6	0.54
1974...	1.5	0.54	0.4	0.35
1975...	1.4	0.47	0.4	0.38
1976...	2.3	0.63	0.6	0.45
1977...	3.2	0.77	0.8	0.55
1978...	3.9	0.82	0.9	0.58
1979...	3.6	0.67	0.7	0.46
1980...	0.8	0.14	−0.2	−0.12
1981...	−4.6	−0.73	−1.4	−0.83
H1...	−1.5	−0.49	−0.5	−0.56
H2...	−3.1	−0.97	−0.9	−1.10
1982-H1	−3.3	−1.01	−0.8	−0.92

Source: Federal Reserve Bulletin, December 1982, p. 726.

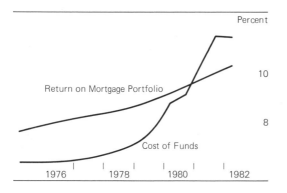

Figure 3–3: Return on mortgage portfolio and cost of funds for insured Savings and loan Associations. (From *Federal Reserve Bulletin,* Dec. 1982, p. 727.)

5. *Access to the Federal Reserve's Discount Window was provided for all depository financial institutions* having transaction accounts and nonpersonal time deposits.

6. *Thrift institutions were given expanded lending powers* and were authorized to invest 20 percent of their assets in consumer loans, commercial paper, and corporate debt securities.

7. *Federal Reserve Services were to be explicitly priced.* Among others, such services include check clearing and collection, wire transfer, and automated clearing house operations.

The thrust of this deregulation and monetary control act was thus to establish a "more level playing field" within the financial sector, to reduce the compartmentalization of depository financial institutions, to allow the monetary authority more control over bank and thrift reserves, and to generally allow greater flexibility within the financial sector.

In accordance with provisions of the act and with decisions of the Depository Institutions Deregulation Committee (DIDC), deregulation commenced. In January 1981, Negotiable Order of Withdrawal (NOW) accounts (transaction accounts which pay interest) became available nationwide and by mid 1982, rate ceilings were removed on certain long-term deposit accounts. But because of continued high market rates, disintermediation continued and money market funds held some $230 billion (about 10 percent of M2) of the nation's funds by early fall 1982. Sizable portions of the financial sector, particularly savings and loan associations and mutual savings banks, remained in jeopardy. Net worth of the savings and loan industry fell by 22 percent between 1980 and 1982 and hundreds of savings and loans were merged (figure 3-4). In the face of this continuing crisis, Congress enacted (October 1982) major legislation to "shore up" savings and loan associations and mutual savings banks. This 1982 act also speeded up

deregulation initiated by the Monetary Control Act of 1980 and generally expanded the deregulatory environment.

The Garn—St Germain Depository Institutions Act of 1982[11]

The Garn—St Germain Act, passed in October, 1982, amended certain sections of the Monetary Control Act of 1980 and provided certain additional powers to depository financial institutions. Important provisions included within this 1982 act were as follows:

1. *Authorized money market deposit accounts (MMDA) for depository financial institutions.* These accounts would be directly competitive with money market mutual funds, were federally insured, were free of interest rate ceilings (with initial and average maintained balances of $2500 or more) and became available 14 December 1982.

2. *Federal, state, and local government were authorized to hold NOW Accounts.* (Previously these accounts were limited to persons and to nongovernment, nonprofit organizations).

3. *Federally chartered savings and loan associations were permitted to offer demand deposits to business and agricultural customers.* (Previously only commercial and mutual savings banks were permitted to accept demand deposits).

4. *Regulation Q-rate differentials were phased out effective 1 January 1984.* (Previously thrifts could pay 0.25 percent above that of commercial banks on most types of deposits.

5. *Federally chartered S&Ls and SBs may make overdraft loans, and importantly, commercial loans.* Authority to make certain other loans and investments was expanded.

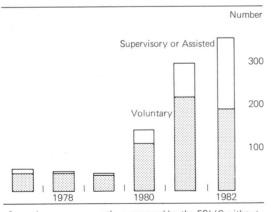

Supervisory mergers are those arranged by the FSLIC without financial assistance.

1982 data are as of September 30.

Figure 3–4: Mergers of FSLIC-insured savings and loan. (From *Federal Reserve Bulletin*, December, 1982, p. 735.)

[11]Discussion in this section relies heavily on Gillian Garcia, et. al., "The Garn—St Germain Depository Institutions Act of 1982," *Economic Perspectives* Federal Reserve Bank of Chicago, (March/April, 1983).

Table 3-4:

**Ratio of Net Worth to Total Assets
at Thrift Institutions Percentage**

Year	FSLIC-Insured Savings and Loans	All Operating Mutual Savings Banks
1975	5.80	6.96
1976	5.58	6.71
1977	5.45	6.77
1978	5.51	6.90
1979	5.58	7.05
1980	5.25	6.63
1981	4.23	5.68
1982[1]...............	3.44	5.34

[1]Data for 1982 are for the end of September.

Source: Federal Reserve Bulletin, December 1982, p. 726.

6. *Thrifts were given wide powers to alter their charters from state to federal and conversely (where state law permits).* They may switch between mutual and stock form and between savings and loan associations and savings bank charters.

7. *State banks and thrifts were empowered to offer variable rate mortgages.* (Federally chartered institutions had been granted this authority previously.)

8. *Regulatory authorities including the FDIC, FSLIC, NCUA were given emergency powers to aid troubled banks and thrifts.* Included in this provision is the authority for regulatory agencies to approve both interstate and interindustry acquisitions and mergers under certain conditions. For example, a banking institution located in New York could acquire a savings and loan association located in Florida.

Passage of the deregulation and Monetary Control Act in 1980 and of the Garn—St Germain Act, resulted in rapid dismantling of the compartmentalization of the financial sector. Many financial institutions expanded their portfolios and moved to take advantage of the new opportunities available to them. New opportunities bring new challenges to the managers of our nation's financial institutions. The old order,

calling for institutional managers to manage narrowly defined portfolios and calling for restrictions that, in many cases, provided strong insulation against competition, is giving way. Managerial implications are substantial. In later pages of this book, as specific financial institutions are examined, much of the discussion will be devoted to development of a conceptual framework designed to set the stage for successful management strategies responsive to deregulation, set in motion and accelerated in the 1980s.

SUMMARY

The United States financial system and its institutions depend on the trust and confidence of the public. As technology, information, and communication systems change, the financial structure must change to meet new needs. Blind adherence to a system based on yesterday's technology and customs will not efficiently and effectively meet today's requirements.

For purposes of analyzing the American financial system, four major historical periods may be identified. The first such period, pre 1913, identifies a time frame where banking functioned as a privately owned, ineffectively regulated industry. The period 1913–1933 witnessed major change in U.S. technology and industrial development. Although the Federal Reserve System had been formed in 1913, the system was largely ineffectual and is believed to have contributed to the financial collapse which occurred in late 1929. The third period, 1933–1980, was one of greater financial stability and of restored confidence in the nation's financial system. Because the financial sector was divided into compartments, it was not sufficiently flexible to respond to innovations brought about by increasingly sophisticated systems of communication and information processing. Also, the system could not satisfactorily respond to high levels of inflation and interest rate. Consequently, a new era was ushered in. This new era was sparked by technological developments and communication improvements, by the increased sophistication of savers in money matters, and by a changing philosophy in government concerning competition within and among industries. Laws were passed in 1980 and 1982 which fundamentally affected the financial sector of the United States, principally through deregulation. Such changes of the 1980s promise new challenges for the managers of today's financial institutions.

QUESTIONS

1. Throughout history, precious metals such as gold or silver have served as money and retained value, while paper money frequently declined in value. Why has this been true?

2. In what way or ways did the First and Second bank of the United States perform functions similar to that of the Federal Reserve System today? In what way or ways was the performance dissimilar?

3. The United States Financial system is based on the trust and confidence of the public. Is it possible for modern economies to have financial systems which are not so based?

4. Identify several defects in the structure of the U.S. financial system that may have contributed to the economic collapse of 1929.

5. By the mid 1930s, some semblance of stability had returned to the United States financial system. How do you explain this return to stability?

6. For the past several decades, the American Financial System has been "compartmentalized." Give examples of such compartmentalization and comment on current trends with regard to compartmentalization of the financial system.

7. Although relatively stable from the mid 1930s to the late 1970s, the American financial system was again threatened as the 1970s drew to a close. How do you account for this condition?

8. Summarize the main features of the major financial legislation discussed in this chapter.

9. From your reading of current newspapers and periodicals, identify new trends or examples of evolutionary change within our financial system today.

SELECTED REFERENCES

Collyns, Charles and Horiguchi, Yusuke. "Financial Supermarkets in The United States." *Finance and Development* 21 (March 1984): 18–22.

Garcia, Gillian, et. al. "The Garn—St Germain Depository Institutions Act of 1982." *Economic Perspectives* 7 (March–April 1983): 3–31.

Kane, Edward J. "Accelerating Inflation, Technological Innovation, and the Decreasing Effectiveness of Banking Regulation." *The Journal of Finance* 36 (May 1981): 355–367.

Reichenstein, William R. and Bonello, Frank S. "Usury Laws Today and Tomorrow." *Issues in Bank Regulation* 7 (Winter 1984): 25–31.

Struck, Peter L. and Mandell, Lewis. "The Effect of Bank Deregulation on Small Business: a Note." *The Journal of Finance* 38 (June 1983): 1025–1031.

Chapter 4

Money Markets

The money and capital markets are similar in that they provide an investment outlet for those with excess funds and a source for those in need of funds. The markets differ with regard to the type of funds involved. As the capital markets deal in long-term securities, they provide a permanent or semi-permanent outlet for funds. The money markets, on the other hand, provide an outlet and source of short-term borrowing; they are primarily liquidity markets.

The money markets are a group of markets in which short-term, generally high-quality credit instruments are bought and sold; money market instruments normally mature in one year or less. Because it is necessary to quickly establish the safety of such an instrument, borrowing within this market is limited to large, safe, well-recognized organizations. Financial institutions, major corporations, and governmental units are the major issuers of money market instruments.

The major securities bought and sold in the money markets include:

1. *Treasury bills*—obligations of the U.S. Treasury with maturities of one year or less.

2. *Agency securities*—obligations of agencies of the United States government.

3. *Commercial paper*—obligations of large, stable corporations and financial institutions. Maturities normally range from a few days to a maximum of 270 days.

4. *Negotiable certificates of deposit*—marketable deposit receipts issued by commercial banks and bearing specified rates of interest for a specified period of time.

5. *Banker's acceptances*—obligations of a firm, guaranteed by a bank. The instruments normally arise through international commerce and carry an average maturity of ninety days.

6. *Federal funds*—loans between commercial banks, typically on an overnight basis.

7. *Repurchase agreement*—sales of securities, normally by a securities dealer, in which the seller agrees to repurchase the same securities within a specified time at a specified price.

8. *Eurodollars*—U.S. dollar denominated deposits held by banks outside the United States, including foreign branches of United States banks.

Each of these instruments as well as other money market instruments will be discussed in greater depth in this chapter.

There is no central physical location which serves as the money market. Separate market structures have developed for each type of instrument and none of these markets have central meeting places. The primary machinery for bringing together borrower and lender (or buyer and seller) consists of approximately forty-six "money market banks" and a handful of specialized dealers and brokers. These "money market banks" include the largest New York banks and banks in other financial centers around the country. There are about twenty government securities dealers, some of which are banks, and about twelve commercial paper dealers. There are also a few banker's acceptances dealers and a number of brokers, such as federal funds brokers. The money markets operate by telephone with brokers and dealers functioning to match supply and demand. The market for each instrument will be discussed in more detail in later parts of this chapter.

The money markets are important because of their volume. In early 1984, the volume of outstanding treasury bills, negotiable certificates of deposit, and commercial paper totalled nearly $3,000 for every person in the United States. Also, the money markets are important because they are a major medium through which the Federal Reserve implements monetary policy. The Federal Reserve increases the money supply by purchasing U.S. government securities and decreases the money supply by reselling these securities.

Many money market instruments do not pay interest directly, but are sold at a *discount*. That is, the instruments are sold at less than their face value with the buyer receiving face value at maturity. Therefore, prices and available returns on money market instruments vary with market conditions and the general level of interest rates. The higher the general level of interest rates, the greater will be the yield necessary for a money market instrument to provide its buyer a competitive rate of return.

Most purchasers of money market instruments are large corporations, institutions, or governmental units. Since most money market transactions involve large volumes of money for short time periods, few individuals have the financial capacity to participate in these markets. The main exception to this generalization involves Treasury bills which are presently sold in denominations as small as $10,000. Even in this market, individual participation is quite small, relative to total volume.

The bulk of this chapter is devoted to a discussion of the various money market instruments—issuers, holders, market, and volume. Final sections of the chapter are devoted to the determinants of interest rates in the money markets and the impact of Federal Reserve policy decisions on these markets.

TREASURY BILLS

The Treasury bill market is the largest single segment of the money market. From the time of their first issue in 1929 until 1984, the volume of Treasury bills outstanding has increased from $100 million to $347 billion. Thus Treasury bills provide an important outlet for temporarily idle funds and an important source of borrowed funds for the United States government. In addition, the trading of Treasury bills in secondary markets is a major tool in the implementation of monetary policy.

A Treasury bill is an obligation of the United States government to pay the bearer a fixed sum at a specified date. Treasury bills are regularly issued in maturities of 91 days, 182 days, and 365 days, with the 182-day or six-month bill representing the largest volume. Treasury bills range in denomination from $10,000 to $1,000,000.

Treasury bills are sold in an auction market with the Federal Reserve System handling the sale on behalf of the Treasury. Treasury bills do not pay interest directly, but are sold at a discount, with the amount of discount being determined by the auction process. The actual interest rate earned depends on the amount of the discount. Suppose, for example, that an average accepted bid for 182-day bills is $94.130 per $100 of face value. The published interest rate is based on the amount of discount and on an assumed 360-day year. The quoted rate (often called the discount interest rate) is

$$\frac{100 - 94.130}{100} \times \frac{360}{182} = 11.611\%.$$

While this method of computing and reporting interest on Treasury bills has become commonplace, it is not comparable to the manner in which the rate is computed for many other instruments. In calculating the yield to maturity on direct interest-bearing issues such as bonds, the denominator is the amount invested rather than the maturity value, and the number of days per year is 365 rather than the 360 used in the above computation. A more accurate measure, called bond-equivalent yield, is

$$\frac{100 - 94.130}{94.130} \times \frac{365}{182} = 12.506\%.$$

Since the former rate is one that is frequently quoted and the latter procedure represents the method of quotation for interest-bearing issues, this difference must be remembered when comparing interest rates.

Treasury bills are auctioned each week by the Treasury department, with bids being collected and tabulated by the Federal Reserve System. Bids for the weekly offering are accepted at Federal Reserve Banks and their branches until 1:30 P.M. (New York time) on Monday. Bids for amounts less than $500,000 may be submitted on a noncompetitive basis. Treasury bills are first allocated to noncompetitive bids. Competitive bids are then accepted in descending order until the week's issue has been fully allocated. Successful bidders pay their bid price, and bills are awarded to noncompetitive bidders at a price equal to the weighted average of accepted bids. Delivery then occurs on Thursday. The average weekly issue is several billion dollars; most of the proceeds go to retire existing issues.

Treasury bills provide an excellent temporary outlet for funds held to meet possible liquidity needs. First, they are considered risk-free because they are obligations of the United States government. Second, there is an active secondary market. Government security dealers continually stand ready with bid and ask prices— prices at which they will buy or sell—for all outstanding issues. The typical spread is four basis points[1] or about 1¢ per $100 of a three-month bill. Third, there is no risk of a large shrinkage if the holder needs to sell Treasury bills quickly to meet liquidity needs. Because of the short maturity, even a large interest rate movement will result in only a relatively small change in the price of a Treasury bill.

As an example of how little value loss is risked, we look at the 182-day Treasury bill used above to see how the interest rate is computed. At the time of issue, that particular bill had a discount interest rate of 11.611 percent and a price of $94.130 per $100 of face value. Normally we would expect the price to rise steadily as the issue gets closer to maturity. However, a rise in the required rate of return or general level of interest rates might prevent this from happening. By the end of thirty days from time of issue, with no change in the quoted interest rate, the price of this issue would rise to 95.098.[2] Suppose, however, that interest rates rise over the thirty-day period to the point that the discount rate is 13 percent, a quite rapid rise in interest rates. The market value would then be 94.511. While this is a small gain over the 94.130 price one month earlier, this price is still above the price originally paid. Thus the chance of a significant loss in market value is quite small.

The identification of holders of Treasury bills is rather difficult, because reporting requirements are such that less than half of total ownership is observed through any kind of reporting requirement. However, it appears that the holders in descending order of importance are the following: Federal Reserve banks, commercial banks, state and local governments, non-financial corporations, and individuals. U.S. government trust funds have been substantial holders but are not at the present time. A substantial volume of holdings is also in the

---

[1]The term "basis point" is a short hand method of describing small fluctuations in interest rates. One hundred basis points represents 1 percent.

[2]$\frac{100 - P}{100} \times \frac{360}{152} = 0.1161; P = 95.098.$

hands of foreign holders, both central banks and others.

The Role of Treasury Bills in Economic Policy

In addition to being the largest of the money markets, the Treasury bill market is important because it is the market through which much of the Federal Reserve's monetary policy is implemented. Increases in the supply of money will generally stimulate economic activity if the economy is operating below capacity. Conversely, decreases in the money supply will decrease the ability of financial institutions to lend money thus decreasing overall demand for goods and services. Through the impact on demand, changes in the money supply also affect the rate of inflation. When the economy is at or near full capacity, an increase in the money supply and a resultant increase in demand will result in an increase in prices. The Federal Reserve System attempts to control the money supply to create a balance that will encourage a healthy, steady rate of economic growth without encouraging inflation.

While there are several ways that the money supply can be controlled, day-to-day control is primarily maintained through the open-market operations of the Federal Reserve. Open-market operations consist of buying or selling U.S. Government securities—primarily Treasury bills. When the Federal Reserve buys Treasury bills, the seller receives payment through credit to his demand deposit account. If the seller is a commercial bank, the payment is in the form of a credit to its account with the Federal Reserve. This is an increase in the bank's reserves and an increase in its ability to loan money. For a non-bank seller, the seller ends up with credit to his demand deposit with his bank; the bank ends up with an increase in its deposit account with the Federal Reserve, again resulting in an increase in its ability to make loans. Conversely, the selling of Treasury bills by the Federal Reserve serves to decrease the money supply. The Federal Reserve buys or sells Treasury bills on a daily basis to change the money supply as needed to encourage stable economic growth and avoid encouraging more inflation. In recent years, the Federal Re-

serve has held between 20 percent and 25 percent of outstanding Treasury bills.

U.S. GOVERNMENT AGENCY SECURITIES

The debt of U.S. government agencies has become increasingly important in the money and capital markets. Debt instruments issued by government agencies can be divided into two groups: those directly guaranteed by the U.S. government and those sponsored but not guaranteed by the government. The principal government guaranteed agency issues include obligations of the Federal Housing Administration (FHA), the Farmers Home Administration, the Government National Mortgage Association (GNMA or "Ginnie-Mae"), the Tennessee Valley Authority (TVA), the Export-Import Bank, and certain obligations of the U.S. Postal Service. The Tennessee Valley Authority and the Export-Import Bank owed $15 billion each at the beginning of 1984. The other guaranteed agencies owed a combined total of only $4 billion, a small volume when compared with the outstanding volume of Treasury bills.

The claims of the federally sponsored agencies represent a larger volume of liabilities. These agencies act primarily as financial intermediaries, raising funds for the purpose of loaning to others. Typically, these agencies were originally owned by the U.S. government, with their stock being later sold to private holders. For example, all of the shares of the Federal Home Loan Banks are now owned by members, primarily savings and loan associations. While most of these agency issues are not directly guaranteed by the U.S. government, many observers believe that the government would come to the rescue of any agency facing default. Thus issues of sponsored agencies are generally considered to be almost as safe as those of guaranteed agencies. Because of their importance, the major sponsored agencies are discussed in more detail in the paragraphs below.

The Federal National Mortgage Association (FNMA or "Fannie Mae") currently represents the largest issuer of nonguaranteed debt. This agency was formed to provide a secondary market for mortgages and issues both short-term and long-term obligations. Thus some of its liabilities qualify as money market instruments. At the beginning of 1984, debt obligations of this agency had expanded to $74 billion.

The Federal Home Loan Bank (FHLB) system was created in part to enhance the flow of credit to the residential housing market. The banks which constitute the system were patterned somewhat after the Federal Reserve System, and were designed to provide a source of liquidity for mortgage lenders (principally savings and loan associations). Funds raised in security markets by the Federal Home Loan Bank System are, in turn, loaned out to member institutions to support mortgage lending activities. The FHLB varies its mixture of long-term and short-term issues in response to market conditions. At the beginning of 1984, FHLB debt outstanding totalled $49 billion.

The *Farm Credit Banks* began issuing bonds on a regular basis in 1979 to replace the separate financing operations of the Federal Land Banks, the Federal Intermediate Term Credit Banks, and the Banks for Cooperatives. The Federal Land Banks make mortgage credit available to farmers while the Federal Intermediate-Term Credit Banks make credit available by purchasing notes from production credit associations. The Banks for Cooperatives were established to encourage the development of farmers' cooperatives for marketing and related purposes. The

total debt of these four agencies was $74 billion at the beginning of 1984.

In addition to these agencies, several smaller agencies owe a total of $10 billion.

Agencies market three specific types of securities: short-term notes (generally discount notes), unsecured bonds, and participation certificates. A participation certificate represents an interest in a pooled group of loans. Rather than selling mortgages to investors, the issuing agency continues to hold the loans and collect payments. The payments are then used to service the participation certificates. Certificates such as these are guaranteed by the federal government and paid from the Treasury if collections from the assets are not sufficient to meet the contractual interest and repayment terms of the certificates.

While agency securities are negotiable and relatively easy to sell, the secondary market for these securities is not as well developed as that for Treasury bills. Thus Treasury bills are more likely to be used for primary liquidity needs. Because of their limited marketability, market interest rates on agency issues are normally a fraction of a percent higher than those for Treasury bills with similar maturities.

Holdings of agency securities are not concentrated in any particular sector. They are fairly well distributed among financial institutions, nonfinancial corporations, state and local governments, and individuals.

To complete this overview, table 4-1 presents

Table 4-1:

Summary of U.S. Government Debt, January, 1984 (in $ billions)

	Short Term	*Intermediate and Long Term*	*Total*
Treasury obligations	$347	$1,089	$1,436
Federal National Mortgage Association			74
Federal Home Loan Bank			49
Farm Credit Banks (and related agencies)			74
Tennessee Valley Authority			15
Export-Import Bank			15
Other			13

Source: Federal Reserve Bulletin.

a summary of the outstanding U.S. government debt.

COMMERCIAL PAPER

The commercial paper market is a uniquely American institution. Canada is the only other country with a commercial paper market of any significance and its market is relatively small. Commercial paper is a short-term unsecured promissory note issued by a corporation with a well-known, impeccable credit rating. Maturities range from a few days to 270 days. Most issuers back their commercial paper by maintaining unused bank lines of credit equal to or approaching the amount of commercial paper outstanding.

Commercial paper has advantages for both issuer and purchaser. For the issuer, the commercial paper rate is normally below the prime rate—the interest rate charged by banks to their best commercial customers. In some recent years, the commercial paper rate has been more than a full percentage point below the prime rate. From the buyer's point of view, commercial paper offers a return above the rate earned on alternate securities such as Treasury bills with only a small amount of additional risk.

Because of its advantages to both buyer and seller, the commercial paper market has grown rapidly since its inception by General Motors Acceptance Corporation in 1920. The amount of commercial paper outstanding reached $5 billion in 1960, $40 billion in 1970, and $185 billion by the beginning of 1984.

Like Treasury bills, the vast majority of commercial paper is sold at a discount and redeemed at face value. The computation used in publishing interest rates is the same as that used for Treasury bills.

Only about 600 firms issue commercial paper, with about two dozen finance companies accounting for approximately half the total. In addition to finance companies, other issuers are bank affiliates and large nonfinancial corporations, especially utilities. This limited number of issuers reflects the nature of the security involved. Purchase of a short-term unsecured obligation cannot realistically be preceded by a lengthy credit investigation if the transaction is to be profitable. This makes it essential that companies issuing commercial paper have well known, impeccable credit ratings.[3]

Commercial paper is sold either directly to lenders (direct placement) or through commercial paper dealers. About 55 percent of the commercial paper is placed directly with almost all directly placed paper being issued by finance companies. The remainder of the commercial paper is sold through dealers. There are about six major dealers in the United States with all but one being New York investment banking houses. The dealers earn their fee in the form of a spread between the price they pay and the price they sell the issue for. The minimum spread amounts to ⅛ of one percent per annum.

The secondary market for commercial paper is quite restricted. Most commercial paper is held to maturity by its original purchaser. However, many direct issuers have "gentlemen's agreements" that they will buy back the paper before maturity (and adjust the interest rate) if the lender suffers severe liquidity problems. The borrowers can do this because they are continually in the commercial paper market in the same way banks continually accept deposits and because they have back–up lines of credit with commercial banks.

Of the $185 billion of commercial paper outstanding at the beginning of 1984, $138 billion was issued by financial institutions and $47 billion was issued by nonfinancial corporations. Primary holders are banks, non-financial corporations, insurance companies, trust funds, and pension funds.

Despite the fact that commercial paper markets have generally not developed in other countries, this type of market has been very useful in meeting the needs of United States borrowers

---

[3]This is not to say that commercial paper has been default free. The commercial paper market was taken by surprise when Penn Central defaulted on its commercial paper in 1970.

and lenders as attested by the significant growth and development of this instrument. With the volume in this market more than doubling in the past decade, it appears to be a stable factor in the country's financial structure.

NEGOTIABLE CERTIFICATES OF DEPOSIT

The market for negotiable certificates of deposit (CDs) is the newest of the large money markets. It began in 1961 when First National City Bank of New York issued the first negotiable certificates of deposit and a government securities dealer agreed to make a second market in them. The outstanding amount was $92 billion in early 1984; negotiable CDs now compete with commercial paper as a top volume money market instrument.

A certificate of deposit is a receipt for a bank deposit with a specified maturity and bearing a specified interest rate. This type of deposit has been around since at least the beginning of this century. It was the conversion to a negotiable (saleable) form and the development of a secondary market that made these instruments important ones in money markets. Negotiable CDs can be sold with a fixed maturity which guarantees the issuing institution funds for that period of time; they can be sold in the secondary market if necessary which provides liquidity to the holders.

Negotiable CDs differ from Treasury bills and commercial paper in that they bear interest payable at maturity rather than being issued at a discount. Further, interest is based on a 365-day year rather than a 360-day year, as is the case with Treasury bills and commercial paper. Because of these computational differences, quoted rates are not strictly comparable. For purposes of rate comparability, the Treasury bill or commercial paper rate discount interest rate must be recomputed to a bond equivalent yield.

Negotiable CDs are insured only up to Federal Deposit Insurance Corporation limits (currently $100,000). Thus the quality of the bank issuing the CDs is a matter of concern. The largest money market banks are normally able to issue their CDs at ⅛ to ½ percentage point below those issued by smaller regional banks. In addition, secondary markets for CDs issued by smaller banks tend to be less active than those for the large, well–known banks. Some corporations divide temporarily idle funds among several different types of money market instruments—Treasury bills, negotiable CDs of major money market banks, and negotiable CDs of smaller banks—thereby providing different levels of liquidity.

Negotiable CDs also differ from other bank deposits in that certificates of deposit in excess of $100,000 denominations are currently not subject to the Federal Reserve regulations which establish ceiling interest rates that institutions may pay on certain deposits. When banks first began issuing negotiable CDs, maximum interest rates were established by regulation. The result was that during periods of tight money (such as those which existed in 1966 and 1969) banks could not offer CD rates competitive with those available on competing money market instruments. The volume of outstanding CDs declined and the ability of commercial banks to compete for funds was threatened. In 1970 regulations were removed for shorter term large denomination CDs and in 1973 they were removed for all CDs of $100,000 or more. Thus today's rates are set entirely by market conditions. The removal of rate ceilings has resulted in greater stability in terms of the ability of banks to issue new CDs. However, wide swings in CD volume and rates may be observed as banks' needs for funds and lending opportunities change.

The buyers of negotiable CDs are primarily nonfinancial corporations. Indeed, negotiable CDs came into existence as a means of competing for corporate deposits that were leaving the banks in search of more attractive outlets for temporarily idle funds. CD holders frequently meet day-to-day liquidity needs by adjusting Treasury bill balances while holding negotiable CDs as a secondary reserve asset. Thus secondary market volume in CDs is considerably less than that for Treasury bills.

As previously indicated, the main issuers of negotiable CDs are large money market banks. The majority of the issues are by banks with assets in excess of $1 billion. Approximately 40 percent of the total volume originates with large New York banks. These banks tend to have substantial loan commitments and enjoy the credit and reputations which facilitate sale of large CDs.

The negotiable CD market is an excellent example of the manner in which financial institutions and instruments evolve to meet economic needs. Negotiable CDs were originated in response to a need to compete for corporate deposits that were being lost to other money market instruments. Legislation and regulation gradually changed in response to market needs. Within a relatively few years, this new instrument rose to challenge commercial paper as the second largest volume money market instrument.

BANKER'S ACCEPTANCES

One of the oldest of money market instruments, banker's acceptances, came into existence primarily through foreign trade. These acceptances provide an alternative to open account credit, primarily when goods are to be shipped across national borders. As banker's acceptances are negotiable, they are money market instruments. They have grown in importance with the growth in foreign trade; their volume outstanding at the beginning of 1984 equalled $78 billion.

To understand this somewhat confusing credit instrument, we begin with an example of an American firm wishing to purchase overseas goods for import. The buyer secures a letter of credit for the order from a well–known American bank, authorizing the seller of the goods to write a draft on the buyer's bank upon shipment of the goods. The draft instructs the bank to pay a specified amount on a specific date.

The seller has two alternatives: one is holding the draft until the date specified for payment; the second, attaching the shipping documents to the draft as evidence of shipment and selling the draft to his bank at a discount from face value. If the second alternative is taken, the seller's bank then forwards the draft and shipping documents to its American correspondent, which, in turn, presents them to the buyer's bank. The buyer's bank examines and removes the shipping documents and stamps the draft "I accept," making it a negotiable instrument guaranteed by the buyer's bank. The draft is now the obligation of both the buyer's bank and the seller. Because of these obligations, they are considered nearly as safe as Treasury bills.

Once the draft has been accepted, a number of things can happen to it. Since the seller's bank bought the draft at a discount, it may simply instruct its correspondent to hold the draft until maturity as an investment, or it may instruct the correspondent to sell the draft immediately. In this case, it may be sold to the buyer's bank or in the market. Thus this accepted draft or banker's acceptance serves as a money market instrument.

This example involves a foreign seller and a United States buyer. Of course, the whole process can be reversed, with the foreign buyer's bank acceptance or guarantee of the draft. Although the greatest growth has been in support of foreign trade, banker's acceptances can also be used as a method of financing domestic trade.

Maturities of banker's acceptances range from 30 to 180 days with 90 being the most common. From the accepting bank's point of view, this procedure represents an attractive means of helping customers with their short-term credit needs. If the accepting bank does not hold the acceptance itself, it is making credit available by lending its name rather than its money. If the accepting bank holds the acceptance itself, it is effectively lending the buyer the amount of the acceptance. However, the acceptance is recorded on the bank's financial statements as a secondary reserve asset rather than as a loan.

Banker's acceptances have not experienced as active a secondary market as have most of the other money market instruments previously discussed. Accepting banks hold about one fourth of all outstanding banker's acceptances and foreign financial institutions hold some 60 percent. The remainder are held by domestic owners and by Federal Reserve banks. The secondary market is made up mostly of a few government security dealers that make a market in these securities. One reason acceptances are attractive short-term dollar investments for foreigners is that they are not subject to American income taxes as is the interest on Treasury bills.

FEDERAL FUNDS

The federal funds (fed funds) market arises from the requirement that commercial banks[4] hold certain levels of liquid reserves, primarily in the form of deposits with their federal reserve banks. A bank with excess reserves can lend these reserves to a bank with insufficient reserves. The lending bank instructs its Federal Reserve Bank via check or wire to transfer ownership of part of its deposit to the borrowing bank. As these loans are almost entirely overnight,[5] the borrowing bank sends an order the next day transferring ownership back to the lending bank.

Although the fed funds market is almost entirely restricted to overnight loans, it is still profitable for a bank with excess reserves to make such loans. The denominations are large; transactions are normally in multiples of $1 million. At an effective annual interest rate of 12 percent, the interest on an overnight loan of $5 million would be in excess of $1,600. Thus it is worth the bank's trouble to make an overnight loan if it has excess reserves. From the borrower's point of view, borrowing in the fed funds market avoids the necessity of less desirable alternatives

such as turning down loan applications or selling marketable securities.

Growth of the fed funds market was stimulated over the past two decades by general increases in the level of interest rates and the resultant opportunity cost associated with idle bank funds. While any particular bank could be a net seller (lender) of funds or a net buyer (borrower), large banks as a group tend to be net buyers; small banks generally, net sellers. While the fed funds market has traditionally served as a means for participating banks to balance reserve requirements, many of the nation's larger banks have been involved as consistent net borrowers that on a daily basis rely on this source of funds.

Federal funds transactions occur primarily on an unsecured basis, because collateral is troublesome for such short-term loans. When security is required, the borrower is typically a smaller bank and U.S. government securities are placed in a special custody account for the one-day period.

The federal funds market, like all markets, depends on some method of bringing buyer and seller together. The role of market maker falls primarily on certain large New York banks because they tend to be net buyers (borrowers) of funds and because most banks throughout the nation maintain a correspondent relationship with a New York bank. Normally the New York banks are willing to borrow the funds themselves and have knowledge of who needs funds. Other banks, a few stock exchange firms, and some institutional money brokers also act as brokers, collecting information on who has excess federal funds and who needs funds. The federal funds market differs from the money markets previously discussed in that the market makers primarily act as brokers, bringing borrower and lender together. For the other money market instruments, market makers act as dealers, actually purchasing and reselling securities. The federal funds market also differs from other money markets in that direct participation is limited to banks and financial institutions with deposits at the federal reserve banks.

Market rates for federal funds are particularly volatile; they react to short-term shifts in supply

---

[4]With the Depository Institutions Deregulation and Monetary Control Act of 1980, other institutions having transaction accounts are being brought under these reserve requirements over a period of several years. Thus they may become participants in this market.

[5]Federal funds transactions occurring on Friday are "three-day" transactions because transactions are not conducted on weekends.

and demand conditions. Banks must adjust their position quickly to meet reserve requirements. In periods of tight money, these adjustments can result in rapid shifts in federal funds rates. Furthermore, a tendency for some banks to look to the federal funds market as a more or less permanent method of meeting funds requirements has caused demand to be heavy and rates to be high during periods of tight money. Conversely, demand and interest rates can fall sharply in recessionary periods. The federal funds rate is closely watched by the monetary authorities as a barometer of supply and demand for bank credit.

Volume in the federal funds market is a bit difficult to measure because banks report federal funds and repurchase agreements in combined form. In early 1984, the sum of these two types of borrowing outstanding on the books of commercial banks was more than $60 billion.

REPURCHASE AGREEMENTS

Repurchase agreements (RPs) are defined as the sale of securities concurrent with an agreement to repurchase them at a later date. The arrangement may call for repurchase at a specific date for a specific price, or it may be open ended with either party able to end the arrangement at any time. In the latter case, the lender would be guaranteed a fixed return per day over the time the agreement remained in effect. Maturities of repurchase agreements range from one day to several months.

While any two parties may enter into a repurchase agreement, this arrangement has served primarily as a method of financing for U.S. government securities dealers. With the growth in U.S. government debt, dealers in U.S. government securities require extremely large sums of money to finance their inventories of securities. These dealers rely primarily on credit, maintaining debt to total asset ratios of 98 percent or more. They meet their financing needs through borrowing and repurchase agreements.

Because U.S. government securities dealers hold billions of dollars in inventories, their need for funds is quite large, and a major part of their daily activity consists of arranging financing at the lowest possible cost. Financing is achieved through direct borrowing, with the securities serving as collateral and through repurchase agreements.

Lenders (purchasers) include New York banks, regional banks, and other institutions, including nonfinancial corporations. Most dealers begin their day by seeking funds from sources located outside New York, as New York rates tend to be slightly higher. Later in the day they complete the financing of their daily needs through the New York banks. Several New York banks post daily rates at which they will meet the dealer financing of any desired volume of government securities. This posted rate varies from one New York bank to another, depending on how eager each bank is to make additional loans.

Since the dealers are in permanent need of funds, they can tailor maturities to the needs of a particular supplier of funds. Thus corporations view dealer loans and RPs as a flexible method of placing temporarily excess funds. Some funds suppliers prefer direct loans; others prefer repurchase agreements. Repurchase agreements are most likely to be employed when funds are to be advanced for more than a few days. The expense of transferring title for very short periods does not make such transfer economical.

The repurchase agreement market is also an important medium for exercise of short-term money supply control by the Federal Reserve. When there is a temporary need for additional funds in the system, the Federal Reserve can buy U.S. government securities under repurchase agreement. The Federal Reserve is assured that there is a specific date when this agreement will end and the supply of funds to the market can be withdrawn. A reverse RP is also used on occasion. In this case, the Federal Reserve sells security under repurchase agreements to temporarily decrease the money supply.

EURODOLLARS

The Eurodollar market is another relatively young market whose development as an active market can be traced to the late 1950s.

Eurodollars are U.S. dollar-denominated deposits held by banks outside the United States, including foreign branches of domestic banks. They represent an important source of funds for businesses and an important market in which banks adjust liquidity.

To come to grips with the operations of the Eurodollar market, we will follow an example of the development and transfer of Eurodollars.

A German exporting company has received payment in U.S. dollars and presently holds a demand deposit with Citibank in New York. Because the company expects to need dollars in the future, it converts its asset by making a dollar-denominated time deposit with a German bank; the German bank receives ownership of the Citibank demand deposit as an offsetting asset. Thus, Eurodollars have been created.

The German bank has received a number of other dollar-denominated time deposits as well, and is paying interest on these time deposits while receiving no interest on its offsetting dollar-denominated demand deposit assets. It will wish to turn these demand deposits to some profitable use.

The German bank may have a customer in need of a dollar-denominated loan. If not, it will lend the demand deposit to another bank, which in turn lends it to a customer. A United States bank continues to have the same demand deposit liability, but ownership of this deposit may change many times.

Like the other money markets, the Eurodollar market has no physical location; it is based on wire communications. However, the center of activity is London, and the London Interbank Loan Rate (LIBOR) is considered the primary "market" rate. Like the federal funds market, the Eurodollar market is primarily an interbank market; banks have deposits from and loans to their customers. Similar markets exist for other major currencies; London is the center for all currencies except the pound.

A particularly important aspect of the Eurodollar market with regard to the domestic money market is the practice by American banks of borrowing from their foreign affiliates in periods of tight money. The foreign affiliates can borrow Eurodollars in the same way that federal funds or

some other short-term credit instrument can be used. The affiliate then deposits the funds with the parent American bank, thereby increasing the parent's reserves of loanable funds. As a foreign borrower, the affiliate (foreign branch) is free of restrictions on the interest rate paid for the Eurodollar deposit; thus, the affiliate is provided an avenue for circumventing interest rate regulation.

Reliable statistics on the Eurodollar market are extremely limited. However, it appears that total volume (net of transactions between banks) is probably in the neighborhood of $800 billion. The Eurodollar market is discussed in more detail in chapter 15.

INTEREST RATES IN THE MONEY MARKETS

The general level of interest rates in the money markets moves with the overall credit markets.[6] Interest rate differentials between money market instruments depend on risk, marketability, and supply or demand conditions in particular submarkets. Among generally available instruments, Treasury bills display the greatest marketability and the lowest risk. Thus, they normally carry the lowest interest rates. Agency securities normally follow, with similar risk but less marketability. Following U.S. government obligations, commercial paper, negotiable certificates of deposit, and banker's acceptances fall close together and are typically grouped at a rate $\frac{1}{4}$ to $\frac{1}{2}$ percent above Treasury bill rates. Their individual rankings change from time to time because they are close together in yield and because market conditions continually change.

Federal funds represent a special submarket. While rates are not divorced from those in other markets, they do respond to a special set of supply and demand conditions, since they represent the method banks use to adjust their overnight reserve positions. In a recession the federal

---

[6]See chapter 7 for a discussion of general levels of interest rates.

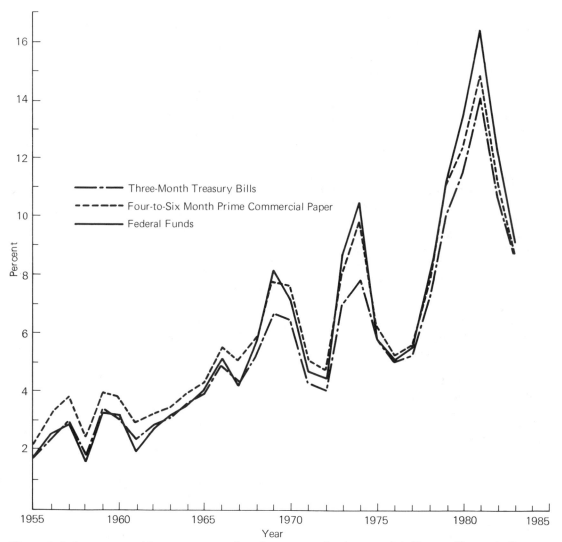

Figure 4–1: Average annual interest rates on selected money market instruments. (Source: *Economic Report of the President, Federal Reserve Bulletin.*)

funds rate will normally lie below all other domestic money market rates. Toward the end of the expansion phase of the business cycle, federal funds typically carry rates above those associated with other domestic money market instruments.

The Eurodollar market represents another special case. Eurodollar rates depend on a host of factors: perceived strength of the dollar, financial conditions in other countries and balance of payment considerations. In recent years the Eurodollar rate has been consistently above domestic interest rates.

A history of interest rate movements for money market instruments and an illustration of the factors discussed in the above paragraphs is

Table 4-2:

Major Money Market Instruments

Instrument	Issuer (Borrower)	Volume*
Treasury bills	U.S. government	$347 bil
Agency securities	U.S. government agencies	240 bil**
Commercial paper	Large finance companies and nonfinancial corporations	185 bil
Negotiable CDs	Large commercial banks	92 bil
Banker's acceptances	Corporations, normally importers (with the guarantee of a bank)	78 bil
Repurchase agreements	U.S. government security dealers	
Federal funds	Commercial banks	61 bil
Eurodollars	They represent liabilities of major banks	800 bil

*Volumes change substantially with economic and money market conditions.

**Including long-term issues.

provided in figure 4-1. This figure illustrates the long-term trend toward higher interest rates that has been associated with increased inflation. While the recent rates seem high, there is no assurance that they have reached a peak.

SUMMARY

The money markets are actually a series of distinct markets in which specific financial instruments are traded. In addition to being regular sources of funds for certain sectors, the money markets provide a medium for liquidity adjustment. The major money market instruments are summarized in table 4-2.

QUESTIONS

1. How could an individual with $10,000 to invest go about purchasing a Treasury bill?

2. Using the *Federal Reserve Bulletin,* find the yields for various money market instruments of three-month and six-month maturity. How do you explain the differences between rates?

3. Why does the Federal Reserve System itself hold large quantities of Treasury bills?

4. Where is the secondary market for Treasury bills located?

5. If a decision is made to increase the money supply, what agency acts? How does the agency act with regard to Treasury bills?

6. What is the primary purpose for which federally sponsored agencies borrow and re-lend money?

7. Why would a company issue commercial paper instead of using bank borrowing?

8. Why would issuers of commercial paper maintain back-up lines of credit with banks?

9. What types of companies are the primary borrowers of funds through the commercial paper market?

10. Why would the regulatory authorities remove interest rate restrictions on large bank deposits (in the form of large denomination certificates of deposit) while maintaining regulation Q ceilings for smaller deposits?

11. For a bank that is "loaned up" and still wants to help a loan customer, what is the advantage of a banker's acceptance?

12. Why are Federal funds rates among the most volatile of money market rates?

PROBLEMS

1. A bid of 97.270 is accepted on three-month Treasury bills. What discount interest rate would be published?

2. For the above Treasury bill, restate the annual interest rate in a way that would make it comparable to rates quoted on bonds (bond equivalent yield).

3. For the Treasury bill in problem 1, assume that the discount interest rate has risen to 12 percent thirty days after issue. What price will the Treasury bills be selling at? What annual rate would the holder have earned if he bought the Treasury bill when it was first issued and resold after thirty days?

4. At a 14 percent federal funds rate, what would be the dollar interest on a three-day (week-end) loan of $10 million in the federal funds market?

5. A 91-day negotiable certificate of deposit is quoted at annual interest rate of 13.8 percent and 91-day Treasury bills are quoted at 14.2 percent discount interest rate. Restate these rates on a comparable basis.

SELECTED REFERENCES

Cook, Timothy Q. ed. *Instruments of the Money Market*. Richmond, Virginia: Federal Reserve Bank of Richmond, 1977.

Fildes, Robert A., and Fitzgerald, M. Desmond. "Efficiency and Premiums in the Short-term Money Market." *Journal of Money, Credit and Banking* 12 (November 1980): 615–629.

James, John A. *Money and Capital Markets in Postbellum America*. Princeton, New Jersey: Princeton University Press, 1978.

Money Market Instruments. Cleveland, Ohio: Federal Reserve Bank of Cleveland, 1970.

Puglisi, Donald J. "Commercial Paper: A Primer." *Federal Home Loan Bank Board Journal* 13 (December 1980): pp. 5–10.

Senchak, Andrew J., Jr., and Heep, Donald M. "Auction Profits in the Treasury Bill Market." *Financial Management* 4 (Summer 1975): 53–62.

Chapter 5

Capital Markets

The capital markets are normally thought of as the markets in which long–term securities, both debt and equity, are bought and sold. The securities involved are corporate stock and bonds; federal, state, and local government bonds and notes; and marketable mortgages. A broader definition would include direct loans, but such a definition is not used here as those aspects of the financial system are covered in other parts of this book. While the money markets are primarily liquidity adjustment markets, the capital markets are primarily markets for long–term funds to meet permanent or semipermanent needs.

Risk is an important factor in the capital markets. Money market instruments are nearly risk–free with regard to default; they involve minimal risks of price fluctuation due to their short–term maturities; yet, both types of risk are frequently present in capital market securities. With the exception of U.S. government securities, all capital market instruments involve some risk of default. Even among those with no risk of default, there is still a substantial risk of price fluctuation with changes in the general level of interest rates. For example, a $1,000 bond with a 6 percent annual interest payment and twenty years to

maturity would decline in market value to $657 if the level of required interest rate for this type of security rose to 10 percent.[1]

Because corporations and government units meet a major portion of their external financing needs in the capital markets, the smooth functioning of these markets is important for both. Because financial institutions hold the majority of all capital market securities, the financial institution manager should have a good understanding of the capital markets. In this chapter, we discuss significant aspects of the capital markets: types of securities, the markets in which they are bought and sold, the users of funds, and the suppliers of funds.

CORPORATE SECURITIES

In addition to private sources of credit such as trade credit and bank loans, corporations rely heavily on the capital markets to meet their needs for capital. They acquire funds by selling bonds and shares in ownership of their business

---

[1]The mathematics of value are discussed in chapters 6 and 7.

(stock). For larger firms, both bonds and stock enjoy active primary and secondary markets. Financial institutions furnish a significant amount of funds to corporations through the purchase of these securities, particularly bonds.

Stock

Stock represents ownership of a corporation. It is sold by corporations at the time of formation and when they need additional equity capital for expansion. It is also regularly resold by investors who need funds or who wish to adjust their investment portfolios. Stock comes in two primary varieties, common and preferred; common stock represents the largest volume.

Common Stock represents residual ownership. The common shareholders own the corporation similar to the way a group of partners would own a business not organized as a corporation. Unlike most other securities, common stock does not promise any particular return to its purchaser. All earnings not specifically owed to others are used for the benefit of the common shareholders, either paid out as dividends or reinvested with the hope of achieving even greater dividends in the future.

Since common shareholders are not promised a specific return, they must have some method of exercising control over the company to enforce their claim. The primary method of exercising control is through the election of a board of directors, who in turn elect the top management of the corporation. In a sense the common shareholders exercise control over the corporation in the same manner citizens of a democracy exercise control over government. In addition to the right to vote for a board of directors, the common shareholders have certain other rights:

1. the right to receive dividends, when voted by the directors;

2. the right to examine the books of the corporation;[2]

3. the right to vote on mergers;

4. the preemptive right—the right to be given the opportunity to buy a proportion of any new equity issue equal to the proportion of existing equity presently held;

5. the right to a list of fellow shareholders.

Thus the common shareholders, unlike creditors, are promised no fixed return but enjoy residual claims and exercise control over the corporation.

Preferred Stock is an intermediate security with some features of debt and some features of common stock. Typically, preferred stock carries a stated dividend rate, but this dividend is not a legal requirement and is paid only if voted each period by the board of directors. Thus preferred shareholders expect a fixed return but cannot force the company to pay the dividend. Usually their interest is protected in two ways. First, most preferred stock is cumulative, meaning that dividends cannot be paid on common stock until dividends not paid to preferred stockholders during previous periods are paid. Second, preferred stockholders generally have the right to elect a minority of the board of directors if dividends have not been paid for a specific number of quarters. While the pressure that can be applied by preferred shareholders is less than that which can be brought by creditors, it is usually sufficient to assure dividends except in times of hardship. Insurance companies are major purchasers of preferred stock because 85 percent of the dividends received by a corporation are normally excluded from taxable income.

The value of new stock sold is much smaller than the value of new bonds (table 5-1). However, the total amount of stock outstanding is several times the amount of bonds. The smaller value of new equity occurs because retained earnings are an important source of equity and because stock does not have a maturity date at which it must be refunded. Furthermore, some debt is convertible to common stock, resulting in a further decrease in the amount of new stock that must be sold to increase the equity base.

Stock is primarily held by individuals (table 5-2). More than two-thirds of all common stock is held by individuals; insurance companies and

---

[2]The courts have normally ruled that a copy of the annual report satisfies this right.

Table 5-1:

Primary Market Volume, 1982 (in $ billions)

	Volume of Issues	Net Increase in Amount Outstanding
Corporate securities		
Bonds	$54	$19
Stocks	31	17
U.S. Government securities		
Bills	629 ⎫	
Bonds and notes	302 ⎭	189
State and municipal	79	36
Mortgages	n.a.	83

Source: Federal Reserve Bulletin, Treasury Bulletin.

pension funds hold most of the rest. Most depository financial institutions hold little or no stock because the residual ownership nature causes it to be excessively risky for their portfolios.

Corporate Bonds

Bonds are marketable debt instruments of corporations. They are long–term promissory notes, normally with maturities between five years and thirty years, normally issued in denominations of $1,000. Bonds represent a major source of external capital to American corporations.

There are two primary documents involved with a bond: the *bond certificate and the indenture*. The bond certificate is the evidence of ownership of the particular claim and states a limited amount of information. For example, the bond certificate states when and how interest and

Table 5-2:

Amounts of Outstanding Securities by Type and Owner, 1982 (in $ billions)

	Issuer				
Holder	Corporate & Foreign Bonds	Corporate Stock	U.S. Government Securities	State & Local Government Securities	Mortgages*
Total	570.6	1,811.7	1372.7	449.4	1,652.1
Households	73.5	1,306.2	360.6	155.3	186.9
Nonfinancial business	—	—	13.0	3.5	—
State & local governments	—	—	124.1	—	45.9
Monetary authority	—	—	148.8	—	—
Commercial banks	9.2	0.1	211.7	158.6	301.7
Nonbank finance	446.5	427.1	361.5	124.5	763.0
Other	41.4	78.3	153.1	7.5	354.6

*Including marketable and nonmarketable mortgages. $302 billion of the mortgage debt is for commercial property, $107 billion is for farms, and the remainder is for residential property.

Source: Board of Governors of the Federal Reserve System.

principal are to be paid. The certificate may be in either registered or coupon form; the registered form is more common. With the registered form, the corporation has a record of who owns each bond and mails interest payments to the bondholder at the times specified, typically semi-annually. Whereas, with the coupon form, a coupon must be cut from the bond and then turned in to the corporation or a financial institution such as a commercial bank that handles coupons as a customer service. Of course, the risk of loss is greater with the coupon form since interest is paid to whoever has the coupon.

The indenture is a lengthy document which often runs to hundreds of pages. It not only specifies the details of the agreement between borrower and lender, but also covers provisions for retiring the issue. Moreover, it contains a detailed description of pledged assets, identifies the trustees, and enumerates the responsibilities of the trustee. In addition to other related matters, it contains a set of restrictive covenants. Examples of such restrictive covenants include; restrictions on the issuance of additional debt, restrictions on the sale of assets, and requirements that a particular level of liquidity be maintained. While the indenture represents an agreement between the company and the lenders, it is not an agreement reached through negotiations with them. The indenture is prepared before the bonds are issued and contains the provisions that are felt to be necessary to successfully sell the issue. The trustee, normally a bank or trust company, acts as the representative of the bondholders in enforcing the provisions of the indenture.

Bonds differ with regard to a number of features. One such feature is *callability*. The company frequently retains the right to retire the bonds before maturity by repurchasing them from the holders. Such a provision is usually seen as important to the issuing company because it gives the flexibility to change the financial structure as necessary. If a bond is callable, the call price that must be paid by the company is normally higher than the face value of the bond by a premium equal to between six months' interest and one year's interest. Thus, bondholders

receive some compensation in the event of early retirement.

Bonds also differ with regard to security offered. A *debenture* is a bond that is secured only by the general good name of the company. Because many debentures are issued by the more credit–worthy companies, the default rate is frequently lower than on bonds secured by the pledge of specific assets. Pledging generally takes one of two forms. The mortgage bond is based on the pledge of specific real assets—land and buildings—as collateral. Equipment trust certificates are based on the pledge of equipment such as railroad cars rather than on land or buildings.

Convertibility is another important feature of many bond issues. A convertible bond can be exchanged for a fixed number of shares of common stock at the option of the bondholder. This feature gives the bondholder the potential for a capital gain if the value of the company's stock rises while still offering the contractual payment of a bond. It is used either as a ''sweetener'' to sell a risky bond issue or as a sequential method of financing for a company constantly in need of funds. As one issue is converted, it provides the equity base for a new debt issue.

Repayment of bonds can take one of several forms; a sinking fund is a common method. With a sinking fund provision, the indenture calls for annual payments to a sinking fund managed by the trustee. Depending on the conditions specified in the indenture, payments are invested in safe securities to accumulate funds for repayment at maturity or used to purchase a certain amount of the issue each year and retire it. If part of the issue is to be retired each year, it will be purchased in the open market if the market price is below the call price; it will be called if the market price is over the call price.

Alternatives to the sinking fund arrangement include a balloon arrangement and serial bonds. Under a *balloon arrangement,* a large portion or all of the issue is repaid at maturity. In such cases, the company frequently issues new debt to retire existing debt. In the case of a *serial issue,* different bonds in the issue have different maturity dates so that the issue is systematically retired over its life. This has an advantage over the use of the call provision in that the buyer knows how long the bonds will be outstanding.

Bonds also differ with regard to risk, which in turn depends on the credit worthiness of the company issuing them and the quality of collateral provided. Investment advisory services (Moody's Corporation and Standard and Poor's Corporation are the best known) rate them according to risk (table 5-3). Interest rates are

---

Table 5-3:

Key to Moody's Corporate Ratings

Aaa

Bonds which are rated Aaa are judged to be of the best quality. They carry the smallest degree of investment risk and are generally referred to as "gilt edge." Interest payments are protected by a large or by an exceptionally stable margin and principal is secure. While the various protective elements are likely to change, such changes as can be visualized are most unlikely to impair the fundamentally strong position of such issues.

Aa

Bonds which are rated Aa are judged to be of high quality by all standards. Together with the Aaa group they comprise what are generally known as high grade bonds. They are rated lower than the best bonds because margins of protection may not be as large as in Aaa securities or fluctuation of protective elements may be of greater amplitude or there may be other elements present which make the long term risks appear somewhat larger than in Aaa securities.

A

Bonds which are rated A possess many favorable investment attributes and are to be considered as upper medium grade obligations. Factors giving security to principal and interest are considered adequate but elements may be present which suggest a susceptibility to impairment sometime in the future.

Baa

Bonds which are rated Baa are considered as medium grade obligations, i.e., they are neither highly protected nor poorly secured. Interest payments and principal security appear adequate for the present but certain protective elements may be lacking or may be characteristically unreliable over any great length of time. Such bonds lack outstanding investment characteristics and in fact have speculative characteristics as well.

Ba

Bonds which are rated Ba are judged to have speculative elements; their future cannot be considered as well assured. Often the protection of interest and principal payments may be very moderate and thereby not well safeguarded during both good and bad times over the future. Uncertainty of position characterizes bonds in this class.

B

Bonds which are rated B generally lack characteristics of the desirable investment. Assurance of interest and principal payments or of maintenance of other terms of the contract over any long period of time may be small.

Caa

Bonds which are rated Caa are of poor standing. Such issues may be in default or there may be present elements of danger with respect to principal or interest.

Ca

Bonds which are rated Ca represent obligations which are speculative in a high degree. Such issues are often in default or have other marked shortcomings.

C

Bonds which are rated C are the lowest rated class of bonds and issues so rated can be regarded as having extremely poor prospects of ever attaining any real investment standing.

Note: Moody's applies numerical modifiers, 1, 2 and 3 in each generic rating classification from Aa through B in its corporate bond rating system. The modifier 1 indicates that the security ranks in the higher end of its generic rating category; the modifier 2 indicates a mid-range ranking; and the modifier 3 indicates that the issue ranks in the lower end of its generic rating category.

Source: *Moody's Bond Record*

affected by rating; the lower ratings carry higher interest rates as compensation for risk. A bond with a Moody's Baa rating will typically carry an interest rate from one to two percentage points above that for a bond with a Aaa rating. (A detailed discussion of these interest rate differentials can be found in chapter 7.)

When a company borrows by selling its bonds, the bonds are normally sold through an investment banker. Purchasers of the bonds who later wish to sell them turn to the secondary markets consisting of both the organized exchanges and the over-the-counter market. The operations of both of these markets are covered in some detail in the following sections of this chapter.

Corporations in virtually every industry category finance part of their operations through bonds. However, the market is restricted to relatively large companies. Fixed administrative costs are such as to rule out small bond issues. On a small bond issue of under $1 million, the cost of issuance can run as high as 20 percent while issue costs can fall to 1 percent or less for an issue of several hundred million dollars.

While individuals do hold corporate bonds as investments, the majority of bonds are held as investments by financial institutions. Only about one sixth of all corporate bonds are held by individuals. Seventy percent of all outstanding bonds are held by either pension funds or insurance companies.

Primary Markets for Stocks and Bonds

Companies normally employ the services of an investment banker for selling both stock and bond issues to private investors and financial institutions. A major exception is private placement of bonds, which involves an entire issue being sold to one or a few financial institutions. Investment banking services are provided by companies that specialize only in investment banking and by many of the larger brokerage houses.

Investment bankers normally act as dealers; they purchase an entire issue from the issuing corporation and resell it in smaller quantities to investors interested in holding it. Occasionally a best efforts arrangement will be used, wherein the investment banker does not buy the entire issue but merely sells as much of it as possible for the issuing company. The steps followed in the issuance of securities through an investment banker are discussed on the following pages. Essentially the same approach applies to the issue of stocks and corporate bonds.

Preunderwriting Conference The company meets with the investment banker to determine if the investment banker is interested in underwriting an issue for it and what type of issue—debt or equity—would be saleable. Investment bankers wish to maintain their reputation and will not sell an issue unless they have carefully evaluated the company and found it to be sound with good prospects for success. In addition, different investment bankers specialize in different types of issues, and a particular investment banking house may not be interested in the issue even though a number of others are. If a general agreement is reached, an *underwriting agreement* is signed between the company and the investment banker.

Registration Statement Once an underwriting agreement has been reached, the issue must be registered with the Securities and Exchange Commission (SEC). The issue cannot be sold until the registration becomes effective—twenty days after the registration statement is filed unless the SEC objects or asks for more time. The SEC uses this period to study the registration statement and determine if the appropriate information is being furnished. The SEC does not rule on the quality of the investment, but on whether appropriate information about the investment is properly disclosed. Although, the investment banker cannot sell any of the issue during this period, the banker can circulate a preliminary prospectus (also called a "red herring") giving all the information in the regular prospectus except the price at which the issue will be sold.

The prospectus is a statement designed to be helpful to a potential investor in deciding whether to purchase some of the securities being offered. It contains a detailed description of the company, detailed financial statements, and a discussion of the way in which the funds will be used. In the case of a debt issue, it also contains the various provisions of the debt instruments such as restrictions on further borrowing or when and how interest is to be paid.

Underwriting Syndicate and Selling Group
Issues worth hundreds of millions of dollars are not uncommon and issues worth several billion dollars are not unheard of. Since the investment banker normally buys the issue and then attempts to resell it, capital is being put at risk. Very seldom can a single investment banker absorb the entire issue. Normally an underwriting syndicate is formed by the originating investment banker. With this arrangement, each of a number of investment bankers buys part of the issue and resells it. Each investment banker has its own selling group—typically a group of brokerage firms—acting as a group of retailers while the investment bankers act as wholesalers. While the selling group handles the actual sale, the underwriters accept the risk of the issue not being sold.

Price Setting and Sale   After the registration becomes effective, the price at which the issue is to be sold is set. Typically this is just before issue time because of market volatility. The selling group then proceeds to sell the issue through public advertisements or contact with investors who may be interested. Since potentially interested investors are notified before the offering via preliminary prospectus, the entire issue is frequently sold in a matter of hours once the registration becomes effective. In any event, the investment bankers hope to sell the entire issue within a few days because they cannot accept the capital commitment and risk of a long-term holding.

Market Stabilization   This is the last act of the managing underwriter. The underwriter stands ready to buy at the offering price any part of the issue that investors attempt to resell before the entire issue is sold. Thus there is not a risk of a decline in market price before the entire issue is sold. However, this price pegging is limited to a

maximum of thirty days. If all the issue is not sold by that time, the investment banker must simply face losses or hold the remainder of the issue and hope the price will rise.

Costs of flotation depend on the size of the issue, the quality of the issuer, and whether it is debt or equity. One study found that the average flotation cost as a percent of net proceeds was 13.4 percent for equity issues of one–half to one million dollars. For equity issues over one hundred million dollars, the average cost was 3.95 percent.[3] As indicated earlier, issue costs can fall to less than 1 percent for a large bond issue. The problem for small issues is that because many costs are fixed, they are very high as a percentage of the issue.

Secondary Markets for Corporate Stocks and Bonds

The secondary markets for corporate securities consist of the organized exchanges, such as the New York Stock Exchange, and the over-the-counter market. The greatest volume of stock transactions in the secondary markets occurs in the organized exchanges, although the vast majority of stocks (eligible for sale and purchase) are not listed on organized exchanges. Stocks of large corporations, particularly those that are frequently bought and sold, are normally listed on an exchange. The majority of corporate bond volume, on the other hand, occurs in the over-the-counter markets.

The secondary market for stock is much more active than the primary market, with annual trading volume equal to twenty times the volume of new issues. Bonds tend to change hands less frequently and are often held to maturity by the original purchaser.

While funds are not furnished directly to users through the secondary markets, these markets are important because they provide liquidity and a continuous test of value. The owner of a

---

[3]Clifford W. Smith, Jr., "Substitute Methods for Raising Additional Capital: Rights Offerings Versus Underwritten Issues," *Journal of Financial Economics* 5 (December 1977).

security can find the current value by checking yesterday's market price in the newspaper and can sell the securities quickly if funds are needed. Thus the existence of an active secondary market makes corporate securities more attractive and makes it easier for the corporation to raise funds. In this section, the secondary markets are discussed in detail.

Organized Exchanges Most resale of stocks occurs on the organized exchanges. The two major organized exchanges are the New York Stock Exchange and the American Stock Exchange, both located in New York City. The New York Stock Exchange accounts for approximately 80 percent of total stock exchange volume and the American Stock Exchange accounts for approximately 10 percent. The concentration of this business on one street in southern Manhattan has led to Wall Street being synonymous with finance. Large regional exchanges include the Midwest, the West Coast, and the Baltimore–Philadelphia–Washington exchanges.

The primary purpose of an organized exchange is to provide a physical meeting place for the buying and selling of securities; exchange members buy and sell either for themselves or for those they represent. Additionally, the exchanges provide communication and bookkeeping systems for recording and reporting transactions. Finally, the exchanges provide sets of rules and enforcement procedures to insure an orderly market place.

The organized exchanges are *continuous auction* markets. The floor of the exchange consists of a number of different posts—meeting places for transactions in a particular group of securities. For example, the New York Stock Exchange provides a market for approximately 2000 different securities and divides them among twenty-seven trading posts.

Transactions are based on bid and ask prices. For example, a broker carrying an order for a client who would like to purchase 100 shares of IBM at $70 per share would go to the trading post for IBM and call out the bid. If someone accepted the bid, a transaction would occur. Someone wishing to sell would call out his ask-ing price in the same fashion. These orders are described as limit orders because the investor only wishes to buy or sell if a certain price can be obtained. A *market order* would instruct the broker to buy or sell at the best price available. The broker would then take the best price available from those at the trading post. Once a sale has been agreed on, the price and quantity are recorded and reported to the public. Thus there is a continuous test of value.

Anyone who visited an exchange, particularly on a brisk trading day, would question the use of the word "organized." To the casual observer, it more closely resembles a melee. People are rushing to and from the various posts to communicate with or join other people there. Trading consists of a group of people shouting at each other in what appears to be a totally unorganized manner. However, to the trained, quick-witted participant, it provides a swift, efficient way of buying and selling securities at the best price currently available in the marketplace.

The people trading in a security at a particular post are of several types. First, there are the brokers trading on behalf of clients around the country who have placed an order to buy or sell through their local brokerage house. Second, there are members who buy and sell for their own accounts, speculating on short–term movements in prices. Third, there are specialists, a group of members who have available to them special information about supply and demand as reflected in unfilled *limit orders*.[4] In exchange for this information, they are required to "make a market" by continually posting both a bid and an ask price. There is only one specialist for each security, although each specialist is responsible for more than one security. The specialist normally quotes an ask price of $0.125 to $0.25 above his bid price. He thus guarantees that a continuous market will exist. In exchange for this service he makes a profit through information about supply and demand, and through selling at an asking price above his bid price.

---

[4]A limit order is one for which the price is specified. The alternative is a market order which instructs the broker to buy or sell at the best price presently available.

Volume of sales on the organized exchanges far exceeds the volume of new stock sold. The stock of a company, once issued, typically remains outstanding for the life of the company. However, the typical owner of stock may hold it for a few years or less, with some purchasers (called floor traders) holding the stock for no more than a few hours. Volume on the New York Stock Exchange alone averages 80 million shares a day. More than one-fifth of the shares listed on the New York Stock Exchange are sold each year.

Over-the-Counter Markets A membership in an organized exchange is referred to as a *seat,* though its owner will find no place to sit on the exchange floor. Likewise, the over-the-counter market (OTC) does not involve a counter. The OTC consists of a group of investment houses acting as market makers in certain securities and a communication network to tie them together. The stocks of large, well known corporations are generally listed on one of the organized stock exchanges.[5] Stocks of lesser known companies and most bonds are bought and sold on the OTC.

In the OTC, one or more investment houses act as market makers which stand ready to buy and sell like the specialist on an organized exchange. Instead of a physical meeting place, market makers and brokers are tied together through the National Association of Security Dealers Automated Quotation System (NASDAQ). A central computer system and telecommunication lines tie this market together. It has been argued that modern technology has rendered physical meeting places obsolete. Indeed, the present NASDAQ system was designed with enough capacity to handle all organized exchange volume.

Eurobonds

Eurobonds are a specialized type of corporate debt issue, designed to increase saleability by decreasing the risk of loss from currency de-

valuation. A Eurobond is defined as a bond denominated in a currency other than that of the country in which it is being sold. Thus an American company doing business in Europe might decide to finance its European operations by selling bonds in Europe but denominating them in dollars.

Eurobonds can be denominated in any currency and some have even given the holder a choice of currencies. Dollars have traditionally been the most popular currency, partly because the Interest Equalization Tax of 1964 encouraged American companies to finance foreign operations by issuing debt overseas.

Like domestic bonds, Eurobonds are issued through investment bankers. The main difference is that they are not advertised to the public; they are sold entirely through direct contact with potential buyers. They are rarely sold through private placement, as is frequently done in the case of domestic bonds.

U.S. GOVERNMENT DEBT

Beginning with borrowing to finance wars and expanding with increases in social programs, the U.S. government has become a major borrower in the capital markets, accounting for $1,667 billion of debt at the beginning of 1984. U.S. government securities are unique in that they are the only securities in the U.S. capital markets considered risk-free with regard to default. Another factor leading to particular importance of U.S. government debt is its use as part of economic stabilization policy.

U.S. government debt is issued in different forms. First, there are the regular Treasury issues: bills, notes, and bonds. Bills have maturities of one year or less, notes have maturities of one to five years, and bonds have maturities of longer than five years. In 1984, 24 percent of the U.S. Treasury debt was in the form of bills, 42 percent was in the form of notes, and 34 percent was in the form of bonds and nonmarketable debt.

In addition to the regular Treasury issues, several U.S. government agencies issue debt.

---

[5]Certain types of companies, particularly banks and breweries, have not been listed by tradition, although it appears that this tradition is beginning to break down.

These agencies were discussed individually in chapter 4. Most of the agencies act primarily as financial institutions, selling securities and using the proceeds to provide funds to the mortgage markets. The proportion of their debts financed by bonds depends on market conditions. In general, though, the bulk of their financing is long-term.

While interest is earned on Treasury bills only through the discount from face value at which they are sold, other securities pay interest based on the face value, normally on a semiannual basis.

Approximately 39 percent of U.S. Treasury debt is held by U.S. government trust funds, state and local governments, and the federal reserve banks. Thus only 61 percent of the total is in private hands, with 10 percent of the total being held by individuals, mostly in the form of savings bonds. A small amount is held by nonfinancial corporations and the rest is held by financial institutions; commercial banks are particularly large holders.

Primary Markets

Unlike corporations, the federal government does not use underwriting. The Federal Reserve acts as fiscal agent, handling the mechanics of sale, but neither underwrites nor markets the issues. Thus it is important that the yield be set so as to make the issues attractive to investors. The yields are usually set with the objective of achieving a slight increase in price following initial issue. If this is done, a type of unofficial underwriting occurs, with U.S. government security dealers and commercial banks acquiring part of a new issue as a short-term holding, thus easing its absorption into the market.

The issue procedure differs from the auction market for Treasury bills. The yield of the issue is set so that the Treasury is relatively sure the bonds or notes will sell. Press releases are given out, and descriptive circulars are sent to potential buyers. The issues are then allocated to those wishing to purchase. On average, approximately two-thirds of the dollar value of new issues goes to commercial banks and U.S. government securities dealers.

Obviously, a large proportion of U.S. government bond sales occur merely to refund maturing issues. Sometimes, because of a desire to increase average maturity of outstanding debt, advance refunding is used. With this technique, new long-term securities of longer maturity are offered in exchange for issues that are close to their maturity date. Yields of the new securities must be higher than those of the existing maturities, since conversion is voluntary and there must be some incentive to convert.

Secondary Markets

While it was once common practice to buy and sell U.S. government bonds and notes in the organized exchanges, the market has shifted to the U.S. government securities dealers. For each issue, the dealers continually post prices at which they will buy and prices at which they will sell. Thus they provide a continuous market for those wishing to buy or sell U.S. government securities.

STATE AND LOCAL GOVERNMENT BONDS

Bonds issued by state and local governments are called *municipal bonds*. They provide a distinct investment opportunity because the interest received from such bonds is exempt from federal income tax.

Municipals may be guaranteed by the *full faith and credit* of the government unit involved or they may be guaranteed only by *revenue* from a specific investment such as a water system or toll bridge. In recent years, approximately 70 percent of the newly issued municipal bonds have been revenue bonds. The building of schools, roads, and other capital projects has traditionally been financed through the issuance of bonds, although some cities—New York is the most notable example—have used debt to finance current spending.

Because of their tax status, municipal bonds can be sold at yields well below those for other securities, with high grade municipal bonds normally selling to yield several percentage points below U.S. government bonds.

Municipal bonds are attractive only to investors facing relatively high tax rates. At a municipal bond rate of 5.75 percent and a corporate bond rate of 9.50 percent, the tax rate necessary to make municipals an attractive investment is found as follows:

$$9.5(1 - T) = 5.75$$
$$T = 0.4$$

In the above example, municipal bonds would be an attractive alternative to corporate bonds if the investor faced a marginal federal income tax rate of 40 percent or greater. The primary holders of municipal bonds are wealthy individuals, banks, and property and casualty insurance companies.

Municipal bonds are sold through underwriting in a manner similar to corporate bonds. An important difference is that banks, which do not underwrite corporate securities, participate in the underwriting of municipals. The underwriter of the original issue also normally makes a second market by acting as a dealer.

Municipal bonds are not risk-free, as illustrated by a number of defaults. The rating services that rate corporate bonds also rate municipal bonds, with yields varying according to rating (table 5-4).

State and local government debt grew rapidly during the 1970s to reach one third of federal debt by the beginning of the 1980s. That growth has abated somewhat in recent years. State and local debt, at $432 billion, was approximately one fourth of federal debt at the beginning of 1984.

FINANCIAL FUTURES

The financial futures markets provide an excellent example of the financial system's ability to adapt to changing needs. In 1975, the Chicago Board of Trade responded to increasingly unstable interest rates by offering a location and procedure for trading in contracts for future delivery of U.S. treasury bonds, mortgages, and other financial instruments. This was a natural extension of the Board's function as a market for spot (immediate delivery) and future delivery contracts in various commodities. Financial futures provided financial institutions and others with a way to decrease risks arising from fluctuating interest rates, and they provided speculators with a new market in which fortunes could be won or lost in hours.

The basic problem (and opportunity) addressed in the financial futures markets is the

Table 5-4:

Sample Bond Rating

State of New Mexico Highway Debentures
Rated "AAA"

RATING RATIONALE: The Highway Debentures are special obligations of the State, payable from gasoline excise taxes, motor vehicle registration fees, and a limited $1.5 million general property tax which has never been levied or used. This issue is part of a $20 million authorization, of which $5.7 million has been issued and retired. The State may not issue any parity debentures beyond the initial authorization. Presently, there are no plans to issue the remaining authorized debentures. Motor fuel taxes and registration fees covered estimated maximum debt service 44.20 times in 1978. Total pledged revenues, including the $1.5 million tax levy, would have covered estimated maximum debt service fifty times during this period. The state has enacted legislation which, effective in 1980, will provide for the escalation of the gasoline tax. The tax rate, which will use $0.07 a gallon as a base, is determined by reference to the average wholesale price of gasoline plus federal excise taxes. The annual incremental increase/decrease may not exceed $0.01 per gallon for each twelve-month period.

Based upon the overwhelming debt service coverage, the limited general property tax pledge and the short maturity schedule, we are rating these bonds "AAA."

PROPOSED ISSUE: $5,000,000 Highway Debentures, Series 1979, selling 26 June 1979.

Dated: 15 July 1979.

Due: Serially 1980–1984; the debentures are not subject to redemption prior to their respective maturities.

Source: Standard and Poor's *Fixed Income Investor*

sensitivity of values of existing fixed-income securities to changes in interest rates. The relationship between interest and value can be briefly illustrated with a perpetual bond, one that provides an interest payment each year forever with the principal never being repaid. As $1,000, 10 percent perpetual bond, for example, pays $100 (0.10 × $1,000) a year forever. Suppose the owner of the bond wants to sell it. The yield to a buyer is

$$\text{Yield} = \frac{\text{Annual Interest Payment}}{\text{Price}} .$$

If interest rates have risen such that investors will not buy unless they can earn a yield of 14 percent, the (current market) price of a $1,000 face value perpetual bond that pays interest at the rate of 10 percent of its face value can be determined using the above equation:

$$0.14 = \frac{\$100}{\text{Price}} .$$

Solving, price equals $714. Thus, the investor who originally bought the bond for $1,000 would suffer a loss of $286 on resale. Similar price movements occur for financial instruments with finite lives. For example, the change in interest rates from 10 percent to 14 percent would cause a thirty-year, 10 percent mortgage to decline in value by 26 percent.[6] The financial futures market provides a way to protect the value of one's portfolio from such risks or to attempt to profit by predicting interest rate movements.

Citizens Savings and Loan illustrates why and how financial futures markets are used to reduce risk. Citizens has agreed with a builder to provide $1 million of mortgages with an interest rate of 12 percent. Citizens intends to sell the package of mortgages rather than hold them. The package would be assembled and ready for sale in six months, and Citizens is concerned about interest rate movements in the meantime. If interest rates rise to 13 percent by that time, a $1 million package of 12 percent mortgages could

be sold for approximately $930,000 which would result in a $70,000 loss. The futures market provides a way for Citizens to eliminate this risk.

Citizens Savings and Loan can eliminate the risk arising from interest rate uncertainty by entering into a futures contract. Citizens is referred to as a *hedger* because it uses the futures market to offset another position, thereby decreasing risk. A *speculator* is one who enters into a futures contract in an attempt to profit by predicting interest rate movements.

Citizens can hedge by finding someone who will agree to purchase $1 million of 12 percent mortgages six months from today with the sale price set today. If interest rates rise, Citizens is protected because the sale price has already been agreed upon. If interest rates fall, the mortgages are worth more than $1 million; Citizens still receives its $1 million, and the other party buys for $1 million mortgages that have a market value greater than $1 million.

Unfortunately, Citizens Savings and Loan would encounter some difficulties in arranging this financial futures contract. First, there is the problem of locating a buyer for this unique package of mortgages. The organized financial futures markets solve this problem by creating a meeting place for representatives of buyers and sellers. Trading is further enhanced by limiting organized trading to a relative handful of financial instruments. Because all financial instruments respond in similar ways to changes in interest rates, Citizens does not need a futures contract to sell its particular mortgages. All that is needed is another futures contract that will provide gains approximately equal to any losses in the value of its own portfolio. As futures contracts are regularly traded for U.S. treasury bills, treasury bonds, and treasury notes as well as certificates of deposit and mortgages (actually GNMA certificates), there are enough choices available to make a good—though not perfect—match.

Another factor allowing Citizens to hedge with similar rather than identical securities is the infrequency of actual delivery of financial instruments in this market. Suppose, for example,

---

[6]Determination of the value of a finite-life financial instrument is covered in chapter 6.

Citizens entered into a contract to sell in six months U.S. Treasury bonds with a $1 million face value and an 8 percent interest rate. Further suppose that the agreed-upon future price was the same as the face value: $1 million. If, at the end of the six-month period, these bonds are actually selling for $930,000 because of a rise in interest rates, the investor who entered into the futures contract to buy will most likely not actually purchase the bonds for $1 million. Instead, the investor will simply pay the $70,000 difference, and Citizens will receive $70,000. Had the bonds increased in value because of falling interest rates, Citizens would have paid the amount by which the bonds increased in value and the investor would have received this amount. Futures contracts are regularly arranged for several securities with price movements similar to the price movements of Citizens' mortgages.

Integrity of contracts is the second problem addressed by the organized futures markets. The use of a clearing corporation assures Citizens that it is contracting with a party willing and able to complete its contract. Although Citizens' broker and the investor's broker strike an agreement with each other, Citizens technically contracts to deliver the package of securities to the clearing corporation and the investor technically contracts to purchase securities from the clearing corporation. Therefore, the clearing corporation has agreed to complete the contract with Citizens even if the investor should default.

Mechanics of the Futures Market

One of the more widely traded financial futures, U.S. Treasury bond futures, are used to explain the technical details of financial futures trading. The standard Treasury bond futures contract calls for delivery of $100,000 face value of 8 percent coupon rate U.S. Treasury bonds with a maturity of fifteen years or more. Treasury bond contracts are traded for delivery in March, June, September, and December going out two and a half years into the future—a total of ten different contracts.

As an example, we will use the September 1984 Treasury bond contract as traded on 12 March 1984. Financial futures are traded in face-to-face meetings on the floor of an exchange whose membership includes speculators as well as brokers representing clients such as Citizens Savings and Loan. The 14 March 1984 daily trading summary for September 1984 Treasury bond futures, is published in the financial press:

open	high	low	settle	change
66–13	66–26	66–12	66–18	+2

yield	change	open interest
12.619	−0.012	13,480

Prices are stated as a percentage of the $100,000 face value, and trading is in increments of $1/32$ of one percent. Thus, the opening contract of the day was for delivery of $100,000 face value of 8 percent Treasury bonds in September 1984 for 66 $13/32$ percent (66.40625 percent) of face value, or $66,406.25. The highest contract of the day was for 66 $26/32$ percent of face value, the lowest price was 66 $12/32$ percent of face value, and the price settled at 66 $18/32$ percent of face value. The price was up $2/32$ of a percent of face value from the price at the end of the previous day. The yield to maturity that would be earned by someone buying the bonds at that price is 12.619 percent, which is down 0.012 percent from the yield at the end of the previous day's trading. Open interest is the number of contracts outstanding. Thus, at the end of this day's trading, there were outstanding contracts for $1.348 billion ($100,000 × 13,480) of face value of Treasury bonds for September 1984 delivery.

Once the contract is agreed to on the floor of the exchange, both parties must post a deposit—commonly referred to as margin. The minimum allowable margin for $100,000 Treasury bond contract is $2,000, but brokerage houses commonly require margins larger than this minimum. If the September 1984 delivery price begins to rise, the buyer will be required to put up more money; and if it falls, the seller will be required to put up more money.

As explained earlier, since each of the parties

technically has a contract with the clearing corporation, either party can cancel out its position by acquiring an offsetting contract. Suppose, for example, that a month has passed and the September delivery price has decreased from 66–18 to 65–16. The person who contracted to sell at 66–18 can place a new order with his or her broker to buy at 65–16. When that transaction is completed, the investor now has two contracts with the clearing corporation—one to sell at 66–18 and one to buy at 65–16. These two contracts cancel each other out and the person receives: $1,062.50 ($100,000 × 66 $\frac{18}{32}$% − $100,000 × 65 $\frac{16}{32}$%) plus the initial margin. Most contracts are settled through the acquisition of an offsetting contract, rather than through the purchase or delivery of $100,000 worth of bonds.

Options

An option contract is like a futures contract, except that one party has the legal right not to carry through the contract. Most option contracts are for common stock, although there are option contracts for U.S. Treasury obligations, foreign currencies, and the values of certain stock market indexes. Thus, a common stock example is used. Sample 12 March 1984, quotes for options on the stock of IBM are given as an example:

Strike Price	Calls			Puts		
	Apr	Jul	Oct	Apr	Jul	Oct
120	$\frac{5}{8}$	$2\frac{7}{8}$	$5\frac{1}{4}$	10	$10\frac{3}{4}$	$11\frac{1}{4}$

Call options give their owner the right to buy at the striking price; put options give their owner the right to sell at the striking price. Three put and three call options (the expiration date of each shown in the column head) were being traded for the 120 striking price. (IBM options with striking prices of $100, $110, $130, and $140 were also being traded on this date.) IBM stock was selling for 110 $\frac{1}{8}$ ($110.125) at the close of trading on 12 March. Thus, a put option expiring in April is valuable at the current price, but it is unlikely that the stock will rise fast enough for the call option expiring in April to have any val-

ue (since the stock can be bought in the open market for less than the striking price). As a result, the April expiration call option is selling for $\frac{5}{8}$ ($0.625) and the April expiration put option is selling for $10. Options with more distant expiration dates are worth more because there is a greater chance that the stock price will move enough to give them value.[7]

Like financial instrument futures, options are traded on a number of exchanges. The trading procedure is similar to that for financial futures. The contracts are standardized to aid trading, and their prices are determined in open auction. Technically, the buyers and sellers contract with the clearing corporation to eliminate the risk of default. Most contracts are allowed to expire without being exercised or are offset by opposite contracts rather than by exercise. A person who sells an October 110 striking price call option for 100 shares at 9 $\frac{7}{8}$ ($9.875) a share and then sees prices rise to 12 $\frac{3}{8}$ can get out of the market by entering into a contract to buy a 100 shares $110 striking price option at 12 $\frac{3}{8}$ a share. Of course, a loss of $2.50 per share is incurred.

Options can be used by speculators, hedgers, and those simply looking to improve return on a common stock portfolio. A speculator buys or writes put or call options on stock he does not own in order to profit if his predictions of future prices are correct. A stockholder who simply wants to improve portfolio return month in and month out in exchange for sacrificing the chance to make really large profits may write call options at striking prices well above the current stock price. Chances are that the stock will not reach the striking price, the option will simply be allowed to expire, and the seller will keep the amount for which he sold the option. If prices do rise rapidly, the option seller can sell the stock for the striking price and also keep the price for which the option was sold—a good profit but not as large as the profit that would have been realized had an option not been written.

As an example of the use of an option contract for hedging, Citizens Savings and Loan has

---

[7]A model for determining the value of an option is explained in appendix 7-B.

made a commitment to a builder to provide mortgage loans at a fixed interest rate, but is not certain the loans will actually be made. If Citizens used a futures contract, the loans were not actually made, and interest rates fell, a substantial loss could be incurred. However, Citizens could purchase a put option rather than entering into a futures contract to sell. There is no traded put option for mortgages, but there is a market for put options on U.S. Treasury bonds. Citizens could purchase a put option on U.S. Treasury bonds, possibly charging the builder a commitment fee equal to the cost of the option. If the loans are made and interest rates have risen, the loss in loan value will be offset by a profit on the put option. If the loans are not made and interest rates rise, the option will still provide a windfall profit as its price will rise. If the loans are made, but interest rates have remained stable or fallen, the option will simply be allowed to expire and its cost will have been an insurance cost. Thus, the option can provide a more effective hedge than a futures contract in certain situations.

SUMMARY

Capital markets are the markets for long-term securities, both debt and equity. The primary instruments bought and sold in these markets are corporate stock and bonds, U.S. government bonds, state and local government bonds, and marketable mortgages. Companies and government units wishing to raise funds turn to a system of primary markets made up mostly of investment bankers, who purchase the issue and resell it. Original purchasers of securities may hold them until maturity or resell them in a secondary market system composed of organized security exchanges, the over-the-counter security market, and a number of dealers who buy and sell for their own inventory.

A review of tables 5-1 and 5-2 is helpful in developing a perspective on the participants in this market and on the importance of various instruments. U.S. government securities dominate in the primary markets, followed by mortgage debt (much of which is not marketable), state and local government obligations, and corporate securities (table 5-1). Within corporate securities, debt instruments clearly dominate equity securities in the primary markets.

A somewhat different picture is seen when we look at total holdings as opposed to new issues and increases in amounts outstanding. Corporations are dominant in terms of the value of total securities outstanding, followed by mortgages, U.S. government securities, and state and local government securities. Within the corporate securities, equity dominates debt in terms of total amount outstanding. However, it should be recognized that much of the equity is not publicly traded and the table does not include $380 billion of bank commercial loans outstanding. Households are the primary suppliers of funds. They hold the majority of equity securities directly. While financial institutions hold the majority of debt securities, they are largely using the funds of households.

These markets for direct ownership of securities are supplemented by options and futures markets, in which contingent claims and claims for future delivery can be traded. These markets increase the set of risk-return opportunities for both borrowers and investors, therefore increasing the well-being of all parties.

QUESTIONS

1. What are the primary types of risk involved in the ownership of capital market instruments?

2. What are the rights of a common stockholder?

3. Explain the differences between common stock and preferred stock.

4. Why are lengthy indentures required for corporate bonds when a similar document is not required for commercial paper issued by the same corporation?

5. Select a bond issue listed in the *Wall Street Journal*. Find the bond's Moody's

rating. Would you recommend this bond to an investor looking for a safe investment?

6. Summarize the process by which a new stock or bond issue is sold.

7. Leading stocks are traded at a physical location (New York Stock Exchange or American Stock Exchange) while there is no central physical location for the purchase and sale of money market instruments. How do you account for this difference in trading arrangements?

8. Why would a company use underwriting for a stock or bond issue? Why does the U.S. government not use underwriting?

9. U.S. government issues are considered risk-free with regard to default. Is there any way an investor can lose money on an investment in U.S. government bonds?

10. Explain the difference between a full faith and credit bond and a revenue bond. Which type is likely to be more risky?

11. Since municipal bonds are generally considered more risky than U.S. government bonds, why do they sell at lower yields?

12. The secondary markets, futures markets, and options markets provide no funds to deficit units. Why are these markets important?

13. Give an example of how a bank could use the futures markets to decrease risk.

PROBLEMS

1. At the beginning of 1984, the yield to maturity on high grade corporate bonds was 12.53 percent while yields on similarly rated municipal bonds were 9.20 percent. For an investor facing a 30 percent federal income tax rate, would corporate or municipal bonds provide a higher after-tax return?

2. The stock of Corporation X is selling for $50 a share and six-month options with a striking price of $60 are selling for $5 ¼. Compute the percent change in the value of the option and the value of the stock if, on the day before the option's expiration, the stock is selling for

a. $50 a share

b. $60 a share

c. $70 a share

SELECTED REFERENCES

Belongia, Michael T., and Gregory, Thomas H. ''Are Options on Treasury Bond Futures Priced Efficiently?'' *Federal Reserve Bank of St. Louis Review* 66 (January 1984): 5–13.

Dunn, Kenneth B. and McConnell, John J. ''Valuation of GNMA Mortgage-Backed Securities.'' *The Journal of Finance* 36 (June 1981): 599–616.

Dunn, Kenneth, B. and Singleton, Kenneth J. ''An Empirical Analysis of the Pricing of Mortgage-Backed Securities.'' *The Journal of Finance* 38 (May 1983): 613–625.

Houthakker, Hendrik S. ''The Regulation of Financial and Other Futures Markets.'' *The Journal of Finance* 37 (May 1982): 481–491.

Kilcollin, Thomas Eric. ''Difference Systems in Financial Futures Markets.'' *The Journal of Finance* 37 (December 1982): 1183–1197.

Kolb, Robert W. and Chiang, Raymond. ''Improving Hedging Performance Using Interest Rate Futures.'' *Financial Management* 10 (Autumn 1981): 72–79.

Kolb, Robert, Corgel, John B. and Chaing, Raymond. ''Effective Hedging of Mortgage Interest Rate Risk.'' *Housing Finance Review* 1 (April 1982): 135–146.

McCabe, George M. and Franckle, Charles T. ''The Effectiveness of Rolling the Hedge Forward in the Treasury Bill Futures Markets.'' *Financial Management* 12 (Summer 1983): 21–29.

Appendix 5-A

Designing a Financial Futures Hedge

A financial futures hedge is designed to decrease the risk of security price fluctuation due to changes in interest rates. A portfolio manager holding U.S. treasury bonds might, for example, wish to hedge his position by entering into a contract for future sale of treasury bonds at a price set today. In a perfect hedge, the profit or loss on the financial futures contract will exactly offset a profit or loss from some other activity. Any gain or loss in the value of the treasury bonds held by the portfolio manager would, for example, be almost exactly offset by gains or losses in the value of the futures contract. The portfolio manager is not betting on interest rate predictions; with a perfect hedge, profit will be the same regardless of the direction interest rates move.

Because there are futures contracts going out to two and a half years in three-month intervals, a hedger's first choice is the appropriate delivery date. A mortgage banker assembling a package of mortgages for sale in three months would have little difficulty in deciding that three months forward was the appropriate delivery date for a futures contract to sell. For others, the decision is not quite so easy. Almost all depository institutions accept an average maturity of liabilities that is shorter than the average maturity of assets. However, a well–managed institution will have

policy concerning the amount of mismatch it is willing to tolerate (see the discussion of gap analysis in chapter 9). When the mismatch begins to exceed the policy limit, action is taken. A savings and loan may, for example, effectively increase the maturity of its six-month certificates of deposit (CDs) to one year by entering into a future contract to sell CDs at the end of six months, at a price (and therefore interest rate) determined today. Likewise, it could enter into CD futures contracts for delivery in one year, one and a half years, etc. to effectively increase the maturity of its six-month CDs up to three years. The exact maturity chosen is a tactical decision to implement the firm's policy with regard to exposure to maturity mismatches; it is not determined exactly by the maturity of any asset.

The second problem faced by a hedger is the choice of the security on which to place a futures contract. If a portfolio manager is holding U.S. Treasury bonds, the fairly obvious hedge choice is a futures contract in U.S. Treasury bonds. However, the Treasury bond futures contracts are based on an assumed 8 percent coupon rate while most bonds carry coupon rates other than 8 percent; a perfect match is impossible. Furthermore, many hedgers find that their risk is related to price movements of securities for which there are no futures contracts. They must therefore use a *cross hedge,* a future delivery contract in some instrument with price movements similar to the movements of the security they are actually interested in. A consequence of these differences between the instrument being held and the instrument involved in the hedge contract is that the best hedge may be for a futures contract of a different amount than the value of the securities being hedged. The determination of the appropriate hedge size is explained in the following paragraphs.

EQUIVALENT PRINCIPAL BALANCE

Using futures contracts for GNMA CDRs as an example, the standard contract is for delivery of $100,000 of face value of 8 percent coupon certificates, or the equivalent. The equivalent face values for some other coupon rates follows. (Similar tables are available for other instruments on which financial futures are traded.)

GNMA Coupon Interest Rate	Face Amount to Be Delivered
7%	$107,816.70
8	100,000.00
10	87,146.00
12	76,792.40
14	68,823.10
16	62,208.40
18	56,737.60

For example, a person who enters into a futures contract for delivery of $100,000 of 8 percent certificates is allowed to substitute $62,208.40 face value of 16 percent certificates. Stated another way, $1.00 of 16 percent GNMA CDRs can be delivered in place of $1.608 (100,000/62,208.4) of 8 percent GNMA CDRs. Thus, a portfolio manager who wants to hedge $100 million of 16 percent GNMA CDRs will enter into future delivery contracts for $160.8 million of 8 percent GNMA CDRs. Since the standard contract is for $100,000 face value, the hedger will need 1,608 contracts.

CROSS HEDGES

A cross hedge is used when there is no futures contract for the instrument the manager wants to hedge. In this case, the hedger enters into a futures contract for delivery of an instrument with similar price movement behavior. For example, there are no traded futures contracts for corporate bonds, and a manager who wants to hedge corporate bonds may choose a futures contract in U.S. treasury bonds.

When a cross hedge is used, it is necessary to determine the relative sensitivity of the security being hedged and the futures contract price. One way to do this is with regression analysis. For example, we might determine that

$$P_T = 0.10 + 0.8 \, P_C$$

where P_T is the price of treasury-bond futures as a percent of face value, and P_C is the price of the corporate bond (or portfolio of corporate bonds) as a percentage of face value. Because treasury bond futures prices (for the particular delivery period) only move in price by 0.8 as much as the corporate bonds, a cross hedge will require a treasury bond contract in an amount greater than the corporate bonds being held. If the manager has $10.0 million face value of corporate bonds, a good cross hedge would require futures contracts to sell $12.5 million ($10 million ÷ 0.8) face value of treasury bonds.

To illustrate how a hedge of this type works, consider a portfolio manager who has developed the above estimation equation and holds corporate bonds with a face value of $10 million and a market value of $8 million. The portfolio manager enters into futures contracts to sell $12.5 million face value of 8 percent coupon treasury bonds at a price of 74–0, or 0.74 × $12.5 million = $9.25 million. Subsequently, the value of the corporate bonds falls to $7 million. If the relationship holds as expected, the treasury bond futures price will fall to 0.10 + 0.8(0.7) = 0.66 times face value, or $8.25 million. The portfolio manager loses $1 million on the corporate bonds, and gains $1 million on the futures contract because he first contracted to sell at $9.25

million and then later offset that contract with a contract to buy at $8.25 million.

It is only fair to point out that things never work out this neatly. While a cross hedge uses securities with highly correlated price movements, one will never find two securities with perfectly correlated price movements. Consequently, the cross hedge is a risk reduction tool rather than a risk elimination tool.

PROBLEMS

A.1 A portfolio manager with $50 million of 14 percent GNMA CDRs wants to be protected from interest rate risk over the next six months. What is the appropriate futures contract?

A.2 An insurance company has a corporate bond portfolio that it wants to hedge from interest rate risk over a one-year period. The bond portfolio has a face value of $100 million and a market value of $90 million. One-year 8 percent treasury bond futures contracts are selling at 85 percent of face value. An analyst has studied the relationship between movement of the corporate bond portfolio and treasury bond futures, and developed the following estimating equation:

$$P_T = 0.04 + 0.9\, P_C.$$

Design an appropriate cross hedge.

Chapter 6

Interest Analysis

Interest plays the same role in financial markets that price plays in the market for goods. Funds are allocated to the uses that can pay the highest rent; thus interest is rent for money. A financial institution manager must have a thorough understanding of its meaning and computation.

Lenders are required to notify borrowers what interest rate they are charging and are sometimes restricted by law as to the interest rate they can charge. Therefore they must understand the impact of such things as service charges on the effective interest rate. Portfolio managers must be able to do such things as determine the interest rate earned on a bond that is purchased for less than its face value. Pension fund and life insurance company managers must be able to determine the amount of money they will have if funds are invested for a set number of years at a particular interest rate. And these are but a few examples of the ways in which managers must use interest analysis. This chapter, then deals with interest definitions, principles, and practices.

INTEREST RATE COMPARISONS

Both actual interest rates and methods of computation vary between markets. It is necessary to distinguish between the various ways in which interest rates are quoted or implied and to develop a methodology by which explicit or implicit interest charges may be calculated and directly compared. The difficulties in comparing the true cost of money over time are illustrated by the following situations:

1. A department store charges 1.5 percent per month on the average outstanding account balance.

2. A commercial bank offers to lease industrial equipment. Monthly lease payments are 3.38 percent of the equipment purchase price on a thirty-six month financial lease.

3. An automobile dealer offers to finance $3,000 of the cost of a new car for three years at an annual add-on interest rate of 6 percent. Repayment terms call for monthly payments. In other words, the dealer charges total

interest of $0.06 \times 3 \times 3,000 = \$540$ and the monthly payment is $(3,000 + 540)/36 = \$98.33$.

4. A mortgage payable monthly over thirty years is negotiated. Although the stated annual interest rate is 8 percent, terms of the mortgage call for payment of a service charge equal to three points (3 percent of the mortgage) at the time loan proceeds are disbursed.

5. A bank negotiates a $1,000 commercial loan with the interest rate stated as 7 percent discount. Loan terms call for repayment of the total loan one year hence. With this arrangement, the borrower receives $1,000 less 7 percent interest, or $930, and pays back $1,000.

6. A security originally issued several years ago may be purchased for $918.90. The holder of the security will receive $30 interest twice each year for the next five years. In addition, par value of the security ($1,000) is payable at the end of year five.

Common to the above situations is the fact that each involves the extension of credit and charging of interest, either explicitly or implicitly. Frequently, the decision maker must calculate the true interest rate inherent in such transactions. Once the true rate is known, the creditor or debtor is in a position to compare credit alternatives.

TIME VALUE OF MONEY: THE MATHEMATICS OF INTEREST

To develop an understanding of the techniques used to compare interest rates, it is first necessary to develop the theory of compound interest. That development is completed in this section.

Compound Value of a Single Payment

The first step in understanding interest rates relates to the concept of compound value. Suppose that $1,000 is deposited in a savings account paying 6 percent interest compounded annually. Interest of $60 will be earned during the first year and the account balance at the end of the first year will be $1,060. If the account is left undisturbed for two years, interest for the second year is $1,060 \times 0.06 = \$63.60$. The account balance at the end of the second year is $1,060 + 63.60 = \$1,123.60$. This process by which interest is computed against both the original principal and previously accumulated interest is known as compound interest. If a financial institution credited interest on the original deposit but did not compound it, the saver could simply remove and reinvest funds once interest had been credited, achieving the same result. Thus compound interest, or interest on interest, is a normal practice in the case of savings accounts and other investment instruments.

If the funds were to be left for a large number of years in the account described above, it would be possible to find the amount to which the account would grow by continuing a series of calculations like those completed for the first two years. However, it is convenient to take a more systematic approach. The amount in the account at the end of the first year is

$$\$1,000 + 0.06(\$1,000) = \$1,000(1.06)$$
$$= \$1,060.$$

The amount in the account at the end of the second year equals

$$\$1,060(1.06) = \$1,000(1.06)^2 = \$1,123.60$$

and the amount in the account at the end of the third year is

$$\$1,000(1.06)^2(1.06) = \$1,000(1.06)^3$$
$$= \$1,191.02.$$

This process can be generalized for the future value (FV_n) of an investment of P dollars at i percent interest per period for n periods:

$$FV_n = P(1 + i)^n \qquad (6\text{-}1)$$

If the previous investment were allowed to continue growing for ten years, the value at the end of ten years would be

$$FV_{10} = \$1,000(1.06)^{10}$$

While the procedure is the same for ten years as for two, the calculations can be tedious if done manually. To alleviate this problem, table 6-1 contains values of $(1 + i)^n$ for various combinations of i and n. Table A-1 in the appendix to this book is a continuation of table 6-1, containing compound values for additional combinations of i and n. The value of the account at the end of ten years is found by locating the intersection of the ten-year row and the 6 percent column in table 6-1. A value of 1.7908 is found and the solution to the problem is

$$FV_{10} = \$1,000(1.06)^{10}$$
$$= \$1,000(1.7908) = \$1,790.80.$$

In the above examples, interest was calculated and added to the account at the end of each year. This is referred to as *annual compounding*. In some cases interest is compounded, or added to the principal, more than once a year. The result of compounding more than once a year is to raise the growth rate slightly. The future value formula when interest is compounded k times per year is

$$FV_n = P\left(1 + \frac{i}{k}\right)^{kn}. \tag{6-2}$$

Thus investing funds for three years at 12 percent per year with semiannual compounding provides the same growth as investing the funds for six years at 6 percent with annual compounding. If $1,000 is invested for three years at a 12 percent annual rate with interest compounded two times per year, the future value is

$$FV_3 = \$1,000\left(1 + \frac{0.12}{2}\right)^{2\cdot3}$$
$$= \$1,000(1.06)^6 = \$1,418.50.$$

Among compounding periods other than annual, monthly compounding is the most important for understanding interest practices. A $100 investment pays interest of 7 percent per year, compounded monthly. By the end of one year the investment will grow to

$$FV_1 = \$100\left(1 + \frac{0.07}{12}\right)^{12\cdot1}$$
$$= \$100(1.0723) = \$107.23.$$

Thus 7 percent compounded monthly would provide the same growth as 7.23 percent compounded annually. Due to the wide use of monthly compounding in such areas as mortgage loan analysis, special tables for monthly

Table 6-1:

Compound Value of a Dollar (Annual Compounding)

Years	6.00%	6.25%	6.50%	6.75%	7.00%	7.25%	7.50%	7.75%
1	1.0600	1.0625	1.0650	1.0675	1.0700	1.0725	1.0750	1.0775
2	1.1236	1.1289	1.1342	1.1396	1.1449	1.1503	1.1556	1.1610
3	1.1910	1.1995	1.2079	1.2165	1.2250	1.2336	1.2423	1.2510
4	1.2625	1.2744	1.2865	1.2986	1.3108	1.3231	1.3355	1.3479
5	1.3382	1.3541	1.3701	1.3862	1.4026	1.4190	1.4356	1.4524
6	1.4185	1.4387	1.4591	1.4798	1.5007	1.5219	1.5433	1.5650
7	1.5036	1.5286	1.5540	1.5797	1.6058	1.6322	1.6590	1.6862
8	1.5938	1.6242	1.6550	1.6863	1.7182	1.7506	1.7835	1.8169
9	1.6895	1.7257	1.7626	1.8002	1.8385	1.8775	1.9172	1.9577
10	1.7908	1.8335	1.8771	1.9217	1.9672	2.0136	2.0610	2.1095
20	3.2071	3.3619	3.5236	3.6928	3.8697	4.0546	4.2479	4.4499
25	4.2919	4.5522	4.8277	5.1191	5.4274	5.7535	6.0983	6.4630

compounding are provided. Table 6-2 contains values of $\left(1 + \dfrac{i}{12}\right)^{12 \cdot n}$ for various combinations of i and n. (Table A-2 in the appendix contains compound values for additional combinations of i and n.)

A \$5,000 investment has a three-year maturity, a 7 percent interest rate and monthly compounding. Principal and interest is payable at the end of the three-year period. To find the amount to which \$1 would grow at the end of three years, we locate the intersection of the three-year row and 7 percent column in table 6-2. The value found there is 1.2329 and in three years the investment will grow to

$$FV_3 = \$5,000\left(1 + \frac{0.07}{12}\right)^{12 \cdot 3}$$
$$= \$5,000(1.2329) = \$6,164.50.$$

Frequently, the tables will not contain the precise interest rate desired. A decision maker wishing to find the compound value of a dollar for ten years at 6.4 percent with monthly compounding is faced with the fact that table 6-2 contains compound value factors for 6.25 percent and 6.50 percent, but not for 6.4 percent.

The compound value factor for 6.4 percent can be estimated using *linear interpolation*. The linear interpolation formula, which is imposing to look at but easy to use:

$$TVF_1 = TVF_b + (TVF_a - TVF_b)\frac{I - I_b}{I_a - I_b} \quad (6\text{-}3)$$

where: TVF_1 = Time value factor for desired interest rate

TVF_b = Time value factor for interest rate below desired rate

TVF_a = Time value factor for interest rate above desired rate

I = Interest rate for which time value factor is desired

I_b = Interest rate below rate for which time value factor is desired

I_a = Interest rate above rate for which time value factor is desired.

Applying the interpolation formula to the above problem, the compound value factor for an annual interest rate of 6.4 percent for ten years with monthly compounding is

Table 6-2:

Compound Value of a Dollar (Monthly Compounding)

Years	6.00%	6.25%	6.50%	6.75%	7.00%	7.25%	7.50%	7.75%
1	1.0617	1.0643	1.0670	1.0696	1.0723	1.0750	1.0776	1.0803
2	1.1272	1.1328	1.1384	1.1441	1.1498	1.1555	1.1613	1.1671
3	1.1967	1.2056	1.2147	1.2238	1.2329	1.2422	1.2514	1.2608
4	1.2705	1.2832	1.2960	1.3090	1.3221	1.3353	1.3486	1.3621
5	1.3488	1.3657	1.3828	1.4001	1.4176	1.4354	1.4533	1.4715
6	1.4320	1.4536	1.4754	1.4976	1.5201	1.5429	1.5661	1.5896
7	1.5204	1.5471	1.5742	1.6019	1.6300	1.6586	1.6877	1.7173
8	1.6141	1.6466	1.6797	1.7134	1.7478	1.7829	1.8187	1.8552
9	1.7137	1.7525	1.7922	1.8327	1.8742	1.9166	1.9599	2.0042
10	1.8194	1.8652	1.9122	1.9603	2.0097	2.0602	2.1121	2.1652
20	3.3102	3.4790	3.6564	3.8429	4.0387	4.2446	4.4608	4.6880
25	4.4650	4.7514	5.0562	5.3804	5.7254	6.0924	6.4829	6.8983

$$CVF_{6.4\%} = 1.8652 + (1.9122$$
$$- 1.8652)\frac{0.064 - .0625}{0.065 - .0625}$$
$$= 1.8934.$$

The same interpolation approach can be used with table 6-1 when appropriate.[1]

Compound Value of an Annuity (Stream of Payments)

The decision maker is frequently interested in the amount to which a single payment or investment will grow; other problems of interest involve the growth of a series of payments. Such problems may be found in areas such as retirement planning, pension fund management, insurance portfolio management, and loan analysis. The procedure used is an extension of that used in the previous section.

A savings program calls for depositing $100 at the *end* of each year for the next three years in an account which pays 6 percent interest compounded annually. The amount in the account at the end of three years can be found as follows:

Value at the end of year 1: $100.
Value at the end of year 2:
         $100(1.06) + $100 = $206.
Value at the end of year 3:
         $206(1.06) + $100 + $318.36.

While this approach provides the correct answer, the calculations would be quite tedious if a large number of years were involved. Again, a table has been provided which contains compound values of $1 per year for selected combinations of years (n) and interest rates (i) with annual compounding (table 6-3). The formula for table 6-3 is[2]

---

[1]A pocket calculator with a power function makes possible an exact solution:

$$\left(1 + \frac{0.064}{12}\right)^{10 \cdot 12} = 1.8933.$$

[2]With some rearrangement of terms, this formula can be reduced to

$$CVA(i,n) = [(1 + i)^n - 1]/i.$$

$$CVA(i,n) = 1 + (1 + i)^1 + (1 + i)^2$$
$$+ \ldots + (1 + i)^{n-1}. \quad (6\text{-}4)$$

The intersection of the three-year row and 6 percent column in table 6-3 yields a compound value factor of 3.184 which, when multiplied by $100, yields (except for a 4¢ rounding difference) the $318.36 found above. If $100 were to be deposited at the end of each year for twenty years, the value at the end of 20 years, based on the twenty-year, 6 percent factor from table 6-4, would be:

$$\$100 \times 36.786 = \underline{\$3,678.60}.$$

A number of lending and investment situations involve monthly payments with monthly compounding. Table 6-4 (and table A-4 in the appendix) contains compound values of $1 per month for n years at an annual percentage rate of i with monthly compounding. The formula for table 6-4 is[3]

$$CVA_m(i,n) = 1 + \left(1 + \frac{i}{12}\right)^1$$
$$+ \left(1 + \frac{i}{12}\right)^2 + \ldots$$
$$+ \left(1 + \frac{i}{12}\right)^{12n-1}. \quad (6\text{-}5)$$

A savings program involves investing $100 at the end of each month for the next twenty years at a 6.5 percent annual interest rate with monthly compounding. The amount in the account at the end of twenty years, based on the twenty-year, 6.5 percent figure from table 6-4 is the following:

$$\$100 \times 490.421 = \$49,042.10.$$

As with compounding of a single payment, interpolation can be used when the desired interest rate is not available. One hundred dollars is to be deposited the end of each month for the next twenty years in an account paying 7.30 percent interest per year with monthly compounding.

---

[3]With some rearrangment of terms, this formula can be reduced to

$$CVA_m(i,n) = \left[\left(1 + \frac{i}{12}\right)^{12n} - 1\right]\Big/(i/12).$$

Table 6-3:

Compound Value of an Annuity of $1 (Annual Payments, Annual Compounding)

Years	6.00%	6.25%	6.50%	6.75%	7.00%	7.25%	7.50%	7.75%
1	1.000	1.000	1.000	1.000	1.000	1.000	1.000	1.000
2	2.060	2.063	2.065	2.067	2.070	2.073	2.075	2.078
3	3.184	3.191	3.199	3.207	3.215	3.223	3.231	3.239
4	4.375	4.391	4.407	4.424	4.440	4.456	4.473	4.489
5	5.637	5.665	5.694	5.722	5.751	5.779	5.808	5.837
6	6.975	7.019	7.064	7.108	7.153	7.199	7.244	7.290
7	8.394	8.458	8.523	8.588	8.654	8.720	8.787	8.855
8	9.897	9.987	10.077	10.168	10.260	10.353	10.446	10.541
9	11.491	11.611	11.732	11.854	11.978	12.103	12.230	12.358
10	13.181	13.337	13.494	13.654	13.816	13.981	14.147	14.316
20	36.786	37.790	38.825	39.894	40.995	42.132	43.305	44.514
25	54.865	56.836	58.888	61.024	63.249	65.566	67.978	70.490

The compound value factor can be estimated by using equation (6-3) to interpolate between the 7.25 percent twenty-year factor and the 7.50 percent twenty-year factor in table 6-4:

$$537.030 + (553.730 - 537.030)$$
$$\frac{0.0730 - 0.0725}{0.0750 - 0.0725} = \underline{\underline{540.37}}.$$

The same interpolation procedure can be used with table 6-3 for appropriate problems.

Present Value of a Future Sum: Reverse Compounding

If a dollar invested today will grow to an amount greater than a dollar at some future date, a dollar received at some future date is less valuable than a dollar received today. Financial institutions acquire and issue securities which provide the holder with one or more future cash payments. Sometimes, securities will have a

Table 6-4:

Compound Value of an Annuity of $1 (Monthly Payments, Monthly Compounding)

Years	6.00%	6.25%	6.50%	6.75%	7.00%	7.25%	7.50%
1	12.336	12.350	12.364	12.378	12.393	12.407	12.421
2	25.432	25.494	25.556	25.618	25.681	25.744	25.807
3	39.336	39.484	39.632	39.781	39.930	40.080	40.231
4	54.098	54.373	54.650	54.929	55.209	55.492	55.776
5	69.770	70.220	70.674	71.132	71.593	72.058	72.527
6	86.409	87.087	87.771	88.463	89.161	89.866	90.579
7	104.074	105.038	106.013	107.000	107.999	109.009	110.032
8	122.829	124.144	125.477	126.829	128.199	129.587	130.995
9	142.740	144.479	146.245	148.038	149.859	151.708	153.586
10	163.879	166.122	168.403	170.724	173.085	175.487	177.930
20	462.041	475.975	490.421	505.397	520.926	537.030	553.730
25	692.993	720.273	748.836	778.746	810.071	842.884	877.260

provision whereby a certain cash payment is to be given the holder at the end of a designated period, with no intervening payments prior to maturity. For example, the prospective purchaser of a certificate of deposit issued by a savings institution may wish to know how much he must invest today in order to have a certain sum two years hence. Similarly, a corporate treasurer may be charged with the responsibility of investing sufficient funds from current earnings to insure the firm's ability to meet construction progress payments due several years hence. Numerous other examples could be cited where the investor knew the amount to be realized in the future and would wish to know what that amount is worth today. Today's value depends, of course, on the interest rate implied in the investment and on the frequency with which interest is compounded.

Suppose an investment will pay $5,000 two years from today. If the investor has alternate opportunities paying 6 percent interest, the amount required to have $5,000 two years from today can be found by restating equation (6-1):

$$P = FV_n \times \frac{1}{(1 + i)^n} \qquad (6-6)$$

$$P = \$5,000 \frac{1}{(1.06)^2}$$

$$= \$5,000 \times 0.8900 = \$4,450.$$

Thus the *present value* of $5,000 received two years from today, given an annual interest or growth rate of 6 percent compounded annually, is $4,450. The present value of $5,000 received five years from today, *discounted*[4] at 7 percent per annum, would be

$$P = \$5,000 \frac{1}{(1.07)^5}$$

$$= \$5,000 \times 0.7130 = \$3,565.$$

This value can be verified by showing that $3,565 invested today at 7 percent compounded annually will grow to $5,000 by the end of five years.

Table 6-5 (and table A-5 in the appendix) contains values of $1/(1 + i)^n$ for selected combinations of i and n. The intersection of the five-year row and 7 percent column in table 6-5 yields the present value factor 0.7130 used above. A payment of $10,000 is to be received twenty years from today. An investor who wishes to earn a return of 7.5 percent compounded annually can find the amount he must pay for the

---

[4]The term "discounted" as used in this section should not be confused with the term "discount rate." The latter is a rate applied to original loan principal as a method of calculating interest charges. The former relates to the use of a simple interest rate so as to reduce the value of future cash payments in order to determine their present value.

Table 6-5:

Present Value of a Dollar (Annual Compounding)

Years	6.00%	6.25%	6.50%	6.75%	7.00%	7.25%	7.50%	7.75%
1	0.9434	0.9412	0.9390	0.9368	0.9346	0.9324	0.9302	0.9281
2	0.8900	0.8858	0.8817	0.8775	0.8734	0.8694	0.8653	0.8613
3	0.8396	0.8337	0.8278	0.8220	0.8163	0.8106	0.8050	0.7994
4	0.7921	0.7847	0.7773	0.7701	0.7629	0.7558	0.7488	0.7419
5	0.7473	0.7385	0.7299	0.7214	0.7130	0.7047	0.6966	0.6885
6	0.7050	0.6951	0.6853	0.6758	0.6663	0.6571	0.6480	0.6390
7	0.6651	0.6542	0.6435	0.6330	0.6227	0.6127	0.6028	0.5930
8	0.6274	0.6157	0.6042	0.5930	0.5820	0.5712	0.5607	0.5504
9	0.5919	0.5795	0.5674	0.5555	0.5439	0.5326	0.5216	0.5108
10	0.5584	0.5454	0.5327	0.5204	0.5083	0.4966	0.4852	0.4741
20	0.3118	0.2975	0.2838	0.2708	0.2584	0.2466	0.2354	0.2247
25	0.2330	0.2197	0.2071	0.1953	0.1842	0.1738	0.1640	0.1547

investment by referring to the 7.5 percent twenty-year interest factor in table 6-5.

$$\$10,000 \times 0.2354 = \$2,354.$$

Table 6-6 (and table A-6 in the appendix) is used for problems of the same type when monthly compounding is involved. If alternate investments pay a 6 percent annual interest rate with monthly compounding, the present value of $1,000 received ten years from today, based on the ten-year, 6 percent factor from table 6-6 is

$$\$1,000 \times 0.5496 = \$549.60.$$

As with future value of a single payment, interpolation using equations (6-3) can be used if the desired interest rate is not available.

Present Value of an Annuity

If a security is to provide a *stream* of future payments, the present value of that stream and thus the market value of the security, can be found in a manner similar to that discussed for a single payment. At a required return of 6 percent, a security which is to provide cash flow or payment of $500 at the end of each year for the next two years would have a present value (PV) of

$$PV = 500 \times \frac{1}{(1.06)} + 500 \times \frac{1}{(1.06)^2}$$
$$= \$916.70.$$

If the investment were to provide the same cash flows each year for twenty years instead of two, the procedure would be the same but the calculations would become quite tedious. Calculations can be aided by generalizing the approach as follows:[5]

$$PV = CF \times \frac{1}{(1 + i)} + CF \times \frac{1}{(1 + i)^2}$$
$$+ \ldots + CF \times \frac{1}{(1 + i)^n} \quad (6\text{-}7)$$
$$= CF\left[\frac{1}{(1 + i)} + \frac{1}{(1 + i)^2}\right.$$
$$\left. + \ldots + \frac{1}{(1 + i)^n}\right]$$

where: PV = Present value (of the security)

CF = The amount to be received at the end of each year

i = The required rate of return

---

[5]With some rearrangement of terms, this formula can be reduced to

$$PV = CF[1 - 1/(1 + i)^n]/i$$

Table 6-6:

Present Value of a Dollar (Monthly Compounding)

Years	6.00%	6.25%	6.50%	6.75%	7.00%	7.25%	7.50%	7.75%
1	0.9419	0.9396	0.9372	0.9349	0.9326	0.9303	0.9280	0.9257
2	0.8872	0.8828	0.8784	0.8740	0.8697	0.8654	0.8611	0.8568
3	0.8356	0.8294	0.8233	0.8172	0.8111	0.8051	0.7991	0.7931
4	0.7871	0.7793	0.7716	0.7640	0.7564	0.7489	0.7415	0.7342
5	0.7414	0.7322	0.7232	0.7142	0.7054	0.6967	0.6881	0.6796
6	0.6983	0.6880	0.6778	0.6677	0.6578	0.6481	0.6385	0.6291
7	0.6577	0.6464	0.6352	0.6243	0.6135	0.6029	0.5925	0.5823
8	0.6195	0.6073	0.5954	0.5836	0.5721	0.5609	0.5498	0.5390
9	0.5835	0.5706	0.5580	0.5456	0.5336	0.5218	0.5102	0.4989
10	0.5496	0.5361	0.5230	0.5101	0.4976	0.4854	0.4735	0.4619
20	0.3021	0.2874	0.2735	0.2602	0.2476	0.2356	0.2242	0.2133
25	0.2240	0.2105	0.1978	0.1859	0.1747	0.1641	0.1543	0.1450

Table 6-7:

Present Value of an Annuity of $1 (Annual Payments, Annual Compounding)

Years	6.00%	6.25%	6.50%	6.75%	7.00%	7.25%	7.50%	7.75%
1	0.943	0.941	0.939	0.937	0.935	0.932	0.930	0.928
2	1.833	1.827	1.821	1.814	1.808	1.802	1.796	1.789
3	2.673	2.661	2.648	2.636	2.624	2.612	2.601	2.589
4	3.465	3.445	3.426	3.406	3.387	3.368	3.349	3.331
5	4.212	4.184	4.156	4.128	4.100	4.073	4.046	4.019
6	4.917	4.879	4.841	4.804	4.767	4.730	4.694	4.658
7	5.582	5.533	5.485	5.437	5.389	5.343	5.297	5.251
8	6.210	6.149	6.089	6.030	5.971	5.914	5.857	5.802
9	6.802	6.728	6.656	6.585	6.515	6.447	6.379	6.312
10	7.360	7.274	7.189	7.105	7.024	6.943	6.864	6.786
20	11.470	11.241	11.019	10.803	10.594	10.391	10.194	10.004
25	12.783	12.485	12.198	11.921	11.654	11.396	11.147	10.907

n = The number of years the cash flows are to continue.

Table 6-7 contains values of this function for selected combinations of i and n (table A-7 in the appendix contains values for additional combinations.) The use of the table eliminates a good deal of tedious calculation. A security will provide cash flows of $5,000 a year for ten years. If the required return is 7 percent, the value associated with ten years and 7 percent in table 6-7 is 7.024 and the present value of the cash flows or value of the security is

$$PV = \$5,000 \times 7.024 = \$35,120.$$

If payments are to be received monthly, with interest compounded monthly, the present value equals[6]

$$PV = CF\left[1\bigg/\left(1 + \frac{i}{12}\right) + 1\bigg/\left(1 + \frac{i}{12}\right)^2 \right.$$
$$\left. + \ldots + 1\bigg/\left(1 + \frac{i}{12}\right)^{12n}\right]. \quad (6\text{-}8)$$

_____
[6]With some rearrangement of terms, this formula can be reduced to
$$PV = CF\left[1 - 1\bigg/\left(1 + \frac{i}{12}\right)^{12n}\right]\bigg/(i/12).$$

Table 6-8 and table A-8 in the appendix contains values of this function for various combinations of i and n.

Suppose a lender wished to grant a loan with monthly payments and an annual interest rate of 7 percent. By referring to table 6-8, the lender could determine that the present value of $1 received each month for twenty years, discounted at 7 percent per annum and compounded monthly, is $128.983. Thus a loan of $128.98 repaid in monthly payments of $1 per month over twenty years yields an annual return on investment of 7 percent compounded monthly. If the loan were to be for a larger amount, say $30,000, we would divide the loan amount by 128.983 to find the monthly payment:

$$\$30,000/128.983 = \$232.59.$$

If a 7.2 percent return was required, interpolation, using equation (6-3), would result in a present value factor of

$$128.983 + (126.522$$
$$- 128.983)\frac{0.0720 - 0.0700}{0.0725 - 0.0700}$$
$$= 127.014$$

Table 6-8:

Present Value of an Annuity of $1 (Monthly Payments, Monthly Compounding)

Years	6.00%	6.25%	6.50%	6.75%	7.00%	7.25%	7.50%	7.75%
1	11.619	11.603	11.588	11.573	11.557	11.542	11.526	11.511
2	22.563	22.506	22.449	22.392	22.335	22.279	22.222	22.166
3	32.871	32.749	32.627	32.507	32.386	32.267	32.148	32.030
4	42.580	42.373	42.167	41.963	41.760	41.559	41.358	41.159
5	51.726	51.416	51.109	50.804	50.502	50.202	49.905	49.611
6	60.340	59.912	59.489	59.069	58.654	58.243	57.837	57.434
7	68.453	67.895	67.343	66.797	66.257	65.724	65.196	64.675
8	76.095	75.395	74.704	74.021	73.348	72.683	72.026	71.378
9	83.293	82.442	81.603	80.775	79.960	79.156	78.364	77.583
10	90.073	89.063	88.069	87.090	86.126	85.178	84.245	83.326
20	139.581	136.812	134.125	131.516	128.983	126.522	124.132	121.810
25	155.207	151.591	148.103	144.736	141.487	138.350	135.320	132.393

and the monthly payment would be:

$$\$30,000/127.014 = \$236.19.$$

DETERMINING INTEREST RATES

Analysis of loan and investment alternatives frequently requires that the decision maker determine the true interest rate associated with a given loan or investment. Insurance companies for example, are often asked to invest in major projects such as proposed shopping centers. In a project of this type, the investor may receive future cash flows based at least in part on rental income derived from shopping center tenants. In this illustration, the decision maker will know the amount of investment required and a reasonable estimate of future cash inflows may be projected. It remains then, to determine the interest rate or return inherent in the transaction. Alternatively, suppose that a security which offers a certain series of future cash flows is available for purchase at a specified price. Such a security could be a new or existing bond, a new or existing mortgage, a negotiable certificate of deposit,

or one of a variety of other financial instruments. The decision to purchase or reject such securities is influenced by the interest rate inherent in the transaction. It is important therefore, that the decision maker be at least conceptually familiar with the process by which the rate is determined. This process involves use of equations and tables previously discussed.

Assume that a particular investment requires $5,000 and will grow in value to $7,000 at the end of five years. The problem can be restated as a simple compound value problem using equation (6-1):

$$\$5,000(1 + i)^5 = \$7,000$$
$$(1 + i)^5 = \$7,000/5,000 = 1.4.$$

Previous use of table 6-1 involved searching for the compound value factor associated with a particular interest rate. Our objective now is to refer to table 6-1 and find the interest rate associated with a particular compound value factor. If we proceed to the five-year row in that table, and look for the interest factor 1.4, a value of 1.4026 is found in the 7 percent column. We conclude that the effective interest rate on the investment is approximately 7 percent compounded annually.

This same procedure can be used when a stream of future payments is involved. An investment requires payments of $100 per month and will grow to $9,000 in six years. The ratio of future value to monthly cash flow is 9000/100 = 90.00. In table 6-4 an examination of the six-year row reveals a compound value factor of 89.866 at 7.25 percent and 90.579 at 7.50 percent. The effective interest rate lies between 7.25 percent and 7.50 percent.

Interpolation can be used to prepare an estimate of the exact interest rate in a manner similar to that used with equation (6-3) when an estimate of exact compound value is desired:

$$I = I_b + (I_a - I_b)$$
$$\frac{TV_1 - TV_b}{TV_a - TV_b} \qquad (6\text{-}9)$$
$$= 0.0725 + (0.0750$$
$$- 0.0725) \frac{90.00 - 89.866}{90.579 - 89.866}$$
$$= 0.0730 \text{ or } 7.3\%.$$

Many times the effective interest rate will be desired for an uneven stream of cash flows. An investment which costs $1,130 today will provide $90 at the end of each year for the next ten years and then $1,000 at the end of ten years. The effective interest rate is the rate which will make the present value of the cash inflows equal to the cost. This rate is found by a trial-and-error process. We decide to start the search with 7 percent. Referring to tables 6-5 and 6-7, we find the present value factors for 7 percent, ten years, and apply these to determine the present value of the cash flows:

Dates	Cash Flow	× PV Factor (7%)	= Present Value
Year 1–10 (annual)	90	7.024	$ 632.16
Year 10	$1,000	0.5083	508.30
		Total Present Value:	$1,140.46

We are seeking an interest rate which would result in a total present value of $1,130. Since a higher interest rate results in a lower present value, we try a higher rate. We decide to try 7.25%:

Dates	Cash Flow	PV Factor (7.25%)	Present Value
Year 1–10 (annual)	90	6.943	$ 624.87
Year 10	$1,000	0.4966	496.60
		Total Present Value:	$1,121.47

Since we are looking for a present value of $1,130, we know the effective interest rate is between 7 percent and 7.25 percent. We can estimate the exact interest rate by interpolation, using equation (6-9):

$$I = 7.0 + (7.25$$
$$- 7.0) \frac{1130 - 1140.46}{1121.47 - 1140.46} = 7.14\%.$$

INTEREST PRACTICES AND EFFECTIVE INTEREST RATES

Having developed the general mathematics of interest, we are now ready to examine specific interest practices. This section has two major objectives. The first is to develop an understanding of interest terminology and payment practices whch are commonly used. The second is to develop a methodology for comparing interest charges which are quoted or computed in different ways.

Annual Percentage Rate

Early in this chapter it was noted that different computational methods sometimes result in different interest charges even though stated interest rates are identical. The annual percentage rate (also referred to as the simple interest rate) is normally used as the standard of comparison. Indeed, truth in lending legislation of recent years requires disclosure of the effective annual percentage rate (APR) in virtually all types of consumer lending.

When we identified or computed effective

interest rates in the previous section, we were dealing with the annual percentage rate. As an example, take a $1,200 note with a 6 percent annual percentage rate, a one-year maturity, and a lump sum payment. Interest on the note will be $72 ($1,200 × 0.06) and the amount due at maturity will be $1,272.00. If this same loan were to be paid in equal installments at the end of each month, interest charged each month would be 0.005 (0.06/12) of the balance due at the beginning of the month. The amount required to retire the loan in twelve monthly payments can be found by referring to table A-8 in the appendix. The present value of $1 per month for one year at 6 percent is found to be 11.619. The monthly payment required is $103.28 ($1,200/11.619). The allocation of the payment between principal and interest is shown in table 6-9.

The same approach to finding the payment and constructing an amortization schedule can be used when the life of the security is greater than one year. To find the monthly payment necessary to amortize an 8.50 percent twenty-year mortgage, the present value factor for 8.50 percent, twenty years (115.231) is first located in table A-8. The amount of the loan is then divided by this present value factor. If the mortgage loan were for $50,000, the monthly payment would be $433.91 ($50,000/115.231). Alternatively, if the loan were to be repaid in *annual* installments, we would find the 8.5 percent, twenty-year figure of 9.463 in table A-7 and the annual payment would be $5,283.74 ($50,000/9.463).

Frequently one wants to know the amount still owed after some number of payments without constructing a complete amortization schedule. Suppose, for example, an individual who took out a 12 percent APR $6,000 three-year automobile loan wants to repay the loan after one year. Using table A-8, the monthly payment would be $6,000 ÷ 30.1075 = $199.29. The balance owed after one year is the present value of the remaining payments. Since there are two years of remaining monthly payments and the loan carries a 12 percent interest rate, the 12 percent, two-year figure from table A-8 is used:

Balance due = $199.29 × 21.2434 = $4,234.

This is the same answer that would have been achieved by constructing an amortization table like table 6-9.

Table 6-9:

Amortization Schedule for a $1,200, 6 Percent, One-Year, Simple Interest Note with Equal Installments Payable at the End of Each Month

Month	Beginning Loan Balance	Monthly Payment	Interest Payment*	Principal Reduction	Ending Balance
1	$1,200.00	$ 103.28	$ 6.00	$ 97.28	$1,102.72
2	1,102.72	103.28	5.51	97.77	1,004.95
3	1,004.95	103.28	5.02	98.26	906.69
.	.	.	.	.	.
.	.	.	.	.	.
.	.	.	.	.	.
12	102.77	103.28	0.51	102.77	0.00
Total		$1,239.36	$39.36		

*Sample interest calculations

	P	×	R	×	t	=	Interest
1st month	1,200.00	×	.06	×	1/12	=	6.00
2nd month	1,102.72	×	.06	×	1/12	=	5.51
3rd month	1,004.95	×	.06	×	1/12	=	5.02

Rule of 78s When a loan is repaid before maturity, some consumer lenders use a method called the rule of 78s rather than the approach described in the previous paragraph (which is called the straight amortization method). When the rule of 78s is used, the finance charge is reduced by

$$\frac{m(m + 1)}{n(n + 1)} \times \text{Total finance charge}$$

where m is the number of payments remaining when the loan is repaid and n is the number of payments called for in the original loan agreement.

For the 12 percent, three-year, $6,000 automobile loan described in the paragraph before last, the monthly payment is $199.29 and the total finance charge is $36 \times \$199.29 - \$6,000 = \$1,174.44$. If the loan is repaid when twenty-four payments are still to be made, the rule of 78s reduction of the finance charge is

$$\frac{24(24 + 1)}{36(36 + 1)} \times \$1,174.44 = \$529.03.$$

The balance due is therefore $24 \times \$199.29 - \$529.03 = \$4,254$, compared to $4,234 that was still owed with straight amortization.

When a loan is repaid before maturity, the amount still due is always higher with the rule of 78s than with straight amortization. This increases the effective APR when the loan is repaid

early. The differences between the two methods are small for loans with short maturities, but can be quite large for loans with long maturities, such as mortgage loans. The rule of 78s is seldom if ever used for these longer maturity loans.

Add on and Discount Rates

Add-on interest rates are frequently used in consumer installment transactions and, to a lesser extent, in business and other commercial loans. Discount rates are also common to both consumer and business transactions. A key distinction between both add-on and discount rates as opposed to annual percentage rates is that calculation of interest charges is based upon the original loan principal and ignores the fact that the principal balance may decline over time as periodic payment of principal and interest is made. The method by which interest charges are calculated can have a dramatic effect on total loan charges (tables 6-10).

Suppose someone wishes to borrow $1,200 and is told that the loan is available at an annual interest rate of 6 percent add-on with repayment in equal installments, one at the end of each month. With the add-on method, the total interest charge will be $0.06 \times \$1,200 = \$72.00$ (compared to $39.36 when the rate was 6 percent simple) and monthly payments will be $106

Table 6-10:

Comparison of Interest Charges and True Annual Interest Rates Applicable to Three Loans, Each Bearing Stated Interest of 6 Percent

	Add-on Method	*Discount Method*	*Simple Interest Method*
Stated Annual Rate	6%	6%	6%
Amount Loaned	$1,200.00	$1,200.00	$1,200.00
Loan Maturity	1 year	1 year	1 year
Repayment Terms	Monthly	Monthly	Monthly
Interest Charges	$ 72.00	$ 72.00	$ 39.36
Loan Proceeds	1,200.00	1,128.00	1,200.00
Time Balance	1,272.00	1,200.00	1,239.36
Monthly Payments	106.00	100.00	103.28*
Annual Simple Interest Rate	10.89%	11.58%	6.00%

*Using Table A-8, $1,200 ÷ 11.6189 = $103.28

($1272/12). The effective annual percentage rate for this loan can be found using table A-8. We know that the time is one year and the ratio of loan value to payment is 11.321 ($1,200/106). Scanning across the one-year row of table A-8, we find the value of 11.344 at 10.5 percent and 11.315 at 11.0 percent. By interpolation, the annual percentage rate is approximately 10.90 percent. Note that this is close to twice the quoted add-on rate.

If the discount method is used, the interest charge of $72 (0.06 × $1,200) is immediately deducted from the amount loaned. In this case, the borrower has initial use of only $1,128. If monthly payments are to be made, they will be $100 per month over twelve months. Interest charges total $72. Obviously, the discount method involves a higher annual percentage rate than the add-on method. With the discount method, the borrower receives $1,128 and pays monthly installments of $100. The ratio of loan to payment is 1128/100 = 11.28. Again, the effective annual percentage rate can be found using table A-8. Present value factors of 11.285 and 11.255 are found at 11.5 percent and 12.0 percent, respectively. Thus the annual percentage rate lies between 11.5 percent and 12.0 percent. By interpolation, the effective simple interest rate is approximately 11.58 percent.

Financial Leases

A specific type of financial instrument and one which has received increased use in recent years is the financial lease. Frequently, financial institutions act in the capacity of a lessor, purchasing assets on behalf of a customer (lessee), and in turn, leasing the assets under terms of a lease agreement. Terms of a pure financial lease differ from those typically associated with an operating or service lease. In the case of the latter, the lessor provides maintenance and other services. Furthermore, operating or service leases are often cancellable on short notice. Financial leases, on the other hand, are simply an alternative method of financing assets. In a financial lease, the lessee assumes all obligations normally associated with ownership. The lessor

merely provides the capital necessary for acquisition of the asset, holds title to the asset, and enters into an agreement whereby the lessee promises to make a series of payments sufficient to provide a return of all costs as well as a profit to the lessor.

Since a lease is not a loan, interest charges are technically nonexistent and are thus unspecified in the lease agreement. However, an interest rate is *implied* in the transaction and a financial lease is frequently an alternative to a loan. Thus, the decision maker should evaluate the lease agreement in terms of the annual percentage rate implied in the agreement.

The information in table 6-11 was drawn from the files of a leasing corporation and provides information relating to one method of quoting lease payments. Specific rates vary over time and the quotations contained in table 6-11 happened to be in effect for that company in the spring of 1973. Suppose that a prospective lessee wished to lease equipment priced at $30,000 from the company whose rates are represented in table 6-11. If the term of the lease were three

Table 6-11:

**Financial Lease Terms
Quoted by a Leasing Corporation**

Asset Cost (including all taxes and charges)	Term (no. of years)	Monthly Rental (% of total cost)
Less than $1,000	1	9.28
	2	5.11
1,000 to 5,000	3	3.53
5,000 to 10,000	3	3.47
	4	2.79
	5	2.44
10,000 to 25,000	3	3.42
	5	2.38
25,000 to 50,000	3	3.38
	5	2.33
50,000 to 100,000	3	3.36
	5	2.30
Over 100,000	3	3.33
	5	2.28

Source: Internal files of a leasing corporation.

years, monthly lease payments would be (3.38% × $30,000) = $1,014.00. Thus, $1,014 represents an annuity to be paid (or received) over a thirty-six-month period. The present value of that annuity is $30,000. Expressed in terms of a dollar, the present value factor is

$$\$30,000/\$1,014 = 29.586.$$

Referring to table A-8 and looking across the three-year row, we find the factor 29.679 associated with 13 percent and 29.259 associated with 14 percent. We conclude that the interest rate inherent in the lease is between 13 percent and 14 percent. Linear interpolation results in an estimate of 13.22 percent. Thus an annual percentage rate of 13.22 percent is implied in the lease agreement.

Points and Service Charges

The collection of a charge payable at the time a loan is granted is a common practice that has the effect of increasing the annual percentage rate. Points will be used as an example although discounts and other service charges have a similar impact. A point, normally used in connection with a mortgage loan is a service charge or discount equal to 1 percent of the value of the loan. Thus a $20,000 mortgage with a three-point charge would require a fee of $600 (0.03 × $20,000). The financial institution would advance a net $19,400 ($20,000 − $600) but would receive payments and calculate interest charges as if the investment had been $20,000. This procedure obviously raises the true rate above that which is stated.

A $20,000 mortgage loan with a thirty-year maturity and an 8 percent stated interest rate would require monthly payments of $20,000/136.284 = $146.75 (from table A-8). Since the net investment is only $19,400, the ratio of loan to payment is $19,400/146.75 = 132.198. In the thirty-year row of table A-8, an interest factor of 133.109 is found at 8.25 percent, a factor of 130.054 is found at 8.50 percent. The annual percentage rate is between 8.25 percent and 8.5 percent. By interpolation, it is approximately 8.32 percent.

While points are of some significance if the loan is carried to maturity, they are of much greater significance if the loan is retired early. In general, the sooner a loan is retired, the greater the true annual percentage rate when points or similar charges had been levied against the original loan.

Frequency of Compounding and Effective Interest Rates

In quoting interest rates on certificates of deposit and other savings instruments, it is common practice to advertise that the use of frequent compounding periods increases the effective interest rate. For example, a bank might advertise that its 10 percent certificate of deposit provides daily compounding for an effective interest rate of 10.515 percent. If interest is compounded k times per year, formula (6-2) shows that the future value is

$$FV_n = P\left(1 + \frac{i}{k}\right)^{kn}$$

where i is the interest rate and n is the number of years. If interest is compounded annually ($k = 1$) and the annual interest rate is 10 percent, the amount a dollar will grow to by the end of the year is

$$FV_1 = \$1\left(1 + \frac{0.10}{1}\right) = \$1.10.$$

If interest is compounded daily, the value at the end of one year will be

$$FV_1 = \$1\left(1 + \frac{0.10}{365}\right)^{365} = \$1.10515.$$

Since a dollar grows to $1.10515 in one year, this is equivalent to an interest rate of 10.515 percent with annual compounding.

Occasionally, the concept of continuous compounding is used. This means that the compounding periods are infinitely short. Using a proof available in most college algebra texts, it can be shown that:

$$\lim_{k \to \infty} \left(1 + \frac{i}{k}\right)^{nk} = e^{in}$$

where $e = 2.71828 \ldots$, the base of the common logarithm. Thus, $1 invested for one year at 10 percent per year, compounded continuously, would grow to $1 \cdot e^{0.10} = \$1.10517$. This is equivalent to an interest rate of 10.517 percent a year with annual compounding.

The continuous compounding approach can also be used to find the present value of a future amount. For example, the present value of $20,000 to be received ten years from today, discounted at an annual interest rate of 12 percent with continuous compounding would be

$$PV = \$20,000 \div 2.71828^{0.12 \cdot 10} = \$6,023.89.$$

Bonds: Value and Yield to Maturity

Bonds are frequently bought and sold by financial institutions and by other investors long after they are issued. Although interest payments and the terminal value of the bond are fixed, the market value of the security may fluctuate depending on shifts in the market interest rate for that type of security. The relationship between par or face value of the bond and the periodic interest payments paid to the holder is called the *stated* or *coupon* interest rate and does not change. The ratio of annual interest payment to current market value is called the *current yield*. However, the current yield is not the true interest rate earned because it does not include the capital gain or loss—the difference between the current market value and the amount that will be repaid at maturity. The *yield to maturity* is the true interest rate earned and is identical with the annual percentage rate. It recognizes both the interest payment received and any capital gain or loss that will occur if the bond is held to maturity. The yield to maturity is thus defined as the interest rate that equates the present value of the future cash flows (interest payments and terminal value) to the current market price of the bond.

A typical bond has a face or par value of $1,000 and pays interest twice a year. Thus a $1,000, 6 percent bond pays $30 each six months and $1,000 at maturity. As previously suggested, bonds frequently trade above or be-

low their face value, making the true interest rate or yield to maturity different than the stated or coupon rate. Market quotations are stated as a percentage of face value: a price quote of 91.89 would mean that a $1,000 bond is being traded at $918.90.

Suppose the above 6 percent bond is five years from maturity and interest rates have risen such that bonds of this type are selling to provide a yield of 8 percent. What is this existing bond worth? We can answer this question by turning to tables A-5 and A-7, assuming semiannual compounding. The 91.89 figure for the above bond is derived using the present value of $1 per year for ten years at 4 percent and the present value of a single payment of $1 in ten years at 4 percent.[7]

$$
\begin{aligned}
\$30 \times 8.111 &= \$243.33 \\
1,000 \times 0.6756 &= \underline{675.60} \\
& \ \$918.93 \\
& \text{ or } 91.893 \text{ percent} \\
& \text{ of face value}
\end{aligned}
$$

A borrower who received $918.93 from a lender and agreed to the series of payments described above would have agreed to a loan with an annual percentage rate (APR) of 8 percent. Likewise, the person who buys the bond for $918.93 will earn an APR of 8 percent. However, the bond trader will not use the term APR; a yield to maturity of 8 percent will be quoted instead.

In practice, the yield to maturity on a bond is normally found using a set of bond yield tables, a sample of which is contained in table 6-12. The bond yield tables contain the sum of the combined values from tables A-5 and A-7. The price of 91.89 is found at the intersection of the 8 percent row and the five-year column. Conversely, the yield to maturity can be determined

---

[7]Tables A-5 and A-7 assume annual cash flows and thus annual compounding. When flows are received semi-annually, these same tables may be used in their evaluation. It is necessary only to divide the interest rate by two and to double the time periods. Thus, cash inflows discounted at 8 percent per annum over five years, when received semiannually, may be evaluated at 4 percent per time period over 10 six-month periods, as in the above illustration.

Table 6-12:

Relationship between Bond Yield to Maturity and Price Face or Coupon Rate: 6 Percent

Yield	1 yr	2 yr	3 yr	4 yr	5 yr	6 yr	7 yr	8 yr
5.00%	100.96	101.88	102.75	103.59	104.38	105.13	105.85	106.53
5.10	100.87	101.69	102.47	103.22	103.93	104.60	105.24	105.85
5.20	100.77	101.50	102.20	102.86	103.48	104.08	104.64	105.18
5.30	100.67	101.31	101.92	102.49	103.04	103.56	104.05	104.52
5.40	100.58	101.12	101.64	102.13	102.60	103.04	103.46	103.86
5.50	100.48	100.93	101.37	101.77	102.16	102.53	102.87	103.20
5.60	100.38	100.75	101.09	101.42	101.72	102.01	102.29	102.55
5.70	100.29	100.56	100.82	101.06	101.29	101.51	101.71	101.91
5.80	100.19	100.37	100.54	100.70	100.86	101.00	101.14	101.27
5.90	100.10	100.19	100.27	100.35	100.43	100.50	100.57	100.63
6.00	100.00	100.00	100.00	100.00	100.00	100.00	100.00	100.00
6.10	99.90	99.81	99.73	99.65	99.57	99.50	99.44	99.37
6.20	99.81	99.63	99.46	99.30	99.15	99.01	98.88	98.75
6.30	99.71	99.44	99.19	98.95	98.73	98.52	98.32	98.14
6.40	99.62	99.26	98.92	98.61	98.31	98.03	97.77	97.53
6.50	99.52	99.08	98.66	98.26	97.89	97.55	97.22	96.92
6.60	99.43	98.89	98.39	97.92	97.48	97.07	96.68	96.32
6.70	99.33	98.71	98.13	97.58	97.07	96.59	96.14	95.72
6.80	99.24	98.53	97.86	97.24	96.66	96.11	95.60	95.13
6.90	99.14	98.35	97.60	96.90	96.25	95.64	95.07	94.54
7.00	99.05	98.16	97.34	96.56	95.84	95.17	94.54	93.95
7.10	98.96	97.98	97.07	96.23	95.44	94.70	94.01	93.37
7.20	98.86	97.80	96.81	95.89	95.04	94.24	93.49	92.80
7.30	98.77	97.62	96.55	95.56	94.63	93.77	92.97	92.23
7.40	98.67	97.44	96.29	95.23	94.24	93.31	92.46	91.66
7.50	98.58	97.26	96.04	94.90	93.84	92.86	91.95	91.10
7.60	98.49	97.08	95.78	94.57	93.45	92.40	91.44	90.54
7.70	98.39	96.90	95.52	94.24	93.05	91.95	90.93	89.99
7.80	98.30	96.73	95.27	93.92	92.66	91.50	90.43	89.44
7.90	98.21	96.55	95.01	93.59	92.28	91.06	89.93	88.89
8.00	98.11	96.37	94.76	93.27	91.89	90.61	89.44	88.35

if the market price is known. If we knew that the market price was 91.89, we could scan down the five-year column until 91.89 was found and observe that the value is associated with an 8 percent interest rate.

Anyone who deals in bonds will have a calculator or a book-length set of bond yield tables readily at hand. If a bond yield table is not readily available, the yield to maturity can be estimated using the approximation formula:

$$Y = \frac{Int + (F - M)/N}{(F + M)/2} \qquad (6\text{-}10)$$

where: Int = Dollar interest payments per year

M = Market value of the bond

F = Face value of the bond

N = Number of years until maturity.

Applying this formula to the above bond, the yield to maturity is approximately

$$Y = \frac{60 + (1,000.00 - 918.90)/5}{(1,000.00 + 918.90)/2} = 7.9\%.$$

SUMMARY

Interest is basic to the operation of the financial system. It is defined as rent paid for the use of money. The general structure of interest rates is a function of the quantity and quality of investment alternatives, future expectations of consumers and businessmen, financial and nonfinancial habits which shift over time, and the level of inflation.

Time Value of Money

Compound Value is the amount to which an investment will grow over a particular time horizon at a given interest rate. The amount to which an investment (P) will grow in n periods with an interest rate of i per period is

$$FV_n = P(1 + i)^n.$$

If interest is compounded or added on k times per year, the amount to which a sum (P) will grow is

$$FV_n = P\left(1 + \frac{i}{12}\right)^{nk}.$$

Compound Value of an Annuity or stream of payments is the sum of the compound values of individual payments. The compound value of an annuity of $1 per year for n years at i percent is as follows:

$$CVA(i,n) = 1 + (1 + i) + (1 + i)^2$$
$$+ \ldots + (1 + i)^{n-1}.$$

Present Value of a Single Payment is the inverse of the compound value of a single payment. With annual compounding, the present value of $1 received n years from today at interest rate i, is

$$P = \frac{1}{(1 + i)^n}.$$

Present Value of an Annuity is the sum of the present values of the individual payments. The present value of $1 per year for n years at i percent is

$$PV = \frac{1}{(1 + i)} + \frac{1}{(1 + i)^2}$$
$$+ \ldots + \frac{1}{(1 + i)^n}.$$

Annual Percentage Rate

Many problems faced by financial institutions involve cases where the cash flows are known and the interest rate is desired. For such problems, the annual percentage rate is the discount rate which makes the present value of the cash inflows equal to the present value of the cash outflows.

QUESTIONS

1. Why is it important to convert all methods of computing interest to some common basis?

2. In competing for deposits, financial institutions have taken to compounding interest more than once a year. Why would they do this instead of simply raising the annual compounding rate directly?

3. Why do lenders charge points on mortgage loans rather than just increasing the stated interest rate?

4. Other things being equal, a long-term investment will carry a higher interest rate than one with a short maturity. Why then do automobile loans frequently carry higher effective interest rates than mortgage loans?

5. Determine the interest rate and points being charged on mortgage loans at a local financial institution. Convert this to an effective interest rate, if necessary, and compare it to the prime rate that is being charged the best

business customers. (The prime rate is published in the *Federal Reserve Bulletin*.) How do you account for the difference?

PROBLEMS

1. A five-year certificate of deposit pays 6.25 percent compounded annually. A $5,000 deposit will grow to what amount in five years?

2. A competing certificate of deposit pays 6 percent interest with semiannual compounding. Which provides the higher return?

3. An investment plan calls for depositing $1,200 at the end of each year for the next twenty years in an account which pays 8 percent interest compounded annually. What will be the value at the end of twenty-years?

4. Another investment plan calls for depositing $1,000 at the end of each month for the next twenty years in an account which pays 8 percent compounded monthly. What will be the value at the end of twenty years?

5. A non-interest bearing second mortgage for $10,000 has a maturity of five years. The holder of the mortgage needs cash for another investment and wishes to sell it today. If similar mortgages yield 10 percent annual compound return, how much could the holder expect to sell the mortgage for?

6. A $1,000 lump sum payment is to be received in one year. What is the present value at 8 percent discounted monthly?

7. A $1,000 bond pays $40 interest at the end of each six-month period and will mature in five years. At 6 percent required return with semiannual compounding what is the value of the bond?

8. Three alternate loan policies involve simple interest of 8 percent, add-on interest of 7.5 percent, or discount interest of 7.25 percent. In any case, retirement will be through thirty-six equal monthly installments. A $10,000 note is signed. Compute the net proceeds of the loan, the monthly payments, and the effective annual percentage rate for each method using the procedure shown in table 6-10.

9. A bond, which pays a face or coupon rate of 6 percent and will mature in eight years, is quoted at 96.32. What is the yield to maturity?

10. What would happen to the price of the above bond if the yield to maturity were to increase to 8 percent?

11. What size equal monthly payments would be required to retire a $30,000, 8 percent mortgage in twenty years? In thirty years?

12. If the above mortgage required a four-point service charge and was to be retired in twenty years, what would be the annual percentage rate?

13. A $50,000 piece of machinery has a five-year life and zero salvage value. A lease with equal annual payments at the end of each year for five years and a 14 percent annual percentage rate is desired. What will be the size of the annual lease payments?

14. A certificate of deposit pays an annual interest rate of 12 percent with continuous compounding. What is the effective annual interest rate?

SELECTED REFERENCES

Bonker, Dick. "The 'Rule of 78.'" *Journal of Finance* 31 (June 1976): 877–888.

Kalay, Avner, and Rabinovitch, Ramon. "On Individual Loans Pricing, Credit Rationing, and Interest Rate Regulation." *Journal of Finance* 33 (September 1978): 1071–1085.

Kau, James B., and Keenan, Donald. "The Theory of Housing and Interest Rates." *Journal of Financial and Quantitative Analysis* 14 (November 1980): 833–847.

Chapter 7

Required Return and Value

In the previous chapter we developed the general principles of interest, frequently referred to as the mathematics of finance. For the manager to apply these principles it is frequently necessary to have an understanding of the factors determining the required interest rate on a particular investment. It is also necessary to have an understanding of the relationship between required return and value. Both topics are developed in this chapter.

There are two related questions in the determination of interest rates. First, there is the question of how the general level of interest rates is established. Second, there is the question of how time until maturity and risk cause interest rate differentials between different securities. In this chapter, we begin with a discussion of factors affecting the general level of interest rates.[1] We then consider certain variables that influence interest rate differentials between securities. Finally, we discuss the relationship between required return and value.

DETERMINANTS OF THE GENERAL LEVEL OF INTEREST RATES

Modern theory recognizes that interest has a role similar to the role of price in determining the supply and demand for other goods. There is a supply curve for money to loan:[2] the higher the interest rate, the more funds will be available for lending. Likewise, there is a demand curve for funds: the lower the interest rate, the more credit will be desired (figure 7-1). In this section, the various factors affecting these supply and demand curves will be examined.

Supply of Funds

The supply of loanable funds available within the economy may be viewed as a schedule relating the various quantities of dollars available for

---

[1]While the "general level of interest rates" refers to a spectrum of rates which tend to move in the same direction over time, it is convenient to speak as if there were a single rate during the early part of our analysis.

[2]For convenience, we limit the present discussion to borrowing and lending. A company may choose to sell stock instead of borrow and some savers may choose to buy stock instead of lend. For purposes of studying the overall supply and demand for funds, stock may be viewed as synonymous with debt instruments.

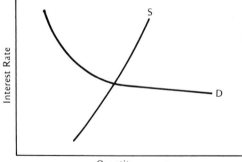

Figure 7–1: Supply and demand for loanable funds.

loan at different interest rates, given existing economic conditions. Determinants of the supply schedule include the following:

> Time preference for consumption
>
> Expectations concerning future income
>
> Desire for money balances
>
> Actions of monetary authorities

Time Preference for Consumption This was the first component of the supply schedule to be recognized by economists. It was assumed that consumers were impatient, thus preferred present to future consumption. One person could consume in excess of his current income only if another consumed less. Compensation in the form of interest would thus encourage one to forego consumption today in return for the prospect of even greater consumption at some future date.

The existence of a multibillion dollar consumer finance industry bears adequate witness to the fact that there are those willing to pay a premium for the privilege of consuming now rather than later. However, it does not necessarily follow that savers are motivated to save primarily by a desire to earn interest. For example, people continue to save even when the real interest rate—the interest rate after adjustment for changes in buying power—is negative. While high interest rates may serve to encourage some savings, interest is clearly not the only motivation for savings.

Expectations Concerning Future Income Another important determinant of the amount of savings is one's income. If it is expected to fall at a future time, savings today assure some level of consumption at that future time. A significant portion of saving is in the form of contributions to various retirement funds to provide income in the retirement years. Uncertainty about future income, caused by factors such as the possibility of a layoff or ill health, also encourages savings. This effect is most frequently seen in terms of increased savings in response to concern about the possibility of a recession. Thus expectations of falling future income or uncertainty about future income may lead to an increased supply of savings.

Desire for Money Balances Sometimes a dollar of savings can result in less than a dollar in loans. Savings may be held in the form of money balances—currency and bank demand deposits—or they may be invested in direct loans and securities. One important reason for holding money balances is transactions demand. If a person is paid on a weekly basis, he will hold money at the beginning of the week to handle transactions later in the week. Likewise, businesses hold money for transaction purposes.

In addition to transactions balances, money is held because of uncertainty. Investment in securities, even U.S. government securities, can result in a loss if the interest rate rises sharply. Thus uncertainty about future interest rates will lead to increased desire for money balances. Uncertainty about future income and future investment opportunities are other factors that may lead to increased desire to hold money balances.

The holding of money balances reduces the availability of credit. Money balances held in the form of currency are obviously not available for lending. More importantly, the requirement that financial institutions hold reserves equal to some portion of transaction account balances means that the decision to hold money balances in any form reduces the supply of credit.

Monetary Authorities Government officials have an impact on the supply of credit. Control of credit availability is an important part of government action to stabilize the economy. One form of control is to change the reserve requirements for commercial banks, thus influencing the proportion of bank deposits available in lending markets. Another, more frequently used approach is for the Federal Reserve System to buy or sell U.S. government securities. When the Federal Reserve System purchases securities, it creates money, thereby increasing funds available to loan in credit markets. Of course, the sale of securities owned by the Federal Reserve System has the opposite effect. Thus the Federal Reserve System acts to increase or decrease the availability of credit in response to current economic conditions.

In summary, the supply of credit is affected by the time preference for consumption, expectations concerning future income, the form in which savings are held, and Federal Reserve actions to control credit. Line *S* in figure 7-1 represents the amount of credit that will be made available at each interest rate under a particular set of economic conditions. The higher the interest rate, the more credit will be made available. A change in conditions can cause *S* to shift. For example, Federal Reserve policy to decrease credit through a change in reserve requirements would cause less credit to be available at each interest rate and would cause the supply curve to shift to the left.

Interest rates are not determined by the supply curve acting alone; they are determined by the interaction of supply and demand. We now turn our attention to the other half of the credit market—demand.

Demand for Funds

The demand for loanable funds within the economy may be viewed as a schedule relating the dollar volume of credit desired at each interest rate, given existing economic conditions. Components of the demand for credit include the following:

Demand for consumer credit

Government borrowing

Acquisition of capital

Demand for Consumer Credit This is generally thought to be relatively insensitive to the interest rate; a rise in interest rates would cause only a small decline in the desire of consumers to borrow. Factors relating to income are believed to have a greater impact. Debt capacity is determined by the ability to make payments. An actual or anticipated increase in income increases the willingness of consumers to borrow so they can enjoy the benefits of that future income today. Stability of income is another factor. If income is viewed as stable, consumers feel more confident of their ability to handle additional debt. Age and family characteristics of the population are also important determinants of the demand for consumer credit. Young people at the family formation age normally demand more consumer credit than older members of the population. While the interest rate had some impact on the demand for consumer credit, these other considerations are of major importance.

Government Borrowing Like consumer borrowing, government borrowing is affected more by revenue expectations and perceived needs than by interest rates. The size of the government deficit is the major determinant of the extent to which government enters credit markets on the demand side. The demand for credit by government is thus insensitive to the rate of interest.

Acquisition of Capital The component of demand which exhibits the greatest sensitivity to interest rates is acquiring capital. Capital goods, such as machinery and factories, make greater production possible. For a capital investment to be attractive, its anticipated return must be at least as great as the interest rate that will be charged. At any time there will be a series of capital investment opportunities, some with higher returns than others. Thus the quantity of credit demanded for the purpose of acquiring capital goods depends on the level of interest rates.

In addition to factories and machinery, another important type of capital good is the residential structure. The quantity of funds demanded for first mortgage loans—characterized by long-term maturities—displays some sensitivity to interest rate movements because the interest rate has a major impact on the monthly cost of owning a home. A small shift in interest rates typically results in a relatively large shift in monthly payments for loans of this type. From 1966 to 1984 the monthly payment per $1,000 of principal value of a mortgage loan nearly doubled, solely because of an increase in the interest rate. Thus interest represents a major portion of the cost of residential real estate.

The shape of the demand curve in figure 7-1 illustrates the shape of a demand curve when some components of demand are sensitive to interest rate levels while other components are relatively insensitive. As interest rates rise to higher levels, demand becomes relatively insensitive to changes in the interest rate, resulting in a near-vertical demand curve at these higher levels.

Inflation and Interest Rates

The impact of inflation on interest rates has been a matter of growing concern. To understand the impact of inflation, it is first necessary to differentiate between real and nominal interest rates. The nominal interest rate is the contract interest rate paid while the real rate reflects changes in buying power. If the nominal interest rate is 7 percent and you have $1.00, the dollar will grow by 7 percent to $1.07 over a year if invested. Suppose that some commodity (basket of goods) costs $1.00 per unit at the beginning of the year. If the inflation rate is 5 percent, the commodity will cost $1.05 at the end of the year. If you purchase today, your dollar will purchase one unit. If you invest the dollar for a year, you can buy $1.07/$1.05 = 1.019 units. The real interest rate is therefore 1.9 percent because you can purchase 1.9 percent more units than you could at the beginning of the year. This definition of the real interest rate can be summarized in a simple formula:

$$\frac{\text{Real}}{\text{Int. Rate}} = \frac{1 + \text{Nominal Int. Rate}}{1 + \text{Inflation Rate}} - 1.0.$$

Applied to the above situation, the real interest rate is computed as $(1.07/1.05) - 1 = 0.019$. As a quick approximation, it is sometimes said that the real interest rate is approximately the difference between the nominal interest rate and the inflation rate, approximately 2 percent for this example.

Traditional theory has held that the real interest rate will not be affected by inflation and that the nominal rate will increase by the expected inflation rate because savers must be compensated in the form of real returns if they are to be encouraged to lend out their money.

INTEREST RATE DIFFERENTIALS

Up to this point we have treated interest rates as if there were one rate applicable to all securities and loans rather than the array of rates that actually exists at any one time. The rates on securities vary with regard to both risk and maturity. Understanding these differentials is vital for dealing with many financial institution management problems. The two types of differentials are taken up in this section.

Term Structure of Interest Rates

The term structure of interest rates represents the relationship between yield and maturity. U.S. government securities can be used to illustrate the impact of maturity as they differ with regard to maturity but not with regard to safety of principal. Figure 7-2 is a yield curve, showing the interest rates on U.S. government securities of various maturities. It represents a more or less typical yield curve, with the interest rate increasing as maturity increases. The three main approaches to explanation of the shape of the yield curve are liquidity premium theory, expectation theory, and market segmentation theory. Each of these is discussed in the following paragraphs.

Liquidity Premium Even though U.S. government securities are considered virtually risk-free with regard to payment at maturity, there is still a risk associated with an early need for funds. If a holder of long-term bonds should need the funds before maturity, the bonds must

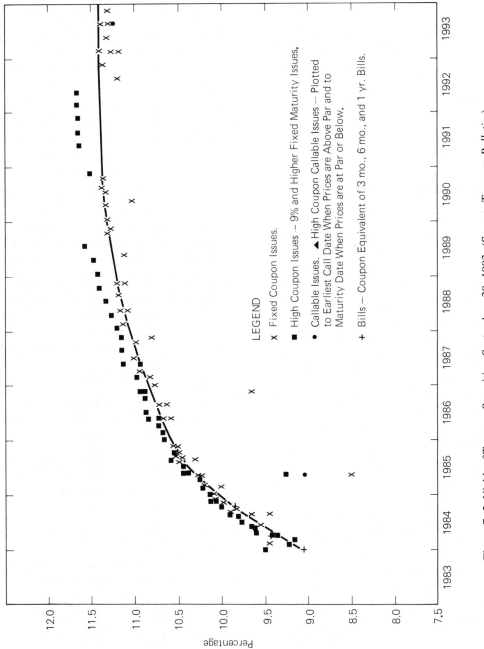

Figure 7–2: Yields of Treasury Securities, September 30, 1983. (Source: *Treasury Bulletin.*)

be sold in the secondary securities market. If the general level of interest rates has risen in the meantime, the price of outstanding bonds will have fallen. The longer the maturity of a bond, the greater will be the change in the price resulting from a change in interest rates.[3] Thus, even among securities that are risk-free with regard to payment at maturity, longer maturities result in greater risk. Under normal conditions, higher return is necessary to encourage people to accept the greater liquidity risk associated with long term securities.

Expectation Theory   Another factor affecting the shape of the yield curve is the set of expectations with regard to future interest rates. In the absence of liquidity risk or market restrictions, the yield curve would represent an average of short-term rates expected over each maturity. Thus the yield curve reflects both liquidity risks and expected changes in the general level of interest rates. Figure 7-3 illustrates a yield curve in which short-term rates are higher than long-term rates. This cannot be accounted for with liquidity premium theory. Expectation theory would argue that the difference in shape between figures 7-2 and 7-3 is explained if September 30, 1983 was a time when investors were expecting a rise in the level of interest rates and 26 February 1982, was a time when they felt interest rates would decline after about a year. If interest rates were expected to fall, borrowers would tend to avoid long-term borrowing and temporarily borrow short-term with the hope of refinancing through issuance of long-term securities when rates fall. Lenders, on the other hand, would be attempting to acquire long-term securities before rates fell. This combination of actions would tend to drive short-term rates up and long-term rates down until each rate equals the average of expected short-term rates over its maturity.

Market Segmentation Theory   A third method is used to explain interest rate differentials. With this approach, the market for funds is looked at as a set of markets, not a single market.

---

[3]A review of bond yield computations in chapter 6 will confirm this.

For example, the short-term maturity market can be viewed as a liquidity adjustment market while the long-term market can be viewed as a market for capital investment funds. To the extent maturity needs rather than interest rate considerations determine maturity, there are separate markets for each maturity and interest rate differentials are determined by supply and demand conditions in the various maturity markets. Using this approach, the inverted yield curve of figure 7-3 would be explained by heavy demand in the liquidity adjustment end of the markets.

It is probably most helpful to look at these three approaches to the shape of the yield curve as complementary rather than competing models. First, it is reasonable to expect some compensation for holding longer maturities and giving up some liquidity. Second, it is reasonable for expectations to be reflected in the term structure because some borrowers and lenders can adjust their maturity structure in response to expected interest rate changes. Third, there is some segmentation in the markets. An example of the impact of this is a fed funds rate well above the rate on maturing Treasury bills. Thus all three reasons should be considered when studying term structure.

Adjusting positions in response to existing and anticipated yield curve shapes can have a substantial impact on profitability. Many borrowers and lenders, particularly portfolio managers of large institutions, study the shape of the yield curves, prepare their own interest rate forecasts, and attempt to pattern their activities in the credit markets in response to these factors.

Duration   In studying the term structure of interest rates and the sensitivity of security prices to interest rates, one is frequently confronted by differences between average life and absolute maturity. Consider, for example, a thirty-year mortgage and a thirty-year pure discount bond—a bond that provides no annual interest payments, but promises only one payment at the end of thirty years to cover both principal and accrued interest. Both of these are thirty year instruments, but half of the mortgage payments are received before the fifteenth year. Thus, the

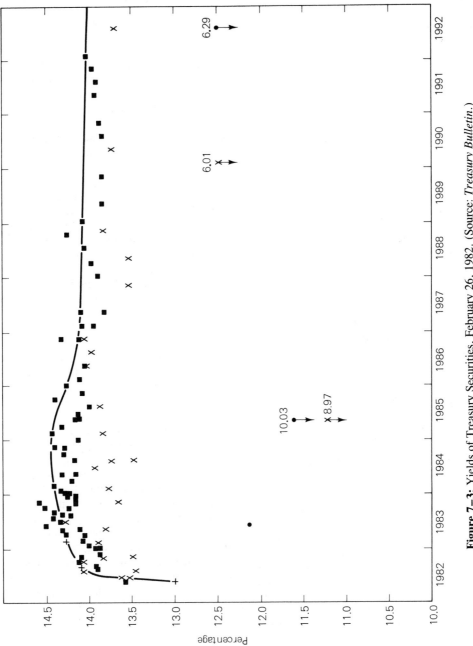

Figure 7–3: Yields of Treasury Securities, February 26, 1982. (Source: *Treasury Bulletin.*)

average time to receipt of cash flow from the mortgage is much less, and the mortgage will be less sensitive to interest rate changes.

Duration is a measure of the average maturity of a security. Its computation is

$$D = \frac{\left[\dfrac{P_1}{(1+r)^1}\right]1 + \left[\dfrac{P_2}{(1+r)^2}\right]2 + \cdots + \left[\dfrac{P_n}{(1+r)^n}\right]n}{\dfrac{P_1}{(1+r)^1} + \dfrac{P_2}{(1+r)^2} + \cdots + \dfrac{P_n}{(1+r)^n}}$$

where P_1 is the cash flow in year 1, P_2 is the cash flow in year 2, etc., with no distinction made between principal and interest payments, and r is the required return. If the security is publicly traded, the denominator in the equation equals the market price of the security.

Example   A $1,000, 10 percent bond calls for three annual interest payments of $100 each and then a $1,000 principal payment at the end of three years. Interest rates have risen so that the required return is 14 percent. The duration is

$$D = \frac{[100/(1.14)]1 + [100/(1.14^2)]2 + [(100+1000)/(1.14^3)]3}{[100/(1.14)] + [100/(1.14^2)] + [(100+1000)/(1.14^3)]}$$

$$= 2469.03/907.14 = 2.72 \text{ years.}$$

Items with the same absolute maturity can have substantially different durations. At a 14 percent required return, for example, a twenty-year bond with a 6 percent coupon rate has a duration of 8.65 years while a twenty-year bond with a 16 percent coupon rate has a duration of 7.44 years. At a 14 percent required return a twenty-year mortgage calling for equal annual payments to cover principal and interest would have a duration of 6.57 years (regardless of the face interest rate on the mortgage). Some of the variations around the yield curves (figures 7-2 and 7-3) are probably accounted for by differences between maturity and duration.

Risk and Required Rates of Return

Another major factor which leads to interest rate differentials is risk[4] with regard to the actual stream of income emanating from a particular security. The value of a share of stock or a bond is a function of the anticipated future cash flows to be derived therefrom and is equal to the discounted present value of these flows. For a debt instrument, the returns are in the form of principal and interest payments, while for stock the return is in the form of dividends. The present value of this stream of returns and thus the price of the security can change because the general level of interest rates (and therefore the required rate of return) changes. The value of the security will also change if there is a change in the stream of cash flow expected, normally caused by a change in actual or anticipated profitability of the firm. When risk increases, the required return also increases. The bond issuers are rated as to the quality of the issue. The most widely known of these rating agencies are Moody's and Standard and Poor (for Moody's rating, see table 5-3).

The rating is one standard measure of the risk level. Figure 7-4 shows average yields of bonds by rating over the past 50 years. The interest rates are higher for more risky bonds, and the size of the spread increases as the general level of interest rates increases (figure 7-4). It is also known that the spread increases with increased uncertainty about the economic outlook.

The data on bond yields do not provide any specific information about the relationship between risk and required return. Studies of the specific relationship between risk and required rate of return have, for the most part, been based on common stock returns, although the results can be generalized to investments of any kind. A major result of these studies—the mean-variance capital asset pricing model—is summarized in appendix 7-A.

---

[4]Risk in this context can be thought of as the probability that the stream of anticipated returns will not be realized. More generally, risk can be thought of as the probability of a financial loss.

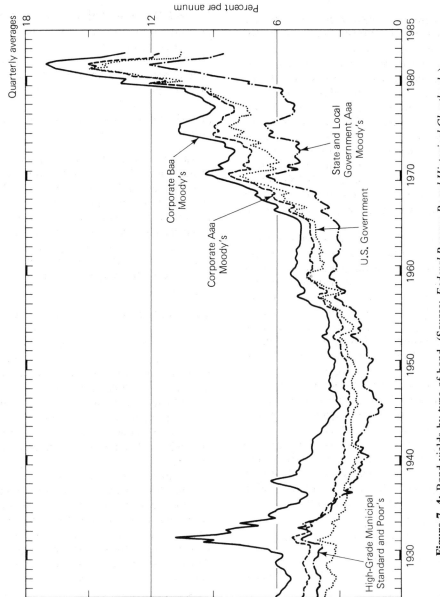

Figure 7–4: Bond yields by type of bond. (Source: *Federal Reserve Board Historical Chartbook.*)

FORECASTING INTEREST RATES

Future interest rate movements are of vital concern to institutions. Profits can be favorably influenced through accurate projection of interest rates followed by appropriate policy decisions. The savings and loan industry has at times found its profits severely eroded by being on the wrong side of a change in interest rates, granting long-term loans while relying on short-term deposits in periods of rising interest rates. The industry has responded to these losses by increasing its efforts to acquire long-term funds, such as long-term certificates of deposit. If this action had been taken earlier in anticipation of rising interest rates, substantial losses could have been avoided.

Most efforts to forecast interest rates concentrate on what is considered the intermediate term by forecasters: from one quarter to several years in the future. Over the intermediate term, interest rates respond primarily to a set of economic variables discussed in this section. Short-term forecasts of a few days to a few weeks are normally prepared by forecasting the recent trend of interest rates. Long-term forecasts involve such factors as changing age characteristics of the population.[5] Both because of the type of factors involved and because of the importance to institutions, this section will concentrate on intermediate-term forecasting.

Methods of preparing forecasts of the general level of interest rates range from application of judgment to mathematical models. Regardless of the method used, the major factors studied in preparing interest rate forecasts are:

1. Federal Reserve policy
2. Changes in Gross National Product
3. The liquidity of the economy
4. The outlook for the supply and demand for funds

5. The inflation rate[6]

Federal Reserve Policy This factor can be measured primarily in terms of the money supply. Target rates of growth are announced by the Federal Reserve and are widely published in the general press. Target growth rates are compared to actual growth rates in preparing forecasts of the money supply. Money supply figures are published monthly in the *Federal Reserve Bulletin* as well as in the business press generally.

Gross National Product Increases in the growth rate of Gross National Product generally cause increased demand for funds for both consumer credit and capital acquisition. Thus increases in the growth rate of Gross National Product cause interest rates to rise while declines in the growth rates typically have a downward impact. Individuals can prepare their own GNP forecasts or obtain them from publicly available sources.

The Liquidity Position of the Economy As was mentioned earlier, savings do not automatically result in a direct increase in the supply of credit. The amount of credit supply increase actually achieved depends on the desires of people and business to hold money balances. For example, if there is a general desire for increased money balances, an effort by the Federal Reserve to increase the money supply may be offset by increased liquid balances, not increased economic activity.

Obviously, the trick here is to forecast the demand for money balances in comparison to present measures of the money supply and to adjust the credit supply forecast accordingly. This is easier said than done. As was discussed earlier in this chapter, desired money balances depend on various factors such as transactions needs and uncertainty about future conditions. A good deal of experienced judgment is required and errors in this area are frequent.

---

[5]See, for example, John S. Burton and John R. Toth, "Forecasting Secular Trends in Long-Term Interest Rates," *Financial Analysts Journal* (September–October 1974): 73–87, or the series of papers on long-term trends in interest rates published in the January, 1970 issue of *Business Economics*.

[6]Francis H. Schott, "Interest Rate Forecasting in Theory and Practice," *Business Economics* 102 (September 1977): 55–60.

Outlook for the Supply and Demand for Credit A major part of the interest forecasting problem, the outlook is usually prepared by using the sources and uses of credit data published monthly in the *Federal Reserve Bulletin*. A condensed version appears in table 7-1. The individual components of the supply and demand for credit can be forecast using the outlook for GNP growth, government budgets, capital spending plan surveys, housing construction forecasts, etc. It is then possible to make a prediction as to whether supply or demand will increase more rapidly, thus whether the pressure on interest rates will be upward or downward.

Table 7-1:

Sources and Uses of Funds in U.S. Credit Markets (in $ billions)

	1981	1982	1983
Users of Credit Funds			
Total credit funds raised	404.4	411.0	528.7
Foreign uses	27.2	15.7	19.2
Total domestic uses of funds	377.2	395.3	509.5
U.S. government uses	87.4	161.3	186.6
Total private domestic uses	289.8	234.0	322.9
State and local government*	9.7	36.3	35.9
Corporate bonds	103.7	72.7	57.4
Households	120.6	86.3	163.6
Farms	16.3	9.0	3.9
Other	39.5	29.7	62.1
Sources of Credit Funds			
Total credit funds raised	404.4	411.0	528.7
Noninstitutional sources			
Lending by U.S. government	72.3	82.0	78.7
Monetary authorities	9.2	9.8	10.9
Foreign lenders	16.0	17.6	25.2
Other	1.7	30.4	45.4
From domestic financial institutions	305.2	271.2	368.5
Commercial banks	103.6	108.5	135.3
Savings institutions	27.2	30.6	128.6
Insurance and pension funds	79.3	94.2	102.1
Other financial institutions	95.2	37.9	2.6
Sources of domestic financial institution funds	305.2	271.2	368.5
Private domestic deposits	211.7	173.4	200.3
Credit market borrowing	38.0	4.4	20.5
Foreign funds	−8.7	−27.7	17.2
Insurance and pension fund reserves	73.2	85.9	88.0
Treasury balances	−1.1	6.1	−6.0
Other	−7.9	29.2	48.4
Memo: Corporate equity issues	16.8	36.6	2.1
not included in above figures			

*Classification of state and local government as ''private'' is the work of the Federal Reserve statisticians, not the authors.

Source: Condensed from *Federal Reserve Bulletin*.

Expected Inflation As indicated previously, the interest rate includes a real return and some compensation for expected inflation; the interest rate will be expected to rise with an increase in the expected rate of inflation. Many forecasting models use an average of inflation rates for previous years to forecast interest rates for the coming period; others use surveys of economists.

The various factors can be weighed in the mind of the interest rate forecaster, who relies on his judgment and past experience to develop actual forecasts, or they can be combined using mathematical models.

VALUE

The pursuit of the profitability objective normally involves two steps: the selection of assets with the highest value relative to their cost, and the management of liabilities to achieve the lowest cost of funds. Valuation principles are used to determine what a financial asset is worth, to determine the quality of collateral, and to determine the vulnerability of an asset's price to interest rate changes. Thus valuation is important for both profitability and risk analysis. It is particularly important for financial institutions because most of their assets are financial instruments.

The valuation principles discussed here are limited to revenue producing assets. We do not deal with approaches such as replacement value (sometimes used in the case of residential property) or aesthetic value (which may have some application in the world of art). We do concern ourselves with market value to the extent that we are discussing the market value of a revenue producing asset.

Valuation principles are primarily an application of interest and required return principles discussed in this and the previous chapter. A financial asset has three primary characteristics for this type of analysis: a stream of expected cash flows, a required rate of return, and a value. If two of these variables are known, the third can be inferred from the other two. Thus valuation is the topic that brings interest and required return analysis together in a useful form.

Fixed Income Assets

To begin the analysis of value, an asset having no maturity and paying a constant stream of cash flows provides a good illustration. An example of this type of asset is the British Consul, a bond issued to finance the Napoleonic wars. It carries no maturity date but pays a fixed amount of interest each year. Preferred stock, of course, has similar characteristics. For such an instrument, the value (V) is based on the annual cash flows (CF) and the required rate of return (r):

$$V = CF/r. \qquad (7\text{-}1)$$

For an instrument with an $80 per year cash flow and a 6 percent required return, the value is

$$V = 80/0.06 = \$1,333.$$

This basic valuation principle can be readily verified from common observation. If a savings account pays 6 percent interest, a $1,333 deposit would yield interest of $80 ($0.06 \times \$1,333$) per year. Thus a promise to pay $80 per year would not be worth more than the amount that you would need to deposit in a savings account to achieve the same result.[7]

The simple problem above can be used to illustrate the relationship among the three characteristics. For example, if we know that the value is $1,333 and the annual cash flow is $80, then the rate of return is found by solving for r (equation 7-1). In this case, the answer would be 6 percent.

The value of an asset with no maturity is particularly sensitive to interest rate changes. If we wanted to test the sensitivity of value to interest rate changes, we could simply solve equation 7-1 for various levels of required return as is done below:

$$V = 80/0.02 = \$4,000$$
$$V = 80/0.06 = \$1,333$$
$$V = 80/0.07 = \$1,143$$
$$V = 80/0.15 = \$\ \ 533.$$

---

[7]This comparison ignores the fact that the savings account would normally carry a lower required return because it is more liquid. Unless the yield curve were perfectly flat, there would be some differences between the required return on the Consul and the savings account interest rate.

Even a one percentage point change in interest rate leads to a 14 percent change in value. Interest rates of such obligations have risen from the 2 percent range to the 15 percent range, resulting in a loss of nearly 90 percent of the previous value with no decline in the credit worthiness of the borrower.

The same general principles apply to the valuation of all financial assets. The value equals the present value of all cash flows, discounted at the required rate of return. However, the existence of a maturity increases the difficulty of computation, requiring the use of the present value tables. A bond with a maturity of ten years, an $80 annual interest paid in semiannual installments, and a $1,000 maturity value will be used as an example. If the required return is 6 percent, the twenty-year, 3 percent tables are used instead of the ten-year, 6 percent tables because payment is semiannual. The value of the bond would be

$$14.877 \times 40 + 0.5537$$
$$\times \ 1,000 = \$1,148.78.[8]$$

To test the sensitivity of the value of this bond to various interest rates, we can simply repeat the calculation at other rates:

2%: 18.046 × 40 + 0.8195 × 1,000
= $1,541.34
6%: 14.877 × 40 + 0.5537 × 1,000
= $1,148.78
7%: 14.212 × 40 + 0.5026 × 1,000
= $1,071.08
9%: 13.008 × 40 + 0.4146 × 1,000
= $ 934.92.

The existence of a fairly limited maturity decreases the sensitivity of value to interest rate changes. In this case one percentage point increase in the interest rate causes the value of the bond to decline by less than 7 percent as opposed to over 14 percent for the perpetual bond.

Sensitivity of the market values of mortgages can be treated in a similar manner. Using table A-8, we find that the monthly payment for a thirty-year, 9 percent, $50,000 mortgage would be $402.31 ($50,000/124.282). If the interest

rate were to rise to 12 percent, the value of such a mortgage would decline to $39,112 ($402.31 × 97.218) (again using table A-8), a loss in value of 22 percent. By way of contrast, a fifteen-year mortgage would have suffered only a 15 percent decline in value under the same circumstances.

Any fixed-income security can be converted to a stream of cash flows and its value can be determined by discounting this stream at the appropriate required return. Alternately, the rate of return can be found if the value and the stream of cash flows are known. This was illustrated for bonds in chapter 6.

Certain nonfinancial assets, such as rental property, can be valued in a similar manner. The value of rental property, for example, equals the present value of the cash flows generated. These include rental income, net of expenses, and terminal value. An income property will cost $25,000 in cash and will require the assumption of an $80,000 mortgage. Annual cash flow, net of all cash expenses including tax and mortgage repayment, would be $3,000 per year and the value of the property at the end of the twenty-year period would be $20,000. At a 12 percent required return, the value would be

$$3,000 \times 7.4694 + 20,000$$
$$\times \ 0.1037 = \$24,482.$$

The value of the cash flows is less than the amount required to purchase the building. Thus it provides a return below 12 percent and would not be an attractive investment.[9]

Equity Securities

While the same principles apply to equity securities, the problem is complicated by the fact that equity securities do not provide a contractual payment, but provide returns based on profits of the firm whose ownership they represent. It is necessary to develop some indirect method of

[8]Based on tables A-5 and A-7. Review the present value methods in chapter 6 if the reasons for this are not clear.

[9]The same approach could be applied to speculative real estate providing no current income. If the required return is 12 percent, the property is expected to be worth $100,000 in five years, and annual holding expense (tax and insurance) is $2,000, the value of the property today is

−$2,000 × 3.6048 + $100,000 × 0.5674 = $49,530

determining value. Two frequently used approaches are discussed here.

The *price-earnings ratio* approach provides one such method of valuation. The price-earnings ratio is simply the ratio of market price to earnings per share for a company's common stock. It can be used as a multiplier like a present value factor. Its use is based on the argument that the earnings, whether paid out or reinvested to provide future dividends, are the return to shareholders. The multiplier applied to these earnings depends on the stability and expected growth of the earnings as well as other opportunities for investment. While the average price-earnings ratio is presently about 10, the range is so broad that ratios of 50 or more are not unheard of.

As an example of the use of this approach, suppose the stock of a company that is not publicly owned is to be given an estimated value. Earnings per share for the company are $3.20. We would begin by looking at the price-earnings ratios for companies in similar business lines whose stock was publicly traded. Suppose that we find a range of 12 to 15. We would then multiply $3.20 by each of these numbers and establish a value range between $38.40 and $48.00. The location of the value within this range would depend on the prospects for this company versus the others in the same business area, as well as factors such as marketability of shares.

The *dividend growth model* is another method of valuing common stock. It is most likely to be applied in a case such as a utility where the dividend level is stable and the growth rate is moderate. In this case, the value of a share of stock equals the present value of the dividends directly:

$$V = \frac{d}{r - g} \qquad (7\text{-}2)$$

where: d = Expected dividends over the next year

r = Required rate of return

g = Anticipated growth rate of dividends.

For example, a company is expected to pay dividends of $2.38 over the next year and dividends are expected to grow at the rate of 4 percent a year. At a required return of 14 percent, the value would be

$$V = \frac{2.38}{0.14 - 0.04} = \$23.80.$$

The use of this approach involves two problems. First, there is the problem of a growth rate. The model assumes a stable, continuous growth rate. Since growth rates greater than the overall economy are not sustainable, it can only be used with low, stable growth rates. Second, there is the problem of determining the appropriate rate of return. The mean-variance capital market model, discussed in appendix 7-A, is frequently used to determine the required rate of return.

The valuation of common stock is made difficult by the fact that there is no accurate way to predict the stream of cash flow. Sometimes these estimating problems are avoided by assuming that the book value per share represents the actual value. This approach ignores the fact that the earnings stream, not historical cost, determines value.

SUMMARY

We have examined both the factors affecting the general level of interest rates and the factors affecting interest rate differentials. The general level of interest rates is determined by supply and demand. The primary factors affecting the supply of credit are

1. Time preference for consumption
2. Expectations concerning future income
3. Desire for money balances

The primary components of demand for credit are

1. Demand for consumer credit
2. Government borrowing
3. Acquisition of capital

The general level of interest rates is also affected by the anticipated rate of inflation. Although the adjustment appears to be less than complete, with the nominal interest rising by less than the anticipated increase in inflation. The interest rate will nevertheless increase in response to an increase in expected inflation.

Interest rate differentials between securities are attributed to risk and time until maturity. The yield curve shows the relationship between interest rate and time until maturity. The shape of the yield curve depends primarily on liquidity preference, expectations concerning future interest rates, and conditions in various sectors of the market for funds.

Interest rate forecasters study the factors leading to changes in interest rates discussed in the first part of the chapter. The five major factors studied are

1. Federal Reserve policy
2. Changes in Gross National Product
3. The liquidity of the economy
4. The outlook for supply and demand for funds
5. The inflation rate

These factors are combined using either the judgment and experience of the forecaster or mathematical models.

Valuation is an application of interest and required return analysis. The value of a financial asset equals the present value of the cash flows discounted at the required rate of return. For fixed-income securities, the calculation is relatively straightforward. For equity securities, the problem is complicated by the fact that cash flows are not known and must be estimated.

Required return and valuation principles are useful to institution managers in gauging profitability and risk exposure. Thus they play a vital role in asset management. As we will see in the following chapter, they also play an important role in management of sources of funds.

QUESTIONS

1. Why does a yield curve generally slope upward? What factors would lead to other shapes?

2. As a library project, trace the volume of demand for funds. Which use—government, consumer, capital investment—appears to be the most volatile?

3. Locate at least two recent articles discussing the expected trend in interest rates. Compare and contrast the conclusions and the reasoning.

4. What are the primary sources and uses of credit in the United States?

5. We rely on the rate of return as the method of allocating funds in a free economy. Does this method lead to any problems? What other methods are possible?

PROBLEMS

1. Construct a figure illustrating the downward sloping demand curve and upward sloping supply curve for funds. Illustrate, by showing shifts in the curve, the impact of

    a. An increase in government deficit spending.

    b. A decrease in the savings rate.

2. Construct a yield curve for the most recent date available using information from the Federal Reserve Bulletin. Do you find evidence of any anticipated changes in interest rates?

3. The nominal interest rate for a particular year was 8 percent and the inflation rate was 5 percent. What was the real rate of interest?

4. Dividends for American Dynamics are expected to be $4 a share next year. The required rate of return is 16 percent. Compute the value of a share of stock for expected dividend growth rates of 8 percent, 4 percent, and 0 percent a year.

5. Two five-year bonds are available. Either will provide a 14 percent yield to maturity. One is selling for its par value of $1,000 and pays interest of $140 a year. The other pays no interest, and simply pays its par value of $1,000 at maturity. This second bond is selling for $519.36. Compute the duration of each bond. Which bond would show the

greatest price change with a change in interest rates.

SELECTED REFERENCES

Cox, John C., Ingersoll, Jonathan E. Jr., and Ross, Stephen A. "A Reexamination of Traditional Hypotheses About the Term Structure of Interest Rates." *The Journal of Finance* 36 (September 1981): 769–799.

Gultekin, N. Bulent, Rogalski, Richard J., and Tinic, Seha M. "Option Pricing Model Estimates: Some Empirical Results." *Financial Management* 11 (Spring 1982): 58–69.

Hessel, Christopher A. and Huffman, Lucy. "The Effect of Taxation on Immunization Rules and Duration Estimation." *The Journal of Finance*. 36 (December 1981): 1127–1142.

Lombra, Raymond E. "The Changing Role of Real and Nominal Interest Rates." *Federal Reserve Bank of Kansas City Economic Review* (February 1984): pp. 12–25.

Roley, Vance V. "The Determinants of the Treasury Security Yield Curve." *The Journal of Finance*. 36 (December 1981): 1103–1126.

Sinkey, Joseph F., Jr. and Miles, James A. "The Use of Warrants in the Bail Out of First Pennsylvania Bank: An Application of Option Pricing." *Financial Management* 11 (Autumn 1982): 27–32.

Appendix 7-A

Mean-Variance Capital Asset Pricing Model

Students of finance have long recognized that the required returns are higher for risky assets. However, conversion from this general observation to a specific relationship between risk and required return proved to be an elusive goal. Mean-variance portfolio theory, developed by Harry Markowitz in the early 1950s,[1] provided the foundation for a more precise approach to risk. The work of Sharpe,[2] Treynor,[3] and Jensen,[4] in the 1960s was largely responsible for building from the foundation provided by Markowitz to a specific model of the relationship between risk and the required rate of return.

The model has proved to have numerous uses in practice. First, it provided a method of adjusting for risk in evaluating returns from investment portfolios. Second, it has been used in determining required returns for investments by profit-seeking corporations. Additional uses have been in areas such as public utility rate case hearings.

The model begins with the observation that investors are, in general, risk averse. Therefore, at any given level of expected return, the typical investor prefers less risk to more. Figure 7A-1 represents the spectrum of all portfolios available to investors at a particular time. Each point in figure 7A-1 represents a given combination of securities (a portfolio) identified as to risk and expected return. Portfolios represented by points B and C, for example, are expected to produce the same return, but portfolio B is more risky. Because investors prefer less risk and more expected return, a particular portfolio will be preferred to any portfolio directly above it or above it and to the left. Portfolio M will be preferred over portfolio B by all investors. However, the choice between M and C is not so obvious. C involves less risk and less expected return. The choice would depend on how risk averse a particular investor is, i.e., his *risk preference function*. A portfolio like M or C, for which there exists no portfolio providing less risk without less return or more return without more risk, is referred to as an *efficient portfolio*. The set of all

[1]Harry Markowitz, "Portfolio Selection," *Journal of Finance* (March 1952): 77–91.

[2]William Sharpe, "Capital Asset Prices: A Theory of Market Equilibrium Under Conditions of Risk," *The Journal of Finance* (September 1964): 425–442.

[3]Jack Treynor, "How to Rate Management of Mutual Funds," *Harvard Business Review* (January–February 1965): pp. 63–75.

[4]Michael Jensen, "Risk, the Pricing of Capital Assets, and the Evaluation of Investment Portfolios," *Journal of Business* (April 1969): 167–247.

Figure 7A–1: Investment opportunity set.

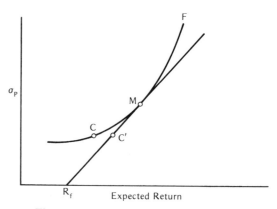

Figure 7A–2: Efficient frontier analysis.

such portfolios is referred to as the efficient frontier.

Thus far we have spoken of risk only in general terms. In practice, standard deviation, a widely used statistical measure, is normally used as a risk measure. The standard deviation of the probability distribution of expected returns (σ_p) is normally used as a measure of risk. The formula for the standard deviation is

$$\sigma_p = \sqrt{\sum_{i=1}^{n} p_i (R_i - E_p)^2} \qquad (7A\text{-}1)$$

where: R_i = Return for the portfolio if outcome i occurs

p_i = Probability of outcome i occurring

n = The number of different possible outcomes

E_p = Expected return for the portfolio.[5]

We now introduce a very important type of investment—a risk-free security such as a Treasury bill. Line F in figure 7A-2 represents the efficient frontier shown in Figure 7A-1. The efficient frontier can be drawn as a line rather than a

series of points because a near-infinite number of different portfolios is possible. By investing a portion of his funds in risky portfolio M and the remainder in a risk-free asset, an investor can create a new portfolio on the straight line connecting M (referred to as the *tangent portfolio*) and point R_f. By varying the proportion of his funds invested in M and putting the remainder in the risk-free asset, the investor can achieve a portfolio anywhere on the line connecting M and R_f. Furthermore, he can achieve points on this line above M if he can borrow at a similar interest rate. Thus, these various combinations of M and the risk-free security provide portfolios superior to all other portfolios on the efficient frontier, such as C. M would be preferred by all investors and they would adjust for their individual degree of risk aversion by varying the proportion of funds invested in M and the proportion invested at the risk-free rate.

As an example, suppose the risk-free rate is 6 percent, the expected return for portfolio M is 10 percent, and the standard deviation of expected returns for portfolio M is 4 percent. Portfolio C′ consists of two thirds of the investor's funds invested in portfolio M and one third invested in the risk-free asset. The expected return and standard deviation for portfolio C′ are

$$\text{Expected return} = \frac{2}{3} \times 0.10 + \frac{1}{3} \times 0.06$$

$$= 8.6\%$$

_____

[5]The expected return for the portfolio is computed as follows:

$$E_p = \sum_{i=1}^{n} p_i R_i$$

Standard deviation $= \frac{2}{3} \times 0.04 = 2.67\%$

Portfolio C' would be preferred over portfolio C by all investors; C' has the same standard deviation but has a higher expected return. Thus an investor wishing to accept a different amount of risk than M would move to a portfolio such as C' rather than a portfolio such as C.

If investors are in agreement about the prospects for particular securities, M must eventually contain all risky securities. The prices of individual securities will rise or fall so that demand for each, as a component of M, is neither greater nor less than the supply available. M is referred to as the *market* portfolio.

From the foregoing analysis it follows that the important aspect of risk for an individual security is its contribution to the risk of the market portfolio. The total risk of a security can be divided into two parts: diversifiable and nondiversifiable risk. For example, the purchaser of stock in one automobile company faces the risk that that company's new model will be unpopular. That risk can be diversified away by dividing funds among all automobile companies. Likewise, the possibility of a change in taste or technology resulting in a shift from products produced by one industry to those of another can be diversified away by including in the portfolio securities issued by firms in different industries. Eventually though, there are risks that cannot be diversified away. The possibility of a recession or restrictive monetary policy leading to decreased return on all security investments can only be avoided by choosing the risk-free security instead. Aggregate risks of the type that tend to affect the economy in general cannot be diversified away.

If a group of stocks had only diversifiable risk, they could be combined in a portfolio and the portfolio would be risk-free. If this risk-free portfolio had a higher return than the risk-free rate, all investors wishing to hold a risk-free investment would choose the portfolio rather than the single risk-free asset. Thus it is necessary for market equilibrium that the return on such a portfolio be the same as the risk-free rate. Therefore, risky portfolios and risky securities pay a higher

return than the risk-free rate as compensation for accepting *nondiversifiable* risk.

Nondiversifiable risk is caused by the tendency of certain factors to affect all securities in the same way. An increase in the general level of interest rates, for example, will cause an increase in required returns for all securities and will drive the prices of all securities down. Likewise, a recession will decrease the profitability and increase the riskiness of most business enterprises. The degree of nondiversifiable risk for a particular security is measured in terms of the tendency of returns for the security to move in the same direction as other securities.

The most widely used method of measuring nondiversifiable risk is *beta*. Beta is a measure of the sensitivity of return for a particular investment to returns for investments in general. The beta can best be explained using a graph illustrating the common stock of a particular company (figure 7A-3). Over a period of time, we observe that when returns on securities in general rise, returns for this particular security rise, and when returns for securities in general decline, returns for this particular security decline. We observed the returns (dividends and price appreciation) a holder of this security would have received during each of a number of periods and observed the return that an investor would have received during each of these periods if he had held some broad-based portfolio, representing all common stocks. Each dot in figure 7A-3 represents one such pair of observations. The line is drawn to fit the dots as closely as possible and represents the

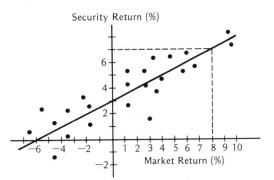

Figure 7A–3: Relation of security to market.

return we might expect from the security at each possible level of return for stocks in general. The greater the slope of this line, the greater the sensitivity of the investment to overall conditions, and the greater the nondiversifiable risk.

Beta provides a measure of the slope of this line, and therefore of nondiversifiable risk. Beta is defined as

$$\text{beta} = \frac{\begin{array}{c}\text{change in expected return}\\\text{for the security}\end{array}}{\begin{array}{c}\text{change in expected return}\\\text{for all stocks}\end{array}} . \quad \text{(7A-2)}$$

Expected return for the security is 3 percent if expected return for stocks in general is 0 percent (from 7A-3). Expected return for the security is 7 percent if expected return for stocks in general is 8 percent. The beta for the security is then

$$\text{beta} = \frac{0.07 - 0.03}{0.08 - 0.00} = 0.5.$$

Obviously, for any particular security during any particular time period, these relationships will not hold precisely. Factors affecting a particular security may cause actual return to be above or below what would be expected based on overall market conditions. For example, return to investors holding the stock of a particular company will depend on acceptance of that company's products as well as on overall market conditions. Once again, a well-diversified portfolio will cancel out the risks associated only with a particular security. However, the expected relationship between the security and securities in general cannot be offset through diversification.

The higher the beta, the greater is the nondiversifiable risk. A beta of two indicates that if returns for stocks in general increase, return for the particular security will be expected to increase twice as much, and if returns for stocks in general decrease, return for the particular security will be expected to decrease twice as much. Betas for publicly traded common stocks are regularly reported by investment advisory services such as Value Line.

As stated earlier, the required return for a particular investment is a function of the general level of interest rates and the nondiversifiable risk associated with that particular investment. The interest rate on risk-free investments, such as U.S. government securities, is normally used as a measure of the general level of interest rates and beta is used as the measure of nondiversifiable risk. Thus, an individual security's beta measures its contribution to portfolio risk. The required rate of return is a function of the interest rate on risk-free assets, return for other risky assets, and the security's beta. It can be shown[6] that the required return, or interest rate necessary to attract investors to a risky asset is

$$K_e = R_f + \beta(E_m - R_f)$$

where: K_e = The required rate of return

R_f = The rate of risk-free securities

β = Beta

E_m = Expected average return for common stocks in general.

The term $(E_m - R_f)$ is the difference between expected average return for all stocks and the risk-free interest rate. It is the average compensation for risk in the security market, or the risk premium. As the formula shows, the risk premium for a particular security is a function of its beta and the risk premium for stocks in general.

Thus we have a concise measure of security risk as well as a concise statement of the relationship between risk and the required return. The model has proved to be quite useful for evaluating portfolio managers and determining the required returns for specific assets.

An Example

First National Bank is considering a new equity issue to expand its capital base. To decide if this action is in the best interest of the present stockholders, the bank must determine whether the return required by equity investors is above

---

[6]A proof and detailed discussion can be found in any advanced investment text. For example, see Jack Clark Francis, *Investments: Analysis and Management*, (New York: McGraw-Hill, 1980).

or below the return it can earn with additional funds. The required return on equity cannot be observed directly in the market place as can the return on Treasury bills or corporate bonds. The returns expected from investments of the latter type can be determined because they carry a fixed, contractual obligation and have an observable market price. Common stock has an observable market price, but does not carry a fixed obligation. Therefore, the return required by investors is not directly observable. It must be estimated using available information about general levels of return and risk premiums.

To estimate the required return, the bank must first develop measures of the risk-free interest rate, the average risk premium for the market in general, and the beta for the bank's stock. Studies covering extensive time periods (up to fifty years) have shown that the difference between the interest rates on long-term U.S. government bonds and the realized return on common stock (the realized risk premium) has averaged approximately 5.4 percent. According to the *Value Line Investment Survey,* the beta for the average commercial bank listed there is approximately 0.90. Assume that the Treasury bond rate is presently 8.6 percent. Thus, the estimate of the required return for common stock in general is

$$E_m = 0.086 + 0.054 = 14\%$$

The required return for the bank's stock would then be

$$K_e = 0.086 + 0.90(0.14 - 0.086) = 13.5\%.$$

Therefore, according to this model, the equity issue would be in the long-run best interest of investors if the bank is successful in producing a return in excess of 13.5 percent for its equity investors.

QUESTIONS

1. Explain the difference between diversifiable and nondiversifiable risk.

2. What are the characteristics of an efficient portfolio?

PROBLEMS

1. Returns for ABC common stock and the market in general for each of the last ten years appear below. What is the beta?

Year	1	2	3	4	5
Mkt.	0.10	0.15	−0.05	0.05	0.00
ABC	0.13	0.20	−0.10	0.05	−0.05

Year	6	7	8	9	10
Mkt.	0.20	0.12	0.06	0.07	0.10
ABC	0.25	0.15	0.06	0.10	0.12

2. Returns for stocks in general are expected to be 12 percent and the risk-free rate is 6 percent. Middle American Finance has a beta of 1.3. Compute the required return for Middle American common stock.

3. Over a particular five-year-period, common stock in general provided an average return of 12 percent per year and the risk-free rate averaged 6 percent. A pension fund managed by Southwest Trust had a return of 15 percent over the same period. It was managed aggressively and had a relatively high beta of 2.0. Evaluate Southwest's performance.

Appendix 7-B

The Black-Scholes Option Pricing Model

The Black-Scholes option pricing model[1] (OPM) was developed in an attempt to understand the pricing of stock options, which were described in chapter 5. The model does, moreover, have fairly general use since a number of other items, such as a call feature on a bond, are essentially options.

On the last day before expiration, the value of a call option is simply the difference between the market price of the stock and the striking price (or zero if the striking price exceeds the market price). The value of the option on earlier dates depends on the probability distribution of its value on the last date before expiration. While most options expire without being exercised because the stock price never reached the striking price, it is the possibility of the stock price passing the striking price that gives them value. A three-month option to buy a stock for $10 above the current market price would be of little value if the stock never changed in price by more than $5 in a three-month period. On the other hand, the option would have value if the stock regularly exhibited price fluctuations of $30 in a three-month period. Thus, the value of the option de-

pends on the variability of price for the security on which the option is written.

The Black-Scholes model quantified this relationship between variability of the underlying stock's price and value of the option in the following formula:

$$\text{Value of option} = P \cdot N(d_1) - \frac{S}{e^{rt}}N(d_2)$$

where:

P = the current market price of the stock;

S = the striking price of the option;

e = the base of the common logarithm: 2.71828;

r = short-term interest rate, continuously compounded;

t = time in years (or fraction of a year) until expiration of the option;

$N(d_i)$ = a value from the table of the normal probability distribution (table A-9) representing the probability of the Z value being less than d_i;

$d_1 = [\ln(P/S) + (r + 0.5\sigma^2)t]/(\sigma\sqrt{t})$;

[1]Fisher Black and Myron Scholes, "The Pricing of Options and Corporate Liabilities," *Journal of Political Economy* 81 (May/June, 1973): 637–654.

$d_2 = [\ln(P/S) + (r - 0.5\sigma^2)t]/(\sigma\sqrt{t})$;

ln = natural logarithm; and

σ = standard deviation of the annual rate of return on the underlying stock, continuously compounded.

An Example

A call option will expire in six months (0.50 years). The stock on which the option is written is presently selling for $100 a share and the striking price is $110. The continuously compounded annual interest rate is 12 percent. The standard deviation of the annual rate of return on the underlying stock, continuously compounded, is 0.20. The value of this option is therefore estimated as follows:

$d_1 = [\ln(100/110) + (0.12$
$\quad + 0.5\ 0.2^2)0.50]/(0.20\sqrt{0.50})$

$\quad = -0.179$

$d_2 = [\ln(100/110) + (0.12$
$\quad - 0.5\ 0.2^2)0.50]/(0.20\sqrt{0.50})$

$\quad = -0.321$

$N(d_1) = 0.50 - 0.0710 = 0.429$

$N(d_2) = 0.50 - 0.1259 = 0.374$

Value of = $100 \cdot 0.429$
option
$\quad - (110/e^{0.12 \cdot 0.50})0.374$

$\quad = \$4.16$

A Note on Continuously Compounded Returns

The concept of continuously compounded expected return and standard deviation is often a source of unnecessary confusion. Continuous compounding in general was explained in chapter 6. If a six-month treasury bill is selling at 95 percent of face value (recall that treasury bills sell at discount rather than pay interest), the continuously compounded annual interest rate (*r*) is found as follows

$\$95e^{0.5r} = \$100.00$

$e^{0.5r} = 100/95$

$\ln(e^{0.5r}) = \ln(100/95)$

$0.5r = \ln(100/95) = 0.05129$

$r = 2 \cdot 0.05129 = 0.10258.$

As an example of continuously compounded standard deviation, consider a stock selling for $100. There are two possible prices a year from now, as shown below:

Probability	Price	Continuously Compounded Return
.4	100.00	$r = \ln(100/100) = 0$
.6	149.1825	$r = \ln(149.1825/100)$ $= 0.40$

Expected continuously compounded return = $.4(0) + .6(0.4) = 0.24$. Standard deviation of continuously compounded return =

$$\sqrt{.4(0 - 0.24)^2 + .6(0.40 - 0.24)^2} = 0.196$$

PROBLEMS

1. For the example used in the text, the value of the option was $4.16. Suppose the price of the stock was $110 when the option was three months from expiration. What would be the value of the option at that time?

2. On 1 May 1984, IBM stock was selling for $116 ⅜ a share. A five-month option at a striking price of $120 was selling for $5 ¾. The continuously compounded annual interest rate was 10.5%. If you felt the continuously compounded standard deviation of annual return for IBM was 25 percent, would you consider the option to be overpriced or underpriced?

Chapter 8

Financial Structure and the Cost of Funds

We have seen that financial institutions differ from other types of business in that they deal primarily in financial obligations, accepting funds for which a return is promised and reinvesting these funds in financial obligations of others. While the cost of funds used is one of many costs faced by the typical nonfinancial business, it is a major cost faced by financial institutions. Thus knowledge of the cost of funds and the factors affecting it are of particular concern to the financial institution manager.

While a nonfinancial business may fail for any number of reasons, such as unacceptance of its major products, the primary danger to the financial institution lies in the structure of the financial obligations. Failure results primarily from the inability to earn a return on assets sufficient to meet obligations to suppliers of funds; in general, the greater the fixed obligations and the shorter the maturity, the greater the risk of failure.

More generally, a financial institution can be considered successful only if it meets fixed obli-gations and provides a return to equity investors that equals or exceeds returns available to these investors elsewhere. Thus the cost of funds consists of fixed obligations and the opportunity cost of funds for which a fixed return is not promised. The total cost of funds, then, represents an important obligation of the institution. The identification of the overall cost of funds is one of the objectives of this chapter.

We are interested in more than understanding the cost of funds and risk of failure associated with a particular financial structure. We are interested in managing and controlling these variables. By varying the financial structure—the proportion of total funds coming from each potential source—management is able to affect both risk and the cost of funds. A second objective of this chapter is to develop the main principles involved in management of the financial mix to control the level of risk and the cost of funds.

This chapter is divided into two main sections. The first section deals with the decision as to what is the appropriate mix of sources of funds and the second section deals with measuring the cost of funds.

FINANCIAL STRUCTURE

By financial structure, we refer to the mix of sources of funds to the institution. These sources can be roughly divided into three main categories. *Short-term liabilities* are those that are due on demand or within a short time period, typically defined as less than one year. *Long-term liabilities* have a maturity of more than one year. *Equity,* the third category, has no maturity at all. For an institution with stockholders, equity consists of the stockholders' direct investments in the firm and the retained earnings. For a firm lacking stockholders, such as a mutual savings and loan association, reserves serve the same function as equity. Sources of funds can also be classified as to whether or not contractually binding payment is required. Contractual—fixed—payments are required in the case of bonds, certificates of deposit, and passbook savings accounts. Returns to stockholders, dividends to holders of life insurance policies, and returns to mutual fund shareholders on the other hand, are related to the return earned on the institution's assets.

When we talk about the debt capacity of an industrial corporation, we normally think in terms of some optimum combination of debt and equity used to support a certain asset structure. For most financial institutions, we tend to think in terms of how much equity is required to support a given set of assets and liabilities. We use the term *capital adequacy.* This difference in emphasis is a result of the management problems faced by the different types of firms. For an industrial corporation, the primary limitation on growth is found in the asset structure. The size of the corporation is normally determined by the ability to find and manage profitable asset investments. The financial structure is developed in response to this set of opportunities. For the financial institution, the liability structure is more likely to be the determinant of the total

size. The total asset level of an insurance company, for example, is largely determined by the ability to sell insurance policies, not by the availability of profitable investments. Likewise, over the long term the size of a bank is heavily influenced by its ability to attract deposits.

While different types of business stress different aspects of the problem, the interactive aspect should not be ignored. The attractiveness of a particular investment depends on both its expected rate of return and the cost of funds. The cost of funds, in turn, depends on the riskiness of assets and the financial structure. The equity capital and liquid reserves judged to be necessary depend on the nature of *both* the assets and liabilities.

Various considerations are included in the financial structure decision:

Regulatory requirements

Cost of funds

Liquidity

Risk of insolvency

Flexibility

Regulatory limitations are frequently stated in terms of minimum acceptable levels of liquid assets and equity capital, as determined by the asset and liability structure of the institution. This section begins with an examination of the relationship between financial structure and the cost of funds. Then the concepts of liquidity, insolvency risk, and flexibility are developed to complete the general principles followed by all financial institutions in developing financial structure policy.

Financial Structure and the Cost of Funds

Central to our analysis is the fact that the average cost of funds is influenced by the mix of funds employed by an institution. One important objective of financial structure management is the minimization of this cost. Decreasing the cost of funds is one method of increasing the spread between the cost of funds and the return on assets, thus increasing profitability.

Fixed liabilities, such as debt and deposit liabilities, normally cost much less than equity or other nonspecific claims. Investors and savers as a group are averse to risks and can be expected to invest in more risky nonspecific claims only when returns anticipated from such claims exceed those available from debt and deposit claims. Furthermore, interest payments to fixed claims are an expense for tax purposes while dividends to equity holders must be paid from after-tax income.

Since debt funds tend to have a lower cost than equity funds, we would expect that the average cost of funds could be decreased by increasing the ratio of debt to equity. Indeed, this will happen over some range. However, as the ratio of debt to total assets continues to increase, the institution's debt becomes an increasingly risky investment and the return required to attract such funds rises.[1] Furthermore, continual addition of debt increases the risk to equity investors, driving up the required return on equity. Thus there are limits beyond which the addition of fixed obligations increases, rather than decreases, the average cost of funds.

While the general relationship between capital structure and cost of funds is fairly well understood, the identification of the exact combination which will minimize the average cost of funds for any given firm is elusive. Numerous studies of financial and nonfinancial corporations have failed to identify such a point.[2] However, what such studies have done is to give us a feel for the shape of the relationship between financial structure and the cost of funds. Figure 8-1 shows two possible relationships between capital structure and the cost of funds. The actual relationship appears to be more like curve *B* than curve *A*. The cost of funds curve appears to be fairly flat over a broad range, indicating that within that range modest changes in the financial structure will not have a major impact on the cost of funds.

---

[1]Of course, many deposits are insured; they do not become more risky. But financial institutions do borrow in the money markets and these loans are not insured.

[2]See, for example, S. D. Magen, *The Cost of Funds to Commercial Banks* (New York: Dunellen, 1971).

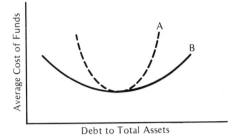

Figure 8–1: Illustrative cost of funds curves.

While the relatively flat cost of capital curve makes it difficult to locate the precise optimum cost of funds, it does indicate that within fairly broad ranges the institution is free to consider other factors in selecting a financial structure. The considerations of liquidity, insolvency risk, and flexibility can be given proper consideration without unduly impairing profitability.

Liquidity

Liquidity refers to the ability to meet financial obligations as they come due. A depository institution must stand ready to meet demand and passbook account withdrawal requests. An insurance company must stand ready to meet claims and the pension funds must make monthly payments on schedule. A company with a strong equity base and a strong profitability position can still face liquidity problems if all funds are tied up in nonmarketable assets.

Historically, liquidity needs have been determined by studying the liabilities, while cash and near-cash items have been relied on to meet these needs. Analysis has traditionally relied on static ratios. For example, an institution might follow a policy requiring cash items equal to 10 percent of passbook accounts, and so on.

More current approaches recognize two important factors. First, liquidity is a dynamic problem which results from instability of cash inflows and outflows, not from the absolute values of certain accounts. Second, many depository institutions have increasingly looked to new liabilities as alternatives to assets in meeting liquidity needs.

Liquidity reserves can be thought of as similar to a reservoir in a water system (Figure 8-2). Water constantly flows into and out of the reservoir, with the net flow being the difference between inflow and outflow. The amount of water needed in the reservoir is determined by the variability of the net flow, not by the absolute level of flow. Furthermore, any reservoir will eventually be drained if inflow steadily lags behind outflow. Thus the reservoir serves to offset difference in flow rates during limited periods of time.

To determine the amount of liquid reserves needed, historical patterns of cash inflows and outflows are studied to determine variability. The degree to which cash inflows and outflows move in the same direction at the same time— the covariance—is an important determinant of variability.

This interactive aspect of the liquidity problem heightens the importance of financial structure in liquidity management. The creation of liabilities which coincide in maturity with assets can greatly reduce the amount of assets which must be held in liquid reserves. Thus, financial structure management has a major impact on the pattern of liquidity demands.

It has been traditional to think in terms of meeting liquidity demands by selling short-term assets. However, many financial institutions frequently use short-term borrowing to meet unexpected liquidity demands. The use of negotiable certificates of deposit during recent periods of credit stringency is probably the most widely advertised example of this use of liability management. Eurodollar loans and commercial pa-

per issued by financial institutions are other examples of the use of liabilities to meet liquidity demands, as is borrowing in the federal funds market. Thus liability management is an important part of liquidity management in terms of both creating and meeting liquidity needs.

Risk of Insolvency (Capital Adequacy)

Insolvency occurs when the liabilities of a business exceed the value of its assets. The amount of shrinkage in assets value that can occur without leading to insolvency is related to the amount of equity capital in the financial structure. Thus the risk of insolvency depends on the risk of asset value shrinkage and the amount of equity in the financial structure.

When one thinks of shrinkage in the value of assets of a financial institution, default or credit risk is normally the first thing to come to mind. A loan, for example, may become questionable in value or worthless if the loan collateral loses its value and the borrower loses his ability to repay. Additionally, interest rate change is an important cause of asset value shrinkage. In chapter 7 it was shown that a rise in the general level of interest rates would cause the value of existing securities to decline. For example, a twenty-year, $1,000 U.S. government bond issued in 1975 had declined in market value to $680 by 1980. This decline in market value was entirely the result of a rise in the general level of interest rates over the five-year period. Fluctuations in the prices of equity securities are even more extreme. For example, the value of an average share of common stock fell 11 percent from 13 October 1978, to 31 October 1978, as a result of rising interest rates and a declining profitability outlook. Finally, operating losses caused by such factors as rising interest and operating expenses lead to erosion of total asset values. Thus all assets except the shortest term, highest quality money market instruments are subject to shrinkage in total value. Many financial institutions have found themselves in the embarassing position of holding an excessive portfolio of long-term securities or loans,

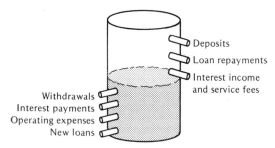

Figure 8–2: The liquidity reservoir.

purchased or made when interest rates were viewed as "high," only to find later that interest rates rose further and the value of these assets fell sharply.

One method of dealing with the risk of loss in value is through matching maturities of assets and obligations. The U.S. government bond previously discussed still has a maturity value of $1,000. The loss in value occurs only if the asset is sold before maturity. By matching maturities of assets and liabilities, this risk of loss can be largely eliminated. Unfortunately, this is not always possible. While the primary assets of a savings and loan company are mortgages with maturities of twenty to thirty years, these firms rely on deposits with much shorter maturities as their primary source of funds.

In the case of loans, fixed assets, and equity securities, the risk of loss in value cannot be escaped. Obviously, such risk can be reduced by selecting higher quality loans and securities, and settling for commensurately lower returns. But risk cannot be eliminated if the institution is to invest in the types of assets which traditionally make up the bulk of its portfolio. Equity must serve to protect the institution's depositors and other creditors from loss in the value of assets.

One approach to determining total equity requirements is to evaluate each category of assets and to estimate the potential decline in value.

The total equity requirement would thus be estimated by computing the equity needed for each category of assets and by summing the results. This approach is commonly used by regulatory authorities for deposit-type intermediaries. The standards set by regulators are minimum standards. The institution seeks to avoid the risk of falling to what regulators consider an inadequate equity position.

Another approach to the capital adequacy problem is the portfolio approach. Just as liquidity reserves can be thought of as a reservoir in the cash flow system, equity capital can be thought of as a reservoir in the income system. If net income after adjusting for gains or losses in the value of assets was positive every period, no equity reserve would be needed. It is variability of net income that leads to the need for equity

capital. Just as the variance and covariance of the various sources and uses of cash determine liquidity needs, variance and covariance of various sources of income and expense determine the equity capital need. For example, assume that an institution makes automobile loans and invests in long-term U.S. government bonds. Losses in the automobile loan portfolio will occur primarily because of defaults while any losses in the bond portfolio's value will arise from market value losses resulting from rising interest rates. In a recession the default rate on automobile loans may rise, leading to losses in this portfolio. However, the general level of interest rates may fall, leading to an increase in the market value of the bond portfolio. Thus the tendency for the market value of the bond portfolio to increase at the time losses are being experienced in automobile loans makes it unnecessary to have equity equal to the entire potential loss in each category of assets. Portfolio analysis is a method of examining the relationships between these various income and expense factors and selecting assets so as to minimize the variance for a particular level of income. Portfolio analysis is taken up in more detail in chapter 9.

We have seen that equity capital is the reserve used to reduce insolvency risk. The amount needed is determined not by a simple ratio of debt to equity, but by the variability of the various income and expense factors as well as their interrelationships. As with liquidity, insolvency risk management is a dynamic and interactive problem.

Flexibility

Flexibility in financial institution management is the ability to deal with unanticipated problems and opportunities that arise from time to time. While attempts to foresee future opportunities and problems are helpful, the simple fact is that the future is unknown. Both unanticipated problems and unanticipated opportunities will arise. Flexibility—the ability to deal with these situations—is very important to both profitability and risk.

The failure of Penn-Central Railroad in 1970

provides an excellent example of the importance of flexibility. The consumer finance companies relied on commercial paper as a means of financing. Because the maturities of their loans were greater than the maturity of commercial paper, they counted on paying off one issue of commercial paper by issuing another. When Penn-Central defaulted on its commercial paper, the entire market for commercial paper virtually dried up overnight. The finance companies were not able to sell new issues of commercial paper in sufficient volume.

This situation would have resulted in massive defaults if it were not for flexibility planning. The finance companies had maintained lines of credit with banks as back-up sources of funds in case of difficulties in the commercial paper market. Thus, when they were faced with this difficulty, there was an alternative source of funds readily available. The banks, with some help from the Federal Reserve System, honored their lines of credit and default was avoided.

While asset management is a major part of flexibility management, management of the maturity structure of liabilities can also contribute to flexibility. Short-term maturities allow the institution to change policy quickly, but carry the risk of liquidity problems if maturing liabilities cannot be replaced with new sources of funds. Again, a distribution of maturities provides the optimum trade-off between flexibility gains and liquidity risks. Additional flexibility can be gained through the use of lines of credit. For example, consumer finance companies normally maintain bank lines of credit equal to their outstanding commercial paper, allowing them to move back and forth between bank debt and commercial paper as market conditions change.

Finally, management of the equity portion of the balance sheet affects flexibility. An institution with the minimum acceptable level of equity capital may find itself unable to take advantage of growth opportunities or may find itself accidentally in violation of regulatory requirements. Flexibility is normally gained by maintaining a capital structure with equity capital somewhat in excess of the minimum required.

Thus, flexibility is an important concept in the management of a financial institution. Flexibility is the response to the uncertainty inherent in a dynamic business environment. It is achieved through careful management of both assets and liabilities so that management has the opportunity to adjust the institution's financial position in response to changing problems and opportunities.

COST OF FUNDS FOR DEPOSITORY INSTITUTIONS

The cost of funds may be thought of as the opportunity cost, or the return stockholders, depositors, and other investors could expect from alternative opportunities of equal risk. The cost of funds provides a standard against which proposed uses of funds and past performance can be measured. If an institution is to successfully compete for funds, it must be capable of providing returns that are at least equal to the returns available from competing instruments available to investors. In order to evaluate investment alternatives, it is necessary to have an estimate of the cost of funds that will be invested. Overall profitability and stability of the institution may depend heavily on the cost of funds estimates.

Several important factors affect the institution's cost of funds. As mentioned previously, the cost of funds is an opportunity cost, or the return that investors and depositors could expect from alternative opportunities of equal risk. One factor in the cost of funds is the general level of opportunities, which influence the overall level of competitive interest rates. Also, investors must expect a higher rate of return if they are to be persuaded to invest in assets subject to risk. The more risk associated with the asset and liability structure of the firm, the higher will be the return necessary to attract funds.

Deposit funds, to the extent insured, are essentially risk free. However, financial institutions derive funds through issuance of securities and creation of liabilities, many of which are not covered or are covered only partially by insurance. Examples of these are large certificates of deposit, commercial paper, capital notes and debentures, federal funds borrowed, Eurodollars, preferred stock, and common stock. The required return for such funds, if all other factors such as size and location of the institution are held constant, may be expected to increase as perceived risk in the asset and liability structure increases.

In this section, the costs of the individual sources of funds are computed and the method of combining these costs to develop a weighted average cost of funds is explained.

Cost of Equity

The cost of equity is the return required by holders of the common stock. This cost is a function of investment opportunities elsewhere and the perceived risk associated with that particular institution's common stock. Unfortunately, it is seldom possible to directly observe the required return for equity investors. Some method for estimating their required return from available information must be used.

One widely used method of computing the cost of equity is the dividend growth model:

$$K_e = \frac{D}{P} + g$$

where: K_e = Required return on equity

D = Dividends expected over the next year

P = Current market price of the stock

g = Constant annual growth rate of dividends (expected to continue indefinitely).

Suppose, for example, that Southwest Bank's common stock is presently selling for $50 per share. Dividends are expected to be $4 per share next year and are expected to grow 4 percent a year thereafter. The cost of equity for Southwest is

$$K_e = \frac{4}{50} + 0.04 = 0.12 \text{ or } 12\%.$$

If dividends grow as expected, an investor purchasing Southwest stock today for $50 will enjoy a 12 percent return on the investment.

Another approach to measuring the cost of equity is the risk-adjusted required-return approach developed in appendix 7-A:

$$K_e = R_f + \beta(E_m - R_f)$$

where: R_f = Rate available on risk-free investments, such as treasury bills

β = Beta, a measure of sensitivity of returns for the particular security to conditions affecting common stock returns in general

E_m = Expected return for securities in general.

The application of the dividend growth model requires stable dividend growth and the risk-adjusted return method requires historical market price data for the stock. Lacking these, an institution may consider returns available on comparable securities for which there is an active market to estimate the returns available to investors in opportunities of equal risk. For mutual institutions there is no possibility of a market price for equity. The reserves of such institutions can be thought of as a form of equity and the required return as a rate that could be earned on equal risk investments elsewhere if the institution did not exist. The returns available on common stocks of comparable risk would be a reasonable basis for an estimate. Suppose, for example, expected return for the market in general were 13 percent and the risk-free rate were 6.6 percent. Citizens Mutual Savings and Loan has no equity, but has reserves which serve that purpose. Equity securities of similar companies have betas of approximately 0.844. The required return for Citizens' is estimated to be

$$K_e = 0.066 + 0.844 (0.13 - 0.066) = 12.0\%.$$

The required return on equity is a return that must be earned after income taxes have been paid. The required return before tax is $K_e \div (1-T)$ where T is the tax rate. Thus, if the income tax rate is 46 percent and the required return on equity is 12 percent, the before-tax required return is $0.12 \div (1-.46) = 22.22\%$.

Cost of Capital Notes and Debentures

The cost of capital notes and debentures (K_b) is the yield to maturity of existing notes or debentures (yield to maturity computation is covered in chapter 6) or the interest rate that would be required to sell new securities of this type. Southwest Bank has a debt series outstanding with a 9 percent yield to maturity. The cost of debt is therefore 9 percent.

Financial institutions frequently have other negotiated cost funds such as Eurodollar borrowings and fed funds. The cost of each such source is computed in the same way as was done for capital notes and debentures.

Cost of Time and Savings Deposit Funds

The direct cost of interest-bearing deposit funds is the annual interest paid divided by the amount of interest-bearing deposit funds. Southwest Bank had average interest-bearing deposits of $100 million during its most recent fiscal year and paid total interest of $5.5 million. The direct cost of deposit funds would be

$$K_{sd} = \frac{5.5}{100} = 5.5\%.$$

This direct cost actually underestimates the cost of deposit funds substantially. First, the cost of attracting and servicing funds should be added to direct interest payments. In addition, reserve requirements limit the amount that is available for investment. To adjust for this, the required reserves should be deducted from the $100 million and any return earned on reserves should be deducted from the cost. For Southwest Bank, the required reserves were $4 million, interest earned on reserves was $40,000, and the cost of serving these deposits was $1.5 million. The cost of interest-bearing deposit funds was therefore

$$K_{sd} = \frac{5.5 + 1.5 - .04}{100 - 4} = 7.25\%.$$

The cost of interest-bearing deposit funds can therefore be summarized in one formula:

$$K_{sd} = \frac{I_e + E - I_r}{S_d - R}$$

where: I_e = Dollar annual interest paid on interest-bearing deposits

E = Annual cost of attracting and servicing accounts

I_r = Annual interest received on reserves, if any

S_d = Average value of interest-bearing deposits

R = Amount of required reserves for these deposits.

Cost of Noninterest-Bearing Deposits

The direct cost of noninterest demand deposits is zero since no interest is paid. The indirect costs of attracting and servicing accounts are real as are the reserve requirements. The cost of noninterest-bearing deposits (K_d) is computed in the same manner as the cost of interest-bearing deposits with the exception that the direct interest expense is zero. Southwest Bank has demand deposits of $60 million. Costs of attracting and servicing these deposits are estimated to be $3 million and required reserves for these deposits are $7 million. No interest is earned on the required reserves. The cost of demand deposits for Southwest is

$$K_d = \frac{3}{60 - 7} = 5.66\%.$$

Weighted Average Cost of Funds

The next step is the computation of an average cost of funds. This requires the combining of individual sources of funds in some manner. Since funds invested are a combination of funds raised from various sources, the cost of funds is an average of the costs of the various individual sources of funds. Since some sources of funds represent a greater portion of the total than others, a *weighted average* must be used. The weighted cost of a source of funds is found by multiplying the after-tax cost by the proportion of total funds represented by that source. The weighted average cost of all sources is found by adding the individual weighted costs. This is illustrated in table 8-1 for Southwest Bank.

A loan, for example, would need to provide an 8.06 percent yield if it were to provide a 12 percent after-tax return on equity. If administrative costs associated with the loan were 3 percent of the average balance outstanding, then it would be necessary for the loan to carry an 11.06 percent APR to provide the 8.06 percent yield to the lender.

Occasionally, one will wish to deal with depreciable assets, municipal bonds, or other items with special tax implications. For these items, the after-tax benefit is evaluated using the after-tax cost of funds, which equals the before-tax cost multiplied by $(1-T)$. If the savings and loan with the 8.06 percent required return on funds and 46 percent tax rate is considering a municipal bond, the bond must yield at least

$$8.06\% \times (1-0.46) = 4.35\%.$$

COST OF FUNDS FOR NON-DEPOSITORY INSTITUTIONS

For many nondepository financial institutions, the problem of cost of capital is altered by the fact that the most important sources of funds fall into neither the equity nor the fixed obligation category. This does not imply that the funds are costless.

While the payouts from many pension funds depend on the rate earned on the fund's investment portfolio, the beneficiaries still have the right to expect a return as high as that available from alternative investments of equal risk. Thus the required return or cost of these funds also depends on the opportunities available elsewhere.

Take, for example, an employee pension fund at Alrite Products Corporation. Contributions to the employee pension fund are divided between mortgages insured by agencies of the U.S. government and common stocks, with half of the funds being invested in each category. If individuals did not contribute to the pension fund, they could invest directly in assets of similar risk. Thus the required return for the pension fund is the return investors could earn by dividing their funds between insured mortgages and a common stock portfolio with equal risk to that of the common stock portfolio held by the pension fund. The evaluation of pension fund performance is covered in more detail in chapter 14.

Insurance companies collect a pool of premiums from which they expect to pay claims. Policy reserves—funds held to meet claims—are the primary source of funds to an insurance company. As an example of the cost of funds to such an institution, we look at a life insurance company writing whole life policies. The whole life policy is generally in force from the time of purchase until the death of the policy holder and pays its face value at the time of death. While the timing of the individual claim is unknown, its eventual payment is certain. Thus the company must build up reserves over the life of the policy holder. As the insured is aware of his eventual

Table 8-1:

Southwest Bank Weighted Average Cost of Funds

Source of Funds	Amount of Funds (Net of Reserves)	Proportion of Total	Before-Tax Cost	=	Weighted Cost
Demand deposits	$ 53 million	0.31	5.66%		1.75
Time and savings deposits	96 million	0.55	7.25		3.99
Debentures	10 million	0.06	9.00		0.54
Common equity	14 million	0.08	22.22		1.78
Total	$173 million	1.00	Wtd. Ave. Cost:		8.06%

death, a policy of this type can be thought of as a combination of a savings plan to provide funds to heirs and insurance against the possibility of death before the savings plan has been completed.

Alternatively, the insured can purchase temporary life insurance at a lower cost and invest the difference directly. The premiums charged and the dividends paid to policy holders depend on the return earned on these reserves. Thus, the ability to compete in the sale of policies depends on these returns. The reserves must earn a return similar to those available on other long-term savings instruments if the company is to be competitive.

While the determination of the cost of funds is somewhat different for a nondepository financial institution, the general principles are still the same. Each type of funds must earn a return that is at least equal to what the furnishers of those funds could have earned from alternative investments.

Management Use of the Cost of Funds

The cost of funds serves two purposes in the financial institution. First, it serves as a standard against which past performance can be measured. The institution should have earned a return on assets at least equal to the cost of funds. An analysis of returns in comparison to the cost of funds can be a regular part of performance review.

Second, the cost of funds represents a standard against which proposed uses of funds can be evaluated. The after-tax cost of funds represents an average return, expressed on an after-tax basis and net of servicing cost, which must be earned on total assets. Some assets, such as highly liquid securities, will normally earn a return lower than the average required. Further, some investments, such as an employee lounge, generate no direct revenue. These low returns must be compensated for with higher returns on other assets so that the weighted average return for all assets equals the weighted average cost of funds. The assignment of these higher costs to specific

asset categories is somewhat difficult and requires a certain amount of managerial judgment.

The concept of spread management is another common application of the cost of funds. For the savings and loan previously considered, the required return on all funds (excluding nonearning reserves) is 8.06 percent. Suppose that 20 percent of funds other than nonearning reserves must be invested in liquid assets earning 6 percent. The required return on the loan portfolio is then found by solving the following equation:

$$8.06\% = 0.20 \times 6.00\% + 0.80 \times \text{return on loans}$$

$$\text{return on loans} = (8.06\% - 0.20 \times 6.00\%) \div 0.80 = 8.58\%.$$

If administrative costs associated with loans equal 1 percent of the loan portfolio, the loans must then carry an average APR of 9.58 percent.

The interest rate paid on deposits was 5.5 percent so the required spread between the APR on loans and the interest rate paid on deposits is $9.58\% - 5.50\% = 4.08\%$. Spread can also be computed in relation to the average interest cost for all nonequity funds.

Required spread is a widely used concept in management of financial institutions that are heavily involved as lenders. The required spread is used in pricing loans, evaluating new loan products, and other aspects of profit planning.

SUMMARY

In this chapter, we have concentrated on the factors guiding decisions with regard to the financial structure of the financial institution. The costs of individual sources of funds and the average cost of funds have been covered. In addition, we have covered the factors guiding the decision as to what particular financial structure an institution will have. These include regulatory limitations, insolvency risk, liquidity needs, and the cost of funds. These various objectives are frequently contradictory. For example, the structure giving the greatest flexibility and lowest risk of default would undoubtedly result in a high average cost of funds and low profitability. The financial structure decision cannot be reduced to a simple formula.[3] The job of management is to weight these various factors and to apply its own judgment and experience in selecting a financial structure which gives adequate consideration to each of these factors.

QUESTIONS

1. Industrial corporations are free to use whatever financial structure they prefer, subject only to the willingness of lenders to furnish funds. On the other hand, the financial structure of a financial institution is closely regulated by government regulatory bodies. Why are the financial structures of financial institutions regulated while the structures of industrial corporations are not?

2. Financial institutions typically have much higher proportions of their total funds furnished by depositors and other lender groups. Such large volumes of fixed obligations are normally considered risky, yet financial institutions typically have lower failure rates than industrial corporations. Why?

3. A typical bank has 15 to 20 percent of its assets in the form of cash and demand deposits with other institutions. A typical savings and loan company, on the other hand, holds only 2 to 3 percent of its assets in similar liquid forms. How do you account for this difference?

4. Why do we emphasize debt capacity when analyzing industrial corporations and capital adequacy when analyzing financial institutions?

5. For which financial institutions is liquidity planning easiest and for which institutions is it likely to be the most difficult? Why?

6. Five types of considerations involved in the financial structure decision are discussed in this chapter. Compare the importance of each of these for financial and non-financial corporations.

7. The cost of funds curve appears to be relatively flat over a broad range. What are the implications of this for managerial decision making?

8. What determines the liquidity needs of a financial institution, and how are these liquidity needs met?

PROBLEMS

1. First City Bank has 300,000 shares of common stock outstanding. The stock is traded in the over-the-counter market (there is a market for the stock through local brokerage firms, but it is not traded on a stock exchange) where the present price is $40 per share. Dividends per share for the next year are expected to be $3 and have been growing at the same rate as earnings, 4 percent a year. The present rate on Treasury bills is 6 percent and the expected future return for stocks in general is approximately 12 percent. First City Bank's stock has a beta of 0.9. Compute the after-tax cost of equity using both the dividend growth model and the risk-adjusted required return approach. Based on a 46 percent tax rate, convert each of these to a before-tax required return on equity.

2. Community Federal plans to raise additional funds through the sale of one-year certificates of deposit. The certificates will carry 9 percent interest, with annual compounding, and the estimated average cost of attracting one $1,000 certificate is $20. The reserve requirement is 10 percent and reserves will earn 4 percent. Compute the cost of this source of funds.

---

[3]One now-successful banker reports that, as an enthusiastic new employee, he developed a massive 800 constraint linear programming model for managing the bank's assets and liabilities. His solution was returned from the president with a short, but unprintable response. The model would have led the bank to failure in less than two years if it had been followed.

3. Old Reliable Life Insurance Company's financial structure consists of $1 billion in policy reserves and $100 million in equity. The before-tax required return on equity is estimated to be 18 percent. It is felt that policy reserves must earn a return at least as high as that available on high-grade bonds; 8 percent at the time. Compute the average cost of funds for Old Reliable.

4. Old Reliable (problem 3) has office facilities, which earn no direct return, of $6 million. In addition, $50 million is put in liquid reserves that earn a return of 6 percent. The remainder of their funds are available for investment. What return must be earned on the remainder of the portfolio if the overall cost of funds is to be met?

5. Neighborhood Bank has total assets of $110 million, with $100 million coming from deposits and $10 million coming from equity. The interest paid on deposit funds is 6 percent and the cost of attracting and administering these accounts equals 1 percent of the average balance of deposits. The before-tax cost of equity is 20 percent. The bank is required to maintain noninterest bearing liquid assets equal to 10 percent of deposits.

    a.   Compute the cost of deposits.

    b.   Compute the weighted average cost of funds available for investment (funds other than those held as required liquid reserves).

6. Neighborhood Bank (problem 5) has the following asset structure.

Required reserves	$10,000,000
Investment securities	30,000,000
Loans	65,000,000
Physical assets	5,000,000
Total assets	$110,000,000

The required reserves earn nothing, the investment securities earn 7 percent, and the

physical assets generate fee income, net of related expenses, of $200,000.

    a. What return must the bank earn on the loan portfolio?

    b.   The annual cost of attracting and administering loans is 1.5 percent of the value of the loan portfolio. To achieve the necessary return on the loan portfolio, the average loan must carry what APR?

    c.   What is the spread between the average APR required on a loan and the interest rate paid on deposits?

SELECTED REFERENCES

Beranek, William. "The Weighted Average Cost of Capital and Shareholder Wealth Maximization." *Journal of Financial and Quantitative Analysis* 12 (March 1977): 17–31.

Biederman, Kenneth R. "Capital Adequacy: Problems and Prospects." *Federal Home Loan Bank Board Journal* 12 (November 1979): 13–15.

Gordon, Myron J., and Gould, L. I. "The Cost of Equity Capital with Personal Income Taxes and Flotation Costs." *Journal of Finance* 33 (September 1978): 1201–1212.

Hehman, David H., and Winger, Alan R. "Measuring the Cost of Money Market Certificates." *Federal Home Loan Bank Board Journal* 12 (July 1979): 8–10.

Koehn, Michael, and Santomero, Anthony M. "Regulation of Bank Capital and Portfolio Risk." *Journal of Finance* 35 (December 1980): 1235–1244.

Pringle, John. "The Capital Decision in Commercial Banks." *Journal of Finance* 29 (June 1974): 779–795.

Santomero, Anthony M., and Watson, Donald D. "Determining Optimal Capital Standard for the Banking Industry." *Journal of Finance* 32 (September 1977): 1267–1283.

Chapter 9

Asset Management

Good asset management has always been important for the profitability and liquidity of financial institutions. In recent years its importance has increased due to shortages of funds, higher interest rates, and more aggressive competition. When there was little competition for funds and lower interest rates, a depository institution could make only the safest loans and invest the remainder of its funds in U.S. Treasury obligations. Today, such a policy would not allow the institution to meet costs, compete for funds, and meet its other obligations. Thus institutions have sought profits through a more aggressive loan and investment policy. Aggressive policy reduces the margin for error and requires greater skill in asset management.

Inflationary pressures and erratic behavior of economic and financial variables, especially interest rates, are other factors which have led to greater importance of asset management. Changes in the prime rate (the interest rate banks charge their best commercial loan customers) provide a good example. From 1950 through 1969, the prime rate changed sixteen times per decade, a significant increase from the two changes that occurred in the period from 1934 to 1949. In the decade of the 1970s, the prime rate changed over 100 times![1] The rapid rate of change in financial variables adds a new dimension to asset management. Flexibility in meeting such changing conditions has become an important consideration.

Another important factor is the increasing emphasis on allocation of assets to uses deemed socially desirable. In recent periods of monetary tightness, the Federal Reserve encouraged banks to allocate credit to firms that could not directly compete for funds. Legislation such as the equal credit opportunity act is aimed at requiring institutions to grant some loans they would not voluntarily choose to make. Other legislation of this type is pending.[2] Responding to these requirements without jeopardizing profitability or unduly increasing risk requires new management skills.

---

[1]James V. Baker, Jr., "Why You Need a Formal Asset/Liability Management Policy," *Banking* (June 1978): 33.

[2]These responsibilities are in addition to the long-recognized social responsibility of all financial institutions: the responsibility to customers and the general public to stay liquid and solvent through careful selection of assets appropriate to the particular liability structure.

TYPES OF ASSETS

Assets of financial institutions vary by maturity, ranging from overnight loans in the federal funds market to long-term securities and fixed assets. They also differ according to whether they are personal debt instruments, such as most loans, or impersonal instruments such as Treasury obligations and corporate bonds (table 9-1).

Various classes of assets are of differing importance to different types of financial institutions. The data in table 9-2 came largely from reports to the government agencies overseeing the institutions. Since each agency consolidates information in a different manner, comparability between types of institutions is somewhat limited. However, some general observations are possible. We note, for example, that commercial banks held substantial cash, deposits, and government securities while savings and loan companies had a substantially smaller percent of their assets in these categories. Traditionally, savings and loan companies have maintained a less liquid asset structure because their sources of funds were more stable. Their deposits are less volatile compared with banks. Note also that

Table 9-1:

Categories of Financial Institution Assets

	Short Term	Long Term
Impersonal	U.S. government	U.S. government
	Treasury notes	Treasury bonds
	Agency notes	Agency bonds
	State and local notes	State and local government
	Commercial paper	General obligation
	Negotiable certificates of deposit	Revenue
	Federal funds	Corporation bonds
	Banker's acceptances	Corporation equity
Personal	Commercial loans	Commercial loans
	Consumer loans	Consumer loans
		Mortgages
Other	Cash and deposits	Physical plant

Table 9-2:

Asset Structures of Major Types of Financial Institutions

	Commercial Banks	Savings & Loan Companies	Mutual Savings Banks	Credit Unions	Life Insurance Companies
Cash	9.7%	13.2%	3.2%		57.1
Securities	21.8		31.6		
Loans	55.6	67.5	60.2	60.5	34.6
Other	12.9	19.3	5.0	39.5*	8.3%*

*Including cash.

Source: *Federal Reserve Bulletin*

equity holdings are low for all depository institutions. The unstable nature of equity security values largely precludes their use as assets for depository financial institutions.

CONSIDERATIONS IN ASSET MANAGEMENT

There are five primary objectives or areas of consideration in asset management. These include profitability, liquidity, risk, flexibility, and regulatory requirements. This same set of considerations guides all businesses, but with different degrees of emphasis.

Profitability

While financial institutions are important to the economy and society, this should not cloud the fact that individual institutions are normally profit-seeking businesses. With certain exceptions, they are owned by stockholders who have invested in the firm with the expectation of earning a rate of return commensurate with the risk involved.[3] If the institution is to attract equity capital, it must earn a competitive rate of return. Thus asset investments must yield certain minimum required rates of return to be acceptable.

Liquidity

Liquidity—the ability to meet all legitimate demands for cash—is more important for financial institutions than for other firms. The public confidence that institutions must have to attract funds is closely related to their ability to meet legitimate demands for cash, such as deposit

withdrawals and insurance claims. While liability sources, including lines of credit and the federal funds market, are frequently used to meet liquidity needs, the primary source continues to be assets that can be sold or converted to cash quickly. Thus, institutions hold a certain amount of funds in cash or in short-term, marketable assets to meet liquidity needs.

Risk

Since most of the typical institution's obligations are fixed and the equity base is generally small, it must be concerned about the risk of shrinkage in the value of its assets. A level of asset value shrinkage that would cause little difficulty in another type of business can reduce the institution's capital to the point where further expansion must be curtailed. Thus the financial institution must pay very close attention to risk.

Flexibility

Flexibility is an important concept related to both risk and return (chapter 8). Flexibility is essentially the ability to respond to unexpected changes, either problems or opportunities for investment. Profitability can be enhanced and risk can be reduced by managing assets so as to provide such flexibility.

Regulatory Requirements

Regulatory requirements are designed to encourage safety and liquidity as well as to promote the accomplishment of certain public policy goals. Regulatory agencies accomplish these objectives in at least three ways:

1. By specifying the nature of the assets which may be held.

2. By specifying certain general relationships among assets, liabilities, and equity capital.

3. By encouraging investment in assets designed to promote goals of a public policy nature.

Regulatory requirements have an effect on the

---

[3] A frequently heard debate about the role of business in society can be avoided by differentiating between the goals and results of business activity. A financial institution can only earn a profit if it provides some service for which society is willing to pay. This service results from the financial institution's pursuit of its profitability objective. For example, the availability of credit to automobile buyers results from conclusions by banks and finance companies that they can profit from these loans.

asset structure of selected categories of financial institutions (table 9-2).

If savings and loan companies with mutual savings banks are used for comparison, the substantial holdings of private debt and equity securities by mutual savings banks and the nearly total absence of these assets from the portfolios of savings and loan companies result from differences in regulations affecting the two types of institutions. Savings and loan companies were created for the purpose of making mortgage money available while mutual savings banks were created as a service to savers.

The regulatory environment has already been discussed in some detail in chapter 3. For the purposes of this chapter, regulatory considerations can be thought of as constraints that may limit the institution's actions in pursuing its objectives.

PRINCIPLES OF ASSET STRUCTURE MANAGEMENT

Once the objectives to be pursued in asset management are identified, the question of how to achieve these objectives must be faced. In this section, some methods of achieving specific objectives and methods of analyzing the asset structure with regard to these objectives are presented. In studying these methods, it must be kept in mind that pursuit of one objective almost always involves a tradeoff in terms of some other objective. The appropriate tradeoff is always a difficult policy question for management.

Profitability

The profitability objective permeates much of what has been discussed. In chapters 7 and 8, the methods of finding the required return and of comparing it to returns on available assets were developed. Thus those two chapters provide the basis for profitability analysis.

In general, the profitability objective requires that the institution invest only in those assets that earn a return higher than the cost of funds.

Among investments meeting this criterion, the highest return possible is desired, all else being equal. Unfortunately, with most investment alternatives, all else is not equal. Problems involving risk and the assignment of costs frequently arise. The assignment of costs is discussed in the following paragraphs and risk is taken up in the next section of this chapter.

The return on an asset is not just the directly computed rate of return. It must be adjusted for the costs of acquiring and servicing the asset. While the administrative costs of acquiring and holding U.S. government bonds are quite small, a loan involves processing costs, credit examination costs, and general office overhead costs in addition to the cost of funds. Failure to consider these other costs will lead to biased decisions.

Example Friendly Neighborhood Savings and Loan is experiencing insufficient demand for first mortgage loans. Alternative investments including second-mortgage lending[4] to existing customers are being considered. While Friendly has not previously been involved in this type of lending, other institutions in the area have, and data on their experience is available. The average second-mortgage loan carries an interest yield of 12 percent, net of bad debt losses, while U.S. government bonds are currently yielding 9 percent. The second-mortgage loans appear on the surface to be more attractive. However, the cost of servicing such loans must be considered.

The loans would be promoted through ''stuffers'' included with statements to regular customers. The cost would be relatively low, an estimated $5 per $1,000 of second mortgage loans made. Credit investigation and other administrative costs associated with granting a loan would average $120 per loan. Ongoing administrative costs would average $0.50 per month per loan. Although management anticipates that the original maturity of a typical second-mortgage loan would be seven years, the experience

---

[4]A second mortgage is a security claim against a property that falls after another claim, the first mortgage, in the event of bankruptcy. Second-mortgage loans on houses are used for remodeling or to borrow money for unrelated expenses such as education or medical.

Table 9-3:

Second Mortgage Profitability Analysis

Monthly payment (7 year, 12%, $8,000 loan)	$141.22
Processing cost	.50
Net monthly payment received	$140.72
Loan amount	$8,000.00
Solicitation cost (8 × $5)	40.00
Processing cost	120.00
Net outlay	$8,160.00
Amount received at the end of three years ($141.22 × 37.975)	$5,362.83

		10.5%		11.0%		11.5%	
Period	Payment	*Present Value Factor*	*Present Value*	*Present Value Factor*	*Present Value*	*Present Value Factor*	*Present Value*
1–36	$ 140.72	30.767	$4,329.53	30.545	$4,298.29	30.325	$4,267.33
36	5,362.83	.7308	3,919.16	.7200	3,861.24	.7094	3,804.39
			$8,248.69		$8,159.53		$8,071.72

of others has shown that the average loan is re-paid after three years. No penalty will be charged to people who repay early.

The profitability analysis is summarized in table 9-3. The monthly payment of $141.22 was found using table A-8. The outlay by the savings and loan equals the $8,000 loan amount plus the solicitation and processing costs for a total of $8,160. The amount still owed (and therefore repaid) at the end of three years is determined using table A-8. It is the present value of $141.22 per month for four years, discounted at 12 percent per year.

The rate earned on these loans is found by taking the present value of the net monthly payments and final payments—using tables A-6 and A-8— at various interest rates to find the rate that generates a present value as close as possible to $8,160. This rate (yield) turns out to be about 11 percent (table 9-3). In other words, after taking into account the additional expenses associated with the second mortgage loan program, a return of 11 percent is expected. The second-mortgage loans are more profitable than U.S. government bonds.

Timing and Profitability In the previous example, an 11 percent return was estimated for a portfolio of second-mortgage loans. In many cases, however, the profit from a new venture will be delayed by start-up costs. These start-up costs must then be recognized in computing the realized return. Suppose that the savings and loan feels that it can generate a $5 million portfolio of second mortgage loans earning an average annual income of $0.11 × \$5$ million = $550,000. However, even though the $5 million must be committed almost immediately, start-up costs will be $450,000 in the first year, holding income before cost of funds to $100,000.

To find the realized return, one simply finds the discount rate that makes the present value of the income stream equal to the initial outlay. If there were no start-up costs, the problem would simply be

$$\$5,000,000 = \frac{\$550,000}{R}$$

$$R = \$550,000/\$5,000,000 = 11\%$$

where R is the realized return.

Since there is an extra start-up cost of

$450,000 in the first year, the present value of this cost must be deducted. This is done using the basic present value of a single payment method explained in chapter 6:

$$\$5,000,000 = \frac{\$550,000}{R} - \frac{\$450,000}{1 + R}$$

Values of R are substituted into this equation until the R that causes the two sides of the equation to equal each other is found. That value of R turns out to be 0.1017; the realized return is 10.17 percent. The start-up costs decreased the return from 11 percent to 10.17 percent. However, the second-mortgage loans are still attractive unless there are alternate investments that will yield more than 10.17 percent or the required return on funds is more than 10.17 percent.

Assignment of Joint Costs

One difficult problem in profitability analysis is the assignment of joint costs. In the above problem, for example, should part of the cost of maintaining the savings and loan building be assigned to second mortgage loans since the existence of the building and other services makes the second-mortgage lending possible? Or should these costs be ignored because they will continue whether or not the institution enters the second mortgage market?

The traditional argument, and probably the appropriate one in this example, is that only the costs that will change—the marginal costs—should be considered. However, the typical financial institution offers a range of services supported by an organization and structure that will not change significantly with the addition or deletion of one service. Although certain costs are fixed, they must still be seen as a cost of the total package of services and must be met through charges for that package of services. Furthermore, certain services are offered below cost as a means of attracting more profitable business. Thus the marginal cost approach must be applied with a strong dose of judgment as the institution must price its services competively and still meet fixed costs from some source.

LIQUIDITY

Although profitability is of paramount importance, the financial institution needs to maintain a sufficient volume of liquid assets. The institution must stand ready to meet all legitimate demands for funds, such as withdrawal demands. Failure to meet such demands on an immediate basis would likely destroy confidence in the institution, without which it cannot survive. On the other hand, liquid assets frequently earn low rates of return, interfering with the profit objective. Thus the institution should seek to maximize profit, but subject to the constraint that adequate liquidity is necessary.

Primary vs. Secondary Liquidity Reserves

In order to evaluate liquidity requirements, it is necessary to differentiate between primary and secondary liquidity reserves. All depository and some nondepository financial institutions are required to maintain some minimum amount of liquid reserves. For example, immediately available cash or "cash-like" assets equal to 12 percent of most transaction account balances must be maintained by commercial banks.

It should be noted that required primary reserves are the minimum level that must be maintained. Use of any of these reserves to meet demands for funds would take the institution below minimum levels and would bring a quick response from the regulatory authorities. Thus primary reserves do not provide a source of usable liquidity for the individual financial institution under normal conditions, although they do provide a certain cushion for the financial system in general.

The funds a financial institution actually uses to meet liquidity needs are called *secondary reserves*. These are assets that earn interest, but can be sold quickly if additional funds are needed. Securities in this category include Treasury bills, bankers acceptances, and federal funds. Financial institutions buy and sell these securities on a daily basis to meet their liquidity needs and primary reserve requirements while avoiding the holding of idle cash.

Liquidity reserves can be viewed from either a "stock" or a "flow" perspective. A stock approach involves looking at the balance sheet and deciding the liquid reserve needs based on the structure of the institution's liabilities. The shorter the maturity of the liability, the higher the proportion of the funds that must be held in liquid reserves. The proportions of each liability that must be maintained in the form of liquid assets is then determined on the basis of past experience. This is the approach used by regulators in determining the amount of required primary reserves. It is also a method used by many institutions in determining the appropriate level of secondary reserves.

A flow approach involves looking at the liquidity reserves as a reservoir (figure 8-2). The inflow may not equal the outflow on any particular day and the reservoir serves to offset temporary differences between inflow and outflow. As with a water reservoir, the liquidity reserve cannot offset a permanent imbalance. It can only offset temporary imbalances.

If the flow approach is used, the variabilities of inflows and outflows are studied to determine the amount of liquid reserves that may be needed. The flow approach is similar to certain approaches used in inventory management, and inventory models have been applied successfully to liquid reserve problems. An approach to the problem has been illustrated in figure 9-1 which shows the cumulative value of net cash flows

(cash inflows minus cash outflows) over time for a particular savings and loan company. There are some periods of time during which cumulative net cash flows decline. These are periods of net cash outflows. Liquid reserves must be held to meet demands for funds during these periods of negative cash flow, or the institution must have some liability source it can call on at such times. For this institution, we see that the largest decline occurred between day 33 and day 43, when cumulative cash flows declined by $76,000. Thus a secondary reserve of $76,000 would have been sufficient to meet demand during the period examined. While the study of data for only two months would not be sufficient for determination of liquidity needs, the method can serve as a useful guide if flows are examined over a sufficiently long time period.

Voluntary vs. Involuntary Outflows

A further refinement is to break down the outflow during the negative flow periods into voluntary and involuntary outflows. An involuntary demand is something like a deposit withdrawal demand, which must be met. A voluntary demand, such as a request for a loan, need not be honored if funds are not available. Cumulative net cash flows, including new loans are contrasted with cumulative net cash flows excluding new loans for the two periods of greatest cash outflow (figure 9-2).

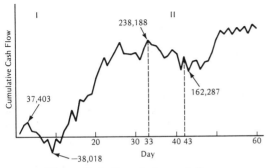

Figure 9–1: Cumulative cash flows.

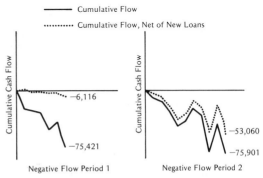

Figure 9–2: Cumulative flow for major negative cash flow periods.

During Period 1 increased loan demand was being met from excess liquid funds. This time period contained no threat to liquidity (figure 9-2). However, period 2 was a period of decreasing deposits. It represented the major test of the institution's liquidity over this time period. Secondary reserves of $53,000 would have been required to meet this demand.

Once the secondary reserve requirement has been determined, the next question is what form these reserves should take. Funds must be held in assets that can be quickly converted to cash without substantial loss. It is also desirable to earn the highest return possible on these funds. Thus secondary reserve assets must be safe, of short maturity, and readily salable. Secondary reserve assets include Treasury bills, bankers acceptances, and other short-term, high quality investments.

In addition to secondary reserves, some temporary liquidity needs can be met through borrowing. Depository institutions can borrow on a temporary, limited basis at the Federal Reserve Discount Window, using such securities as U.S. government bonds as collateral. Depository institutions can also borrow from each other in the federal funds market. Some nonbank financial institutions maintain lines of credit at commercial banks to meet their liquidity needs. For example, finance companies frequently raise funds through the sale of bonds and commercial paper while using bank lines of credit as a back-up source of liquidity.

There are certain dangers inherent in the planned use of borrowing as a means of meeting liquidity needs. Banks and thrift institutions, for example, tend to experience net deposit outflows when market interest rates rise above regulation *Q* ceilings. When one institution faces heavy withdrawal demand, it is quite likely that other institutions are facing similar problems. Thus it may be very difficult to borrow to meet liquidity needs at the time when these needs are greatest.

Because secondary reserves frequently earn a low return, a reduction in needed secondary reserves will often result in increased profitability. There are several things that can be done to reduce the amount of secondary reserves needed.

One method has already been mentioned: arranging lines of credit to provide emergency liquidity. Improved forecasting is another approach. The more accurate the institution in predicting cash flows, the less reserves it needs for potential outflows.

Another frequently used approach to minimizing the secondary reserve need is hedging. Hedging involves matching the maturities of assets and liabilities. To the extent that maturities do match, secondary reserves are not necessary. Unfortunately, the nature of the financial institution limits the degree to which this can be achieved. Deposit funds can frequently be withdrawn on demand while loans are granted for specific maturities. Thus the institution must develop asset management policies based on the stability of particular sources of funds, with less reliance on the absolute maturity of funds sources.

RISK

Because of the small proportion of equity in their capital structures, financial institutions are particularly sensitive to the possibility of asset value shrinkage. Both prudent management and regulatory requirements dictate that risk be held to a relatively low level. The recognition, management, and control of risk are important roles of management in all financial institutions. There are two important sources of asset value shrinkage for a financial institution: interest risk and credit or business risk.

Interest Rate Risk

Interest risk refers to the fact that the value of a fixed stream of returns from a financial asset declines as the general level of interest rates rises. For example, the value of a perpetuity of $100 a year would be $2,000 at a required return of 5 percent, but only $1,000 if the required return rose to 10 percent. Thirty-year U.S. government bonds were issued in November 1972 with a face interest rate of approximately 5.4 percent. In January 1981, the market interest rate on such bonds was approximately 12 percent and the market value of these bonds had declined to less than 50 percent of face value. While the face value could still be realized by holding the bonds until maturity, anyone wishing to sell one in 1981 would lose over half the original investment.

With increased inflation and the accompanying instability of interest rates, interest risk has become an increasingly serious problem for financial institutions. The problem is aggravated by the fact that the assets of a financial institution frequently have longer maturities than the sources of the institution's funds. Savings and loan companies that made twenty-five year loans at 5 percent in the early 1960s found themselves paying in excess of 5 percent on virtually all funds sources before these loans matured.

Interest rate risk is difficult to eliminate for many financial institutions. Hedging—matching the maturities of assets and liabilities—is one method of eliminating interest rate risk. Unfortunately this is a difficult task for many financial institutions. An important service of depository financial institutions has traditionally been the provision of immediate liquidity to savers while assuring borrowers of a longer term source of credit (asset transmutation was the name given to this activity in chapter 1). The problem is particularly severe for mortgage lenders such as savings and loan companies. They face demand for loans with twenty-year to thirty-year maturities while the depositors are generally unwilling to commit their funds for similar periods, particularly at a fixed interest rate.

Depository institutions have tried to deal with the problem by seeking longer term deposits in recent years and have succeeded in increasing the average maturity of deposit funds. They have also worked to reduce the average maturities of their assets. For example, a savings and loan may decide to increase its efforts to market second mortgage loans and take advantage of the 1980 legislation to enter other shorter term lending such as automobile loans. While complete hedging is probably not possible, institutions can take steps to bring the maturity of their assets and liabilities into closer alignment.

Another approach to minimizing interest rate risk is the variable rate loan, a loan with the interest rate tied to some general indicator of interest rates. This type of loan has gained acceptance in several countries and is used on a limited scale by some long-term commercial and mortgage lenders in the United States. A variation is the balloon mortgage loan which is technically due in a few years, but is actually renegotiated to the current market interest rate at its due date. The balloon note has been used increasingly in recent years.

Gap Analysis

Gap analysis is a useful tool for measuring and controlling interest rate risk. The duration gap is the difference between the average duration of assets and liabilities. Maturity is often used instead of duration, but duration is a more accurate measure. The duration should be based on the time until the asset or liability is eligible for repricing rather than the nominal amortization schedule. For example, a thirty-year adjustable rate mortgage may have a duration of only a year if it can be repriced in one year. The objective of gap analysis is not the maintenance of zero gap, but the measurement and control of risk, as measured by the gap.

Following is a duration gap analysis for a highly simplified savings and loan.

		Duration
Cash & Short Term Inv.	$2,000	0.5
Mortgages	8,000	5.0
Total Assets	$10,000	4.1

Av. Duration of Assets =
$0.2 \times 0.5 + 0.8 \times 5.0 =$ <u>4.1</u>

		Duration
Short-Term Deposits	$4,000	0.5
Long-Term Deposits	5,000	6.0
Equity[5]	1,000	8.0
T. L. & N. W.	$10,000	4.0

Av. Duration of Sources =
$0.4 \times 0.5 + 0.5 \times 6 + 0.1 \times 8 =$ <u>4.0</u>

The duration gap is $4.1 - 4.0 = 0.1$ years. This would suggest that this institution faces very little interest rate risk. This gap can be compared to other companies in the industry, to the gap for previous years, or to a policy standard. It is particularly useful as a tool for spotting trends in risk exposure.

Unfortunately, the simple duration gap measure cannot be used for definitive analysis because it obscures important interest rate risks. Greatest among these is the risk of a shift in the shape of the yield curve. Suppose, for example, that short-term rates rose sharply while long-term rates remained stable. The institution has $4,000 of liabilities and only $2,000 of assets coming up for repricing at the higher rate; its profit will decline. A financial institution can face considerable risks of this type even if the overall duration gap is zero.[5]

To overcome this problem, institutions frequently measure the dollar gap in each of a number of maturity or duration categories. Assuming that short-term items will be received in less than one year, the institution might perform a simple gap analysis like the following:

Due Date	Assets	Sources	Dollar Gap
Under 1 year	$2,000	$4,000	−$2,000
Over 1 year	8,000	6,000	2,000

This analysis tells management that while the average duration of assets is approximately the same as the average duration of the sources of funds, there are serious imbalances within categories. Recognizing this risk, the institution may wish to adjust assets, adjust sources of funds, or enter into a futures contract to decrease the dollar disparities within due date categories. For example, a futures contract to sell a financial instrument would help offset the imbalance between short term assets and liabilities.

Institutions frequently compute dollar gaps for four or five different maturity or duration ranges in an attempt to accurately measure their risk exposure. Other refinements include the recognition of the portion of a long-term asset such as a mortgage that will be received in each maturity range as part of that range's maturities rather than simply categorizing these long-term assets according to duration. With these refinements, and others discussed in the references at the end of this chapter, gap analysis has found a place as a simple and extremely useful tool for assessing interest rate risk.

Credit or Business Risk

Credit or business risk is associated with potential variability of the stream of cash flows from the asset itself. For a debt instrument, credit risk is the risk that the creditor will not meet his obligations under the debt contract. For equity investments such as common stock, the holder faces the risk that the company may suffer from reduced profitability, resulting in a decline in the value of the equity.

Credit or business risk can be controlled by investing in less risky securities, such as U.S. government obligations. Unfortunately, risk-free securities may pay lower returns and a complete portfolio of these would require that the institution essentially forego its profit objective. Risk can be controlled while still allowing reasonable profits through the use of portfolio analysis.

Portfolio Analysis

The central theme of the portfolio concept is that the assets of the institution should be thought of as part of a unified whole, not as the sum of a group of individual entities. By proper management of the asset mix, it is possible to create a group of assets, the total risk of which is less than the sum of the risks of the individual assets. While this concept has long been recognized, it has received particular attention in recent years.

An example serves to highlight both the

___
[5]One might think that the duration of equity would be infinite, but this is not the case. It is not difficult to show that for a nongrowth stock, the duration is approximately $1/K$ where K is the required return on equity. The computation is more complex for a growth stock, but the duration is still finite.

potential and limitations of portfolio analysis in controlling risk. While 5 percent of the loans made by a particular consumer finance company are expected to default under normal conditions, the portfolio of loans is riskless with regard to these losses. The defaults on 5 percent of the loans are simply one of the costs reflected in the interest rates charged. Thus what first appears to be a group of risky loans can be combined in such a way that the particular risk is virtually eliminated. However, the portfolio is only riskless with regard to this normal level of losses. The company still faces the risk of the loss rate being higher than the anticipated 5 percent. This can occur because of a recession or other economic problem, resulting in higher unemployment among the borrowers. Thus the risk related to individual securities can be eliminated through construction of a portfolio, still certain overall risks remain. We refer to the risk that can be overcome through the use of portfolio approaches as *diversifiable* risk and that which cannot be eliminated in this manner as *nondiversifiable* risk.

To further illustrate the essential nondiversifiability of certain risks, consider the consumer finance company just discussed. While it is possible for the loan company to invest in assets other than consumer loans, the same risks remain. The high default rates occur during periods of economic downturn. At the same time, stock prices normally decline and other types of investments are subject to increased defaults. Thus, further diversification is likely to be unsuccessful in eliminating this type of risk. Nondiversifiable risk can be eliminated only by movement to low-return risk-free securities.

The recognition of diversifiable and nondiversifiable risk can be formal or informal. With the informal approach, we begin by identifying the types of risk involved and determining which are and are not diversifiable. The diversifiable risks must be estimated as carefully as possible so that they can be accurately treated as a cost factor. The degree of nondiversifiable risk can be measured by studying past patterns, if historical data are available, or by estimating the impacts of various conditions.

Example The consumer finance company discussed above makes two general types of loans: loans secured by the item being purchased, such as installment loans for appliance purchase; and unsecured loans for purposes such as medical expenses and bill consolidation. The company has one half of its funds in each category. Under normal conditions, default rates for the secured loans average 4 percent while default rates for unsecured loans average 6 percent. Normal conditions include a 5 percent unemployment rate. As the primary nondiversifiable risk is associated with unemployment, the default rates experienced for each type of loan during past unemployment periods are shown in table 9-4.

The company is considering a change in its mix of loan types. Obviously, average default rates at each unemployment rate depend on the mix of loans. For example, with 30 percent of the funds in secured loans and 70 percent in unsecured loans, the default rate at an 8 percent unemployment rate would be

$$0.30(5.6\%) + 0.70(8.1\%) = \underline{7.35\%}$$

Expected average default rates for a range of unemployment rates and various loan portfolios are shown in table 9-5.

The information contained in table 9-5 does not tell the finance company what mixture of secured and unsecured loans would be optimal. However, it does provide a concise summary of the risks associated with each combination. Using the informal approach, the risks for each

Table 9-4:

Default Rates at Various Levels of Unemployment

Unemploy-ment Rate	Default Rates		
	Secured	Unsecured	Average
5%	4.00%	6.00%	5.00%
6	4.50	6.60	5.55
7	5.00	7.30	6.15
8	5.60	8.10	6.85
9	6.30	8.90	7.60

Table 9-5:

Average Default Rates for Alternative Loan Portfolio Mixes

	Proportion of Funds in Secured Loans				
Unemployment Rate	.3	.4	.5	.6	.7
5%	5.40%	5.20%	5.00%	4.80%	4.60%
6	5.97	5.76	5.55	5.34	5.13
7	6.61	6.38	6.15	5.92	5.69
8	7.35	7.10	6.85	6.60	6.25
9	8.12	7.86	7.60	7.34	7.08

combination are judgmentally compared to the expected returns in choosing a preferred loan portfolio mix.

The formal approach uses statistical techniques to develop more precise guidelines. The use of beta, first described in chapter 7, provides one such example. Recall that beta (b) was a measure of sensitivity of returns for the particular asset to conditions affecting common stock returns in general, r_f is the rate available on risk-free securities such as Treasury bills, and E_m is expected return for securities in general. The required return for equity was then

$$K_e = r_f + b (E_m - r_f)$$

This formula was used to develop an estimate of the cost of equity capital. It can also be used to estimate required return for particular assets.

Example The required before-tax return for the loan portfolio of the consumer finance company discussed above is 12 percent. The portfolio has a beta of 1.2 computed by comparing returns for the portfolio to returns in the securities market in general for a number of years. The risk-free rate is 8 percent. What would be the required return if the portfolio beta were reduced to 1.0? By definition, security returns in general (E_m) have a beta of 1. Thus we only need to solve for E_m:

$$12\% = 8\% + 1.2(E_m - 8\%)$$
$$E_m = 11.33\%$$

Using this value of E_m, we can then find the required return for any beta. The secured loans

have been found to have a beta of 1.0 while the unsecured loans have been found to have a beta of 1.4. Thus the required returns for the two types of loans are

Secured: $0.08 + 1.0(0.1133 - 0.08)$
    $= 11.33\%$

Unsecured: $0.08 + 1.4(0.1133 - 0.08)$
    $= 12.67\%$

Using this approach, the company would then compare expected returns for each type of loan with the required return for that type of loan and invest in opportunities exceeding their required return.

One limitation of this approach is that it assumes that diversifiable risk has been eliminated through the holding of a large number of assets (loans in this case). When only a few assets are to be held, or when there is other reason to be concerned about whether diversifiable risk has been eliminated, the mean-variance portfolio model can be used directly. It is briefly summarized in appendix 9-A.

FLEXIBILITY

Flexibility is the ability to respond to changing conditions. Because of the inherent unpredictability of events, the ability to respond to unanticipated changes in business and economic conditions is an important ingredient of good asset management. An unexpected increase in loan demand (and interest rates) is an example of a situation in which planning for flexibility would be rewarded. Such a situation presents the institution with the opportunity to make highly profitable loans and to gain new customers, if funds are available to lend.

A necessary level of flexibility can be attained through proper management of assets and liabilities. In general, flexibility in asset management is achieved through the management of the maturity structure of securities and loans, and through the holding of marketable assets.

In general, shorter security and loan maturities result in greater flexibility because the institution can make new investment decisions at more frequent intervals. However, this flexibility does not come without cost. Shorter term loans and securities frequently carry lower interest rates. Furthermore, some institutions face only limited demand for short-term credit. A savings and loan company, for example, has little choice but to hold the bulk of its assets in the form of long-term mortgages.

A portfolio with staggered maturities—one with certain proportions of loans or other securities maturing each period on a planned basis—is one method of gaining flexibility without foregoing longer term, higher yielding assets. Properly distributed maturities assure a continued flow of cash to be used in making new loans or investments.

Finally, the existence of marketable securities and loans within the total portfolio increases flexibility while allowing investment in longer term assets. Long-term securities can be sold in the open market if the institution faces a need for funds or if a particularly attractive opportunity for investment becomes available. The existence of interest rate risk and the associated risk of loss in the market value of securities, however, frequently precludes the conversion of this type of asset to cash.

others. They can be classified according to whether they are personal or impersonal and whether they are short-term or long-term. We also noted that the mixture of assets varied by type of institution, depending on institutional objectives, liability structure, and regulatory requirements.

The primary considerations in asset management are

Profitability—Most financial institutions are private, profit-seeking enterprises.

Liquidity—The ability to meet all obligations on schedule and to meet withdrawal requests immediately is very important for financial institutions. Both regulatory requirements and the need to maintain public confidence make adequate liquidity imperative.

Risk—Loss in asset value is particularly damaging to financial institutions because of their low ratios of equity to total assets. Risk can be recognized through informal methods or through statistical portfolio analysis techniques.

Flexibility—Flexibility is the ability to respond to unanticipated changes in the form of either problems or opportunities. It is achieved primarily through management of maturity structure and marketability of assets.

Regulatory Requirements—Regulatory requirements are designed to control risk and see that the institution provides the service for which it was created.

Regulatory requirements can be thought of as constraints—conditions that must be met. Given the necessity of meeting these constraints, asset management is guided by the desire to achieve the best possible trade-off between the other considerations.

SUMMARY

In this chapter we identified the primary types of assets held by financial institutions. The assets consist primarily of financial obligations of

QUESTIONS

1. Why is the percentage of commercial bank assets held in the form of cash items

substantially higher than the percentage of thrift institution assets held in this form?

2. The Financial Institution Deregulation and Monetary Control Act of 1980 instructed the regulatory authorities to move toward equal cash reserve requirements for commercial banks and thrift institutions. Why would it be deemed appropriate for banks and thrift institutions to move toward similar liquid asset percentages?

3. Explain the difference between primary and secondary reserves.

4. Do required reserves provide a source of liquidity to the financial institution? Why?

5. Why is it so difficult for thrift institutions to eliminate interest rate risk?

6. For a life insurance company, list as many types of risk as you can think of. Categorize these risks as to whether they are diversifiable or nondiversifiable.

7. By studying the current news, find an example of a financial institution that has profited from maintaining flexibility or has suffered losses due to the absence of flexibility.

PROBLEMS

1. The Financial Institution Deregulation and Monetary Control Act of 1980 allowed savings and loans to invest up to 20 percent of their funds in assets other than liquidity reserves and real estate mortgage loans. Community Federal Savings and Loan is considering automobile loans. The average automobile loan is for 36 months and carries an

Cash Flows Experienced by the Employee's Federal Credit Union

Week	Deposits	Withdrawals	Loan Repayments	New Loans
1	10,000	7,000	3,000	7,000
2	10,600	7,400	3,000	6,000
3	10,900	7,600	3,100	7,000
4	11,800	7,400	3,100	8,000
5	11,600	7,800	3,150	7,000
6	12,000	8,200	3,150	7,000
7	13,000	8,500	3,150	8,000
8	12,500	8,700	3,170	7,000
9	10,000	9,200	3,175	5,000
10	9,600	9,800	3,180	5,000
11	9,400	10,200	3,180	4,000
12	9,200	10,500	3,185	4,000
13	8,400	11,300	3,190	3,000
14	6,400	11,800	3,190	1,000
15	5,200	14,200	3,195	500
16	4,000	15,800	3,195	500
17	4,200	16,200	3,200	300
18	4,400	15,300	3,200	200
19	5,000	12,800	3,200	200
20	5,000	11,700	3,205	0
21	5,200	11,000	3,210	0
22	5,400	10,300	3,210	200
23	5,600	9,000	3,210	200
24	6,000	7,900	3,210	500
25	5,800	6,400	3,210	1,000
26	6,400	6,400	3,215	2,000

interest rate of 14 percent, compared to 12 percent for a first mortgage loan. It costs approximately $50 for promotion and $50 for processing for each loan granted. In addition, it costs Community Federal approximately $0.40 to process each monthly payment. To allow for expected bad debts, Community assumes that actual payments received will be 99 percent of contractual payment amounts. The average automobile loan is expected to be $6,000 and Community's cost of funds is 9 percent.

    a.   Are the proposed automobile loans profitable for Community Federal?

    b.   Are there any intangible benefits associated with loans of this type by a savings and loan company?

    c.   Do you anticipate any problems for savings and loans entering into lending of this type?

2.   On page 146 is information on cash flows experienced by Employee's Federal Credit Union over a twenty-six-week period. Analyze these flows and determine the maximum amount of liquid reserves that would have been needed over this period.

3.   Giant National Bank (GNB) is considering the purchase of an existing company as a way to enter the automobile lending market in the southeast. The company being considered has a $100 million loan portfolio. As a buyer of dealer paper, its other assets are negligable. Income after operating expenses but before taxes and the cost of funds is 12 percent of the loan portfolio each year. To acquire the company, GNB must pay a premium of 5 percent over the book value of loans. In addition, conversion during the first year of GNB's ownership will cost around $1 million. GNB's required return on funds is 11 percent. Should GNB acquire the automobile lender?

4.   A balance sheet summary for First National Bank appears below. Compute the duration gap and prepare a dollar gap analysis. Suggest ways First National can decrease its interest rate risk.

Amounts Due	Value	Av. Duration
Assets		
Within 30 days	$3,000	0.05 years
31–180 days	$2,000	0.30
181–365 days	2,000	0.75
366 days–5 years	5,000	2.00
Over 5 years	3,000	8.00
Liabilities & Equity		
Within 30 days	$4,000	0.04
31–180 days	3,000	0.30
181–365 days	1,000	0.75
366 days–5 years	4,000	2.50
Over 5 years	3,000	9.00

SELECTED REFERENCES

Babcock, Builford. "The Roots of Risk and Return." *Financial Analysts Journal* 36 (January/February 1980): 56–63.

Bates, Timothy, and Bradford, William. "An Analysis of the Portfolio Behavior of Black-Owned Commercial Banks." *Journal of Finance* 35(June 1980): 753–768.

Ferguson, Robert. "Performance Measurement Doesn't Make Sense." *Financial Analysts Journal* 36(May/June 1980): 59–64.

Francis, Jack Clark. *Investments: Analysis and Management.* 3d ed. New York: McGraw-Hill, 1980.

Ibbotsen, R. G., and Sinquefield, R. A. "Stocks, Bonds, Bills and Inflation: Updates." *Financial Analysts Journal* 35(July/August 1979): 40–44.

Kane, Edward, and Buser, Stephen A. "Portfolio Diversification at Commercial Banks." *Journal of Finance* 34(March 1979): 19–34.

Kaufman, George G. "Measuring and Managing Interest Rate Risk: a Primer." *Economic Perspectives* 8(January–February 1984): 16–29.

Appendix 9-A

The Mean-Variance Portfolio Model

The mean-variance portfolio model is a formal method of recognizing risk in the construction of asset portfolios. It is discussed briefly here, but is presented in more detail in many investments texts.[1]

The mean-variance approach is based on the assumption that investors will choose an investment portfolio with the objective of maximizing expected return and minimizing risk, measured as the variance of the probability distribution of expected returns.[2] The particular combination of risk and expected return chosen depends on the individual's attitude toward risk. However,

everyone will be expected to choose a portfolio that provides the lowest variance for its level of expected return. Thus the objective of mean-variance portfolio analysis is the identification of the lowest variance portfolio for each possible expected return.

The expected return for a portfolio can be stated as a weighted average of the expected returns for individual assets:

$$E_p = \sum_{j=1}^{n} p_j E_j \qquad (9A\text{-}1)$$

where: E_p = Expected return for the portfolio

p_j = Proportion of funds invested in asset j

E_j = Expected return for asset j

n = Number of assets in the portfolio.

The computation of the variance for the portfolio is complex. It depends on the covariance, a measure of the degree to which the returns for two assets move together. The covariance between two securities is a measure of the tendency for their returns to be similarly affected by changes in the environment. The formula for the covariance is

---

[1]See, for example, Jack Clark Francis, *Investment Analysis and Management,* 3d ed. (New York: McGraw-Hill, 1980).

[2]The variance (σ^2) is a measure of dispersion. Thus a greater variance indicates a greater range of possible outcomes. Specifically, the variance is computed as follows:

$$\sigma_p^2 = \sum_{i=1}^{m} X_i (R_{pi} - E_p)^2$$

where: σ_p^2 = Variance of the portfolio

X_i = Probability of condition i occurring

R_{pi} = Return for the portfolio if condition i occurs

E_p = Expected return for the portfolio

m = Number of possible outcomes.

$$\sigma_{jk} = \sum_{h=1}^{m} X_h(R_{jh} - E_j)(R_{kh} - E_h) \quad (9A\text{-}2)$$

where: m = Number of different conditions that may occur in the environment

X_h = Probability of condition h occurring

R_{jh} = Expected return on security j if condition h occurs

R_{kh} = Expected return on security k if condition h occurs.

The variance for a portfolio is a function of these covariance terms:

$$\sigma_p^2 = \sum_{j=1}^{n} \sum_{k=1}^{n} P_j P_k \sigma_{jk} \quad (9A\text{-}3)$$

Equations 9A-1 and 9A-3 are then the two key equations used in the mean-variance portfolio model. For each possible expected return, we wish to identify the portfolio that minimizes variance. The set of such portfolios is what we identified as the *efficient frontier* in appendix 7-A. The institution can then choose from among these combinations of risk and return to choose the trade-off between risk and return it feels is most desirable.[3]

We need not concern ourselves with the question of how to actually find the various combinations of expected return and risk that are on the efficient frontier. Computer programs are read-

___
[3]A significant body of finance theory would argue that the optimum portfolio is one that maximizes the ratio:

$$(E_p - r_f) \div \sigma_p$$

where: r_f = Risk free interest rate, such as that available on Treasury bills

σ_p = Standard deviation, the square root of the variance

ily available for this purpose, given the set of expected returns and covariances for the assets.

The main problem in using this method is the set of inputs required. For each asset, the variance and the covariance with each other asset must be computed. For five assets, there are 15 covariance terms required, and for twenty assets, 210 covariance terms are required. To consider 1,000 assets we would require 500,500 covariance terms! Thus the number of covariance terms that must be estimated become quite large if more than a few assets are being used.

One way to overcome the large number of covariance terms needed is to use beta as a risk measure. In doing this, we assume that diversifiable risk will be eliminated by a large number of assets without any attention required. If this assumption is valid, the variance of a portfolio can be computed as follows:

$$\sigma_p^2 = \sigma_m^2 \left[\sum_{j=1}^{m} P_j b_j \right]^2 \quad (9A\text{-}4)$$

where: σ_m^2 = Variance of probability distribution of expected returns for a portfolio consisting of all available securities. Variance of returns for an index of stock market returns is normally used as this measure.

b_j = Beta for investment j.

Using this approach, the large number of covariance terms can be replaced with one beta for each asset. This approach is applicable when a large number of assets is being considered, such as in a portfolio of bonds and common stock. Again, computer programs are readily available for the purpose of identifying the set of efficient frontier portfolios if expected return and beta for each asset have been computed.

Chapter 10

Bank Management

Like industrial corporations, commercial banks are private businesses operated for the benefit of their owners. The process of establishing management policies in pursuit of this objective is different and, in many ways, more complex than that of a nonfinancial corporation. Along with responsibilities to owners, management must consider the unique responsibility of a commercial bank to its community and the constraints imposed by the regulatory environment. It is thus necessary to consider the special objectives and constraints of commercial banks in developing management principles.

BANK OBJECTIVES AND CONSTRAINTS

Banks as Private Enterprises

Banks, like other private enterprises, establish policy aimed at achieving their primary objective: profitability. Profitability is more than simple profit; it is the level of profits relative to the assets committed. A satisfactory level of profitability is necessary to assure proper returns to creditors and owners.

Like all business firms, banks generate liabilities and assets. Those who provide funds to banks do so by purchasing debt or equity securities issued by the bank or by placing funds on deposit. They provide funds for the purpose of receiving benefits in the form of services or expected future income. Thus banks are liable, as are other private businesses, to those from whom funds have been provided. They are liable to pay interest and ultimately return funds in the case of deposits and debt instruments issued. In addition, they are expected to meet dividend payments on equity as investor expectations dictate. Accordingly, management obligations to those who have provided funds are essentially comparable for commercial banks and private nonfinancial firms.

It stands to reason then, that bank funds must be invested in those assets that, when taken as a group, generate returns sufficient in amount to satisfy the legal requirements and expectations of depositors, creditors, and owners. A well-managed bank will generate a return on assets which not only covers minimum legal requirements and expectations, but also provides retained earnings for support of future growth.

As is true in a nonfinancial private enterprise,

proper management of assets and liabilities is critical to success and growth of commercial banks.

Competition

In a free enterprise system, external constraints are placed on private firms through the mechanism of competition. In competitive markets, firms bid for land, labor, capital and management talent. The interaction of supply and demand determines market prices for those resources. Similarly, prices for products and services are set by the forces of supply and demand. Thus, banks are not immune from competitive pressures. If wage levels are set below those offered in comparable employment circumstances, a bank will not be able to attract and retain competent personnel. Similarly, if compensating balance requirements and loan interest rates consistently exceed those charged by competing institutions, qualified loan customers can be expected to seek accommodations elsewhere. Thus, bank policy must reflect competitive forces in ways which are frequently similar to responses of nonbank firms.

Regulation

As discussed in chapters 2 and 3, the need to protect the safety of the public's funds has led to financial institutions' being more heavily regulated than most other types of business. Although the 1980s have witnessed a continued trend toward deregulation of the financial sector, no serious student of the financial system would agree that commercial banking regulations should be completely eliminated.

The need for banking regulations has long been justified on the grounds that unbridled competition would lead to massive bank failure and ultimate economic chaos. Consequently, the number of different banks and banking offices in the marketplace has been restricted. A new bank or branch will not be permitted by the regulatory authority if its existence would threaten the solvency of other banks in the market area. Similarly, to help maintain the solvency of the finan-

cial system, bank costs were held to artificially low levels. Prior to the Monetary Control Act of 1980, banks were largely prohibited from paying interest on transaction accounts and competing financial institutions were largely prohibited from offering transaction accounts. This condition, together with Regulation Q restrictions on interest payments for time and savings deposits amounted to a government-imposed cost subsidy that favored commercial banks and that favored borrowers at the expense of savers.

Although the Monetary Control Act of 1980, together with the Garn-St Germain Act, signalled a shift toward greater reliance on competition in allocating financial resources, the commercial banking industry is still subject to a huge network of regulations. Many of these regulations deal with questions of equity and social justice in credit allocation decisions. Such regulation, in addition to competitive forces and community responsibility, forms the complex of external constraints within which bank assets and liabilities must be managed.

Community Responsibility

In a nonregulated industry, competition is relied upon to assure that needs of society are met. The acceptance of a charter to operate a bank carries with it certain community responsibilities which management must recognize and respond to. Economic growth and stability of an area may depend on the willingness of banks to make necessary credit available. But neither competition nor regulation will assure that community needs are met. One of the most challenging problems for bank managers is the achievement of a proper balance between responsibility to owners and responsibility to the community.

CHOICE OF CHARTER

A group seeking to form a bank must first decide whether to seek a charter from the state or federal government. While most businesses can receive a corporate charter only from the state government, banks and certain other depository institutions may choose to apply for either a state or a national charter. This decision was traditionally made in light of the regulatory environment of the particular state vs. regulations by the federal government. If all else were equal, the bank would prefer the charter giving it the greatest freedom.

The second question faced by a bank has been whether or not to be a member of the Federal Reserve System. A national bank was required to be a member while a state bank had a choice. Prior to the Monetary Control Act of 1980, the primary advantage of membership was that the member bank could use the Federal Reserve System's services, such as borrowing at the Discount Window, wire transfer service, and check clearing. The primary disadvantage was that reserve requirements set by the Federal Reserve System applied only to member banks. Nonmember banks had their reserve requirements set by state banking authorities, with state requirements frequently being more lenient than those established by the federal government.

Increasingly, a number of smaller banks and some relatively large ones found that services provided by the Federal Reserve System did not justify the opportunity cost of required reserves. Indeed, the percentage of all commercial banks that were members fell from 49 percent in 1947 to 37 percent by 1980. The proportion of deposits held by member banks declined from 85 to 71 percent. By 1980, it was believed that this decline in membership, together with the growth in funds held by nonbank financial institutions, was impairing the ability of the Federal Reserve System to effectively implement monetary policy.

The Monetary Control Act of 1980 changed this picture by creating uniform reserve requirements for all depository institutions and by requiring that the Federal Reserve System establish prices for its services as well as make those prices available to all depository institutions. Thus the advantages of one chartering system over the other have diminished. By 1984, the proportion of banks which were Federal Reserve members had increased slightly and the share of deposits held by member banks was comparable to the 1980 level.

ASSET MANAGEMENT

Asset management in commercial banks is subject first and foremost to the constraint that assets must be highly liquid. Unlike a nonbank business which might forestall or delay payment without serious consequence, commercial banks must constantly be prepared to meet expected and unexpected demands for cash by depositors. Inability or even suspicion of inability on the part of banks to meet the demand for funds by depositors could lead to general distrust of commercial banks and ultimately to economic chaos. Hence, it is thus necessary that a large proportion of bank assets must be held in cash or in assets easily convertible to cash.

This results in a dilemma of some magnitude for the bank manager. On the one hand, there is the need to keep large sums in cash and low-yielding "near cash" assets. On the other hand, there is the need to meet community credit needs and to generate the levels of earnings necessary to meet costs. Such earnings provide a return to owners and retain some earnings to sustain future growth. This liquidity-profitability trade-off is the central focus of bank asset and liability management.

Asset Structure of Commercial Banks

The first level of asset management policy deals with the allocation of funds among the major categories of assets: cash, investments, and loans. Other assets, including physical facilities, amount to a small proportion of total assets for the typical commercial bank.[1] Cash assets, which earn little or no return, are required to

---

[1]For large banks, however, the proportion of "other assets" has grown rapidly in recent years. Such growth reflects investment in foreign affiliates and other activities associated with growth of international banking.

meet withdrawal demand from depositors. Investments, primarily in the form of short and intermediate-term U.S. government and municipal securities, provide some income and can be quickly sold to provide additional cash. Loans, which are much less liquid assets, serve the credit needs of the community and provide the greatest source of profit. Shifts in the relative distribution of these asset categories have occurred in recent decades (figure 10-1).

Over the total period covered in figure 10-1, cash assets declined from 23.9 percent of all assets to 9.7 percent. Moreover, investments declined in relative importance from 44.0 percent of total assets to 21.8 percent. Loans, which in aggregate traditionally yield a higher return but are less liquid, became increasingly important in relative terms. The data suggest that commercial banks, as a group, expanded their loan portfolio and in the process, reduced liquidity over this time period. These changes reflect more aggressive management. As will be seen later, they also reflect an increase in the proportion of funds obtained from time and savings deposits, which are less volatile than demand deposits.

Cash Management

The most liquid of assets held by banks or any firm or institution is cash. But while cash is unsurpassed as a form of liquidity, the cost of hold-

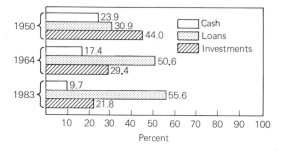

Figure 10–1: Asset structure for all commercial banks, 1950–1983. Graph excludes "other assets." Loans include federal funds sold and securities purchased under agreements to resell. Source: *Federal Reserve Bulletin,* December 1983 and Board of Governors of the Federal Reserve System, *Banking and Monetary* Statistics, 1941–1970.

ing cash is equivalent to the income which could have been earned through investment in alternative assets. Cash is held primarily for reserve requirements, day-to-day transactions, and as compensating balances with other banks in exchange for services. Unexpected cash needs are normally met through sale of certain liquid assets or through other methods rather than through the use of reserves. Since minimum reserve levels are generally fixed by law to assure the solvency of the banking system and to accommodate monetary policy, they are not available for routine liquidity needs.

Effective cash management involves minimizing cash balances over and above minimum required reserves without compromising liquidity. This necessitates management procedures designed to minimize cash balances held for transaction needs and for compensating balance agreements.

Components of Cash   The total cash on the balance sheets of commercial banks is divided into four main categories:

1. Coin and currency inside the bank

2. Funds on deposit with federal reserve banks

3. Funds on deposit with other banks and depository institutions

4. Cash items (principally checks) which are in the process of being collected

As shown in table 10-1, cash represented 10.8 percent of all assets by March 1983. Currency and coin maintained on the premises represented 9.1 percent of those assets classified as cash. In other words, banks as a group found it necessary to maintain only about 1 percent of total assets in the form of currency and coin on the premises to accommodate day-to-day transactions. Typically, coin and currency deposited in a given day is sufficient to accommodate cash disbursements, although local community needs and seasonal factors may result in temporary departure from such a generalization. Funds on deposit with Federal Reserve Banks, funds on deposit with other banks and depository institutions, and cash items in the process of collection

Table 10-1:

**Cash Assets by Domestic Offices
of Insured Commercial Banks,
31 March 1983 (in $ billions)**

Cash Assets Held	Amount	Percentage
Total cash assets	201.6	100.0%
Currency and coin	18.3	9.1
Reserves with federal reserve banks	23.3	11.5
Balances with other banks and institutions	91.5	45.4
Cash items in process of collection	68.5	34.0
Memo: All assets and proportion held in cash	1,866.6	10.8

Source: *Federal Reserve Bulletin,* August 1983

constituted a far larger component of total cash than did currency and coin on hand.

Reserve Requirements Prior to the passage and implementation of the Monetary Control Act, the question of membership in the Federal Reserve System was a significant influencing factor in bank profitability. Advantages of membership were weighed against requirements placed on member banks, chief among which was the stipulation that certain minimum cash balances (required reserves) be maintained. These required balances were usually stricter than those imposed by the states on nonmember banks.

The Monetary Control Act addressed these differences. An important provision of the act concerned reserve requirements and virtually eliminated the impact of the Federal Reserve System membership decision on bank profitability. Effective November 1980, sterile reserves were required of all banks, members and nonmembers alike. Sterile reserves are those which earn no interest. They must be held as cash in the vault or as direct or indirect[2] deposits with the Federal Reserve.

The quantity of required reserves for individual banks depends on the types and amounts of deposit liabilities maintained. These include transaction accounts, nonpersonal time deposits, and Eurocurrency liabilities. Transaction accounts include demand deposits, negotiable order of withdrawal (NOW) accounts, automatic transfer service (ATS) accounts, share draft accounts, and accounts permitting telephone or similar transfers for payments to third parties. Nonpersonal time deposits are defined as time deposits which are transferable *or* as time deposits held by corporations or by other institutions. Percentage reserve requirements before and after November, 1980 are summarized in table 10-2.

The purpose of uniform reserve requirements for all depository institutions was to increase Federal Reserve control over the monetary system. The effect was to reduce reserve requirements for member banks and to impose sterile reserve requirements on nonmember institutions. In order to provide for an orderly transition, the new reserve requirements were to be phased in over a period of several years, ending in September 1987.

Deposits with Other Banks Virtually all banks own funds left on deposit with other commercial banks. Generally, such funds are held in the form of demand deposits. If Bank A deposits funds with Bank B, Bank A does so in return for services which Bank B is expected to provide. Bank B may act as a clearing point for checks drawn on Bank A; Bank B may provide other services such as advice and assistance in purchase, evaluation, or sale of securities. In fact, Bank A may hold deposits with a large number of other banks (called correspondent banks) in return for a variety of services offered by these correspondents. These deposits are referred to as compensating balances[3] and the size of such balances, theoretically, is a function of the value of compensatory services performed.

---

[2]Indirect deposits are those which are "passed through" the correspondent network, e.g., Bank A maintains its required reserve balances in the form of deposits with Bank B.

Bank B, however, "passes through" these balances by depositing them with the Federal Reserve System.

[3]Compensating balances refer to demand account balances which are required as a condition in many commercial loan transactions. The balances are to remain idle in the demand account.

Table 10-2:

Depository Institutions Reserve Requirements (Percentage of Deposits)

Type of Deposit, and Deposit Interval (in $ millions)	Member Bank Requirements Before Implementation of the Monetary Control Act		Type of Deposit and Deposit Interval	Depository Institution Requirements After Implementation of the Monetary Control Act	
	Percentage	Effective Date		Percentage	Effective Date
Net demand			*Net transaction accounts*		
0–2	7	12/30/76	$0–28.9 million	3	12/29/83
2–10	9½	12/30/76	Over 28.9 million	12	12/29/83
10–100	11¾	12/30/76	*Nonpersonal time deposits*		
100–400	12¾	12/30/76	By original maturity		
Over 400	16¼	12/30/76	Less than 1½ years	3	10/6/83
Time and savings			1½ years or more	0	10/6/83
Savings	3	3/16/67	*Eurocurrency liabilities*		
Time			All types	3	11/13/80
0–5, by maturity					
30–179 days	3	3/16/67			
180 days to 4 years	2½	1/8/76			
4 years or more	1	10/30/75			
Over 5, by maturity					
30–179 days	6	12/12/74			
180 days to 4 years	2½	1/8/76			
4 years or more	1	10/30/75			

Note: The Monetary Control Act of 1980 requires that the amount of transaction accounts against which the three percent reserve requirement applies to be modified annually in accordance with an index established by the Act. The original base in 1980 was $0–$25 million.

Source: *Federal Reserve Bulletin.*

Prior to November 1980, nonmember banks could generally include compensatory balances held with other banks when computing reserves. For this reason, balances held with other banks constituted a far larger proportion of cash assets for nonmember banks as compared to members. One consequence of the Monetary Control Act was the fact that compensating balances may no longer be counted for reserve purposes by nonmember state banks. Analysis of the value of services provided in relation to the opportunity cost associated with noninterest earning compensating balances is a particularly important component of cash management.

Methods of determining the cost of funds were developed in chapter 8. If management determines that the cost of balances held in return for services provided is greater than the value of the service, either the size of such balances should be renegotiated or the services should be acquired on a direct payment basis. Evaluation of compensating balances should be an ongoing process and appropriate management policies and procedures providing for their analysis must be developed within the overall framework of cash management.

Evaluating Transaction Needs Just as bankers expect their customers to plan for future cash needs through development of pro forma financial statements and cash budgets, banks should also plan for their own future cash needs. The volume of cash required for transactions is frequently predictable on the basis of past experience and future expectations. Too much idle cash results in income foregone; too little cash may result in forced sale of securities or in expensive borrowing in the money market. In both instances, the impact of poor planning for transaction needs can have a significant impact on profitability. The importance of good forecasts cannot be overemphasized. Good forecasting permits management to determine not only the appropriate size of the secondary reserve, but of the maturity distribution of securities included therein. Since longer term securities normally carry higher yields, knowledge of cash requirements for anticipated future transactions permits management the opportunity to maximize income through investment of excess funds.

Techniques used in projecting transaction needs vary from a simple analysis of seasonal fluctuations based on the experience of prior years to highly sophisticated methods such as construction of econometric models. The appropriate forecasting technique for any given bank depends primarily on the institution's size and on the nature and magnitude of variables which influence changes in the composition of its assets and liabilities.

Loan and Investment Management

The amount of total funds allocated to loans and investments is basically total assets less fixed assets and cash items. By the mid 1980s, three fourths or more of all bank assets were in the form of loans and investments.

The liquidity-profitability tradeoff is most evident in these areas of asset management. Loans provide the primary source of bank earnings and community support. However, loans cannot be converted to cash quickly and economically; and we have seen that required cash reserves are not available to meet expected or unexpected deposit withdrawals. Thus, investments, which normally provide lower returns than loans, must be relied on as the main source of liquidity. Loan

and investment policies must therefore be established in light of both profitability and liquidity needs.

Although no two banks are identical in the relative distribution of loan and investment portfolios, all banks must formulate loan and investment policies in relation to liquidity considerations. Liquidity is defined as the ability to meet demands by depositors and to satisfy reasonable loan demands without the necessity of incurring losses or undue expense in the conversion of assets. Variables influencing liquidity requirements for individual banks include the following:

1. Seasonal fluctuation of loans and deposits

2. Quality and structure of bank assets

3. Proportion of large borrowers and depositors

4. Trend and distribution of liabilities

5. Market area competition for the available money supply

6. Trend and distribution of earnings

7. Capital adequacy

8. Local and national economic conditions

9. Monetary policies of the Federal Reserve Board

10. Long-range economic trends of the market area

Close examination of the above factors indicates that liquidity policy and hence investment and loan policies cannot be formulated in a vacuum. Investment and loan strategies depend not only upon one another, but upon variables which are influenced both internally and externally. The influence of certain factors may be predicted with reasonable certainty, e.g., seasonal fluctuations. Others require careful study and analysis of conditions based on data generated both internally and externally. It is sufficient to say at this point that variables influencing liquidity policy are constantly changing, and that the well-managed bank is one which is not only informed of such changes, but one which adapts loan and investment policies accordingly. Thus careful analysis of variables which influence liquidity will provide management with the basis for decisions leading to the appropriate mix of loans and securities.

Investment Management Commercial banks maintain investments represented almost entirely by obligations of federal and other governmental units. Reasons for holding these investments include income, liquidity, diversification of assets, and flexibility.

Under normal economic conditions, returns available through investment in securities of comparable quality vary directly with maturity schedules. Thus, investment in Treasury bills maturing in less than one year frequently promises a return lower than that available in Treasury securities maturing several years hence. The primary purpose of investing in short-term securities is to provide for liquidity while earning at least some minimal return. Short-term securities of high quality may be sold quickly in the secondary market without serious risk of capital loss and serve as a backup measure in the event that cash is suddenly needed.

On the other hand, the well-managed bank should also maintain a portfolio of longer-term investment securities. Securities which mature over a period of several years, in addition to providing higher returns relative to short-term investments, provide for asset diversification and offer an outlet for funds still remaining after anticipated loan demand and secondary reserve requirements have been met. Long-term securities may be thought of also as an additional line of defense in the event that a totally unexpected need for cash developed and if such need could not reasonably be met through other alternatives. In this unlikely situation, long-term securities could be converted to cash quickly through sale in the secondary market. Typically, however, longer term investments should be purchased for the purpose of providing asset diversification and reasonably high yields. Forced sale of long-term securities purchased during a period of generally rising interest rates will like-

ly result in capital losses detrimentally affecting bank earnings.

Included in table 10-3 is a summary of asset structure for a sample of commercial banks as of 31 December 1982. For the institutions represented in table 10-3, investments amounted to about 40 percent of assets for small banks and about one third of assets for the largest bank category. For all banks, nontreasury investments consisted almost entirely of obligations issued by federal state, and other governmental units.

Notable in table 10-3 is the tendency for smaller banks to rely heavily on treasury securities in calculating their investment strategy. Larger banks, on the other hand, having access to greater investment expertise in evaluating investment alternatives, rely to a greater extent on investment in security issues of state and local governmental units. Noteworthy also in table 10-3 is the fact that large banks calculated an investment portfolio proportionally smaller than that calculated by smaller and intermediate-sized banks. This tendency is explained by three considerations. First, large banks are members of the Federal Reserve System with a larger proportion of their deposits subject to the higher range of reserve requirements.[4] Thus, a smaller proportion of assets are available for investment in other alternatives. In addition, as bank size increases, the capability to facilitate credit needs for loan customers, particularly those of large and prime corporate borrowers, is improved. Finally, the largest banks have the capability to invest in certain assets, such as domestic and foreign affiliates. Thus, a greater opportunity exists on the part of large banks to acquire higher yielding loans and other assets instead of investing in securities.

Because commercial banks restrict their investment portfolios to high-grade debt securities issued primarily by governmental authorities, the risk of loss due to default of interest and principal payments is small. For this reason, and

---

[4]This condition will continue to prevail through late 1987 when reserve requirements will ultimately be equalized in accordance with the Monetary Control Act of 1980.

Table 10-3:

Percentage Distribution of Assets and Liabilities for a Sample of Commercial Banks

Assets	214 Banks Deposits Up to $50M	308 Banks Deposits $50M–$200M	86 Banks Deposits Over $200M
Cash	6.7%	6.6%	8.5%
Treasury securities	16.2	14.7	11.7
Other investments	23.4	24.0	22.3
Loans	49.7	50.3	50.4
Other assets	4.1	4.4	7.2
Total assets:	100.0	100.0	100.0
Liabilities & Capital			
Demand deposits	26.0%	24.0%	25.8%
Time and savings deposits	60.3	59.3	52.8
Borrowings	0.8	1.9	3.8
Other liabilities	4.0	6.3	10.0
Capital accounts	9.0	8.4	7.6
Total liabilities & capital	100.0	100.0	100.0

Note: Totals may not add to 100 because of rounding.

Source: Board of Governors of the Federal Reserve System, *Functional Cost Analysis: 1982 Average Banks, p. 3.*

because most such securities may readily be converted to cash through sale in secondary markets, potential returns on these securities are less than returns available on loans of comparable maturity. Thus the primary source of earnings for commercial banks, and a primary reason for their existence, is to provide funds to borrowers in the form of loans. It is this important component of asset management, bank lending, to which we now turn.

Loan Management The central focus of commercial banking concerns the acquisition and servicing of loans. Indeed, commercial banks are the primary, if not the only, source of loans for most small and medium-sized business firms. But while commercial banks provide a vital service to business organizations and to the community as a source of loans, they are not charitable organizations and cannot be expected to provide loans which may have widespread

social merits but which may or may not be repaid. Indeed, banks have primary responsibility to those depositors who have entrusted their funds for safekeeping. Banks also have a responsibility to those who have provided debt and equity capital; thus banks are expected to operate profitably. It is through returns to equity holders in the form of dividends and through retained earnings that banks are able to continue in operation and to grow along with the communities they serve. Accordingly, the well-managed bank must institute loan policies designed to insure that adequate control exists in the approval and disbursement of loans and that outstanding loans are monitored so as to insure compliance with terms of the loan and ultimate repayment of principal and interest.

Table 10-3 contains information concerning the distribution of loans at 31 December 1982. Notable in Table 10-3 is the recognition that loans represent the largest single category of assets for commercial banks and amounts to about half of the total.

Table 10-4 contains a summary of yields realized on selected categories of loans by banks grouped according to deposit size for 1982. While variations in realized yields occur over time, the data presented in table 10-4 are helpful in the interpretation of bank lending practices and the relative profitability of different categories of bank lending.

Real estate mortgage loans: Real estate mortgage lending has long been an important component of commercial bank lending. At year end 1982, commercial banks held about 18.2 percent of all real estate mortgages outstanding and about 29.5 percent of mortgages held by financial institutions.

The largest banks, which tend to be located in major money market areas, invest most heavily in loans for commercial and industrial purposes while smaller banks, many of which are located in rural and agriculturally oriented communities, invest heavily in non-real estate loans to farmers in support of agriculture.

For 1982, real estate loans provided gross yields of about 11 percent, a return generally lower than that associated with other loan categories. Market mortgage interest rates for much of 1982 were in the 15 to 16 percent range. Real estate yield data in table 10-4 reflect fixed-rate loans made in former (lower interest) periods. However, bank expenses associated with making and administering real estate loans in relation to loans outstanding, was substantially lower than that associated with other loan categories. Because of the low expense of administration per dollar invested, real estate lending provided net yields (after allowing for administrative costs) in excess of 10 percent.

While real estate lending can provide acceptable sources of revenue for commercial banks, the long-term nature of such lending contains inherent risk. Since the cost of generating and servicing such loans is relatively low per dollar outstanding, money cost and possible future increases thereof play a dominant role in the continued profitability of mortgage loans generated in previous years. In 1982, money cost hovered in the range of 9 percent. Should money cost increase dramatically in any given period, the net yield after money cost associated with real estate loans would obviously decline. The experience of recent years has served to illustrate this point. It is, of course, in the best interest of bank managers to guard against such risk, either through the introduction of variable rate morgages, where mortgage interest rates would automatically move up or down with the cost of money—or through use of contractual mortgage agreements where interest rates would be renegotiated at fixed time intervals, e.g., every three to five years.

Installment loans: Over the years, installment lending by commercial banks has become an attractive source of revenue for commercial banks. Traditionally, and prior to World War II, commercial banks did not seek significant amounts of installment receivables and displayed little interest in consumer lending.[5] Following World War II, however, it became evident that yields available on consumer installment receivables were attractive in comparison with those available on commercial and other bank loans. Percentage rates quoted on installment loans were almost always quoted in terms of ''add-on'' or ''discount'' as opposed to simple interest. For example, a loan of $1,000 for a one-year period with interest and principal payable in equal monthly installments, and with a rate of 10 percent applied to the initial amount loaned ($1,000), produced a return of $100. But since the lender's original investment of $1,000 declines steadily over the time period, the true annual yield is substantially greater than 10 percent and approaches 18 percent (as explained in chapter 6). In addition, because of the short-term nature of installment loans, typically maturing within a few years or less, the size of the monthly payments are not materially affected by changes in the interest rate. The evidence suggests that consumers are not particularly sensitive to changes in installment loan interest rates and that such rates do not move freely with money market

---

[5]While installment loans may be made to business firms, most installment lending represents loans to consumers.

Table 10-4:

Yields on Selected Loan Categories, 1982

| | *Bank Size* | | |
| | *(Total Deposits for Reporting Banks)* | | |
Loan Category	*214 Banks* *Under $50M*	*308 Banks* *$50M–$200M*	*86 Banks* *Over $200M*
Real Estate Mortgage Loans			
Gross yield	11.678%	11.194%	10.885%
Less: expense	1.003	0.839	0.780
loan losses	0.125	0.106	0.103
Net yield	10.550	10.249	10.002
Installment loans			
Gross yield	16.366%	15.885%	15.868%
Less: expense	3.636	3.608	3.345
loan losses	.673	0.607	0.562
Net yield	12.057	11.670	11.960
Credit card			
Gross yield	25.020%	24.891%	24.984%
Less: expense	15.568	14.483	10.745
loan losses	1.323	1.886	2.042
Net yield	8.129	8.523	12.197
Commercial and other loans			
Gross yield	15.601%	15.274%	15.109%
Less: expense	2.002	1.797	1.712
loan losses	0.838	0.855	0.930
Net yield	12.761	12.622	12.466
Money cost	8.987	9.194	9.090

Note: Money cost is defined as the cost of processing demand deposits, time deposits (including interest expense), and nondeposit funds less any service charge or fee income. It is calculated as a percent of available funds. Net yield shown above is before money cost.

Source: Board of Governors of the Federal Reserve System, *Functional Cost Analysis: 1982 Average Banks*, p. 2.

and mortgage interest rates. By 1984, commercial banks had captured 46 percent of the market for consumer installment receivables. This compares with 30 percent in 1960 and 13 percent at the beginning of the post World War II era.

Net yields for installment loans were higher than those associated with mortgage loans in 1982 (table 10-4). In addition, the previous discussion suggests that gross yields could be adjusted as necessary by increasing rates for new installment loans to compensate for increased money cost. Thus the interest rate risk associated with installment loans is not nearly so significant

as that associated with fixed rate real estate lending.

Credit card loans: Credit card loans are among the most recent innovations in bank lending practices. Bank credit cards provide the holder with a preauthorized line of credit in some specified amount. Such cards may be used to acquire cash directly from a bank or to acquire merchandise from participating merchants. Gross yields available through credit card loans far outstrip those available through alternative lending categories (table 10-4). The high expense associated with bank credit cards reflects mainly the fact that average loan balances are small and administrative costs high per dollar outstanding. Also, credit card loss chargeoffs are higher than chargeoffs for other forms of bank lending. But while administrative costs are high in bank credit card lending, significant potential exists for reduction of such costs over the long term. It is in lending programs such as credit card operations, characterized by large volumes of routine transactions, that technological economies may prove to be significant. As technological improvements in this area continue, credit card lending may generate increased contributions to commercial bank profitability.

Commercial and industrial loans: Loans for commercial and industrial purposes have always been the principal domain of commercial banks. While banks have sought to increase market shares for consumer installment receivables and have expanded operations to include credit card loans, commercial lending continues to represent the largest single component of bank lending practices. By 1984, commercial and industrial loans constituted about one fourth of all loans outstanding for the industry.

Traditionally, commercial banks have preferred short-term business loans, designed to meet seasonal needs for working capital purposes. Rates are tied to the prime lending rate with large and established customers borrowing at the prime or best available rate. Loans to less established firms are typically made at interest rates that exceed prime by a margin judged sufficient to compensate for the increased credit risk.[6]

Commercial and industrial loans are essentially of two types. The first and traditional type represents those made for working capital purposes as discussed above. Risk associated with fluctuating interest rates is minimized in this type loan because maturities are relatively short, averaging a few months at most and with rates adjusted in the event of loan renewal. The sec-

ond major type of commercial and industrial loans is the *business term loan*. Term loans are those with original maturities of more than one year and are frequently made for the purpose of financing the acquisition of fixed assets. While data describing the extent of term lending in the banking industry are sketchy, available data suggest that the volume of term lending included in commercial and industrial loans increased in the post-war era. Traditionally, term loans have been made at fixed rates somewhat higher than those charged for short-term working capital loans. Higher rates are justified on the grounds that longer term maturities represent increased exposure to the risk of fluctuating money cost.

Beginning with the experience of the early 1970s, when bank money costs increased dramatically as the result of severe fluctuations in money market rates, many banks turned to the practice of allowing term loan rates to vary with money market conditions. Thus many term loans are made with original maturities of several years but with interest rates tied to prime or to some other index with rate adjustments frequently occurring several times per year. Indeed, with the continuing erratic behavior of interest rates in the late 1970s and early 1980s, an increasing proportion of all business loans were made with floating rates. Results of a Federal Reserve survey conducted in November 1983, indicated that about 37 percent of all short-term commercial and industrial loans were made with floating rates, even though maturities averaged less than three months. Almost three fourths of the long-term loans had floating rates.[7]

LIABILITY MANAGEMENT

In recent years, commercial banks have devoted increased attention to the concept of liability management. As money costs climbed, and as the demand for bank loans increased, commercial bank managers became increasingly aware of the need to acquire funds to support

---

[6]With the volatility of interest rates prevailing in recent years, some banks began the practice of charging less than prime for some short-term loans to certain large business customers. The extent of such lending was unknown.

[7]*Federal Reserve Bulletin,* February 1984, p. A-25.

asset expansion. Thus there developed a general awareness of the fact that desired levels of expansion could be met only through new means of attracting funds. Consequently, the management of commercial bank liabilities took on an importance comparable to that of asset managment.

The nature of liabilities and liability management by commercial banks shifted markedly over the decades of the 1960s, 1970s, and into the 1980s. Over that period, in response to rising market interest rates and continued loan demand, bankers shifted from a passive role as money gatherers to a role involving active competition for funds in the market place. In 1950, almost three fourths of liabilities for all commercial banks were represented by noninterest-bearing demand deposits. The ratio of demand to time deposits was almost 3:1, and rates paid on time and savings accounts were low by today's standards. Loan demand during the previous decade was largely supported by available liabilities and by converting investment securities accumulated during the war and during the post-

war period. Thus the efforts of bank managers were devoted primarily to asset management with little attention paid to the availability and structure of liabilities.

The Changing Nature Of Bank Liabilities

Aggregate liabilities of commercial banks for 31 December 1950, 31 December, 1964, and for 30 June 1983 have been summarized (figure 10-2). While noninterest-bearing demand deposits dominated the liability structure in 1950, *time and savings deposits* became increasingly important with the passage of time. By 1983 time and savings deposits were clearly the most important source of funds for commercial banks. At the same time, the proportion of funds represented by demand deposits had declined from 73.8 percent in 1950 to 20.5 percent by 1983. Commercial bank borrowings, virtually nonexistent in 1950 had risen to 19.2 percent of total liabilities. Factors influencing this condition

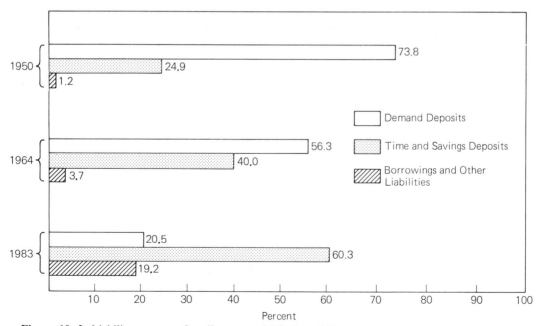

Figure 10–2: Liability structure for all commercial banks, 1950–1983. (Source: same as figure 10-1.)

included a number of innovations in liability management which occurred. Included among these were the following:

1. Development of a secondary market for large denomination certificates of deposit (CDs)
2. Issuance of consumer-type CDs
3. Expansion of the federal funds market
4. Eurodollar borrowings
5. Repurchase agreements

Development of a Secondary Market for CDs   A certificate of deposit (CD) issued by a bank is a receipt for funds placed on deposit. The funds must be left on deposit for the time specified on the certificate and bear interest at a rate established at the time of issuance. Prior to 1961, CDS were issued by a few banks. Total CD outstandings prior to 1961, however, constituted little more than 1 percent of total liabilities and less than 4 percent of total time and savings deposits.

While commercial banks had authority to issue CDs prior to 1961, many felt that to do so would encourage corporations and other large depositors who were precluded by law from holding passbook savings accounts,[8] to transfer funds from noninterest-bearing demand deposits to interest-bearing CDs. But beginning in early 1961, several large banks began to issue large CDs in negotiable form. At the same time, major securities dealers agreed to make a market for them. Thus the availability of negotiable CDs in large denominations and the liquidity provided by the ready availability of a secondary market provided corporations and other large investors with an alternative and highly liquid means for investment of temporary excess funds. Individual banks found that by varying rates for new issues slightly in relation to current market yields, the volume of new time deposits attracted could be substantially increased or decreased in accordance with current or projected needs for

funds. Hence the ability of commercial banks to manage liabilities was improved dramatically with this turn of events.

Prior to 1973, however, liability management through issuance of new CDs was constrained somewhat by the Federal Reserve's Regulation Q. Regulation Q sets maximum rates payable on time and savings accounts and is applicable to insured commercial banks. At times, throughout the 1960s and early 1970s, liability management was hindered by the fact that market interest rates exceeded statutory rates permissible for new CDs. This condition caused difficulties for bank managers in attempts to raise funds through issuance of new CDs for the purpose of retiring maturing ones or for the purpose of supporting further asset expansion. Although ceiling rates on certain CDs were modified or partially eliminated from time to time, it was not until mid 1973 that Regulation Q ceilings were suspended for all CDs issued in amounts of $100,000 or more.

Issuance of Consumer Type CDs   While large negotiable CDs played an important role in bank liability management during the 1960s and 1970s, consumer type CDs (savings certificates, nonnegotiable CDs, and negotiable CDs in denominations of less than $100,000) took on increasing importance following a change in Regulation Q in late 1965. In December of that year, ceiling rates under Regulation Q were increased for time deposits while rates for passbook savings accounts were held at 4 percent. Subsequent changes in Regulation Q during the 1960s and 1970s maintained and in some cases expanded the rate differential between consumer savings and time deposits. Finally, because of disintermediation caused by increasingly higher yields on open-market securities beginning in 1977, the federal regulatory agencies authorized the sale of certain new consumer-type certificates effective 1 June 1978. The most important of these was the six-month money market certificate, available in minimum denominations of $10,000 and with interest yield tied to the Treasury bill rate. Thus banks were in a position to provide a variety of time certificates in various denominations

---

[8]Effective 10 November 1975, corporations, partnerships, and other profit-making organizations were permitted to hold savings accounts of up to $150,000 per depositor.

and maturity. Finally, the Monetary Control Act of 1980 provided for a gradual phase out of Regulation Q ceilings. Effective 1 October 1983, restrictions on maximum rate ceilings for all categories of time deposit accounts maturing in more than thirty-one days were removed. At this writing, all remaining regulation Q ceilings will have been phased out by 31 March 1986. Maximum interest rates payable on time and savings deposits for commercial banks in early 1984 are summarized in table 10-5.

Expansion of the Federal Funds Market
Previous discussion has emphasized the need for commercial bank managers to maintain an appropriate balance between liquid investments and higher-yielding loans. It has also been suggested that profitability objectives require that a minimum of excess cash over and above required reserves be held. Cash in the vault and deposits with federal reserve banks that exceed necessary requirements may represent evidence

of inefficient management. So are balances held with correspondents in excess of that expected or required in return for services provided. On the other hand, it is not realistic to expect loan demand and investment requirements to precisely match the quantity of funds available for the purpose of meeting such demand or requirements. While the volume of deposit liabilities may be managed through variation in interest rates and in the maturity range of offerings, and while lending and investment policies and activities may be adjusted to affect the level and composition of assets, it is likely that too much or too little cash will be available for desired purposes at any given point in time. Further, it may be expected that divergences from the optimal level and composition of assets and liabilities would be an occurrence expected almost daily.

Throughout the 1960s and 1970s and into the 1980s, as interest rates rose and competitive conditions intensified, commercial banks responded to the need for finer adjustment in asset and

Table 10-5:

Maximum Interest Rates Payable on Time and Savings Deposits at Federally Insured Institutions (percentage per annum)

Type of Deposit	Commercial Banks, Savings and Loan Associations, and Mutual Savings Banks
	In Effect Jan 31, 1984
	Percentage
1. Savings	5½%
2. Negotiable order of withdrawal (NOW) accounts	5¼%
3. Negotiable order of withdrawal accounts ($2500 or more)	—
4. Money market deposit accounts	—
Time Accounts by Maturity	
5. 7–31 days of less than $2500	5½%
6. 7–31 days of $2500 or more	—
7. More than 31 days	—

Notes: 1. Effective 1 October 1983, restrictions on the maximum rates of interest payable on various categories of deposits were removed.

2. Effective 1 January 1984, the 0.25 percent rate advantage traditionally allowed thrift institutions was eliminated.

Source: *Federal Reserve Bulletin*, February 1984.

liability management. A significant mechanism to provide for such adjustment was the *federal funds market*.

Federal funds are deposits held by commercial banks with the Federal Reserve System. The federal funds market refers to the exchange of claims between banks against such balances. Such exchange takes place through the loan of deposit balances by one bank to another. The bank which has borrowed federal funds is said to have "purchased" such funds and the bank which has loaned fed funds is said to have "sold" such funds. From the point of view of the "selling" bank, fed funds constitute an asset and from the point of view of the "buying" bank, a liability.

While federal funds and the federal funds market have existed for a considerable number of years, growth and development of the market began in earnest during the 1960s and was spearheaded, as were many major banking innovations, by major money market banks located principally in New York City. Federal funds transactions are commonly ones which represent loans for a period of only one day, although the length of time may be expanded if desired by the participating parties. Whether or not a bank is a member of the Federal Reserve System is not material insofar as market participation is concerned, since transactions may be handled through a correspondent.

Traditionally, federal funds were looked upon as an alternative to direct borrowing from the Federal Reserve System for the purpose of meeting reserve requirements. Thus banks needing reserves would borrow from other banks only if such funds were available at lower cost. But in 1965, in the face of strong loan demand and tight money, the federal funds rate began to exceed the discount rate (rate of interest charged by federal reserve banks to member banks). As more and more banks became aware of the convenience and potential of the federal funds market, participation in the market and the volume of transactions increased dramatically.

Available data suggest that small banks tend to be net sellers of federal funds (lenders) while large banks are net buyers (borrowers). In one recent year, for example, banks with total assets of less than $50 million, while important sources for federal funds, did little borrowing in the market. On the other hand, the largest banks, particularly those with assets exceeding $1 billion, were heavy borrowers of federal funds. In effect, the federal funds market was functioning as a conduit whereby excess funds of small banks were utilized to support cash needs of large banks. Thus, from the viewpoint of bank managers, the federal funds market affords a convenient and flexible means to improve asset and liability management in promoting the goal of profit maximization.

Eurodollar Borrowings Another highly significant development within the framework of liability management occurred with the spectacular growth in Eurodollar borrowings.

Eurodollars are deposits denominated in U.S. dollars and held by any bank located outside the United States—including foreign branches of U.S. banks. Dollars may be on deposit with foreign banks for a variety of reasons. They may exist for the purpose of facilitating trade or they may have been deposited outside the U.S. so as to earn a higher rate of return. Most Eurodollar deposits are held in the form of short-term time deposits and thus earn interest.

Growth in this market became significant in the latter half of the 1960s. Impetus to this growth was provided by tight money conditions that prevailed at times over the past fifteen years or so, and by Regulation Q ceilings which restricted the ability of banks to acquire desired levels of funds domestically. Hence large banks turned to foreign markets in search of additional funds.

Since Eurodollars represent borrowings rather than deposits, domestic banks were not restricted by interest rate ceilings. Thus a supply of funds from this source was virtually assured for large banks when funds were needed.

Initially, Eurodollar borrowings were not subject to reserve requirements, thus adding to the desirability of this source from the viewpoint of individual banks. However, reserve requirements were imposed on certain Eurodollar borrowings in 1969, and the percentage requirement has changed from time to time in accordance with Federal Reserve System objectives.

Given the continued internationalization of business affairs and the expansion and growing importance of U.S. banks in foreign lands, as well as growth in the presence of foreign owned banks in the U.S., it may be expected that Eurodollars will continue as an important non-deposit source of funds for commercial banks.

Repurchase Agreements A "repurchase agreement" (RPs or "repos") is a financing method by which a bank can acquire relatively large amounts of cash for short-term periods, frequently from its corporate customers. A repurchase agreement occurs when a bank sells securities, such as treasury bills, to a securities dealer or to a corporation with an agreement to repurchase the securities at a stated price and a specified time. The sale is usually over a period of a few days. A bank manager may adjust his banks's reserve position by selling securities to a

corporation on Friday with an agreement to repurchase these securities on Monday. The transaction, in this example, would have the effect of increasing the bank's average cash balance for the reserve period. A repurchase agreement is frequently preferable to sale of the securities in the open market with the intent to buy the same securities a few days later because the risk of price fluctuation and brokerage commissions are both avoided.

The use of RPs as a source of funds for commercial banks increased with the surge in short-term interest rates in the late 1970s and early 1980s. The value of security repurchase agreements exceeded $80 billion by 1984.

Bank Profitability

Analysis of income and expense data for a sample of commercial banks reveals that loan

Table 10-6:

Percentage Distribution of Revenue and Expense Items for a Sample of Commercial Banks

Revenue	214 Banks Deposits Up to $50M	308 Banks Deposits $50M–$200M	86 Banks Deposits Over $200M
Loan interest and discount	54.9%	55.2%	58.5%
Investment income	38.9	38.4	33.7
Service and handling charges	4.3	3.5	3.8
Other income	1.9	3.0	3.9
Total revenue:	100.0	100.0	100.0
Expense			
Salaries and fringes	13.4	12.9	13.9
Other operating expenses	15.1	14.6	16.2
Interest expense	54.9	58.2	56.4
Total expense:	83.4	85.8	86.5
Net current earnings (before tax)	16.6	14.2	13.5

Notes:

1. Totals may not agree because of rounding.

2. Tax-exempt income has been converted to a taxable basis to permit comparability among banks with different amounts of tax-exempt income.

Source: Board of Governors of the Federal Reserve System, *Functional Cost Analysis: 1982 Average Banks*, p. 5.

interest income as a percent of total income was proportionally greater for large banks as compared to their smaller counterparts (table 10-6). Investment income for small banks was proportionally larger as was revenue derived from service and handling charges. Other income, reflecting revenue derived from trust services, computer service fees, fees derived through letters of credit, safe deposit box rentals, and other activities increased with bank size.

Analysis of expense data for the sample group reveals that interest expense was clearly the dominant expense item. Although the midsized bank group had the greatest interest expense, midsized banks also had proportionally smaller salary and other operating expenses which tended to offset the larger interest expense (table 10-6).

Profitability data for all commercial banks show that the banking industry, unlike thrifts, maintained profitability as deregulation commenced (table 10-7). The decline in profitability commencing in 1980 cannot necessarily be attributed to a deregulatory environment, since various influencing conditions, including a world-wide recession were in progress. Rather, the data suggest that bank managers, benefiting from diversified fund sources and having the capability to adjust loan and security portfolios (unlike their thrift manager counterparts) were able to maintain respectable levels of profitability. With the introduction, effective 14 December 1982, of money market deposit accounts and with the introduction of *Super NOWS*[9] effective 5 January 1983, bank managers were increasingly subject to a more sensitive cost structure.

BANK CAPITAL

One of the most important issues which commercial bank managers must face is the question of capital adequacy. We have noted the growth

---

[9]Money Market Deposit Accounts are discussed in chapter 2. Super NOWs (Negotiable Order of Withdrawal) are NOW accounts with more than $2500 average balance. Super NOW accounts are available only to individuals, governmental units, and certain nonprofit organizations.

Table 10-7:

Profitability of Insured Commercial Banks

| Year | Net Income as Percentage of | |
	Total Assets	Total Net Worth
1978	0.76%	12.9%
1979	0.80	13.9
1980	0.79	13.7
1981	0.76	13.2
1982	0.71	12.2

Source: *Federal Reserve Bulletin*, July 1983, p. 498.

and changing composition of bank assets and liabilities that occurred throughout recent decades. Many trends noted thus far suggest that the general composition of bank assets has become less liquid. And with the substitution of a greater volume of loans for cash balances and liquid investments, some would argue that asset structure is characterized by a greater degree of risk as the result of this process.

In addition, increased reliance on CDs, Eurodollars, and other forms of ''purchased'' funds together with the general reduction in the proportion of funds acquired through interest-free demand deposits, has contributed to upward pressure on the cost of bank funds. Indeed, by the mid 1970s the number of banks closed because of financial difficulties began to exceed the number closed in any given year since 1949 (table 10-8). Continued high money costs, combined with a deregulation environment resulted in relatively large numbers of bank failures in 1982 and 1983. Thus bank managers, regulatory agencies, and large depositors have expressed increasing concern over the question of capital adequacy.

For commercial banks, as is true for other business enterprises, capital provides the cushion against which temporary losses may be absorbed. Although the Federal Deposit Insurance Corporation (FDIC) provides protection against loss to depositors for all but a tiny fraction of commercial banks, such protection is subject to an absolute ceiling ($100,000 at

Table 10-8:

Number of Banks Closed Because of Financial Difficulties 1934–1983

1934	61	1951	5	1968	3
1935	32	1952	4	1969	9
1936	72	1953	5	1970	8
1937	84	1954	4	1971	6
1938	81	1955	5	1972	3
1939	72	1956	3	1973	6
1940	48	1957	3	1974	4
1941	17	1958	9	1975	14
1942	23	1959	3	1976	17
1943	5	1960	2	1977	6
1944	2	1961	9	1978	7
1945	1	1962	3	1979	10
1946	2	1963	2	1980	10
1947	6	1964	8	1981	10
1948	3	1965	9	1982	42
1949	9	1966	8	1983	48
1950	5	1967	4		

Source: *Annual Report,* Federal Deposit Insurance Corporation.

present) for each deposit account. Thus insurance protection above that sum is not available through FDIC for holders of large CDs or for holders of savings or demand accounts. Large depositors therefore look to capital as an important factor in evaluating financial strength for individual banks.

The Nature of Bank Capital

Depending on the purpose for which it is calculated or classified, commercial bank capital may be represented in one or more of the following forms:

Equity Capital

Common Stock

Preferred Stock

Surplus

Undivided Profit

Reserve for Securities

Reserve for Bad Debts

Other Capital Reserves

Debt Capital

Capital Notes and Debentures

There are, of course, fundamental differences between equity capital and debt capital. In the case of equity capital, there is no legal requirement that payments or dividends be made to holders of equity securities. Thus payment of dividends may be delayed or postponed indefinitely if conditions warrant. In the case of capital notes and debentures, interest must be paid in accordance with legal requirements and the securities must ultimately be retired in accordance with the terms of their issue. But since capital notes and debentures are subordinate to deposit liabilities and other debt obligations of commercial banks, such notes and debentures provide a cushion similar to equity in absorbing losses and asset shrinkage in the event of failure.

Capital Adequacy

There is disagreement as to the optimal level of capital which should be maintained by commercial banks. As the casual observor might surmise, regulators would like to see greater levels of capital in relation to assets or deposits for many banks, while at the same time, managers of these same banks frequently believe that existing levels are high enough and perhaps too high. While some would argue that capital should be sufficient to provide for a zero level of bank failures and deposit losses, others suggest that inefficiencies traceable to excessively high capital positions and excessively conservative operating practices would be more harmful to the overall economy than would a limited number of bank failures. Indeed, the evidence suggests that the cause of most bank failures is related to management weaknesses, fraud, embezzlement, speculation, and other factors rather than to an inadequate capital structure.[10]

Differing Views of Capital Adequacy
Whether or not a given level of capital is

[10]For a detailed discussion of bank failures see George W. Hill, *Why 67 Insured Banks Failed—1960 to 1974*. Federal Deposit Insurance Corporation.

adequate for any particular bank depends upon the vantage point from which the question is viewed. Thus the question must be evaluated from the standpoint of three distinct groups. These include 1) bank regulators and examiners, 2) commercial bank managers, and 3) large depositors.[11]

Bank Regulators and Examiners: Regulatory bodies such as the Federal Reserve System and the Federal Deposit Insurance System are understandably concerned with the question of capital adequacy. The major function of these regulators is to protect the solvency of the banking system. If the record of bank failures for any given period is zero, regulators may point to such a record as evidence of the fact that their principal responsibilities are being discharged in an optimum fashion. On the other hand, if the number of bank failures looms large, regulators become subject to the criticism that examination procedures are inadequate and that their responsibilities are not being discharged efficiently. Given this system of rewards and penalities, one might expect that regulators would demand capital levels sufficient to provide solid protection against bank failure casued by continued and extensive operating losses.

Commercial Bank Managers: While bank managers are concerned with the solvency of their banks and of the banking system in general, their point of view is tempered by the knowledge that increased levels of capital may detrimentally affect returns to holders of bank equity securities. Bank managers may be reluctant to sell additional equity securities if the market for such securities is perceived to be depressed and if earnings dilution may likely result. Management is also aware of the unfavorable reaction of stockholders which may be expected if dividends are restricted for the purpose of strengthening the capital position. Thus, the view of bank managers necessarily takes into account the

effect on profitability which may be associated with any effort to strengthen bank capital. The authority of regulators to order increased capital levels for any given bank is not absolute, and regulators must frequently rely on logic and persuasion in inducing compliance with recommendations concerning capital expansion.

Commercial bank managers, then, can be expected to interpret capital as being adequate if its level is sufficient to protect depositors in the event of normal losses, but not in the event of unexpected, continued, and extensive operating losses.

Large Depositors: Small depositors including most households and those business firms with deposit balances completely or substantially covered by FDIC insurance protection have little cause to worry about loss of deposit funds in the event of bank failure. Large depositors, on the other hand, must rely on the financial strength of banks in which they hold deposits in excess of FDIC insurance ceilings (currently $100,000). Thus a corporation which purchases negotiable CDs, which represent substantial investments, has cause for concern over the issuing bank's continued solvency. Large investors, therefore, can be expected to consider the question of capital adequacy in deciding whether deposits should be maintained with any given bank. Indeed, the rates which different banks must pay to attract purchasers of large certificates of deposit are not identical with respect to CD size and maturity. Of course, other factors such as the quality of bank management, bank size, and the range of services made available to large customers are important components in the decision of large investors to place funds with any particular bank. But while conclusive evidence is not available, it is reasonable to believe that the preference of large depositors in terms of capital adequacy would lie somewhere between those of regulatory authorities and commercial bank managers.

Standards of Capital Adequacy Standards of capital adequacy can be classified in terms of two groups: qualitative and quantitative. In evaluating the adequacy of capital for any given

---

[11]We are indebted to Harvey Rosenblum for his analysis of these views, See "Bank Capital Adequacy," *Business Conditions,* Federal Reserve Bank of Chicago, September 1976.

bank, both groups of measures must be considered.[12]

1. Qualitative Measures

   a. Management

   b. Assets

   c. Earnings

   d. Deposit Trends

   e. Fiduciary Business

   f. Local Characteristics

2. Quantitative Measures

   a. Ratios of Capital to Total Assets

   b. Ratios of Capital to Risk Assets

Qualitative measures:

1. *Management*—The ability, attentiveness, integrity, and record of management is critical in the evaluation of a bank's ability to withstand risk. Prudent managerial practices and policies are vital in the protection of depository funds.

2. *Assets*—The general character, quality, liquidity, and diversity of assets influence the acceptability or non-acceptability of any given level of capital.

3. *Earnings*—The earnings capacity of a bank and the bank's dividend policy are important aspects in evaluating the adequacy of its capital. Earnings applied to the elimination of losses and depreciation and then to the establishment of suitable reserves prior to disbursement of dividends provide protection against capital impingement.

4. *Deposit trends*—If deposit trends are upward, and if retained earnings reflect the same upward movement, internal additions to capital may be sufficient to support asset expansion. On the other hand, if additions to capital have not kept pace with deposit expansion, and if growth is expected to continue,

capital should be augmented through whatever means possible.

5. *Fiduciary business*—The volume and nature of business conducted in a fiduciary capacity must be considered in evaluating capital needs. Contingencies in this area must be carefully appraised.

6. *Local characteristics*—The stability, diversification, and competitive situation of local industries must be considered in the evaluation of capital adequacy.

Quantitative measures:

1. *Ratios of capital to total assets*—The ratio of total capital to total assets or alternatively, the ratio of equity capital to total assets, represents the percent by which the value of such assets could decline without causing losses to depositors. Both the ratio of total capital to total assets and the ratio of equity capital to total assets declined rather consistently from the early 1960s until the mid 1970s and stabilized thereafter. By 1984, the ratio of equity capital to total assets for all domestic insured commercial banks was about 7 percent.

2. *Ratios of capital to risk assets*—Ratios which are perhaps even more descriptive in terms of a bank's ability to withstand losses include the ratio of total capital to risk assets and the ratio of equity capital to risk assets. Risk assets equal total assets less cash and due from banks, less U.S. Treasury and government agency securities.

The Optimal Level of Capital Presumably, the optimal level of capital for the banking system as a whole is one where capital is sufficient to maintain overall confidence in the banking system but not so high as to permit a zero level of bank failures. A zero level of bank failures would imply overly restrictive policies and high social costs. From the point of view of bank managers, the capitalization decision must be one which incorporates the goal of profit maximization consistent with the recognition of an acceptable level of risk. Indeed, the bank which seeks to take no risk and to maintain capital

---

[12]For an analysis of capital requirements from the bank examiners view, see Board of Governors of the Federal Reserve, *Bank Holding Company Supervision Manual*, Section 400, June 1982.

ratios sufficient to cover all possible contingencies is performing a disservice to its owners, to its customers, and to the community which it serves.

FUTURE EXPECTATIONS

Commercial banking has long been characterized by competition, but banking has been a regulated and protected industry also. Thus, some contend competition in banking has not been the keen, vigorous, intense type which is found in many less regulated industries. Banking, as a regulated industry, has been protected from complete price and service competition in the market place. By law, nonbank financial institutions were formerly prohibited from offering many bank services, such as checking accounts.

The Monetary Control Act of 1980, together with the Garn-St Germain Act of 1982 will result in continued and greater competition over the next several years. Today's bank manager should be alert to the competitive threats represented by the recent expansion and aggressiveness of foreign banks, by expanded activities of investment banking firms, by the likelihood of interstate branch banking, by the continued expansion in new electronic technology, by the expanded powers now held by nonbank financial institutions, and by ever increasing price competition for sources of bank funds.

The 1980s hold much promise for well-managed banks that anticipate and plan for these challenges. Banks that do not anticipate these competitive challenges and that do not develop appropriate strategic responses may well become casualties in this new competitive environment.

SUMMARY

The objective of commercial bank managers continues to be one in which the welfare of the bank and hence the bank's stockholders is maximized. But because of the nature of commercial banking, managers must respond to a number of constraints to which their nonbank counterparts are not subject. A major implication to be drawn in any analysis of bank asset and liability management is the fact that no aspect of such management can stand alone. Asset management policies depend upon the nature and structure of liabilities and capital. In turn, decisions affecting liabilities and capital depend not only upon asset distribution but upon their relationship to one another.

Discussion contained in this chapter illustrates the changing nature of commercial banking, and the need for continued advancement of sound management policies and practices. Successful managers of commercial banks may no longer merely gather funds from inexpensive sources and invest in assets which may be conveniently available. To the contrary, the changing nature of commercial banking implies the need for more and greater expertise in the traditional functions of planning, organizing and control.

QUESTIONS

1. In what way is asset management for commercial banks similar to that of industrial firms? In what way does it differ?

2. What are the three main categories of assets for commercial banks? To what extent have these categories shifted over the past decades? How do you account for this shift?

3. What are sterile reserves? How did the Monetary Control Act of 1980 influence the quantity of sterile reserves required of member banks? Of nonmember banks?

4. What are some differences in *investment* management policies for small banks vs. large banks? How do you account for these differences?

5. What are some differences in *loan* management policies for small banks vs. large banks? How do you account for these differences?

6. Comment on the use of fixed- vs. variable-interest rates for commercial and

industrial loans by commercial banks. Why has the use of variable rates increased in recent years?

7. What were the major innovations in banks' liability management which occurred in recent decades. In general, why did liability management take on such increased importance?

8. Contrast the view of bankers, regulators, and large depositors with regard to the issue of capital adequacy for commercial banks.

PROBLEMS

1. County Bank had the following Income Statement and balance sheet at 31 December 1982

Income Statement (in $ thousands)

Revenue	
Loan Interest and Discount	$18,400
Investment Income	15,500
Service and Handling Charges	700
Other Income	1,400
Total Revenue:	$36,000

Expense	
Salaries and Fringes	$ 5,000
Other operating expenses	6,150
Interest expense	21,600
Total Expense:	32,750
Net Current Earnings Before Tax.	$3,250

Balance Sheet (in $ millions)

Assets		Liabilities	
Cash	$ 50	Demand	$105
Treasury Securities	70	Deposits	
		Time and Savings Deposits	281
Other Investments	124		
		Borrowings	18
Loans	220	Other Liabilities	50
Other Assets	36	Capital Accounts	46
Total Assets	$500	Total Liabilities & Capital	$500

a. With reference to text tables 10-3, 10-6, and 10-7, analyze County

Bank's financial performance. The tax rate is 50%.

b. Assuming that one half of County's time and savings deposits are subject to reserve requirements, calculate County Bank's required reserves using reserve requirements imposed by the Monetary Control Act of 1980 and contained in table 10-2.

c. Formulate a set of policy recommendations that might improve County's financial performance.

2. Mercantile Bancorporation, a large Bank Holding Company had a 1982 loan portfolio as follows (in $ millions).

Real Estate Mortgage Loans	$20
Installment Loans	45
Credit Card Outstandings	35
Commercial and Other	100
Total:	$200

Using data contained in table 10-4, calculate the net interest spread (net yield less money cost) for the loan portfolio.

SELECTED REFERENCES

Flannery, Mark J. "Market Interest Rates and Commercial Bank Profitability." *The Journal of Finance* 36 (December 1981): 1085–1101.

Goldberg, Michael A. "The Impact of Regulatory and Monetary Factors on Bank Loan Charges." *Journal of Financial and Quantitative Analysis* 16 (June 1981): 227–246.

Ho, Thomas S. Y., and Saunder, Anthony. "The Determinants of Bank Interest Margins: Theory and Empirical Evidence." *Journal of Financial and Quantitative Analysis* 16 (November 1981): 581–600.

James, Christopher. "An Analysis of Bank Loan Rate Indexation." *The Journal of Finance* 37 (June 1982): 809–825.

O'Hara, Maureen. "A Dynamic Theory of the Banking Firm." *The Journal of Finance* 38 (March 1983): 127–140.

Siegel, Jeremy J. "Bank Reserves and Financial Stability." *The Journal of Finance* 36 (December 1981): 1073–1084.

Chapter 11

Finance Company and Consumer Financial Service Management

While consumer financial services are offered by a broad array of institutions, finance companies have long served as an important source of credit for American households. Traditionally, finance companies have differed sharply from commercial banks and other deposit-type financial intermediaries. On the one hand, finance companies had far greater flexibility in the acquisition of assets and liabilities. Yet, generally they did not have access to lower cost deposit funds and their funds cost were subject to prevailing rates in money and capital markets.

The events of recent years however, have blurred traditional distinctions between finance companies and depository financial institutions. The phaseout of Regulation Q ceilings has narrowed the cost of funds advantage historically enjoyed by depository financial institutions. This and other regulatory developments and technological innovations have encouraged competition by finance companies in mortgage lending and in other markets, markets traditionally reserved for depository financial institutions. Indeed, terms such as *Consumer Banking,*

Nonbank Banks, Loophole Banks, and similar terms—virtually unheard of a few years ago, fill the pages of financial newspapers and journals today. This new terminology is indicative of turmoil in the financial services industry, turmoil unleashed with deregulation of the industry in the 1980s.

We begin our discussion with a review of the traditional structure of the consumer finance industry. Following this review, we consider the events of recent years where finance companies have played a major role in the evolutionary expansion of consumer financial services.

TYPES OF FINANCE COMPANIES

Although all finance companies are similar in that their principal function is to make loans, they differ in terms of the loans they specialize in. Some are predominantly *consumer loan companies,* with their principal activity the granting of direct cash loans to individuals or households.

Other finance companies are referred to as *commercial loan companies* with all or a major proportion of their loans being made to business units. Still others are *sales finance companies* whose principal function is to purchase retail time sales contracts from nonfinancial businesses. Although most finance companies began by focusing entirely on one of the activities described above, many individual finance companies today offer a broad range of financial services to businesses and consumers alike.

Finance companies are "stock" companies in the sense that they are privately owned entities with ultimate control vested in their owners. The nature of ownership differs however. Some are operated as units of bank holding companies or as subsidiaries of conglomerates, and others are "dependent" or "captive" finance companies formed by parent firms to finance the sale of goods manufactured by the parent. Perhaps one of the more familiar dependent or captive finance companies is General Motors Acceptance Corporation. Still other sales finance companies are "independent," ranging in size from a single office to multiple offices located throughout the nation.

The asset and liability data for domestic finance companies at 31 December 1983 show that loan receivables (spread almost evenly between consumers and businesses) accounted for about 80 percent of gross assets (figure 11-1). The data also show that finance companies are highly leveraged, with debt representing about 87 percent of the capital structure. Clearly, finance company profitability is highly dependent upon the difference (spread) between the cost of borrowed funds and interest revenue earned from loan receivables.

GROWTH AND DEVELOPMENT OF FINANCE COMPANIES

Unlike commercial banks and thrift institutions, finance companies are not dependent on deposits as a source of funds and have had far greater flexibility in choosing the types of loans and investments to be acquired. In addition, banks and thrift institutions are generally precluded from branching across state lines while many finance companies operate nationwide. Also, although most states severely restrict the number of branches which may be maintained by depository institutions within the state, states don't restrict the number of finance company offices. In contrast to depository financial institutions, finance companies have been relatively free to innovate and to seek out various types of loan and other investment portfolios.

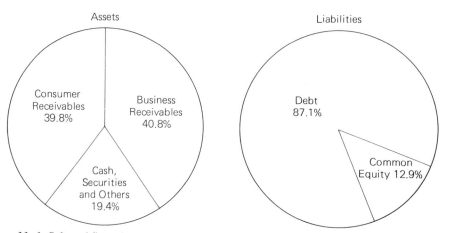

Figure 11–1: Selected financial data for domestic finance companies, December 31, 1983. (Source: *Federal Reserve Bulletin,* March, 1984, p. A37).

In some cases, finance companies have paved the way in developing profitable lending innovations and in establishing the relative safety of many types of lending operations. Examples of lending activities of this type include direct consumer lending and the development of retail time sales lending activities. However, once the industry developed successful lending programs such as the financing of retail automobile time sales contracts, it experienced severe competitive pressures from other financial institutions such as banks and credit unions. In many cases, other lending institutions entered and eventually overtook certain traditional finance company lending markets once the finance companies had established the relative safety and profitability of those markets.

Following World War II, households expanded their debt obligations not only in an absolute sense but also in relation to their incomes (table 11-1a). Installment debt obligations, which totaled $2.5 billion and represented less than 2 percent of disposable income in 1945, grew dramatically over the next three decades.

Table 11-1(a):

Consumer Installment Credit by Holder
(in $ millions)

Year	Total	Comm. Banks	Finance Companies	Credit Unions	Misc. Lenders, Retailers & Others
1945	$ 2,462	$ 745	$ 910	$ 102	$ 705
1950	14,703	5,798	5,315	590	3,000
1955	28,906	10,601	11,838	1,678	4,798
1960	42,968	16,672	15,435	3,923	6,938
1965	71,324	28,962	24,282	7,324	10,756
1970	101,161	41,895	31,123	12,500	15,643
1975	162,237	78,703	36,695	25,354	21,485
1980	313,472	147,013	76,756	44,041	45,662
1984	336,488	177,641	96,471	53,882	58,454

Table 11-1(b):

Consumer Installment Credit by Holder
(Share of the Market)

Year End	Total	Comm. Banks	Finance Companies	Credit Unions	Misc. Lenders, Retailers & Others
1945	100.0%	30.3%	37.0%	4.1%	28.6%
1950	100.0	39.4	36.1	4.0	20.4
1955	100.0	36.7	41.0	5.8	16.6
1960	100.0	38.8	35.9	9.1	16.1
1965	100.0	40.6	34.0	10.3	15.1
1970	100.0	41.4	30.8	12.4	15.5
1975	100.0	48.5	22.6	15.6	13.2
1980	100.0	46.9	24.5	14.0	14.6
1984	100.0	46.0	25.0	13.9	15.1

Note: 1984 data are for January. All other data are for 31 December.

Source: *Federal Reserve Bulletin*, various issues.

By 1984, consumer installment credit represented 16 percent of consumer disposable personal income.

Although finance companies participated in this post war growth of consumer credit receivables, the industry's share of total market receivables began to decline (table 11-1b). This decline began to appear by the mid 1950s as commercial banks and credit unions experienced ever increasing market domination. Beginning in the 1950s, commercial banks and credit unions became more aggressive in consumer credit markets. This, combined with their ability to attract lower cost (deposit-type) funds and therefore offer consumer financing at lower rates, resulted in a strong competitive advantage for commercial banks and thrift institutions.

ASSET MANAGEMENT

A review and discussion of the major categories of consumer and business receivables held by finance companies is useful in the development of an understanding of finance company operations (table 11-2). Each of these will be discussed in turn.

Consumer Receivables

Retail Passenger Automobile Paper Retail passenger automobile paper refers to receivables generated through the sale of new or used automobiles under terms of a conditional sales (or similar) contract. Receivables such as these are originated through automobile dealers and are subsequently sold or assigned to a financial institution. A typical procedure is as follows:

1. The automobile dealer negotiates the selling price and trade-in allowance for a new or used car with the purchaser.

2. Following agreement on these cash sales terms, the dealer may offer to finance the automobile with the customer to pay monthly payments over time. Given an extended payment arrangement, the sale would be termed a "time sale" as opposed to a "cash sale."

3. The customer at this point may choose to (a) pay the cash price from his own funds, (b) arrange financing directly through a lender of his choice, or (c) accept the dealer's offer to finance the automobile.

4. If the dealer's financing offer is accepted, the customer will complete a credit application.

Table 11-2:

Major Types of Credit Outstanding Held by Finance Companies

Consumer Receivables	*Business Receivables*
Retail Passenger Automobile Paper	Wholesale Paper
Mobile Homes	Automobiles
Revolving Consumer Installment Credit	Other consumer goods
Personal Cash Loans	Equipment and industrial
Second Mortgage Loans	Retail Paper
Other Consumer Installment Loans	Commercial vehicles
	Business, industrial, and farm equipment
	Lease Paper
	Automobile paper
	Business, industrial, and farm equipment
	Other Business Credit
	Loans on commercial accounts receivable
	Factored accounts receivable

5. Information concerning the transaction—e.g., price and description of the automobile, down payment, requested contract maturity, and credit information—is telephoned or otherwise transmitted to the lending institution.

6. On the basis of information submitted, the lending institution will (verbally) approve, reject, or suggest modification of contract terms (required down payment, maturity, comaker, etc.).

7. If the contract is approved by the lending institution, the sale is consummated. The contract is endorsed by the dealer and sold or assigned to the lender, who in turn issues the dealer a check for the principal balance financed.

Certain features of the time-sales contract and its subsequent sale or assignment to the lender are noteworthy and influence the potential risk and profitability of the transaction.

First, the nature of the dealer's endorsement influences the level of risk inherent in the transaction. The contract may be endorsed "without recourse," with "full recourse," or in some other way so as to partially protect the lender in the event of customer default. If the endorsement is "without recourse," the dealer has no responsibility in the event of customer default and any collection or collateral repossession expense must be borne by the lender. If a "full recourse" endorsement is used, credit risk for the lender is substantially reduced or eliminated, and the dealer is committed to absorb the losses in event of customer default. Under terms of a "partial repurchase" or other limited recourse agreement, the dealer is obligated to absorb losses up to some fixed sum or is perhaps obligated only until a given number of payments have been paid by the customer.

Hence, the nature of contract endorsement is important from a managerial aspect. Obviously, if all else is equal, the financial institution would prefer to have all contracts endorsed on a "full recourse" basis. Even in the case of full recourse endorsements, however, the financial institution

faces certain risks. Full recourse endorsement by financially unsound dealerships may provide little protection to the lender. Even in the case of financially sound dealerships, risk exposure may be substantial if the institution relies excessively on dealer endorsements and relaxes credit standards or regularly accepts contracts with cash advancements in excess of the "quick" or wholesale value of the collateral. The extent to which recourse endorsements may be required by financial institutions varies over time as well as with the nature of the collateral and the geographic location. In larger urban areas where lenders compete vigorously in the retail automobile paper market, a lender who wishes to participate in this market may have little choice other than to purchase the paper on a nonrecourse basis, particularly with regard to contracts secured by new automobiles. On the other hand, dealers in rural areas tend to have fewer financing outlets and must frequently endorse time sales contracts on a recourse basis.

A second feature associated with time sales financing and one with considerable influence on potential profitability associated with the financing of retail paper involves the tradition of dealer participation in finance charges. Because competition among financial institutions for retail auto receivables has been intense, particularly in the postwar era, most financial institutions which seek those receivables offer some program whereby a portion of finance charges from times sales contracts are shared with the dealer. For example, a particular lender might establish a (retail) rate to the public of, say, 7 percent add-on. If the amount financed were $5,000 over thirty-six months, total finance charges would be $1,050 ($5,000 × 7% × 3 years). Suppose the same institution established a net rate of 6 percent add-on (net rate is the rate retained by the lender). The financial institution would seek to net $900 ($5,000 × 6% × 3 years) and the difference of $150 ($1,050 − $900) would be paid to the dealer as an incentive for offering the contract to the lender. This dealer participation in finance charges is frequently referred to as "dealer reserve." Also, the proportion of total finance charges received by the dealer is influenced by the type of collateral, contract maturity, competition, and other factors.

When the contract is sold or assigned to the lender, the lender may issue an additional check to the dealer in the amount of the finance charge participation. More commonly, however, the dealer reserve is entered as a liability on the lender's books and paid at periodic intervals. Frequently, the reserve account is established in such a way that the account may be charged to cover losses arising through defaults on contracts that had been partially or fully guaranteed by the dealer.

From a managerial point of view, competitive conditions frequently dictate dealer participation in finance charges. The amount of participation and the terms under which reserves are available to offset credit losses should be carefully monitored. Changes in competitive conditions and analysis of the profitability of retail paper should influence policy decisions regarding relationships between the lender and dealers.

Mobile Home Financing Although mobile homes may be financed through mortgage instruments in ways that are similar to the financing of residential real estate, finance companies have traditionally financed mobile homes in a manner similar to that of automobiles: through use of conditional sales (or similar) contracts.

Several aspects of the financing of mobile homes by finance companies differ from those of new automobile financing (table 11-3). Principal differences include higher finance rates and larger average amounts financed. Maturities for mobile home loans have averaged about thirteen years in recent times (*not* shown in table 11-3). This compares to average maturities of about forty-six months for new cars and about forty months for used cars by 1984. By early 1984, consumer mobile home installment credit receivables held by all lenders were about $20 billion. Of this, commercial banks held almost $10 billion while finance companies and savings and loans each held $5 billion. A small amount of this market (about $0.5 billion) was held by credit unions.

Like automobile financing, conditional sales contracts for mobile homes may be subject to full

Table 11-3:

Finance Rates and Average Amount Financed for Finance Companies

Average Finance Rates	1977	1982	1984
Personal Loans	20.5%	23.1%	—
Automobiles			
New	13.1	15.8	14.18%
Used	17.6	20.8	17.54
Mobile Homes	13.6	18.8	—
Other Consumer Goods	19.2	22.6	—
Average Amount Financed			
Personal Loans	$1,521	$2,683	—
Automobiles			
New	4,990	8,173	9,099
Used	2,720	4,740	5,392
Mobile Homes	9,174	14,364	—
Other Consumer Goods	563	990	—

Note: 1977 and 1982 data are average for the respective years. 1984 data are for January. Missing data are not available as of this writing.

Source: Data for 1977 and 1982 from American Financial Services Association, *1983 Finance Facts Yearbook*. 1984 data from *Federal Reserve Bulletin*, March, 1984, p. A41.

or partial dealer recourse arrangements. Dealer participation in finance charges is common within the industry. Because mobile homes (unlike residential real property) have traditionally been subject to rapid depreciation, and because of the greater complexity and potential loss in the sale of mobile homes in the event of customer default, management should exercise considerable care in establishing relationships with individual dealers, evaluating credit applications, and selecting terms.

Revolving Consumer Installment Credit During the 1970s, revolving credit was the fastest growing single segment of the consumer credit market. According to a 1977 Federal Reserve Survey dealing with consumer credit, almost 63 percent of all families surveyed had at least one credit card.[1]

---

[1]Board of Governors of the Federal Reserve System, *1977 Consumer Credit Survey*, 1978.

Although the bulk of revolving credit receivables are held by commercial banks and retailers, some finance companies have developed revolving credit programs of their own in recent years. In lending programs of this type, customers are given advance approval for credit extensions up to some maximum limit and may draw against this limit by executing notes and forwarding these to the finance company office. In some programs, arrangements have been developed whereby finance company credit is extended through use of Visa cards. As the movement toward electronic funds transfer systems continues, scale economies and innovative marketing techniques may well stimulate further expansion by the consumer finance industry into the market for revolving consumer installment credit.

Personal Cash Loans   Personal or direct cash loans constitute a major portion of finance company consumer receivables. Loans of this type have amounted to about 36 percent of all finance company consumer receivables in recent years.

Unlike other types of loan receivables such as those secured by automobiles or mobile homes, direct cash loans are typically small in size. They may be secured by household goods and other miscellaneous assets, or may be unsecured. Finance rates for personal loans in excess of 20 percent are common within the industry (table 11-3). Although these rates have traditionally been high compared to the finance rates associated with automobile or mobile home loans, finance company personal loans tend to be relatively small in size and are costly to administer. Also, because of competitive pressures, increasing funds costs, and state-mandated interest rate ceilings, the relative profitability of personal loans by finance companies has fallen over the years.

A particular problem area for finance company management with regard to small personal loans is the fact that finance companies must compete for funds in money and capital markets where interest rates are not regulated. At the same time, maximum rates for personal loans are fixed by the various states. In a 1978 study of the consumer finance industry in Missouri, the authors found that the combination of high funds costs and fixed state interest-rate ceilings had resulted in a decline of the industry in Missouri.

From a management perspective, the future attractiveness of the market for relatively small personal loans is questionable at best. It is likely that commercial banks and credit unions will continue to increase their respective market shares. On the other hand, as Regulation Q ceilings continue to be phased out, the cost of deposit funds for commercial banks and credit unions will increase, with a consequent reduction in the competitive advantage these institutions traditionally have had over finance companies.

Second-Mortgage Loans   A second-mortgage loan (sometimes called "home equity loan") is one secured by real estate but where the real estate collateral is subject to some prior lien. The prior lienholder has priority in the event of foreclosure and liquidation of the real estate collateral.

Information concerning the total volume of second-mortgage lending is relatively sketchy and frequently inconsistent. There is, however, general agreement that consumer lending of this type has been among the fastest growing forms of credit to consumers. Estimates of outstanding and market shares by lenders for 1971 and 1976 were developed by Commercial Credit Economic Services (table 11-4). Of all lenders represented in the table, finance companies held the largest single share of second-mortgage receivables by 1976.

Reasons for growth in second-mortgage lending markets were first cited during testimony before the Federal Trade Commission in December 1977, by C. Stuart LaDow, a director of the *National Second Mortgage Association*. Those same reasons continue to hold today:

1.   As housing prices climb, homeowners find that they have increased equity in their homes—equity which may be used as loan collateral.

2.   Homeowners who might otherwise have been in the market for new homes are staying where they are and taking out second mortgage loans to make improvements and repairs on their existing homes.

Table 11-4:

Estimated Value of Second-Mortgage Loans Outstanding for the United States (in $ millions)

	1971		1976	
	Amount	*Percentage*	*Amount*	*Percentage*
Individuals	$1,477	33.6	$2,379	26.1
Finance Companies	797	18.1	2,433	26.7
Commercial Banks	461	10.5	1,407	15.4
Savings & Loans	442	10.1	712	7.8
Mortgage Companies	261	5.9	420	4.6
Credit Unions	130	3.0	525	5.8
Others*	826	18.8	1,248	13.7
Total	$4,394	100.0	$9,124	100.0

*Others include real estate and construction companies, mutual savings banks, federal agencies, insurance companies, retirement funds, state and local pension systems, private pension plans, nonprofit organizations and organizations and trust accounts administered by banks.

Note: According to Federal Reserve Survey data, Finance Company second mortgage Real estate receivables had grown from $1.9 billion in 1975 to $11.8 billion in 1980, and to $13 billion by 1981.

Source: "Monthly Perspective and Insight on Consumer Financial Behavior," (Vol. 2, Number 3), Commercial Credit Economic Services, March 1977, p. 8.

3. Many of those who can afford a new home are finding that they cannot afford the higher down payments and closing costs, so they turn to a second mortgage to finance those items.

The representative of the National Second-Mortgage Association, in emphasizing the fact that second mortgage loans tended to be relatively large in size, cited average loan sizes made by three of the group's members. Average loan sizes that were cited ranged from $10,000 to $12,900 and loan maturities ranged from seventy-two months to ninety-nine months.

The typical second-mortgage borrower appears to be a middle-income person approximately forty years of age with considerable residential and job stability. The two primary reasons for second-mortgage borrowing are home improvement and consolidation of short-term consumer loans. Borrowers appear to take out second mortgage loans only after a period of contemplation averaging several months. Delin-

quency rates for these loans appear to be quite low.

Maximum interest rates for second-mortgage loans are established by state law. Some states also specify maximum loan amounts and maturities.

Second-mortgage lending offers finance companies certain advantages over the more traditional cash loans offered by the industry. Lending of this type offers cost economies since handling and processing costs per dollar loaned are significantly less. Also, credit risk associated with lending of this type is reduced, given customer stability and the nature of the collateral. Finally, it is a market that is growing much more rapidly than the market for other types of loans.

Other Consumer Installment Loans Other consumer installment loans include finance receivables secured by personal property such as refrigerators or television sets. Goods such as this are sold and financed in a manner similar to that described in the financing of retail passenger automobile paper.

Example Telcom Finance Company has developed cost and revenue data concerning personal cash loan operations for all company activities within a particular state (table 11-5). The maximum APR under the state usury statute for direct cash loans is 15 percent and Telcom's cost of funds is currently 10 percent. Is Telcom's personal cash loan business profitable?

Analysis of data contained in table 11-5 reveals that Telcom's interest rate spread is insufficient to cover operating expense and produce a profit. The average spread provides revenue of $100 (0.05 × $2,000) per account, thus failing to cover operating costs by $14.74 ($100 − $114.74). The company is losing $692,854 (47,005 × $14.74) per year on operations within the state. Management strategies to improve performance and restore profitability within the state include the following:

Reduce annual operating costs to a point below $100 per account

Increase average loan balances (perhaps

through a second mortgage or auto loan program)

Improve the mix of funds sources in an effort to reduce funds cost

Undertake activities, perhaps in conjunction with industry trade associations to increase permissable APRs for direct cash loans

Given the existing average outstanding cash loan balance of $2,000, the existing operating cost structure and current funds cost of 10%, an APR of 15.737% [$2,000 × (APR − 10%) = $114.74] would represent the breakeven APR.

Evaluating Consumer Credit Applications

The analysis of consumer credit applications is similar to business credit evaluation in some respects and different in others. In both cases, the three Cs of credit (character, capacity, and collateral) must by considered.

Character refers to the reputation of the potential borrower in terms of his perceived reliability in repaying the loan. Finance companies, as do other consumer lenders, contact prior or existing creditors, the names of which are typically disclosed by the applicant in his credit applications. These credit references are asked to furnish information concerning the applicant's record with them. In addition to direct contact with creditors, the lender might communicate by telephone or teletype with the local credit bureau or lenders' exchange, where a file containing the applicant's credit repayment history is maintained. This file frequently contains employment history and residence information in addition to an evaluation of loans and other credit repayment history. The credit evaluation agency will have accumulated this credit information as the result of the applicant's prior requests for credit and subsequent inquiries from other lenders.

Capacity refers to the applicant's potential ability to repay the loan from current income or existing resources. The credit manager must evaluate the applicant's ability to repay the loan,

Table 11-5:

Personal Cash Loan
Loan Profitability Analyses

Annual Operating Expense	$ Total	$ Per Account
Advertising	170,091	$3.62
Bad debts (net)	1,537,121	32.70
Legal	153,898	3.27
Postage and printing	109,346	2.33
Rent and utilities	366,850	7.80
Salaries	1,539,618	32.75
Administration	1,028,948	21.89
Telephone	195,756	4.16
Other	292,500	6.22
	$5,394,128	$114.74
Average number of accounts		47,005
Average outstanding balance		$2,000
Maximum permissable APR		15%
Annual cost of funds		10%
Interest rate spread		5%

in view of the borrower's existing financial obligations and income limitations.

Finally, *Collateral* represents the security to which the lender may turn in the event of loan default. Collateral repossession in order to liquidate a loan is viewed as a last resort by finance company lenders. In 1981, almost three fifths of all finance company loans to consumers were secured by automobiles, household goods, or by other chattels. One fourth was unsecured, and the remainder was secured by co makers, real estate, and other considerations.[2]

Business Receivables

Wholesale Paper Wholesale paper refers to trust agreements or similar legal documents which arise during the course of inventory financing. To induce sellers of "large ticket items" such as automobiles, heavy duty trucks, farm equipment, and other items which are frequently sold on time sales contracts to offer these contracts to a particular lender, a finance company (or other lender) may offer to finance the wholesale value of the dealer's inventory. Such financing—also referred to as "floorplanning"— is typically provided as an accommodation to the dealer.

Suppose that a franchise for a new car or truck dealership is awarded to a businessman in the local area. The dealership will be expected to develop a certain amount of retail time sales finance paper and it is likely that a number of financial institutions will have an interest in purchasing this retail paper. The dealer, on the other hand, will likely carry large inventories of the product and these inventories must generally be financed. Typically, one or more lenders would approach the dealer and offer to finance the inventory in exchange for the opportunity to finance the retail contracts. The lender may agree to establish a "floor plan line of credit" whereby the dealer maintains inventory financed by the lender up to the amount of the established credit line. Once the floorplan arrangement has been

negotiated, the manufacturer will be authorized to draft on or bill the lender for subsequent shipments of inventory items to the dealer. As the dealer sells the floor planned units, he is expected to remit payment for sold items promptly to the lender.

Because of competitive conditions, wholesale dealer paper is typically financed at breakeven interest rates, with the interest rate tied to the prime lending rate plus, say, 1 percent. Since finance companies frequently borrow at rates which are only slightly less than the floorplan rates offered to dealers, floorplanning in and of itself is not a particularly profitable operation. Wholesale financing accommodations are generally provided to the dealer with the expectation that the dealer will offer "compensating retail paper" to the lender. On the basis of experience, the lender knows that a considerable portion of "big ticket items" such as new cars, trucks, etc., are financed. Since the dealer is in a position to control the placement of a certain proportion of the retail time sales paper, the dealer is expected to offer this paper to the lender who has provided the floorplan accommodation. Of course, if the floorplanning lender rejects a particular financing transaction, the dealer may well seek to sell the time sales contract to some other lender.

Floorplanning can involve considerable risk to the lender and considerable management attention should be given to its control. Even relatively small dealers may require floorplan lines amounting to several hundred thousand dollars. For large dealerships, the value of floorplanned inventory can amount to a million dollars or more; amounts which may be far in excess of the dealer's equity investment.

The risk of potential loss through wholesale financing is perhaps greatest during depressed economic periods when dealer sales volume may be low. Indeed, examples abound where particular dealers, faced with high fixed costs and working capital requirements, have defaulted on inventory trust agreements. The default may go undetected by the lender for a considerable period of time because the dealer simply defers payment on sold inventory items and enters into a

---

[2]American Financial Services Association, 1983 Finance Facts *Yearbook*, 57.

floorplan "float." The float may at first involve a delay in payment of sold inventory items for a few days with the proceeds from current sales used to pay the lender for floorplanned units sold in the prior time period. If depressed economic conditions continue, the float may build gradually over time, reaching the point where the lender suffers considerable losses.

Although the nature of wholesale financing is such that the risk of a dealer being "out of trust" is always present, controls can be instituted to minimize potential losses. Frequent unannounced floorplan inventory checks by the lender are a critical component of such controls. Insistence on the timely preparation and submission of dealer financial statements, followed by analysis of such statements on an ongoing basis, is another means of control.

Finally, management should systematically evaluate the quantity and profitability of the compensating retail paper purchased from individual dealers. If the quantity and quality of the retail paper is insufficient to justify the investment and risk associated with the dealers' wholesale receivables, and if this condition cannot be improved, the floorplan line should be terminated.

Retail Business Receivables In addition to time sales contracts secured by consumer durables, finance companies also purchase time sales contracts secured by commercial assets such as heavy duty trucks, farm equipment, and other industrial products. Frequently, commercial time sales contracts secured by assets such as these are purchased from dealers in ways that are similar to the procedure described for retail passenger automobile paper.

On the one hand, the financing of commercial equipment carries with it the prospect for enhanced profitability. The amount financed under individual contracts tends to be substantial when compared with consumer durables such as automobiles or household products. On the other hand, collateral such as heavy duty trucks and other types of industrial products is difficult to dispose of in the event of foreclosure. Because of the large balances financed and the lack of a readily available secondary market for most types of industrial equipment, there exists considerable risk of loss on individual time sales contracts.

Large finance companies with branches located throughout the nation have competitive advantages in the financing of certain types of industrial equipment. First, it is possible to diversify portfolio holdings of this paper on a geographic basis, reducing the impact of credit losses caused by regional economic slowdowns. Second, commercial banks are reluctant to purchase contracts secured by "on the road" commercial vehicles such as tractor-trailers financed for "owner-operators," because the equipment may be far away and physically difficult to repossess in the event of default. From a practical point of view, the lender must have the capability to enforce terms of the time sales contract, and as a last resort, to take physical possession of the collateral when it appears that the purchaser is unable or unwilling to meet his contractual obligations. Large finance companies with a national network of branches have this capability.

LIABILITY MANAGEMENT

On average, finance companies carry seven to eight dollars in debt for each dollar of equity capital. Lacking deposit funds as a major source of debt, they must bid for funds in a competitive market place. With the cost of these funds being a major part of their total costs, finance companies depend on skillful liability management to minimize interest expense and achieve a satisfactory level of profitability.

However, minimizing the cost of funds is only one consideration in liability management. A second major factor is interest rate risk. The average finance company loan has a maturity of several years. A shorter liability maturity exposes the finance company to the risk of having to refinance maturing liabilities at interest rates higher than the net rates being earned on loans. In a period of falling interest rates, liability maturities longer than loan maturities can leave the institution in the position of being committed to high-cost sources of funds while competition is driving down the rates charged on loans. Thus interest rate risk is a major consideration in liability management.

Finally, availability of funds is a major consideration for finance company management. Money and capital markets are quite impersonal; they make no commitment to provide funds. Past experience such as collapse of the commercial paper market following the Penn Central default confirms the importance of assuring that some source of funds will always be available to finance existing loans.

A summary of the liability structure of finance companies at year-end 1983 can be found in figure 11-2. Each of the major sources of funds covered there is discussed in the following paragraphs.

Bank Loans

Finance companies have traditionally relied on commercial banks as key sources of funds and frequently borrowed against revolving credit lines. Such reliance is particularly true for the smaller finance companies which lack access to national credit markets.

For the industry as a whole, bank loans were about 9 percent of total liabilities and capital at year end 1983. The aggregated data (contained in figure 11-2), however, obscure the fact that liability structure differs markedly for finance companies depending on firm size.

In fact, of some 2,800 finance companies surveyed by the Federal Reserve System in 1980, less than 2 percent were responsible for some 80 percent of total industry liabilities.[3] These larger firms tend to rely proportionately less on commercial bank loans and proportionately more on commercial paper. Regional and small firms, however, draw heavily on bank credit lines in financing their operations. More than half the outstanding debt of smaller finance companies (those with receivables of $25 million or less) was owed to commercial banks in 1980, compared to only 11 percent of the debt owed by large finance companies.

Bank borrowing is frequently accomplished by drawing down on a prenegotiated revolving line of credit. This source of borrowing has the important advantage of assuring availability. However, interest rates on such lines are frequently tied to prime rate; the cost of bank credit varies from the prime rate for the soundest companies to three or four percentage points over prime for the smaller firms. Thus the interest rate may vary, and the benefit of assured availability is offset by exposure to interest rate risk. Normally, credit arrangements of this type require a compensating balance, and/or a fee of about 0.5 percent of the credit line. Charges or balances are frequently required regardless of whether or not the line is used. Therefore, a price is paid for availability which makes bank credit a sometimes expensive source of funds.

Finance company managers using bank credit should seek to minimize the cost of these funds.

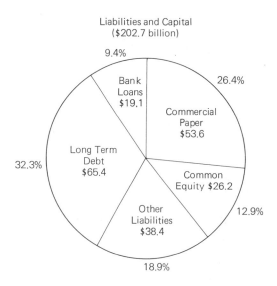

Liabilities and Capital
($202.7 billion)

Figure 11–2: Liability structure for domestic finance companies, December 31, 1983 ($ billions). (Source: *Federal Reserve Bulletin,* March 31, 1984, p. A37.)

---

[3]Results of a 1980 survey of finance companies were reported in the *Federal Reserve Bulletin* (May 1981) 398–409.

It may be possible, for example, to negotiate a reduced commitment fee—or a lower compensating balance—in return for the firm's payroll account. Alternatively, the finance company might suggest a smaller compensating balance, but one which would be kept in the form of a noninterest bearing time deposit (one on which the bank would be required to hold proportionately smaller reserves). In short, the cost of bank credit is an important component of finance company cost and new innovative financing techniques can have important implications for company profitability.

Commercial Paper

The commercial paper market is a major source of funds for large finance companies. According to data contained in figure 11-2, financing of this type represented about 26 percent of the industry's financial structure in 1983. In fact, finance company paper constitutes more than half the entire domestic commercial paper market.

The use of short-term bank loans and commercial paper in financing such a large part of operations is consistent with the principle of matching the maturity of assets and liabilities. Finance companies, as our previous discussion indicated, hold large volumes of short-term self-liquidating retail and wholesale receivables. The commercial paper and bank loans, combined with long-term debt, provide a liability structure with an average maturity similar to that of the assets.

Financing of this type also provides flexibility. The volume of financing requirements can be adjusted on a daily basis, principally by varying the rate of interest that the issuing company is willing to pay.

Of course, a principal reason for the popularity of commercial paper among finance companies is the fact that interest rates for the paper are consistently below the bank prime rate. It should be noted, however, that the rate of interest applicable to commercial paper does not represent the entire cost. Smaller issuers generally place their paper through dealers, who charge a fee. Larger firms place commercial paper directly with investors; thus large firms are faced with the expense associated with the maintenance of commercial paper managers and staff.

In addition to selling costs, commercial paper issuers face the cost of maintaining back-up, unused lines of bank credit, as expected by the investment community. Under normal circumstances, maturing commercial paper is redeemed through issuance of new paper. However, there may exist market conditions under which the issuer would find it difficult to "roll over" maturing paper and would be forced to rely on bank credit to redeem it. Since these lines of credit are paid for with noninterest compensating balances or by direct payment of fees, part of the cost savings of commercial paper is offset by the cost of assuring availability of funds through banks.

Bonds and Other Long-Term Debt Financing

Like industrial corporations, finance companies rely on bonds and other long-term debt as sources of financing. Long-term sources have the advantage of assuring the availability of funds at a fixed interest rate for a specific period of time. Thus they provide a solution to the availability problem.

One major disadvantage of long-term debt is that it has historically been more expensive than short-term funds. However, this disadvantage is somewhat offset by the fact that most bonds are callable; they can be retired early, at the option of the issuer, typically with the payment of a call premium. If interest rates rise after a bond has been issued, the issuer continues to pay interest at the prior low rate. On the other hand, if market interest rates fall, the bonds can be called and replaced with a new, lower interest rate issue. Thus the higher average cost of long-term debt is at least partially offset by inclusion of the call feature or by other features that provide flexibility in adjusting to changes in interest rates.

Given the advantage of assuring availability

of funds, and with the cost and interest rate risk problems mitigated by callability, bonds have been an important source of funds to finance companies. Bonds and other long-term debt totalled 32 percent of finance company sources of funds (figure 11-2).

Equity Capital

Finance companies differ from most other financial institutions in that regulators do not impose a minimum equity level requirement on them. They are free to choose a debt-to-equity ratio in keeping with market forces and their own objectives.

Finance companies face two major considerations when choosing a financial structure. First, like any company, they recognize that the value of the owner's investment is affected by financial leverage. A higher debt-to-equity ratio can lead to a higher return on equity if funds are invested in assets which earn a rate of return greater than the cost of debt. However, beyond some point, further increases in debt increase the risk of insolvency, which drive up both the interest rate on debt and the required return on equity. Finance companies with less risky and better diversified asset portfolios can use proportionately less equity. The larger finance companies with total assets over $25 million had equity equal to 14 percent of total assets in 1980. At the same time, finance companies with total assets under $5 million had equity of some 46 percent of total assets. These smaller companies normally concentrate in limited types of lending in narrow geographic areas and are not nearly so diversified as the larger firms.

In addition to the threat of insolvency, finance companies must consider the effect of their equity ratios on their access to the debt markets. Finance companies that allow the equity cushion to fall too low may find it difficult or impossible to market commercial paper. Similarly, a low equity ratio may impair the firm's ability to acquire other short- or long-term debt funds at reasonable cost.

FINANCIAL SERVICES IN TRANSITION: MANAGERIAL IMPLICATIONS

The foregoing discussion emphasized the traditional role and structure of the consumer finance industry. Data presented early in this chapter, and specifically market share data contained in table 11-1 suggest that finance companies reached their peak in the 1950s and that their share of consumer finance receivables declined over the next two decades. This trend appeared to reverse itself in the 1980s, and finance company market shares began to increase once again. While it is too early to draw conclusions as to the ultimate structure of the market for financial services in general, and consumer financial services in particular, this section will analyze developments in consumer financial markets which have occurred over time and which appear to have accelerated dramatically in the 1980s.

Consumer Banking, Nonbank Banks, and Loophole Banking

In 1970, Congress, in amending the Bank Holding Company Act, defined a *commercial bank* as a company that *accepts demand deposits and makes commercial loans*. Also, the Bank Holding Company Act, as amended, required companies that owned one or more banks to register with the Federal Reserve. These *registered bank holding companies* were then subject to rules and supervision by the Federal Reserve. Activities in which they could engage were restricted.

A key restriction faced by banks and by bank holding companies concerned their ability to expand across state lines. The principle statutory restrictions on geographic activities of banks are contained in the *McFadden Act* of 1927 and the *Douglas Amendment to the Bank Holding Company Act*. The McFadden Act prohibits interstate branching and permits each state to set branching restrictions within the state for national as well as for state banks within its borders. The Douglas Amendment prohibits bank holding companies from acquiring banks in other states unless the state in which the acquired bank is located has specifically provided for such out-of-state entry.

Although bank holding companies were prohibited from owning and operating commercial banks across state lines, they were not prohibited from owning and operating certain other businesses, including finance companies, which may expand across state lines.[4] Beginning in the 1970s, some large bank holding companies (including Bank of America, Citicorp, Manufacturers Hanover, Security Pacific Corporation, and others) acquired finance companies. In some cases, the finance companies so acquired began to appear more "bank like." Market Research conducted by one major bank holding company showed that people liked banks because they had a full product array, low rates, and were reputable and stable, but disliked banks because of their impersonal atmosphere, inconvenient hours, and the belief that it was difficult to get money from them. Finance companies were viewed by these same consumers as easy places to borrow money, as convenient, and as more personal. But finance companies were also viewed as not reputable and as high-rate lenders. A number of such finance companies began to emphasize home equity (second mortgage) loans and simultaneously deemphasized small cash loans and other traditional finance company markets. Also, as inflation mounted and as deregulation of the financial sector proceeded in the early 1980s, some large savings and loan associations failed and were acquired, in some cases, by finance company subsidiaries of bank holding companies.[5] Finally by 1984, a major

"loophole" surfaced which appeared to open the door to substantial interstate banking activity. In March of that year, the Federal Reserve approved the application of United States Trust Corporation of New York to convert its Florida Trust Subsidiary to an institution that could accept consumer deposits and make consumer loans—a consumer bank.[6] Within weeks, a large number of major bank holding companies applied for permission to conduct similar operations across state lines. Clearly, the floodgates had been opened. Dramatic changes in traditional methods of providing consumer financial services were anticipated.[7]

Managerial Implications

Managerial implications associated with the impact of deregulation of the consumer finance industry are enormous. The traditional business of a large component of the consumer financial services industry—the making of small loans to consumers—is no longer a particularly viable activity. Innovations of recent years, including the expanded use of bank credit cards which carry cash advance privileges, has rendered some components of the traditional consumer finance industry obsolete. Finance company managers must respond to this new environment through a planned strategy.

---

[4]A 1970 amendment to the Bank Holding Company Act restricted bank holding companies activities to those "closely related to banking or managing or controlling banks as to be a proper incident thereto . . . ." See table 3-1 for a list of permissable bank holding company activities.

[5]In 1982, acting under emergency conditions, the Federal Reserve Board and the Federal Home Loan Bank

Board authorized both interstate and interindustry mergers. The most notable (and controversial) of these involved Citicorp's (a New York based bank holding company) acquisition of Fidelity Federal Savings and Loan Association of Oakland, California. The Garn-St. Germain Depository Institutions Act of October 1982 specifically authorized such acquisitions under certain specified conditions.

[6]At this writing, the Federal Reserve decision had been appealed in the courts, and the Federal Reserve had asked the Congress to enact legislation dealing with Consumer Banks.

[7]The "loophole" concerned the definition of a bank which was contained within the Bank Holding Company Act (a company that accepts demand deposits and makes commercial loans). It was argued that if an institution engaged in all banking activities *except* commercial lending *or* acceptance of demand deposits, then the institution was not by definition a bank.

SUMMARY

Traditionally finance companies have differed sharply from their major competitors—banks and thrifts. Events of recent years, however, have sharply reduced these traditional distinctions. The advantages that finance companies have traditionally enjoyed—the ability to expand without geographic restriction, the ability to open or close branches virtually at will, the reduced level of regulatory supervision (compared with banks and thrifts)—have served to identify finance companies as a major catalyst by which the regulatory geographic constraints imposed on depository institutions can be circumvented. It seems certain that the market for consumer financial services will become increasingly competitive and that new products and innovations will be introduced by the market leaders. Successful managers within the consumer financial services industry will successfully identify the conditions which surround them and formulate policy decisions based on this environment.

QUESTIONS

1. Beginning in the late 1950s, the market share of installment credit held by finance companies declined. How do you account for this decline?

2. Should consumers finance large purchases, such as a new or used car, directly through the dealer? Why might this be to the customer's advantage or disadvantage?

3. Distinguish between the various ways in which a time sales finance contract may be endorsed before being sold to a financial institution by a dealer.

4. What is meant by the term "Dealer Reserve"?

5. Why have finance companies emphasized second mortgage lending in recent years?

6. Define the term "floorplanning" and comment on the inherent riskiness of this type of financing from the lender's point of view.

7. Certain types of equipment, such as heavy trucks and trailers, are financed by finance companies. Why might finance companies pursue this type of lending while depository and thrift institutions do not?

8. In addition to interest charges, there may be certain additional costs implied when finance companies borrow from banks. Comment on these.

9. Why are finance companies such heavy issuers of commercial paper? Are there significant costs associated with the issuance of commercial paper above and beyond interest paid to purchasers of the paper?

10. Suppose that the balance sheets of a large bank were contrasted with that of a large finance company. Would the proportion of assets financed by equity capital tend to be greater for the finance company as compared to the bank? Why or why not?

11. What is meant by the term "loophole banking" or "nonbank banks"?

12. Identify the major legislative restrictions on the geographic expansion of banks and bank holding companies.

13. What were some of the significant developments of recent years that may ultimately lead to interstate banking?

PROBLEMS

1. General Finance Company is subject to a state usury ceiling. The present ceiling is 18 percent APR. The company has operating costs per account of $125 per annum. In addition, General's cost of funds before tax is 12 percent and average loan balances are $2200.

    a. Is General Finance Company's cash loan portfolio profitable?

    b. If General's cost of funds increased to

13 percent, would cash loan operations be profitable?

2. National finance, a large sales finance company requires a before-tax return of 10 percent on its portfolio of retail auto finance receivables. Given average loan advances (proceeds) of $8,000, administrative costs of $10 per auto loan per month, a typical dealer reserve of $180 per transaction (which is paid to the dealer "up front" together with the loan proceeds), and average loan maturity of thirty-six months, calculate:

    a. The minimum average monthly payment necessary to earn the required rate of return.

    b. The retail rate (APR) charged to the public which corresponds to your answer to a. above.

    c. If the dealer reserve were eliminated, what would the monthly payment and APR be?

3. Padberg Financial Services, Inc., a large diversified financial services company has a capital structure comparable to that of the industry (figure 11-2). Padberg's long-term bonds carry a yield to maturity of 13 percent; bank borrowing is at the prime rate (currently 11 percent) and the commercial paper rate is 10 percent. The company calculates a required rate of return on equity capital of 20 percent. Other liabilities include items such as deferred taxes and accounts payable.

These other liabilities, from a practical point of view, are seen by the company as "costless."

    a. calculate the weighted average (before tax) cost of capital for Padberg.

    b. Is Padberg correct in assuming the other liabilities to be costless?

SELECTED REFERENCES

Benston, George. "Graduated Interest Rate Ceilings and Operating Costs by Size of Small Consumer Cash Loans." *Journal of Finance* 32 (June 1977); 695–708.

————. "Rate Ceiling Implications of the Cost Structure of Consumer Finance Companies." *Journal of Finance* 32 (September 1977); 1169–1194.

————. "Risk on Consumer Finance Company Personal Loans." *Journal of Finance* 32 (May 1977); 593–607.

Boczar, Gregory. "Competition Between Banks and Finance Companies: A Cross-Section Approach." *Journal of Finance* 33 (March 1978): 245–258.

Hamburger, Michael J., and Zwick, Burton. "Installment Credit Controls, Consumer Expenditures and the Allocation of Real Resources." *Journal of Finance* 33 (December 1977); 1557–1570.

Wiginton, John C. "A Note on the Comparison of Logit and Discriminant Models of Consumer Credit Behavior." *Journal of Financial and Quantitative Analysis* 15 (September 1980): 757–770.

Chapter 12

Thrift Institution Management

The thrift institutions—savings and loan companies, mutual savings banks, and credit unions—rank second only to commercial banks in total assets held by a financial institution category. With assets of over $1 trillion in 1984, they provide an outlet for savings of individuals as well as an important source of real estate and consumer credit.

The cumulative balance sheets of these institutions provide a quick overview of their characteristics (table 12-1). All three types of thrift institutions have liability structures composed primarily of savings deposits. Both savings and loan companies and mutual savings banks hold the bulk of their assets in the form of mortgage loans. Their mortgage loan holdings are double those of commercial banks and account for approximately 45 percent of all mortgage debt not held by government agencies. In contrast, credit unions invest most of their funds in consumer loans, with mortgage loans making up only a small proportion of total assets.

As depository financial intermediaries, the thrift institutions have many characteristics in common with commercial banks. In fact, as a consequence of the monetary control act of 1980 and the Garn—St. Germain Act of 1982, the similarity is increasing as their services have expanded to include transaction accounts and a wider variety of lending. However, they are more vulnerable to interest rate changes than are commercial banks. With an average asset maturity substantially longer than average deposit maturity, the thrift institutions, and particularly savings and loans, suffered from the effects of rising, unstable interest rates. Thus they have a unique set of management problems.

CHARACTERISTICS OF THRIFT INSTITUTIONS

Savings and Loan Companies

Little more than a decade ago, a savings and loan could be characterized as an institution that accepted passbook savings deposits, paying a maximum rate set by federal regulation, and then used these funds to make mortgage loans for the purchase of homes. As late as 1970, mortgage loans represented 85 percent of S&L assets while passbook savings represented 60 percent of total sources of funds to these institutions. Sheltered

Table 12-1:

**Total Assets and Liabilities of All Thrift Institutions, January 1984
(in $ millions)**

	Savings and Loans	Mutual Savings Banks	Credit Unions
Cash		$ 6,252	
U.S. Government Securities	$102,260	15,349	
Other Securities		45,766	
Mortgage Loans	497,746	97,368 ⎫	
Other Loans		19,120 ⎬	$50,306
Other Assets	174,949	9,662 ⎭	
Total Assets	$774,955	$193,517	$83,182
Savings Deposits	$641,762	$172,639	$76,068
Other Liabilities	102,362	2,119 ⎫	
Capital	30,831	18,759 ⎬	7,114
Total Liabilities and Net Worth	$774,955	$193,517	$83,182

Note: Missing data are a result of differences in reporting requirements and certain data are preliminary.

Source: *Federal Reserve Bulletin.*

by regulation and serving a vital need for housing credit, S&L's saw their assets grow from one tenth those of commercial banks in 1950 to 45 percent of commercial bank assets in 1980.

By 1980, however, pressures for change were inescapable. Rising, unstable interest rates had led savers to move their money elsewhere in search of interest rates higher than the low, regulated rates paid by depository institutions. To make matters worse, the S&Ls held many old mortgages that were paying interest rates below the current cost of funds. In response to these problems and a general demand for decreased regulatory protection of business, the Depository Institution Deregulation and Monetary Control Act of 1980, the Garn—St Germain Act of 1982, and subsequent regulatory changes have given S&Ls the authority to offer a broad range of services while both requiring and allowing them to compete for funds by paying market rates.

A typical S&L at present has a liability structure consisting of checkable deposits (accounts on which checks can be drawn), a series of certificates of deposits paying competitive market interest rates, and borrowed funds; passbook savings are a nearly insignificant source of funds. The typical S&L's asset structure now consists of 64 percent mortgages, down from 85 percent mortgages in 1970. The S&L offers an entire market basket of mortgage products rather than the one or two alternatives that were offered to the borrower a decade ago. It has taken advantages of increased investment authority to increase its security holdings, particularly corporate securities. It has also increased investment in commercial mortgages, has begun offering consumer loans, and has or will begin offering credit cards. And although few savings and loans are doing so at this time, a S&L is also authorized to make limited nonmortgage commercial loans.

These changes in asset and liability structure have led to important changes in industry structure. Because larger S&Ls have an advantage in offering a broad range of service, the number of S&Ls has declined 27 percent in the last ten years, to about 3800 institutions. Despite the decrease in the number of S&Ls, the total assets of S&Ls have continued to grow modestly, although the growth rate has been far below that of commercial banks in the last few years. In addition to consolidation, there have been important changes in the ownership of savings and loans. The Garn—St Germain Act of 1982 established a procedure subject to regulatory approval, whereby commercial banks and S&Ls could cross state lines and acquire S&Ls in imminent danger of insolvency. As a result, major bankholding companies, especially Citicorp, have moved aggressively to acquire a national network of S&Ls, hence they have entered markets they were not previously allowed to enter. Savings and loans provide an excellent case study of an industry in transition.

Savings and loan companies are chartered by either the federal government (through the Federal Home Loan Bank Board) or the state in which the institution wishes to set up business. Over half of the savings and loans are presently state chartered.

A savings and loan may have the more common mutual form or the stock form of ownership. The depositors and borrowers of a mutual savings and loan elect a board of directors who oversee the company as would any other corporate board of directors. With the stock form of ownership, stockholders own the company, select the directors, and face returns and risk as do stockholders in other firms. Some existing savings and loans have switched from mutual ownership to stock ownership in recent years, primarily to raise capital by selling more stock. It has also been argued (with some statistical support) the the existence of a group of stockholders interested in profitability leads to greater efficiency.[1]

The primary regulatory body for savings and loans is the Federal Home Loan Bank Board. It examines all federally chartered savings and loans and all state chartered savings and loans that have joined the federally chartered institutions in having their depositors' funds insured by

the Federal Savings and Loan Insurance Corporation (FSLIC). Over 98 percent of savings and loans assets are held by institutions insured by the FSLIC. Deposits are presently insured up to $100,000.

A somewhat confused regulatory structure exists with this dual chartering system. Federal regulations may apply to only federally chartered savings and loans or to all federally insured savings and loans. State regulations may apply to all state chartered savings and loans or only those not insured by the FSLIC. For example, variable rate mortgages began in California with state chartered savings and loans being allowed to grant variable rate mortgages. The Federal Home Loan Bank Board did not try to stop insured state chartered institutions from extending variable rate mortgages, but federally chartered institutions were not given authority to enter the market until six years later.

In addition to acting as a regulatory agency, the Federal Home Loan Bank System acts as an important source of credit for savings and loans. The Federal Home Loan Bank System was formed in 1932 and organized into twelve regional banks. These banks, which are public corporations similar to the Federal Reserve Banks, grant savings and loan companies direct loans with maturities from a few months to ten years.

The Federal Home Loan Banks have three sources of funds to loan to member savings and loans. Capital is supplied by member savings and loans, which must purchase capital stock equal to 2 percent of their mortgage loan balances. In addition to capital stock, members are encouraged to make deposits of excess funds. Federal Home Loan Bank capital stock and deposits totalled about 3 percent of savings and loan assets in 1980. Supplementing these funds, the system sells consolidated debentures which are the joint obligations of the twelve banks.

Federal Home Loan Bank lending is supplemented by Federal Home Loan Mortgage Corporation purchases of mortgages from savings and loans and mutual savings banks. The Federal Home Loan Mortgage Corporation finances these purchases by selling public bond issues secured by packages of mortgages purchased

---

[1]David L. Smith, Donald M. Kaplan, and William F. Ford, "Profitability: Why Some Associations Perform Far Above Average," *Federal Home Loan Bank Board Journal* (November 1977): 7–13.

from savings and loans. Federal Home Loan Bank debentures and mortgage backed bonds outstanding totalled $49 billion at the beginning of 1984. Thrift institutions also gained the right to borrow from the Federal Reserve System under provisions of the deregulation act.

Mutual Savings Banks

Mutual savings banks presently serve purposes similar to those of savings and loans, but have some differences resulting from their historical development. The savings and loans were formed by people who wanted to purchase homes. In some cases, the savers even drew lots to determine when each one would be allowed to borrow. The mutual savings banks, on the other hand, were started to serve small savers and encourage thrift.

Savings banks operate in only seventeen states, with 90 percent of their deposits being in five Northeastern states: New York, Massachusets, Connecticut, Pennsylvania, and New Jersey. All savings banks presently operate under state charter, though federal charter is available. Their total asset size—25 percent of that of savings and loans— indicates that they are an important factor in the few states in which they do have substantial operations. However, their growth has not been dramatic; it approximately parallels that of commercial banks and falls well behind that of savings and loans.

In contrast with savings and loans and most other corporations, the savings bank board of directors is not elected by owners. It is a self-perpetuating organization with existing members of the board electing a new board member if a former member resigns. While this situation may seem unusual, new board members of other businesses are frequently selected by management or the existing board, with the vote of the shareholders being little more than a rubber stamp. In any case, the board of a savings bank is held accountable under the standards of fiduciary responsibility.

The liabilities of savings banks are similar to those of savings and loans. They offer passbook savings accounts as well as various time deposit accounts. They were the first institutions to offer NOW accounts.[2] Like the other thrift institutions, their deposits are insured to $100,000.

Savings banks show more significant differences in their asset mix. Mortgage loans comprise less than 50 percent of their assets compared to about 65 percent for savings and loans. They commit approximately 20 percent of their funds to corporate securities, both debt instruments and stock. The proportion of their funds invested in mortgages has increased gradually over recent years, making them more like savings and loans in asset structure. As the Deregulation Act goes into effect, differences between savings and loans and mutual savings banks will probably decrease further.

Credit Unions

Credit unions have been the fastest growing type of depository financial institution in recent decades, with assets in 1984 being seventy-five times their 1950 level. However, in total assets, credit unions are still only 4 percent of the size of commercial banks and 11 percent of the size of savings and loans. Like the other thrift institutions, their growth has tapered off in the last several years.

The key requirement for a credit union is *commonality*. All members of the credit union must have some common bond, with the most frequent bond being place or means of employment. A physical location is frequently provided by the employer and much of the work is contributed by the employee members. It is also common practice for loans to be repaid through withholding from the borrower's pay, thereby minimizing collection problems. Credit unions have been exempt from taxes, with federal taxation of their income becoming effective in 1984. With minimal operating costs, no taxes, and limited collection problems, credit unions have been able to offer competitive interest rates on deposits yet still provide loans at rates below those available from other lenders. With these advantages, it is little wonder that their growth has been rapid.

---

[2]Negotiated Order of Withdrawal accounts. These essentially serve as checking accounts and are now included in the general heading "transaction accounts."

While the type of credit union described above still exists, another type has also evolved. This other type serves interest groups with many thousands of members, such as all people who are employed by educational institutions in a major city. In at least one case, residence in a particular state senatorial district has been used as the common bond. Credit unions of this type have offices resembling those of other depository institutions and rely on professional managers. Their cost structures are also more closely aligned with those of the other depository institutions.

Credit unions may be chartered by the state or federal government, with slightly over half of the charters presently being federal. Charters, supervision, examination, and deposit insurance are provided by the National Credit Union Administration. Depositors are protected by deposit insurance provided by the National Credit Union Association for up to $100,000 per account. Credit unions can borrow from the Federal Intermediate-Term Credit Bank.

As with other thrift institutions, credit unions take deposits from their members and make loans to them, investing liquid reserves and excess funds in other securities, primarily U.S. government obligations. Credit unions offer time and passbook savings accounts like the other thrift institutions. They also offer share draft accounts, which serve as checking accounts for members.

The credit unions differ sharply on the asset side. While they have authority to make mortgage loans, only about 3 percent of their assets are presently invested in mortgages, primarily because they generally lack the capital to make such loans. They concentrate on consumer loans, with automobile loans being the most common.

MANAGEMENT PRINCIPLES FOR THRIFT INSTITUTIONS

As with any other business, the financial management of a thrift institution involves a profitability/risk trade-off. Profitability is the primary motive for most business ventures and additional risk is frequently the cost of added profit. Like other businesses, the thrift institution faces various alternatives, each with different risk and return characteristics. The appropriate risk/return combination is both a management decision and a matter for regulatory control.

At first glance, there may be some question about the appropriateness of the profitability objective as there are seldom any stockholders to benefit from such profitability. However, as economists have long pointed out, competition forces all business in the direction of profitability maximization. In perfect competition, each business will operate in such a way as to minimize its cost per unit of output, and market competition will force the price to a level just sufficient to meet these lowest possible production costs plus a profit sufficient to attract the necessary capital. In perfect competition, individual firms cannot affect selling price. They can affect profitability only by minimizing unit production cost. In such an environment, only firms that maximize profitability will earn enough to continue producing.

Recent experience of thrift institutions has underscored the effectiveness of market forces in requiring profitability maximization. When general interest rates rose rapidly and the interest rates that financial institutions were allowed to pay on passbook deposits were not increased correspondingly, savers removed their funds from thrift institutions and invested them directly with purchases such as Treasury bills. When Treasury bills in denominations of less than $10,000 were eliminated to discourage disintermediation, money market mutual funds arose to serve the needs of small savers by offering each investor an interest in a large portfolio of money market instruments. Institutions then found themselves bidding in relatively free markets for funds held by the money market funds. Regulation was not very successful in protecting the thrift institutions from competitive forces.

Even the limited protection from competition provided by past legislation is being phased out with the 1980 Deregulation Act and subsequent legal and regulatory changes. In addition to broadening lending authority, the law phases out most limitations on interest rates paid and some limitations on interest rates charged by institutions, leaving the setting of these rates to market forces. With interest income and expense now being set by market forces, the profitability objective will become increasingly dominant for financial institutions.

Risk for the thrift institution arises from three sources. *Default risk* refers to the failure of borrowers to repay loans. Default losses on first mortgage loans must be held to very low levels because of the small margins traditionally existing between the cost of funds to thrift institutions and the interest rates on these loans. *Interest rate risk* arises from the fact that thrift institution loans are frequently for longer maturities than are their liabilities. Rising interest rates have forced thrift institutions to pay more for some deposits than is being earned on many of the older loans that are still on the institutions' books. With rising and fluctuating interest rates in recent years, interest rate risk has been greater than default risk. It permeates almost every aspect of thrift institution management. *Liquidity risk* also arises from the short-term nature of liabilities. While an industrial corporation may be a few days late with its payments and experience no substantial difficulties, a thrift institution would be seriously damaged if it were unable to meet withdrawal demands. The risk of being unable to meet withdrawal demand must be kept in mind when developing the asset structure.

Finally, the *service obligation* of a thrift institution creates another problem and set of trade-offs for management. Charters are not granted for the benefit of institution stockholders or managers. They are issued for the benefit of the community the institution is expected to serve. The supposed purpose of deposit interest rate regulations was not to insure a happy level of profitability, but to assure the safety of depositors' funds and to assure a steady supply of money to the housing industry. Laws such as the Community Reinvestment Act are aimed at assuring that thrift institutions meet their social responsibility as defined by legislators. Should a thrift institution pursue its own profitability within the constraints created by such laws? Or should it go beyond this and make its own judgments about the social objectives it should be striving for? These issues have been frequently debated but never settled. However, growing competition decreases the ability of institutions to make decisions on other than profitability grounds.

In pursuing its objectives, the thrift institution must answer five primary asset and liability management questions:

1. Which loans should be made?

2. What quantity and specific type of liquid reserves should be held?

3. What investment outlet(s) should be used for funds not committed to loans or liquid reserves?

4. What mix of liabilities should be used?

5. How much equity capital is needed?

While these various questions represent separate areas of management within the institution, the policy decisions are not made in isolation. For example, interest rate risk depends on the relative maturities of assets and liabilities. The investments chosen as outlets for idle funds should be considered in light of the asset/liability mix to decrease overall risk. These and other interrelationships must be considered in developing policy so that the sum of the management decisions in the various areas results in a harmonious whole. These interrelationships are stressed in the following discussion.

Loan Management

As indicated earlier, thrift institution lending is dominated by mortgage loans. Thrift institutions also dominate mortgage lending by financial institutions and are an important factor in mortgage lending overall (table 12-2). Consumer loans, the second important category, are discussed in detail in chapter 11 and are discussed here only in terms of the contribution to the risk/returns characteristics of the overall loan portfolio.

Table 12-2:

**The Mortgage Loan Market
(in $ millions, 1 Jan 1984)**

	Dollars	Percentage
Commercial banks	329,745	18.1
Mutual savings banks	133,325	7.3
Savings and loan companies	492,857	27.1
Life insurance companies	150,192	8.3
Federal agencies* (General)	144,890	8.0
Federally guaranteed mortgage pools*	285,666	15.7
Individuals and others	283,680	15.6
Total	1,820,445	100.0

*Government National Mortgage Association, Federal National Mortgage Association, Farmers Home Administration, Federal Home Loan Mortgage Administration, FHA and VA direct loans.

Source: *Federal Reserve Bulletin.*

Types of Mortgage Loans The most common mortgage loan made by a thrift institution is the *conventional mortgage.* Conventional mortgages involve no guarantee by a third party such as a public or private insurance agency. The institution relies on the credit worthiness of the borrower and on the value of the property. A 20 percent down payment is normally required, but loans for up to 95 percent of the value of the property are permitted by regulators if the amount over 80 percent is insured by a separate agency or is covered by a special reserve account. Loans for over 80 percent of property value frequently carry higher interest rates.

A typical conventional loan has traditionally involved a fixed-interest rate and equal monthly payments for a maturity of up to 40 years. However, there have been some recent changes—the so-called alternate mortgage instruments—aimed at dealing with current market conditions. The *graduated payment loan* is one such adaption, designed to help house buyers deal with the higher house payments associated with inflation and higher interest rates. With the graduated payment loan, the payments are smaller during the early years. Typically, interest only is paid during the early years, up to five years. Payments necessary to amortize the mortgage begin after this initial period.

The *adjustable rate mortgage* loan (ARM) is a type of conventional loan designed to protect the lender from problems caused by fluctuating interest rates. The lender can adjust the interest rate as frequently as once each month, with the rate tied to an agreed-upon index of market interest rates. The interest rate must be decreased if the index falls and the interest rate change can be accommodated by extending loan maturity, changing the payment, adjusting the principal loan balance through negative amortization, or some combination of these.

Variable rate mortgage arrangements do not eliminate interest rate risk; they simply pass it on to the borrowers. Even a two percentage point increase in the interest rate can result in a 20 percent increase in monthly payments. As long as short-term deposits are used as a source of funds for long-term loans, someone must bear the interest rate risk.

While indexing the mortgage rate has been widely heralded as the solution to the thrift institutions' interest rate risk problem, its future is still in doubt. In California, where state chartered institutions have been allowed to offer variable rate mortgages, the precursor to the adjustable rate mortgage, for some years, results have been mixed. A study of the California experience showed that variable rate mortgages peaked in 1976 with only 17 percent of California savings and loans offering variable rate mortgages and 46 percent of the mortgages granted by these institutions being variable rate. The use of variable rate mortgages in California declined from 1976 to 1978, when the study ended. One reason for the decline was that institutions were only willing to offer beginning interest rates approximately 0.25 percent lower for variable rate mortgages. Because this was not enough to encourage voluntary selection of a variable rate mortgage, variable rate mortgage borrowers tended to be lower income, lower down payment borrowers who had no alternative in a tight market.

If variable rate mortgages were to be issued to people other than poorer credit risks, and be issued when money was readily available, it was necessary that they be made attractive somehow.

Many institutions have responded to this challenge by offering adjustable rate mortgages at interest rates tied to an index of short-term interest rates. This might mean an initial interest rate of 2 percent or more below the fixed mortgage rates available in certain market conditions. Other institutions have offered adjustable rate loans with the initial rate 5 percent or more below rates on fixed rate loans, with the rate being raised each year until it parallels some index of market interest rates. This latter type of loan is designed to encourage first-time home buyers by keeping the initial payment low as well as to encourage the use of variable rate mortgages. The low interest rate in the first few years is offset by a subisdy by the home seller or by a high enough interest rate later to cover the early losses. These various incentives have achieved the desired result: between 30 and 40 percent of new mortgages in recent years have been adjustable rate. An unfortunate side effect is an unmeasured increase in default risk as borrowers face sharply increased monthly payments. This potential problem is particularly severe with the mortgages that carry initial interest rates deeply discounted from prevailing interest rates.

In addition to conventional first-mortgage loans, the thrift institutions also make second-mortgage loans. Second-mortgage loans are based on a claim to the property which is subordinate to a first-mortgage loan against that same property. These loans are used for purposes such as remodeling, educational expenses, and investment. They are normally of shorter maturity than first-mortgage loans, thereby reducing interest rate risk.

Besides conventional mortgages, thrift institutions also make Federal Housing Administration (FHA) and Veterans Administration (VA) insured loans. These loans are granted by private lenders, but are insured by the U.S. Government so that the lenders are protected in the event of default. The primary objective of these insurance programs was the provision of mortgage credit to those without sufficient funds to make the down payments required for traditional mortgage loans. These insurance programs made it possible to buy a house with a down payment of a few percent or less.

It turned out that the FHA and VA programs served two purposes in addition to direct aid to borrowers. Because these mortgages are insured with regard to default risk and are otherwise standardized, they are readily marketable. Thus, these insurance programs aided in the development of a secondary market for mortgages. These insurance programs also demonstrated that even people who made very small down payments were unlikely to default. As a result, private insurance plans also developed and lenders began making loans with down payments of 5 percent and 10 percent without FHA or VA insurance.

Credit Analysis Mortgage loans differ from other consumer lending in their long-term nature and in the narrow margins between interest rates paid on deposits and interest rates charged. Credit analysis is based on the standard three Cs of credit: character, capacity, and collateral. But the application of these factors is different primarily in that the focus must be long term and losses must be held to a very low rate.

Character analysis is little different than that for other loans. Past character is the best evidence concerning future character. The lender checks with the local credit bureau and other financial institutions with which the applicant has dealt to determine if other financial obligations have been treated seriously and honestly. It has been frequently argued that the mortgage payment is the last payment people will default on, while medical bills are about the first category to suffer. Whether these differences result from different senses of obligation or from the importance of protecting the home from foreclosure is not certain, but it is a factor to consider in character analysis. Therefore, special emphasis is placed on any past mortgage loan experience. Of course, it is illegal to consider matters such as sex, marital status, or race in any aspect of the loan analysis. Lenders may not extend their character analysis to pass moral judgment on such things as living arrangements. The character analysis must focus on the handling of financial responsibilities.

Capacity deals with the ability to meet loan payments. Standard policy for an institution may be that mortgage loan payments cannot exceed 25 percent of income, for example, or that total loan payments cannot exceed 35 percent of income. These policies are based on past experience with regard to default rates. In addition to present income, the stability of income in the future must also be considered. A past record of employment instability or employment in a profession suffering from frequent periods of high unemployment would be a negative factor even if present income were satisfactory. The equal credit opportunity act requires that sex not be considered in evaluating the stability of income and that alimony be considered as income. Questions about childbearing plans are not allowed in evaluating income stability.

Collateral takes on special importance with mortgage loans because it is difficult to forecast an individual's income over the long time periods involved. The loan decision involves both the appraised value (discussed below) and the loan-to-value ratio. Collateral provides protection if an individual's income declines, but the depression of the 1930s showed that it is of little help if everyone's income declines sharply. Experience with VA and FHA loans in the last 30 years has convinced lenders that they can safely lend 90 percent and even 95 percent of the face value. These loan-to-value ratios have not been tested in a depression, but 50 percent loan-to-value ratios provided no protection for the financial system in the 1930s.

The Credit Decision The loan decision is technically made by a loan committee made up of officers of the institution. However, efficiency and regulatory requirements make relatively standardized policy necessary. The loan committee does not have the time or expertise about individual cases to provide carefully considered judgments in each case. In addition, legislation such as the Community Reinvestment Act and the Equal Credit Opportunity Act require the credit policy be consistent and fair, not arbitrarily considering factors such as race, sex, or property location. In addition, institutions are required to give an answer if an individual inquires as to why his or her application was turned down. A general statement such as "our loan committee voted against it" is usually not adequate. If the institution has specific policy, it can make loan decisions efficiently and without illegal bias.

Institutions do not normally vary the interest rate by risk class, with the exception of variation by down payment size. This is a matter of tradition as well as a matter of regulation. Regulators discourage risk-taking by quickly downgrading delinquent loans and requiring extra capital to support them, thereby decreasing the ability to make further loans. In addition, it is illegal to quote different rates or terms based on race, sex, marital status, or property location. The institution can protect itself from inadvertently developing an illegal policy by quoting the same terms for all first-mortgage loans.

Market forces also discourage the offering of different rates for different risk classes. Because more than 90 percent of applicants are typically approved, higher rate, high-risk loans would have to come from this additional 10 percent. Many of these would not be acceptable credit risks at any additional rate they could possibly afford to pay. In addition, credit analysis is not so precise an art as to make risk classification precise, opening up problems of bias charges and general ill will. In competitive markets, these are costly problems.

Setting credit standards that are expected to result in low default rates has traditionally been a matter of judgment based on senior management's experience (and bias) as to what characteristics lead to default. Recently, this approach has been supplemented by statistical studies aimed at increasing the objectivity and accuracy of policy determination. The most widely used statistical approach is *discriminant analysis*. The analysis begins with loans that have been made in the past and classifies them as good or bad based on payment experience. For each of these loans, information is collected on a number of factors that are believed to be important in determining failure rates. Based on a statistical procedure beyond the scope of this discussion, but readily available on most computers, a *discriminant function* is developed. Rakes[3] developed the following discriminant function for a group of mortgage loans:

$$Z = 1.647 - 0.442I - 0.0398C + 0.218A$$
$$- 0.136E + 0.066W$$

where: I = Loan-to-income ratio

C = Number of unsatisfactory credit indications from previous creditors

A = 0 if the wife is as old as or older than the husband
1 if the husband is older than the wife

E = 0 if a borrower is classified as having stable employment
1 if a borrower is classified as having unstable employment

W = Wife's age

If the Z score is above 0.5, the loan is expected to be good and if the score is below 0.5, the loan is likely to be bad. This particular model was developed by testing a large number of variables, most of which did not turn out to be good predictors. The model should be taken as illustrative only since it was based on data from one city and is based only on applications from families. In addition, the two age variables might be considered unfair discrimination under present laws.

Statistical methods have the benefit of potential increases in accuracy and increased objectivity which increase the fairness and profitability of credit decisions. The fact that losses continue to occur is an indication of the limits of precision. Nobody can predict exactly who will lose their job, suffer ill health, etc. It is only possible to predict these things in terms of probabilities.

Appraisal Because collateral is important, and because houses are not standard units like stocks or bonds, an accurate estimate of property value is necessary. As loan-to-value ratios have risen, the accuracy of the appraisal has become increasingly important. The fact that most defaults occur early in the life of the mortgage increases the importance of accurate value estimation. The appraisal is normally performed by a professional appraiser who either works for the institution or works independently, performing appraisals for various institutions. There are various approaches to appraisal, depending on the situation.

Replacement cost is an approach that can be used with newer properties. If similar structures are being built, the replacement cost is both easily determined and relevant. The appraiser examines construction costs and land costs in the area, making adjustments for any particular features of the individual property. The replacement cost can also be adjusted for depreciation, if any. The approach is of little use in evaluating older homes, many of which are selling at fractions of their replacement costs.

Present value of benefits is an approach used primarily for income properties. Essentially, the appraiser estimates the useful life of the property, the rental income over that life, and the expenses that will be incurred. The value of the property then equals the present value of the benefits minus the present value of expenses.

Market value is the ultimate objective of all lender appraisals since the lender wants to estimate what the property could be sold for if the borrower were to default. With an older house, a direct market value appraisal is often the only method that can be used. The property is not expected to generate income and may be selling below its replacement cost because houses of its type are not being built any more. The appraiser begins by studying recent transactions in the area to determine the prices other properties have sold for. Adjustments are then made for differences between the particular property and others in the

---

[3]Ganas K. Rakes, "A Numerical Credit Evaluation Model for Residential Mortgages," *Quarterly Review of Economics and Business* (Autumn 1973): 73–84.

area. Price per square foot is an important part of this approach, with adjustments then being made for location and other features of the property. Needless to say, the skill and experience of the appraiser is very important in going from prices other properties have sold for to an estimate of the likely market value of the property under consideration.

Appraisers have frequently been accused of contributing to the decline of older neighborhoods by appraising property at less than a potential buyer is willing to pay, making it impossible to obtain a loan. Appraisers do consider the present condition of the neighborhood and apparent trends in property condition in preparing their estimates. Therefore, it is likely that a previously deteriorating neighborhood will find appraisals lagging behind redevelopment efforts. Critics of appraisal practices argue that property is worth what someone will pay for it, and therefore cannot be appraised at less than the currently agreed-to sale price. However, the lender is interested in the price the property could be sold for if the buyer should default.

Interest Charges Interest charges on mortgage loans are set in light of the institution's profitability objective. The limit on how much the institution can charge is set by competitive market forces. If the institution sets its interest charges on mortgage loans above those for competing institutions, it is likely to attract only those high default-risk borrowers who do not qualify for a loan at another institution. The lowest rate that could possibly be charged is determined by the cost of funds to the institution plus costs of processing, administering, and collecting loans. Again, competition causes these charges to be quite similar for institutions. The average cost of funds and interest rate charged by savings and loans illustrate the relatively stable relationship between the cost of funds and the interest rate charged (figure 12-1).

In addition to direct interest charges, points are a common requirement with mortgage loans, conventional or otherwise. Points are a form of initial service charge for granting a loan. Each point is 1 percent of the loan amount. Points raise the effective interest rate, especially if the loan is repaid early.[4] Thus they provide a means of assuring recovery of fixed costs when a loan is repaid soon after being granted. They also provide a means of raising the effective interest rate if there is some reason it cannot be raised directly. Points and service charges fluctuate from year to year. They presently average 3 percent, which, in effect, raises interest rates by 0.45 percent. Points and service charges are included in the loan interest rates in figure 12-1. Prepayment penalties of six months or more of interest may also be required if the loan is prepaid.[5]

Escrow payments provide both decreased risk and a bit of extra return. In addition to loan repayment, the borrower pays an amount each month equal to one twelfth of the estimated annual tax and insurance expense for the property. Escrow payments decrease risk by assuring that borrowers are saving money to pay insurance and taxes. Since interest is not normally paid on these funds, they provide interest-free deposits.

Mortgage Loan Risk An analysis of mortgage loan risk requires that a distinction be drawn between diversifiable and nondiversifiable risk. Because a life insurance company can accurately predict the number of deaths among a group of insured each year, benefit payments are an expense rather than a risk. The same thing could be said for mortgage loans if the loss rate were steady from year to year. The risk of default for an individual loan would simply be an expense for the portfolio of loans. Unfortunately, the chargeoff rate may be three times as high during a recession as during periods of economic expansion. The loss rates during normal times are a diversifiable risk and can be treated as an expense, but the fact that default rates vary with economic conditions cannot be diversified away within the conventional loan portfolio.

Other risks may be related to specific lending

---

[4]See chapter 6 for a detailed discussion of this relationship.

[5]Federal Home Loan Bank Board regulations prohibit prepayment penalties for adjustable mortgage loans (AMIs) made by member institutions.

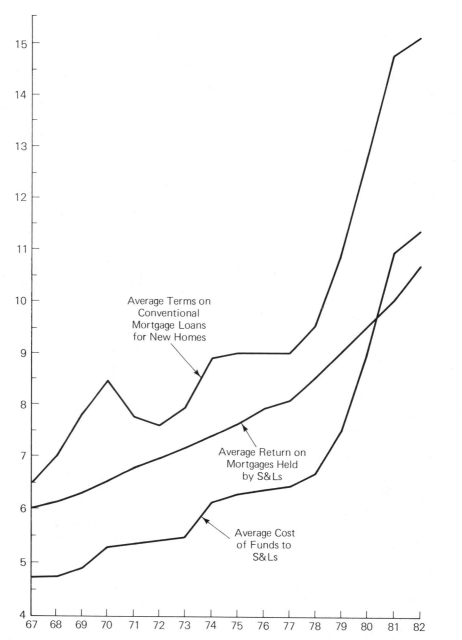

Figure 12–1: Average mortgage interest rates and S&L cost of funds. (Source: *Federal Home Loan Bank Board Journal.*)

areas. In the 1950s, some thrift institutions that were heavily committed to lending in the older parts of cities suffered large losses as those neighborhoods declined with migration to the suburbs. At other times, lenders have suffered losses because a factory or industry in their area suffered a decline. This happened in Cape Canaveral with one phasing down of the space program. This type of risk can be at least partially diversified away by investing some funds in non-mortgage loans and by investing in mortgages over a broader lending area.

As indicated earlier, interest-rate risk is another type of risk that is of particular importance to thrift institutions. In the 1950s and early 1960s, thrift institutions received most of their funds in the form of short-term passbook deposits and loaned an increasing proportion of these deposits in the form of long-term mortgage loans. During this period, the yield curve generally had a "normal" shape: short-term rates were below long-term rates. The institutions earned steady profits by taking deposits at the short-term rates and making loans at the higher long-term rates. Beginning in the mid 1960s, a period of rising and volatile interest rates developed and the nation experienced many periods in which short-term rates were higher than long-term rates. To keep deposits, the institutions found it necessary to pay interest rates which were, at times, more than double the interest rates on older loans. If the older loans were sold to meet withdrawal demand, they could only be sold at substantial discounts from their face values. The value of an outstanding mortgage loan can easily decline by 30 percent or more if the general level of interest rates rises (figure 12-2).

This type of risk cannot be eliminated through diversification since a rising interest rate affects all outstanding fixed-interest rate loans in the same general manner. However, it can be evaluated using gap analysis and controlled through adjustable rate loans, diversifying into other types of loans (with shorter maturities), bidding for deposits with longer maturities, and the use of financial futures contracts.

While wishing to maximize profitability, the

Figure 12–2: Percentage decrease in the value of a 10 percent mortgage loan with various required rates of return.

thrift institution also desires to minimize risk. This can be partially achieved by eliminating diversifiable risk through diversification. However, interest-rate risk and non diversifiable default risk remain problems that are dealt with at least partially through a profitability/risk trade-off.

Mortgage Loan Documents   Once it has been decided that the risk and costs associated with a mortgage loan are low enough to make the loan profitable at the interest rate that can be charged, the necessary documents must be prepared.

The lender is first concerned with the title to the property, wishing to be sure that the borrower has a clear title. This is normally provided by a title company which searches the records at the county recorder's office for liens or other claims and provides a certificate of insurance against any undiscovered claims. Of course, the new mortgage must also be filed in the recorder's office if the lender's claim is to be protected.

The borrower's debt is represented by a simple promissory note indicating the amount owed, interest, and repayment schedule. The note also makes reference to the mortgage. The mortgage is essentially a transfer of title to the lender with the provision that the transfer is voided if the borrower repays the loan and interest as called for in the note. Court decisions have interpreted the mortgage as only giving the lender the right to satisfy his claim through sale of the property. Any excess over the debt and reasonable expenses must be returned to the borrower.

Consumer Loans Except for credit unions, thrift institutions have had little experience with consumer loans. However, the Deregulation Act and subsequent legal and regulatory changes have given them expanded authority. The authority to make consumer loans makes the profitability/risk aspects of these loans of interest.

There seems to be a general misperception that consumer loans are much more profitable than mortgage loans because their face interest rates have been higher. However, analysis of the profitability of consumer finance companies does not bear this out. The higher interest rates charged are offset by higher loan origination and servicing costs plus higher default rates. Profits end up being similar to those of other financial institutions.

However, consumer loans have an attraction other than high profitability. If they provide profits as high as those of mortgage loans, they can be useful as a source of risk reduction. First, they may provide some limited diversification with regard to default risk. Though mortgage and consumer loans both suffer default rates during economic downturns, consumer loans provide some diversification from risk associated with the value of real property in a specific lending area. This diversification is, however, likely to be limited by the fact that many consumer loans are made to existing mortgage customers. Consumer loans may also provide some diversification in times when demand for real estate loans is limited. However, consumer loan and mortgage loan demand tend to be correlated, again limiting the diversification advantage.

The major contribution of consumer loans to risk reduction is not from diversification, but from reducing the interest rate gap. The average maturities of consumer loans are a fraction of those of mortgage loans. These shorter maturities can reduce the average maturity of the loan portfolio, matching it more closely to the maturity of the institution's liabilities. Consumer loans may prove to be an important source of interest rate risk reduction.

Investment Portfolio Management

A depository institution faces the expenses associated with having an office facility readily accessible to the public. One way of recovering these expenses is by making direct loans at rates above what could be earned by investing in securities. A depository institution simply could not earn enough to survive by taking deposits and investing only in securities. However, depository institutions do place part of their funds in securities for a number of reasons. First, institutions hold securities as a source of liquidity because they can be sold quickly if cash is needed to meet withdrawal demand. Institutions may also hold securities as a means of decreasing interest rate risk or default risk. Finally, institutions invest in securities when they do not have sufficient loan demand for all their funds. The excess is invested in securities until needed.

Recent changes in authorization to hold securities other than U.S. government securities have increased the usefulness of the investment portfolio as a source of diversification. Unfortunately, the fact that all credit losses vary with the business cycle tends to limit diversification to specific risks associated with real estate values in limited geographic areas. Like consumer loans, securities make their greatest contribution to risk reduction by reducing the average maturity of the institution's assets, thereby decreasing interest rate risk. Since interest rates on short-term assets are lower than those for longer maturities during most time periods, the shorter maturities and associated decreases in interest risk come at the expense of lower returns. The thrift institution that does not recognize this when short-term rates are low will find these securities of no help in dealing with interest rate risk.

Liquidity Reserves

The liquidity needs of thrift institutions have traditionally been less than those of commercial banks because their deposit levels have been more stable. However, that situation will bear close watching in the years ahead. Transaction account services, into which thrift institutions are expanding, normally represent unstable account balances. In addition, depositors are showing increasing willingness to move their funds in response to a small change in interest rates.

The thrift institutions have constant inflows from loan repayments and interest payments. Likewise they have constant, predictable outflows in the form of expenses and interest on deposits. They also have less predictable cash flows in the form of loan demand and net deposit flows (deposits less withdrawals). Since the institution can reject all loan applications if it lacks funds, these may not seem like a source of unexpected liquidity demand. However, institutions prefer to meet loan demand in their area when possible. Failure to meet loan demand will detract from their present ability to attract deposits and their future ability to attract loan applications. A net outflow of deposits represents a higher priority liquidity demand. Failure to respond instantly to any withdrawal demand would seriously jeopardize the institution's ability to attract funds.

Liquidity needs can be set by ratio standards, such as a certain percentage of total deposits or certain percentages of each type of deposit. However, this type of approach does not really capture the cash flows experienced by an institution. A cumulative cash flow chart, as illustrated in figure 12-2 is a more useful approach. Past experience as illustrated in the chart can be modified by adjusting for changes in the asset and liability structure. For example, daily cash inflow will be greater if the institution has changed its loan mix to reduce the average maturity.

Likewise, outflow can be reduced through a change in the mix of deposits, with increases in long-term deposits leading to decreased outflows and increases in transaction accounts to increased potential outflows. Increased liquidity reserves invested at low interest rates are one of the costs of short-term deposits. Net deposit

flows of savings and loans (figure 12-3) give an illustration of the cash flow effects of various economic conditions. With their asset and liability mix undergoing rapid change, the thrift institutions will need to reexamine their cash flow assumptions carefully in the years ahead.

When the thrift institution faces a demand for liquidity, it can sell securities. The first act would normally be to sell short-term securities as these can be sold at or near their face value. Longer-term securities can also be sold, but they will be sold at a loss if interest rates have risen since they were purchased. The institution can also bid for extra funds by raising the interest rates on deposits. The institutions can also borrow money from their respective federal credit sources—e.g., the Federal Home Loan Bank— and from the Federal Reserve System. The institutions can also sell loans. FHA and VA loans have traditionally been the most salable because they are guaranteed and standardized. However, the Federal Home Loan Mortgage Corporation is increasingly moving into the purchase of conventional loans.

Regulatory liquidity requirements are probably of more importance for monetary policy and system liquidity than for the liquidity of the individual institution. They are based on relatively simplistic ratio approaches.

Liability Management

In the last three decades, liability management at thrift institutions has undergone two revolutions and is in the midst of the third. In the 1950s and early 1960s, interest rates remained relatively steady and rate ceilings on deposits were not significantly below market rates, if at all. Thrift institutions profited from the yield curve by paying the market rate for passbook savings accounts and loaning these funds to purchasers of residential real estate at the higher long-term rates.

Beginning in the mid 1960s, the environment changed in five important ways:

1. Interest rates began an upward trend.

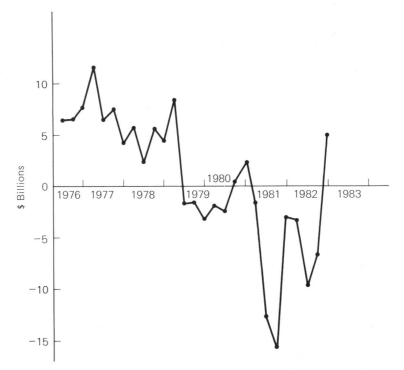

Figure 12–3: Net new retail savings flows at insured savings and loans. (Source: *1983 Savings and Loan Sourcebook.*)

2. Because interest rate ceilings were not increased correspondingly, the rate paid on deposits became fixed by regulation rather than determined by market forces.

3. Free market interest rates fluctuated substantially from year to year.

4. In the absence of ability to compete for funds, the thrift institutions experienced erratic deposit flows.

5. There were many periods in which short-term interest rates rose above long-term rates.

These changes caused frequent periods of sharp savings outflows and sometimes pushed the cost of funds above the interest rates on loans still outstanding. It was a major change in the liability management environment from a stable, free market to an administered, erratic market.

Following the change in market stability, a revolution in liability maturity developed. The thrift institutions and commercial banks asked for and received authorization to offer large denomination and long-term certificates of deposit at higher interest rates to allow them to compete for funds. While rate ceilings for these accounts existed, these ceilings reached levels almost triple those for passbook accounts. Certificates of deposit for more than $100,000 carried no interest rate ceilings at all. The differences in interest rate ceilings resulted in major changes in the liability structure of thrift institutions. For example, passbook accounts, which accounted for 90 percent of savings and loan deposits until the mid 1960s, accounted for less than 20 percent in 1980. Savers have moved their funds to the longer-term deposits or to money market funds which can pool funds and purchase the $100,000 certificates of deposit without interest rate restrictions.

With the phasing in of the Deregulation and

the Garn—St Germain Act, a third revolution in liability management is nearly complete. With the removal of most interest rate restrictions, thrift institutions are free to bid for funds over the full yield curve. This presents major new challenges and opportunities in the area of liability management.

The new laws give thrift institutions the opportunity to integrate asset and liability management to a greater extent. With a complete yield curve available, the thrift institution can bid for funds of any maturity and price loans of each maturity in relation to the cost of funds of that maturity. The thrift institution can act as a financial intermediary, offering the borrower the full range of maturities and rates available in the financial markets. For example, savings and loans are increasingly offering fixed rate mortgages at the cost of long-term money and variable rate mortgages at the rate presently charged for short-term funds. The borrower can decide whether to pay the long-term rate or pay the short-term rate and take the risk of rates rising later.

Active liability management, use of adjustable rate mortgages, diversification of loan portfolios, and the use of financial futures have allowed thrift institutions to combine asset and liability management to control risk. However, two problems remain. First of all, many institutions are still saddled with old mortgages made at lower interest rates. These loans will continue to be a burden for some years. Second, accomodation of the maturity needs of both borrowers and savers is one of the important services provided by financial institutions. If the thrift institutions do not provide this service, they will face great difficulty in attracting customers. Therefore, management of interest-rate risk rather than the total elimination of risk is the challenge facing thrift institution managers.

Capital

Determining the amount of capital needed and the method of acquiring it is an especially difficult problem for most thrift institutions. Nonfinancial corporations that raise both debt and equity capital in relatively unrestricted markets can observe the market's response to changes in their proportions of debt and equity. Most thrift institutions have no stock, so there is no equity market to observe. Since deposits are insured, it is difficult to observe the debt market's reaction to risk. Thrift institution managers rely on their own judgment and on regulatory requirements.

As in any other business, capital serves to protect creditors in the event of shrinkage in asset value. Shrinkage can derive from loan defaults, interest rate risk, fraud and mismanagement, or declining volume of business in the institution's market area. Since most deposits are insured, the primary losers from any such shrinkage would be the deposit insuring agencies.

The question of the appropriate amount of capital is not different in concept than that of the appropriate quantity of liquidity reserves. Just as the liquid assets serve in periods in which cash outflow exceeds cash inflow, capital serves in periods in which expenses (and asset value shrinkage) exceed income. The two key factors that are watched in this regard are loan losses over the business cycle and interest rate risk exposure.

Historically, the profits of thrift institutions have averaged approximately 0.5 percent of assets. A relatively small change in loan defaults such as that which routinely occurs at the bottom of the business cycle can quickly turn profit to loss. By estimating the worst loss rate that might occur during a business downturn, the necessary cushion for loan default can be estimated. Loan default rates rarely exceed 1 percent for thrift institutions, with losses being a small fraction of defaulted amounts. Thus a relatively small equity capital base would protect against defaults.

Interest rate risk holds the potential for larger losses. This, coupled with the fact that interest rate risk and default risk are not positively correlated causes interest rate risk to be the dominant factor. As shown in figure 12-2, the percent shrinkage in asset value with a rise in the general level of interest rates can be substantial. Suppose a thrift institution has 80 percent of its assets in loans and the rest in short-term investments. All but 20 percent of the loans for this institution are offset by equity or liabilities of a maturity similar to that of the loan. The remaining 20 percent of loans—16 percent of assets—has an average maturity of 20 years. As figure 12-2 shows, a 5 percent rise in interest rates would cause a 26.7 percent decline in the value of these loans. This would be a 4.3 percent (0.16 × 0.267) decline in total asset value. Obviously, the percent of assets not covered by maturity hedging and their average maturities has a major impact on the equity capital needed.

While the institution may develop its own estimates of its capital needs based on measurements of its own potential asset shrinkage, the regulatory authorities make their determinations based on ratio analysis.

Once the amount of equity capital needed has been determined, the method of raising it must be decided. This is particularly troublesome since most thrift institutions cannot sell equity capital. Presently, the primary source of capital is retention of profits. However, rapid growth in recent years has eroded the ability of thrift institutions to create adequate capital through this source. If an institution earns 0.5 percent on assets and wishes to maintain equity equal to 5

percent of assets, it can grow at only 10 percent per year. If no other source is available, the institution would then need to limit growth to this rate. For savings and loans, another approach is to convert to stock form and sell additional equity. It is not coincidental that conversions have been most frequent in areas experiencing rapid growth. A final approach would be the issuance of capital notes. However, thrift institutions are not authorized to offer such notes at present.

DETERMINANTS OF PROFITABILITY

The profitability of a thrift institution comes from two main sources: spread and the ratio of operating expenses to total assets. The spread is simply the difference between the average interest earned (as a percent of assets) and the average cost of funds. Other factors affecting profitability are the ratio of other income to total assets, the tax rate, and the ratio of net worth to total assets. The relationships among the major factors affecting profitability are captured in figure 12-4.

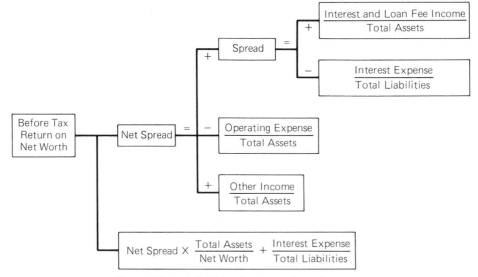

Figure 12–4: A thrift institution profitability system.

Other income tends to be minor, and regulatory considerations frequently govern financial leverage. Thus, spread and the operating expense ratio are controllable by the institution. Operating expense control depends on careful use of people, automation, branch locations, promotional activities, etc. Spread depends on interest income and interest expense.

Because higher interest is normally earned on loans than on investments, a high loan-to-total-asset ratio generally helps the spread. Minimizing assets that do not earn interest also improves the spread. On the other side of the balance sheet, deposits generally cost less than borrowed funds. Therefore, a high deposit-to-total-liability ratio generally improves the spread.

A major factor leading to decreased spread in recent years is the mismatch between maturities of assets and liabilities. With interest rates rising and deposits coming up for renewal while low-interest rate loans remained outstanding, many otherwise well-managed thrifts have found the spreads declining and even turning negative. Thus, it is now clear that maturity management, using tools like gap analysis, is an important part of spread management.

SUMMARY

Historically the thrift institutions have specialized in taking passbook deposits and making loans: real estate loans for savings banks and savings and loans and consumer loans for credit unions. However, the deposit mix has increased to include transaction accounts and time deposits. Recent legislation expanding the lending authority of savings and loans gives most thrift institutions the authority to serve all of the typical family's deposit and lending needs. These traditional limited scope depository institutions are undergoing transition to complete family financial centers.

Like all financial institutions, the thrift institutions are regulated. The regulatory agencies for the various thrift institutions are as follows:

1. Savings and loans: Federal Home Loan Bank Board

2. Credit unions: National Credit Union Administration

3. Savings banks: Various state authorities

However, the Federal Reserve System is taking over the setting of reserve requirements. Regulation has concentrated on assuring safety of depositors' funds by requiring certain liquid asset and equity capital ratios. In addition, safety has been pursued through regulation of the interest rates depository institutions could pay. However, these interest rate regulations are in the last stages of a phase out.

Like all businesses, the thrift institutions seek to maximize profitability. This can be achieved by minimizing the cost of funds, maximizing return on assets, and maximizing operating efficiency. Unfortunately, increased asset return frequently results in increased default risk. Increasing the spread between asset return and funds cost frequently requires the acceptance of interest rate risk and liquidity risk. These risk-return trade-offs are a major factor in thrift institution management.

QUESTIONS

1. Find the most recent asset and liability structures for thrift institutions in the *Federal Reserve Bulletin*. Have the proportions changed since the 1984 data reported in table 12-1? If so, what do you think has caused these changes?

2. What are the major differences in financial structure between savings and loans and savings banks? What has caused these differences?

3. Visit a thrift institution in your area and ask for a copy of its balance sheet. Compare its asset and liability proportions to those shown in table 12-1. How do you account for the differences? Go back to the institution and inquire if necessary.

4. If you were a depositor at a savings bank and were unhappy with some management decision, what could you do? What

would be your most likely reaction if you were unhappy with the management of a savings and loan at which you had an account?

5. We noted that the cost of funds differed moderately between different savings and loans. Is this evidence that competition is working to effectively control rates paid on deposits, or evidence of an absence of competition?

6. Why did the government want to regulate the interest rates paid on deposits, and why has the effort to regulate these rates been abandoned?

7. Describe the types of risk faced by a thrift institution.

8. Do you feel that a thrift institution has a service obligation beyond things specifically required by law? Why? If your answer is yes, what obligations do the thrift institutions have?

9. It was once believed that a down payment of up to 50 percent was needed for a mortgage loan. Now thrift institutions are willing to make mortgage loans for up to 95 percent of appraised value. How do you account for this change in attitude?

10. Explain the difference between graduated payment and adjustable rate loans.

11. Describe the three methods of appraisal. Which method is most important for existing single-family housing?

12. What courses of action are available to a thrift institution wishing to reduce interest rate risk?

PROBLEMS

1. A 9 percent, twenty-year loan with annual payments carries a service charge of 3 points. If the loan is repaid after the second annual payment, what is the effective interest rate? (see table 6-9 and the discussion on page 88 for a methodology in computing unpaid principal balance for installment loans).

2. A 7 percent thirty-year loan for $50,000 was made ten years ago. The loan called for equal monthly payments. How much is still owed today? If the current interest rate level for this type of loan is 12 percent, what could this loan be sold for? What is the percentage decrease from face value?

3. The financial statements of Arco Savings and Loan appear below. Use the profitability system in figure 12-4 to determine whether profitability has increased or decreased, and why.

Year	1980	1981
Interest income	$12,286	$14,559
Interest expense	8,976	11,118
Operating expense	1,869	2,120
Other income	−7	32
Earnings before tax	1,434	1,353
Tax	656	568
Net income	778	785
Loans	$117,650	$129,855
Other assets	25,043	28,370
Total assets	$142,693	$158,225
Deposits	$124,199	$134,887
Borrowed funds	10,489	14,351
Net worth	8,005	8,987
Tot. liabilities & NW	$142,693	$158,225

SELECTED REFERENCES

Dann, Larry Y. and James, Christopher M. "An Analysis of the Impact of Deposit Rate Ceilings on the Market Value of Thrift Institutions." *The Journal of Finance* 37 (December 1982): 1279–1275.

Deshmuck, Sudhaker D., Greenbaum, Stuart I. and Thakor, Anjan. "Capital Accumulation and Deposit Pricing in Mutual Financial Institutions." *Journal of Financial and Quantitative Analysis* 17 (December 1982): 705–725.

Dunham, Constance. "Thrift Institutions and Commercial Bank Mergers." *New England Economic Review.* (November/December 1982): 45–62.

Gould, Julius. "The Merging of the Savings and Loan Industry." *Federal Home Loan Bank Board Journal* 16 (January 1984): 6–13

Mills, Dixie, and Suggs, Guerry A. "Developing a Commercial Lending Strategy: Key Issues for Savings Institutions." *Federal Home Loan Bank Board Journal* 16 (May/June 1983): 26–31.

Murray, John D., and White, Robert W. "Economies of Scale and Economies of Scope in Multi Product Financial Institutions: a Study of British Columbia Credit Unions." *The Journal of Finance* 38 (June 1983): 887–902.

Puglisi, Donald J., and McKenzie, Joseph A. "Capital Market Strategy for Thrift Institutions." *Federal Home Loan Board Journal* 16 (November 1983): 2–11.

Smith, Donald J.; Cargill, Thomas F.; and Meyer Robert A. "An Economic Theory of a Credit Union." *The Journal of Finance* 36 (May 1981): 519–528.

Smith, Gary, and Brainard, William. "A Disequilibrium Model of Savings and Loan Associations." *The Journal of Finance* 37 (December 1982): 1276–1293.

Walker, David A. "Effects of Deregulation on the Savings and Loan Industry." *The Financial Review* 18 (February 1983): 94–110.

Winger, Alan R. "On the Importance of Functional Cost Data to Thrift Institutions." *Federal Home Loan Bank Board Journal* 16 (December 1983): 4–7.

Chapter 13

Insurance Company Management

The primary business of insurance companies is the elimination of certain financial risks for individuals. Most events insured against occur to a stable, predictable percentage of a certain population group on a regular basis. The events may represent risk for individuals, but they are a predictable expense for the population as a whole. The insurance company serves by converting the individual's risk to an individual expense. The premiums it charges those who choose to be insured are sufficient to pay benefits to that proportion of the insured group that suffers the loss insured against.

In addition to the insurance function, many insurance companies also serve a financial intermediary function. A whole life insurance policy is an important example of this function. Since the whole life policy normally remains in force until death and pays a benefit at death, the eventual payment for each insured person is a certainty. The only real insurance provided is against the financial loss associated with premature death. Thus the policy serves as both an insurance against premature death and a savings program. In this provision of a savings program, the insurance company acts as a financial intermediary, accepting and reinvesting savings.

Because of these dual roles, there are two distinct management areas in an insurance company. The insurance function is typically the most visible and employs the greatest number of persons. It involves the retail sale of insurance as well as the determination of the probabilities of certain events, payment of claims, and the recording of the millions of transactions involved. The other aspect of management deals with equally large sums of money, but is less visible and requires fewer employees. This is the management of the nearly $900 billion in assets, which place insurance companies above savings and loans in total asset size.

Like all financial institutions, insurance companies are dealing with deregulation and changing markets. In response, they have expanded services to compete with other institutions, innovated the design of insurance products, and changed their marketing methods. Thus, they are full participants in the financial services revolution.

SCOPE OF THE INSURANCE BUSINESS

Insurance Concepts

Diversifiability is the essential concept underlying most insurance activity. Death may result in financial hardship to a family. Since no one knows if he or she will die in the next year, the family faces financial risk. This risk can be eliminated through a type of group diversification. For example, one could get together with a group of other people of the same age and agree that each will contribute to a pool with the funds being divided among the dependents of those who do die during the year. Under normal conditions, the percentage of a particular age group that dies during a year remains quite stable (unless, for example, the cooperating group were all serving on the same battleship in wartime). Therefore, one could predict the amount his or her dependents would receive in the event of death, and the individual risk would be converted to an expense.

In earlier times, associations such as burial societies did collect funds from their members and redistribute the funds like an insurance company. However, this service is now provided primarily by insurance companies who estimate the percentage of the population that will suffer some particular financial loss. They then sell policies to individuals. An appropriate price is set that will insure benefits to those who suffer the loss, cover operating expenses, and provide a reasonable profit.

While diversification is the key to most insurance, we should note that there are insurance policies written in cases where the risk is not really diversifiable. Lloyds of London frequently provides insurance in cases in which there may not be enough people facing the risk to provide diversification. Wealthy individuals simply place large amounts of capital at risk, betting on such things as the possibility of rain in Sikeston on the day of the Bootheel rodeo. However, this is a relatively small part of the total insurance picture. Even Lloyds does most of its business in the more mundane field of marine insurance. Earthquakes and floods represent more important areas in which diversification is difficult to achieve. Frequently the participation of government has been necessary in order to provide insurance in such cases.

As do all companies, the insurance companies wish to maximize return and minimize risk. Income comes from premiums and from return on the investment portfolio. The insurance company's risk is not that of an individual claim; this is a programmed expense. The primary risks arise from possible loss in investment portfolio value and the possibility that the company's estimates of total claim payments for the population insured are too low. If their estimates of the dollar claims paid out are wrong, the insurance companies can suffer large losses. For example, a particularly severe winter combined with a rapid inflation of health costs can cause a health insurance company to experience more claims than predicted and a higher dollar cost per claim. Since rising interest rates have caused the value of some outstanding stock and bond issues to decline in value 50 percent or more, the risk of portfolio value loss is also great.

Types of Insurance Companies

Insurance companies can be classified according to the type of insurance provided. Some insurance companies specialize while others are willing to insure life, health, home, automobile, and business. Multiple offerings are frequently handled through wholly owned subsidiaries. For example, Prudential Insurance Company sells life insurance; its subsidiary Prudential Property and Casualty Company sells property and liability insurance.

Insurance companies can also be classified according to how they market their services. Some companies serve only a special group and promote their services only to members of that group. Teachers' Insurance and Annuity Association is one such example of this. Other companies have a group of agents that sell only insurance offered by them. Still other companies market their insurance through general agencies that sell their insurance plus that offered by other companies. This latter approach is particularly common for companies that do not offer a full range of insurance. A growing amount of insurance is sold through group sales, particularly to groups of employees. Some group sales are handled by agents and some are handled by employees of the insurance company involved. Group sales lower the sales cost per insurance dollar and create the opportunity to price insurance according to the characteristics of a particular group rather than the general population.

Insurance companies can also be classified according to type of ownership. A *stock insurance company* is formed like most other corporations. Common stock is sold to investors who risk the loss of all or part of their investment if the insurance company does not profit, and enjoy the benefits of higher returns if the company does profit.

Mutual insurance companies have no stockholders and are owned by the policy holders. They typically charge a higher premium than a stock company to provide a cushion for larger than expected losses, but then pay a dividend each year based on the actual loss experience for that year. Since the policy holders accept the risk of greater than expected loss experience in this manner, they enjoy lower insurance costs when loss experiences are favorable. In the life insurance field, where mutual insurance companies are most important, 93 percent of the companies are stock companies, but 43 percent of the face value of policies and 57 percent of the assets are held by mutual companies.

Types of Insurance

Insurance business can be divided into three broad categories: life insurance, property and liability insurance, and health and disability insurance.

A comparison of the relative importance of these types of insurance can be made in terms of assets held or premiums received (figure 13-1). Life insurance dominates in terms of assets held because life insurance business involves receipt of premiums during one year with payments from those premiums to occur many years in the future. Many other types of insurance involve collection of premiums during a year and payment of claims from those premiums during the same year.[1] A look at premiums received yields a different picture. Life insurance premiums are far less than those for property and liability insurance.

Life Insurance. Life insurance policies can be broken down according to the method by which they were sold. The categories are

> *Ordinary:* Life insurance sold to an individual by an agent or employee of the life insurance company, with premiums normally being paid by mail monthly, quarterly, semi-annually, or annually.

---

[1]Assets of health insurance companies are not reported separately because health insurance is written by life insurance companies and property and liability companies as well as by separate companies.

Figure 13–1: Selected financial data for life and nonlife insurance companies. (Source: *Statistical Abstract of the United States.* Health insurance data excludes Blue Cross–Blue Shield and certain other plans.)

Group: Life insurance sold to cover all members of some group. The most common group would be all employees of a firm, who receive the insurance as a fringe benefit. The group policy may still give some options to individual members of the group.

Credit: Life insurance sold in connection with a loan. The policy is normally for the amount of the loan and is normally marketed to borrowers by lenders. The lender may or may not own a captive insurance company for the purpose of selling these policies.

Industrial: Insurance sold in small amounts to relatively low income buyers. Collection of premiums is normally on a weekly basis with the agent calling on the insured rather than relying on them to mail in premiums.

As shown in the last column of table 13-1, ordinary and group sales together accounted for 96 percent of all life insurance in force in 1982. Group sales represented the fastest growing sales category and industrial insurance sales declined over the time period considered in table 13-1.

Probably more important than method of sale, life insurance differs in type of coverage and pattern of payment. *Whole life* insurance is expected to remain in force for the life of the insured and pay the contracted-for benefit upon death. *Straight life,* which represents nearly 80 percent of the whole life insurance in force, re-

quires payment each period (year, quarter, and so on) until death.

Limited pay life requires payment for a certain number of years and then continues to provide coverage until the insured dies and benefits are paid. Of course, premiums are higher for limited pay life than for straight life.

Since benefits are paid at eventual death, the payment of benefits from these policies is a certainty unless the policy is cancelled. In the early years of the policy, when very few people in the age group are dying, most of the premiums must be invested to provide funds to pay claims as the insured people get older and the death rate for that group increases. Total lifetime premiums are frequently less than death benefits because the life insurance company has the premiums to invest for most of a century. Most of these policies have cash values based on these savings that are being built up. The insured member can normally either cancel the policy and receive the cash value or borrow against the cash value and keep the insurance in force, with any amount borrowed being deducted from the benefit in the event the insured person dies while the loan is outstanding. Many people who purchase such policies keep them in force until retirement, when their dependents no longer need protection from the financial loss of their death, and then cash them in. Thus these policies serve as both insurance programs and savings programs. From

Table 13-1:

Growth of Life Insurance in Force
(in $ billions)

	Whole Life		Endowment		Term		Total		
	1974	*1981*	*1974*	*1981*	*1974*	*1981*	*1974*	*1981*	*1982*
Ordinary	654.0	1,166.0	43.0	52.0	312.0	760.1	1,009.0	1,978.1	2,216.4
Group	6.6	8.9	0.1	0.1	820.9	1,879.4	827.6	1,888.4	2,066.4
Industrial	33.1	29.0	2.9	2.0	3.4	3.5	39.4	34.5	32.8
Credit	—	—	—	—	109.6	162.4	109.6	162.4	161.1
Total	693.7	1,203.9	46.0	54.1	1,245.9	2,805.4	1,985.6	4,063.4	4,476.7

Source: *Life Insurance Fact Book.*

the other side, these policies put the insurance company in the position of acting as a financial intermediary, accepting funds that it must return to the insured persons at some later date and investing these funds to earn a profit in the meantime.

Endowment policies also put the insurance company in the position of acting as a financial intermediary. An endowment policy pays the insured a specific amount at a specified future date. If the insured dies before this date, the same amount is still paid. These policies are frequently sold as a combined savings program to help sons and daughters with their education and insurance programs to guarantee that funds for education will be there in the event the parent dies before the children reach college age.

Term policies are pure insurance. If the premium is paid on a term policy and the insured does not die during the year, there is no cash value, although the policy may frequently be extended simply through payment of another premium. In brief, term insurance is similar to automobile, health, and home insurance in that the only benefit received is insurance against certain risks over the period covered by the premium.

From the buyer's point of view, term and whole life insurance can be compared by subtracting the cost of term insurance from the cost of whole life insurance to determine the amount effectively being placed in a savings plan. The cash value at the time the policy will likely be cashed in can be compared to the effective savings plan contributions embedded in the whole life premium and the rate of return earned on the savings plan can be measured. One insurance company, for example, quotes the following first-year premiums for a $100,000 life policy, for a twenty-two year old person.

Insurance Type	First-Year Premium
Whole life	$532
5-year renewable level term	134
20-year decreasing term	83

If an individual buys the whole life policy and dies after ten years, the person's dependents re-

ceive $100,000. If the same individual buys term insurance and invests the difference between the whole life and term premium each year, the insured's beneficiaries may then be entitled to receive both the insurance and the value of the investment. Therefore, the insurance portion of whole life may be viewed as decreasing term insurance covering the difference between $100,000 and the accumulated cash (savings) value of the policy. For this reason, whole life can be compared to decreasing term; of the $532 premium for whole life insurance, $449 ($532 − $83) is actually a contribution to a savings plan. Using table A-3, one notes, for example, that $449 invested each year for thirty years at 10 percent would grow to $73,858. ($449 × 164.494). This can be compared to the cash value of the whole life policy after thirty years to determine whether the whole life policy pays an effective interest rate of more or less than 10 percent.

The move toward term insurance meant that life insurance companies were losing one of their products; instead of selling insurance and savings programs, they were selling only insurance. Furthermore, the growth of group sales meant a declining market share for companies geared toward individual sales which require a more expensive marketing effort. The insurance industry has responded to these problems by developing two new products: variable life and universal life.

Variable Life Insurance   Variable life insurance, introduced in the United States in 1971, addresses one of the competitive disadvantages of whole life insurance. The life insurance company needs to guarantee certain cash values to the insured and cannot count on interest rates remaining high. Therefore, the life insurance company must assume a low return on invested funds in designing its policies. This means that in periods of high-interest rates the implied return on a whole life policy is well below that available on other investments. The variable life insurance policy is a variation on whole life insurance that addresses this problem by allowing the insured to participate in both risk and return.

Like whole life insurance, the variable life insurance policy has premiums based on a conservative return assumption such as 4 or 5 percent. As with whole life, the insured's annual premium, after the cost of administration and the mortality cost (approximately equal to the cost of one-year term insurance) is invested. At the end of each year, any excess return over the low, assumed return is used to purchase additional paid up whole life insurance. Consequently, the amount of insurance depends on the return earned by the company on invested funds.

From the buyer's point of view, the problem with variable life is that it seldom fits insurance needs. The returns earned by the insurance company's investments are primarily dependent upon the general level of interest rates. For most individuals, the amount of life insurance needed is not determined by the general level of interest rates. While variable life insurance has grown rapidly in recent years, it still represents less than 1 percent of whole life insurance in force.

Universal Life Insurance Universal life insurance is an attempt to allow policyholders to participate in higher returns when they are earned while packaging the form of participation to better fit the insured's needs. The universal life policy is like a straight life policy, except that returns earned in excess of the low-assumed return accrue to the benefit of the insured through adjustment to the cash value of the policy. In addition, the insured may vary both the amount of insurance and the amount of premiums from time to time. This type of policy has certain tax advantages in that the return earned accumulates tax-free to the insured unless the policy is cancelled. This type of policy allows the insured to participate in market interest rates while also having the ability to alter insurance and cash payments to fit changing needs. Universal life is a much newer type of policy than variable life, having been introduced in 1979. However, universal life in force at the end of 1982—over $40 billion—was ten times the amount in force a year earlier and six times the amount of variable life insurance in force.

Life insurance companies also offer *annuity plans*. The purchaser of an annuity makes a single payment or a series of payments for which the life insurance company then agrees to make monthly payments for the rest of the insured's life. Annuities are used primarily as a means of providing retirement income. They are purchased by individuals who want more retirement income than that provided by their employers or by small employers as a means of providing a pension plan. In addition to providing a regular savings program, the annuity may allow greater monthly income than the individual could achieve by investing funds elsewhere. For a sixty-five year-old retiree, a conservative (from the annuity payer's viewpoint) life expectancy is twenty years. If the interest rate on Aaa rated bonds is 10 percent, a retiree with $100,000 could invest in high grade bonds and receive $10,000 a year without reducing the principal. As shown in table A-7, $100,000 at 10 percent would provide $11,746 a year with the principal being gone by the end of the twenty years. An individual, not knowing when he will die, cannot really afford to consume the principal of his funds if he wishes to be sure of the income for his entire life. However, the insurance company can make payments based on average life expectancy, with losses from those who live longer being offset by gains from those who die sooner. Even after subtracting its operating expenses, the insurance company may be able to offer a greater payment than could be earned by private investment. With whole life policies, it is generally possible to exchange the cash value for an annuity at age sixty-five. Annuity plan premiums received by life insurance companies were $33.6 billion in 1982, or 68 percent of life insurance premiums. This is an increase from 15 percent of life insurance premiums in 1969, with much of the increase being in the form of pension plans for small companies. These pension plans are discussed in chapter 14.

Property and Liability Insurance The property and liability insurance field provides protection against financial losses to property and against lawsuit. Most things insured against in this category would be considered accidental, though theft is certainly not an accident to the thief, and negligence of some type is normally argued in liability cases.

As previously noted, premiums for property and liability insurance exceeded those for life insurance. A detailed listing of types of property, liability, and allied insurance and annual premiums appears in table 13-2.

Automobile insurance is the single largest category, accounting for a large portion of total property and liability insurance. Included is protection against damage to the policy holders and their own automobiles in an accident, as well as insurance against lawsuits arising from an accident.

Multiple peril and fire and allied lines make up a group of insurance programs protecting property owners from financial loss from fire, theft, storm damage, etc. The trend among these policies is for writing single policies providing combined coverage for storm, theft, and certain other risks as well as fire.

Workers' compensation is insurance by the employer against claims for injuries by workers. Benefits provided are determined by state law, and employers are required to carry this insurance in most cases.

Liability, including malpractice but excluding worker's compensation and automobile, is an important source of premium income. This

Table 13-2:

Premiums for Selected Property, Liability, and Allied Insurance, 1982 (in $ millions)

Type of Coverage	Premiums
Automobile	$40,088
Liability other than automobile	6,048
Fire	4,882
Homeowners multiple peril	10,973
Commercial multiple peril	6,975
Workers' compensation	13,957
Inland Marine	2,475
Other	18,186

Source: Statistical Abstract of the United States.

includes personal liability insurance carried by many professionals.

Marine insurance covers risks its name implies. Protection against financial loss from theft, storm damage, and other types of risk is provided for ships and their cargoes. Insurance against political loss is covered separately (see chapter 15).

Surety and fidelity insurance generally provides a guarantee that a certain course of action will be carried out. This may be required when late or inadequate completion of work would cause serious financial losses to one party to a contract. In such a case, insurance may be required to protect one party to a contract from loss if the other party should fail to complete work as agreed to.

Health Insurance. Health insurance covers medical expenses and income loss associated with accident and illness. Insurance premiums in this field have increased rapidly in recent years, with increases in the number of people insured and increase in medical expenses.

Blue Cross and Blue Shield organizations presently account for slightly under half of total health insurance premiums. Blue Cross was started by hospitals as a means of decreasing their collection problems and Blue Shield was started by doctors for the same purpose. The plans are incorporated separately in each state, with premiums and benefits varying by state. The point is sometimes made that these programs are not technically insurance, but are prepayment programs started by hospitals and doctors with payments to them rather than the insured. However, this is an irrelevant technicality from the point of view of the insured who receive protection from unexpected medical expenses. Life insurance companies are the dominant factor in health insurance not written by Blue Cross and Blue Shield.

Property and liability insurance companies provide the remainder. Approximately 13 percent of health insurance benefits paid by life insurance companies are to replace lost income. Blue Cross and Blue Shield provide no loss of income protection.

General health insurance is primarily sold in the form of group policies. Group sales account for 80 percent of private health insurance and a higher percentage for Blue Cross and Blue Shield. "Special" policies such as cancer insurance are more frequently sold as individual policies.

REGULATION OF INSURANCE COMPANIES

Most regulation of insurance companies is carried out by the individual states. Each state creates its own laws and regulates insurance companies selling insurance within its boundaries as well as those with headquarters there, causing national insurance companies to face fifty different sets of regulations. While specific rules vary from state to state, the same general areas—finance and investment policy, premium rates, contract provisions, and sales practices— are regulated in all states.

Finance and investment policies are regulated to assure that funds will be available to honor claims. Minimum amounts of capital and surplus are needed to start selling insurance and certain ratios of capital, surplus, and reserves must be maintained for all additional insurance written. In addition, the types of investments the insurance company can make are regulated. Life insurance companies are generally required to invest in bonds and mortgages, with only a limited investment in equity securities. Property and liability insurers, on the other hand, are normally allowed to invest in equity securities in amounts up to the value of the company's capital and surplus.

Premium rate regulations require that rates be adequate but not excessive. In addition, rate structures must not discriminate unfairly. In some states, all rates must be approved by the insurance commissioner in advance. In other states, rate increases do not need to be approved in advance, but the insurance commissioner can reduce premiums retroactively if they are found to be unjustified.

Rate regulation does not assure that each company will offer the same rate for the same insurance; each company may adjust its rates for its loss experience. In light of these rate differences, there has been some movement toward letting market forces play a bigger role in the rate setting process.

Contract provision regulation has resulted in a good deal of standardization across states. Regulation in this area followed complaints from people who filed claims and found out too late that the "fine print" excluded many things they thought were covered. Comparison shopping for policies is much easier when standard language is used.

A new aspect of the regulation of premium rates and contract provisions is the unisex requirement. Important federal court rulings in recent years have held insurance and benefit plans with difference costs or benefits for men and women to be discriminatory, even if based on sound actuarial evidence about differences in life expectancy between the sexes. The result has been a movement toward unisex rate tables which mean that women experience reduced pension costs (or increased benefits) and increased life insurance costs. The reverse is true for men.[2]

The United States Congress is presently considering legislation to clarify this issue and set standards. One aspect of this legislation is that it moves the federal government more deeply into the regulation of insurance companies. The federal government's intervention has traditionally been limited to issues such as antitrust and fraud.

Sales practices are also regulated, although it is not always clear whether the purpose of regulation is to protect consumers or those in the insurance business. Laws banning deceptive advertising are clearly for the purpose of protecting

---

[2]Many companies are already using new unisex tables that average the mortality projections for men and women. Since the proportion of men to women in a particular group is not equal, a simple way to prepare a unisex table is for example, to take a weighted average of the deaths per thousand in a particular age group, with the weights being based on the proportion of men and women in the group.

consumers. However, the benefit from laws that forbid agents from returning part of their commission to the policyholder as a means of price competition is not so clear. Laws requiring testing and licensing of those who would sell insurance are supposed to assure that insurance agents are knowledgeable, but the tests in some states are so easy as to be of little value.

MANAGEMENT CONSIDERATIONS

Management of an insurance company involves the actuarial job of accurately determining the risks involved, the marketing job of selling insurance to groups or the public, the operations management job of processing premiums and claims as efficiently as possible, and the financial management job of investing funds and maintaining an appropriate capital base.

Operations Management

The insurance company essentially acts as an intermediary by accepting premiums, deducting its expenses and a reasonable profit, and returning the remaining funds in the form of benefits. While the exact amount to be paid in benefits is not known in advance, premiums are set in light of anticipated operating expenses and benefit expenses. Operating and marketing expenses can be a substantial portion of total premiums. Holding these costs to a minimum is an essential part of successful insurance company management. Insurance companies have dealt with these costs by being leaders in the use of such things as computerized data processing and lockbox collections[3] to operate at maximum efficiency.

Marketing Management

Successful marketing involves packaging the insurance in forms that are attractive to custom-

---

[3]A lockbox collection plan involves establishment of a post office lockbox where customer payment is received. The firm's bank picks up the checks, notifies the firm, and begins the check-clearing process, thereby reducing check collection time and speeding cash flow.

ers and reaching the customers in the most cost-efficient way possible. A major portion of total operating costs can relate to the marketing effort. For example, 40 percent of life insurance company operating costs are for commissions to agents, who may receive 100 percent or more of the first year's premium as the commission for selling a whole life policy. Agent commissions are only part of the marketing expense, as they do not include advertising or the expense of the marketing staff that helps to design policies, supervise and train agents, and so on.

As insurance buyers have become sophisticated and price conscious, the emphasis has switched from developing attractive packaging methods to the development of efficient marketing methods. Group insurance has shown substantial increases in market share because of the economies of scale involved. A group life insurance program can be sold to 2,000 employees of a company in a small portion of the time required to sell a policy to each individual. Physical examination costs are eliminated for health and life insurance policies since a large group is involved and the group's health characteristics can be estimated without individual physicals.

Group life insurance increased from 20 percent of life insurance in force in 1950 to 46 percent in 1982, and sales to groups have actually increased faster than these numbers indicate. Technically, a group sale consists of a single contract with the group. Of the ordinary whole life insurance in force at the end of 1982 $23.3 billion was sold to groups on a wholesale basis with a separate policy written for each group member. Group health insurance has also grown dramatically, and group automobile insurance is being promoted.

The role of other financial institutions in the sale of insurance remains an unanswered question. Many financial intermediaries have recently made important steps toward becoming financial supermarkets, with banks having gained, for example, the right to offer stock brokerage services.

Since lenders have traditionally sold credit life insurance and credit disability insurance in connection with their credit granting activities, it would be a short step for them to begin selling other types of insurance. Furthermore, a lender would have a marketing cost advantage in selling a homeowner's policy or automobile insurance to a person arranging financing for a house or an automobile. The lender would also offer the convenience of one-stop shopping for financial services.

One reason financial intermediaries have been restricted from expanded insurance sales rests with the argument that they would have an unfair competitive advantage; borrowers would feel intimidated in making their insurance decisions and would not shop for the best price. With companies like Sears offering checkable money market funds, stock brokerage services, and insurance, pressure may begin to build from financial intermediaries for the right to expand their insurance offerings. Consequently, we may be on the verge of another revolution in the marketing of insurance and even in the structure of the insurance industry.

Actuarial Science

The work of the actuary is key to the profitable operation of an insurance company. The actuary is primarily a statistician, working with past loss experience and other factors to predict future losses for a particular group. For example, table 13-3 contains widely used projections of life expectancy and annual death rates for the population as a whole. The life insurance company can use this information to set rates for life insurance.

If actuaries only worked with experience for the total population (such as that in table 13-3) there would be little need for the thousands of people presently employed as actuaries. The actuaries must deal with several subgroups of the population and use this information to construct policies that will be cost-competitive in the marketplace and profitable to the company. For example, it is recognized that college professors have lower mortality rates than the population as a whole (despite the wish of an occasional student). A separate mortality table for this particu-

lar profession makes it possible to market a policy specifically to this profession at a premium cost below what would have to be charged to the general population and still make a profit. The growing importance of group sales has heightened the importance of separate actuarial computations for each group. Likewise, the sale of insurance to special low-risk groups means that the general population not included in some low-risk group has a higher incidence of loss than the total population, including these various low-risk groups. Thus the expected loss rate for the general population changes continually and must be watched carefully.

Variations in loss ratios are not limited to life insurance. For example, automobile insurance rates incorporate a number of factors that result in higher or lower loss experience. Classifying people as lower accident risks than they actually are will result in losses for the company. Classifying them as higher risks than they actually are will result in the policy being overpriced and business being lost to competing companies.

In addition to predicting the incidence of unfortunate events, the actuary must also predict their costs. The amount to be paid is fixed for most life insurance policies, but must be estimated for health insurance and property and liability insurance. The importance of the actuary in these areas has been particularly important during periods of rapid inflation.

In addition to predicting costs, it is also necessary to predict security returns. Because many life insurance policies and annuity plans involve a period of many years between premium receipt and benefit payment, premiums are based on assumptions about the rate at which funds can be invested. One thousand dollars invested for forty years at 10 percent per year will grow to $45,259 while the same amount invested for the same time period at 15 percent would grow to $267,864. A company's profits and losses can be dramatically affected by failures in these projections.

A discussion of the skills necessary to perform competently as an actuary is well beyond the scope of this book. Many universities have

Table 13-3:

Mortality Tables

	Commissioners 1980 Standard				1983 Individual Annuity Expectation of Life (years)		United States Total Population	
	Male		Female					
Age	Deaths per 1,000	Expectation of Life (years)	Deaths per 1,000	Expectation of Life (years)	Male	Female	Deaths per 1,000	Expectation of Life (years)
0	4.18	70.83	2.89	75.83	—	—	20.02	70.75
5	0.90	66.40	0.76	71.28	74.10	79.36	0.51	67.43
10	0.73	61.66	0.68	66.53	69.22	74.42	0.31	62.57
15	1.33	56.93	0.85	61.76	64.36	69.47	0.82	57.69
20	1.90	52.37	1.05	57.04	59.50	64.55	1.40	53.00
25	1.77	47.84	1.16	52.34	54.66	59.64	1.47	48.37
30	1.73	43.24	1.35	47.65	49.83	54.75	1.55	43.71
35	2.11	38.61	1.65	42.98	45.03	49.87	2.09	39.07
40	3.02	34.05	2.42	38.36	40.25	45.02	3.14	34.52
45	4.55	29.62	3.56	33.88	35.57	40.20	4.84	30.12
50	6.71	25.36	4.96	29.53	31.07	35.46	7.38	25.93
55	10.47	21.29	7.09	25.31	26.77	30.83	11.36	21.99
60	16.08	17.51	9.47	21.25	22.62	26.32	16.95	18.34
65	25.42	14.04	14.59	17.32	18.63	21.98	24.95	15.00
70	39.51	10.96	22.11	13.67	14.96	17.87	36.61	12.00
75	64.19	8.31	38.24	10.32	11.72	14.02	55.52	9.32
80	98.84	6.18	65.99	7.48	8.96	10.61	83.94	7.10

Source: Life Insurance Fact Book.

degree programs in actuarial science, and there are a number of professional associations devoted to maintaining high standards of actuarial practice. The primary actuarial associations are

American Academy of Actuaries, 208 South Lasalle St., Chicago, Ill. 60604

American Society of Pension Actuaries, 1413 K St., N.W., Washington, D.C. 20005

Conference of Actuaries in Public Service, 500 Park Blvd., Itasca, Ill. 60143

Society of Actuaries, 500 Park Blvd, Itasca, Ill. 60143.

ASSET AND LIABILITY MANAGEMENT

Liabilities and Capital

An understanding of the liabilities of insurance companies is necessary to develop an appropriate approach to management of assets. The dominant liabilities for both life and nonlife insurance companies are reserves based on the fact that premiums are collected as much as a year ahead for nonlife insurance companies and most of a lifetime ahead for life insurance policies. The amounts expected to be paid out over the period covered by the premium is carried as a reserve when that premium is first received. As claims are paid, both cash and reserves are reduced. If claims exceed reserves, capital and surplus are decreased, and vice versa. The long lives of many life insurance policies versus those of nonlife insurance companies result in much larger policy reserves for life insurance companies.

In addition to the higher absolute amount of reserves, life insurance companies have a much higher ratio of reserves to equity. The lower capital levels for life insurance companies result from both management decisions and regulatory requirements. They are based on recognition of the fact that life insurance obligations are easier to predict than the obligations of most other insurance companies. In addition, the accumulation of funds for certain death benefits means that the dollar value of liabilities per face value of insurance is higher for life insurance than for other insurance. Therefore, a higher ratio of liabilities to equity does not necessarily mean a higher ratio of insurance face value to equity. Accident rates and the amount of settlement per accident have varied. This has been particularly true with high inflation.

The size of the equity base has important implications for asset management. With a limited equity base, the life insurance companies can endure less asset value shrinkage than can nonlife companies.

Assets

The primary assets of insurance companies are investment portfolios in the form of government and corporate securities (table 13-4). Investment portfolios are held for two reasons. Because the insurance companies collect premiums with insurance coverage provided for some time after collection, they have these funds to invest until they are paid out as benefits. On the liability side, this shows up as reserves. The second category of funds are held as protection against losses due to factors such as excessive benefit expense or shrinkage in the value of assets. On the liability side of the balance sheet, these funds

Table 13-4:

**Asset Structure
of Life Insurance Companies, 1983
(in $ billions)**

Assets	Amount	Percentage
Government securities	$47.2	7.2
Corporate securities		
Bonds	260.4	39.9
Stock	65.4	10.0
Mortgages	148.9	22.8
Real estate	22.3	3.4
Policy loans	54.4	8.3
Other assets	54.4	8.3
Total	$652.9	100.0

Source: *1980 Life Insurance Fact Book* and Board of Governors of the Federal Reserve System, *Assets and Liabilities Outstanding, 1969–1979.*

are represented by surplus and equity accounts. The investment policy is determined by the two purposes the portfolio serves.

The liquidity needs from the investment portfolio are minimal. Most insurance companies are continually expanding in size, with premiums received during any month being more than sufficient to meet all cash outflows for that month. Actual sale of securities would be necessary only if premium revenue declined. The company will add to its portfolio and reserve accounts from month to month unless its volume declines or disintermediation occurs. The allocation of the life insurance dollar for U.S. life insurance companies for 1982 is shown in table 13-5.

This is not to say that day-to-day cash management is not an important function in an insurance company. A large insurance company will have cash flows of several million dollars a day. A company may be able to improve profit by half a million dollars a year or more by reducing idle cash equal to one day's cash flow. Therefore, the companies follow cash flow over the week and month very closely to keep as much cash as possible invested. If premiums for a particular company tend to come in around the first of the month, with claims paid at an even rate over the

Table 13-5:

Life Insurance Company Dollar 1982: U.S. Life Insurance Companies

Income

Premiums	71.5¢*
Net investment earnings and other income	28.5
	100.0

How Used

Benefit payments and additions to funds
   for policyholders and beneficiaries

Benefit payments in year	46.6¢
Additions to policy reserve funds	32.4
Additions to special reserves and surplus funds	1.9
	80.9

Operating expenses

Commissions to agents	6.1
Home and field office expenses	9.6
	15.7

Taxes	2.3
Dividends to stockholders of stock life insurance companies	1.1**
	100.0

*Premiums were 20.1% of total assets.

**For stock companies only, this ratio would be 2.0¢ per dollar.

Source: *1983 Life Insurance Fact Book*, p. 61.

month, the company will have idle cash during the early part of the month. These funds will be invested in money market instruments, with adjustments being made on a daily basis. Because these day-to-day cash flows vary with such things as mail delivery and are not totally predictable, there may be short-term liquidity demand that requires the sale of money market instruments. This short-term money management problem is linked to management of the investment portfolio only to the extent that the company must decide how much to invest in money market instruments for liquidity reserve purposes.

Liquidity demands of a more serious nature arise from disintermediation. Whole life and endowment policies normally give the holder the right to borrow a large portion of the reserve attributed to the policy at an interest rate stated in the contract. With rising interest rates, people have found these *policy loans* to be a low-cost source of funds and have borrowed heavily, either to meet credit needs or to invest at higher interest rates. In addition if a whole life or endowment policy is cancelled, the insured is paid most of the reserve associated with that policy. This is the *cash value* spelled out in such policies. Cancellation of whole life policies, to be replaced with term policies, has also occurred during periods of high interest rates. The relative stabilities of cash flow demands for death benefits and loan and cash surrender payments are shown in figure 13-2. Downturns in loan and cash surrender demand are in periods when interest rates are falling, while rapid increases in this demand are during periods of rising interest rates. Outflows have not been sufficient to cause net outflows for all insurance companies, but they have been sufficient to lead to substantial net outflows for individual companies.

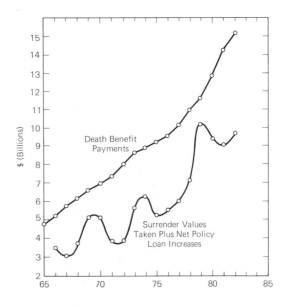

Figure 13–2: Cash outflow demands on life insurance companies. (Source: Based on data in *1983 Life Insurance Fact Book.*)

The pressures to earn returns on portfolios come from two sources. First, insurance companies are clearly profit-seeking ventures, and portfolio return is an important source of revenue, equalling 28.5 percent of the life insurance dollar in 1982. Unlike mutual thrift institutions, even mutual insurance companies pay profit-based dividends to members who also elect directors. Thus, virtually all insurance companies are overseen by directors elected by people who share in the profits. In addition to direct profitability to the owners, investment portfolio return indrectly affects profitability through the ability of the company to price policies compretively. For all insurance companies, and particularly for a life insurance company, the premiums depend on an assumption about rates of return on the firm's investments and on an assessment of risks. For a $10,000 benefit payment fifty years in the future, the annual investment necessary to accumulate this amount is $8.59 if the interest at which funds can be invested is 10 percent and $1.39 if the interest rate is raised to 15 percent. If a 20 percent rate of return could be assumed, the payment would fall to $0.22. Premiums required for some life insurance policies are therefore quite sensitive to the return that can be earned on the investment portfolio. The assumption of a low long-term investment return at a time when interest rates were high was one factor leading to the increased portion of the life insurance premium dollar going to term insurance.

For life and nonlife insurance companies, the amount of new insurance which a particular company can write is limited by the amount of equity and surplus. Return on the investment portfolio increases the amount of surplus.

Tax considerations differ by type of insurance company and lead to different policies with regard to the investment portfolio. The two main forms of tax paid are state premium taxes—a percentage of all premiums collected in a particular state—and income tax. Income tax is the most important of the taxes for both life and nonlife companies. All insurance companies are taxed at standard corporate income tax rates (presently 46 percent). However, the tax base income to which this rate is applied varies according to the type of insurance being sold.

Life insurance companies can allocate half their underwriting profits[4] for each year to policyholders' surplus with the balance being allocated to a shareholders' surplus account. The amount allocated to the policyholders' account is recognized as taxable income only if it is transferred to the shareholders' account. Since it would be transferred to the shareholders' account only if it were to be used to pay dividends, the life insurance company can effectively retain half of its underwriting earnings without paying income tax on them. Other insurance companies pay tax on all their profits, whether or not they are retained. In effect then, the marginal federal income tax rate for a life insurance company can be half that for a nonlife company or industrial corporation.[5]

Because of this difference in tax treatment, nonlife companies hold a substantial proportion (almost half) of their assets in the form of state and local government obligations while life insurance companies hold less than 2 percent of their assets in this form. State and local government securities pay lower returns than do other securities, but returns associated with these municipal securities are not subject to federal income tax. The yield spreads between municipals and other securities are such that they are attractive only to investors with effective income tax rates in the neighborhood of 40 percent or higher. Thus they are attractive to nonlife companies but not to life insurance companies.

Regulation of portfolio policy by state authorities is aimed at protecting the insured by protecting the portfolio from shrinkage in value. Life insurance companies are severely restricted

---

[4]Underwriting profits (or losses) are premiums earned less losses and expenses. They do not reflect investment earnings.

[5]For a detailed discussion of insurance company tax treatment, see Keith Tucker and Dennis Van Mieghem of Peat, Marwick, Mitchell & Co. *Taxation of Insurance Companies—Problems and Planning* (Englewood Cliffs, N.J.: Prentice Hall, 1981).

with regard to investment in equity securities, direct investment in real estate, and with regard to other investments perceived to be risky. Nonlife companies are usually allowed to invest in equity securities up to the amount of their own equity and surplus. However, the attractiveness of equity securities is decreased by procedures the regulators use in computing the insurance company's equity and surplus. Equity securities are carried at their current market values; bonds can be carried at their face values or original costs. If rising interest rates cause both stock and bond values to decline, the company holding only bonds will not suffer a decline in portfolio value from the regulators' viewpoint, but losses will be recorded for the company with equity investments. The consequent reduction in recognized capital can impair the company's ability to sell additional insurance since certain ratios of capital to insurance face value are required. Nonlife insurance companies hold 18 percent of their assets in equity securities while life insurance companies hold 9 percent of their assets in this form.

Risk   As with any other company, the insurance company cannot think of the riskiness of a single security in isolation from the investment portfolio, nor can the investment portfolio be viewed in isolation from the other aspects of the company's business. An insurance company faces four major types of risks.

Excessive benefit costs are the first type of risk. They can occur because of a natural disaster, because inflation drives average claim amounts to higher than anticipated levels, or simply because the company's original estimates of losses were wrong.

Sales declines represent the second type of risk. They can occur because a severe economic downturn eliminates either the ability to pay for premiums or the need for certain types of insurance. Business insurance would be the most obvious example as the need for it decreases during a recession when business activity declines or businesses close. Demand for life insurance, particularly whole life, may also decline in infla-

tionary periods as people look for investments that will provide some protection from inflation.

Portfolio value loss is a risk that results from a similar set of factors. As inflation rates rise, the general level of interest rates rises as well. A rise in the general level of interest rates results in a decline in the market value of existing fixed-income securities. In addition, common stock returns have been negatively correlated with the inflation rate in recent years. An economic downturn can also have a negative impact on portfolio value through defaults on bonds and mortgages, and through a reduction in common stock values as profits decline. Default rates on the types of securities that insurance companies hold have remained low even in economic downturns, but losses in market value have been substantial. For example, a bond with an 8 percent coupon rate and twenty years to maturity would be selling at 70 percent of its face value if the general level of interest rates for this risk class were to increase to 12 percent. Likewise, but less surprisingly, we have seen the average value of a share of common stock decline 40 percent or more. With their low ratios of equity capital to total assets, the insurance companies cannot absorb large losses of this type.

Cancellation and policy loan risks are primarily problems faced by companies offering whole life or endowment policies. These withdrawals generally occur during periods of high interest rates, but could also occur in severe economic downturns. Of course, high interest rate periods and economic downturns are both periods when the values of securities may be low. For fixed income securities, the maturity value is not affected by a decline in current market value. The decline in market price is significant because: 1) it reflects an opportunity loss in that higher yielding securities are currently available, and 2) if the company should need cash, the bonds would have to be sold at a loss. As indicated earlier, a loss in the value of equity can have an immediate negative impact on equity and surplus ratios, even in the absence of a need to sell the securities at depressed prices.

The conditions which might lead to each of

the various types of losses are summarized as follows:

Problem	Causes		
Excessive claim losses	natural disasters	inflation	
Sales declines		inflation	economic downturn
Losses in investment portfolio		inflation	economic downturn
Policy loans and cancellations		inflation	economic downturn

Since inflation and economic downturn are factors influencing most types of losses, particularly for life insurance companies, the investment portfolio does not provide significant opportunity to diversify away risks from other aspects of the business.

Portfolio Strategy   Because of this limited opportunity for diversification, insurance companies pursue a conservative portfolio strategy. Long-term fixed-income securities are the primary investment for both life insurance and nonlife companies. Because of previously discussed tax differences, life insurance companies hold large quantities of corporate bonds and mortgages while nonlife insurance companies hold larger quantities of state and local government securities. There has been a switch in emphasis in mortgage holdings, away from FHA and VA mortgages and toward commercial mortgages. In addition to higher return, commercial mortgages create the opportunity for "equity participations" through which the insurance company can participate in profits if the venture is successful.

Within the investment portfolio, the normal principle of eliminating diversifiable risk is followed to the extent possible. Unfortunately, legislation designed to assure safety may actually increase the difficulty of achieving proper diversification. Regulations are based on the view that high-grade, fixed-income securities are nearly risk-free. Restricting insurance companies to heavy investment in these securities and restricting them from such areas as direct investment in real estate has left them exposed to the full effect of interest rate risk associated with inflation. Portfolio managers have sought to diversify

within these regulatory limits. The movement to commercial mortgages with equity participations is one such example, giving some of the diversification benefits of real estate ownership without violating restriction on direct real estate ownership or direct common stock purchase. Convertible bonds are another investment medium providing similar opportunities.

To deal with interest rate risk, it must be remembered that the life insurance companies base their premiums on expected investment return. If management knew the policy would not be cancelled or borrowed against, investment maturity could be based on expected eventual payment date, therby insuring a rate of return. This would not be entirely possible for payments expected to be made sixty years in the future, but forty-year maturities are available and would be sufficient to cover most commitments. Unfortunately, the picture is complicated by a number of uncertainties, including the fact that bonds can be called and policies can be cancelled or borrowed against. The problem of high-yield bonds and mortgages being repaid when interest rates fall could be dealt with through increased holdings of U.S. government securities, which are generally not callable. However, with the experience of more than two decades of rising interest rates and almost no bonds being called, the insurance industry seems content to accept call risk. Convertible bonds and equity participation in real estate loans provide at least some diversification in this regard.

Portfolio strategy to deal with the possibility of excessive withdrawals through loans and cancellations is primarily dealt with through a balancing of the maturity structure so that any demand can be met through maturing securities rather than by selling securities at a discount. This has been combined with some movement toward raising the policy loan interest rate in new contracts or making it a floating rate tied to some money market indicator.

An insurance company that temporarily finds itself with an insufficient supply of shorter term securities can hedge in the financial futures markets. By entering into forward contracts to sell, it can effectively convert some long-term U.S. government securities or mortgages to short-term securities.

In summary, insurance companies face significant risks tied to the inflation rate and economic conditions. These risks cannot be very effectively diversified away, but they are problems of the short and intermediate term, in which securities might have to be sold below cost. If a company has its maturity structure designed evenly so that it can avoid the necessity of selling securities before maturity, the risks are manageable. A poorly designed maturity structure could quickly result in insolvency in the face of withdrawal demand.

SUMMARY

Insurance companies act as intermediaries for risk. They do so by collecting funds from all members of a large group in order to pay benefits to certain members of the group who suffer some consequence. This consequence is diversifiable from the point of view of the general population but not from the point of view of individuals. The three main types of insurance and annual 1981 premiums are

Life insurance	$46 billion
Property and liability insurance	99 billion
Health insurance	80 billion

The life insurance companies are a larger factor than these premium levels indicate. Life insurance companies receive almost half the health insurance premiums and billions more in payments toward annuity plans. In addition, life insurance company assets are much greater than those of all nonlife insurance companies.

Insurance companies also act as financial intermediaries in collecting savings from individuals and reinvesting them. Their investments of some $600 billion make them an important source of investment capital.

Regulation is left almost entirely to state governments. Regulations vary by state, with insurance companies required to meet regulations of states in which they sell insurance. Regulations cover investment and finance policies, premium rates charged, contract provisions, and sales practices.

Like most companies, insurance companies are guided by the profitability objective in the four main areas of management: operations management, actuarial science, marketing management, and financial management. Operations management consists of efficiently and economically handling the millions of transactions involved. Actuarial science consists of accurately estimating the percent of the population that will suffer a particular insurable event. Marketing management involves designing policies that fit buyers' demands, but increasingly involves the development of cost efficient methods of sales. Financial management consists of determining and maintaining the proper amount of equity, and managing the investment portfolio.

The portfolio manager attempts to maximize profitability while dealing with four types of risk: 1) excessive benefit costs; 2) sales declines; 3) portfolio value loss; 4) cancellation and policy loan demands. These risks must be met within the constraints of regulations which affect investment policy. Such regulations tend to restrict equity investments and tax laws have the effect of favoring state and local government securities for nonlife insurance companies but not life insurance companies. The fact that most types of potential losses tend to occur in periods of high inflation or economic downturn make them difficult to eliminate through any portfolio strategy, especially in the face of regulatory restrictions. Balancing maturities to avoid the necessity of selling securities at a loss and purchasing fixed-income securities with equity participation options are important strategies.

QUESTIONS

1. What pressures would cause a mutual insurance company to pursue a profitability objective? How do these pressures differ from those on a mutual savings and loan company?

2. Why do life insurance companies dominate in asset size, even though they receive less than half of total insurance premiums?

3. For regulatory purposes, bonds can be counted at their face value even if their current market price has declined. If bonds were revalued to current market price, some insurance companies would be insolvent.

   a. Which type of company—life or nonlife—would be more likely to be pushed into insolvency by a revaluation of fixed income securities to current market value?

   b. What is the effect of this situation on the protection offered to policyholders?

4. As a regulator, what portfolio management rules would you suggest to improve diversification by insurance companies?

5. Why is it difficult to purchase insurance for damage due to acts of war?

6. For an insurance buyer, which type of insurance company—stock or mutual—would be expected to provide lower total costs if claims expense is lower than anticipated? Higher than anticipated?

7. Why can a life insurance company operate with a higher liability-to-equity ratio than a nonlife insurance company?

8. Under what conditions would a property and liability insurance company find it necessary to sell assets from its portfolio? What is the appropriate maturity structure for property and liability insurance company assets?

PROBLEMS

1. New Horizons Life Insurance company has equity equal to 8 percent of total assets. The company's assets are as follows:

Item	Maturity	Coupon or Face Rate	Yield to* Maturity	Face Value
Bonds	30 yrs	8.0%	10.0%	$2,000,000
Bonds	10 yrs	9.0	9.5	3,000,000
Bonds	5 yrs	9.0	9.25	3,000,000
T bills	90 days	8.0	8.0	5,000,000
Mortgages**	20 years	8.0	10.0	5,000,000

*Based on market price; assume annual interest payments for bonds.

**These involve monthly payments over the twenty-year period.

   a. If these assets were revalued to market value, would the company be solvent?

   b. If yields to maturity on all securities rose one more percentage point, would the company still be solvent?

   c. If requirements were changed to require that fixed-income securities be carried at market value, what would be likely to happen to the average maturities of insurance company assets?

2. Your insurance company can invest funds at 4 percent. 90 percent of the first year's premium is paid as a sales commission and operating expenses are 10 percent of premiums. For someone who lives for thirty years (and pays thirty-one premiums, with the first being paid today):

   a. What would be the annual premium necessary for a straight life insurance policy for $20,000?

   b. What would be the annual premium necessary for a twenty-year limited payment life insurance policy for $20,000?

   c. Rework a. and b. on the assumption

of a 7 percent return on invested funds.

3. Following are financial statements for Old Reliable Life Insurance company. The board of directors has noted that the profitability of the company is below average. Compare the financial statements of Old Reliable to those for life insurance companies in general, and suggest methods for improving profitability.

Old Reliable Life Insurance
Income Statement
Year Ending 31 December 1980
(000,000 omitted)

Premium revenue	$146
Investment portfolio income	44
	190
Benefit payments and reserve additions	145
Operating expenses	41
Income tax	1
Net income	$ 3

Balance Sheet
31 December 1980
(000,000 omitted)

Demand deposits and currency	$ 8
Corporate equity	70
Treasury bills	12
U.S. government bonds	40
State and local government bonds	21
Corporate bonds	281
FHA and VA mortgages	190
Commercial mortgages	20
Policy loans	60
Other assets	40
Total assets	$742
Policy reserves	$550
Other liabilities	50
Equity and surplus	142
Total liabilities and net worth	$742

SELECTED REFERENCES

Borch, Karl. "Additive Insurance Premiums: A Note." *The Journal of Finance* 37 (December 1982): 1295–1298.

Campbell, Ritchie A. "The Demand for Life Insurance: An Application of the Economics of Uncertainty." *Journal of Finance* 35 (December 1980): 1155–1174.

Foster, George. "Valuation Parameters of Property-Liability Companies." *Journal of Finance* 32 (June 1977): 823–836.

Geehan, Randall. "Returns to Scale in the Life Insurance Industry." *The Bell Journal of Economics and Management Science* 8 (Autumn 1977): 497–514.

Kraus, Alan and Ross, Stephen A. "The Determination of Fair Profits for the Property-Liability Insurance Firm." *The Journal of Finance* 37 (September 1982): 1016–1028.

Chapter 14

Pension Fund Management

"If 'socialism' is defined as 'ownership of the means of production by the workers'—and this is both the orthodox and the only rigorous definition—then the United States is the first truly 'Socialist country.' . . . Indeed, aside from farming, a larger sector of the American economy is owned today by the American worker through his investment agent, the pension fund, than Allende in Chile had brought under government ownership to make Chile a 'Socialist country,' than Castro's Cuba has actually nationalized, or than had been nationalized in Hungary or Poland at the height of Stalinism.''
Peter Drucker[1]

Private pension plans have assets of $573 billion, while combined assets of public and private pension plans total $932 billion. Among financial institutions, only commercial banks have more assets than pension funds.

The growth in importance of pension funds has been a recent phenomenon. In the 1930s pension fund assets amounted to only about $2.5 billion, and as late as 1950 private pension fund assets amounted to only $12 billion. However, these assets had grown to $138 billion by 1970, making pension funds major financial institutions. From this level, the growth rate increased sharply following Labor Day 1974 when ERISA—the Employee Retirement Income Security Act—was signed into law, increasing required pension fund reserves and leading to projections of a continued high rate of growth in pension fund assets.

As Drucker points out, even these growth numbers may understate the importance of pension funds to the United States economy and society. In combination, the pension funds hold controlling interest in the common stock of most large American corporations.[2] Their continued growth and potential use of that control could lead to major changes in the economic structure of the country. Proper management of pension funds is a matter of concern for the welfare of the country, not to mention the welfare of the individuals covered by the plans and the companies contributing to them.

---

[1]Peter Drucker, *The Unseen Revolution*, (New York: Harper and Row, 1976).

[2]Ibid., p. 20

TYPES OF PENSION FUNDS

Pension plans are operated by private companies, private associations, insurance companies, state and local governments, and the federal government. Government sponsored funds are normally controlled by legislation of the sponsoring government unit while private funds are regulated through ERISA. Regardless of the sponsor or guiding legislation, certain common principles underlie the management of the assets of any pension fund. Following an overview of the types of funds and types of regulation, the principles of fund management will be developed.

As a prelude to examining the various types of funds and sponsors, it is necessary to understand the difference between a funded and an unfunded pension plan. A funded plan maintains assets sufficient to meet its remaining obligations over the lives of the persons covered by the plan. The plan's obligations rise from payments already received, and it would be in a position to meet those obligations if no further contributions to the fund occurred. All private pension plans and some government sponsored plans are now of the funded variety. An unfunded plan counts on current payments to meet current obligations and maintains assets sufficient to meet obligations for only a short time. Because it can guarantee payment through its taxing ability, the U.S. government can sponsor unfunded pension plans. However, private firms and most state and local governments have no way other than funding to guarantee that commitments will be honored.

Social Security

Social Security (Old Age, Survivors, and Disability Insurance Program) is, of course, the broadest pension program, presently paying benefits averaging $450 a month to each of 36 million individuals. It was started as a program to provide a floor level of retirement income to contributing workers; it has been expanded to serve a number of other needs including disability and survivors' dependent benefits. Many private pension plans are designed to mesh with social security, providing a supplement to fill the gap between social security and some desired level of retirement income. Social security payments are adjusted for inflation each year. Such adjustment is an important consideration and a source of security in periods of high inflation. Because portfolio value may not increase with inflation, few private plans are in a position to promise payments adjusted for inflation. Social security obligations are primarily unfunded, with total assets of the social security trust fund presently being equal to only a few months of benefit payments.

Civil Service Retirement System

Federal civilian employees are covered by the United States Civil Service Retirement System, which presently has approximately 1.8 million retired recipients. Civil service employees do not participate in the social security system. The civil service retirement system is one of the few plans with benefits completely adjusted for inflation.

The Civil Service Retirement System is designed to be a fully funded system, with contributions by both the United States government and its employees. Unfunded liabilities are to be made up from appropriations over a thirty-year period. At the present time the fund has assets of $38.6 billion and the discounted present value of unfunded liabilities is approximately $108 billion. Thus the bulk of its liabilities are actually unfunded at this time. The assets of the fund are invested in U.S. government securities.

State and Local Government Pension Funds

Pension plans of state and local governments have increased in importance with the increase in the number of persons employed by state and local government. Legislation in 1950 and 1954 made state and local government employees eligible to participate in social security and most have done so. State and local governments have been slow to integrate their pension plans with social security, thus some government employees can actually increase their income by retiring. State and local government pension plans are not covered by all the federal laws that govern the management of private pension funds. They are controlled primarily by state and local legislation. For private plans, the idea of investing corporate pension funds in the company involved has been largely rejected because of the risk of the employee if both the company and the pension fund fail. However, state and local employees do not seem to have similar protection. Their assets have sometimes been used to underwrite unsound fiscal policies by purchasing the debt instruments of the local government when other lenders were unwilling to hold the debt.

Private Pension Funds

Private funds represent the bulk of pension fund assets to be managed, though they do not provide coverage to as many people as does the Social Security System. Private plans can be further divided into the following categories:

Insurance company sponsored plans

Noninsurance company plans

Single company plans

Multicompany plans

Life insurance-related plans are normally used by small firms as these firms have found the costs of managing their own plans to be excessive. The plan sponsored by a life insurance company has the advantage, particularly for the small fund, of being guaranteed by the life insurance company itself and not merely by the assets of the particular fund. The most common life insurance arrangement is the "group deferred annuity." With this plan a paid up annuity[3] is

purchased for each employee each month and the policies are held by a trustee (usually a bank or trust company). The employee is protected by the pension plan and the plan requires minimal management time on the part of the company. Assets of life insurance related funds are approximately one third of all private pension plan assets. Approximately 17 million people are covered by such plans.

The nonlife insurance funds represent $344 billion of assets, including both single company and multicompany funds. Contributions to private plans are made by employers (or employers and employees) with the contribution typically being made to a fund administered by a bank or trust company. Because these plans are designed to be fully funded, their assets are quite extensive. The trustee invests the funds and makes payments to the retirees in accordance with the provisions of the plan. Some large companies have their own investment staffs that handle the investment of the fund directly. The amount of contribution and the investment policy are directed by legislation as well as company policy and possible agreements between employer and union. Because funds are invested in relatively safe assets, employees can expect to receive their pensions even if the company should fail. Like life insurance-sponsored plans, these plans cannot make commitments unless they can be justified by actuarial experience and the value of the assets on hand.

Multicompany plans normally arise from union contracts, although there are exceptions such as the Teacher's Insurance and Annuity Association, started by the Carnegie Foundation to provide a multiemployer pension plan for teachers. Multicompany plans are particularly popular in industries where employees tend to continue in the industry for long periods of time, but change employers frequently. The multicompany plan provides job mobility—a desirable feature from an economic efficiency viewpoint—without jeopardizing pension protection. Industries with multiemployer plans include construction, motor transportation, trade (wholesale and retail) and some service industries. With a multiemployer plan, contributions

---

[3]An annuity is a simple promise to pay a specific amount per month for life, beginning at a particular age. A paid up annuity requires no further payments on the part of the recipient. As an example, suppose a company buys a $1 paid up annuity for each employee each month. An employee who works forty years before retirement will receive $480 per month at retirement.

are made to a pension fund managed by a board of trustees. The board may be made up of representatives of both management and labor.

Unfortunately, several major multicompany pension funds have been racked with scandal resulting from misappropriation of funds to the benefit of trustees. A number of prison sentences have been imposed for improper use of funds. Despite some problems and the necessity for continuous supervision, these funds provide needed pension protection in mobile professions.

Keogh plans are a special arrangement allowed to individuals who are self-employed or are not covered by a pension plan at their place of employment. An individual is allowed to deduct from his or her taxable income contributions to a private pension plan in amounts up to 15 percent of earned income (up to a limit of $1,500 for an employee and $7,500 for a self-employed person). Funds may be placed with a bank or thrift institution, a life insurance company, a mutual fund, or in certain government bonds.

REGULATION OF PENSION FUNDS

Most pension fund regulation now in effect traces from the 1974 Employee Retirement Income Security Act (ERISA). The objectives of the act were the encouragement of increased pension benefits and protection of benefits. The act does not require employers to have pension plans, but sets standards for plans that do exist. The act covers seven major areas:

1. Who must be covered by pension plans.

2. Status of accrued benefits when an employee leaves an employer (vesting).

3. The pension rights of an employee's spouse.

4. The amount of assets that must be accumulated to vest projected pension benefits (funding).

5. Standards of conduct and responsibility

for pension fund managers (fiduciary responsibility).

6. Plan termination insurance to protect employees in the event a cancelled plan has insufficient assets to meet its commitments.

7. Reporting and disclosure requirements.

Who Must Be Covered A very important feature of the coverage aspect of the legislation is that it does not require employers to have pension plans. It also does not require that existing plans be continued. It only requires that any plan that does exist meet certain standards. Basically, a plan must cover any full-time employee who has worked for the company one year and is twenty-five or older.[4] While issues such as the definition of ''full time'' are sufficient to keep a battery of attorneys employed, they need not concern the reader interested in the general principles guiding pension fund management.

Vesting An employee is vested on the day his or her right to pension benefits becomes certain. Before ERISA, there were cases of companies discharging employees in their early sixties to negate forty years of accumulated pension benefits. Under present legislation, there are several allowed vesting plans. The simplest is complete vesting of all employees no later than ten years after beginning employment with the particular employer. Other plans are permitted to include age as a factor when setting the time vesting must occur or be phased in, starting no later than the fifth year of employment.

Vesting does not guarantee benefits at retirement equal to what would have been earned if the employee had stayed with the company. Most pension plans base benefits on years of employment and income. The vested employee receives benefits based on the amount of service up to departure from the employer. For the employee who receives vested rights in the form of a cash settlement when leaving the employer, the law allows the employee to defer tax on the payment if it is reinvested in an individual retirement annuity or invested in the new employer's plan.

---

[4]If a plan provides immediate vesting, it can require three years of employment before eligibility.

Spouse Rights An employee covered by a pension plan must be given the option of providing that pension benefits be paid to the surviving spouse. Of course, choosing this option results in smaller benefits; the amount of adjustment is determined by the relative ages of the two people and other actuarial factors.

Funding Private pension funds are required to maintain assets equal to the present value of future benefits. This requirement is designed to assure that benefits will be paid as provided. Unfunded plans simply pay current benefits from current operating revenues. If the company sponsoring an unfunded plan ceased operation, employees and retirees would simply lose their benefits. Thus ERISA required that all plans be funded. Pension plans are given thirty years to amortize obligations for past services and become fully funded. Because determining the amount of funds needed and the best method for achieving funding are major management problems, these topics will be considered in a separate section.

Fiduciary Responsibility This refers to the standards that must be followed in managing pension funds assets. A fiduciary is a trustee, investment adviser, or other person who has the authority to make decisions with regard to investment of the fund's assets. First, fiduciary responsibility standards prohibit transactions that would involve a conflict of interest. A fiduciary cannot invest the funds for any purpose other than the benefit of those covered by the plan. Specifically, transactions from which the trustee may personally gain are prohibited.

The second aspect of fiduciary responsibility is the "prudent man" rule. The fiduciary is required by the law to act "with care, skill, prudence, and diligence under the circumstances then prevailing that a prudent man acting in a like capacity and familiar with such matters would use. . . ." Managing the investment portfolio in consideration of this rule and other objectives is another major aspect of pension fund management and will be discussed as a separate section.

Plan Cancellation Insurance ERISA called for the creation of the Pension Benefit Guarantee

Corporation (PBGC) to protect pension fund beneficiaries in the event a plan was terminated and its assets were not sufficient to meet its future obligations. The PBGC was modeled after the Federal Deposit Insurance Corporation which guarantees bank deposits. The employer is responsible for unfunded liabilities at plan termination time up to a limit of 30 percent of net worth, with the PBGC making up the difference.

Like the FDIC, the PBGC charges insurance premiums that are sufficient to cover isolated failures. Because the PBGC has had to pay a number of claims, it has not been able to accumulate enough capital to handle a really major pension fund failure. A really large failure would require the Federal government to step in if commitments were to be honored.

Reporting and Disclosure Requirements Disclosure regulations, like other aspects of ERISA, arose from prior abuses. Employees were often surprised to find that after thirty years of employment, they had no vested interest when a plan was terminated or they were dismissed; they had built their retirement security upon a false assumption about their pension coverage. Additionally, the lack of oversight to assure that fiduciary standards were being met resulted in millions of dollars in benefits being lost. The present reporting requirements set standards for reports to both the government and covered employees. Plans must now submit to the Secretary of Labor each year an audited financial report similar in detail to the reports companies issue to their shareholders. Employees must be given a description of the plan, written in language that the average person can understand. The employee must be given a new copy of the description every ten years if no changes have occurred and every five years if changes have occurred.[5]

The reporting requirements have been frequently criticized. The cost and time required for an annual audit has been blamed for the cancellation of many plans. In response, plans with fewer than 100 participants have been exempted

---

[5]Of course, participants must also be notified of any changes as they occur.

from a large portion of the reporting requirements; plans with individual benefits fully guaranteed by an insurance company have been exempted from the auditing requirement. Reporting requirements continue to be an area of debate; several changes have occurred and more are likely to occur.

MANAGEMENT POLICY

Pension fund assets have become large relative to total corporate assets; pension fund expenses have become a substantial portion of total labor expense. Additionally, many people depend on pension plans as an important employee benefit and source of retirement security. From the points of view of both employees and the company, proper management decisions are important. In this section, we discuss the four major areas of management policy:

1. Benefits to be received
2. Vesting procedures
3. Funding of liabilities
4. Investment policy for the fund portfolio

Benefits

Interestingly, government regulation has much less to say about the benefit formula than other aspects of the pension plan. This is partly explained in terms of the types of problems prompting ERISA. Failure to receive expected benefits was the major problem addressed. In addition, full disclosure and assurance of ability to meet commitments has been the thrust of most financial regulation.

The government's main interest in benefit formulas relates to recently raised issues of sexual discrimination. Benefit payments in some plans were adjusted for life expectancy; a woman retiree would receive a smaller monthly pension check than a man with the same employment experience because her life expectancy was greater and she could expect to receive more checks. This practice has been ruled discriminatory in recent court rulings and a bill to clarify this issue is presently before the U.S. Congress.

Since there is considerable freedom in establishing a benefit formula, this provides a rich area for gains through proper decision making by management. Most pension plans are tied to years of service and there is an increasing trend toward tying the plan to income levels as well. The exceptions to income relationship normally occur in plans negotiated with unions where income levels do not vary greatly. Where benefits are tied to income, there is the additional question of whether it should be tied to average income for all years of employment or only the few years immediately preceding retirement. Additional problems involve integrating with social security and dealing with inflation.

To begin, there is the basic question of what amount of income a retiree needs. Many experts feel that a retired person needs income, including social security, of 60 percent to 70 percent of preretirement income to maintain the preretirement standard of living. Savings come from decreased taxes and elimination of the expenses associated with going to work. Higher income employees need a lower replacement ratio as they consume a smaller portion of their take-home pay and will recognize greater tax savings in retirement.

While needs do not necessarily depend on years of employment, most benefit programs are based on income and length of service. After all, wages themselves are based on service rather than need. Programs are normally designed to provide a "satisfactory" level of retirement income to an employee who has spent a large number of years with the employer or covered by the multiemployer plan.

A major problem in benefit plan development is the question of how to integrate the plan with social security. A company sponsoring a plan will reasonably view its contributions to the pension fund and to social security as a package of retirement benefits. Companies that started pension plans years ago with no effort to integrate them with social security have found their total pension costs rising sharply as social security benefits and taxes have increased. In some cases, the situation has reached the point where employees can increase their after-tax income by retiring. Thus the need to integrate pension benefits with social security is widely recognized. There are three approaches to integration: the excess approach, the offset approach, and the cap approach.

The excess approach ties pension benefits to the social security contributions made by the employer. Social security taxes are based on income up to a certain level, referred to as the base. A typical excess formula for annual pension income is

$$P = 0.01I_1 + 0.02I_2$$

where: P = Annual pension benefit

I_1 = Total income earned during employment to which social security tax was applied

I_2 = Total income during employment to which social security tax did not apply (income above the base)

The formula might be modified to consider average income for the last few years of employment multiplied by years of employment instead of actual total income. When the pension is based on income for the last few years, it is also common practice to redefine I_1 and I_2 in terms of income above and below the base during the last few years of employment. Regardless of the precise formula used, the objective of the excess approach is to integrate employer pension fund and social security expenses.

The offset approach is designed to integrate employee social security income and pension income. A typical offset formula would be

$$P = 0.04I - S$$

where: I = Total income during employment

S = Annual social security benefits

Modifications would involve using average income for recent years or only subtracting some percentage of social security benefits.

On first glance, an offset approach might seem more fair to the employee in that it focuses on achieving a total employee income goal rather than a total company expense goal. However, an offset approach results in serious distortions during a period of rapid inflation. Social security benefits are tied to the cost of living, thereby providing at least some protection from inflation. The offset approach eliminates this protection by decreasing the company pension by an amount equal to any increase in social security cost of living adjustment. At recent inflation rates, the offset approach would move a pension plan participant from a comfortable level of income to poverty within a normal postretirement life span. Thus the offset method appears to be unsuccessful in either assuring retirement income or integrating company costs.[6]

The cap approach is a modification of the offset approach. A typical cap formula would be

$$P = 0.02I \text{ or } (0.8I/n) - S,$$ whichever is less

where: n = Number of years of employment

Again, income for recent years might be used in place of total income. This approach effectively establishes a cap on total benefits, becoming an offset approach when combined benefits would otherwise exceed some percentage of preretirement income.

As with the regular offset approach, the cap approach leads to serious distortions during inflationary periods. If the cap is at 80 percent of preretirement income and the consumer price index triples during a participant's retirement years, the total benefit ceiling, in real dollars, would fall to approximately *one fourth* of preretirement income. Under present social security practices, this would mean a complete halt in pension income. Like the offset approach, the cap approach fails to integrate company expenses or provide retirement income security.

Inflation is, of course, the problem that makes the development of a sound benefit formula so difficult. Failure to include an inflation

---

[6]For an argument in favor of the offset method, see Lloyd S. Kay, "The Pension Benefit Formula: An Element in Financial Planning," *Financial Executive*, (July 1978); 24–30.

adjustment provision in the benefit formula leaves the employee exposed to the risk of having retirement income eroded by inflation. However, it is very difficult for a pension plan to provide inflation protection. If a company knew that the plan would continue indefinitely and the ratio of workers to retirees would remain stable, pension benefits could be tied to salary and paid on an on-going basis, as is done with social security. However, pension plans must be funded on the assumption there will be no new employees and existing commitments must be paid from an investment portfolio. There is no sound actuarial basis for determining the amount of expected inflation to use in computing future benefits and present fund contribution needs. In addition, there is a dearth of investments whose value will grow at the inflation rate. Therefore, adequate inflation protection is very difficult to provide.

A number of approaches have been used to attempt to offset the effect of inflation. One of these is the variable annuity approach under which pension income depends on returns earned on the pension plan investment portfolio. Unfortunately, portfolio returns have tended to be low during periods of high inflation, compounding the retiree's problems. The use of an excess rather than an offset approach helps to decrease the bite of inflation somewhat and still produces a predictable cost structure. Basing retirement income on income the last few years before retirement rather than overall years of employment serves to provide protection against inflation occuring before retirement. Finally, some pension plans simply promise to adjust pension benefits for inflation. However, it is not clear what resources they would have with which to meet such promises in the face of high rates of inflation, low investment porfolio returns, and a declining ratio of working participants to retired participants.

Development of a benefit formula is much more than a question of how much should be spent on pension benefits. It involves questions of who should receive the greatest share, how other sources of retirement income should be considered, and how to deal with inflation. The development of a rational benefit plan—one that is equitable and safe for both the company and the employee—is the first, and possibly the most important decision, facing the pension fund manager.

Choice of Vesting Plans

The choice of a vesting plan involves the desire to control costs, the desire to retain qualified employees, and the desire to provide an equitable program. The cost of a pension plan and the benefits that the employer can afford to provide are affected by the vesting arrangement chosen. Within a given dollar cost constraint, the employer can choose between more generous benefits or more generous vesting. ERISA sets the minimum standards that must be met, with some plans providing vesting in excess of the minimum. The plan must meet one of three minimum standards:

1. Total vesting after ten years on the job.

2. Vesting of 25 percent of accrued rights after five years of employment, with vesting being increased by 5 percent each year for the next five years, then 10 percent each year for the following five years.

3. Vesting of 50 percent of accrued rights after age plus service equal 45, or after five years of service, whichever comes later. The 50 percent vesting must occur after ten years of employment even if age plus employment are still less than 45. After vesting begins, it is then increased 10 percent each year for five years to achieve 100 percent vesting.

Choice of vesting plan has an effect on the rate at which vesting is achieved (table 14-1). An employer wishing to minimize cost should choose the plan that would produce the lowest level of vesting for his particular group of employees. The age-plus-service formula provides the slowest vesting for young employees and the fastest vesting for older employees (table 14-1). The relative costs of the ten-year and phased-vesting plans would depend on turnover patterns within the particular company or industry, though phased vesting would seem to be more equitable.

Table 14-1:

Percentage Vesting Under Alternative Formulas

Years of Employment	4	5	6	7	8	9	10	11	12	13	14	15
10-year full vesting							100	100	100	100	100	100
Phased-in vesting		25	30	35	40	45	50	60	70	80	90	100
Age/Employment												
Hired at 21							50	60	70	80	90	100
Hired at 31				50	60	70	80	90	100			
Hired at 41		50	60	70	80	90	100					

We can see (table 14-1) that the choice of minimum vesting standard does not matter for the employee who leaves before the fifth or after the fifteenth year. However, it is important for the employee leaving between the fifth and fifteenth year. The benefit impacts of the various vesting choices are illustrated below for a worker beginning employment at age twenty-one. The law allows pension funds to exclude income earned before age twenty-five and during the first year of employment in computing benefits, though time for vesting of benefits begins with the date of actual employment. The company's formula for annual pension benefits is

$$P = V \times 0.02 \times I$$

where: P = Annual pension benefit, beginning at age 65

        V = Vesting percentage from table 14–1

        I = Total income earned after twenty-fifth birthday

If the employee leaves at age twenty-seven, after six years of employment at a salary of $1,000 per month, cumulative eligible income (I) is $24,000. We see that the vested percentage is 0.30 after six years, using phased-in vesting, and 0 otherwise (table 14-1). Thus, with phased-in vesting, the employee who starts at age twenty-one, earns $1,000 per month, and leaves after six years, will be eligible for an annual pension at age sixty-five of

$$P = 0.30 \times 0.02 \times \$24,000 = \$144$$

Vested pension entitlements for this employee under various minimum vesting standards are summarized in table 14-2.

Since funding must equal the present value of vested benefits, the cost of the employee's service is clearly affected by the benefit vesting plan chosen. Suppose the company were to choose a more generous program such as complete immediate vesting. At the end of six years, the vested annual benefit for the employee used

Table 14-2:

Illustrative Vested Monthly Benefit Payments Under Alternative Formulas
(in $)

Years of Employment	4	5	6	7	8	9	10	11	12	13	14	15
10-year vesting							120	140	160	180	200	220
Phased-in vesting		5	12	21	32	45	60	84	112	144	180	220
Age/Employment							60	84	112	144	180	220

in the previous example would be

$$P = 1.0 \times 0.02 \times \$72,000 = \$1,440$$

Thus the vested annual benefit for the employee could be between $0 and $1,440 using the same basic benefit computation but varying eligibility and vesting rules. Cost differences could be increased manyfold by changing vesting provisions for a plan with high turnover in the early years.

Choosing the right combination of benefits, eligibility, and vesting is indeed difficult. First, it is necessary to ascertain the preferences of employees; within a total pension benefit budget, what combination of benefits, eligibility, and vesting would they prefer. Second, it is necessary to carefully estimate cost impacts of all alternatives, based on estimates of employee income and turnover. Third, it is necessary to consider questions of equity. Fourth, it is necessary to consider risk; a plan involving high benefits offset by slow vesting could be disastrous if turnover declined sharply. Finally, it is necessary to develop the plan within the constraints of the requirements of ERISA.

Types of vesting continue to vary substantially from plan to plan, with some plans offering complete vesting after three years. However, complete immediate vesting is rare and the trend appears to be toward ten-year vesting, a method that delays vesting about as long as is allowed. Ten-year vesting also has the advantage of being easy for employees to understand.

Funding of Liabilities

A problem of more concern to pension fund sponsors than managers, but worthy of a brief discussion, is that of the funding of pension obligations. Basically, ERISA requires that pension funds hold assets equal in value to the present value of all future benefits earned to date. Contributions must be sufficient to meet current obligations and amortize past obligations over a thirty-year period for a single employer plan and forty years for a multiemployer plan. In theory, most plans would gradually become fully funded.

Several problems have arisen in the funding area. First, contractual changes in benefit formulas and actuarial assumptions have created new unfunded liabilities. Second, the falling prices of securities have reduced the level of funding. Third, there are various questions as to the definition of an unfunded liability. While ERISA provides for insurance to protect beneficiaries from losses due to insufficient funding, companies are at least partially liable for the unfunded liabilities in the case of plan termination and must make contributions sufficient to amortize the unfunded liabilities as discussed above. Among other problems, credit ratings are adversely affected by unfunded liabilities.[7]

The assets needed to meet funding requirements depend on actuarial assumptions about employee turnover and beneficiary life span. Fortunately, actuaries have excellent life span data and reasonably good turnover data to work with. Unfortunately, the same cannot be said for salary growth and investment return assumptions. A recent survey revealed that the median salary growth assumption was 5 percent and the median investment return assumption was 6 percent.[8] With salary growth being substantially greater than investment return in those years, contribution formulas proved inadequate, creating a stream of new unfunded liabilities.

Without getting into complex details, we should take a brief look at the problem of defining unfunded liabilities. If we hire an employee and ignore, for simplicity of illustration, the possibility of his leaving employment before retirement, we can compute the present value of eventual benefits using appropriate actuarial assumptions. At any given time, some of the amount needed will be on hand with the rest to be accumulated from future contributions. Thus, the present value of projected benefits is divided between assets on hand and present value of future contributions. Most of, a small percentage of, or none of the present value of future

---

[7]Patrick J. Regan, "Credit Ratings and Pension Costs," *Financial Analysts Journal* (March/April, 1979): 6–7.

[8]*Pension and Investments,* January 2, 1978.

contributions may appear as an unfunded liability,[9] depending on accounting method selected. While we are certain, given our actuarial assumptions, what the present value of future needed contributions is, the accounting conventions give wide latitude in choosing what portion of this present value should be assigned to unfunded liabilities and what portion should be considered "present value of future normal pension costs." While it is generally agreed that not all of the present value of future benefits should be considered a present liability—since much of it is dependent on assumed future employee income—there is substantial room for disagreement.

While the problem of defining unfunded liabilities remains troublesome, it is clear that by most definitions unfunded liabilities have increased rather than decreased. The increases—resulting from changing benefit formulas, poor portfolio performance, and inflation induced wage increases—present a difficult problem. These liabilities decrease value in mergers, decrease cash flow available for reinvestment, and create a potential national problem in the event of a major economic downturn. Methods of dealing with these problems have proven to be elusive.

Managing the Pension Fund Portfolio

The classic risk/return trade-offs of finance are most clearly seen in the area of portfolio management. A high return on the portfolio can serve to lower pension fund expense to the company and/or increase employee pension benefits. Unfortunately, increased expected return is normally achieved only by accepting increased risk (chapter 7). If risks are taken and the fund suffers losses, increased contributions are required or pensions are jeopardized. The fund must be guided by a portfolio management policy that gives adequate operational guidelines with regard to risk and return.

In establishing policy, the first thing that must be decided is who will have primary management responsibility. Where the pension plan is negotiated with a union, there is frequently a board of trustees consisting of members from both management and labor. In the case of some large funds, the sponsoring company decides to manage the funds directly, paying investment advisers to provide recommendations and banks to provide custodial services. However, most companies assign funds to a trustee, either providing general policy statements or leaving the trustees to develop their own policies. The division of funds among several trustees is common practice; funds are periodically reallocated among trustees according to their past performance. When several trustees are used, each may be given different guidelines. For example, an insurance company may be given funds to invest in real estate; a brokerage firm, given funds to invest in common stock.

Parties serving as trustes include banks, insurance companies, brokerage firms, and investment counselors such as those who manage mutual funds. Banks, the institutions that traditionally dominated this area, have experienced increasing competition from these other groups. Services are heavily marketed and competition to achieve the best performance is intense, sometimes leading to concerns about unsound investment policy.

Factors to consider in all the choice of trustees include:

Investment skill

Costs

Administrative skill

Size and financial strength[10]

In addition to the obvious need to invest profitably and prudently for a reasonable fee, the trustee has complex record keeping responsibilities. Failure to keep proper records and maintain

[9]Paul A. Gerwitz and Robert C. Phillips, "Unfunded Pension Liabilities . . . The New Myth," *Financial Executive* (August 1978): 18–24.

[10]Patrick J. Davey, *Financial Management of Pension Plans* (New York: The Conference Board): 46.

proper administrative controls led to multi-million dollar losses of securities in the late 1960s and early 1970s.[11] Finally, the standards of fiduciary responsibility cannot be effectively enforced unless the trustee has the size and financial strength to provide at least some backing to commitments made.

Regardless of who accepts responsibility for managing the portfolio, a management policy must be developed. The policy typically specifies, among other things:

Types of investments

Risk levels

Performance objectives

Restrictions on investment in sponsoring company's securities

Modern mean-variance portfolio theory provides a logical starting point for the development of management policy. For these purposes, there are two primary lessons from portfolio theory:

1. Risk should be viewed in the context of a portfolio rather than for each security separately.

2. Higher expected return is normally associated with greater risk.

The portfolio approach to risk is based on the observation that some risks can be diversified away—effectively eliminated—when risky securities are combined in portfolios. For example, the risk that one automobile design will be favored over others can be diversified away by owning stocks in all automobile companies. However, even a well-diversified portfolio will move up and down in value with market conditions in general. Thus risk associated with market conditions in general cannot be eliminated through diversification. Portfolio theory argues that rational people will eliminate diversifiable risk by constructing portfolios consisting of a number of different investments. Opinion varies on the number of securities necessary to construct a well diversified portfolio, but most writers agree that no more than thirty securities are required.

A closely related body of literature argues that markets are *efficient,* meaning that no investor has superior information or superior ability to evaluate information. Thus the *efficient market hypothesis* argues that the investor cannot expect higher returns except through the acceptance of greater risk.

The implications of the above analysis for pension fund portfolio management are quite significant. First, the portfolio should not contain diversifiable risk since there is no reward for such risk. Thirty is probably a sufficient number of securities to achieve this objective unless the thirty are concentrated in certain industries.

We might also consider the point of view in determining risk. To the extent benefits are not insured, risk should be examined from the point of view of the beneficiary. For example, a concentration in real estate would not provide reasonable diversification if most beneficiaries had real estate investments in the form of their homes and did not own other assets. Heavy investment in the sponsoring company would not be wise, as income risk to the employees is already tied to the well-being of the company.

Finally, plans and objectives must consider the risk-return trade-off and should not be based on the assumption that the fund manager can regularly achieve superior results without accepting greater than average risk. Stating return objectives without reference to risk may simply lead to greater risk being accepted in keeping with the risk-return trade-off.

This problem has sometimes been handled in the pension fund area by specifying a weighted average beta[12] level and specifying that the portfolio be well diversified, then attempting to maximize return within these constraints.

ERISA creates a set of standards that must be considered in applying the principles of portfolio theory. Of particular interest are ERISA's standards of fiduciary responsibility:

1. The fiduciary must act only for the

---

[11]For an interesting discussion of these problems, see John Brooks, *The Go-Go Year* (New York: Weybright and Talley, 1973): 182–205.

[12]Recall that beta measures the sensitivity of returns for a security of portfolio to returns for securities in general.

purpose of providing benefits to the fund's participants and defraying reasonable costs.

2. The fiduciary must act "with the care, skill, prudence, and diligence under the circumstances then prevailing that a prudent man acting in a like capacity and familiar with such matters would use in the conduct of an enterprise of a like character with like aims."

3. The fiduciary must diversify the portfolio to minimize the risk of large losses.

4. The fiduciary must comply with the plan's documents if they are consistent with ERISA.

The prohibition on conflict of interest, requirement that plan documents be followed, and the instruction to diversify cause little difficulty. In fact, portfolio theory tells us something about how to achieve diversification. Unfortunately, the prudent man rule, as presently interpreted, causes some confusion. In its earlier history at common law, the prudent man rule was interpreted as prohibiting equity investments of any type. However, the application has changed over the years and the concept of investment vs. speculative securities has developed. A frequent interpretation is that only the stocks of very safe, well-established companies can be included in a portfolio.

While common stock is recognized as a reasonable investment medium, the full benefits of diversification are not recognized. The trustee may be held accountable for each investment individually. Thus the portfolio manager who achieves a normal risk level by holding a few high-risk stocks offset by a large group of low-risk stocks might have problems if one of the high-risk stocks does poorly, even if the portfolio as a whole does well.[13] The portfolio manager would be free of liability if he invested entirely in conservative, well-established companies and the portfolio performed poorly. Portfolio theory suggests that portfolio risk should be the appropriate risk guideline, but the prudent man rule does not adequately differenti-

ate between diversifiable and nondiversifiable risk.[14]

Under ERISA, there has been an attempt to reinterpret the prudent man rule in light of portfolio theory. Unfortunately, it takes years for an adequate base of case law to be built and portfolio managers cannot wait to act. As a practical matter, they frequently limit equity investments to a narrow list of well established companies held by numerous other institutional portfolios. The equities of some companies were "institutional favorites" in March 1984 (table 14-3). Investing in such "favorites" provides excellent protection from liability under the prudent man rule. However, the practice results in a two-tier market consisting of a small group of stocks favored by the institutions and the rest of the market, largely ignored by institutions.

One problem with limiting all investment to a list of older, stable companies is that it may not provide complete diversification. Diversification does not come entirely from large numbers of securities. Holding stock of all steel companies would clearly leave the portfolio undiversified with regard to factors affecting the steel business. Likewise, the holding of only old, stable companies and the complete exclusion of innovative newer companies leaves portfolios exposed to risks unique to established companies and may limit returns by excluding highly profitable opportunities.

From society's viewpoint, the use of a list of institutional favorites has important implications for resource allocation. With the growing importance of pension funds and other institutional portfolios, the favored companies have ready access to new capital while other companies are virtually shut off from the capital markets. Specifically, the innovative new companies that traditionally provide a major source of economic growth have had their access to the capital markets severely restricted.

As the above discussion shows, the prudent

---

[13]Because ERISA is fairly new, this guideline has not been tested well through case law.

[14]For an excellent discussion of this problem, see Roger D. Blair, "ERISA and the Prudent Man Rule: Avoiding Perverse Results," *Sloan Management Review* (Winter 1979): 15–23.

Table 14-3:

Stocks Currently Favored by Institutional Portfolios

Company Name	Number of Institutions Holding*
American Express	538
Atlantic Ritchfield	892
Citicorp	531
Coca Cola	540
Digital Equipment	580
du Pont de Nemours	575
Eastman Kodak	880
Exxon	962
General Electric	1,015
General Motors	912
GTE Corp.	629
Haliburton Co.	598
Hewlett Packard	535
IBM	1,507
Johnson & Johnson	614
Merck & Co.	668
Minnesota Mining & Manufacturing	698
Mobil	716
Pfizer	644
Phillip Morris	666
Phillips Petroleum	555
Procter & Gamble	577
Reynolds (R, J) Ind.	515
Schlumberger, Ltd.	840
Sears, Roebuck	583
Standard Oil of California	686
Standard Oil of Indiana	755
Texaco	584
Union Pacific	577
Xerox	536

*Standard and Poors Stock Guide, March 1984. While the data are based on a survey of 2400 institutions, excluding pension funds, it is believed that pension funds do not differ from the other institutions with regard to which particular stocks are favored at a given time.

man rule sets requirements that would be considered unneccessary and even harmful from the perspective of portfolio theory. Because case law is an evolutionary type of law, we can expect that portfolio risk will come to be fully recognized.

In addition to portfolio theory and fiduciary responsibility, the pension fund manager can also expect certain standards to be set by the sponsoring company. The following is a typical example of a performance objective.

The portfolio should earn an average return over a five-year period of at least 20 percent greater than the S & P 500 stock index and at least 10 percent per annum.

A beta range may also be specified, though this is less common.

Performance standards of the type illustrated are particularly difficult to meet in light of what we know about portfolio theory, efficient market theory, and fiduciary responsibility. If everyone is to purchase securities from the same restricted list, everyone has the same information, and nobody has superior ability to analyze available data, earning a superior return is going to be a most difficult project. In fact, the theory would tell us that higher return can be earned only through the acceptance of higher risk. There is no evidence that objectives of the type illustrated are attainable. Moving funds from portfolio manager to portfolio manager in search of "superior" performance is likely to be unproductive.

The considerations discussed above have led to some degree of consensus as to what should be included in a pension fund portfolio. The mix of pension fund portfolio assets has developed over the years (table 14-4). From a time when equity was almost entirely excluded from trusteed portfolios, thought on the subject evolved to the point that by the end of the 1960s—a decade in which stock prices rose sharply—common stock became the dominant asset. The poor stock market returns of the 1970s caused a further rethinking, with a growing interest in the asset that performed well in the 1970s: real estate.[15] There has also been a limited move to internationally diversified portfolios designed to decrease risk and increase return. The consensus as to what a

---

[15]Elbert Bressie, "When Will Pension Funds Enter the Real Estate Market?" *Financial Executive* (April 1979): 26–29.

Table 14-4:

Assets of Private Noninsured Pension Funds at Market Value
(in $ millions)

	1955	1960	1965	1970	1972	1974	1976	1978	1979*
Cash and deposits	415	546	940	1,804	1,857	4,286	2,199	8,110	8,609
U.S. gov. securities	2,938	2,655	2,913	2,998	3,700	5,582	14,918	18,767	21,516
Corporate & other bonds	7,702	14,629	21,949	24,919	26,232	30,825	37,858	48,633	51,261
Preferred stock	624	718	768	1,631	1,869	703	1,212	1,162	1,099
Common stock	5,461	15,827	39,986	65,456	113,369	62,582	108,483	106,732	122,703
Mortgages	321	1,034	3,391	3,504	2,427	2,063	2,160	2,554	2,664
Other assets	592	1,398	2,950	4,422	4,908	5,681	7,073	15,585	17,336
Total assets	18,053	37,077	72,898	104,737	154,363	111,724	173,906	201,545	225,188
Common stock as a percentage of total assets	30%	43%	55%	62%	73%	56%	62%	53%	55%

*This series was discontinued after 1979.

Source: Security and Exchange Commission, *Annual Report 1979* and *Statistical Bulletin*, May, 1980.

"prudent man" would invest in continues to evolve with changing market conditions.

Portfolio Performance Measurement Both for purposes of analyzing past performance and for projecting future returns, performance measures must be developed. First it is necessary to compute an annualized rate of return. This problem is made a bit difficult by the fact that funds are added and deducted periodically. It is necessary to separate performance of the portfolio from the impact of additions and withdrawals of funds. The problem is illustrated below for two pension funds over a two-year period.

	Fund A	Fund B
Starting market value	$1,000	$1,000
Cash contributed at the start of the first year	1,000	0
First-year return	80%	80%
Cash contributed at the start of the second year	0	1,000
Second-year return	10%	10%
Ending value	$3,960	$3,080

Each fund started with $1,000 and received $1,000 in additional contributions over the two-year period. Can we conclude that fund A was better managed because the terminal value was higher? More careful examination shows that return earned by each fund was identical for each year. The higher ending value for A was a result of the timing of contributions from sponsors, not differences in performance by portfolio managers.

The *geometric mean return* (time weighted rate of return)[16] is a method used to put returns on a comparable basis. The geometric mean return for a portfolio is computed using the following formula:

$$G = \sqrt[n]{(1 + r_1)(1 + r_2) \ldots (1 + r_n)} - 1 \quad (14\text{-}1)$$

where: G = Geometric mean or time weighted rate of return

---

[16]In financial analysis, the geometric mean of a series of annual returns over time is viewed as the annual compound rate of growth inherent in the series of returns.

r_i = Return (price appreciation and dividends) during period i

n = Total number of periods over which evaluation is to occur

For the portfolios illustrated above, the geometric mean return is

$$G = \sqrt[2]{(1 + 0.8)(1 + 0.1)} - 1 = \underline{40.7\%}$$

The geometric mean return, not being affected by the timing of contributions, is the same for each portfolio. Thus it measures the performance of the portfolio manager, not the effects of contribution and withdrawal timing.

While the geometric mean return is a useful method of evaluating returns, it does not include any method of recognizing differences in risk accepted. Based on portfolio theory, a widely used risk adjustment measure is the reward to variability ratio:

$$\frac{R_p - R_f}{\sigma_p} \quad (14\text{-}2)$$

where: R_p = Average return for the portfolio over the periods for which performance is being evaluated

R_f = Average return on risk-free investments over the same period

σ_p = Standard deviation of returns for the portfolio over this period

For one portfolio to outperform another, it should have a higher ratio (equation 14-2).

SUMMARY

Pension fund management involves three sets of trade-offs and one set of contradictions. The first trade-off involves the desire to provide maximum benefits at a minimum cost. The second trade-off involves the desire to provide maximum benefits to individuals and the desire to provide coverage to as many people as possible. Within a particular total cost limit, various combinations of vesting, participation rights, and benefit formulas are possible. The choice involves legal constraints of ERISA, employee desires, union labor contract provisions, and management judgment. The third trade-off is the classic risk-return trade-off faced in virtually all portfolio management problems. Higher returns reduce cost and allow improved benefits, but involve greater risk of loss. Most pension funds are managed quite conservatively with regard to risk. Finally, there is a conflict between portfolio risk as recognized by modern portfolio theory and individual security risk as defined through the prudent man rule. Pension fund management consists of developing both benefit and portfolio management policy in line with these off-setting and contradictory considerations.

QUESTIONS

1. Why have pension fund assets grown so rapidly since the passage of ERISA?

2. Do you feel it is appropriate for the federal government to sponsor unfunded pension plans? Why? Do you feel it is appropriate for state and local governments to sponsor unfunded pension plans? Why?

3. While pension funds together own enough stock to exercise effective voting control over many major U.S. corporations, they have not done so. What reasons can you think of for their failure to attempt to exercise control?

4. What groups of people are *not* protected by ERISA?

5. What factors should be considered in developing a vesting formula?

6. Should a pension fund sponsor give the fiduciary standards such as "outperform the stock market average by at least 2 percent"? Why?

7. It has been claimed that the prudent man rule "discourages true diversification." Comment on this claim.

8. In light of efficient market theory, can international diversification of the pension fund portfolio be considered "prudent"?

PROBLEMS

1. An employee retires after working twenty years and earning total wages of $200,000, with social security being paid on half of this amount. After retirement, the employee will receive $4,000 a year in social security payments. Inflation is expected to average 10 percent per year. How much pension benefit will the employee receive in the first and tenth year under

   a. the excess approach, with annual benefits equal to 1 percent of total income on which social security was paid and 2 percent of total income on which social security was not paid?

   b. the offset approach, with annual pension benefits equal to 4 percent of total income minus social security benefits?

   c. the cap approach, with annual benefits equal to 2 percent of total income or

   $$\frac{0.8 \times \text{total income}}{\text{number of years employed}}$$

   − social security benefits,

   whichever is less?

2. You begin to work for a company at age twenty. Thereafter, you change jobs every ten years, just prior to completing your tenth year of employment, until you retire just before reaching age seventy. Assuming your income did not change, you would be vested for what percent of total benefits from all employers using

   a. ten-year full vesting?

   b. phased-in vesting?

3. A pension fund portfolio received $100,000 from the sponsor at the beginning of the first year. Through investment return, this amount grows to $120,000 by the end of the first year. It then receives an additional contribution of $30,000 from the sponsor, bringing the total value up to $150,000. Through investment return, the value grows

to \$160,000 by the end of the second year. What is the geometric mean return?

SELECTED REFERENCES

Blair, Roger D. "ERISA and the Prudent Man Rule: Avoiding Perverse Results." *Sloan Management Review* 20 (Winter 1979): 15–23.

Babbel, David F. and Staking, Kim B. "A Capital Budgeting Analysis of Life Insurance Costs in the United States: 1950–1979." *The Journal of Finance* 38 (March 1983): 149–170.

Drucker, Peter. *The Unseen Revolution.* New York: Harper and Row, 1976.

Feldstein, Martin, and Seligman, Stephanie. "Pension Funding, Share Prices and National Savings." *The Journal of Finance* 36 (September 1981): 801–824.

Rosen, Kenneth. "The Role of Pension Funds in Housing Finance." *Housing Finance Review* 1 (April 1982): 147–177.

Winter, Ralph A. "On the Rate Structure of the American Life Insurance Market." *The Journal of Finance* 36 (March 1981): 81–96.

Chapter 15

International Aspects of Financial Institution Management

The topic of international finance is extremely broad, including the problems of exchange rate and balance of payments policy, the myriad international financial institutions, and the international aspects of financial management. In keeping with the purpose of this text, we concentrate on the international aspects of financial institution management and the role of financial institutions in facilitating international business. We concentrate on the primary financial problems and needs encountered by business and financial institutions dealing in the international sphere, and discuss the institutions, instruments, and conventions that have been developed to meet these needs.

DEVELOPMENT OF INTERNATIONAL BUSINESS

Economic history is characterized by growing interdependence. The industrial revolution led to interdependence between people and busi-

ness units, and the growth of international business has led to growing interdependence between nations. The result has been a rising standard of living and a growing challenge to financial managers and policy makers.

Reasons for International Business

When asked why international business has expanded so rapidly, economists are quick to cite the *theory of comparative advantage*. Just as income within countries has been increased through specialization by individuals, world income can be increased through specialization by countries. For example, a country with a limited population and substantial potential for hydroelectric energy might concentrate on manufacturing processes requiring high energy inputs and purchase products requiring extensive manual labor from a country with a large, low-skill population. Both countries would gain from the exchange.

The theory of comparative advantage certainly accounts for a substantial amount of export and import activity in a world in which raw materials, energy, capital, labor, and technology are so unevenly distributed. The advanced economies have primarily sold goods requiring highly skilled labor and capital intensive production. Their imports, by comparison, have been raw materials and products requiring a substantial input of low-skill labor.

Technological advantage is a type of comparative advantage which deserves special attention. A country may have a technological advantage because of a sudden break-through, a highly educated population, or a heavy investment in a particular technology. It could be argued that United States' domination of the international computer market for a number of years depended on some important conceptual breakthroughs as well as on a heavy investment in engineering development and on a highly educated population. By comparison, the development of a new class of airplane, such as the Anglo-French Concorde, depends primarily on an engineering application of known technology. The fixed cost of converting this known technology to a tested airplane is measured in billions of dollars. The country that takes the initial risk in making this investment has a decided cost advantage over other countries considering their own production. Had the Concorde proved commercially feasible, the United States and Russia are the only other countries that could have been expected to make the investment necessary to develop a competitive airplane. Other countries wishing to own such airplanes would have purchased them from one of these countries, selling other goods to obtain the necessary funds.

Moving from import-export to internationalization of production, technological advantage again comes to play. A company with developed technology may take advantage of that technology by producing at home or in other countries. The production of foreign designed automobiles in the United States is one such example. The construction of United States designed calculators in developing countries for sale in the United States is an even more striking example of companies roaming the globe in search of comparative advantage in any one phase of their operation.

Differences in capital accumulation rates and in investment opportunities represent other reasons for foreign business. Other things being equal, investors will place their funds where the highest return can be earned. If a country has a mature economy, a nongrowing population, and a high savings rate, domestic investment opportunities are likely to be limited and businesses will look overseas for opportunities paying higher returns. Frequently, these may be found in countries with growing populations and limited savings. The overseas investments of oil producing countries can also be explained in terms of an inability to find domestic investments paying a high rate of return. Their economies cannot absorb such huge amounts of capital efficiently.

Diversification and risk control are other motivations for foreign business. Investments or business operations in numerous countries help to diversify away risks unique to a particular country. Both business cycle risks and risks associated with government instability can be at least partially diversified away through international expansion.

Finally, much international business activity is motivated by the desire to avoid taxes or government regulation. For example, production may be moved to a country with minimal pollution laws. By operating in several countries, it is frequently possible, through altering methods of cost allocation, to shift at least some profits to the country with the most favorable tax structure.

Growth of International Business

International business is of growing importance to the United States (table 15-1). Particularly in the period since World War II, the United States has grown to be a major power in the international marketplace. Concurrently, the international marketplace has grown to be a major factor in the United States economy.

While the growth in international business is itself impressive, the changing nature of

Table 15-1:

**Exports, Imports, and Capital Flows
of the United States
(in $ billions)**

Year	Exports	Imports	Capital Outflow	Capital Inflow
1946	12	5	1.6	2.1
1950	10	12	1.4	1.9
1955	14	12	1.5	1.5
1960	20	15	4	2.3
1965	26	22	6	0.7
1970	42	40	9	6
1975	107	98	40	16
1976	115	124	51	37
1977	121	152	36	51
1978	142	175	61	64
1979	182	212	62	38
1980	224	250	86	54
1981	236	264	109	78
1982	218	250	123	94

Source: Department of Commerce, Bureau of Economic Analysis, and summarized in *Economic Report of the President.*

international business is of even greater significance. The trend has been away from the traditional import-export form of business toward truly multinational business, characterized by capital, technology, materials, and people moving across national boundaries with increased freedom. The dollar value of foreign investment by the U.S. in foreign countries and by foreign countries in the U.S. is shown in table 15-1.

Since World War II, exports and imports have grown at a more rapid rate than has the Gross National Product; inflows and outflows of capital have grown at an even faster rate.

Analyses of these international accounts and their rates of growth tend to underestimate the internationalization of business; they do not capture foreign control of capital raised and invested within a country. For example, the building of a Volkswagen plant in the United States financed with borrowing in the United States, shows up as neither import nor capital flow. Thus, the growth

of international business has been much more rapid than the growth of the domestic economy.

Banking provides yet another exmple of the growth of international business. In 1960, eight U.S. banks had overseas branches, and assets in these branches totaled $3.5 billion. By 1982, 163 U.S. banks had overseas branches, with assets totaling $376 billion.

Before leaving this overview, we should note that for all this growth, international business remains much less important to the United States than to most other developed countries. The international business of some other countries can be compared to the United States (table 15-2). Because of its internal resources and diversity, the United States depends on foreign trade much less than any other developed capitalistic country.

SPECIAL PROBLEMS ENCOUNTERED IN INTERNATIONAL BUSINESS

The company involved in international business faces a number of problems not faced by the domestic company. First, there is the problem of

Table 15-2:

**Exports as a Percentage
of Gross Domestic Product, 1978**

Israel	43
Korea	40
West Germany	34
Sweden	33
Great Britain	27
Italy	26
France	22
Japan	17
Brazil	9
USA	8
India	7

Source: *International Financial Statistics,* International Monetary Fund.

managing exchange rate risk arising from the fact that different currencies are involved and the relative values of those currencies are subject to unexpected change. Second, the exporter or importer faces noncompliance risk arising from distance and lack of familiarity with the customer or supplier. Third, those involved in international business face country or sovereign risks— those risks related to the economy, political, and social factors in a given country. Finally, the truly international business faces the problem of raising and investing money in the international money and capital markets. Financial institutions aid nonfinancial businesses with each of these problems and use the international markets to make investments and raise funds for themselves. Each of the main problem areas of international business is discussed in the following sections.

EXCHANGE RATE RISK

One of the major problems in international finance results from the fact that the value of one currency relative to another is continually changing. Any international contract involving future payment requires that one side agree to transact in a currency other than that of his native country and accept the risk that the amount involved will, when converted to his own currency, be different than anticipated.

While we usually expect risk to decline as we gain experience in a particular area, foreign exchange risk has increased concurrent with the increased volume of international business. From the end of World War II until the late 1960s, exchange rates were held nearly constant by international agreement. The cornerstone of the agreement was the U.S. commitment to buy or sell any amount of gold at $35 an ounce. Imbalances between exports and imports were cleared through purchase and sale of U.S. dollars or gold. The lack of gold stock growth in relation to business growth led to problems in the 1960s; the first major break in stability was the devaluation of the British pound in 1967. What has happened since then is illustrated in figure

15-1, using the British pound and the German mark as examples. While the dollar has generally strengthened against the pound and weakened against the mark, it has become more volatile against both currencies. International business continues to grow in the face of this instability because methods of dealing with these risks have been developed.

Managing Exchange Rate Risk

The possibility of a change in the relative values of currencies creates two primary types of risk: *translation risk* and *transaction risk*. These risks and methods of dealing with them are discussed in the following paragraphs.

Translation risk arises primarily from accounting conventions. A U.S. firm with interests in several countries must somehow convert all of its assets to dollar values for the purpose of preparing annual reports. The current rules on translation are spelled out in *Financial Accounting Standards Board Statement #52 (FASB #52)*.

As a very simple example of what happens under current accounting rules, consider a U.S. firm that owns securities denominated in Deutsch Marks (D.M.) and also owes money payable in D.M. The securities are valued at 2,000 D.M. and the debt is for 1,200 D.M.; the company's D.M. monetary assets exceed its D.M. monetary liabilities by 800 D.M. If the D.M. is worth $0.50 at the beginning of the year and $0.40 at the end of the year, the company will be required to report a loss of $80 (0.50 × 800 −

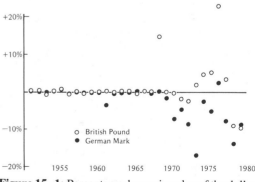

Figure 15–1: Percentage change in value of the dollar with respect to other currencies.

0.40 × 800) for the year, even though it did not sell the securities or pay the debt. The risk of having to report a loss because of the rules used in translating foreign assets, liabilities, and income to U.S. dollars is referred to as *translation risk*. Translation problems can also arise in areas like depreciation computation and inventory/cost of goods sold calculations when business is conducted in more than one country.

The situation becomes more complex when the U.S. firm has subsidiaries operating in various countries. Current rules may require the company to report an exchange rate loss even if one subsidiary has D.M. monetary assets and another subsidiary has D.M. monetary liabilities of exactly the same amount. Under FASB #52 these D.M. asset and liability positions are not necessarily netted against each other in consolidation when they are housed in different subsidiaries. Thus, there is the potential for the company to be exposed to translation risk if any subsidiary has a mismatch between financial assets and liabilities denominated in other currencies.

Transaction risk represents a more immediate and more real risk. Transaction risk occurs when there are outstanding contracts calling for payment or receipt in a currency other than that of the home country. They occur because of purchase or sale on credit as well as from contracts for future delivery with the price agreed upon today. Suppose a U.S. firm agrees to purchase French goods for one million francs at a time when the exchange rate is 0.1231 dollars per franc. The goods are to be delivered and paid for in ninety days and the importer has contracted to resell them for $125,000 in the United States. At the present exchange rate, the goods would cost $123,100 (1,000,000 × 0.1231). Thus the importer expects to sell the goods for $1,900 above cost. However, if the exchange rate should rise to above 0.125 by the end of the ninety-day period, the products will be sold at a loss instead of a gain. Clearly, some method of eliminating these risks is desirable.

Balance sheet hedging (also referred to as money market hedging) provides an effective method of controlling exchange rate risk. It is most widely used to control translation risk, although it can be used to control transaction risk. Essentially, a company (or each subsidiary of a company) strives to have a net financial assets in each currency exactly equal to financial liabilities in that currency. We started this example with a company that had D.M. assets $800 in excess of its D.M. liabilities. A balance sheet hedge would consist of arranging an $800 loan denominated in D.M. and using the proceed to make investments denominated in dollars. The company that contracted to pay for French goods in ninety days could hedge by buying Francs today and investing them in French bank certificates of deposit or other French Franc denominated investments. This would, however, have the disadvantage of tying up funds for ninety days.

Currency futures provide another widely used method of hedging against exchange rate risks. Currency futures, or forward exchange contracts, are handled in a manner similar to forward contracts for commodities. Two parties enter into a contract, agreeing to exchange a certain amount of one currency for a certain amount of another currency at a specified future date. If we enter into a futures contract for French francs, we assure ourselves a certain number of francs at a specified price while the other party is being assured of a certain amount of dollars at a fixed price in francs.

The use of a forward exchange contract can be illustrated with the French franc example from above. The forward exchange quotes from the *Wall Street Journal* appear in table 15-3. Our purchaser of French goods sees that he can purchase ninety-day forward exchange contracts for French francs at 0.1224. In other words, he can contract to purchase francs at $0.1224 each. This assures him a total cost of $122,400 and secures a profit on the purchase and resale of goods.

The forward exchange market operates in a manner similar to the over-the-counter securities market. There is no central meeting place.[1] The

---

[1]An exception is the Chicago Board of Options Exchange, which maintains a physical location for dealing in currency futures.

Table 15-3:

Foreign Exchange

Monday, April 16, 1984

The New York foreign exchange selling rates below apply to trading among banks in amounts of $1 million and more, as quoted at 3 p.m. Eastern time by Bankers Trust Co. Retail transactions provide fewer units of foreign currency per dollar.

Country	U.S. $ equiv. Monday	U.S. $ equiv. Friday	Currency per U.S. $ Monday	Currency per U.S. $ Friday
Argentina (Peso)	.03017	.03017	33.142	33.142
Australia (Dollar)	.9173	.9185	1.0902	1.0887
Austria (Schilling)	.05394	.05414	18.54	18.47
Belgium (Franc)				
Commercial rate	.01856	.01861	53.895	53.745
Financial rate	.01812	.01810	55.200	55.250
Brazil (Cruzeiro)	.0007496	.0007496	1334.00	1334.00
Britain (Pound)	1.4210	1.4295	.7037	.6995
30-Day Forward	1.4235	1.4319	.7025	.6984
90-Day Forward	1.4289	1.4369	.6998	.6959
180-Day Forward	1.4369	1.4444	.6959	.6923
Canada (Dollar)	.7811	.7820	1.2803	1.2787
30-Day Forward	.7814	.7824	1.2798	1.2782
90-Day Forward	.7815	.7825	1.2796	1.2780
180-Day Forward	.7817	.7825	1.2793	1.2780
Chile (Official rate)	.01134	.01134	88.18	88.18
China (Yuan)	.4821	.4821	2.0742	2.0742
Colombia (Peso)	.01059	.01059	94.47	94.47
Denmark (Krone)	.1031	.1037	9.6950	9.6460
Ecuador (Sucre)				
Official rate	.01685	.01685	59.34	59.34
Floating rate	.01120	.01120	89.25	89.25
Finland (Markka)	.1775	.1782	5.6350	5.6125
France (Franc)	.1231	.1238	8.1250	8.0880
30-Day Forward	.1229	.1236	8.1350	8.0910
90-Day Forward	.1224	.1230	8.1675	8.1270
180-Day Forward	.1214	.1219	8.2400	8.2020
Greece (Drachma)	.009556	.009606	104.65	104.10
Hong Kong (Dollar)	.1281	.1281	7.8080	7.8085
India (Rupee)	.0924	.0925	10.8225	10.8108
Indonesia (Rupiah)	.0009980	.0009980	1002.00	1002.00
Ireland (Punt)	1.1635	1.1660	.8595	.8576
Israel (Shekel)	.005938	.005992	168.40	166.90
Italy (Lira)	.0006125	.0006160	1632.50	1623.50
Japan (Yen)	.004435	.004448	225.47	224.80
30-Day Forward	.004453	.004465	224.58	223.95
90-Day Forward	.004488	.004499	222.82	222.26
180-Day Forward	.004544	.004553	220.07	219.62
Lebanon (Pound)	.1795	.1795	5.57	5.57
Malaysia (Ringgit)	.4367	.4372	2.2900	2.2875
Mexico (Peso)				
Floating rate	.005587	.005571	179.00	179.50
Netherlands (Guilder)	.3365	.3373	2.9720	2.9645
New Zealand (Dollar)	.6586	.6597	1.5184	1.5158
Norway (Krone)	.1318	.1324	7.5850	7.5525
Pakistan (Rupee)	.07463	.07463	13.40	13.40
Peru (Sol)	.0003694	.0003694	2707.11	2707.11
Philippines (Peso)	.07133	.07133	14.02	14.02
Portugal (Escudo)	.007496	.007496	133.40	133.40
Saudi Arabia (Riyal)	.2841	.2843	3.5195	3.5175
Singapore (Dollar)	.4797	.4802	2.0845	2.0825
South Africa (Rand)	.8055	.8060	1.2415	1.2407
South Korea (Won)	.001260	.001260	793.40	793.40
Spain (Peseta)	.006680	.006702	149.70	149.20
Sweden (Krona)	.1277	.1283	7.8320	7.7940
Switzerland (Franc)	.4565	.4591	2.1905	2.1780
30-Day Forward	.4593	.4619	2.1771	2.1650
90-Day Forward	.4649	.4674	2.1508	2.1394
180-Day Forward	.4733	.4757	2.1128	2.1020
Taiwan (Dollar)	.02506	.02506	39.90	39.90
Thailand (Baht)	.04349	.04349	22.995	22.995
Uruguay (New Peso)				
Financial	.02015	.02015	49.63	49.63
Venezuela (Bolivar)				
Official rate	.1333	.1333	7.50	7.50
Floating rate	.07112	.07112	14.06	14.06
W. Germany (Mark)	.3787	.3807	2.6405	2.6265
30-Day Forward	.3804	.3824	2.6291	2.6153
90-Day Forward	.3837	.3856	2.6061	2.5932
180-Day Forward	.3888	.3906	2.5719	2.5599
– – –				
SDR	1.05779	1.06094	.945366	.942562

Special Drawing Rights are based on exchange rates for the U.S., West German, British, French and Japanese currencies. Source: International Monetary Fund.

z-Not quoted.

Source: Reprinted by permission of the *Wall Street Journal* © Dow Jones & Company, Inc. 17 April, 1984. All rights reserved.

market consists of a few large banks and a handful of foreign exchange dealers and brokers who make a market among each other. The banks then transact with customers either directly or through their correspondent banks. Participants in the market include industrial corporations as well as financial institutions covering their own positions and speculators hoping to make a profit by correctly predicting the direction of forward exchange rates.

The forward exchange market is quite limited. There are only a few major currencies involved and the longest contract normally available is for 180 days.

Currency options provide yet another—and rapidly growing—approach to controlling exchange rate risks. Like other option contracts, the currency option gives its holder the right, but not the obligation, to purchase a stated amount of a particular currency at a fixed price prior to a specified expiration date. A U.S. company with a D.M. liability could eliminate its exchange rate risk by purchasing an option to acquire D.M. at a fixed price. The option contract is particularly popular when the future obligation is uncertain; an offer to purchase something with payment in D.M. has been made, for example, and there is still a question about whether the offer will be accepted. Unlike stock options which are heavily traded by individual investors, most currency options are written by large banks and purchased by corporations.

The European Currency Unit (ECU) is another vehicle for decreasing exchange rate risk. The ECU is a package of currency consisting of stated amounts of the currency of each of the countries in the European Economic Community. If a loan or other contract calling for future payment is stated in ECUs, the portfolio effect reduces the exchange risk associated with any single currency.

Interest Rates and Exchange Rates

The relationship between exchange rates and interest rates is an excellent example of how the opportunity for arbitrage serves to remove market differentials. The "spot" or current U.S. dollar equivalent for French francs is 0.1231 while the 180-day future rate is 0.1214 (table 15-3). This reflects an expectation that the value of the franc will fall relative to the dollar. International finance theory would suggest that changes in exchange rates are strongly affected by differences in inflation rates between countries. A future rate for the franc below the spot rate is evidence that investors expect the French inflation rate to be higher than the U.S. inflation rate over the next 180 days.

Since interest rates normally increase when expected inflation increases, we would expect interest rates to be higher in France than in the United States. However, the forward exchange rate sets a limit on how much higher or lower this rate will be. Suppose, for example, that 180-day U.S. Treasury bills are presently selling at a discount sufficient to provide a 5.5 percent return over the 180-day period (an equivalent yield of 11 percent on an annual basis). If 180-day French government obligations were selling to yield 6.5 percent per 180-day period, a French investor or financial institution could improve return with no increase in risk by purchasing a U.S. Treasury bill and selling U.S. dollars on a 180-day forward contract. The return on a 7,699,976 French franc investment would be as follows:

Purchase dollars at current spot rate (7,699,976 × .1231)	$947,867
Purchase U.S. Treasury bills with a face value of $1,000,000, discounted to yield 5.5 percent over a 180-day period	$947,867
Simultaneously purchase a forward contract for $1 million worth of French francs in 180 days at $.1214 per franc: $1,000,000/.1214	8,237,232 ff
Hold Treasury bills until maturity and receive face value	$1,000,000
Complete forward contract to purchase francs	8,237,232 ff
Return earned [(8,237,232/7,699,976) − 1] =	6.98%

If French government 180-day obligations are selling to yield less than 6.98 percent per 180-day period, the French investor can improve his position by investing in U.S. Treasury obligations and using a forward exchange contract to protect himself from exchange rate risk. The reverse is also true. If the rate in France were over 6.98 percent, an American investor could improve his position by purchasing French government obligations and hedging against exchange rate risk by contracting to sell francs in 180 days.

The calculation of the interest rate that would prevent investors from either country gaining by investment in the other country can be found using a simple formula instead of the extensive calculation above:

$$R_r = \frac{S}{F}(1 + R_d) - 1 \qquad (15\text{-}1)$$

where: R_f = Interest rate for the period on risk-free obligations in the foreign country

S = The spot value of a unit of the foreign country's currency

F = The forward value of a unit of the foreign country's currency

R_d = The domestic risk-free interest rate for the period

Applying the formula to the previous example, we confirm the previous solution and the correctness of the formula:

$$R_f = \frac{0.1231}{0.1214}(1 + 0.055) - 1 = 6.98\%$$

Of course, the fact that everyone could take advantage of this risk-free opportunity to increase return is likely to decrease or eliminate such opportunities. A flow of capital from France to the United States and the offsetting demand for future contracts to buy francs would drive the French interest rates up, the U.S. interest rates down, and the forward value of francs up until the potential profit disappeared. Thus we would expect to find the relationship between interest rates and exchange rates shown in equation 15-1 to hold in general.

FINANCING EXPORTS AND IMPORTS

The purchase and sale of goods across international borders involves several problems that do not exist or are much less difficult to handle for domestic sales. First, a contract calling for future payment requires that payment be specified in some currency. If the contract calls for payment in the importer's currency, the exporter must accept the risk that an unfavorable movement in the exchange rate between the two currencies will result in his receiving less than anticipated, and vice versa. Second, the problem of dealing with noncompliance—failure to deliver goods according to contract or failure to make payment according to contract—is more difficult to deal with because of distance, unfamiliarity, and different legal systems. Third, credit is needed for longer periods of time because of distances and shipping times involved. Exchange rate risk was treated as a separate topic. The second two problems are treated in this section.

Assuring Compliance (Banker's Acceptances)

Every domestic seller of goods on credit must make the sale decision based on knowledge of the credit worthiness of the potential buyer. The decision is normally based on substantial personal knowledge of the buyer or readily available credit information sources. In the international marketplace, information on credit worthiness is limited by distance, language barriers, infrequency of trade, and other factors. Furthermore, a domestic firm's credit manager is likely to be quite knowledgeable with regard to the status of a claim in the courts in the event of a payment default. In the international marketplace, the status of a claim in the courts, and even the proper jurisdiction, is likely to be subject to question. Thus legal remedy is uncertain and expensive. Finally, the distances involved in shipment frequently make longer credit periods necessary, again increasing risk exposure.

From the buyer's point of view, there are also increased risks. A failure to ship goods per contract specifications on a domestic order can be remedied by returning goods or turning to a familiar court system. Again, great distances and unfamiliar court systems decrease the buyer's confidence in his ability to achieve adequate remedies in the case of default. The problem is again complicated by lack of direct knowledge about the seller. The problems cited above must be overcome if international trade is to flourish. The procedures that have evolved for dealing with these problems are outlined in the following paragraphs.

Transaction procedures must deal with the uncertainties suffered by both exporter and importer. Essentially, the procedures that have evolved recognize two facts:

1. Trust, not the availability of legal remedies, is the foundation for most transactions.

2. A promise to pay by a major international bank will be accepted with little or no question.

The process involved in substituting the bank's credit for the individual importer's credit is outlined in figure 15-2.

First, of course, importer and exporter must come to an agreement on product, price, shipping method, etc. Second, the importer applies to the bank for a letter of credit. The letter of credit authorizes the seller to write a draft on the buyer's bank for a specified amount upon shipment of the goods. Upon receipt of the letter of credit, the seller ships the goods. The seller then forwards the draft and the bill of lading (proof of shipment) to the seller's bank. The seller's bank forwards this material to the buyer's bank, possibly going through a correspondent if the two banks do not have a correspondent relationship. The buyer's bank examines the documents to assure that the shipment was consistent with the letter of credit. If the draft is a sight draft, the buyer's bank then pays the seller's bank by crediting its account. More typically though, the letter of credit authorizes a draft payable on a specified date up to 180 days after shipment. If this is the case, the buyer's bank marks the draft "ACCEPTED" or "I ACCEPT" and returns it to the

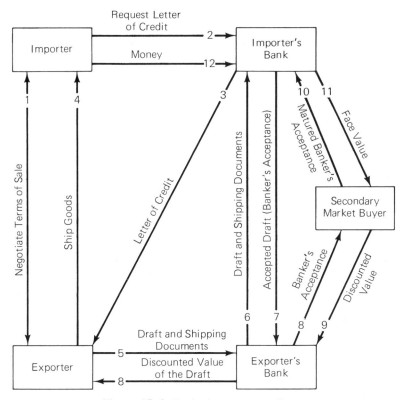

Figure 15–2: Banker's acceptance flow.

seller's bank. The draft is now referred to as a *banker's acceptance* because it has been accepted and is virtually certain to be paid upon maturity.

Upon receipt of the accepted draft, the seller's bank will ask the seller for instructions. The seller may want to hold the draft until maturity and receive the full face value. Or instead, the seller may instruct the bank that it wants to receive its money right away. In this case, the amount the seller will receive is the discounted value, an amount enough below the face value to provide a competitive return to whoever holds the banker's acceptance until maturity. The seller's bank may hold the draft until maturity and then receive the face value, earning the difference between the face value and what it paid the seller.

If neither the seller nor the seller's bank wants

to hold the draft, two alternatives remain. The buyer's bank may simply pay the discounted value immediately; thus, it will pay out less than it will collect from the buyer and will earn a return similar to what it could have earned elsewhere. Most banker's acceptances are held by either the buyer's bank or the seller's bank. However, if neither of these banks has funds available to invest, the draft can be sold in a limited second market. In a sale in the second market (figure 15-2), the seller's bank will receive the discounted value immediately, and the second market buyer will receive the face value at maturity. This secondary market sale would be handled by the seller's bank, which would contact one of the several government securities dealers who also make markets in banker's acceptances. Of course, the banker's acceptance could, like any money market instrument, be sold again before maturity if the original borrower needed funds. Many banker's acceptances sold in the secondary market are held by commercial banks as secondary reserves.

In addition to handling the problem of assuring compliance, banker's acceptances have become an important method of financing imports and exports. One reason they are popular as a financing method is that they allow the buyer's bank to provide credit to a customer even when it is fully loaned up. The letter of credit and the marketable banker's acceptance provide a way to finance a purchase without the seller, the buyer, or the buyer's bank being required to tie up funds. Banker's acceptances outstanding in the United States totaled $78 billion at the beginning of 1984.

Export Credit Insurance

Export credit insurance provides a method of dealing with both country risk and risk associated with a particular customer. In the United States, export credit insurance is provided primarily through the Foreign Credit Insurance Association (FCIA), an association of insurance companies working in conjunction with the Export-Import Bank of the United States. FCIA provides insurance against both commercial risk and political risk on American products sold abroad for credit. Commercial risks involve delayed payment or failure to pay for reasons covering the gamut of factors leading to failure to pay in domestic trade. FCIA has paid off in cases of failure running from competitive difficulties to theft, fire, and earthquake. Political risk covers war, expropriation, cancellation of import and export licenses, and so on. Insurance can be provided for short periods of time or for credit terms up to seven years in certain cases. Policies are normally sold for all shipments over a period of time rather than for just one shipment. The percent of loss covered by the policy varies from 90 percent to 98 percent. Premiums depend on length of time involved, category of country, and the riskiness of the credit involved.

Special Sources of Import-Export Credit

While the banker's acceptance has proved to be a very useful method of handling transactions and a satisfactory source of short-term credit, it does not meet all the needs of exporters for extended credit terms. Most developed countries have some government agency which provides credit to encourage exports. In the United States that organization is the *Export-Import Bank*. The Export-Import Bank was started in 1934 to aid companies in importing and exporting. Actually, it was started to encourage the development of trade with Russia.

The Export-Import Bank is a quasi-public agency with a president and vice-president appointed by the President of the United States. The bank is financed through the purchase of equity, all of which is owned by the U.S. Treasury.

The Export-Import Bank's primary mode of activity involves support of commercial banks. The Export-Import Bank guarantees intermediate term export obligations with maturities of six months to five years. Additionally, the Export-Import Bank purchases debt obligations of foreign borrowers from United States banks. Both short-term and intermediate-term obligations are purchased in this manner. Through these two routes the Export-Import Bank provides funds or support to banks lending money to exporters.

In addition to the support of banks, the Export-Import Bank also makes direct loans to foreign purchasers of U.S. goods. These direct loans are primarily participation loans with other financial institutions. Finally, the Export-Import Bank makes loans to foreign financial institutions that in turn loan money to small businesses purchasing United States goods.

As the above brief outline shows, the Export-Import bank acts primarily in conjunction with other financial institutions. It serves to increase the ability of financial institutions to serve the needs of their customers rather than as a source of competition to financial institutions. The private financial institution can frequently provide greater credit service at lower risk by using the services of the Export-Import Bank.

The Private Export Funding Corporation (PEFCO) can reasonably be thought of as another extension of the services of the Export-Import Bank. The PEFCO was formed in 1970 through the efforts of the Bankers' Association for Foreign Trade. It makes loans to foreign purchasers of U.S. goods. All of its loans are guaranteed by the Export-Import Bank. Because it is privately owned—primarily by a group of large banks—PEFCO provides another source of credit, drawing on the Export-Import Bank guarantee to increase the supply of export credit available. PEFCO borrows in the long-term security markets, issuing secured notes.

INTERNATIONAL CAPITAL MARKETS

Along with the change from concentration on export-import operations to multinational production has come an increased tendency to turn to international capital markets for funds. Companies are motivated to use the international capital markets by considerations of balance sheet hedging, cost, and tax considerations. Funds are raised through Eurobonds, foreign bonds, and financial institutions specializing in international lending.

A *foreign bond* is issued primarily in one country, denominated in the currency of that country, and is the obligation of a corporation headquartered in another country. For example, a foreign automobile producer such as Toyota or Volkswagen might issue dollar-denominated bonds in the United States for the purpose of building a plant in the United States. These would be foreign bonds because they are denominated and sold in the United States, but are an obligation of the foreign manufacturer. Such a bond issue might be motivated by cost of capital considerations or a desire for exchange rate hedging.

Foreign bond issues are sold through the services of financial institutions normally handling bond underwritings in the country in which the issue is being sold. In the United States, this would be an investment banking firm. In most other countries, commercial banks are allowed to provide this service and are the institutions primarily involved.

A *Eurobond* is in a sense a more truly "international" issue. The Eurobond is sold principally in countries other than the country of the currency in which it is denominated. It is usually underwritten by an international syndicate of underwriters: major European banks, European branches of United States banks, and banks from other major financial centers. For tax and other reasons, the issue is usually sold to people who are not citizens or residents of the country of denomination. These bonds are usually sold on general reputation rather than financial analysis or bond ratings. Thus, only the best known international firms are able to use this source of funds. Approximately two thirds of the amount of Eurobonds outstanding is denominated in U.S. dollars. Not infrequently, companies headquartered outside the United States use the Eurobond market to raise funds in other nonUnited States countries, denominated in U.S. dollars.

U.S. companies selling bonds overseas were hampered by a U.S. withholding tax requirement and are still hampered by a requirement that they identify foreign purchasers of their bonds. These rulings have been circumvented through the use of an offshore finance subsidiary. The finance subsidiary is incorporated in a tax haven country such as Switzerland, the Bahamas, or the Netherland Antilles. The subsidiary is wholly owned by the United States company and its sole purpose is to borrow money through the sale of bonds and re-lend it to the parent company, thereby paying interest from a foreign country and avoiding the United States regulations.

In addition to the above mentioned bond markets, there are a number of financial institutions that specialize in providing capital on an international basis. Most of these specialize in loans to countries, but some also participate in purchases of private debt and equity. Foremost among these is the World Bank Group. The primary institution of the World Bank Group is the International Bank for Reconstruction and Development, also called the World Bank. The World Bank makes loans only to countries. The International Finance Corporation, another member of the World Bank Group, specializes in direct investments in businesses in developing countries. It specializes in participation equity investments in basic industries such as steel and cement. Finally, there are a number of national development banks and private development banks that specialize in private loans. The Atlantic Development Group for Latin America (ADELA) is a good example of these. It is owned by more than 200 large corporations and invests in participations in private business enterprises in Latin American countries.

Country Risk

Country risk has always been a problem faced by international businesses. It has become a problem of growing concern in recent years as banks and other private companies have become more involved in loans or joint investment projects with foreign governments. Country risk, at its most obvious level, deals with the political and social stability of the country. Revolutions or social upheavals occur with sufficient frequency to be considered real risks to international businesses.

Other country risks relate more to the economic position of the country. For example, direct loans and joint investments with a foreign government become risky if that government is so heavily in debt that its ability to make payments is in question. Problems of this type have arisen with regard to bank loans to foreign governments. Some governments borrowed heavily in the late 1970s and early 1980s in anticipation of increased exports or of higher oil prices. These did not occur, and the governments were left with no way to repay their foreign debts without applying such stringent internal economic policies that they would risk revolution. One recent example of this type of problem was

an eleventh-hour loan package that allowed Argentina to narrowly escape a default on its interest payments.

Country risk can also occur with loans or credit sales to businesses within a foreign country. If the country together with its businesses are heavily in debt, a business may find it impossible to acquire the foreign exchange with which to make payments. Even worse, the government may respond to heavy demand for foreign currency by freezing assets and not allowing payments to foreigners. Because of these problems, the lender or credit seller must look beyond the particular company to the political and economic situation in the country.

Export credit insurance is one response to country risk. By acquiring export credit insurance, a company can eliminate or sharply decrease both credit and country risk.

Another response to both credit and country risk is the rise of the international banker as a provider of information. A U.S. company considering a sale to a Brazilian company can use the services of Citibank or another of the international banks. Citibank's local office in Brazil will be able to provide information about the specific company involved that would not be readily available to the exporter from other sources. In addition, Citibank can provide important information about political and economic conditions so that the exporter can better guage both near-term risk and the likelihood of the business relationship's becoming permanent. A major part of the activity of international bankers is the provision of information of this type to their customers.

INTERNATIONAL BANKING AND INTERNATIONAL CREDIT MARKETS

In the previous parts of this chapter, international banks have been mentioned in relation to various aspects of the solution of international business problems. In this section, we focus directly on the development and operation of these international banks.

European banks became active in the international markets during the period of colonization and have therefore had several centuries of experience. United States banks, on the other hand, were largely restricted from international activities until the Federal Reserve Act of 1913. However, this authorization did not lead to a rush toward international banking; by 1919, only one bank had established an overseas branch. The Edge Act of 1919 further expanded the authority of banks to engage in international activity. This act did not lead to a rush either. As late as 1960, only eight banks had overseas branches, and these branches had assets totalling $3.5 billion.

Growth of U.S. international banking remained modest through 1965 but then accelerated rapidly. By 1970, there were seventy-nine banks with foreign branches, assets held by these branches totaled $46.5 billion. By 1982, there were 163 banks with overseas branches. Overseas branches totaled 830; assets held by these branches totaled $376 billion. Since 1960, the number of banks involved has increased twentyfold and assets involved have increased a hundredfold.

This rapid growth occurred for two reasons. First, growth of international business was rapid during this period (table 15-1). U.S. businesses expanding their international activities needed new services, and U.S. banks moved to provide those services. Second, various capital flow constraints were introduced by the U.S. and other governments when they experienced balance of payments deficits. Thus, it became quite difficult for a bank to serve its customers' needs from a domestic base. Overseas branches made it possible to raise money in other markets, thereby avoiding capital flow restrictions.

International Banking Offices

Banks wishing to enter into international activities have a number of choices with regard to the types of arrangements they can use. These range from simply establishing correspondent relationships with foreign banks to operation of full service facilities.

Correspondent Relationships Correspondent relationships with other banks are an important part of banking in the United States. Similar correspondent relationships are maintained with foreign banks. Because banks maintain deposits with their correspondents, the correspondent relationship can be used to clear checks or drafts and transfer funds by adding to or subtracting from each other's account balances. Correspondent banks can also be used for foreign exchange needs and to provide information about local conditions. As will be seen later in this chapter, the correspondent relationship is a key factor in the operation of the Eurodollar market.

Representative Offices Representative offices provide a low-level method for a bank to have a direct presence in another country. The representative office has no assets other than furniture. However, it provides an important contact point to gain the information necessary to keep customers informed about the country where the office is located. The representative office also provides a facility for soliciting business and maintaining contact with correspondent banks.

Shell Branches Shell branches are used to enter into foreign transactions such as Eurodollar transactions, currency transactions, and participations in syndicated loans that would be more heavily regulated in the home country or would be taxed if carried out in the home country. Nassau and the Cayman Islands are popular locations for shell branches. Actions carried out through these branches normally reflect decisions made at the home office and are simply executed by wire from the branch location. Over half of the banks with overseas operations have only shell branches. In addition, banks with more extensive overseas operations also have shell branches to avoid taxes or regulation.

Foreign Branches Foreign branches operate as branches of the domestic parent bank and are located in foreign countries. Because the foreign branch is a legal part of the parent bank, it is subject to reserve requirements and other regulations that apply to the parent. In addition, these branches are subject to the banking laws of the country in which they operate. Because of their status as a legal part of the parent, foreign branches are viewed as very safe by depositors because they have the full credit of the parent behind them. Foreign branches are an extremely important vehicle for provision of international banking services. They make loans, take deposits, handle funds transfers and foreign exchange, and provide information to businesses wishing to do business overseas.

Edge Act Corporations Edge corporations were first allowed under the Edge Act of 1919. They are established as subsidiaries of banks, and are allowed to engage in international financing activities prohibited to the parent corporation. Edge Act corporations may own foreign banking subsidiaries (banks can only have foreign branches) and are also allowed to make equity investments. Edge Act corporations are used to finance long-term industrial projects by providing long-term debt and equity capital.

Consortiums and Syndicates Many loans are too big for any single bank to handle. A standard method of handling larger business has been the syndicate. This is simply an agreement among a number of banks for each bank to grant a business or a country a specified amount of the total loan for which it has applied. Syndicated loans are common in both domestic and international lending. A consortium bank, on the other hand, is a separately incorporated bank owned by a number of other banks and used as a vehicle. Nordicbank, for example, is a consortium bank organized by a number of banks located in Scandinavian countries to carry out international banking activities.

INTERNATIONAL PAYMENTS SYSTEM

Like the domestic payment system, the international payment system depends on instructions to banks to transfer ownership of deposits rather than on physical transfer of currency or metal. The process can be illustrated with a draft cre-

ated through import of goods to the United States. Let us say that German goods were purchased with a letter of credit authorizing the German firm to write a draft of $1 million on Morgan Guaranty Trust, the United States purchaser's bank. The German exporting company deposits the draft with its bank, Deutsche Bank, acquiring a $1 million deposit denominated in dollars. Deutsche Bank gains an asset of $1 million in the form of a deposit with Morgan and a $1 million liability in the form of a customer deposit. The German exporter may now use the dollar deposit to pay dollar obligations, to convert it to marks, or to hold it as a dollar investment.

Suppose the German firm owes $1 million to a British firm that wants payment in the form of a deposit at National Westminster Bank in London. The German firm instructs Deutsche Bank to transfer the $1 million to National Westminster in payment. Deutsche Bank carries out this instruction by wiring Morgan in New York to transfer ownership of a $1 million deposit to National Westminster. Morgan then notifies National Westminster by wire that the $1 million has been credited to its account and National Westminster notifies its customers, completing the transaction.

If the German business had no dollar debts, it could decide to convert the funds to Deutsche marks. The German firm would instruct Deutsche Bank to convert the dollars to marks. As a major money market bank, Deutsche Bank will have an inventory of dollar deposits for trading purposes and will be able to immediately quote the German firm a rate. Assuming the conversion rate in table 15-3, the German firm will be able to exchange a $1 million deposit for 2,640,500 marks (minus the fee charged by the bank). Payment will be made by deducting $1 million from the German firm's dollar deposit balance and adding 2,640,500 to its mark balance. Because the bank made the exchange based on its own position, its dollar deposit assets have remained constant while its dollar liabilities have decreased. Deutsche Bank still has the $1 million deposit with Morgan.

As a continual buyer and seller of deposits

denominated in various currencies, Deutsche Bank may decide to simply hold the dollar deposit in its own inventory. If, on the other hand, Deutsche Bank now feels that it is holding excess dollars, its trading department will use its telephone networks to exchange some dollars for marks. Suppose Deutsche Bank feels that its dollar holdings are excessive and Credit Lyonnais in France—one of the money market banks with which Deutsche Bank is in constant contact—feels that its mark holdings are excessive and its dollar holdings are low. Credit Lyonnais' holdings of marks are in the form of a deposit with Dresdner Bank in Germany. Credit Lyonnais and Deutsche Bank agree to an exchange at the presently quoted rate of 2.6405 marks per dollar. Credit Lyonnais wires Dresdner Bank to transfer ownership of a 2,640,500 mark deposit to Deutsche Bank and Deutsche Bank wires Morgan to transfer ownership of a $1 million deposit to Credit Lyonnais which completes the transaction.

The number of banks acting in the foreign exchange market in this manner is quite limited. In the United States, only about two dozen banks maintain positions in the leading currencies. Other banks serve their customers' needs by dealing with one of these leading banks. The leading banks adjust their positions by buying and selling between one another, primarily through one of the six brokers that deal in foreign exchange. Normally, banks within a particular money center, such as New York, would contract most of their exchanges with other banks in the same area. However, traders in foreign exchange departments will constantly watch rates in other money market centers and be ready to buy or sell in one of those markets if the rate is different than that in the local market. Thus while most trades occur within a local market, there is a parity between rates quoted at different locations around the world.

A third alternative is also possible. Either the German exporter or Deutsche Bank may decide to hold the dollar deposit and loan it out to earn interest. When this is done, a Eurodollar deposit is created. The Eurodollar market represents a special international money market, worthy of additional attention.

Eurodollar Markets

The Eurodollar, as an investment or loan source, follows from the international payment system as described above. The German exporting company has received payment in the form of a demand deposit with Morgan Guarantee Trust which has been credited to the account of Deutsche Bank. The German firm decides to convert the dollar demand deposit to a time deposit with its bank rather than to convert it to marks or to use it for payment purposes. Thus, Deutsche Bank, the German firm's bank in this example, continues to have a dollar-denominated liability and an offsetting dollar-denominated asset in the form of a deposit with Morgan Guaranty Trust. The relevant accounts for the three entities are summarized in the following T-accounts.

German Exporter

Time deposit with Deutsche Bank	$1,000,000	

Deutsche Bank

Demand deposit with Morgan	$1,000,000	Time deposit from German exporter	$1,000,000

Morgan Guaranty Trust

	Demand deposit from Deutsche Bank	$1,000,000

At this point Eurodollars have been created. A Eurodollar is defined as a U.S. dollar-denominated deposit held by a bank outside the United States, including a foreign branch of a United States bank. Deutsche Bank is now paying interest on a time deposit and holding a noninterest bearing demand deposit. One possible course of action is for Deutsche Bank to exchange the demand deposit for a certificate of deposit, at the interest rate presently being quoted by Morgan. If this is done, the only change in the above T-accounts is the change of the Deutsche Bank deposit with Morgan from demand to time. Deutsche Bank may decide to loan the Morgan demand deposit to another bank. This is the point where the funds enter the active Eurodollar market. The loan to another bank may be for as short as overnight or for as long as six months.

The center of the Eurodollar market is in London, with the London Interbank Offer Rate (LIBOR) being the primary Eurodollar rate. Like the federal funds rate in the United States, the LIBOR represents the rate paid by banks on large ($500,000 or more) deposits from other banks. Besides London, there are active markets in Frankfurt, Paris, Amsterdam, Zurich, Geneva, Basle, Milan, Vienna, Toronto, Luxembourg, Montreal, and Singapore.

Suppose Deutsche Bank, lacking a direct dollar borrower, decides to deposit the funds with Barclays, a London bank, at the current LIBOR. Deutsche Bank will contact Barclays by wire to arrange for the desired maturity. Barclays, a major money market bank, stands ready to make Eurodollar loans or accept Eurodollar deposits. After making arrangements with Barclays, Deutsche Bank wires instructions for the transfer to Morgan. These transactions have not caused any changes in the financial statement of the German exporter, which still holds a dollar-denominated time deposit with Deutsche Bank. However, the accounts of the other parties have changed as shown in the following T-accounts.

Deutsche Bank

Time deposit with Barclays Bank $1,000,000	Time deposit from German exporter $1,000,000

Barclays Bank

Demand deposit with Morgan $1,000,000	Time deposit from Deutsche Bank $1,000,000

Morgan Guaranty Trust

	Demand deposit from Barclays Bank $1,000,000

Of course, Barclays will want to find a profitable use for the Morgan demand deposit as quickly as possible. Suppose Barclays loans the money to Brazil, an oil importing country, by crediting Barclays demand deposit. The only accounts that change are those of Barclays, which now appears as follows:

Barclays Bank

Demand deposit with Morgan $1,000,000	Time deposit from Deutsche Bank $1,000,000
Loan to Brazil $1,000,000	Demand deposit from Brazil $1,000,000

How much time is required to complete this series of transactions? The funds can flow from the German exporter to Brazil in a few hours through the use of wire transfers.

Brazil will most likely use the funds to pay an oil exporting country in dollars.

Thus Brazil instructs Barclays to transfer ownership of the deposit to the exporter. After this transaction, the accounts of all parties appear as follows:

German Exporter

Time deposit with Deutsche Bank	$1,000,000		

Deutsche Bank

Time deposit with Barclays	$1,000,000	Time deposit from German exporter	$1,000,000

Barclays Bank

Demand deposit with Morgan	$1,000,000	Demand deposit from oil exporter	$1,000,000
Loan to Brazil	$1,000,000	Time deposit from Deutsche Bank	$1,000,000

Brazil

		Loan from Barclays	$1,000,000

Oil Exporting Country

Demand deposit with Barclays	$1,000,000		

Morgan Guaranty Trust

		Demand deposit from Barclays	$1,000,000

We should now observe several points about the Eurodollar market. First, its entire growth was based on an underlying dollar-denominated demand deposit at Morgan. Total credit granted never exceeded the amount of this deposit. All Eurodollar transactions involved transfer of ownership of deposits based on this Morgan account back to the United States.

Another point we should notice is that the banks were never exposed to exchange rate risk. Their dollar assets and liabilities were always equal. Exchange rate risks are borne by the Ger-

man exporter and British importer. These two parties could, of course, eliminate their risks through transactions in the foreign exchange futures market.

There is also the question of why Eurodollar transactions occur at all. The German firm could have held a Morgan time deposit itself, and Morgan could have made a loan to the British importer. This does not occur for reasons that include knowledge and convenience of transaction. It is more convenient for the German exporter to deal with its bank and the British importer to deal with its bank. More important, the arrangement allows the banks to circumvent regulations aimed at limiting interest rates and money expansion. We showed Deutsch Bank lending the entire amount of its dollar deposits. In reality, the banks act on a fractional reserve basis, receiving many Eurodollar deposits and loaning out less than they receive in deposits, with the remainer held as reserve. However, reserve requirements are minimal compared to regulations in the United States.

We should also note that the phrase Eurodollar market is a misnomer in two senses. First, the market is not limited to Europe. A dollar deposit in a United States bank owned by anyone outside the United States meets the definition of a Eurodollar. There are active markets outside Europe, particularly in Asia. Additionally, market activity of this type is not limited to dollars. There are active markets in deposits of all major currencies outside their home countries. The market for all currencies is referred to as the *Eurocurrency market*.

Bank Use of the Eurodollar Market

Thus far, we have treated the Eurodollar market as a market in which banks serve the deposit and credit needs of their customers. The Eurodollar market also serves as an important money market in which banks can borrow funds to meet liquidity needs and invest idle funds at a profit.

An American bank facing a liquidity problem can attempt to adjust reserves by using the federal funds market or other sources within the United States. Alternatively, the bank can turn to the Eurodollar market for funds. This is done through an overseas branch of the American bank. Let us go back to the situation as it occurred immediately after Deutsche Bank received the time deposit from the German exporter. Instead of depositing funds in Barclays, Deutsche Bank could have deposited the funds with an overseas branch of an American bank. Suppose Citibank in the United States is presently in need of funds. The London branch of Citibank may accept the deposit from Deutsche

Bank and gain, as an asset, the demand deposit with Morgan. The London branch of Citibank then notifies Morgan by wire that it wants the demand deposit transferred to Citibank. We should note that no increase in bank deposits occurred. Citibank simply used its overseas branch to bid for deposits presently with other U.S. banks. While the bidding for funds results in no direct increase in deposits in the United States, it may result in an indirect increase as interest rates are bid up and holders are encouraged to hold their Eurodollar deposits longer.

Instead of a shortage, suppose Citibank has an excess of funds. Suppose further that Eurodollar rates are presently more attractive than domestic money market rates. Citibank can loan funds to its London branch, showing a demand deposit as an asset and a loan as an offsetting liability. The London branch can then loan this demand deposit in the Eurodollar market, earning a favorable rate of return.

The agressiveness of banks in using the Eurodollar market to invest idle funds can be illustrated by the example of a typical bank operating a branch in Luxumbourg, one of the major international banking centers in Europe. From opening time until late in the afternoon, the branch stands ready to accept overnight deposits or lend on an overnight basis, charging slightly more on loans than the rate it pays on deposits. Late in the afternoon, the Luxumbourg branch has overnight deposits in excess of overnight loans. The Luxumbourg branch then transfers the idle funds to the bank's New York branch. It is six hours earlier in New York, so the New York branch has a good chance to find an outlet for the funds. As the banking day draws to a close in New York, the New York branch transfers idle funds to a branch located farther west to gain additional business hours. This process continues until the idle funds are finally transferred to the Singapore branch where a profitable overnight loan is found. The transfer of this deposit in a series of steps all the way from Luxumbourg to Singapore was done to avoid the loss of one day's interest. Such actions are feasible because wire transfers are inexpensive and one day's interest on $1 million is frequently over $300. Over the course of a year, a bank could increase its profit $1 million by placing an average of $10 million each banking day in this manner.

SUMMARY

With the increased volume of international business, financial institutions have become increasingly involved in the international financial markets. They are involved in these markets both to serve the needs of their customers and to meet their own liquidity and profitability objectives.

Financial institutions help their customers complete international transactions through such approaches as the letter of credit, draft, bill of lading, and through other specialized arrangements. Financial institutions help their customers exchange one currency for another and hedge against exchange rate risk through their foreign exchange departments. They also help customers in using international money markets to create balance sheet hedges. Additionally, financial institutions provide export credit insurance and certain institutions specialize in providing export credit.

Financial institutions also aid their customers in tapping the international capital markets. While there is no truly international equity market, there are two types of international bonds. A foreign bond is issued primarily in one country, is denominated in the currency of that country, and is the obligation of a corporation headquartered in another country. A Eurobond is sold principally in countries other than the country of the currency where it is denominated. In addition to these international bond markets, certain firms specialize in long-term loans, particularly in developing countries.

The Eurocurrency markets represent the primary international money markets. The Eurodollar is defined as a dollar deposit in a United States bank owned by a person, business, or institution outside the United States. In addition to helping customers through this market, banks use it as a source of liquidity adjustment and temporary investment.

The history of financial system development on the international front is similar to that for the domestic financial system. Institutions and instruments have developed in response to specific needs and the profit opportunities they created. While the growth of international business was not caused by financial institutions, it probably would not have occurred without them.

QUESTIONS

1. Give an example of international business activity that can be explained through the theory of comparative advantage.

2. Capital flows *into* the United States have increased sharply in recent years (table 15-1). What factors have led to this increased inflow?

3. What are the main financial problems faced in international business that are not encountered in domestic enterprise?

4. International business is relatively less important for the United States than for other developed countries (table 15-2). What are the reasons for this?

5. What is translation risk? How does a company normally protect itself from translation risk?

6. Translation risk only involves accounting entries. Why would a company be concerned about translation risk?

7. What factors have caused exchange rates to become less stable in recent years?

8. Find the most recent spot and ninety-day rate for Japanese yen. Are people expecting the yen to increase or decrease in value relative to the dollar in the next 90 days?

9. An American company will sell goods to a German company, agreeing to grant one-year credit terms and accept payment in marks. How can the company hedge against exchange rate risk?

10. It is common practice for sales between

businesses in the United States to be on an open-account basis. Why is this not common practice in international trade?

11. Explain the difference between a foreign bond and a Eurobond.

12. Most domestic payments are made through paper order, in the form of checks. How are international payments normally made?

13. How would a business go about raising funds in the foreign bond market?

14. Explain how a bank uses the Eurodollar market to adjust its liquidity position. Can the banking *system* adjust its liquidity through the Eurodollar market?

PROBLEMS

1. A Danish subsidiary of a U.S. company has Japanese yen monetary assets of 10-million yen, and has no yen liabilities. A German subsidiary of the same U.S. parent has a 10-million yen liability and no yen assets.

    a. Is the consolidated company exposed to exchange rate risk?

    b. If the answer to a, is yes, specify the transactions that could be used to eliminate exchange rate risk.

2. Find the present yield for ninety-day United States Treasury bills. Also find the spot and ninety-day exchange rate for the British pound. What would the equilibrium rate for ninety-day British government obligations be under these conditions?

3. British government obligations with 180 days to maturity are selling to provide an 8 percent annual yield while U.S. government obligations of similar maturity are selling to yield 8.5 percent. Is the relationship between these two interest rates in equilibrium (table

15-3)? If not, what type of transaction would take advantage of this disequilibrium?

4. An Italian exporting company receives a $1 million payment from a United States importer in the form of a deposit in the name of the Italian firm's Roman bank—in dollars at Citibank. The Italian firm converts its deposits to a time deposit with a London bank; the London bank in turn loans those deposits to a customer in the form of a dollar demand deposit with the London bank. Show the status of the relevant accounts of the Italian exporting company, the London bank, the London borrower, and Citibank.

SELECTED REFERENCES

Crystal, K. Alec. "A Guide to Foreign Exchange Markets." *The Federal Reserve Bank of St. Louis Review* 66 (March 1984): 5–18.

Dufey, Gunter, and Srinivasulu, S. L. "The Case for Corporate Management of Foreign Exchange Risk." *Financial Management* 12 (Winter 1983): 54–62.

Feder, Gershon, and Ross, Knud. "Risk Assessments and Risk Premiums in the Eurodollar Market." *The Journal of Finance* 37 (June 1982): 679–691.

Fieleke, Norman S. "International Lending in Historical Perspective." *New England Economic Review*. (November/December 1982): 5–12.

Langetieg, T. C., Findlay, M. C. and DaMotta, L. F. J. "Multiperiod Pension Plans and ERISA." *Journal of Financial and Quantitative Analysis* 17 (November 1982): 603–631.

Levin, Ronald, and Roberts, David L. "Latin America's Prospects for Recovery." *Federal Reserve Bank of New York Quarterly Review* 8 (Autumn 1983): 6–13.

Nadler, Paul S. "Troubled World Loans in Perspective." *Bankers Monthly* 51 (February 15, 1984): 10–13.

Shapiro, Alan C. "Risk in International Banking." *Journal of Financial and Quantitative Analysis* 17 (December 1982): 727–739.

Case 1

Identifying Financial Institutions

In general, the financial statements of financial institutions are similar in appearance to those of nonfinancial, manufacturing, and retailing corporations. Both types of business firms have assets, liabilities, revenues, and expenses, etc. However, for the most part the assets and liabilities differ significantly. For many financial institutions, the primary profit-making assets are financial in nature and are normally held in the form of loans and/or investment securities. Revenue is generated from these assets in the form of interest income. The financing of these assets (liabilities) often occurs in part in the form of customer deposits, some of which may receive interest (or dividends). The interest expense from these deposits and other liabilities often is a major expense item to the firm.

All financial institutions are playing an increasingly important role in the everchanging economy. In addition, regulation is slowly reducing the distinctive differences between financial institutions. For example, commercial banks may now pay interest on demand deposits, savings and loan associations may issue drafts

This case was prepared by Professor Ernest W. Swift of Georgia State University as a basis for classroom discussion and not to illustrate either effective or ineffective handling of an administrative situation.

Copyright © 1979 by Ernest W. Swift, Georgia State University.

similar to checks; credit unions may issue credit cards, etc. Although the expectation of a further reduction in distinguishable characteristics is not unreasonable, some differences remain. Common-sized balance sheet and income statement data for the eleven financial institutions listed alphabetically below can be found in tables 1 & 2. See if you can match the financial statements with the appropriate financial institutions.

1. Bank Holding Company—Consolidated
2. Bank Holding Company—Parent
3. Commercial Bank
4. Credit Union
5. Domestic Finance Company
6. Investment Companies
7. Life Insurance Company
8. Mutual Property—Casualty Insurance Company
9. Mutual Savings Bank
10. Private Pension Funds
11. Savings and Loan

With the exceptions listed below, the statements reflect aggregate industry averages as of 31 December 1977. The BHC–Parent and Consolidated statements are for a major regional banking corporation.

Table 1:
Balance Sheet

Firms

Assets	A	B	C	D	E	F	G	H	I	J	K
Cash assets	7.3%		18.1%	7.5%	2.5%	14.5%	1.7%	1.6%	2.9%	0.7%	2.0%
Total investments	91.4	55.5%	19.8	4.9	1.9	19.4	86.1	25.9	17.9	47.2	90.3
U.S. government securities	2.9	5.0	9.8	2.8	1.9	4.5	9.0	6.2	10.1		11.1
State & municipal securities	5.0	1.7	8.5			5.5	43.3	1.9			
Other fixed-income securities	14.4	39.2	0.8			9.4	15.8	14.6		1.0	25.1
Stock and equity investments	69.1	9.6	0.7	2.1			18.0	3.2	7.8	46.2	54.1
Total loans (including rec.)		35.3	57.7	85.2	82.9	60.0	6.3	69.9	77.1	49.8	1.4
Commercial			22.7		46.5	31.4		2.3	0.6	49.8	
Mortgage		27.5	18.0	83.0		10.8	0.3	65.5			1.4
Consumer (incl. installment)		7.8	16.9	2.2	36.4	17.8	6.0	2.1	76.5		
Real estate, bldgs., & equip.		3.2	1.4	1.7		2.6	2.2	1.2			
Other assets	1.3	6.0	3.0	0.7	13.7	3.4	3.7	1.4	2.1	2.3	6.3
Total Assets	100.0%	100.0%	100.0%	100.0%	100.0%	100.0%	100.0%	100.0%	100.0%	100.0%	100.0%
Liabilities, Reserves, & Equity											
Demand, or currently payable (AP)	0.4%	3.0%	28.3%		28.4%	38.2%	2.0%		2.6%		
Time, or short-term payables (NP)			55.1	84.3%	11.6	50.0		91.0%	91.6	49.7%	
Contingent liabilities		1.7	7.3	6.0			21.8	0.4			
Other liabilities, or payables		8.8	3.0	4.2	11.0	3.2	4.0	1.8		5.3	
Long-term debt			0.4		34.5	3.6		0.2		11.5	
Reserves		79.9	0.1			0.7	45.3	6.6	4.5	0.9	
Total liabilities & reserves	0.4	93.4	94.2	94.5	85.5	95.7	73.1	100.0	98.7	67.4	
Capital and surplus	99.6	0.6	3.6	5.5	14.5	2.5	26.9			19.4	100.0%
Retained earnings		6.0	2.2			1.8			1.3	13.2	
Total owners' equity	99.6	6.6	5.8	5.5	14.5	4.3	26.9		1.3	32.6	100.0
Total Liabilities, Reserves, & Equity	100.0%	100.0%	100.0%	100.0%	100.0%	100.0%	100.0%	100.0%	100.0%	100.0%	100.0%

Table 2:
Income Statement

Firms

Income	A	B	C	D	E	F	G	H	I	J	K
Investment income											
Interest											
Loans	62.0%	22.2%	73.4%	80.8%	78.7%	64.0%	99.8%	66.1%	83.1%	43.7%	19.0%
Investments	38.0		16.7			19.2	⎬	32.1	15.7		
Dividends			0.1								
Fees		73.8		4.6						26.7	80.6
Commissions			3.0			3.1				28.8	
Service charges			4.7			11.5					
Other income		4.0	2.1	14.6	21.3	2.2	0.2	1.8	1.3	0.8	0.4
Total income (100%)	100.0%	100.0%	100.0%	100.0%	100.0%	100.0%	100.0%	100.0%	100.0%	100.0%	100.0%
Expenses											
Interest	14.3%		49.3%	71.0%	24.7%	39.8%		73.9%	3.5%	47.8%	
General administrative											
Salaries & employee benefits	7.4	6.5%	18.1	7.4	20.3	22.5	13.8%	17.5	12.0	18.0	1.0%
Occupancy expense				1.7	1.4	5.7			4.7	1.7	
Other		9.3	5.5	8.2		8.1	1.3		1.8	3.1	
Other expenses	0.2	79.1	14.3		34.9	14.5	62.1		15.5	5.2	46.4
Total expenses	21.9%	94.9%	87.2%	86.6%	81.3%	90.6%	78.3%	93.4%	37.5%	75.8%	47.4%
(percentage of income)											
Net income before taxes	78.1%	5.1	12.8%	13.4%	18.7%	9.4%	22.7%	8.6%	62.5%	24.2%	52.6%
(percentage of total income)											
Income taxes (or tax credit)	0.8%	4.2%	3.1%	4.0%	5.6%	2.8%	2.7%	1.0%		(2.1)	
Net income	77.3%	0.9%	9.7%	9.4%	13.1%	6.6%	20.0%	7.6%	62.5%	26.3%	
(percentage of total income)											

Case 2

Auburn Bank and Trust Company
The Charter Application

Auburn, Alabama is fairly typical of small university towns. With a population of just 23,000, it is economically dependent on Auburn University (enrollment: 15,000). At the same time, the university community relies on the town to provide the necessities and luxuries of life. (Montgomery, the state capital, is fifty miles away, too far to travel except for major purchases.)

Immediately adjacent to Auburn is the city of Opelika, whose economy is based on light industry and whose population is about 19,000. Recent growth of both towns has made their combined population large enough to attract the interest of larger retail establishments based elsewhere. The most viable result of this interest is a new enclosed shopping mall opened in 1973.

Early in 1972, the banking situation in Auburn closely resembled that prevailing in many towns of its size. There were two banks in town of virtually equal size (just under $20 million total assets), neither of which, in the opinion of many business and individual customers, showed any inclination toward aggressive competition. Loan standards seemed excessively conservative; maximum rates on savings deposits were not paid; free checking accounts were not offered; and the banks were not open evenings or Saturdays. The potential for change was also present, however. Alabama law permits countywide branching. Opelika had three banks; two had more liberal loan standards as evidenced by their loan-to-deposit ratios (exhibit A-9). The most aggressive of the three had opened a branch in Auburn, but it could not be said that the Opelika banks had made a major effort to penetrate the Auburn market.

Another latent force in Auburn banking was a group of business and professional people who were not entirely satisfied with the service provided by the existing banks. Led by a prominent local businessman who had long desired to become active in banking, they considered the possibility of obtaining a charter for a new bank.

This case was prepared by John H. Hand, associate professor of finance, Auburn University. It is a basis for classroom discussion and is not intended to illustrate either effective or ineffective handling of an administrative situation.

Presented at a Case Workshop and distributed by the Intercollegiate Case Clearing House, Soldiers Field, Boston, Mass. 02163. All rights reserved to the contributors.

The first decision they faced was whether to apply for a state or a national charter. The possession of federal charters by both Auburn banks and all three Opelika banks was the major factor in the decision to explore a state charter first. (The First State Bank of Smiths, the only other bank in the county, had a state charter, but it was located twenty-five miles from Auburn. Because of its distance and small size, this bank was not a significant factor in the Auburn market.)

In spring 1972, those of the interested businessmen who had tentatively agreed to serve on the board of directors went to Montgomery to discuss the prospects for a new bank with the state banking supervisor. They recognized that the supervisor could not make any firm commitments, but at least they might find out whether it would be worth the time and expense of filing a formal application. If the supervisor had been negative, the men could have dropped the project with no further expense. As it happened, the official was receptive to their plans, and suggested that they file a formal application. The market research department of a large bank in the state was recommended for preparation and analysis of supporting data.

The organizers were not ready to formalize the structure of the proposed bank. A critical decision was selection of officers and directors. Whether or not these people would impress the banking authorities would be a critical factor in the success or failure of the application. Needless to say, these same people would be responsible for the survival and growth of the new bank if the application were successful. All officers and directors must be legally and financially "clean." The top officers should be experienced in banking and have local connections. The primary criterion for selection to the board was being of substantial importance in the town. Not only would the directors bring their own business to the bank, but they could also influence others to do the same. The organizers found little difficulty in drawing up a slate of officers and directors who met these criteria, and their qualifications were never an issue in the application.

The initial capitalization of the bank was set at $750,000. The legal minimum was $500,000, but the state banking officials suggested the larger figure. The stock was to sell at $20 per share, with a par value of $10 per share.

While these preliminaries out of the way, the directors were ready to take the first step of the formal application process. The law requires that a notice be printed in the local press for fifteen days announcing the intentions of the undersigned individuals to open a bank with stated capitalization. This notice serves two purposes: to ascertain public interest in the venture, and to allow the existing banks to prepare their opposition to the application if they so desire. Existing banks rarely fail to object to introduction of new competition, and this application was no exception. Banking authorities are interested in public reaction; this reaction determines if the new bank can attract enough business to survive. Also, the authorities prefer banks to have a broad public participation in ownership. The willingness of the public to purchase stock is a significant test of community interest in a new bank. In this case, the stock issue was oversubscribed by a wide margin.

The structure of the application document and all supporting data is the language of Section 6 of the Federal Deposit Insurance Act of 1950, presented in exhibit 1. The Federal Deposit Insurance Act is important even in a state application because nearly every bank—including this one—considers federal insurance of its deposits a necessity. Thus, the application must be considered by two sources: the state banking supervisor and the Federal Deposit Insurance Corporation. The sixth requirement of the Federal Deposit Insurance Act (that the bank's corporate powers be consistent with the purposes of the Act) forces the state to adopt essentially the same standards. Since Alabama requirements are in conformity with federal law, FDIC approval is virtually automatic if the state approves the charter.

The first FDIC criterion, the financial history and condition of the bank, is a simple matter for a proposed new bank. Its history is nonexistent, and its present condition, that is, its current financial condition includes nothing beyond the capital account. This provision is important

Exhibit 1:

An Act

To amend the Federal Deposit Insurance Act (U.S.C., Title 12, Sec. 264), Section 12B of the Federal Reserve Act, as amended, is hereby withdrawn as a part of that Act and is made a separate Act to be known as the "Federal Deposit Insurance Act."

Sec. 6. The factors to be enumerated in the certificate required under Section 4 and to be considered under Section 5 shall be the following: The financial history and condition of the bank, the adequacy of its capital structure, its future earnings prospects, the general character of its management, the convenience and needs of the community to be served by the bank, and whether or not its corporate powers are consistent with the purposes of this Act.

Source: *U.S. Statutes at Large* V 64: 1, 1950–51.

mainly for banks already in business which might apply to join the FDIC. The second criterion, the adequacy of the bank's capital structure, is also more appropriate for banks already in operation. Whether the bank's capital is capable of supporting its liabilities is moot when the organization has no liabilities. The question is extended to assess the likelihood of the capital being adequate to cover future liabilities. Since the major part of a bank's liabilities are deposits, a forecast of deposits is needed. A three-year forecast is usual. The applicants reported that they expected total deposits to be $2 million after one year, $4 million after two years, and $6 million after three years. No formal estimation techniques were used to derive this forecast.

The future earnings prospects of a proposed bank are documented by three-year estimates of income and expenses. Revenue estimates are dependent on the deposit forecast. Given the deposit forecast, the amount of loans outstanding are estimated by applying a loan-to-deposit ratio that is reasonable for a bank of its size. In this case, loans were estimated at $1.1 million, $2.2

million, and $3.3 million for the first three years, implying a loan-to-deposit ratio of 55 percent—about average for banks with deposits between $2 million and $5 million. Given an estimate for loans outstanding, revenue from loans can be forecast by multiplying loans by the anticipated average interest yield. A similar procedure for interest and dividends on securities generates an estimate of income from that source. The technique can also provide an estimate of the interest that must be paid on time deposits. Wage and salary expenses were calculated by determining the number and type of employees that would be needed and assuming they would be paid about the average amount prevailing in the area. These calculations showed that the bank could expect to make a small profit even in the first year (a rather unusual feat for a new business), and that profits would expand sharply the following two years; thanks to favorable operating leverage.

The applicants also estimated the costs of the land and building, the office furniture, and such expenses of organization as the filing fee, attorney fees, and advertising. The land and building could not cost more than 40 percent of the bank's capital, but recent inflation of construction costs led the banking authorities to be flexible about that requirement. The total of these expenses was estimated as in excess of $450,000.

The FDIC's "convenience and needs" criterion essentially asks the question "Does this town need another bank?" Two types of evidence are brought to bear on this issue, the potential for economic growth in the area and the state of competition among banks already there. The first type calls for analysis of population, industries (including agriculture), income, and the labor force. This information would determine whether the region could support a new bank. The second type shows whether the present banks are providing adequate service to the community. The most important test of service adequacy is the lending practices of the banks: are they providing the financial backing for the area's economic growth? The task of marshalling the needed evidence was assigned to the marketing research consultants. The text of their report and some of the supporting data are presented in the appendix.

The application form was completed and the supporting data assembled by the end of the summer. The application was formally filed on 7 September 1972. The state would take about six weeks to reach a decision, and until then the would-be bankers could only wait and hope. In the meantime, the other banks had been preparing their opposition, and were ready to carry their case to the state.

QUESTIONS

1. Evaluate the data provided in support of the proposed new bank. What additional kinds of data would be helpful in developing support for a bank charter application?

2. Review the arguments for a state vs. national charter. Should any additional factors be considered before deciding on a state vs. national bank charter?

3. Outline a program for promoting the bank's services during its first year of operation. What promotional methods and which specific services do you believe would prove most effective?

4. If you had responsibility for approving or denying the proposed charter, based on data provided within the case, what would be your decision?

Auburn Bank and Trust Company

Appendix: Economic and Market Research Study

INTRODUCTION AND PREFACE

For the purposes of this study, Lee County in general, and the Auburn-Opelika area specifically, will be the topics under consideration since it is consistent that a new bank market its services throughout most of this county. It is realized that bank business could also accrue from adjoining counties; however, this is not taken as a matter of reference in this text.

The data and statistics used in this report are from reputable secondary sources and are as up-to-date as possible. It is the contention of this study that Auburn could use an additional banking outlet. This text is prepared simply as an additional source for the proper banking authorities to make this decision.

Trade Area of the Proposed Auburn Bank and Trust Company

Lee County is the industrial and commercial center of East Alabama. It is surrounded by Chambers and Tallapoosa counties to the north, Macon and Russell counties to the south, and the Chattahoochee river, which serves the Alabama-Georgia border, to the east. The county contains 612 square miles.

Auburn is the largest city in Lee County and adjoining Opelika is the county seat. Because of its central location in Lee County, the trade area for the proposed new bank will be defined as the entire county. Although it is not reasonable to expect any great overflow of bank business from the surrounding counties, including Georgia, some business will accrue from these areas.

A look at Auburn and Lee County economic indicators will be a reasonable framework in which to analyze the convenience and needs of the community for the proposed Auburn Bank and Trust Company.

Lee County

The principal trade centers in Lee County are Auburn and Opelika, a smaller portion of the trade going to Marvyn and other small communities. Items that cannot be obtained within Lee County are secured from nearby trade centers such as Montgomery and Columbus, Georgia. The good road system throughout the county, plus main roads leading to these centers, furnish a means of rapid transportion both within the county and outside it.

Lee County has had an increase in population of 23.1 percent from 1960 to 1970 and Auburn had an increase of 40 percent during the same period.

The remainder of this section will present in table form an excerpted overview of the economy and characteristics of Lee County.

Competition for the Proposed Auburn Bank and Trust Company

Data will be given on competing banks within Lee County.

The loan/deposit ratios for Auburn and Lee County are somewhat low (exhibit A-9). Also, there has not been a bank chartered in the major trade areas of Auburn or Opelika since 1923 and presently, there is not a state bank in either of these areas. With the economic development activity that needs to be started now and in the future, the Auburn Bank and Trust Company expects to actively solicit loans and keep a vigorous loan/deposit ratio that is more in keeping with a growing and economically potent trade area.

In addition to the banks, other agencies make loans in the county. The Farmers Home Administration has an office located in the county, and makes loans to rural residents. Their loans include operating loans, farm ownership loans, water and waste disposal system loans to small communities under 5500 population, loans to rural groups for soil and water conservation and shifts in land use, rural housing loans, emergency loans, and water economic opportunity loans. These loans vary from one-year loans for production expenses, to long-term loans for farm ownership and other uses.

The Production Credit Association makes loans to farmers for the production of crops, livestock and the purchase of machinery and equipment. Loans from this agency are usually short-term and intermediate type loans up to seven years. The Federal Land Bank also makes loans to farmers. These include real estate, crop and livestock and general farm improvement loans.

The length of the loans depends on the type, usually ranging from five to thirty-five years.

The Bank for Cooperatives makes loans to farm marketing, service and supply processing and purchasing cooperatives. Length of loans and terms depend on the type of loans made.

The Small Business Administration, Economic Development Administration, Department of Housing and Urban Development, Federal Housing Administration, and the Department of Health, Education and Welfare have loans for certain types of commercial, industrial, public utilities, and recreational enterprises. Insurance companies, the Veterans Administration, and individuals also make loans in the area.

SUMMARY

This report has given data on the convenience and needs of the community for the proposed Auburn Bank and Trust Company.

Statistics on Lee County, Auburn, and financial competition have been presented. It is the contention of this study that:

1. Lee County is an agricultural and industrial area capable of sustaining and increasing economic growth.

2. Auburn is showing good population and economic growth. It is the largest city in the county. However, Auburn, with a larger population, has a combined deposit/population ratio of only $1,529 per person while Opelika has a combined deposit/population ratio of $2,509 per person with a smaller population. This is a possible indicator of an outflow of deposits to Opelika and other cities.

3. New shopping malls, plazas, and industrial parks are being built in the Auburn area (example: Village Mall, $5 million investment, proposed opening date March 1973). The Auburn-Opelika area is also fast becoming a medical services center for eastern Alabama.

4. All present economic barometers seem to indicate that the Auburn-Opelika trade area will become one of Alabama's major trade centers. In fact, this area is presently in the top ten trade areas in the state.

5. As a sidenote, during the spring 1972

Student Government Association elections at Auburn University, one of the SGA presidential hopefuls indicated on his platform that the improvement of bank services and bank relations to the student body would be one of his "planks." The proposed Auburn Bank and Trust Company will hopefully meet their needs.

6. Based on the preceding report, we submit that Auburn can support the proposed Auburn Bank and Trust Company and that this new bank will more than meet the convenience and needs of the community, while providing increased banking competition, increased economic activity, and the ever worthwhile factor of resulting benefits to the people of Auburn and Lee County.

Exhibit A-1:

Population of Primary Trade Areas for Auburn Bank and Trust Company
(Lee County Subdivisions 1960–1970)

Area or Town	1970 Population	1960 Population	Population Increase	Percent Change
Auburn	22,767	16,261	+6,506	+40.0%
Opelika	19,027	15,678	+3,349	+21.4%
Loachapoka - Roxana	4,242	3,977	+ 265	+ 6.7%
Beauregard - Marvyn	3,557	3,646	− 89	− 2.4%
Opelika - Rural - Pepperell	4,034	3,789	+ 245	+ 6.5%
Smith's Station - Salem	7,641	5,227	+2,414	+46.2%

Source: U.S. Dept. of Commerce

Exhibit A-2:

Per Capita Income in Lee County,
Alabama
1960 to 1970

Year	Per Capita Income	Percentage Change from 1960 to 1970
1960	$1,257	
1970	$2,362	+87.9%

Source: U.S. Dept. of Commerce

Exhibit A-3:

Estimated Nonagricultural Wage and Salary
Employment for Lee County, Alabama
September 1971

Category	Unit (000)
Total Wage Salary	$18,020
Manufacturing	$ 6,790
Mining and Quarries	—
Construction	$ 610
Transportation, Communication and Utilities	$ 570
Wholesale and Retail Trade	$ 2,480
Finance, Insurance and Real Estate	$ 510
Services and Miscellaneous	$ 1,760
Government	$ 5,300

Source: Alabama Dept. of Industrial Relations

Exhibit A-4:

Basic Labor Market Information
for Lee County, Alabama
September 1971

Category	Unit
Civilian Work Force	23,620
Total Unemployment	870
Unemployment Rate	3.7
Total Employment	22,750
Non-agricultural Employment:	
Wage and Salary	18,020
All other	3,840
Total	21,860
Agricultural Employment	890

Source: Alabama Dept. of Industrial Relations

Exhibit A-5:

Effective Buying Income Estimates
by Households, Lee County, Alabama
1970

Breakdown	Percentage of Households
$0 − $2,999	26.3%
$3,000 − $4,999	17.0%
$5,000 − $7,999	20.5%
$8,000 − $9,999	11.6%
$10,000 and over	24.6%

Source: *1971 Survey of Buying Power, Sales Management Magazine*

Exhibit A-6:

General Characteristics of Lee County, Alabama 1970

General Characteristics:	Data
Number of Households	17,600
Effective Buying Income	$156,476,000
Total Retail Sales	$ 73,019,000
Effective Buying Income Per Household	$ 8,891

Source: *1971 Survey of Buying Power, Sales Management Magazine*

Exhibit A-7:

General Housing Characteristics of Auburn (Lee County) Alabama

Category	Unit
Total Population	22,767
Total Housing Units	6,490
Median Number of Persons per Unit	2.3
Percent Owner Occupied	44.8
Owner Median Value (dollars)	$21,800
Renter Median Contract Rent (dollars)	$ 80

Source: *General Housing Characteristics (Alabama)*, U.S. Dept. of Commerce

Exhibit A-8:

Retail Sales, Lee County, Alabama

Kind of Business	1971 ($1,000)	1970 ($1,000)	Percentage Change 1970 to 1971
Food	11,556	9,413	+22.8%
General Stores with Food & Gas	1,228	1,574	−22.0%
General Merchandise	4,868	6,321	−23.0%
Apparel	3,461	3,336	+ 3.7%
Furniture, Furnishings & Appliances	2,393	2,215	+ 8.0%
Automotive	15,728	11,832	+32.9%
Gasoline Service Stations	5,669	5,211	+ 8.8%
Lumber & Building Materials	4,419	3,615	+22.2%
Hardware & Farm Implements	898	794	+13.1%
Eating Places	8,800	7,834	+12.3%
Drug Stores	2,203	2,099	+ 5.0%
All Other Retail Concerns	6,518	5,929	+ 9.9%
Total Retail Sales	67,739	60,172	+12.6%

*Percent of state sales at Retail for 1971 equals 1.1%

Source: Bureau of Business Research, University of Alabama

Exhibit A-9:

Lee County, Alabama, Bank Competition

31 December 1971

Bank	City	County	Established (Year)	Offices	Total Deposits	Total Loans	Loans/ Deposits	Total Resources
Auburn National Bank	Auburn	Lee	1907	1	$17,821,553	$ 6,289,982	35.3%	$19,865,813
First National Bank of Auburn	Auburn	Lee	1923	2	$17,559,807	$ 7,277,370	41.4%	$19,268,565
First National Bank of Opelika	Opelika	Lee	1886	1	$12,587,939	$ 5,319,323	42.3%	$13,891,535
Farmers National	Opelika	Lee	1909	1	$16,994,608	$ 9,297,036	54.7%	$18,854,555
Opelika National Bank	Opelika	Lee	1869	3	$20,058,377	$14,127,903	70.4%	$22,676,546
First State Bank	Smiths	Lee	1970	1	$ 1,200,000	$ 689,000	57.4%	$ 1,500,000

Source: *Published Call Reports* December 31, 1971

Jackson County Bank

"It is obvious that the biggest reason we want a branch bank is that our competition has one," said Martin Thomas, member of the Board of Jackson County Bank, as he left a board meeting in early spring 1972. Thomas served as vice-president and cashier of the bank. Some weeks earlier he had been appointed to spearhead a task force to report back to the board on the desirability of alternate locations for a proposed new branch. In giving him this assignment, Randy Holland, chairman of the board, told the members:

"I feel that it is now necessary for us to begin placing branches in different areas, in order that we may not only better serve our customers, but also that we may keep pace with our competition."

Following Holland's comments, the board went on to decide that branching was necessary to insure the continued growth of the bank. Board members felt that a branch should be prof-

This case was prepared by Professors Larry E. Price and Lynn E. Dellenbarger, Jr., of Georgia Southern College as a basis for class discussion rather than to illustrate either effective or ineffective handling of an administrative situation.

Presented at a Case Workshop and distributed by the Intercollegiate Case Clearing House, Soldiers Field, Boston, Mass. 02163. All rights reserved to the contributors.

itable in its own right and should not be operated at a loss. Nathan Beasley, president of the bank, assured Thomas that he would support the task force study by assigning needed clerical help so that the job of gathering facts and figures for a report to the board could go forward. Because some board members had only recently been elected, Thomas felt it would be helpful to begin his report with a recap of the history of the bank as well as a capsule of the local economic picture. The information he gathered included this rundown:

The Jackson County Bank is located in the county seat of Carnes, Georgia. The bank began operations in 1934 following the reorganization of an earlier failed bank. Local businessmen perceive the bank as being more conservatively managed than its competitor, the Adams State Bank. Adams, for example, has already entered the branching field by establishing a branch near the campus of Eastern Georgia College located on the southern edge of Carnes. Adams State has also recently opened a new elaborate downtown home Office just two blocks from the older and less attractive facility of Jackson County.

The town of Carnes, as well as Jackson County, has experienced a period of growth and prosperity during the 1960s. The population of the county rose to 31,585 at the last census. The city population was 14,616, not including the college community. Student enrollment in the current term is at an all-time high of 6,027. The college enrollment has caused state funding to be made available for an extensive building program on campus with four major buildings under construction and two more in the early planning stages.

Carnes is not reliant solely on the college. Several branch plants of major industries have located in the area. Figures supplied by the local Chamber of Commerce show that the six largest employers have a payroll of over $9 million annually. However, the County remains primarily an agricultural center. Some of the more important crops include tobacco, peanuts, corn, soybeans, pecans, timber, and livestock. Estimated agricultural sales for 1970, the latest figures that Thomas could locate, were $25 million.

Because three major highways intersect in Carnes, a substantial tourism related business growth has been experienced. There are thirteen motels and one hotel located in town. The twelve local restaurants have a total seating capacity of 1,944. Thomas considered this to be quite remarkable in a town of only 14,000 population.

Thomas next briefed Mr. Beasley on the background information he developed. After reviewing the facts presented, Beasley remarked, "I think we have all been surprised at how rapidly our area has progressed recently, I am particularly surprised at the large revenue from farming. Between agriculture, industry, and the college, I believe that Carnes and Jackson County have a very promising future."

Beasley went on to explain that the action of Adams State Bank in establishing a branch near the college had convinced the board that they must place a branch *somewhere* because of the action of their competitor. As Beasley put it, "There is really no way to know how everyone would feel if the Adams Bank didn't have a branch, but I feel sure that this strong desire of the directors for a branch is quite successful." As Beasley explained it, "Adams definitely got the jump on us with that branch. Now we are trying to find a place to put a branch that will be

equally or more effective than *their* branch. After all, that's the name of the game."

Since the Adams branch has been started, the total assets of Adams have outdistanced Jackson County by about $3 million. Thomas was convinced, however, that at least some part of this increase was window dressing of the Adams reports in order to make the operation of their branch seem even more successful than it had really been. The year end statement of condition for Jackson (exhibit 1) showed resources of about $14 million while Adams was claiming footings of $17 million.

Thomas began a search of the community for possible branch bank locations. One area immediately came to mind. Although it was not yet generally known in the community, Thomas had learned about a shopping center to be built. This new College Plaza Shopping Center would be located about one-fourth mile from the Eastern Georgia College campus. This was on the south side of town, the area that experienced the largest building growth during the last decade. The shopping center site was alongside a major U.S. highway and only about one mile from the center of town. The center, when completed, would have space for twelve stores. Leases had been signed so far with only four businesses, but Thomas believed that as soon as the plans were announced to the business community that some specialty shops would quickly be lined up to fill out the vacancies. Just adjacent to the shopping center was the empty building previously used by a national franchise fast food restaurant that had failed. Only the vacant building was left and Thomas knew that it would be available at a reasonable price.

If Jackson County wanted to place a branch near the shopping center, but not actually in the center proper, a good possibility might be the purchase and conversion of the building into a branch bank. It would be possible to construct a short road that would run from the rear of the building directly into the shopping center parking lot, which would enable customers to go from one lot to the other without entering the major highway. This was an important factor to Thomas because he feared that although a lot of customers would be in the immediate area, traffic congestion might discourage the use of the branch bank. The State Highway Department was working on plans to enlarge the highway at the point where it passed the shopping center. This would make it much easier to enter and leave the parking lots and would probably relieve some of the congestion.

Thomas wished to prepare a proforma statement of the proposed branch if it were located in the College Plaza Center. Since it was uncertain how many stores, and which ones, would occupy the plaza, he felt that the uncertainties precluded constructing any kind of meaningful estimated statements.

Thomas was able to locate only one other possible site for the proposed branch. The Carnes Mall was nearing completion. The mall was located about three miles from the center of town in an easterly direction. As in the case of the plaza shopping center, the mall was located on a U.S. highway. The mall was inconveniently located for students at Eastern Georgia College. It was far from some areas of town but was quite convenient to many county residents in the eastern section of Jackson County. Several national chain stores were located in the mall. Although the mall was not yet open to the public for retail sales, the stores were near opening date. Thus, employees had been hired and were already at work stocking shelves and learning the company procedures of their new employers. Thomas talked with several of the store managers as well as with the officials of the newly formed Mall Merchants Association.

Mall merchants projected total retail sales for the first year of operation at $10–12 million. Based on this information Thomas attempted to prepare an estimated statement for a branch located at the mall. Using some figures taken from averages furnished by his state bankers association, he estimated that the branch would generate $700,000 in demand deposits and $300,000 in time deposits. He concluded that the branch would garner 675 new demand deposit accounts and 115 new time deposit customers. He incorporated these estimates (exhibit 2) which he prepared for presentation to the Board of Directors.

One important factor of concern to Thomas was the distance from the mall to the college. He wished he had a way of measuring the likely success of drawing students the three miles from the campus to the mall branch. As Thomas observed to his assistant, "It's not the most convenient location for the students, but since the mall will be open long before College Plaza, maybe they will get in the habit of driving out to the mall for shopping."

Thomas estimated that it would cost the same amount to place a branch bank at either location. After consulting bank equipment dealers, he figured that the cost of the branch would be about $125,000. He thought the board would seek the funds from an additional issue of stock offered to existing holders of the bank's common.

After spending several days at his desk looking over all of the data he had gathered, Thomas went into President Beasley's office to see if the two of them could finalize a recommendation for the next meeting of the Board of Directors.

QUESTIONS

1. On the basis of information developed in the case, what should Martin Thomas recommend to the Board of Directors of Jackson County Bank?

Exhibit 1:

Jackson County Bank
Condensed Statement of Condition

	December 31, 197X
Assets	
Cash & Due from Banks	$ 1,726,814.67
U. S. Government Securities	2,671,819.89
Other Bonds & Securities	1,151,251.50
Federal Funds Sold	None
Loans & Discounts	7,917,236.91
Banking House	247,899.77
Furniture & Fixtures	67,453.93
Other Real Estate	None
Accrued Interest Receivable	48,926.80
Other Assets	5,781.50
Total Assets	$13,837,184.97
Liabilities	
Capital	$ 300,000.00
Surplus	400,000.00
Undivided Profits	136,137.08
Reserves	223,508.63
Reserves for Taxes, Expenses, etc.	108,842.49
Unearned Discounts	193,963.46
Deposits	12,474,733.31
Total Liabilities	$13,837,184.97

Exhibit 2:

Jackson County Bank
Mall Branch Proforma Income Statements

	197X + 1	*197X + 2*	*197X + 3*
Demand Deposits	$700,000	$900,000	$1,200,000
Time Deposits	300,000	400,000	550,000
Number of New Accounts			
Demand	675	1,020	1,560
Time	115	165	225
Total Deposits	$925,000	$1,225,000	$1,625,000
Gross Income	61,050	80,850	107,250
Net Income	8,420	18,665	31,063

Case 4

Town and Country Bank
Employee Cost Management

Thomas Coyn, the major stockholder of the Town and Country Bank, had expressed his displeasure to Bill Williams, the bank's president, during the January Board of Directors' meeting. He was concerned about the bank's mediocre earnings performance for the year ending 1977. He had anticipated that 1977 would be an exceptionally good year for the bank, but this had not been the case. Coyn was particularly annoyed at the steadily growing amount of funds the bank was spending on salaries and on officer and employee benefits. He felt that this spending area was largely to blame for the depressed profit performance.

Whether the expenses of salaries and officer and employee benefits have been abnormally high has been an issue of incessant disagreement between the bank's major stockholders and management for the last few years. With assets of $18 million and forty-one employees, Town and Country currently has a 2.28 ratio of employees per million dollars in assets. The national average of employees per million dollars in assets is 1.50. It is this variance that has been the subject of much debate.

To add even more strength to Coyn's argument is the fact that of the five other banks in which he is a major stockholder, none has more than one employee per million dollars in assets, and two banks have a ratio that is less than one.

Williams and Joe Church, his executive vice-president, have always maintained that the bank's salary and officer–employee benefits expense account is not out of line. The higher figures are due merely to the bank's aggressive posture which it must maintain if it is to remain competitive. The extended hours, number of facilities, and volume of customer traffic do indeed require additional employees; the bank's management think that there is very little that can be done to reduce the number of employees.

Coyn was never fully convinced that the Town and Country Bank was all that different from his other banks and thought perhaps that there was a weakness in its management. He told Williams that by the February board meeting he

This case was prepared by James J. Baptist, Barbara Bugal and James L. Hall, graduate students under the supervision of Dr. Lewis E. Davids; Illinois Bankers Professor of Bank Management, Southern Illinois University, Carbondale.

wanted to see good hard evidence that forty-one employees were fully justified.

After the meeting, Williams got together with Joe Church to brief him on what had transpired. He said, "Joe, we've got a problem here. You and I have always agreed that this bank is not overstaffed. Now we must prove it. Tom wants us to reappraise our situation and brief him next month on our conclusions. See what you can get together."

Jefferson State Bank, later to become known as The Town and Country Bank, was chartered on 13 January 1919, in the small town of Jefferson in downstate Illinois. It was a community-owned bank which operated primarily for the small farming community of Jefferson township. At this early date, Jefferson was a major grain shipping center for Jackson County. Jefferson State Bank did not set any tremendous growth records but was a good solid bank. Initially, it started with $25,000 in capital, sixty-two shareholders, and two employees, including a cashier and a clerk.

By 1962, some of the older shareholders were ready to retire, and they sold their interest to Fred Matthews. Matthews later bought out most of the other shareholders to gain controlling interest. Most of the stock purchased was in the name of Banker's Investment, Inc., a subsidiary of Matthews Real Estate agencies, Matthews Insurance agency, and a law firm. In addition, Banker's Investment, Inc. bought the First National Bank of Gotham, Illinois.

The first promotional effort of Jefferson State Bank was the advertisement that it would pay the highest interest on time deposits in Southern Illinois. This action tripled the bank's time deposits in less than one year.

The years of 1964 and 1965 saw great progress in loan growth. By 1966, it became apparent that some of the loans the bank had so eagerly made through its related real estate agencies, through Banker's Investment, Inc., and through First National Bank of Gotham were not that good. However, along with these loans, the borrower was also sold life insurance and mortgage insurance. With these sales and Fred's son doing the legal work, the initial operation was able to reap profits from all around, despite the bad loans.

The loan policy eventually became very loose; people were given loans when all other sources had turned them down. Because of this, bank examinations became more frequent and demanding, until in 1968 when the bank was given sixty days to obtain more capital or be closed.

At this time, the bank had four employees—cashier, assistant cashier, and two clerks. Everyone did teller work and bookkeeping. All CDs, passbook accounts, statements, etc. were calculated manually. Later, another employee was hired to assist primarily with CDs and checks.

As a result of the capital shortage (assets of $4.238 million) the bank was sold to Coyn in December 1968. One of Coyn's first acts as bank owner was to petition the Commissioner to move the bank twenty miles south to University City and to change the bank's name to The Town and Country Bank.

University City is the largest community in Southern Illinois with a population of just over 25,000. Over the years, University City has become a major trade center for all of Southern Illinois. University City's prosperity is due largely to the presence of a major state university and its 20,000 students. The social and economic influence of the university is felt throughout Southern Illinois, and it offers the area residents and businessmen many opportunities. It also presents many problems. These opportunities of growth attracted Jefferson State Bank to University City.

Permission was finally granted to move to University City which had only three banks at that time. The only other banks in the area that would be major competitors for Town and Country were the Big National and Little National Banks in Stokerville, located only seven miles to the west. It should be noted that none of these existing banks filed to prevent Jefferson State Bank from moving into University City, an indication that they felt the new bank's presence would be of little consequence.

The official opening date was scheduled for 28 December 1970. In preparation for the move, a loan officer, secretary, and bookkeeper were hired on 1 November 1970. On this first day of business, these eight employees opened 118 new accounts.

In the last month at Jefferson, the bank lost $400,000 in demand deposits, about half of the total demand deposits. Some people withdrew their money because it would not be feasible for them to drive to University City. Others withdrew out of spite.

Promotional tactics at the new location included no charge checking, free checks, and no service charges on checking for the first year.

The year of 1971 was eventful in many ways. The first big change was putting demand deposit accounts on computer. Lee Johnson and Daniel Shore were hired as cashier and vice-president, and as president, respectively; shortly thereafter two loan officers were added. In addition, plans were begun for a new drive-in facility located at Walnut and Washington to take advantage of the city's east-bound traffic flow. In late 1971, Bill Williams was added as executive vice-president in public relations. He had been with another bank in town for five years and brought twenty-four years of banking experience to The Town and Country Bank.

At the end of Town and Country's first year, demand deposit accounts had grown to $1.377 million and assets had grown from $4.173 million to $7.164 million. By January 1972, the other banks in University City had begun to feel the effects of the growth of The Town and Country Bank, and decided that a change in tactics was needed. It was then that they made the first change in service charges in over twenty years.

The Town and Country Bank continued new promotional efforts throughout 1972 and 1973. February 1972 marked the beginning of $200 minimum free checking accounts. The new drive-in facility was opened in May. The facility was equipped for two tellers, but was usually manned by one individual. In 1973, 6 percent interest was paid on CDs. Also, prepaid interest was paid on CDs.

The bank then began to use a number of give-away schemes. In response to all the giveaways, people first wanted to know what was being given away before they bought a CD. Nevertheless, The Town and Country Bank did get its name before the public, and people came to recognize it.

Furthermore, in January 1972, the employees were promised an expense-paid weekend in New Orleans if the goal of $9 million in assets was reached. By September, the goal was accomplished.

A six-day work week from 9:00 to 6:00 was established in May 1973; these hours held until January 1975, when they were cut back to 5:00 p.m.

In December 1974, Williams was promoted to president of The Town and Country Bank. Joe Church was brought in from one of Coyn's other banks in August 1975 as executive vice-president.

Town and Country struck hard at its competitors in November 1976, when it opened a facility in the shopping mall at the east edge of town. The opening of Town and Country's mall facility made it not only the only bank on the whole eastern side of the city, but also the only bank in town to offer banking services seven days a week and evening hours until 8:00 p.m. six days a week. Such was the convenience of this banking facility that all but seven of the forty-eight businesses in the University Mall opened accounts with Town and Country.

The University Mall shopping complex of forty-four retail stores and four movie theaters had opened three years earlier and has become a tremendously popular place to shop in Southern Illinois. It did an astounding volume of retail business and was said to draw heavily from a sixty-mile radius of the city.

Initially the opening of the mall facility required the hiring of four additional full-time employees; the hours of two part-time people had to be extended. A short time later, however, three other part-time employees had to be added to the staff to help meet the large increase in customer volume. The attached traffic study illustrates this growth in the mall facility's customer volume.

Town and Country's current total staffing consists of seven officers, eighteen tellers, four receptionists (new account clerks), one loan clerk, three proof operators, and eight book-keepers. No department considers themselves even slightly overstaffed.

The Town and Country Bank is one of four commercial banks in University City. The other banks were established well before Town and Country moved from Jefferson. There has always been keen competition among these and the two banks in Stokerville for the area's business, but Town and Country (as of yet) is the only bank to offer extended facilities, seven-day banking, and evening hours six days a week. Under the circumstances, The Town and Country Bank has done quite well in University City since it opened its doors for business in December 1970. The bank's growth and success, however, has not come easily, and it has fre-quently been forced into banking practices that were previously untried in Southern Illinois. The question at hand is whether or not these practices are now forcing the bank into the realm of diminishing returns.

QUESTIONS

1. Thoroughly analyze the Jackson County Bank using whatever analytical tools you deem appropriate.

2. On the basis of your analysis, develop recommendations concerning earnings performance.

Key Comparisons of Six Major Area Banks

	T&C (1)	Lawyers (1)	Old Bank (1)	Big Bank (1)	Big National (2)	Little National (2)
Number of savings accounts as of 31 December 1977	3,112	3,200	2,487	6,371	6,505	3,188
Number of checking accounts as of 31 December 1977	6,082	4,103	3,741	8,307	5,493	2,997
Number of employees as of 31 December 1977	41	38	21	50	45	25
Daily average of proof items for year ending 31 December 1977	12,518	8,088	9,763	16,879	10,500	5,218
Daily average on us items for year ending 31 December 1977*	5,932	3,506	2,891	6,289	8,500	563
Ratio of salaries and employee benefits to total expenses 31 December 1977	26.8%	20.8%	31.0%	21.5%	17.7%	20.1%
Number of banking facilities	3	1	1	1	1	1
Number of hours of operation per week	74	38.5	39	35.5	35.5	36.5
Number of days a week open	7	6	6	5	5	5
Saving and checking account computer maintenance	outsider servicer	outsider servicer	outsider servicer	outsider servicer	inhouse	outsider servicer

*Checks drawn on subject bank only.

(1) University City Banks.

(2) Stokerville Banks.

Comparison of Six Major Banks Growth Records 1973–1977
(in $ thousands)

Town and Country Bank

	1973	1974	1975	1976	1977
Total loans	7,020	7,751	7,183	8,230	9,307
Demand deposits	3,966	4,008	3,896	4,910	5,864
Time deposits	7,210	7,670	8,516	8,849	10,721
Equity capital	850	892	1,047	1,079	1,202
Total assets	12,599	13,246	13,955	15,082	18,037

Lawyers Trust & Savings Bank

	1973	1974	1975	1976	1977
Total loans	8,253	10,807	12,169	13,325	14,959
Demand deposits	10,686	7,878	7,309	7,547	9,028
Time deposits	7,371	9,310	11,184	11,392	12,671
Equity capital	996	1,119	1,248	1,358	1,385
Total assets	19,293	18,653	20,238	20,432	23,618

The Old National Bank

	1973	1974	1975	1976	1977
Total loans	4,066	4,340	4,591	5,203	5,548
Demand deposits	7,153	7,238	7,496	7,672	8,506
Time deposits	5,356	5,659	6,061	6,757	6,980
Equity capital	2,342	2,522	2,734	2,878	3,078
Total assets	15,020	15,621	16,375	17,495	18,773

Big Bank and Trust

	1973	1974	1975	1976	1977
Total loans	10,648	12,861	13,965	14,790	18,635
Demand deposits	10,037	10,372	11,726	12,659	14,256
Time deposits	17,417	20,120	23,686	23,429	26,225
Equity capital	2,673	2,920	3,181	3,260	3,678
Total assets	30,728	34,443	39,454	39,780	44,412

Big National Bank

	1973	1974	1975	1976	1977
Total loans	15,509	16,547	18,125	20,198	24,120
Demand deposits	9,104	9,426	9,627	10,736	11,755
Time deposits	21,140	23,622	26,167	30,247	31,011
Equity capital	2,306	2,571	2,939	3,070	3,444
Total assets	33,522	36,704	40,081	44,577	46,710

Little National Bank

	1973	1974	1975	1976	1977
Total loans	7,951	8,570	8,707	8,806	10,159
Demand deposits	5,129	4,960	5,612	6,824	6,036
Time deposits	12,484	14,179	15,151	17,200	17,999
Equity capital	961	1,294	1,359	1,416	1,559
Total assets	18,876	20,676	22,434	24,647	25,848

Balance Sheet 31 December 1977
(in $ thousands)

Assets

Cash and due from banks	1,926
U.S. treasury securities	0
Obligations of other U.S. government agencies and corporations	2,122
Obligations of state and political subdivisions	1,096
Other bonds, notes and debentures	460
Corporate stock	0
Trading account securities	0
Federal funds sold	2,550
Total loans (excluding unearned income)	9,307
Less reserve for possible loan losses (valuation portion)	15
Net loans	9,292
Direct lease financing	0
Bank premises, furniture and fixtures	368
Real estate other than bank premises	0
Other assets	223
Total assets	18,037

Liabilities

Demand deposits IPC	4,756
Time and savings deposits IPC	7,620
Deposits of U.S. government	114
Deposits of states and political subdivisions	3,869
Deposits of foreign governments	0
Deposits of commercial banks	0
Certified and officers' checks	226
Total deposits	16,585
Total demand deposits	5,864
Total time and savings deposits	10,721
Federal funds purchased	0
Other liabilities for borrowed money	0
Mortgage indebtedness	0
Other liabilities	250
Total liabilities	16,835
Subordinated notes and debentures	0

Equity Capital

Common stock (par value) 2,500 shares authorized and outstanding	250
Surplus	250
Undivided profits	702
Reserve for contingencies and other capital reserves	0
Total equity capital	1,202
Total liabilities and equity capital	18,037

Statement of Income and Expense 1973–1977
(in $ thousands)

	1973	1974	1975	1976	1977
Interest and fees on loans	550	604	644	690	780
Interest on balances with banks	0	0	0	0	0
Income on federal funds sold	106	93	66	32	119
Interest on U.S. Treasury securities	8	3	5	25	1
Interest on other U.S. govt. securities	125	186	192	233	190
Interest on state and political subdivisions	8	26	48	64	66
Interest on other bonds, notes and debentures	60	68	63	55	43
Service charges on deposit accounts	33	44	63	85	127
Other service charges, commissions and fees	16	33	2	5	4
Other income	8	6	11	4	10
Total Operating Income	914	1,063	1,094	1,193	1,340
Salaries and employee benefits	172	194	202	247	323
Interest on CDs of $100,000 or more	93	111	135	76	123
Interest on other deposits	281	335	387	431	445
Expense of federal funds purchased	0	0	0	0	0
Interest on other borrowed money	0	0	0	0	0
Occupancy expense of bank premises	17	47	30	29	44
Furniture and equipment expenses	17	15	16	25	37
Provision for possible loan losses	0	0	39	16	12
Other expenses	220	243	177	252	222
Total operating expenses	800	945	986	1,076	1,206
Income before taxes and securities gains or losses	114	118	108	117	134
Applicable income taxes	28	21	8	10	9
Income before securities gains (losses)	86	97	100	107	125
Securities gains (losses) gross	0	3	(13)	0	12
Applicable income taxes	0	1	6	0	3
Securities gains (losses) net	0	2	(7)	0	9
Net income	86	99	93	107	134
Other increases in capital accounts	5	6	56	0	17
Other decreases in capital accounts	39	55	50	3	28
Net change in total capital accounts	52	50	99	104	123

	Selected Operating Statistics for Town and Country Bank 1973–1977					Median Value–1977 BAI Index of Bank Performance 1977 State of Illinois (All Banks)		
	1973	1974	1975	1976	1977	Lower ¼	Median	Upper ¼
Operating performance—percentage of assets								
Interest income*	7.26%	7.85%	7.53%	7.85%	7.42%	7.06%	7.42%	7.75%
Interest expense	3.14%	3.49%	3.71%	3.44%	3.35%	3.81%	3.50%	3.11%
Salaries & employee benefits	1.45%	1.52%	1.43%	1.67%	1.90%	1.57%	1.31%	1.07%
Occupancy expense	0.14%	0.37%	0.21%	0.20%	0.26%	0.27%	0.18%	0.12%
Other expense	1.99%	2.03%	1.37%	1.88%	1.53%	1.20%	0.90%	0.69%
Return on assets—operating income	0.71%	0.76%	0.71%	0.73%	0.74%	0.72%	0.94%	1.19%
Return on assets—net income	0.73%	0.77%	0.66%	0.73%	0.79%	0.74%	0.97%	1.20%
Loan loss data								
Net charge offs as percentage of average loans	0.22%	0.09%	0.33%	0.21%	0.13%	0.29%	0.12%	0.04%
Yields and rates								
Yield on earning assets*	8.12%	8.68%	8.43%	8.74%	8.55%	7.88%	8.21%	8.59%
Yield on loans	8.63%	8.13%	8.61%	8.90%	8.92%	8.07%	8.58%	9.04%
Yield on taxable securities	6.23%	8.04%	7.31%	7.53%	8.03%	6.76%	7.20%	7.60%
Yield on tax exempt sec.*	9.20%	10.31%	12.79%	11.86%	11.88%	8.77%	9.42%	10.28%
Rate on total interest funds	5.30%	5.90%	6.50%	5.78%	5.70%	5.25%	5.50%	5.72%
Salaries & employee benefits as percentage of total expense	21.50%	20.53%	20.49%	22.96%	26.78%			
Occupancy expense as percentage of total expense	2.13%	4.97%	3.04%	2.70%	3.65%			
Other expense as percentage of total expense	29.63%	27.41%	19.57%	25.74%	21.48%			
Balance sheet data								
Earning assets as percentage of total assets	89.41%	90.43%	89.40%	89.80%	86.87%	88.02%	90.32%	92.29%
Loans as percentage of total assets	53.57%	58.12%	53.04%	52.57%	51.53%	42.40%	50.61%	58.19%
Taxable sec. as percentage of total assets	26.04%	25.00%	25.13%	28.17%	17.17%	15.68%	22.63%	31.48%
Tax exempt sec. as percentage of total assets	1.37%	3.79%	4.73%	7.03%	6.30%	7.88%	11.94%	15.75%
Total deposits as percentage of total assets	88.69%	88.07%	89.23%	91.43%	91.82%	88.29%	90.53%	91.97%
Time deposits as percentage of total assets	59.29%	59.11%	57.09%	59.49%	58.67%	63.88%	69.26%	73.75%
Equity as percentage of total assets	7.04%	6.90%	7.04%	7.30%	6.85%	6.56%	7.59%	9.00%
Number of employees	27	30	32	36	41			

*Calculated using full tax equivalent.

Comparison, January 1977–1978 Mall Traffic Patterns

Per Hour Traffic

Time	1977 Customers	1978 Customers	1977 Av. per Hr.	1978 Av. per Hr.
9:30–10:00	199	401*	8.29*	16.04*
10:00–11:00	356	665	14.83	26.60
11:00–12:00	378	937	15.75	34.70
12:00–1:00	609	1,183	22.56	40.79
1:00–2:00	669	1,253	24.78	43.21
2:00–3:00	581	1,250	21.52	44.64
3:00–4:00	542	1,254	20.07	43.24
4:00–5:00	690	1,360	25.56	48.57
5:00–6:00	732	1,562	30.50	65.08
6:00–7:00	510	1,162	21.25	48.42
7:00–8:00	419	1,057	17.46	44.04
	5,685	12,084	20.32	41.39

Per Day of Week Traffic

Day	1977 Av. # of Cust. per Day	1978 Av. # of Cust. per Day	1977 Av. per Hr.	1978 Av. per Hr.
Monday	180	362	17.14	34.48
Tuesday	171	404	16.29	38.47
Wednesday	170	377	16.19	35.90
Thursday	170	337	16.19	32.10
Friday	281	552	26.76	52.57
Saturday	306	626	29.14	59.62
Sunday	192	312	38.40	56.72

Accounts Opened at Mall

January 1977 (Approx.)		January 1978	
Checking	106	Checking	83
Savings	71	Savings	83
	177		166

*Only ½ hour.

Largest counted day to date: 3 February 1978. On that day 821 people used the mall. On that same day between the hours 4:00 to 5:00 there were 140 people who used the mall facility.

Note: January may not be a truly representative month since the bad weather in January 1978 drastically hindered automobile travel.

Case 5

A Bank IS a Bank—Is a Bank?

More than 700 stockholders were represented when an application for authority to organize a bank in Pensacola, Florida, was filed in May 1976. This was the largest group that had ever applied for a bank charter in Florida. The application was unusual also because the seven persons whose names appeared on it were all women. The major purpose of the bank was to serve the financial needs of women. Filing for a charter represented a culmination of intense effort over a ten-month period from August, 1975 to May 1976. The announcement of the decision by three women to organize a bank appeared in *The Pensacola News Journal* on 24 August 1975. The news item presented this action of the women as another example of feminine progress in fields traditionally dominated by men. It stated that the first all-women's bank was chartered in Cleveland in 1935. Two such groups in Florida—this one and another in Tallahassee—were working for a bank charter.

This case was prepared by Professor Eleanor Casebier with the collaboration of Professor Manning Hanline at The University of West Florida. It is designed to be used as a basis for class discussion rather than to illustrate either effective or ineffective handling of decision making.

Justification for the action can be seen from statements in the newspaper article containing quotes from the three women:

Helen Hunter: "We feel the community is ready for it . . . and the brilliant caliber of women right here in this community will help make this a success."

Mary Colleen Moore: "Women are not given the same consideration in the trust department. . . . The male trust officers don't feel you know enough as a woman to make decisions on what to do with your money. They give advice, instead of listening to any ideas women might have."

Margie Hadley: "That's right . . . A man in a pair of pants feels he knows more. But I've been in the business world long enough to know better."

Both Hadley and Moore were realtors. Hunter worked for the city.

Further evidence of a felt need for improving credit facilities for women was the new federal law which was a part of the Equal Credit Opportunity Act passed in October 1975. The law states, "A creditor shall not discriminate against any applicant on the basis of sex or marital status with respect to any aspect of a credit transaction."

According to the December (1975) issue of *American Teacher,* "the ECOA marks the first legislation written to deal with the rampant discrimination against women by banking and loan companies. Some of the regulations go into effect immediately; others will be phased in gradually until February, 1977. Sexist credit applications have to be changed by next 30 June. Creditors won't have to explain why they reject a woman's application until next year."

Also, Regulation B, issued by the Federal Reserve Board on 28 October 1975, expressly states: "A creditor shall not discriminate against any applicant on the basis of sex or marital status with respect to any aspect of a credit transaction." Section 202.4 (b) says: "A creditor shall not refuse, on the basis of sex or marital status, to grant a separate account to a credit-worthy applicant."

It appears from the foregoing comments that women have been discriminated against in matters pertaining to credit. A need for the bank in Pensacola could be based on patterns of population growth, as well. Statements supporting this need are quoted from the Pensacola paper under the dateline of 26 November 1975.

A case analysis is made of the decision points which occurred in the organizational period. It is well to keep in mind that the decision-making group was an interim board of directors that varied in size over time. There were twenty board members at the time the charter application was filed. Only one of them had previous experience in banking, yet their backgrounds included many years of business experience.

The ultimate goal was to obtain a bank charter, and this could be accomplished only after an application had been filed. Before that could happen stock subscriptions had to be acquired in the amount of $1 million. A feasibility study and site analysis had to be completed. Raising required capital was not an easy task, especially since there were no women of great wealth on the interim board for most of the time in which stock subscriptions were sought. Financial strength came from hundreds of individuals (mostly women) in the community who saw the project as an opportunity both to lend support to

EXHIBIT 1:

Population Expansion Calls for Planning

A POPULATION projection for the Pensacola metropolitan area predicted for the next five years by *Sales Management* magazine, forcefully points up the urgency for sound planning, both economic and environmental.

The Pensacola area, which includes Pensacola Beach and Gulf Breeze in Santa Rosa County, is listed twelfth in growth in Florida, with a 15.1 percent increase by 1980 and a population of 325,400, of which 265,200 would reside in Escambia County.

If the magazine's projection is accurate, there will be an influx of approximately 50,000 new residents, most of them living in the extreme southern portion of Escambia County between Pensacola and Perdido bays.

And if this projection is incorrect, it most certainly errs on the conservative side.

Increasing numbers of people seek the mild climate of the South, both the old in search of retirement homes and the young attracted by year-round recreational opportunities, and they all endeavor to get as near the Gulf Coast as possible.

a women's group and also to make a wise investment.

Obviously, legal requirements had to be met. Most of the activity that is described in this case was an effort to comply with the state laws for organizing a bank. The following steps are necessary to get a charter:

1. Application. The application must be in compliance of regulation (Charter) 659. It must include proof of need and a reasonable promise of success.

2. Field investigation. This is done by the comptroller's office and the FDIC. The State will be looking at the site, speaking to local bankers and businessmen. The FDIC does the same.

3. Actual investigation. This is a very thorough investigation of the charter applicants.

4. Public meeting. This is designed to let residents of the area speak for or against a

new bank. This was presented as a great opportunity for local feedback and an opportunity to use the rules advantageously by getting minority groups to come to the meeting and speak positively about a women's bank.

5. Evaluation. The reports from the field investigation (in the community) are sent back to Tallahassee for evaluation of the business expertise and ability of the proposed charter applicants to manage a bank. Simultaneously, reports of public meeting (pros and cons) are submitted for evaluation. Both of these reports are open for public review.

6. Comptrollers' conference. The comptroller or deputy comptroller hears arguments from each side concerning the advisability of the bank. There is no cross examination. The applicants, the protestants, and public attend.

7. Order. The decision on the application is called the order and the order is made after the comptroller's conference.

Before a charter will be granted, the comptroller must be convinced of three things—management, capital and need. A reasonable chance of success must be proved and the burden of proof is on the applicant. One factor that caused concern was that a branch banking law had been passed and would take effect in 1977. A copy of the senate bill revising the law follows:

EXHIBIT 2:

Chapter 76–142
Senate Bill No. 711

AN ACT relating to industrial savings banks; amending s. 656.071(1), Florida Statutes; providing for the establishment of branch banks, the relocation of a parent or branch bank, and the merger of banks; providing an effective date.

Be it Enacted by the Legislature of the State of Florida:

Section 1. Subsection (1) of section 656.071, Florida Statutes, is amended to read:

(Substantial rewording of subsection. See S. 656.071(1), F. S., for present text.)

656.071 Place of transacting business; drive-in facilities.—

(1) (a) Any bank heretofore or hereafter incorporated pursuant to this chapter shall have one principal place of doing business as designated in its articles of incorporation; in addition, with the approval of the department and upon such conditions as the department shall prescribe, including a satisfactory showing by the bank that public convenience and necessity will be served thereby, any bank may establish up to two branches per calendar year within the limits of the county in which the parent bank is located and, in addition, may establish branches by merger with other banks located within the county in which the parent bank is located. The location of a parent bank or of a branch bank may be moved if the department determines that public convenience and necessity will be served by such move, but the location of a parent bank or of a branch bank may not be moved beyond the limits of the county in which it is located. The term "parent bank" shall be construed to mean the bank or banking office at which the principal functions of the bank are conducted. An application for a branch bank shall be in writing in such form as the department prescribes, supported by such information, data and records as the department may require to make findings necessary for approval. The department shall not act upon a branch application until it has completed consideration of any bank application pending when the branch application was filed if the proposed locations for such branch and bank are within one mile of each other. Provided however, that action upon a branch application shall not be delayed more than six months after its filing due to the pendency of such a prior bank application. When the department has approved an application, it shall issue a certificate authorizing the operation of the branch bank and specifying the date on which it may be opened and the place where it will be located.

(b) This subsection shall be construed to allow the merger of banks within the same county and the operation by the merged company of such banks, and to allow the sale of any bank to, and the purchase thereof through merger by, any other bank in the same county and the operation of such banks by the merged bank, provided that the Department of Banking and Finance shall be of the opinion and shall first determine that public convenience and necessity will be served by such operation.

Section 2. This act shall take effect January 1, 1977.

Approved by the Governor June 15, 1976.

Filed in Office of Secretary of State June 16, 1976.

REPRODUCED by FBA

JULY, 1976

Applications take anywhere from one to seven years but can be done in 270 days or nine months. Because the branch banking law was passed, speed in preparing the application was imperative. The decision-making group felt extreme pressure in relation to time. Since *need* for additional banking facilities had to proved, a stronger case could be made for this bank with an application filed prior to those that certainly would be made by existing banks for establishing branches.

Decision Point 1 The first decision was that of the three women to organize a bank which was to be owned, managed, and operated mainly for the benefit of women. After a public announcement in the newspaper, there was quite a lot of interest in the project. Many persons contacted the three women organizers and indicated a wish to support the effort or to be employed by the bank.

Decision Point 2 An open meeting was held for the first time on Monday 7 October 1975. Prior to that time several decisions had been made by the organizers. There had been agreement on a proposed name and location as well as on preliminary plans for design of the building to house the bank. Other areas covered were requirements for directors, proposed capital structure, and statement of purpose. Seven women had been selected to serve on the Interim Board. These early decisions were made primarily by Hunter, her husband, who acted as attorney for the group, and Bette Imus, who was comptroller of a local motel. At subsequent dates and decision points, many of these items were changed.

The first meeting was conducted by the interim board of directors which was made up of five realtors, Imus and Hunter. It was well attended and there was obviously great interest and enthusiasm about the bank. Women present were lawyers, teachers, professors, realtors, government employees, and homemakers. At the meeting there was a general discussion of the bank project, followed by a distribution of stock subscription forms. Capital stock had a par value initially of five dollars a share—later increased to ten dollars. A subscription fee of 5 percent was assessed at the time of the agreement. This money was to be used as a contingency fund for paying legal fees, application fees, and other expenses incurred in the organization phase. Subscriptions were to be paid in full at the time the charter was granted. Subsequent meetings held from time to time followed the same general format.

Decision Point 3 During October, the number of women named to the Interim Board of Directors was increased from seven to thirteen. One of these was a newcomer to the community, with several years of experience in banking. Two of the new directors were black, both prominent educators. One woman was quite active in state politics and in the women's movement. The number was increased again in March in an effort to include women whose names might be helpful in applying for the charter.

Decision Point 4 On 6 November 1975, a "Notice Required For Proposed New Financial Institution" was mailed to the Division of Securities, Tallahassee, Florida. According to state banking laws, this had to be done prior to application, and renewal was possible in the event that an application was not forwarded within ninety days. One of the benefits of having filed a formal notification was that the Board could deposit checks received as payment for stock subscriptions. Checks were made payable to Ed O. Hunter, Trustee, and the money could not be used prior to the formal notification.

Decision Point 5 A dinner meeting was held for a few interested women on 25 November at the home of Mary Baker, corresponding secretary. Several matters of concern were discussed. One of these had to do with the question of selling stock to men. Some of those present felt quite strongly that the bank stock should be owned only by women. Yet, it was obvious that this would be discriminatory and therefore illegal. A decision was made to accept stock subscriptions from men. This policy change was approved by the board on 12 January. The formal motion carried a stipulation that the percentage of stock held by male stockholders would be restricted.

Decision Point 6 Completion of a market study and site analysis was required as a part of the application for a charter. The decision to award a contract for this proved difficult for the board. The problem became an issue in November and was finally solved in late December. Three proposals were examined. One was submitted by the marketing department of the local university. Their price was $10,000 and the proposal was rejected because it was too costly. Another bid for the contract was submitted by the management department of the same university; their proposal was also rejected. The contract was awarded to a professional team from Miami. Mike Barth, an economist, had ten years of experience in economic and market consulting and had worked on many charters throughout the country, most of them successfully. Neil Hansen, an attorney, had been general counsel to the State of Florida comptroller's office and helped draft existing rules that applied to this charter. The bank attorney indicated his hearty approval of this choice in a memorandum to the interim board on 23 December 1975. Fees for Barth and Hansen were established at roughly $6,500 each.

Decision Point 7 Barth told the board members that they must make a decision as to whether they intended to be a member of the Federal Reserve System or apply for membership in the Federal Deposit Insurance Corporation. He advised that there are advantages to being a member of the Federal Reserve System but a nonmember is less closely regulated. The group voted to apply for membership in FDIC.

Decision Point 8 A pressing problem came to the attention of the board in January and February. On 2 December subscriptions amounted to about a half-million dollars. On 12 January, a financial report was submitted showing the bank

had about $540,000 in subscriptions. By February the increase had amounted to only $50,000. This represented too little progress and members were disappointed. A decision was made to use a new approach in an effort to acquire the needed minimum of $1 million in subscriptions. The board decided to spend money in fairly generous amounts in an effort to increase subscriptions. They began a program of luncheons and parties to attract subscriptions.

On 26 February there was an open meeting at a local country club held in the evening. Coffee was served as well as several kinds of hors d'oeuvres. About 200 attended and the number who showed an interest in subscribing to stock was gratifying. There was a distressing situation that developed in relation to this meeting. The bill from the country club was $700. Board members felt it was excessive for the service rendered. This was a learning experience and was not to be repeated.

Luncheon meetings were held almost weekly. The guest list was provided by various members of the board. The number attending the luncheon was between fifteen and twenty. Two or three members of the board would explain the bank project and solicit subscriptions. Sales of stock picked up very rapidly and by 22 March it was reported that in excess of $800,000 had been subscribed.

Decision Point 9 A site had to be chosen before an application could be prepared. Barth was responsible for assisting in this decision based on an exhaustive economic study of the area. Several sites were available and were investigated. One of these was a building formerly used as a brewery. It was rejected because that location was not considered to be a favorable one. It was in an old, rundown neighborhood and on a street with only an average traffic flow. A second site was an abandoned grocery store building, available for $360,000. It was on a 1.57-acre tract of land directly across from a major bank. One drawback to this location was that on two of the three access streets there was only a one-way traffic flow.

A third possibility consisted of a four-acre

tract of land in a large, new shopping center. The land was available for $310,000, part of which could be paid in stock. Interest payments of $6,000 would be needed quarterly to reserve the tract.

A fourth site carried with it an opportunity to substantially increase stock subscriptions. It was described as "a parcel of land located in the southeast quadrant of the intersection of Bayou Boulevard and 170 feet on the north side of Dodson Drive." It was near a huge shopping complex in the center of the metropolitan area. This possibility was made known to the board on 24 March. Jim and Christy Sons, a wealthy couple who owned this site, had offered to make it available for the bank. They had agreed to subscribe to $400,000 in stock, pay the required 5 percent fee, or $20,000, and in return accept $30,000 as lease payment for one year. Rental for the property was $30,000 annually and the lease agreement was to be for ten years. There was no building on the property.

Board members were concerned about two aspects of this offer. First, there had been an early agreement that no one person would control the bank as a result of holding more than 10,000 shares of stock. It was obvious that the Sons family, with one-third of the capital stock, could easily get enough votes to control all matters including membership on the board of directors as well as chairmanship of the board. This was resolved, on paper at least, by issuing 10,000 shares of stock to each of four members of the Sons family—husband, wife, and two children. The other major concern was that a ten-year lease was insufficient for the purpose of obtaining a mortgage to build a bank structure. This was resolved by obtaining an option to renew the lease for an additional thirty years. With these decisions clearing away any further objec-

tions, the offer was accepted and subscriptions were closed at $1.2 million.

One would have expected some members of the board to increase their stock subscriptions after hearing about the Sons' offer. In fact, during the twenty-four hour period following the disclosure of the offer of the Sons family, two board members increased their subscriptions. One member subscribed to 100 shares and the other subscribed to 300 shares.

A stockholder's meeting was called for the following Monday evening, 29 March, at which time affidavits were signed and notarized which was another legal requirement before the charter application could be finalized. On this same date there was a board meeting, and an announcement was made that the sale of stock to the Sons family had been finalized, and the lease agreement had been signed. Christy Sons was introduced as a member of the interim board. Members of the board planned a dinner party to celebrate acquiring a charter.

QUESTIONS

1. In your opinion, did there exist a legitimate need for a bank owned, managed, and operated for the benefit of women in 1975? Today?

2. Summarize the various steps and decisions involved in the acquisition of a bank charter.

3. Are there any potential conflicts associated with acceptance of the Sons' subscription for $400,000 in bank stock?

4. In general, evaluate the potential profitability and success of the proposed bank.

Case 6

First Hawaiian Bank
Formation of a Bank Holding Company

There is not supposed to be any such thing as a free lunch in this world, but it certainly looks like one may have arrived in the mail this morning. A letter and prospectus from First Hawaiian Bank, a company in which you own stock, announced that a special stockholders' meeting would be held on 19 April 1974. At the meeting stockholders will be asked to approve a merger of First Hawaiian Bank into a subsidiary of a bank holding company. Each share of stock in the bank would be exchanged for a share of stock in First Hawaiian, Inc., the bank holding company. Instead of holding stock in the bank only, you would own stock in a larger organization, the holding company which included the bank as a subsidiary.

In the letter to stockholders, John Bellinger, president of First Hawaiian Bank, pointed to several advantages of the proposal and to the unanimous recommendation for approval by the Board of Directors. The proposal may result in greater growth potential due to an expansion of the banking operations and other financial services currently offered by the bank. There will be new alternative ways to raise funds in financial and monetary markets not now available to the bank. Also, the holding company will have the ability to establish or acquire certain other financial enterprises as authorized recently by the Federal Reserve Board.

In forming a bank holding company, First Hawaiian is following the course taken by its major competitor, the Bank of Hawaii. In 1972 the Bank of Hawaii formed Hawaii Bancorporation, a bank holding company. Rival Hawaii Bancorporation has already set up two new subsidiaries with the bank and issued commercial paper in its own name; one subsidiary provides computer services while the other is in the leasing business.

First Hawaiian proudly claims to be the "Bank that says, 'yes.'" What you have to decide is whether you want to be the stockholder who says, "Yes." The proposal certainly looks good. There has been a great deal of talk lately in the financial press about the rapid expansion of

This case was prepared by Professor Steven Dawson of the University of Hawaii as a basis for class discussion rather than to illustrate either effective or ineffective handling of an administrative situation.

the bank holding company movement, and you have seen numerous references to other bank holding companies moving into areas which are closely related to banking yet denied to banks themselves. On the other hand, there might be some disadvantages to the proposal. After all, except for Bank of Hawaii, none of the other banks in Hawaii has set up a bank holding company. Before the April stockholder meeting you plan to consider thoroughly all the advantages and disadvantages so that you can make an intelligent decision.

FIRST HAWAIIAN BANK

First Hawaiaan Bank is the oldest bank in the State of Hawaii; it was established in 1858. Known then as Bishop and Co., it was founded by Charles Reed Bishop and William Aldrich. It was a one-room bank in the Makee Building on Kaahumanu Street. For the next twenty-seven years it was the only bank chartered in Hawaii until Claus Spreckels and Co. came along in 1885. Over the past century the bank has grown and prospered, and has acquired other banks and added branches until it now has forty offices.

Today, First Hawaiian offers a broader range of financial services than any other bank in Hawaii's tough competitive environment. The bank is an active lender in the commercial, consumer, and real estate loan markets. Demand, savings, and time deposits are accepted. Unlike its major rival, the Bank of Hawaii, it has a trust department which handles a full range of trust services. The International Banking Department finances international trade, principally in the Pacific Basin area.

First Hawaiian is the second largest bank in the state with assets well above American Security, the next largest (exhibit 1). Only the Bank of Hawaii is larger, but it wasn't always that way. Back in 1956, First Hawaiian Bank was the state's largest bank. Being second biggest is not an easy thing to accept, even if it is big enough to rank 117th nationally; thus, a number of competitive moves have been taken in recent years. At the start of 1969 the bank switched

EXHIBIT 1:

Asset Size of Hawaii's Banks
31 December 1973

	Assets $000	Percentage of Total
Bank of Hawaii	$1,024,219	37.3%
First Hawaiian Bank	887,972	32.4%
American Security Bank	214,900	7.8%
Central Pacific Bank	208,415	7.6%
City Bank	141,757	5.2%
Liberty Bank	138,174	5.0%
Hawaii National Bank	114,120	4.2%
Bank of Honolulu	13,631	0.5%
	$2,743,189	100.0%

Source: Bank Examiner Reports, State of Hawaii Department of Regulatory Agencies.

from a national to a state charter and gave up its membership in the Federal Reserve System. This added substantially to the funds available for use as loans or investments. As a Federal Reserve member, the bank could not count money deposited with correspondent banks as part of its required reserves. With a state charter, these deposits do count toward the requirement. Later in 1969, the bank introduced the Master Charge credit card to Hawaii. In 1970 the bank entered the field of international banking when it became a member of Allied Bank International. This consortium of eighteen U.S. banks is organized to compete effectively with the international banking giants such as Chase Manhattan, First National City, and Bank of America.

Of course, the Bank of Hawaii has not been standing still. In 1972 it became the first bank in Hawaii to form a bank holding company.

BANK HOLDING COMPANY LEGISLATION

In 1956, Congress passed the Bank Holding Company Act. The Federal Reserve was concerned at the time that holding companies were being used to evade the intent of the Banking Act of 1933. Banks were not supposed to engage in business activities unrelated to banking, yet bank holding companies or their affiliates were doing what their subsidiary banks were prohibited from doing. The 1956 act sharply limited the nonbank activities. Only those which were "a proper incident to" banking or managing or controlling banks and which were "of a financial, fiduciary or insurance nature" could be undertaken. Holding companies were given a choice of relinquishing all but one of their banks or getting rid of their nonbanking interests. Significantly, the law applied only to multibank holding companies. This was because many organizations, including Goodyear Tire and Rubber, Hershey Foods, the United Mine Workers, and even Dartmouth College owned small and relatively insignificant banks.

Exclusion of one-bank holding companies meant they could engage in unrestricted types of business activity. It was not long before this loophole was discovered and exploited. By the end of the 1960s the number of one-bank holding companies and their nonbank activities increased greatly. The 1970 amendments to the Bank Holding Company Act restored control over bank holding companies. There were two key aspects of the amendments. First, one-bank holding companies were now included. Second, in a liberalization of the 1956 Act, the Federal Reserve Board, which administered the Act, was directed to determine acceptable nonbanking activities for holding companies. Holding companies could not, however, return to earlier ways since these activities were to be "so closely realted to banking or managing or controlling banks as to be a proper incident thereto." Missing was the earlier phraseology "Financial, fiduciary, or insurance [in] nature."

By early 1974 the list of permitted activities for bank holding companies (designated Regulation Y) included the following:

1. Mortgage banking
2. Finance company (consumer or commercial)
3. Insurance
4. Leasing of real and personal property
5. Data processing
6. Factoring
7. Community development
8. Industrial banking
9. Trust services
10. Investment or financial advising

In announcing its intention to form a bank holding company, First Hawaiian stated that the holding company had no present intention to acquire other banks. It might engage through subsidiaries in those activities which are permitted by the Bank Holding Company Act and the regulations of the Board of Governors of the Federal Reserve System, but according to the letter to shareholders, there are currently "no definite plans" to do so. A newspaper report noted that Bellinger was legally barred from discussing possible holding company ventures, but "the bank wouldn't be setting up the holding company unless it had some specific ideas, with prospects for near-term results."

THE PROPOSAL

At the meeting called for 19 April 1974, the stockholders would be asked to approve the merger of First Hawaiian Bank into a subsidiary of a bank holding company, First Hawaiian, Inc. The technical details of the transaction would call for First Hawaiian Bank to merge with the newly organized (state) FHB Bank whose common stock except for directors shares is owned by First Hawaiian, Inc. After the merger, FHB Bank would change its name to First Hawaiian Bank, thereby continuing the name of the present bank. The bank subsidiary would carry on the same banking activities as before and keep the same officers and directors.

Exchange Ratio The 3,045,360 shares of bank stock could be exchanged on a one-for-one basis for shares in First Hawaiian, Inc., the holding company. An additional 24,640 shares of authorized holding company stock would be available for future acquisitions or other corporate purposes.

Required Vote The formulation of the holding company was approved earlier by the Federal Reserve Board. The merger has been approved by the Department of Regulatory Agencies of the State of Hawaii. An application is on file with the FDIC. This application will be acted upon if there is a favorable vote from holders of two thirds of the bank stock.

Stockholders who reject the exchange Stockholders who do not want to exchange their bank stock for holding company stock may exercise their right to receive the appraised cash value of the bank shares as provided for in section 404-10 of the Hawaii Revised Statutes. This option is available only to stockholders who vote against the proposal. The amount paid for these shares will be established by the new bank subsidiary and it will represent what is considered to be the fair market value at the time of the stockholders' meeting. If this value is not acceptable to the dissenting stockholders, a second appraisal will be made by three appraisers. One each will be selected by the dissenting stockholders and by the bank directors, with these two appraisers selecting a third.

This plan differs from the offer made by Bank of Hawaii when it formed a holding company. The Bank of Hawaii made a tender offer to existing stockholders. Those who did not accept (about 0.5 percent of the stock outstanding) kept their bank shares.

Reasons for the plan The prospectus distributed to shareholders contains the following statement in support of the proposal:

> The directors and principal officers of the bank believe that a bank holding company will be able to enter into more diversified financial activities than the bank can do directly or through bank-owned subsidiaries. A bank holding company may provide more alternatives in the raising of funds required by the Continuing Bank, or by other subsidiaries of the holding company under changing conditions in financial and monetary markets. A holding company also has greater flexibility than the bank in structuring the establishment or acquisition of banks and other financial enterprises. A bank is not permitted by law to engage in certain businesses, even though they are closely related to banking. Similarly, it may not own subsidiaries engaging in such businesses. A holding company may do both.

Income tax consequences Shareholders who receive holding company shares will not pay taxes on the exchange and will continue to have the same tax basis as with the bank stock. Dissenting shareholders who elect to receive cash will be liable for taxes due on any realized gain.

COMPARISON OF BANK STOCK WITH HOLDING COMPANY STOCK

Dividends Until other subsidiaries become part of the holding company, dividends of the continuing bank will be the only source of dividends for the holding company. The ability of the bank to legally pay dividends remains the same.

Voting rights Hawaii laws require that stockholders in state banks have cumulative voting rights. Stockholders in the holding company will not have cumulative voting rights.

Liquidation rights In liquidation, stockholders receive pro rata any assets distributed. There is no change.

Amendments to by-laws Bank stockholders must approve any changes in the by-laws of the bank. The by-laws of the holding company may be amended by the board of directors without stockholder action.

STOCKHOLDERS AND MARKET TRADING

There are approximately 2,250 stockholders who own the 3,045,360 shares of First Hawaiian Bank stock. The bank's officers and directors own a total of 36,910 shares. In addition four of the directors are trustees for the estate of S. M. Damon, which holds 700,000 shares (23 percent) of stock. There are no other stockholders who own more than 10 percent of the stock. The stock has unlisted trading privileges on the Honolulu Stock Exchange and it is traded on the over-the-counter market. The latest closing bid price at the Honolulu Stock Exchange was $23.50. This is just above its recent low of $21 and well below its 1973 high of $36. More detailed stock prices as well as information about Hawaii Bancorporation stock, the holding company for the Bank of Hawaii is listed in exhibit 3.

RELATIONSHIP OF BANK TO OTHER AFFILIATES OF THE HOLDING COMPANY

There would be no direct relationship between the bank and other affiliates of the bank holding company. If the holding company should start or acquire, for instance, a leasing affiliate, the leasing company would be a subsidiary of the holding company and not of the bank. The only factor the bank and the leasing company would have in common would be their common ownership by the holding company.

The ability of the bank to flow funds to other affiliates would also be limited. There are three main devices by which funds could be transferred; by loans to affiliates, through dividends to the holding company, and by the purchase of assets. Each of these has its limitations.

Loans to Affiliates These are limited by the Federal Reserve Act as amended and by the Banking Act of 1933 as amended. Loans of insured banks to individual affiliates may not exceed 10 percent of the bank's capital and surplus. Loans to all affiliates combined are limited to 20 percent. Furthermore, these loans must usually be secured by collateral which has a market value in excess of the amount of the loan.

Dividends Dividends cannot be paid to the parent company which would endanger the bank. As a state bank, First Hawaiian cannot pay dividends greater than its undivided profits.

Purchase of Assets A bank could try to bail out a troubled affiliate by purchasing assets. There are, however, limitations on the kinds of assets banks can buy. For insured banks, there are laws restricting loans to affiliates which are so broadly defined that the Federal Reserve Board has taken the position that *it* covers the purchase of assets in this situation.

Commenting on the separation of the bank from the other bank holding company activities, one observer notes "It is in the interests of depositors, examiners, and shareholders alike for the capital accounts of individual banks to be protected as much as possible from the risk associated with innovation—and yet innovation is absolutely essential if banks are to keep up with the changing times. The bank holding company structure serves both purposes."

STUDIES OF HOLDING COMPANY PROFITABILITY AND RISK

Although every proposal to change from a bank to a bank holding company is probably a unique situation, it is interesting to look at what has happened in other such situations. A number of studies have examined the change in profitability for banks affiliated to bank holding companies. None of the evidence reported so far, however, concerns bank holding companies that acquired nonbank subsidiaries. The performance studies conclude that profitability does not improve significantly. The common methodology of the studies was to identify a set of acquired banks and compare them with a control group of "similar" nonacquired banks. Rose and Fraser, who have published a review of these studies, conclude that "Bank holding companies seem to have much less effect on the performance of their affiliated institutions than both the supporters and the critics of the holding company movement would have us believe."[1]

We've all heard of the statement that a growth

---

[1] Peter S. Rose and Donald R. Fraser, "The Impact of Holding Company Acquisitions on Bank Performance," *The Bankers Magazine* (Spring 1973): 91.

EXHIBIT 2:

B.H.C. Activity	Av. Profits to Capital	Variability	Risk Index	Correlation to Bank Profits
Commercial banks	5.49%	1.21	0.220	—
Insurance agents and brokers	15.40%	2.71	0.176	−.44
Business credit agencies	8.95%	1.98	0.221	0.49
Personal credit agencies	9.44%	1.23	0.131	0.36
Lessors of agricultural and public utility property	8.51%	1.53	0.180	0

company and a growth stock are not necessarily the same thing. Let's look at what happened to stockholder returns. There are two studies available with conflicting results:

1. Upson and Jessup have concluded that for the 1957–1971 period bank, holding companies provided significantly higher returns to investors than did banks.[2] Their study compared a group of banks with a separate group of bank holding companies over the same time period.

2. Brewer and Dukes used a different approach and concluded that stockholders who exchanged their bank stock for bank holding company stock between 1965 and 1973 have generally faced a decline in returns, an increase in market risk, or both.[3] Return was measured for seventy-eight weeks before and after a bank's becoming a holding company and was adjusted for changes in Standard and Poor's Bank Index. In thirty-four of forty-one cases the bank stock provided the higher return. The mean return during the bank stock period was 2.39 percent compared to −1.10 percent for the bank holding companies. The respective standard deviations were 2.14 and 4.58. Ten of forty-one sample companies had a significant change in their beta value after becoming a bank holding company. Eight of the ten were increases in market risk.

Sketchy information is available about the level of risk in some of the areas opened up to bank holding company affiliates. The data are difficult to obtain but Heggestad has compiled several measures of risk using 1953–1967 figures published by the Internal Revenue Service.[4] These are presented below in exhibit 2.

Risk has traditionally been measured by the variability of profit rates with greater variability being associated with greater risk. The data for profitability (exhibit 2) are the ratio of net income after taxes to equity capital. This is the relevant measure for bank holding companies since it indicates the return on their investment in affiliates. Variability is measured by the standard deviation of the average industry profit rate over the period 1953–1967. The risk index is the industry's variability divided by its profitability. Two industries with similar profit variability but different profit levels do not have the same risk characteristics. The last risk measure in exhibit 2 is the correlation of industry profits with bank profits.

OTHER ASPECTS

Some other stockholders have been grumbling a little about the one-for-one exchange they are being offered. When the Bank of Hawaii stockholders voted to change to a bank holding company they received four shares of new stock in the bank holding company for each share of bank stock. "Sure they are a bigger bank, but

[2]Roger B. Upson and Paul F. Jessup, "Returns from Bank Holding Companies," *The Banker's Magazine* (Spring 1972): 59–62.

[3]Virgil L. Brewer and William P. Dukes, "Empirical Evidence on the Risk-Return Relationship Between Banks and Related Bank Holding Companies," *Review of Business and Economic Research* (Spring 1976): 56–65.

[4]Arnold A. Heggestad, "The Economist's Corner," *The Banker's Magazine*, (Winter, 1976), pp. 109–12.

EXHIBIT 3:

Market Price of Bank Stock

| | *Average of High and Low Bid* | | |
Date	*First Hawaiian*	*Bank of Hawaii*[1]	*S&P Bank Stock (outside NYC) Index*
1971	$26.375	$15.875	88.85
1972			
First Quarter	32.125	16.41	95.2
Second Quarter	33.625	19.00	102.4
Third Quarter	34.00	18.50	111.3
Fourth Quarter	33.625	19.00	117.3
1973			
First Quarter	33.875	18.062	110.3
Second Quarter	28.625	16.375	99.0
Third Quarter	27.50	15.688	105.0
Fourth Quarter[6]	26.625	15.50	107.6
1974			
to March 22	22.25	14.188	106.0
May 27, 1971[2]	28.50	16.125	86.2
January 31, 1972[3]	31.25	16.37	90.1
October 19, 1973[4]	28.50	17.50	115.1
March 22, 1974[5]	23.50	13.50	110.0

[1]Hawaii Bancorporation after April 3, 1972. Adjusted for 4-to-1 split.

[2]Bank of Hawaii announced it would form a bank holding company.

[3]Bank of Hawaii on January 31, 1972, informed stockholders about the bank holding company proposal details.

[4]First Hawaiian Bank's Board of Directors voted on October 20 to form a bank holding company.

[5]Latest price available.

[6]Book value as of December 31, 1973, was $17.18 for First Hawaiian and $8.92 for Hawaii Bancorporation.

they certainly aren't four times as big," was the way one First Hawaiian stockholder put it. Another pointed to the two-for-one split ups of First Hawaiian stock in August 1972, and early in 1969 as an explanation for the one-for-one exchange. A shareholder already had four bank shares for every one held in early 1969. It wouldn't be fair to reward relatively new stockholders the same as the long-term investors who had been with the bank for a number of years. A third stockholder stated that the one-for-one ex-change was actually preferable since it would result in less dilution of earnings.

TIME FOR A DECISION

It certainly seemed that the bank holding company was the current trend in banking, and First Hawaiian should follow along. In 1956 when the First Bank Holding Company Act was passed there were fifty-three bank holding

EXHIBIT 4:

Earnings and Dividends per Share

	First Hawaiian Bank		Bank of Hawaii	
	EPS	Divi-dends	EPS	Divi-dends
1971	$2.32	$1.08	$1.18	$.625
1972	2.49	1.22	1.27	.65
1973	2.74	1.27	1.49	.65

companies owning 428 banks and controlling 7.5 percent of total bank deposits. At the end of 1971, the year the amendments to the 1956 Act were passed, 1567 holding companies owned 2420 banks and 58 percent of all bank deposits. Still more banks have made the switch in the last two years.

Nevertheless, a nagging doubt still remains about switching to the holding company strategy. Just because others were doing it doesn't mean it will be good for First Hawaiian's stockholders. Lemmings probably think they are headed in the right direction too. What about the fact that Bank of Hawaii was the only other bank in the state to form a holding company? Another legitimate question is why those specified activities can't be conducted by the bank directly or through a subsidiary of the bank?

Shareholders need to make up their minds before the stockholders' meeting. Those who do not want to exchange bank shares for holding company shares will need to cast a negative vote. Unless an affirmative vote of two thirds of the shares is obtained, the transaction is defeated. If it is passed, anyone who voted no has the right to claim the cash surrender value of his or her shares.

QUESTIONS

1. Why has the bank proposed the formation of the bank holding company?

2. Are the objectives of bank management compatible with the objectives of the stockholders?

3. What are the favorable and unfavorable aspects of the proposal from the stockholder's view?

4. Would you recommend that the stockholders vote *for* or *against* the proposal?

Case 7

Southeast Imported Auto Loans (A)

By 1984, opportunities that provided both rapid growth and good profits were becoming increasingly hard to find. Managers at Universal Bank were therefore excited about auto-lending opportunities presented by the imported-auto market as it existed in the Southeastern United States. This market was consistent with Universal's strategy of national expansion in consumer lending. In addition, Universal's experience in the automotive credit market would minimize the cost of entry into this market.

The overall automobile market had shown little growth in recent years. However, sales of foreign cars continued to grow. Furthermore, automotive lending competition in the foreign car market was not so severe as in the domestic car market because the automobile manufacturers' captive finance companies had emphasized domestic auto financing. Thus they had not moved aggressively in the market for foreign car finance receivables. Universal's managers were convinced that they could sign up a large number of imported car dealers in the Southeast. They based their projections on the success they had enjoyed in the Western and Midwestern mar-

kets. It was estimated that average customer net finance receivables[1] would grow from $38 million in the first year to $500 million in the seventh year. Beyond this, little or no growth was anticipated.

The market could be served from a single branch in Atlanta. The foreign car dealers would handle the customer contact; Universal would approve the credit and buy the sales finance receivables from the dealers. It was also believed that Universal's other experience in automobile lending could be used to project branch costs. The typical size of a branch for automobile lending was $188 million in customer assets, and the operating cost for a typical branch was $119,000. It was estimated that branch operating cost would not be less than $119,000 a year even if customer assets were less than $188 million. However, experience with larger branches indicated that the so-called fixed costs varied with branch size; a $750 million branch had operating costs of $250,000. Exhibit 1 is a graphical representation of the apparent relationship between branch operating costs and customer assets.

The Atlanta branch would require a capital asset investment of $200,000 and personnel

---

This case was prepared by Neil E. Seitz, Department of Finance, Saint Louis University.

[1]Net of unearned finance charges.

EXHIBIT 1:

Branch Operating Costs and Customer Assets

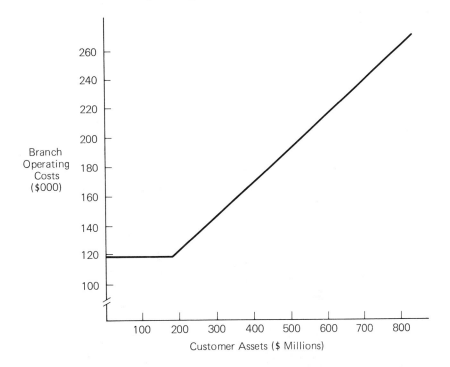

expenditures for start up would be $100,000. From recent studies, the company had determined that the variable costs for attracting and processing a new loan were $83.31. These costs were in addition to the branch operating costs and the fees (dealer reserves) paid to dealers for originating loans. Moreover, bad debt expense was expected to average 0.40 percent of net finance receivables. It would cost $4.64 to process a payment.

A typical automobile sales finance transaction would require disbursement of $8,000 in loan proceeds and would carry a four-year maturity, with monthly payments. Very few loans would be repaid early as foreign cars were not traded in quickly. These loans were expected to carry a 14.53 percent interest rate, and dealers would be paid a $56 fee (dealer reserve) at the time the sales finance contract was acquired. At steady state, the average customer net receivable

would be $4,466.18. Thus, there would be an average of 111,952 ($500 million/$4,466.18) loans outstanding and 27,988 (111,952/4) loans made each year.

The cost of borrowed funds was estimated to be 11 percent, and equity would be 4 percent of total assets. The tax rate would be 46 percent.

QUESTIONS

1. Estimate the operating cost of a branch once the $500 million customer net receivable level is achieved.

2. The required steady state accounting return on equity is 20 percent. Will the imported auto business achieve this 20 percent return?

EXHIBIT 2

Proforma Financial Statements

Year	0	1	2	3	4	5	6
Av. net loan balance		38038985	135657786	275767815	400481797	469507020	496072521
Ending equity	1529559	5434311	11038713	16027272	18788281	19850901	20008000
Change in equity	1529559	3904752	5604401	4988559	2761009	1062620	157099
No. loans made		9324	18648	27988	27988	27988	27988
Cost per loan		176	156	139.31	139.31	139.31	139.31
Pmts rec'd		60606	233100	517586	853442	1138016	1310702
Interest income		5527065	19711076	40069064	58190005	68219370	72079337
Interest expense		4038037	14346582	29142201	42311998	49601061	52406378
Bad debt		152156	542631	1103071	1601927	1878028	1984290
Operating costs							
Making loans	136752	1746696	2991581	3899008	3899008	3899008	3899008
Collect pmts		281212	1081584	2401599	3959971	5280394	6081657
Branch oper.	100000	119000	119000	139450	168508	184590	190780
Total operations	236752	2146908	4192165	6440057	8027487	9363993	10171446
Earnings before tax	−236752	−810036	629698	3383734	6248593	7376288	7517223
Tax	−108906	−372617	289661	1556517	2874353	3393093	3457923
NI	−127846	−437419	340037	1827216	3374240	3983196	4059301

3. Compute the accounting return on equity with equity equal to 5 percent of total assets.

SOUTHEAST IMPORTED AUTO (B)

Questions were raised about the realized return (internal rate of return) on equity in light of the fact that the steady state would not be reached until the seventh year. The cost of attracting and processing new customer finance receivables (loans) was almost certain to be higher during the start up phase. It was estimated that the cost of attracting and processing a new loan would be $120 in the first year of operations and $100 in the second year. The cost of processing a payment would be $4.64 from the beginning.

To address the concerns about realized return, projections for each of the first six years were prepared (exhibit 2). To avoid tedious projections and complex calculations that do little to improve accuracy, the projections are based on the assumption that equity equal to 4 percent of average total assets for the year must be committed at the beginning of the year.[2] In general, it is assumed that all income and expenses for the

------

[2]An exact realized return computation would require a month-by-month cash flow analysis. The use of annualized data in this example results in an error of approximately .1 percent.

year occur at the end of the year. The one exception to this generalization is that one twelfth of the costs of acquiring loans, including processing costs and fees paid to dealers, occur at the beginning of the year (end of the previous year). This adjustment is used because the costs of making loans begin one month before payments begin.

QUESTIONS

1. Find the cash flow to the owners (net income minus increases in equity) each year for years zero through seven.

2. Cash flow each year after year seven will be the same as for year seven. If projects are required to produce a 20 percent realized return on equity, would the Southeast imported auto business be attractive?

3. If the company were to start in the Southeast at the beginning of this year and in one new region (with the same patterns of income and expense growth) each year thereafter, what would be the accounting return on equity for imported automobiles six years from this year, assuming 4 percent equity?

4. What adjustments would you make in your program to move toward a 20 percent realized return on equity?

Case 8

The Missouri Financial Services Association

In January 1978, a major concern of the Missouri Financial Services Association was the restrictive interest rate structure applicable to direct cash loans imposed on lenders through the Missouri Usury Statute. Consequently, representatives of the consumer finance industry had gathered in Jefferson City to analyze the political climate and to discuss strategy in an effort to seek rate relief through the Missouri legislature. The discussion focused on a bill, recently introduced in the Missouri State Legislature and endorsed by the Missouri Financial Services Association, which would increase the small loan base from $500 to $1200.

THE MISSOURI FINANCIAL SERVICES ASSOCIATION

The Missouri Financial Services Association is an industry trade group consisting of member finance companies operating within Missouri.

This case was prepared by Fred C. Yeager and Neil Seitz, Department of Finance, Saint Louis University.

The authors are grateful to the Missouri Financial Services Association, and particularly to Tom Harvey, former Chairman of the Association's Executive Committee, for invaluable assistance in developing the necessary data for this case.

Member firms varied in size from small companies with only one office to large national companies such as Household Finance, CIT, Commercial Credit, Associates Corporation, and others with branch operations throughout the United States. In terms of structure, state consumer financial services associations are similar to state banking associations, savings and loan leagues, and credit union associations. Their purpose is to pursue objectives common to the industry; objectives which frequently involve state legislation.

Day-to-Day operations of the Missouri Financial Services Association were guided by Harry Gallagher, the executive vice-president of the association; policy matters were determined by an executive committee drawn from the ranks of member finance companies. In 1978, 111 firms were members of the consumer financial services association in Missouri. Although most of the members were small companies with one or only a few offices, about 15 percent of them were large finance companies that operated two thirds of all consumer finance offices in the state and about one half of all consumer finance offices in the nation. The main operating expenses of the state association included salaries for the executive director and the small staff, rent, newsletter printing, and other office-related expenditures. These operating expenses were paid through membership fees and through assessments against member finance companies.

RATE REGULATION OF CONSUMER CREDIT

Early interest-rate theory, dating back to Aristotle, held that interest was primarily a means of exploiting those who were forced by temporary hardship to resort to borrowing. It was this view of interest that led to legal and religious restrictions on interest charges that existed through much of the history of our western culture.

In the United States, the first general usury statute (essentially being inherited from England) was enacted by Massachusetts in 1641, which fixed maximum interest rates at 8 percent. Usury statutes quickly spread throughout the American Colonies. Because the mandated rate ceilings were set at artificially low levels, a legal installment loan market was effectively outlawed.

By 1900, almost every large city in the United States had loan companies. All the companies were operating illegally, many were charging annual rates of 200 percent or more, and some were employing collection tactics which could at best be described as unbusiness like.[1]

The Russell Sage foundation, established in 1907, sponsored studies of consumer lending activities. Disclosures of illegal lending practices and related activities led to development of the first Uniform Small Loan Law which initially set maximum interest rates for small loans (up to $300) at 42 percent per year. In subsequent years, this law or a modification thereof, had been adopted by all states except Arkansas, thus creating an exception to the general usury ceiling.[2]

RATE REGULATION IN MISSOURI

Missouri usury law in 1978 specified a maximum annual interest rate of 6 percent when no other rate had been agreed upon by the parties. For written contracts, the maximum agreed rate was 10 percent. Over the years, however, the state legislature had provided for a number of "exceptions" to the general usury ceiling. Higher rates were allowed for various types of credit including credit card balances, time sales financing, and certain other consumer related receivables. Most business loans were exempt from rate regulation as were loans above $5000 secured by specified securities. Unlike many states, where usury exceptions pertain to certain types of lenders, e.g., finance companies but not banks, the Missouri state constitution provided that the usury statute and exceptions pertain to the type of loan. The maximum contract rate for residential real estate loans, for example, was 10 percent regardless of the lender class (bank, savings and loan, finance company, etc.).

Of particular interest to the Missouri Financial Services Association was the exception in the statute that dealt with direct cash loans of up to $500 to consumers. That particular exception, unchanged since 1959, permitted negotiated rates of up to 15 percent add-on, or at the equivalent simple interest rate of 2.218 percent per month (26.616 percent per annum assuming a one year maturity) for loans of up to $500.[3] Under the statute, direct cash loans of any amount could be made to consumers. However, interest charges on loan balances in excess of $500 were subject to maximum rates of 0.833 per month (10 percent per annum).[4]

THE PROBLEM

Statistical data concerning the consumer finance industry in Missouri is provided in tables

---

[1] One collection procedure was known as the "bawlerout" technique, whereby female loan company employees would visit the delinquent borrower at his place of employment and bawl him out in front of his colleagues.

[2] See appendix for theories of rate regulation.

[3] See chapter 6 of this text for a discussion of add-on and simple interest rates.

[4] In 1976, the maximum contract rate was increased from 8 percent to 10 percent. While this change provided significant rate relief for residential real estate lenders, the impact on finance companies was inconsequential.

TABLE 1:
Average Net APR Earned by Licensed Lenders in Missouri
(000s omitted for all dollar figures)

Year (1)	Average Loans Outstanding[1] (2)	Interest Collected (3)	Recoveries of Charged Off Loans (4)	Loans Charged Off (5)	Reserve for Bad Debts (6)	Net Interest (3) + (4) − (5) − (6) (7)	Net APR (2) ÷ (7) (8)
1976	360,828	59,401.72	879.73	6,080.06	5,723.92	48,477.47	13.44
1975	358,409	59,631.65	812.88	5,397.82	5,634.10	49,394.61	13.78
1974	356,913	57,984.04	755.14	3,890.40	5,737.32	49,111.46	13.76
1973	360,079	53,860.14	924.51	5,203.68	4,024.40	45,556.57	12.65
1972	342,476	53,013.54	842.82	4,482.71	4,501.47	44,872.18	13.10
1971	323,985	50,162.05	801.83	4,161.77	4,191.40	42,610.71	13.15
1970	331,998	52,246.46	766.39	4,996.30	3,814.06	44,202.49	13.31
1969	337,888	52,847.28	766.80	3,940.14	3,772.89	45,901.05	13.58
1968	325,215	51,098.41	833.31	3,095.44	4,264.96	44,571.32	13.71
1967	312,085	50,929.88	734.53	3,358.73	3,868.78	44,436.90	14.24
1966	296,259	47,691.24	1,100.33	3,165.23	4,679.99	40,946.35	13.82
1965	271,278	45,307.41	753.48	2,641.56	5,007.10	38,412.23	14.16
1964	252,274	40,459.92	550.97	3,162.94	4,218.56	33,629.39	13.33
1963	267,069	37,812.22	391.11	3,308.87	3,613.71	31,280.75	11.71
1962	251,507	35,728.95	406.91	1,942.60	3,281.95	30,911.31	12.29
1961	204,422	33,041.25	401.35	1,657.97	2,970.22	28,814.81	14.10

Source: Division of Finance, State of Missouri.

[1](Beginning net loans + ending net loans) ÷ 2.

and charts 1 through 6. There was a relatively stable level of APR from 1961 through 1976 (tables 1 and 2 and chart 1). However, debt cost for the industry almost doubled over the same time span. Also, consumer income and inflation more than doubled over the time periods contained in the tables and chart. Between 1965 and 1976, for example, the national average loan made by a consumer finance company increased from $558 to $1,384.

As a result of financial constraints faced by the industry, and beginning in the early 1970s, many firms began to curtail business operations in Missouri. Also, the legislature had recently enacted legislation reducing maximum pre-

TABLE 2:

Cost of Debt—Finance Co.

Year	S & P High Grade Corp. Bond Index[1]	Fin. Co. Comm. Paper Rate[2]	Est. Cost of Fin. Co. Debt[4]
1976	8.36%	5.22%	7.81%[3]
1975	8.63	6.16	8.24[3]
1974	8.25	8.62	8.31
1973	7.56	7.40	7.53
1972	7.26	4.52	6.79
1971	7.38	4.91	6.96
1970	7.84	7.23	7.74
1969	6.93	7.16	6.97
1968	6.05	5.69	5.99
1967	5.53	4.89	5.42
1966	5.13	5.36	5.17
1965	4.47	4.22	4.43
1964	4.37	3.77	4.27
1963	4.24	3.40	4.10
1962	4.29	3.07	4.08
1961	4.36	2.68	4.07

[1]S & P trade and security statistics.

[2]Federal Reserve Bulletins.

[3]*NCFA Research Report on Finance Companies in 1976*, National Consumer Finance Association: Washington, D.C., 1977.

[4]P(8.36) + (1 − P)5.22 = 7.81; P = 0.82.
P(8.63) + (1 − P)6.16 = 8.24; P = 0.84.
Average P = (0.84 + 0.82) ÷ 2 = .83.
Cost of fin. co. debt = 0.83 (High grade corp. bond rate) + 0.17 (fin. co. commercial paper rate).

miums for credit life insurance, commissions from which had kept a number of finance company offices afloat (table 3 and chart 2). By 1978, the effect of inadequate profitability had begun to threaten the continued existence of the consumer finance industry in Missouri. While the number of loan offices in the United States remained relatively constant, the number in Missouri declined by 40 percent between the late 1960s and 1978. From 1973 through early 1978, 300 loan offices closed. Per capital loans by consumer finance companies had declined (chart 3) and a consumer credit gap had developed (table 4 and chart 4). A recent study of the industry concluded that "had Missouri per capita cash loan (from all lenders) and bank credit card receivables grown at the national rate, such receivables would have been greater in 1976 by approximately $151 million."

THE PROPOSED SOLUTION

Maximum permissible cash loan rate data for Missouri, contiguous states, and the nation are contained in table 5 and chart 5. The data (table 5 and chart 5) reveal that maximum allowable APRs were lower for Missouri finance companies relative to the national average and relative to the average for contiguous states at all loan sizes. Legislation which was recently introduced in the state legislature would increase the small loan base to which the rate of 2.218 percent per month (26.616 percent per annum) could be applied from $500 to $1200. If approved by the legislature (and signed by the governor), interest rate ceilings would be as shown by table 6 and chart 6.

As the executive committee of the Missouri Consumer Financial Services Association pondered these matters, they were keenly aware that attempts to gain rate relief had failed in previous years. They knew that critics of their industry would fight every move to seek higher interest rates for small loans. The rate relief bill had been assigned to committees in the State House of Representatives and in the state senate. The executive committee knew that a strategy to insure passage of the legislation must be developed.

QUESTIONS

1. Should ceiling interest rates be set by law for the various categories of credit to consumers?

2. From the point of view of the Missouri Financial Services Association, develop a strategy designed to maximize prospects for passage of the legislation proposed in the case.

3. If you were a member of the Missouri State Legislature, would you vote for the proposed legislation?

CHART 1:

Average Annual Percentage Rate Earned and Cost of Debt for Missouri Finance Companies

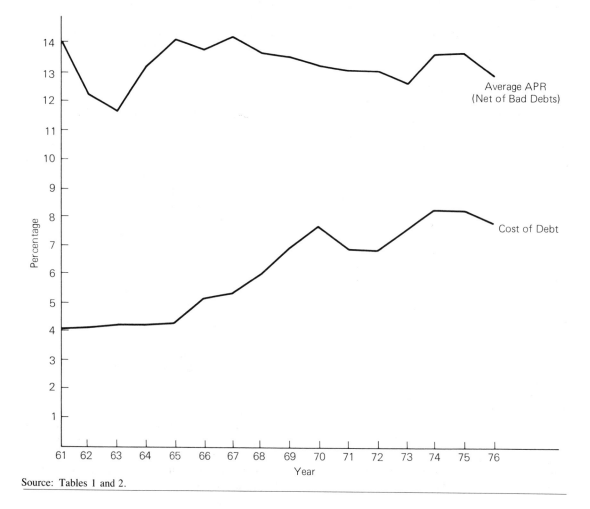

TABLE 3:

Return on Asset Analysis of Licensed Lenders in Missouri
Total Missouri Business

Year (1)	Total Assets (000) (2)	Net Operating Income Excl. Ins. Comm.[1] (000) (3)	ROA Excl. Insurance (3) ÷ (2) (4)	Insurance Commissions (000) (5)	Net Operating Income Incl. Ins. Comm. (000) (6)	ROA Incl. Insurance (6) ÷ (2) (7)
1976	414,290	20,353	4.91%	14,985	35,338	8.53%
1975	429,235	17,147	3.99	15,139	32,286	7.52
1974	407,886	19,273	4.73	14,783	34,056	8.35
1973	455,963	19,264	4.22	15,014	34,278	7.52
1972	446,058	18,821	4.22	15,047	33,868	7.59
1971	394,793	16,761	4.25	13,543	30,304	7.68
1970	386,797	21,220	5.49	13,504	34,724	8.98
1969	399,247	18,522	4.64	14,212	32,734	8.20
1968	396,010	17,604	4.44	13,995	31,599	7.98
1967	372,600	16,376	4.93	13,155	29,531	7.93
1966	368,238	15,300	4.15	12,899	28,199	7.66
1965	329,337	15,708	4.76	11,834	27,542	8.36
1964	[2]					
1963	288,600	11,801	4.09	10,248	22,049	7.64
1962	272,954	13,201	4.84	9,545	22,746	8.33
1961	256,597	13,124	5.11	8,948	22,072	8.60
1960	232,685	5,838	2.51	9,118	13,955	6.00

[1]From annual report to Missouri Finance Division.

[2]The 1964 data are not compatible.

CHART 2:

Return on Assets for Missouri Finance Companies

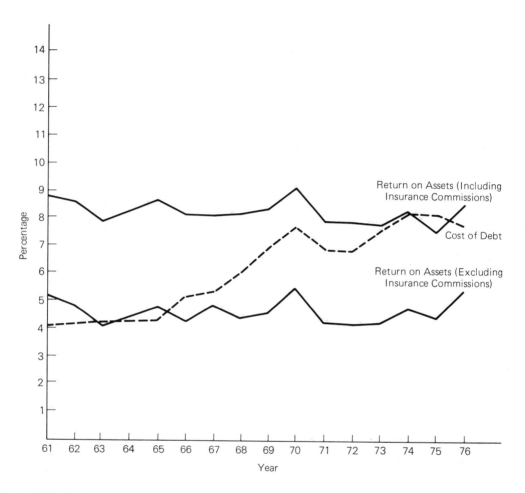

Source: Tables 2 and 3.

CHART 3:

Per Capita Loans by Consumer Finance Companies (1967 $)

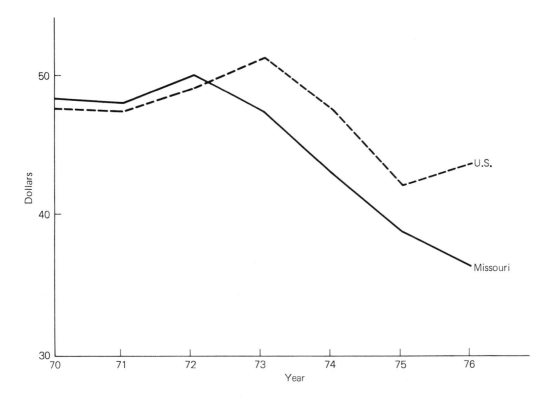

Source: Missouri data based on Consolidated Annual Reports, Division of Finance, State of Missouri. U.S. data furnished by Research and Law Departments, Household Finance Company.

TABLE 4:

Per Capita Cash Loan Balances and Credit Card Balances in Missouri and the United States

	Missouri			*United States*		
Year	*Cash Loans*	*Bank Credit Cards*	*Total*	*Cash Loans*	*Bank Credit Cards*	*Total*
1965	127.93	NA	NA	144.06	NA	144.06
1970	260.96	15.59	276.55	283.84	17.22	301.06
1971	284.66	18.65	303.31	319.20	20.10	339.30
1972	319.40	24.17	343.57	350.21	22.32	372.53
1973	334.43	31.27	365.70	381.35	29.73	411.08
1974	358.96	39.51	398.47	420.48	36.13	456.61
1975	374.66	43.25	417.91	436.98	38.90	475.88
1976	402.86	50.59	453.45	490.56	46.39	536.95

Source: Research and Law Departments, Household Finance Company.

Note: Cash loan data includes cash loans made by all lenders.

CHART 4:

Per Capita and Bank Credit Card Credit for Missouri and the United States

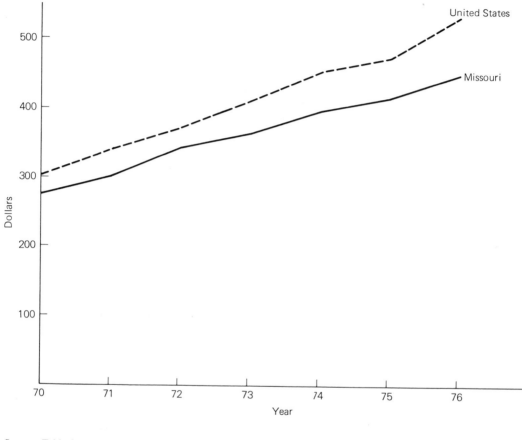

Source: Table 3.

CHART 5:

Existing Interest Rate Ceilings for Missouri and Average Ceilings for Other States
(excluding Arkansas and Tennessee which do not have consumer loan laws in effect)

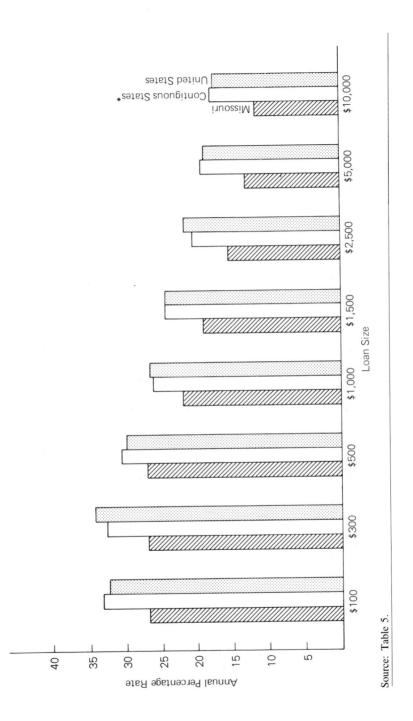

Source: Table 5.

CHART 6:

Proposed Interest Rate Ceilings for Missouri and Average Ceilings for Other States
(excluding Arkansas and Tennessee which do not have consumer loan laws in effect)

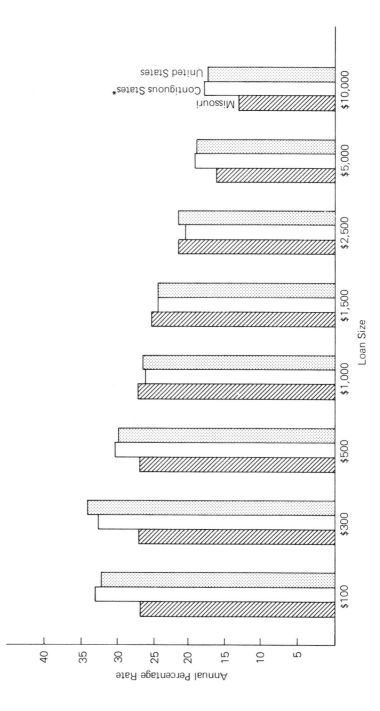

	TABLE 5:					TABLE 6:		
	Distribution of Maximum Permissible Interest Rates (APRs) for Loans Subject to State Consumer Loan Laws (Existing Median Rates—January 1978)					**Distribution of Maximum Permissible Interest Rates (APRs) for Loans Subject to State Consumer Loan Laws (Proposed—January 1978)**		

Loan Size	Missouri	Contiguous States[1]	All States		Loan Size	Proposed Missouri	Contiguous States*	All States
$ 100	26.62	33.00	35.08		$ 100	26.62	33.00	35.08
300	26.62	32.71	34.22		300	26.62	32.71	34.22
500	26.62	30.45	30.00		500	26.62	30.45	30.00
1,000	21.89	26.03	26.23		1,000	26.62	26.03	26.23
1,500	18.70	24.30	24.33		1,500	25.64	24.30	24.33
2,500	15.58	20.02	21.67		2,500	21.54	20.02	21.67
5,000	12.93	18.83	18.58		5,000	16.57	18.83	18.58
10,000	11.50	18.79	18.00		10,000	13.47	18.79	18.00

Source: Internal files of a National Consumer Finance Company.

[1]States contiguous to Missouri include Arkansas, Oklahoma, Illinois, Iowa, Kansas, Nebraska, Kentucky and Tennessee. Above data excludes Arkansas and Tennessee. Arkansas has no consumer loan law and consumer finance companies do not maintain loan offices within the state. Tennessee's Industrial Loan and Thrift Act was declared unconstitutional 22 August 1977 and a constitutional referendum was then pending. Inclusion of Tennessee's rates as they existed prior to 22 August would raise the median slightly for loan categories of $1,500 and more. Median rates for loan categories of $300 through $1,000 would be reduced slightly. It is further noted that State small loan ceilings of $3,000 and $7,500 exist in Nebraska and Kentucky, respectively. Thus, Nebraska is excluded in the above computations for loan sizes of $5,000 and $10,000 while Kentucky is excluded at the $10,000 loan size level.

*See note—table 5.

The Missouri Financial Services Association

Appendix: Theories on Rate Regulation of Consumer Credit

In the United States each state has set some type of restriction on interest rates which may be charged on consumer loans. This approach contrasts sharply with that taken in other developed countries. Canada permits interest rates on loans in excess of $1,500 to be set by free market forces. Consumer loan rates in England, Germany, France, Austria, and Switzerland are determined—for all practical purposes—by free market forces. Belgium is one of the few European countries to limit finance charges for personal loans and installment credit.

There are two basic and conflicting views concerning the method by which reasonable rates should be set for consumer credit. One view holds that prices for credit should be set by market forces, unhindered by government interference. The other view supports "decreed rates" which set price ceilings on consumer credit. Professor Milton Friedman (formerly) of the University of Chicago states:

I know of no economist of any standing . . . who favored a legal limit on the rate of interest that borrowers could pay or lenders receive - though there must have been some . . . (p. 91).

On the other hand, Economist Leon Keyserling says:

I find it deplorable that we feel bound to set an 18 percent interest rate ceiling for these people, which is three times the rate at which . . . a powerful corporation can borrow money . . . (p. 91).

In its 1972 report to the President and Congress, the National Commission on Consumer Finance identified four theories on rate regulation of consumer credit. These included:

1. To redress unequal bargaining power

2. To avoid overburdening consumers with excessive debt

3. To administer credit grantors as public utilities

4. To assure that consumers pay fair rates for credit.

The commission pointed out that "the rate of charge is only one of a number of features

<hr>

Information developed in this appendix relies heavily on *Consumer Credit in the United States: Report of the National Commission on Consumer Finance*, U.S. Government Printing Office, December, 1972, pp. 91–108.

embodied in an offer of credit, just as price is only one of the considerations in the purchase of an automobile.'' The commission went on to identify some of the characteristics bound up with an offer of credit. These included:

1. Rate of charge

2. Maturity

3. Down payment (if any)

4. Security required (if any)

5. Availability of irregular payment plans

6. Willingness of credit grantors to assume risk of default

7. Convenience of location

8. Status of credit grantor in view of consumer

9. Collection methods

10. Delinquency and deferral charges.

With regard to theories on rate regulation, the commission addressed each in turn.

To Redress Unequal Bargaining Power

Advocates of low rate ceilings on consumer credit often argue that the unequal bargaining power of debtors versus creditors will allow debtors to charge what the traffic will bear—the ceiling rate. Through staff studies, the commission found that assertions that rates always rise to the ceiling are incorrect except when the price ceiling is set at or below the market rate for the particular form of credit placed under price control. The commission found persuasive evidence that rates do *not* inevitably rise to the ceiling. This finding was supported by a commission study of rates prevailing for various forms of consumer credit during the second quarter of 1971. Among other conclusions, the commission noted that finance companies—competing in the area of higher credit risk—succeed or fail on the basis of their skill in making personal loans to applicants who will repay and separating them from others who will probably default. The commission went on to say that ''conventional wisdom would have us believe that 100 percent

of installment loans of finance companies will be at the ceiling.'' However, when that hypothesis was tested by evaluation of personal loans made by finance companies during the last two weeks of the second quarter of 1971, the commission found that while a considerable portion (of the finance company personal loans) were made at or near the ceiling rates, not all had ''APRs equal to or greater than 90 percent of the rate ceiling.'' The commission concluded:

1. If the legal rate ceiling is set above the market rate, the market rate prevails and average rates of charge do not rise to the ceiling.

2. Even in the cash loan market served by finance companies where the emphasis is on nonprice competition, rates do not always rise to the ceiling.

3. If price ceilings are set at or below the market rate, rates will generally be at the ceiling. The precise impact of this upon consumers has yet to be examined.

The commission reported that ''Commission studies had provided some support for the notion that consumers are not wholly knowledgeable about finance charges and APRs, nor do they appear to shop as intensively for credit as they do for the goods financed.'' The commission further noted however, that ''it is well-established that perfect knowledge and intensive shopping behavior are not required to make a market workably competitive—for the market to offer opportunities for credit at reasonable rates'' (p. 99).

To Avoid Overburdening Consumers With Excessive Debt

The second theory of rate regulation identified by the commission postulates that consumers cannot estimate how much debt they can carry when acquiring a good or service. On the basis of this theory, some argue that rate ceilings are needed so as to prevent consumers from becoming over-burdened with debts and subject to abusive collection tactics. The commission points out that a discussion turning on excessive use of consumer credit should establish what is meant by "excessive." For some, it means a consumer-used credit, possibly at a fairly high APR, to acquire something—a color TV set or a big car—that the critics consider unwise because of the consumer's economic or social status. To prevent this "prodigal" from such an unwise decision, a low rate ceiling might force down the APR to the point that he is denied credit. The Commission found it to be "repugnant" to force a denial of credit on many credit worthy borrowers by the imposition of another's value system.

On the other hand, another meaning of "excessive," according to the commission, is simply an accumulation of debt that a consumer is unable to repay in accordance with the terms of his credit agreements. The commission concluded that the placing of rate ceilings on consumer credit does not accomplish the objective of preventing consumers from becoming overextended. The commission recommended that this problem may better be treated by placing emphasis on the need to provide creditors with every incentive to avoid overburdening consumers by limiting creditor remedies and outlawing harsh collection practices.

To Administer Credit Grantors as Public Utilities

A third theory of rate regulation in the area of consumer credit suggests that an alternate purpose of setting rate ceilings on consumer credit transactions would be to assure that consumers are charged rates sufficient to allow creditors a fair return on assets used to provide an "adequate" service to consumers. According to the commission, this might be termed the "public utility approach" to rate regulation. This approach is rejected by the commission on the ground that there are substantial differences in the market for consumer credit as compared to the market for services provided by a public utility. The commission noted:

Most regulations of public utilities limit the prices that may be charged by a firm to which some governmental body has granted a franchise. Usually, public utilities are monopolies . . . but credit grantors are not granted franchises. They generally compete with one another more vigorously than most public utilities. Each city typically has a number of banks, credit unions, finance companies, and retailers offering consumer credit. In addition, a consumer may be able to obtain a loan by mail, borrow on his life insurance policy, or use one or more credit cards. In contrast, a consumer wishing to light his home has no realistic alternative to using electricity and only one source of electric power.

The commission concluded that the "public utility approach to the regulation of consumer credit grantors is theoretically neither sound nor feasible" (p. 102).

To Assure That Consumers Pay Fair Rates for Credit

The final theory of rate regulation considered by the commission postulates that consumers pay "fair" rates for credit. But theoretical and practical problems with this approach are enormous. Consumers belong to a variety of risk classes. A "fair" rate for one consumer may be substantially different than a "fair" rate for another consumer belonging to a different risk class. If legal interest rates are set at maximum rates deemed to be "fair" by some legislative body and if the rate is set at a level too low to accommodate certain risk classes, the effect would likely be twofold. First, the total volume of credit available to consumers would fall. Second, sellers of goods on credit would likely raise the price of such goods, effectively transferring a portion of finance charges into the cost of goods and services.

Case 9

Modern Financial Services Company

It was mid September 1975, and the problem was a troublesome one for Bill Teal, regional vice-president of Modern Financial Services Company, a consumer finance company headquartered in Missouri. An interesting interpretation of Missouri usury law had come to his attention only two weeks ago—a business opportunity had become apparent. If this interpretation was legally correct, then large balance, direct cash loans secured by real estate (second-mortgage loans) could be made to Missouri consumers. The vitality and profitability of company lending operations in Missouri could be restored. On the other hand, what if this interpretation was incorrect? What were the risks of entering this potentially profitable home equity lending market in Missouri? As Teal weighed these potential benefits and consequences, he reviewed certain events of recent months and years, and he considered the current status of his industry.

THE CONSUMER FINANCE INDUSTRY

The traditional business of consumer finance companies—the making of direct cash loans to young, typically working class households—was on the decline. Bank credit cards with cash advance privileges and competitive gains by credit unions were eroding the market share of finance companies for consumer loans. While the market for consumer installment receivables had more than doubled in the last ten years, finance companies had not kept pace with that growth (exhibit 1). Within Missouri, one of the states over which Teal exercised management authority, the problem was particularly acute. The impact of restrictive state usury laws[1]

---

[1]Effective 9 January 1975, the maximum annual interest rate applicable to direct personal cash loans in Missouri was 26.6 percent for the first $500 outstanding principal and 10 percent for principal balances beyond $500. This Consumer Finance Law is an exception to the statutes governing general interest rates. Prior to 1975, the maximum allowable rate on balances beyond $500 was 8 percent. (See Case 8 for additional background data on the Missouri consumer finance industry).

This case was prepared by Fred C. Yeager, Department of Finance, St. Louis University.

EXHIBIT 1:

Consumer Installment Credit by Holder
(in $ millions)

Year End	Total	Comm. Banks	Finance Companies	Credit Unions	Misc. Lenders, Retailers & Others
1945	$ 2,462	$ 745	$ 910	$ 102	$ 705
1950	14,703	5,798	5,315	590	3,000
1955	28,906	10,601	11,838	1,678	4,798
1960	42,968	16,672	15,435	3,923	6,938
1965	71,324	28,962	24,282	7,324	10,756
1970	101,161	41,895	31,123	12,500	15,643
1974	155,384	75,846	36,208	22,116	21,214

Consumer Installment Credit by Holder
(Share of the Market)

Year End	Total	Comm. Banks	Finance Companies	Credit Unions	Misc. Lenders, Retailers & Others
1945	100.0%	30.3%	37.0%	4.1%	28.6%
1950	100.0	39.4	36.1	4.0	20.4
1955	100.0	36.7	41.0	5.8	16.6
1960	100.0	38.8	35.9	9.1	16.1
1965	100.0	40.6	34.0	10.3	15.1
1970	100.0	41.4	30.8	12.4	15.5
1974	100.0	48.8	23.3	14.2	13.7

Source: *Federal Reserve Bulletin,* various issues.

together with steady increases in the cost of funds for the industry had triggered an exodus of the industry from the state (exhibits 2 and 3). Large numbers of finance company offices had been closed within Missouri and some firms had simply sold their Missouri portfolios and departed the state.

A recent internal analysis of sixty-eight Modern branch offices had resulted in identification of the ten best, the middle forty-eight, and the ten worst performing offices in terms of profitability (exhibit 4). Four of the five offices in Missouri ranked with the lower portion of the middle forty-eight and one was included with the ten worst. This profitability study confirmed what Teal's nineteen years of experience with Modern had already told him. Profitable branches:

Operate within a favorable legal environment

Do well in business development

Are more leveraged in terms of accounts and dollar revenue per employee

Have cleaner portfolios

Have more effective managers

In reviewing the results of this profitability analysis, Teal noted the small average loan sizes for Missouri offices. He knew that operating expenses of 9.2 percent and accounts per branch employee of 181 would be difficult to further leverage. New customers tended to be in their early twenties and were attracted to and accepted by banks once their credit history was established. Given the legal limitations of a 10 percent APR on Missouri loan balances beyond $500,

EXHIBIT 2:

Return on Assets for Missouri Finance Companies

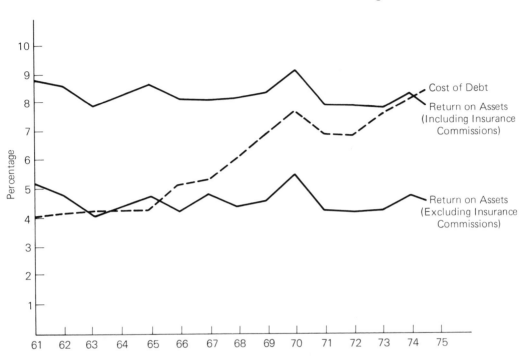

Source: Return on Assets calculated from data contained in consolidated annual reports of Missouri Finance Companies, which are submitted to the Division of Finance, State of Missouri. Cost of finance company debt estimates based on finance company commercial paper and high grade corporate bond rates weighted to reflect aggregate industry debt structure.

attempts to increase loan sizes would reduce portfolio yield. Offices were small, and the traditional consumer finance business was dying. Industry lobbyists had been unsuccessful in getting rate relief through the Missouri legislature. But higher rates for small loans, thought Teal, were not really the answer. The answer was in repositioning; the production and marketing of a wide variety of consumer financial services at reasonable rates; a new image, a new kind of financial institution. It had been two years now since Modern was acquired by World Bancshares, a large bank holding company; two years since the repositioning of Modern had commenced in earnest. Modern was on its way as a new kind of financial institution. But until now,

Missouri did not fit the mold; the legal environment had not been right. Core new products, particularly second-mortgage loans, could not profitably be marketed in Missouri.

THE MODERN FINANCIAL SERVICES CONCEPT

That the traditional business of consumer finance companies—small personal loans to working class families—was declining, was apparent to the new owners of Modern. Early research showed that people liked banks because they had a full product array, offered low rates,

EXHIBIT 3:

Per Capital Loans by Consumer Finance Companies (1967 $)

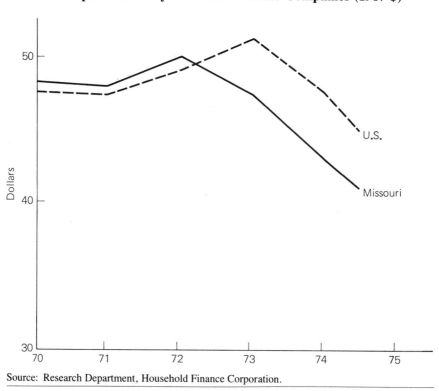

Source: Research Department, Household Finance Corporation.

and were reputable and stable; people disliked banks for their impersonal atmosphere, for their inconvenient hours, and for their alleged reluctance to give out loans. Finance companies, on the other hand, were viewed by these same consumers as friendly, convenient places willing to lend money, though somewhat disreputable and expensive lending places.[2] The repositioning strategy then, was one where the best features of banks and the best features of the finance companies could be combined. This repositioning strategy, or Modern Financial Services concept, was to rely heavily on the strongly consumer-oriented package goods concept of product man-

agement. Consumer financial services were to be thought of in terms of products designed to meet a particular consumer need. Home equity loans, closed-end loans, revolving credit lines, pattern pay plans, balloon notes, sales financing, mobile home loans, sheltered financing, bridge loans, insurance services, travelers checks, financial planning seminars, and other "products" would be immediate or eventual components of the repositioning. Rather than simply offering these new products at existing Modern offices, the repositioning was to be "tested" in four states.

By July 1974, Modern "Financial Centers" had been opened in four western cities. The new offices were highly visable, attractive, and expensively refurbished. Unlike the traditional

_____

[2]See exhibit 5 for rate data—banks vs. finance companies.

EXHIBIT 4:

Modern Financial Services Corporation Office Profitability Analysis (in $ Thousands, 1974)

	Best 10	*Middle 48*	*Worst 10*	*Missouri*
Average ANR[1]	$647	$542	$340	$493
Average loan size				
Direct	$1.581	$1.531	$1.219	$1.049
Sales finance	0.356	0.346	0.422	0.417
Operating expenses/ANR	8.0%	9.2%	13.2%	9.2%
Accounts per employee	240	200	154	181
Portfolio yield	19.5%	21.3%	21.4%	19.3%
Chargeoffs/ANR	1.0%	2.3%	6.1%	1.9%
Branch controllable contr.[2]	10.1%	5.6%	1.5%	4.0%

[1]Annual Net Receivables.

[2]Branch controllable contribution represented branch profit before home office overhead (2 percent) and before taxes (50 percent × branch net profit after home office overhead was deducted). The minimum acceptable branch controllable contribution was 4.4 percent if World's requirement of 1.2 percent RORA (Return on Risk Assets) was to be achieved.

Note: World's 1974 equity was 6 percent of total capital. A controllable contribution of 4.4 percent less 2.0 percent equals 2.4 percent before taxes and 1.2 percent after taxes. 1.2%/6% = 20%.

finance company office with closet-like cubicles designed to connote privacy but which, according to company research, contributed to customer anxiety—Modern Financial Centers contained round tables, designed to create a sense of

EXHIBIT 5:

Finance Rates for Selected Types of Consumer Installment Credit (Average Rates in Effect for December 1974)

Average Finance Rates	*Commercial Banks*	*Finance Companies*
Personal loans	13.6%	20.7%
Credit card plans	17.21%	NA
Automobiles		
New	11.62%	13.1%
Used	NA	17.9%
Mobile homes	11.7%	13.6%
Other consumer goods	13.3%	19.5%

Source: Federal Reserve Bulletin.

equality and to reduce customer anxiety. The core product offered by the Modern Financial Centers was the second-mortgage loan.[3] By June 1975, it was clear that the test was successful. These Financial Centers had attracted high quality customers in sufficiently large numbers, in accordance with profit models previously developed for the various financial products. The decision was made to convert all Modern offices to Financial Centers.

The Modern Financial concept, particularly second-mortgage lending, had caught on. But

[3]As housing prices climbed in the early 1970s, homeowners found that they had increased equity in their homes—equity which could be used as collateral for relatively large loans. Real estate (home equity) borrowers tended to demonstrate considerable income, employment, and residential stability. Average loan sizes were $10,000 or more and delinquency rates were low. Because of reduced administration expenses per dollar loaned, combined with low delinquency rates, the Modern Financial Centers were able to offer such loans at rates considerably less than those associated with small personal loans.

the company operated in states that did not permit the tested products (particularly home equity loans) to be offered at all. In Missouri, the products could not be offered at competitive rates given the original interpretation of Missouri law. It was against this background when, on 2 September 1975, an excited young marketing manager, Terry Means, burst into Teal's office and announced that Enterprise Loan Company was marketing home equity loans in Missouri. "I heard their commercial on the car radio on my way to work," he said.

THE DECISION

The same day, after receiving Means's message, Teal conferred with Tom Harris of Modern's legal department. Harris contacted the legal department of Enterprise to learn the basis of its second mortgage program. Tom then reviewed chapter 10 of the Revised Missouri Statutes; the chapter concerning interest rates. Section 10.02 concerning "Residential Real Estate," "Residential Real Estate Loan," and section 10.01 concerning real estate loans

EXHIBIT 6:

Chapter 10   Interest Rates

Section 10.00   Contract Rate

After 9 January 1975, parties may agree, in writing, for the payment of interest, not exceeding ten percent per annum, on money due or to become due upon any contract.

Section 10.01   Unlimited interest, when allowed

Notwithstanding the provisions of Section 10.00, it is lawful for the parties to agree in writing to any rate of interest in connection with any

1. Loan to a corporation;
2. Business loan of five thousand dollars or more, but excluding loans for any agricultural activity;
3. Real estate loan, other than residential real estate loans and loans secured by real estate used for an agricultural activity.

Section 10.02   Definitions

1. "Business Loan" shall mean a loan to an individual or a group of individuals, the proceeds of which are to be used in a business or for the purpose of acquiring an interest in a business. The term shall also include a loan to a trust, estate, cooperative, association, or limited or general partnership.
2. "Corporation" shall mean any corporation, whether for profit or not for profit, and including any urban redevelopment corporation.
3. "Lender" shall include any bank, savings and loan association, credit union, corporation, partnership, or any other person or entity who makes loans or extends credit.
4. "Residential real estate: shall mean any real estate used or intended to be used as a residence by not more than four families.
5. "Residential real estate loan" shall mean a loan made for the acquisition, construction, repair, or improvement of real estate used or intended to be used as a residence by not more than four families. The term shall also include any loan made to refinance such a loan. No loan secured by residential real estate shall be considered to be a business loan.

Section 10.03   Penalties for Usury

If a rate of interest greater than permitted by law is paid, the person paying the same or his legal representative may recover twice the amount of the interest thus paid, provided that the action is brought within five years from the time when said interest should have been paid. The person so adjudged to have received a greater rate of interest shall also be liable for the costs of the suit, including a reasonable attorney's fee to be determined by the court.

exempted from any interest rate ceiling were of particular significance (exhibit 6). It was the interpretation of these statutory provisions by Enterprise that consumer loans could be secured by real estate without rate restrictions, so long as the loans were not made for the "acquisition, construction, repair, improvement, or refinancing" of residential real estate.

Over the next few days, the statute was evaluated within Modern's legal department. A review of Missouri law did not reveal any previous decisions which defined "real estate loan." There was a federal statute that defined a real estate loan to be a loan secured by real estate, but this was not necessarily a precedent to be followed by Missouri courts. Although the state banking department was contacted, it had not yet taken a position on the matter. Contact was made with several legislators to see if any of them could shed light on the legislative intent. Some were sure that it was not intended to open the door to unlimited rates on second mortgages while others thought that a "loop hole" existed for such loans.

Was Enterprise's interpretation correct? Was there legal authority to make Missouri home equity loans for certain purposes (e.g., college tuition or short-term debt consolidation) with no legal interest ceiling? On the one hand, Harris argued that the company should not venture into this business (Missouri home equity loans) because from a practical standpoint, the use of the loan proceeds cannot be controlled. On the other

hand, Harris believed there were significant reasons that could support a legal argument that there was a "loop hole" in the law. He thought the statute had been ill-drafted. But given that, on its face it appeared to permit the activity; though there was no apparent legislative history to support a contention that the Missouri legislature intended to allow such loans to be made at rates exceeding 10 percent. However, no one could judge how a Missouri court would decide if the same question was put to it.

Although Russ Pluta, Modern's CEO was the ultimate decision-maker, Teal knew that Pluta would follow his recommendation. He knew also that he must decide soon. Competitive pressures were mounting. Other finance companies were beginning to enter the market. If Modern were to enter the Missouri home equity market, then newspaper and radio advertisements must be prepared. It was either "join" or "get out of the business in Missouri."

QUESTIONS

1. Identify the key issue or issues represented by this case.

2. Should Modern begin making second mortgage loans in Missouri? If yes, identify any apparent risks and develop a management strategy to minimize or eliminate these risks.

Case 10

FHI Financial, Inc.
Bank Holding Company Diversification

The problem was troubling all three people, each in a different way. Six months ago the Department of Regulatory Agencies denied First Hawaiian, Incorporated's application for a de novo industrial loan license. First Hawaiian, a holding company for the second largest bank in the state, will be appealing this denial next week, the end of May 1975. Wayne Minami, the newly appointed director of Regulatory Agencies, must decide whether to continue the existing ban on bank holding company entry into the industrial loan company market.

The other two key participants in this encounter are Teruo Himoto, spokesman for The Hawaii Consumer Finance Association and also president of Commercial Finance, Limited, and Phillip Ching, vice president of First Hawaiian, Inc. and First Hawaiian Bank.

This case was prepared by Professor Steve Dawson of the University of Hawaii as a basis for class discussion rather than to illustrate either effective or ineffective handling of an administrative situation.

Copyright © 1975 by Steve Dawson.

Distributed by the Intercollegiate Case Clearing House, Soldiers Field, Boston, Mass. 02163. All rights reserved to the contributors.

Himoto and the other members of the Hawaii Consumer Finance Association are determined that bank holding companies must be kept out of the industrial loan market. Their entry would likely lead to unequal competition and could cause serious problems for the more than 200 industrial loan licensees. The holding company's earlier application was denied and the governor subsequently spoke out against bank holding company entry, but stopping the appeal still might not be easy. The holding company has apparently strengthened its position considerably.

At this same time, Ching and others at the bank holding company are putting together their appeal position. The 1970 amendments to the Bank Holding Company Act gave them new authority under Federal law and regulations to enter bank related activities, including the industrial loan company market. Many other applications around the country were successful in the last two years. Ching knew that he must prepare effective counter arguments to the points raised in last year's denial ruling. In addition, he must be prepared to respond to arguments raised by the Consumer Finance Association.

FIRST HAWAIIAN BANK

First Hawaiian Bank is the oldest and second largest bank in the state. It is a state bank, chartered under the laws of the state of Hawaii and is not a member of the Federal Reserve System. In 1974, the bank reached a major milestone as assets rose above the $1 billion level. The Bank of Hawaii continues to be slightly larger. Together these two banks control 71 percent of the assets and 70 percent of the deposits held by the state's eight banks (exhibit 1).

First Hawaiian Bank offers a broader range of financial services than any other bank in Hawaii. The bank is an active lender in the commercial, consumer, and real estate loan markets. Demand, savings, and time deposits are accepted. The bank manages the Master Charge credit card system in Hawaii. Recent customer service innovations include the OTTO automatic twenty-four-hour tellers, the Yes-Check plan which covers checks written above the account balance, and an individual automobile leasing plan. The trust department handles a full range of trust services, including living trusts, fiscal management of apartments, probates, life insurance, and employee benefit trusts. The enactment of the Employee Retirement Income Security Act of 1974 promises increased participation as a trustee for employee benefit accounts. In the international area, the bank works with both U.S. and foreign companies that are trading and investing in the Pacific Basin market.

On 1 July 1974, First Hawaiian Bank was reorganized as a holding company. First Hawaiian, Inc., the holding company, owns all the stock of First Hawaiian Bank except for Directors' qualifying shares. During 1974 the holding company began to issue commercial paper, temporarily using the proceeds to acquire time certificates of deposit from First Hawaiian Bank. The bank in turn paid dividends to the holding company of $6.098 million during 1974. Total dividends paid by the holding company to its stockholders were $4.110 million.

According to regulations issued by the Federal Reserve System, bank holding companies are permitted to operate industrial loan companies as authorized by state law. Within a week of its formation, the holding company applied to the State Department of Regulatory Agencies for permission to operate an industrial loan subsidiary under the name of FHI Financial, Inc.

HAWAII'S FINANCIAL INSTITUTIONS

Competition in banking in Hawaii is intense. The bank must compete for deposits and loans with seven other banks located in Hawaii and

EXHIBIT 1:

Banks in Hawaii, 31 December 1974
Assets, Deposits, and Capital Accounts
(in $ millions)

	Total Assets	Total Deposits	Total Capital
Bank of Hawaii	$1,061	$944	$82
First Hawaiian Bank	1,008	855	76
Central Pacific Bank	220	202	14
American Security Bank	218	190	18
Liberty Bank	137	119	9
City Bank	133	117	11
Hawaii National Bank	123	109	8
Bank of Honolulu, N.A.	18	16	2
	$2,918	$2,553	$220

with mainland banks when interest rate differentials arise. The Bank of Hawaii is a regional bank which has a relatively high level of mortgage and other long-term loans outstanding. The major money-center banks in New York and Chicago which concentrate on relatively shorter term loans are better positioned to adjust their interest rates. In 1974 corporate deposits tended to move to the mainland money center banks; First Hawaiian Bank's deposit growth was modest, producing less funds for lending than was desired. The 1974 Annual Report goes on to note that outside borrowings were also cut due to the cost of money. "During the second half's [1974] general shortage of lendable funds it was necessary to dampen the growth of our real estate loan portfolio but we continued to serve essential needs even when it necessitated outside borrowing."

There is active competition in Hawaii for savings and time deposits. Savings and loan associations, industrial loan companies, and credit unions are all actively seeking funds, and they are permitted to pay higher rates of interest than banks for individual accounts. The eleven sav-

ings and loan associations are more than twice the national average in asset size. Over the last ten years Hawaii's banks have experienced a slower growth of savings deposits than each of the other three financial institutions. In 1974 the savings and loan associations actually exceeded the banking institutions in terms of total time and savings deposits. Although they continue to be much smaller, the industrial loan companies have demonstrated a rapid rate of growth (see exhibits 2 and 3).

Industrial loan companies are often called finance companies or consumer finance companies. Counting all the branches, Hawaii has about eighty companies operating around 230 offices. Some of Hawaii's industrial loan companies are associated with large national firms such as Household Finance, CIT Financial, Beneficial Finance, and GMAC. Others are very small organizations with capital near the $15,000 level required by the state for getting a license.

Industrial loan companies are far less regulated than the commercial banks. Like the banks they make both personal and business loans. In

EXHIBIT 2:

Savings in Hawaii's Financial Institutions
1965–1974
(in $ millions)

Year	Bank Time Deposits	S&L Withdrawable Shares, Deposits and Investment Certificates	Industrial Loan Investment Certificates	Credit Union Shares	Total Institutional Savings
1965	$ 394.4	$ 378.1	$ 24.7	$114.8	$ 912.0
1966	427.7	399.5	25.9	123.5	976.6
1967	495.4	450.2	33.3	133.4	1,112.3
1968	566.9	502.4	40.6	146.9	1,256.8
1969	592.6	553.3	56.9	162.0	1,364.8
1970	713.9	625.9	99.7	182.6	1,622.1
1971	791.6	780.5	143.8	216.0	1,931.9
1972	891.7	957.6	191.7	248.6	2,289.6
1973	1,022.7	1,080.0	245.9	278.0	2,626.6
1974	1,111.2	1,190.6	319.0	313.2	2,914.0

Sources: *Credit Union Yearbook* and *Bank Examiner Reports*

EXHIBIT 3:

Hawaii's Financial Institutions
Percentage Shares of Savings

Year	Bank	S&L	Industrial Loan	Credit Union
1965	43.2%	41.5%	2.7%	12.6%
1966	43.8	40.9	2.6	12.6
1967	44.5	40.5	3.0	12.0
1968	45.1	40.0	3.2	11.7
1969	43.4	40.5	4.2	11.9
1970	44.0	38.6	6.1	11.3
1971	41.0	40.4	7.4	11.2
1972	38.9	41.8	8.4	10.9
1973	38.9	41.1	9.4	10.6
1974	38.1	40.2	10.9	10.7

Source: Calculated from Exhibit 2

general both the risk and rate of interest are higher on the industrial loan company's loans. The area of rapid growth has been the real estate mortgage loan market (see exhibit 4). In 1969 these loans totaled $36 million and 12 percent of total assets. At the end of 1974 the real estate loans were $292 million and 41 percent of assets. Much of the real estate loans are second mortgages at simple interest rates of up to 18 percent a year for terms of up to six years. Banks and S & Ls are not allowed to make second-mortgage loans. Rising mortgage interest rates have made second mortgages very attractive for homeowners seeking to raise money against a rising equity value in their property.

Almost half the total funds available in industrial loan companies are raised by investment certificates (see exhibit 4). These deposits are not insured but investors are attracted by the interest rates which exceed those offered by other financial institutions. Another major source of funds is borrowed money, supplied primarily by commercial banks.

BANK HOLDING COMPANY LEGISLATION

Bank holding companies have existed since before 1900, but it was not until 1956 that specific powers were given to the Federal Reserve Board to regulate them. Despite a reduction in the number and importance of bank holding companies following the widespread bank failures during the depression, the Federal Reserve Board contended that holding companies were being used to evade the intent of the Banking Act of 1933. Although, banks were not supposed to engage in business activities unrelated to banking, bank holding companies or their affiliates were doing what their subsidiary banks were prohibited from doing.

In 1956 Congressional concern about the growth of bank holding companies led to the passage of the Bank Holding Company Act which gave the Federal Reserve Board the power to regulate bank holding companies. The act limited nonbanking activities to the performance of services that were "a proper incident to" banking or managing or controlling banks and, in addition, were "of a financial, fiduciary or insurance nature." Surprisingly, the act applied only to multibank holding companies controlling two or more banks, and one-bank holding companies were excluded.

Exclusion of the one-bank holding companies meant they could engage in unrestricted types of business activity. At first their activities were primarily confined to financial activities, but in the late 1960s both the number of one-bank

EXHIBIT 4:

Industrial Loan Companies in Hawaii
Balance Sheet Data on 31 December
(in $ thousands)

	1969 $	1969 %	1974 $	1974 %
Assets				
Real estate mortgage loans	$ 35,936	12.3%	$291,566	41.0%
Retail installment contract	27,431	9.4	31,245	4.4
Character loans	49,609	16.9	62,766	8.8
Collateral loans	64,609	22.0	89,029	12.5
Auto & trade financing loans	9,054	3.1	16,878	2.4
All other loans	27,572	9.4	51,250	7.2
Total loans	$214,088	73.0	$542,733	76.3
Judgments & Repossessions	162	0.1	126	0.0
Premises, furniture & fixtures	3,122	1.1	6,184	0.9
Cash	9,474	3.2	22,152	3.1
All other Assets	66,186	22.6	140,408	19.7
Total Assets	$293,031	100.0%	$711,604	100.0%
Liabilities & Capital				
Borrowed money	$100,673	34.4%	$151,761	21.3%
Debentures	47,308	16.1	41,685	5.9
Invest. cert. outstdg.	56,906	19.4	318,978	44.8
Other liabilities	9,997	3.4	52,910	8.2
Unearned interest	26,238	9.0	30,444	4.3
Capital	27,422	9.4	47,835	6.7
Surplus & undivided profits	19,944	6.8	49,996	7.0
Reserve for losses	4,542	1.5	12,995	1.8
Total	$293,031	100.0%	$711,604	100.0%

holding companies and their nonfinancial activities increased greatly. In 1970, in order to preserve the basic separation of bank activities from other business activities embodied in federal law since the Glass-Steagall Act of 1933, Congress passed a series of amendments to the Bank Holding Company Act of 1956. The principal purposes of the amendments were to regulate the one-bank holding companies and to broaden the range of activities in which regulated holding companies could engage.

Section 4 (c) (8) of the amendments established two tests which must be met in order for an activity to be permissible. First, the Federal Reserve Board must determine that the activity be "so closely related to banking or managing or controlling banks as to be a proper incident thereto." Second, the board must determine whether the activity "by an affiliate of a holding company can reasonably be expected to produce benefits to the public, such as greater convenience, increased competition, or gains in efficiency, that outweigh possible adverse effects, such as undue concentration of resources, decreased or unfair competition, conflicts of interests, or unsound banking practices."

The 1970 amendments to the Bank Holding Company Act did not change section 7 which reserves the right of the states to exercise their present and future powers and jurisdiction with respect to banks, bank holding companies, and their subsidiaries.

Bank holding companies were quickly given permission to acquire finance company subsidiaries. From January 1971 through June 1974 the Federal Reserve Board approved applications to purchase seventy-seven existing finance companies and denied only eleven applications. Four hundred thirty-one de novo finance subsidiaries were also authorized.[1]

Writing in the *Banking Law Journal,* Rose and Fraser have summarized several Federal Reserve Board preferences with regard to finance company subsidiaries:

1.   Acquisitions of small finance companies or de novo entry are clearly favored over applications which seek to take over a substantial creditor in the market area.

2.   There is little competitive overlap between small loan operations and commercial banks. Consumer finance companies make a wider variety of loans and service different risk classes of customers.

3.   With holding company management and capital, finance company subsidiaries are able to enter new geographic markets, expand their loan volume, offer larger and more diversified loans, and be more effective competitors.

4.   Several applications were turned down because they would result in undue concentration of resources or adverse effects on existing competition in the consumer finance field.

5.   All applications must be subjected to the so-called "balancing test." The holding company must show that any potentially adverse effects on competition must be offset by public benefits. This may be shown through new services being offered, reductions in fees charged on loans, or increased access to sources of capital to support future growth.

---

[1]Peter S. Rose and Donald R. Fraser, "Bank Holding Company Diversification into Mortgage Banking and Finance Companies," *Banking Law Journal* (November 1974): 977.

FIRST HAWAIIAN'S APPLICATION FOR A FINANCE SUBSIDIARY

On 5 July 1974, First Hawaiian, Inc., filed an application on behalf of FHI Financial, Inc., a proposed wholly owned subsidiary which intended to conduct an industrial loan business under chapter 408 of the Hawaii Revised Statutes. The application stated the management of the proposed subsidiary would be directed by the senior officers of First Hawaiian, Inc., which in most instances comprises the senior officers of First Hawaiian Bank. The subsidiary would concentrate in the real estate loan market and, more specifically, in the taking of junior liens on real property. Under current Hawaii statutes, banks cannot make such junior liens, and they may represent a substantial potential for consumer borrowing.

On 26 August 1974, Hawaii Bancorporation, Inc., also filed an application for an industrial loan subsidiary. It is a one-bank holding company for the Bank of Hawaii, the largest bank in the state.

Chapter 408-8 of the Hawaii Revised Statutes establishes three conditions which must be demonstrated before the application could be approved by the Director of Regulatory Agencies. The conditions are

1.   That the financial responsibility, experience, character, and general fitness of the applicant and of the officers or members thereof are such as to command the confidence of the community and to warrant belief that the business will be operated honestly, fairly, and efficiently within the purposes of this chapter;

2.   That allowing the applicant to engage in this business will promote the convenience and advantage of the locality or community in which the business of the applicant is to be conducted; and

3.   That the applicant has available for the operation of this business at the specified location capital of at least $100,000.

INFORMATION SUPPORTING THE APPLICATION

A hearing was held before the Director of Regulatory Agencies on 18 October 1974. A second hearing was also held on 15 November to consider supplemental information filed by First Hawaiian, Inc. In the section which follows information presented at these hearings and in the application will be summarized or reported in part. Certain issues which primarily dealt with the proposed location will not be included in this case. This case is not concerned with the location of the subsidiary. The question at issue is whether a bank holding company should be authorized to establish an industrial loan subsidiary in the State of Hawaii, regardless of its location within the state.

Prior to the hearings, Ching, a vice-president of both the holding company and the bank, sent the following information to the director of Regulatory Agencies.

1. *Background.* First Hawaiian, Inc., a bank holding company, has filed an application on behalf of FHI Financial, Inc., a proposed Hawaii Corporation, which will be a wholly owned subsidiary of First Hawaiian, Inc., to conduct an industrial loan business under chapter 408, Hawaii Revised Statutes. . . . The application to conduct an industrial loan business . . . is a permissible activity under the Bank Holding Company Act of 1956 as amended in Regulation Y of the Federal Reserve Board.

2. *Convenience and Advantage to the Community in Which Applicant's Business Is to Be Conducted.*

a. Growth of industrial loan companies. In the recent past Hawaii has seen a substantial increase in loans made by industrial loan companies which indicates tremendous growth potential. Annual loan growth rates for Hawaii's industrial loan companies, savings and loans, and banks are as follows for the period June 1969 to June 1974. For the industrial loan com-

panies, 21.1 percent; savings and loan, 18.6 percent; banks, 11.5 percent.

b. Real estate loans. FHI Financial intends to emphasize the real estate loan area, particularly the making of second-mortgage loans on real property. FHI Financial will also offer all the services of an industrial loan company dependent on the demands and needs of its clients in the community in which it will conduct its business.

"We believe that the potential for second mortgages in Hawaii is substantial. In view of the fact that we have had in recent years tremendous increase in real estate values, statistics compiled by the Multiple Listing Services of the Honolulu Board of Realtors show the following average prices of residences on the Island of Oahu. For 1971 for the period August to December—because this is the only time that the Hawaii Board of Realtors had started tabulating on single-family residences—average price for that period for single-family residences was $60,160; for condominiums for the same period, $42,616. For the year 1972, single-family residence, $65,704; condominiums, $44,136. 1973, $85,912; condominiums, $49,312. For six months of 1974, the single-family residence average sales prices was $85,951; condominiums, $54,902.

"This may result in a wide gap between current market value and current balances on first mortgages thus giving the property owner the capability of making a second mortgage. Refinancing of existing mortgages would be impractical due to current high mortgage interest rates which would make such long-term refinancing costly. High prices for homes represent another potential market for second mortgages due to the fact that in many instances purchasers are unable to meet the substantial down payment for a home, though their income is adequate for the entire debt services. Banks are currently restricted to a maximum loan-to-value ratio on mortgages.

First Hawaiian Bank has been forced to turn down mortgage loans which otherwise represent prudent desirable loans solely because they were in excess of the permissible loan-to-value ratio. Entry into the industrial loan field would permit FHI Financial to make such loans which ordinarily would have been made by First Hawaiian Bank or other banks but for the loan-to-value restrictions.

c. Benefit to the community. "We intend to conduct business on the basis beneficial and convenient to the public. We propose to implement innovative programs through FHI Financial such as Pay Any Day of the month, simple interest calculation, and no prepayment penalty on all loans. It is our understanding that these are not generally available throughout the industrial loan industry. These programs should result in lower borrowing costs to our customers

"FHI Financial will provide another competitive entity in the industrial loan field. We feel that we will be able to compete effectively with other industrial loan companies. This should result in benefit to the community in better service and competitive pricing of our services."

3. *Financial Responsibility and General Fitness of the Applicant.*

". . . We propose to capitalize FHI Financial at $1 million fully paid in. We intend to staff FHI Financial with experienced financial officers who will be identified at a later date."

Hearing on the Application

At the opening session of the hearings. John Bellinger, president of First Hawaiian, Inc., made the following statement to start the bank's presentation:

"Mr. Chairman, I just have a brief statement. I would like to go on record in reply to the brief that was filed by the Hawaii Consumer Finance Association, which lists both Bank of Hawaii and ourselves as applicants, that this is our application, and Bank of Hawaii is not being heard today. They had a holding company for a couple of years and if they decide to file an application a month after us, that is their problem, but ours is a separate problem and I would prefer that this is handled in that manner. This is our application and should be looked upon as our application and not the two banks'."

"Secondly, I think that with the application we have submitted, we can offer to the consumer public better service than they are receiving now. It is obvious that the growth of some of the finance companies and industrial loan companies, in the last five years has been tremendous and that there is room for additional companies. We intend to offer services which we cannot afford in the bank. We will include those we think are convenient to the public, and if our application is approved we will offer the public simple interest loans and also the opportunity of our Pay Any Day Plan."

"We do not believe that our entering this field will in any way damage or hurt the other finance companies. Competition is always healthy. Thank you."

The hearings continued throughout the day. Questions were asked by Wee, the senior bank examiner, Honda, the director of Regulatory Agencies, Wheelan, an attorney for the Hawaii Consumer Finance Association, and several members of the audience. The following are excerpts, occasionally paraphrased, from these exchanges.

Mr. Honda: You say that you do not feel that your entry into the business will hurt others. Whom do you mean by "others"?

Mr. Bellinger: I meant the other finance companies that are objecting.

Mr. Honda: How do you arrive at that conclusion?

Mr. Bellinger: Well, because of the growth of the overall totals of the finance companies in the last five years. I think there will be continued growth and those that are hustling and working for the business will continue to grow. I think that some of those that do not really get in and work are going to maybe stay status quo and not have the growth. We think that there is room.

★ ★ ★

Mr. Wee: Would this be a vehicle for referring down the second mortgage? In other words, an individual goes to the bank and makes an application for a first-mortgage loan and is referred to your subsidiary.

Mr. Bellinger: Probably would.

★ ★ ★

Mr. Ching: We have stated in our application we intend to stress second mortgages, but we have also stated that as a collateral matter dependent on the clients we will engage in the other activities permitted to industrial loan companies. Our main intent in applying for industrial loan license is to do those things which we cannot do now under the bank. It would be, I think, somewhat imprudent as a general business practice to actively solicit consumer loans in our industrial loan company when in fact we are conducting that business as a bank. We would be fighting against each other in a sense. And so it is our intent to concentrate in the second mortgage area and as a collateral matter as a benefit, you know, where a guy comes in and he happens to be a one-stop shopping in finance, if he happens to need a consumer loan, fine, but we are not going to be pursuing it on an active basis.

★ ★ ★

Mr. Ching: One of the unfair competitive advantages cited by the Consumer Association is that the bank, which now provides lines of credit to some of the financial companies, would begin to favor FHI Financial and this would provide unfair competition. As a matter of practicality, the FHI Financial will be considered an affiliate under the Federal Deposit Insurance Act of the Federal Reserve, and as such, any lines or borrowings by FHI Financial would have to be fully collateralized depending on the class of the collateral whether it be securities or governments or municipals; but, in any event, it would be at least fully collateralized, any loans. Now, we have analyzed this and considered it and we have concluded that this is totally impractical to conduct our business as FHI Financial by borrowing from the bank and we are not looking to borrowings from the bank or First Hawaiian Bank lines to finance the activities of FHI Financial.

Mr. Schutte (Bank Attorney): The banks in the state of Hawaii have total assets of $2.875 billion. Our information indicates that Household Finance consolidated assets are $2.985 billion; CIT's consolidated assets of 31 December 1973 were $3.961 billion; Beneficial Finance at 30 June 1974 reported consolidated assets of $2.399 billion. And we are turning loose, depending on how you look at it, a million dollar company in that area. Or, if you use our consolidated assets, about a $900 million company taking on $2 and $3 billion dollar companies. So we don't believe solely in competition among equals. We are willing to go in as a pigmy and fight our way with the giants.

Mr. Honda: Where would the proposed finance company be obtaining funds from?

Mr. Ching: Initially, of course, the million-dollar capitalization; but, in addition, First Hawaiian, Inc., has recently gone into the commercial paper market, and we intend to downstream funds to the finance company. Outside bank borrowing from mainland banks would be another source of funds for our finance company's operations. At the present time the commercial paper market is within the state. However, it is our intention to market it outside of the state on a national basis.

Mr. Pingree (Bank Officer): We find that while we are marketing our commercial paper locally, we are really competing for mainland dollars because we found that many of the people who are traditionally in the paper market are using mainland sources, so in that sense in essence when we market our paper locally we are bringing dollars back to Hawaii because that money would traditionally stay on the Mainland in other types of paper.

Mr. Ching: An additional source of funds ultimately will be the issuance of investment certificates and/or debentures as has been the case for other industrial loan companies.

Mr. Honda: So you will be in that sense competing for funds with many of the existing institutions?

Mr. Ching: Certainly.

★ ★ ★

Mr. Schutte (Bank Attorney):   I take it that the question addresses itself to will FHI Financial borrow from First Hawaiian Bank. To respond very briefly, the answer is no; but, here is the answer why the answer is no: First Hawaiian Bank is a State nonmember insured bank, deposits which are insured by the Federal Deposit Insurance Corporation. As such it is subject to the Federal Deposit Insurance Act. Section 18 (j) of the Federal Deposit Insurance Act makes section 23(a) of the Federal Reserve Act applicable to all sate nonmember banks. Section 23 of the Federal Reserve Act prohibits loans between banks and their affiliates unless certain conditions are met. Affiliates are specifically defined in section 23(a) as amended now in force to include the subsidiaries of bank holding companies; that is to say, every subsidiary of the bank holding company is an affiliate of every other subsidiary of a bank holding company under section 23(a).

Section 23(a) says that a bank shall not lend to an affiliate unless: One, there are certain maximum loan amounts observed in terms of percentage of capital to surplus. But the really significant thing is that they cannot lend except on collateral. If the collateral is securities other than U.S. governments, government agencies and municipals, the collateral must equal 120 percent of the amount of the loan. If the collateral is municipal, state and local government obligations, the collateral must be 110 percent of the loan. If the collateral is United States government and government agencies, then the statute simply requires that the loan be collateralized.

I suggest to you, Mr. Director in response to this question also that if there is a local industrial loan licensee who has stock exchange, government or municipal collateral sufficient so that he could put up that kind of backing for his bank loan, it is either the richest industrial loan license in the world or it is headed for bankruptcy, one of the two.

A voice: Will you get a loan from the Bank of Hawaii? Can your subsidiary get a bank line from Bank of Hawaii?

Mr. Schutte: Legally, the answer is legally it could. To the best of my knowledge and belief, we do not own Bank of Hawaii or any controlling interest in it so that we wouldn't be an affiliate of Bank of Hawaii. It would be legally permissible; whether our No. 1 competitor would be delighted to give us the money with which to compete with them, I don't know.

Prior to the November resumption of hearings, First Hawaiian submitted additional material which established the following points:

1.   It is generally uneconomical to refinance an existing mortgage loan bearing a low rate of interest since the entire loan will be rewritten at current rates. In Hawaii there is both a low percent of second mortgages and a large homeowner equity in homes which provide a tremendous market for second mortgages.

2.   All applicants for second mortgages do not receive them and 63 percent of the downtown industrial loan companies are not currently making second-mortgage loans. This is hardly meeting the public's need for second mortgage loans.

3.   We will be able to benefit the public through lower borrowing costs.

Counter Arguments Presented by the Hawaii Consumer Finance Association:

The Hawaii Consumer Finance Association and its attorneys submitted a statement to the Director of Regulatory Agencies which strongly objected to the First Hawaiian application. The following are excerpts from the conclusion section of this statement.

The proposed entry of the Bank of Hawaii and First Hawaiian Bank into the industrial loan company market poses several serious problems:

1.   Bank of Hawaii and First Hawaiian Bank, by virtue of being the two largest banks in the state, have the potential to direct a tremendous amount of business to their proposed industrial loan company subsidiaries. This would tend to monopolize control and related activities

within the banking field and the industrial loan company market.

2. Bank of Hawaii and First Hawaiian Bank are regulated by the state and federal governments, and accounts are insured by an agency of the federal government. Industrial loan companies are not insured by any governmental agency, and are only subject to state regulation. It is probable that industrial loan company customers will confuse the identity of these banks and their respective proposed industrial loan companies. The banks and their proposed industrial loan companies have a number of common incidents: common ownership, common directors, common names, etc. These factors will lead customers to believe that the bank and its proposed industrial loan company are one and the same. This gives the bank's proposed industrial loan company an unfair edge in competition. It misleads the customer. It perhaps exposes the bank and its assets to liability arising out of the industrial loan company operations by ''piercing the corporate veil.''

3. If, as the banks project, there is increased demand for real estate second-mortgage money, an important source of industrial loan company operating funds to meet this demand derives from the banks. Diversion of bank lines from existing industrial loan companies would unfairly and illegally affect the future of existing industrial loan companies to meet this demand.

4. Although the banks' applications for industrial loan company licenses do not specify whether the proposed companies will issue thrift certificates or debentures, state law permits issuance of such debt instruments. The banks take various forms of deposit which yield various returns. The industrial loan companies receive nondemand funds by issuance of certificates or debentures which generally produce higher yields than can be obtained from the banks. The banks will be in a position to divert public monies which would otherwise be deposited with the banks to their proposed industrial loan companies by issuing certificates or debentures.

The banks may also divert public monies which would otherwise be invested with other industrial loan companies to the banks' proposed industrial loan companies. Such activity would be illegal and unfair to the existing industrial loan companies. The public is aware that bank deposits are insured by an agency of the federal government.

Teruo Himoto, the president of Commercial Finance, Limited, and a director of the Hawaii Consumer Finance Association, also presented a statement at the hearings.

''I appear before this hearing with mixed emotions. I have worked very closely with the two major banks that have applied for industrial loan licenses under chapter 408, Hawaii Revised Statutes, while employed by three separate companies that I have worked for during the past twenty-three years. These two banks have been very good to me and assisted me with our financial needs.

''On account of the good business relationship that we have with these two banks, many of the members of the Hawaii Consumer Finance Association are reluctant to testify at this hearing in order that these relationships would not be severed. If none of us spoke up to express our true feelings and thoughts when our very livelihood depended on the outcome of whether or not bank holding companies may be permitted to operate industrial loan companies and eventually put many of us present industrial loan license operators out of business, we are definitely shirking our responsibility to our investors and the public.''

''The management of the industrial loan companies as well as the staff of the Bank Examiner's Office are entrusted with the responsibility of protecting the public monies invested in the various industrial loan companies. We both must make every effort to see that such public funds do not deteriorate through poor management operation or unfair edge in competition by the entries of two giant banks into our industry.''

''Why did the federal and the individual states throughout the country create three major categories of financial institutions; namely, banks, savings and loan associations and industrial loan companies? Each of these financial institutions has a specific function to perform to serve the financial needs of the public. Under the Banking Act, the banks were prohibited from operating a savings and loan or an industrial loan company; so why should they be permitted to operate an industrial loan company under the Bank Holding Company Act? Isn't it one and the same thing?''

''Under our free enterprise system, I welcome good healthy competition, but am strongly opposed to unfair competition. As you are all aware these two major banks dominate the market in this small financial community of ours, operating only as a bank. What will happen if they were permitted to enter the industrial loan area and later into the savings and loan industry. Do you think our free enterprise system will be in operation then? The answer is *no*! They will definitely monopolize and control the banking and other financial markets.''

''First Hawaiian, Inc. has indicated that the second-mortgage loan market has grown substantially during the past few years and quoted the amount of second mortgages closed in 1973, and the first five months of 1974. Who has provided the funds for such second mortgages? It is the present existing industrial loan companies that have met the needs of the public and will continue to meet these needs of the public.''

''Until a few years ago, the industrial loan companies were primarily making consumer loans, such as installment sales contracts, auto loans, character loans and loans on personal property; but when the need for second mortgages arose, we were able to take care of the public demand. We were able to meet the public demand for such needed funds and we are prepared to satisfy the needs of the public for such demands in the future, without the banks entering into this field.''

''The public convenience and advantage will not, in any legitimate way, be served by approving the application of First Hawaiian, Inc. The present industrial loan companies have in the past, and will continue to meet the demands of the public. . . . No convenience or advantage will be served granting the application when there would be the potential for unfair competition and monopolistic trade practices. The public convenience and advantage will be much better served if the existing industrial loan companies are permitted to maintain the healthy and strong competitive market which presently exists. Entry of the banks into this market would seriously distort competition

and jeopardize the financial health of the industrial loan company industry in Hawaii.''

Initial Decision of the Director of Regulatory Agencies

On 27 November 1974, the Director of Regulatory Agencies denied the application for an industrial loan license. After considering all the facts, information, and relevant laws, the director determined that

1. Allowing the applicant to be licensed as an industrial loan company under chapter 408, Hawaii Revised Statutes, through a wholly owned subsidiary will not promote the convenience and advantage of the locality or community in which the business of the applicant is proposed to be conducted, based on the fact that First Hawaiian Bank, a principal subsidiary of the applicant, presently possesses under section 478—4, Hawaii Revised Statutes, the same rights conferred upon industrial loan companies operating under chapter 408, Hawaii Revised Statutes, as to charge, contract for, receive, collect in advance, or recover interest, discount, and other charges at the same rates and in the same amounts as permitted by law in the case of loans made by industrial loan companies licensed under chapter 408, Hawaii Revised Statutes.

2. Since applicant's principal subsidiary, First Hawaiian Bank, is not permitted under the present statutes to make second-mortgage loans, applicant should not be permitted to accomplish this through an indirect route.

3. The consumer loan activity of applicant conducted through its subsidiary, First Hawaiian Bank, will not be adversely affected without an industrial loan license.

4. Applicant's earnings will not be substantially affected without an industrial loan license.

5. Approval of the subject application would result in undue concentration of resources due to the resources of applicant's principal subsidiary, First Hawaiian Bank, as of 30 June 1974, being 1.392 times the total resources of all industrial loan companies in Hawaii.

6. Approval of the subject application would create a competitive inequality, to some degree, in the field of mortgage loans where first mortgage loans are made to the borrowers by applicant's principal subsidiary, First Hawaiian Bank, and the second mortgage loans are directed to its proposed industrial loan licensee.

7. At this time, there are no compelling mitigating circumstances of competitive or other hardships which applicant or any of its subsidiaries will suffer vis-a-vis comparable institutions which are chartered by other than state agencies.

"Based on the foregoing, it is ordered that the application of First Hawaiian, Inc. for a license to engage in the business of an industrial loan company through a subsidiary be and is hereby denied at this time."

SUBSEQUENT EVENTS

During the 1975 session of the State Legislature a bill was introduced which would prevent banks and savings and loan associations from getting into the industrial loan business. This attempt to deny entry created considerable controversy in the Lesiglature.

A spokesman for First Hawaii, Inc., testified before the Legislature that:

1. The Federal Reserve Board permits bank holding companies to operate industrial loan companies in the manner authorized by state law. The bill would prevent other financial institutions from engaging in the industrial loan business.

2. The bill will eliminate potential competition and the possibility of lower borrowing costs to the public.

3. There is a definite need for additional financing alternatives in the second mortgage market.

Late in the Legislative session Governor Ariyoshi sent a letter to the Speaker of the House of Representatives which outlined his support of the bill:

"There is a present prohibition against the enumerated firms from directly engaging in the industrial loan business. I do not believe that they should be permitted to do indirectly through a holding company that which they could not do directly. I am therefore very strongly in support of the concept of the bill to prohibit all banks, savings and loan associations, and trust companies from engaging in the industrial loan business."

"I also believe that this prohibition should apply equally to all legal entities, whether they are organized and doing business in or out of our state. It is therefore my hope that the bill passed by the House will be amended to reflect a total prohibition."

"I want to assure you that I feel very strongly about this matter. I feel equally strongly that such action should be taken during this session of the Legislature. To delay may result in the need to "grandfather" more firms than are presently involved. Your consideration of this matter would therefore be greatly appreciated."

Despite the governor's support, the bill failed to pass.

From the viewpoint of the bank holding company it was fortunate they were attempting to secure approval for an industrial loan subsidiary rather than a real estate investment trust. Nationally a combination of high interest rates and a slow housing market had pushed many REIT's close to financial bankruptcy. Within the last year the Fed had informally suggested that banks extend credit generously to the endangered REIT's so as to avert a total collapse. The 19 May 1975 issue of *Business Week* reported that the Chase Manhattan Bank subsequently encountered difficulty with its REIT affiliate:

"Of all the banks involved, Chase Manhattan Bank, the $1 billion REIT's sponsor, advisor, and with $150 million in the credit lines, biggest creditor, has the most at stake. It does not own the trust or have any legal obligation to stand behind it, but Chase's name is on the line. And any default to the public bondholders by the trust could do incalculable damage to the bank, to Chase Manhattan Corp., the bank's holding company parent, and to the holding company's various nonbank subsidiaries."

There are thirty-eight industrial loan licensees in the downtown Honolulu area. The research personnel at First Hawaiian in the latter part of 1974 conducted a poll which asked the question: Are you making consumer and/or second-mortgage loans? Only fourteen of the thirty-six said they are currently making second-mortgage loans. The results of this poll were reconfirmed by a more recent poll.

APPEAL HEARING

As provided for in state statutes, First Hawaiian, Inc., appealed the denial of its application. The three-person appeal board was composed of Wayne Minami, the newly appointed director of Regulatory Agencies, Attorney General Ron Amemiya, and State Comptroller Hideo Murakami.

The appeal hearing was scheduled for late May.

QUESTIONS

1. Evaluate the arguments presented by the Bank Holding Company and by the Hawaii Consumer Finance Association with regard to the Bank Holding Company entry into the industrial loan market.

2. Would approval of FHI's application to enter the industrial loan market be in the best interest of the public? Fully support your position.

Case 11

Independence Savings and Loan Association

Four months ago the Independence Savings and Loan Association had contracted Don Sandiman of Financial Research Corporation to provide them with a feasibility study on a proposed branch office. Don founded Financial Research with three other colleagues from the business school at State University seven years ago. Among his consulting activities, he had participated in many similar feasibility studies for Independence, other savings organizations, and various banks. He was especially pleased with this report since all signs were favorable for a new branch office in Adamson.

Adamson is a small township located in a semicircle of medium-to-large cities in a southern sunbelt state. Adamson lies ten miles south of Lofton, the state capital, a city with a population of over 250,000. Mason, a city of 24,000 lies eight miles due east of Adamson with the towns of Pilgrim City (population 15,000) and

This case was prepared by Professor B. J. Campsey of the University of Virginia, and Professor G. K. Rakes of Ohio University as the basis for class discussion and not to illustrate either correct or incorrect business practices.

Copyright © 1976 by G. K. Rakes and B. J. Campsey

Presented at a Case Workshop and distributed by the Intercollegiate Case Clearing House, Soldiers Field, Boston, Mass. 02163. All rights reserved to the contributors.

Stafford (population 36,000), seven and twelve miles respectively, to the south. Historically Adams County, in which Adamson is located, has been a farming and rural residential area. Beginning in the late 1950s, however, the area began a pattern of population increase which continues today.

As he reviewed his research, Don felt sure the Federal Home Loan Bank in Atlanta would approve the application for a new branch of Independence Savings and Loan in the area. He knew an application based on his study for Independence would have to show a present and increasing need for a new branch savings institution and that a new office would not cause harm to existing thrift and home-financing institutions. Support for these assertions would have to come from population and per capita increases in incomes and from savings potential in the proposed area.

The major cause for the population increase in the portion of Adams county to be served by the proposed Adamson branch is due to the area's location between two urban land masses. On the northern boundary of the proposed market area lies Lofton, the state capital, with all the attending agencies and departments of government. To the south and east lie the more industrialized cities of Mason, Stafford, and Pilgrim City with a combined population of over 75,000. While some industries are contemplating the construction of new facilities in the proposed market area for the new branch, a metals manufacturer employing between 900 and 1000 and a Department of Defense facility employing eighty-five are the area's only major current employers. Even so, Adams County is one of the state's fastest growing counties. Between 1970 and 1974 Adams County recorded a gain of 20,600 new residents, earning it a number-three ranking out of the state's 105 counties in terms of absolute population growth. Moreover, Adams County's nearly 27 percent rate of growth earned it a ranking of number one of all the counties in the state that grew by 5000 or more during the period. The portion of the county which will be served by the proposed savings and loan branch office has historically grown at approximately the same rate as the county. The county and market area's growth is particularly impressive when compared to the decreases in population in most of the surrounding cities (exhibit 1). The continued growth in the area may be anticipated from the building permit data (exhibit 2).

The growth in population in the area has been accompanied by a concomitant increase in income for the country and proposed market area.

Total personal income in Adams County grew 80.5 percent between 1970 and 1974 (exhibit 1).

The analysis of the market area by Sandiman indicated an estimated $51 million in deposit-type savings potential. The estimate was derived by finding the per capita savings deposits for the state, multiplied by the market area population. Thus, with savings and loan deposits in the state equaling $4.8 billion and time deposits in commercial banks of $8.4 billion, the combined savings deposits in the state equal $13.2 billion. With a state population of 4.906 million, the per capita savings deposit for the state is $2,690. Applying this per capita savings deposit figure of $2,690 to the current market area population of 19,200 persons results in an existing savings potential estimate of $51,648,000.

Sandiman further estimated that during the first year of operation the proposed branch should attract an approximate 5 percent share of the savings potential. Therefore the first-year savings at the new branch should amount to slightly over $2.5 million. In future years, savings flows at the proposed branch office should increase as additional savings are created out of the incomes of existing savers, and as new families move into the market area bringing with them their accumulated savings.

In addition to the income and population

EXHIBIT 1:

Population and Income Data

Jurisdiction	Population	Changes 1970–1974			1974 Per Capita Personal Income
		Total Personal Income	Per Capita Personal Income	
Adams County	26.7%	80.5%	40.2%		117%
Proposed Market Area in County	23.8%	80.5%	40.2%		117%
Lofton	−5.5%	30.3%	39.8%		121%
Pilgrim City	11.7%	50.7%	35.3%		107%
Mason	−1.1%	38.5%	40.5%		89%
Stafford	−3.7%	41.7%	52.0%		95%
State	5.5%	51.3%	44.0%		100%

EXHIBIT 2:

Selected Items

Building Permit Data* Single Family	
1975	2,064
1974	1,520
1973	1,931
1972	2,144
1971	1,662
1970	1,038
Total	10,359

*Approximately 16% of this activity is located in the market area of the proposed branch.

Savings and Loan Deposit Growth*

Conservative Federal Savings
(Chartered 1960)

Dec. 31, 1972	$ 7,063,000
Dec. 31, 1973	7,457,000
Dec. 31, 1974	8,033,000
Dec. 31, 1975	9,472,000
July 31, 1976	10,544,000

Adams Savings and Loan
(Chartered 1974)

Sept. 30, 1974	$ 187,000
Sept. 30, 1975	1,001,000
July 31, 1976	2,012,000

*Total time and savings deposits in commercial banks (5 offices) totaled $11,424,000 as of June, 1976.

Offices Per Capita*
Market Area

Year	Savings and Loan Offices	Population
1970	1	15,515
1976	2	19,200

State

Year	Savings and Loan Offices	Population
1970	132	4,651,487
1976	337	4,973,000

*As of 1976 there was one banking office for each 3,440 persons in the state.

increases which argued for an additional savings institution, Sandiman felt there was an imbalance of savings and investment in the area for Independence. Total loans outstanding in the proposed market area from Independence Savings and Loans's branches is slightly less than $5 million. Even though Independence has a large dollar volume of investments in the proposed market area, it has been able to attract only about $1 million in savings from that portion of the county. Thus, Sandiman's analysis showed a clear deficit of nearly $4 million in the area. That is, the firm is attracting nearly $4 million less in savings accounts from the area than it is investing in mortgages there. Because of its heavy mortgage activity in this part of Adams County, Independence Savings and Loan felt that when it opened a branch in Adamson it would be able to attract a larger volume of savings from the area which will enable it to balance out its mortgage investment there.

Sandiman's report to Independence also argued for the branch on the grounds that there was an imbalance between the number of savings and loan offices and banks in the proposed market area. There were five commercial banks and, in contrast, only two savings and loans.

QUESTIONS

1. Evaluate the population and income growth in the relevant market for financial services and their impact on the need for the proposed branch office.

2. On the basis of deposit and other data provided for the relevant market, evaluate Don Sandiman's estimate of $2.5 million in first year deposits for the new branch.

3. Comment on the validity of Sandiman's assertion to the effect that an imbalance of savings and investment argued in favor of the proposed branch.

4. If Independence Savings and Loan Association applied for a new branch charter on the basis of facts provided in this case, should it be granted?

Case 12

Coronet Savings and Loan

The monthly management review at Coronet Savings and Loan was of special interest to John Burke. It was his first monthly review meeting as he had joined Coronet as treasurer less than a week earlier. In addition, the results for the previous year had just become available and were to be discussed. He anticipated that this meeting would be extremely helpful to him in developing his plans. Furthermore, Susan Wingate, the president, had indicated her desire to get his assessment of things while he still had the fresh perspective of an outsider.

The meeting opened with a presentation of the annual financial results (exhibit 1) by the controller, Ronald Schmitz. Schmitz noted that Coronet's profits had recovered nicely from the previous year, when high interest rates combined with an inverted yield curve had resulted in a large loss. Schmitz had assembled some preliminary industry average ratios (exhibit 2) by using the financial results of a dozen competitors that had released their results earlier. Again, he noted good news. Coronet's return on equity was well above the industry average, while it had

been well below the industry average in the previous year. Schmitz finished an otherwise rosy analysis with a note of concern: he was worried about interest rate risk resulting from reliance on fixed-rate loans and short-term deposits. "Coronet has been burned by this strategy before," he concluded.

Robert Parrish, the chief loan officer took strong exception to Schmitz's comments on fixed-rate loans. "Interest rate risk is part of this business," he said. "We've beaten our competitors in new loan growth, asset growth, deposit growth, and profitability. The primary reason is our firm commitment to the fixed-rate mortgage while others are trying to push variable rates. We are a market-oriented business, and the product the customer wants is the fixed-rate mortgage."

Burke had been asked to give a brief presentation of financial market conditions. As part of his presentation, he displayed the current yield curve (exhibit 3).

There were general statements of pleasure that for most of the past year the yield curve had had a "normal" upward slope. "As long as this shape holds," said Parrish, "we're in great shape."

This case was prepared by Neil E. Seitz, Department of Finance, Saint Louis University.

EXHIBIT 1:

Coronet Savings and Loan
Balance Sheet and Annual Income Statement
(in $ millions)

Interest income	$211
Interest expense	144
Operating expense	36
Other income	−3
Earnings before tax	28
Income tax	11
Net income	$ 17

Cash	$ 23	Passbook deposits	$ 290
Investments	197	Time deposits	1,186
Loans		Borrowed funds	351
Real estate	1,590	Deferred income tax	32
Other loans	82	Other liabilities	58
Other assets	119	Net worth	94
Total assets	$2,011	Tot. Liab. & NW	$2,011

"If it doesn't," replied Schmitz, "we'll be the Laclede Avenue branch of BankAmerica."

"Accountants are all the same," exclaimed Parrish. "If we listened to them, we'd be the Laclede Avenue phone booth!"

Wingate interrupted the conversation: "We've gone over this strategic issue a dozen times, and we're not going to resolve it with mutual unpleasantries. We need to take a hard look at this whole issue, and it's a top priority of

EXHIBIT 2:

Industry-Average Ratios

Return on net worth	0.137
Ratios to total assets:	
Loans	0.820
Investments	0.104
Deposits	0.812
Borrowed funds	0.091
Net worth	0.051
Interest & fee income	0.106
Operating expense	0.015
Other income	0.001

mine. Burke has a fresh perspective here, but he's been around this business a while. Burke, I want you to give top priority to a thorough study of this issue of matching or not matching asset and liability maturities."

After discussion of a few noncontroversial points, the meeting broke up.

Later in the day, Parrish stopped into Burke's office. "I want to be sure you don't start with false notions about our position," he said. The mortgage market is very competitive in this town. We've managed to keep the interest rate on our fixed-rate loans about half a percent below the average rate for the city and still maintain a profit by not pushing adjustable rates. Our competitors are charging as much as 2.5 percent less for adjustable rate loans, compared to our 1.75 percent difference. And they're not getting rid of any risk. Many of those loans have such steep interest buy-downs from the builders that monthly payments will double in a couple of years. Default rates will skyrocket when that happens. Our approach creates no more risk, and greatly improves our competitive position. We owe our growth and profit to this strategy."

EXHIBIT 3:

Current Yield Curve

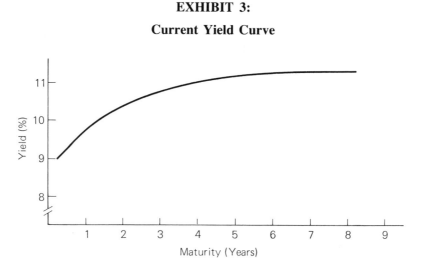

Burke heard Parrish out while trying to be both courteous and noncommital. It was clear to Burke that any suggestions involving a change in loan policy would net him a powerful enemy. The next day, Burke received a memo from Schmitz (exhibit 4) reiterating his concern about the risk of current policy.

QUESTIONS

1. Use ratio analysis to compare Coronet to the industry. Identify Coronet's strengths and weaknesses.

2. Prepare a gap analysis.

3. Recommend policy.

EXHIBIT 4:

Memo

TO: John Burke, Treasurer

FROM: Robert Schmitz, Controller

TOPIC: Asset and Liability Maturity

After yesterday's meeting, I am certain you will be needing information about the maturity structure of our assets and liabilities. I have been keeping track of that situation, as the summary below illustrates.

Maturity Schedule
(in $ millions)

Maturity[a]	Investments	Loans	Deposits	Borrowed Funds
Less than 6 mo.	78	53	602[b]	236
6 mo.–1 year	53	53	503	62
1 year–2 years	48	100	166	
2 years–3 years	16	105	89	32
3 years–4 years	2	112	53	21
Over 4 years		1,249	63	
Total	197	1,672[c]	1,476	351

[a]Maturity time for each dollar of principal is the date on which that dollar must be repaid or the rate must be readjusted to market rates.

[b]Including $290 million of passbook deposits and NOW accounts.

[c]Duration equals 8.5 years.

It is obvious that we have a serious mismatch between asset maturity and liability maturity. In my opinion, this spells excessive risk.

As you need additional information, just let me know.

Case 13

Western Savings and Loan

Western Savings and Loan's 30 June 1982 balance sheet showed a net worth of $534,000, a decline of almost $32 million in one year. By the end of 1982, Western's net worth had declined to minus $22.5 million, and the Federal Home Loan Bank Board (FHLBB) declared Western insolvent. The company was reorganized and operated under the direction of a CEO appointed by the FHLBB.

Of course, the FHLBB did not intend to run the company indefinitely; it began seeking a buyer. In the past, the only choices would have been rescuing Western through an infusion of capital from the FSLIC, merging Western with another savings and loan, or liquidation. However, the Garn—St Germain Act, passed in 1982, provided a new option. The act allowed interindustry acquisitions in times of emergency. Thus, the FHLBB was able to accept bids for Western from a variety of financial institutions.

The FHLBB began accepting bids in early 1983. In the past, the value of an insolvent savings and loan had generally been negative. Because of this negative value and to induce profitable savings and loans to bid for failed ones, the

This case was prepared by Neil E. Seitz, Department of Finance, Saint Louis University.

Federal Savings and Loan Insurance Corporation (FSLIC) would sometimes purchase poor quality or low earning assets at par from the failed institution. Thus the bidding process revolved on the question of which assets the FSLIC would have to acquire at par prior to the merger. However, in the case of western, regulators hoped that enough financial institutions would be interested in entering the market to avoid or to at least minimize such losses. Of course, the successful bidder would be required to provide a capital infusion to return Western to a reasonable level of solvency.

One of the companies considering a bid was FirstAmerica, one of the largest bank holding companies in the United States. Although FirstAmerica had traditionally concentrated on commercial banking, several years ago it had begun an aggressive expansion into consumer banking. FirstAmerica presently owned insurance companies, consumer finance companies, credit card companies, and two savings and loans that had been acquired under provisions set forth within the Garn—St Germain Act. FirstAmerica's managers wanted to expand further in the savings and loan business, and they were aware that Garn—St. Germain might provide only a temporary window. Thus, they were eager to move quickly. In addition, Western would provide statewide access in an important growth market. Offsetting these advantages was the fact that Western had been described as a "mess."

Western's headquarters were located in the largest city of a sunbelt state. The company had thirty-four branches located throughout the state. The warm, dry climate was popular with retired people, and this had resulted in rapid population growth. Not only retirees but also younger people were attracted by the climate and by the economic opportunities as well. The economic opportunities stemmed from the service needs of retirees and from the relocations by several high-tech companies which were attempting to increase their appeal to technically trained people. The population growth was expected to continue as energy problems recurred and as the population continued to age. Total deposits in financial institutions in the state were expected to grow at approximately 8 percent to 10 percent per year.

Because statewide branching of savings and loans was allowed, the market tended to be dominated by a few large competitors. Although there were over 100 savings and loans in existence in the state, Western was the fifth largest; it held 15 percent of all savings and loan deposits in the state. In comparison, branching by banks was severely restricted which gave savings and loans a strong competitive edge in the state.

Western had been founded as a mutual association in 1952. The company remained under the management of its founder, George Green, until the take-over by the FHLBB. Green had watched the institution grow to $1.98 billion in assets. He had also converted the company from mutual to stock form. Although the company experienced minor problems in 1966 and 1975–1976, it continued to maintain an impressive growth rate through most of the 1970s.

The late 1970s and early 1980s found Western, like many other savings and loans, without a strategy for dealing with rising and unstable interest rates. While all savings and loans suffered from imbalance of maturities between assets and liabilities, Western's problems were worse. Western's asset maturity was toward the long end of the savings and loan spectrum; its liability

structure was a little shorter than average. In addition, the recession slowed growth sharply which reduced the opportunity to increase the average interest rate on loans by making new loans. One analyst estimated that Western's loan portfolio would be worth $138 million less than book value if the stream of payments was discounted at current interest rates.

Western's response was too little and too late. In 1981, the company began a policy of making primarily adjustable rate mortgages (ARMs) and variable rate mortgages (VRMs). The policy was introduced at a time when demand for housing loans was going slack anyway. Thus, the volume of these loans was fairly small. By 30 June 1982, these loans accounted for only 9 percent of the loan portfolio. Furthermore, they had not helped the company up to this point. Interest rates rose only slightly after the policy was introduced and declined thereafter. Western also entered consumer lending, but second-mortgage loans were only $35 million and consumer loans were only $16 million.

Although the published financial statements looked bad, FirstAmerica's analysis showed the situation to be even worse. Analysis of various investments showed that these items were being carried at book values which were $54.5 million over market value. In addition, Western did not have an adequate reserve for loan losses. Using standards normally applied by FirstAmerica, an additional $2.25 million in reserves for loan losses was needed.

Offsetting these unfavorable factors was FirstAmerica's strategy of expanding into a nationwide consumer banking operation and the opportunity to acquire a franchise as well as statewide offices. Management was certain that FirstAmerica's ownership would restore public confidence in Western and that FirstAmerica could provide the necessary management.

The question of how to set a price was particularly difficult in this case. Price is frequently based on a multiple of the book value of equity. But it was hard to use this approach when book value was negative. In addition, there was the fact that a franchise was for sale and several other financial institutions, like FirstAmerica, were eager to gain footholds in as many consumer banking markets as possible.

QUESTIONS

1. Evaluate the financial statements of Western. What are the company's financial strengths and weaknesses?

2. On the basis of past financial data when did a problem first become evident?

3. How much new capital would be needed to give Western a stable financial picture in keeping with the evaluations of rating services such as Standard and Poors?

4. Prepare an offer, remembering that you are bidding against other companies that want this company.

5. Suppose Western were acquired by First-America and you were appointed CEO. What policies would you implement?

EXHIBIT 1:

Western Savings and Loan Selected Financial Data

(Thousands Omitted Except per Share)	Year Ended 30 June				
	1982	1981	1980	1979	1978
Income:					
Interest on loans	$ 181,616	$ 145,972	$ 103,988	$ 72,145	$ 52,125
Loan points and earned discounts	6,066	7,417	4,048	2,382	1,422
Commitment fees	6,922	8,206	5,717	2,584	2,823
Interest on investments	18,177	17,011	15,327	10,444	3,743
Other	5,470	513	275	190	153
Total income	218,251	179,119	129,355	87,745	60,266
Expenses:					
Interest on savings	203,230	155,675	102,359	61,945	40,789
Interest on borrowings	25,635	10,172	7,544	5,947	2,899
Operational and administrative	27,087	23,784	17,824	11,267	9,129
Total expenses	255,952	189,631	127,727	79,159	52,817
Income (loss) before income taxes	(37,701)	(10,512)	1,628	8,586	7,449
Income taxes (credit)	(5,823)	(3,654)	256	2,585	2,394
Net income (loss)	$ (31,878)	$ (6,858)	$ 1,372	$ 6,001	$ 5,055
Selected balance sheet items:					
Total assets	$1,852,078	$1,784,267	$1,431,924	$1,100,522	$831,828
Loans receivable, net	1,716,647	1,593,930	1,286,972	942,671	744,960
New loans	177,140	380,028	408,894	286,306	318,977
Total savings	1,540,880	1,588,926	1,318,172	979,237	698,970
Savings increase (decrease)	(48,046)	270,754	338,935	280,267	193,720
Borrowed funds	283,837	141,315	45,368	59,236	84,691
Stockholders' equity	534	32,412	39,837	39,814	34,501
Number of shares outstanding	1,875	1,875	1,861	1,234	1,203
Book value per share	$ 0.28	$ 17.29	$ 21.40	$ 21.51	$ 19.13
Earnings (loss) per share	(17.00)	(3.67)	0.73	3.23	2.81
Dividends per share	—	0.40	0.80	0.70	0.55
Yields earned and rates paid					
Yield on loans	10.96%	10.17%	9.33%	8.67%	8.45%
Yield on investments	15.82	15.44	13.58	10.31	6.79
Combined weighted yields earned	11.25	10.52	9.70	8.84	8.32
Rate paid on savings	12.59	10.70	9.03	7.40	6.67
Rate paid on borrowings	14.66	14.22	11.62	8.58	7.10
Combined weighted rates paid	12.79	10.86	9.17	7.49	6.69

EXHIBIT 2:

Unaudited Consolidated Statements of Income

	Six Months Ended 31 December	
	1982	*1981*
Income		
Interest on loans	$ 96,391,000	$ 87,886,000
Interest and dividends on investments	4,631,000	10,460,000
Loan points and earned discounts on loans purchased	1,937,000	3,428,000
Commitment fee income	628,000	5,449,000
Other income	894,000	860,000
Total income	104,481,000	108,083,000
Expenses		
Interest expense:		
Interest on savings accounts	93,450,000	103,926,000
Interest on borrowings	19,303,000	9,405,000
Total	112,753,000	113,331,000
Operational and administrative expenses:		
Compensation	6,391,000	5,366,000
Occupancy	4,027,000	3,556,000
Advertising	1,997,000	2,763,000
Other	2,364,000	1,800,000
Total	14,779,000	13,485,000
Total interest, operational and administrative expenses	127,532,000	126,816,000
Loss before income taxes	(23,051,000)	(18,733,000)
Income tax credit		(3,414,000)
Net loss	$(23,051,000)	$(15,319,000)
Loss per common share (note A)	$(12.30)	$(8.17)
Weighted average shares	1,874,629	1,874,629

EXHIBIT 3:

Statements of Consolidated Financial Condition

Assets	31 December 1982 (Unaudited)	30 June 1982
Cash	$ 16,045,000	$ 7,269,000
Investments:		
Time deposits and certificates of deposit	3,310,000	5,310,000
Federal funds	61,925,000	56,556,000
Total investments	65,235,000	61,866,000
Accrued interest receivable	19,407,000	21,499,000
Income tax refund receivable	1,404,000	1,835,000
Loans receivable:		
Total loans	1,760,642,000	1,725,823,000
Less: deferred points and fees	(2,991,000)	(3,393,000)
deferred discounts on mortgage loans purchased	(1,441,000)	(1,717,000)
unearned interest on consumer loans	(12,939,000)	(4,066,000)
Net loans receivable	1,743,271,000	1,716,647,000
Office properties and equipment	10,364,000	10,615,000
Federal Home Loan Bank stock—at cost	16,459,000	16,459,000
Real estate held for development and sale	5,431,000	5,151,000
Other assets	12,400,000	10,737,000
Total	$1,890,016,000	$1,852,078,000

Liabilities, Deferred Income and Stockholders' Equity		
Savings accounts:		
NOW accounts	$ 11,420,000	$ 7,931,000
Passbook accounts	99,073,000	105,979,000
Certificate accounts	1,616,622,000	1,426,970,000
Total savings accounts	1,727,115,000	1,540,880,000
Advances from the Federal Home Loan Bank	105,250,000	239,500,000
Securities sold under agreements to repurchase	28,455,000	11,860,000
Mortgage-backed bond	42,000,000	42,000,000
Note payable	477,000	477,000
Accrued interest payable on borrowings	2,059,000	1,886,000
Undisbursed portion of loans in process	197,000	1,230,000
Advances by borrowers for taxes and insurance	3,475,000	9,696,000
Other liabilities	2,824,000	2,788,000
Deferred income tax payable	195,000	195,000
Total liabilities	1,912,047,000	1,850,512,000
Deferred commitment fee income	486,000	1,032,000
Stockholders' Equity:		
Preferred stock, $0.01 par value; authorized 4,000,000 shares; outstanding, none		
Common stock, $0.01 par value; authorized 5.000,000 shares; outstanding 1,874,629	19,000	19,000
Paid-in capital in excess of par value	14,845,000	14,845,000
Deficit	(37,381,000)	(14,330,000)
Total stockholders' equity	(22,517,000)	534,000
Total	$1,890,016,000	$1,852,078,000

EXHIBIT 4:

Industry Average Ratios for Savings and Loans

Year	1978	1979	1980	1981	1982
Total assets (TA)	471446	530310	583348	626475	668125
Investments/TA	8.73	8.43	8.73	9.41	10.82
Loans/TA	82.45	82.07	80.66	82.81	82.91
Deposits/TA	85.01	83.25	82.46	81.09	80.03
Borrowed funds/TA	7.35	9.07	10.06	12.00	13.70
Net worth/TA	5.61	5.68	5.54	4.83	4.00
Int & fee inc/loans & inv.	9.45	10.13	10.77	11.28	11.00
Int & fee inc/TA	8.61	9.17	9.63	10.40	10.31
Cost of deposits	6.50	7.29	8.66	10.65	10.96
Cost of borr. funds	7.70	8.94	9.88	12.26	12.74
Cost dep and borr. funds	6.59	7.45	8.79	10.86	11.22
Operating expense/TA	1.31	1.34	1.36	1.43	1.51
Other income/TA	0.00	0.02	0.07	0.15	0.84
ROTA (net income/TA)	0.83	0.68	0.13	−0.74	−0.64
Return on equity	14.82	12.01	2.42	−15.37	−15.99

Note: Ratios involving balance sheet items are income or expense for the year to the average balance sheet value for the year.

Case 14

Warren Federal Savings and Loan Association

In February 1977, Marion Lyman, president of Warren Federal Savings and Loan Association, was preparing a report for the Association's board of director's meeting. At the last meeting the board had discussed several economic forecasts for 1977 and the forecasts' implications for the association. The economic forecasts predicted rising interest rates for 1977 beginning in the spring, if not earlier, with one exception—mortgage rates. These were expected to continue in a mild decline for quite a while. The forecasts were also quite bullish for housing. The economic reports were predicting a 15 to 20 percent increase in new housing starts in 1977, coming after a 33 percent increase in 1976. After the discussion of the economic reports, the meeting had adjourned with a request that Mr. Lyman recommend possible courses of action available to the Association in light of these forecasts and the Association's financial resources.

HISTORY OF WARREN FEDERAL

Warren Federal was founded in Bowling Green, Kentucky in 1961 by Richard Hawes, a local real estate broker and builder, and several of his business associates and close friends. Since there was only one other savings and loan association in the city, the association grew quite rapidly from its inception until 1970, paralleling the growth of Bowling Green. By 1970, the total assets of the association were $19 million. From 1970 until 1976 the growth of the association slowed considerably but continued with total assets reaching $27 million in 1976 (exhibit 1).

The association has its headquarters approximately three blocks from downtown Bowling Green in a new modern building with ample parking facilities. The new building was erected in 1972 after the association's initial building proved to be too small. The association maintains one branch in the downtown area of Bowling Green. This branch, located in a remodeled storefront, was started in 1975 as a service for

This case was prepared by Harold D. Fletcher, Booz, Allen & Hamilton, Inc., William W. McCartney, University of Central Florida, and Philip M. Van Auken, Baylor University, as a basis for class discussion rather than to illustrate either effective or ineffective handling of an administrative situation.

the association's downtown customers. Although the branch's performance proved to be disappointing, it was continued for public relations purposes. Its location between the two largest financial institutions in the city was thought to enhance the visibility and prestige of Warren Federal.

THE COMMUNITY

Bowling Green, Kentucky, the fifth largest city in the state of Kentucky, is a growing city with a greater metropolitan population of approximately 70,000 people. The city is also the county seat of Warren County. There are no other major urban areas in Warren County, the remaining incorporated areas being small farming villages. The city has grown quite rapidly in recent years. Since the 1960 census the average rate of population growth has been between 2.5 to 3 percent per annum. The projected population figure for the early 1980s is approximately 100,000 people.

The economy of Bowling Green is diverse. The city and the county area adjacent to the city are the homes of a number of manufacturing and assembly facilities producing such products as chemicals, fertilizers, air conditioning equipment, automotive parts, textiles, clothing, and heavy equipment. The city is also the home of a state university with a student enrollment of 13,000.

The economy has expanded at a rapid rate since the early 1960s. Before 1960, Bowling Green was a typical, small, sleepy southern town with very little manufacturing except some textiles and clothing manufacturing. Beginning in the early 1960s, the city (with the judicious use of municipal bond financing) was able to persuade several disgruntled northern companies to locate plants in the area. Initial successes by these plants provided the encouragement for additional companies to relocate in the Bowling Green area. Also during this period, the university increased enrollments and expanded its facilities. Enrollments rose from approximately

5,000 students in 1960 to approximately 13,000 students in 1976.

The combination of increasing population, growing industry, and an expanding university created problems for the city of Bowling Green. Rapid growth fostered the development of several new suburban neighborhoods and shopping centers. However, the city street system and city services such as sewage, water, and fire protection were not expanded to meet the growing needs. The school systems, city and county also have felt the effects of this growth. The county schools in particular did not have the resources to meet increased enrollment.

Given these increased service demands, the city and county tax base was forced upward in the face of taxpayer opposition. These increased taxes raised the costs of doing business in Bowling Green, obviously lessening some of the previous advantages of locating and living in Bowling Green.

In recent years additional problems developed. While demands for increased city services continued, the city faced increased competition from other cities for new plant locations. The rush of new plants to Bowling Green slowed considerably in mid 1970s, leaving the city no choice but to extract higher taxes from existing plants instead of obtaining new taxes from new plants.

Another concern for the city was the decline of the downtown area. The rise of suburban shopping centers with new stores and available parking discouraged downtown shopping. After the closing of several downtown stores, the remaining businesses financed the renovation of the town square, the construction of new sidewalks and benches, and the planting of trees. Parking meters were removed. Unfortunately, the results of the renovation were considerably less than expected. Businesses continued to close and pedesterian traffic continued to decline.

The rapid growth rate of the city has also reduced the "quality of life" in Bowling Green. The cost of housing, the cost of services, and other consumer costs have been forced up to levels found in Louisville, Kentucky's largest city, which is more than ten times the size of Bowling Green. Thus the city has lost some of the appeal and its image of a small town that is a nice place to live. The city is faced with the same complex of urban problems as any other city.

Furthermore, the stabilization of the university enrollments had its effects on the city. The stable student enrollment has resulted in fewer new university employment opportunities, decreased building construction, and less stimulus to the local economy in general.

MANAGEMENT

Warren Federal is headed by Marion Lyman, who is both president and chairman of the board of directors. Lyman, fifty-two-years old, has been with Warren Federal since its inception. He had originally been a partner of Hawes in the real estate business and joined Warren Federal as vice-president at its creation. He became president in 1966 upon Hawes' death. He became chairman of the board of directors in 1968.

The association is operated on a very informal level. In addition to Lyman, the association is managed by Anthony Colt, forty-eight years old, and James Haskell, sixty-one years old. Both Colt and Haskell have been with the association from its creation and now carry titles of vice-president. Colt handles mortgages including all appraisals and other details, while Haskell concentrates on internal operations, including personnel. Haskell, a member of an old-line Bowling Green family, also does considerable public relations and civic work.

The three officers have offices next to each other and all decisions are made through a process of informal consultation. In practice, the three men handle all problems as the problems arise as if there were no separately defined areas of responsibility.

In addition to the three executive officers, the association also employs Bonita Jagers, forty-five years old, in an executive position. Jagers originally joined the association at its creation as a bookkeeper and currently carries the title of treasurer. She works in the areas of accounting and also does considerable work in the mortgage area. As in the case of the other executives, Jagers is a member of the board of directors and participates in all management decisions.

The association also employs twelve other people, primarily as tellers and bookkeepers. The ranks of tellers change fairly rapidly as the tellers leave for better paying jobs or for marriage and family. The tellers were all women until last year when a younger male teller was hired. All record keeping is done with accounting machines since computers are considered too expensive.

The association is governed by a board of directors that includes four officers, Lyman, Colt, and Haskell, and Jagers, and ten local residents. The local members are business and professional people, including an attorney, who is also the legal counsel of the association, a university dean, several local builders, a local real estate broker, a local doctor, several local manufacturers, and Viola Lee Hawes, the founder's widow. The board meets monthly and several members are also members of the Association's loan committee.

OPERATING POLICIES OF WARREN FEDERAL

The association has grown rapidly from its organization in 1961 until 1970 when its assets reached $19 million. Since 1970 the growth has been far less spectacular. During 1969 and 1970, the association suffered from the effects of tight money, recession, and severe savings competition from local financial institutions. The association found that while loan demand continued at high levels because of the momentum of the local economy, the influx of savings ceased as savers placed their funds in higher yielding financial instruments. This problem of strong loan demand and slow growth of savings continued to plague the association throughout the 1970s. The association raised saving rates in 1973 when allowable, but this did little to alleviate the problem since other institutions raised their rates also. By 1976, the assets had reached $26 million, but the problem of differential rates of growth of loan demand and savings was still unresolved (exhibits 1, 4, and 5).

Beginning with Richard Hawes' tenure as president, the association has sought growth within a simple framework. It had been his opinion that a savings and loan association had one simple objective: to gather the savings of many small savers and to promise them the utmost safety through lending their savings to build homes. This objective was reinforced when Lyman became president and coined the Association's motto, "Save safely and help build the community." These twin concepts of safety and home building have continued to dominate the asset and liability management policies of the association in recent years.

The asset portfolio reflected this philosophy of safety and home building by emphasizing single family mortgages and the purchase of FHA and VA guaranteed mortgages. The association did not actively seek any kind of mortgage other than mortgages on single-family dwellings. The officers preferred not to make apartment building loans, unless for an old customer, because they felt that apartment lending was riskier than home mortgages. The government-guaranteed mortgages, which were purchased from outside of the area, were maintained for reasons of safety. Although the yields on these guaranteed mortgages were below conventional rates, the association felt that the increased safety obtained was worth the price. It was the association's policy to hold all mortgages obtained by either lending or purchasing until maturity (exhibit 3).

It was felt that the savings and loan business involved long-term lending and therefore a savings and loan association should not move in and out of various types of assets like a commercial bank. Its function was to lend for home building, not to make short-term loans like a bank. The association therefore did not seek some of the newer types of loans made by other savings and loan associations. It did not make mobile home loans, and kept a tight hold on short-term construction loans and other types of nonmortgage loans.

The association set mortgage rates at as low a level as possible in order to make single homes affordable to as many people as possible. In theory, the mortgage rates were set to yield a high enough return to pay adequate dividends, cover costs, and increase reserves without excess profits. In recent years, the association's mortgage rate was approximately 0.25 percent to 0.5 percent below that of its competitor. In addition, the association did not force borrowers to pay property taxes monthly into escrow accounts. Thus the association's rate-setting policies did not yield any significant increase in profits to build reserves. Almost all profits were paid to savers in the form of dividends (exhibit 2).

The association's liability management policy was also structured around the concepts of safety and home building. The association sought savings from a variety of savers, but concentrated its efforts on the passbook type of saver. The association paid competitive rates on passbook savings although it tended to lag behind other institutions in raising its saving rates. The officers felt that savings rates should be raised when prudently possible and when the higher rates could be maintained. Rates should not reflect up and down variations in the financial markets. The longer term and more costly savings certificates were not aggressively sought by the association. These sources of funds were considered to be too expensive and too volatile. Therefore, the liability policy concentrates on the small saver. The association has no well-defined marketing or advertising strategy to support its liability management policies other than to run advertising in the local newspaper periodically.

PROBLEMS CONFRONTING WARREN FEDERAL

As a first step in making recommendations to the board, Lyman outlined the major problems the Association faced. After discussion with Haskell, Colt, and Jagers, the following concerns were identified as requiring immediate action. These included:

1. *Increased Competition.* Warren Federal faces considerable competition from the other financial institutions in Bowling Green. The major competition is from the three commercial banks, $100 million, $90 million, and $50 million in total assets, respectively, and the other savings and loan association which has assets of $95 million. The commercial banks in particular have been very aggressive in seeking the small saver. The smallest commercial bank has just recently instituted an ''Insta-Teller'' service in which funds are automatically transferred from the customer's saving account to his checking account by phone. The larger banks will in all likelihood offer this service during 1977 also. The savings and loan competitor has begun a new advertising campaign on local radio and television stressing its higher rates on longer term saving certificates.

2. *Increasing Savings Inflow.* The economic forecasts predict a high level of housing starts, implying greater mortgage loan demands for the Association. This demand can be met only if savings inflow increases. Yet, if interest rates increase as predicted, savings will leave the Association because of disintermediation. The total number of savers at the Association has declined from 6,580 savers with an average account balance of $3,052 in 1975 to 6,420 savers with an average account balance of $3,200 in 1976. The January 1977, cash flow (exhibit 6) emphasizes the problem of both high savings withdrawals and high mortgage loans as reflected in changes in cash. If the remaining forecasts of cash flow are also wrong, major revisions in management policies will be necessary. The slower growth trend in saving deposits presents a major area of concern.

3. *Increasing the Profitability of the Association.* The association's profitability has proven to be disappointing in recent years. Operating expenses and interest on borrowed money are considered to be too high (exhibit 2). The additions to net worth (exhibit 2) have not increased in proportion to other balance sheet items. This does not meet the safety objective of the association. Without profits, dividends to savers cannot be maintained at a high enough level to attract savers.

With these three specific problem areas in mind, Lyman is considering potential courses of action. Lyman believes the Association must continue to emphasize safety and home building while attracting increasing savings and improving investment performance. These goals must be implemented in the face of changing economic activity and discrepant community needs.

QUESTIONS

1. Compare the financial statements of Warren Federal with the industry data. What are the significant differences?

2. Describe the organization structure of Warren Federal.

3. Discuss the imbalance between Warren Federal's maturity structure of its assets and liabilities. How does this imbalance weaken its ability to compete with other financial intermediaries in times of rising interest rates?

4. Discuss the relative merits of Warren Federal's policy of holding conventional and VA and FHA mortgages from the point of safety and profitability.

5. Suggest some changes in Warren Federal's asset and liability structure that might strengthen its competitive position in relation to other financial institutions.

6. Evaluate Lyman's motto ''Save safely and help build the community.'' Can a better motto be suggested? Can any of Warren Federal's problem be associated with the goals of Warren Federal as expressed by Lyman?

7. What courses of action for 1977 should Lyman recommend to the board of directors?

EXHIBIT 1:
Warren Federal Savings and Loan Association
Statement of Condition (31 December of Each Year)
(in $ thousands)

	1970	1971	1972	1973	1974	1975	1976
Assets							
Mortgage Loans	$16,631	$17,784	$18,237	$19,942	$20,765	$21,876	$22,612
Loans on Savings	113	117	116	117	121	122	124
Other Loans	40	42	51	61	75	42	54
Investments and Securities	1,943	2,018	2,761	2,451	2,614	2,941	3,198
Cash on Hand and in Bank	577	672	615	418	782	725	773
Office Building (net)	375	361	384	372	368	371	369
Office Equipment (net)	76	81	91	90	93	97	101
Other Assets	83	92	76	69	78	55	68
Total Assets	$19,838	$21,167	$22,331	$23,520	$24,896	$26,229	$27,299
Liabilities and Net Worth							
Total Savings	$16,562	$17,656	$17,614	$18,652	$19,260	$20,084	$20,547
Borrowed Money	773	891	1,442	1,684	2,487	2,997	3,464
Notes Payable - Office Building	150	150	150	150	150	150	150
Loans in Process	393	412	671	703	738	571	710
Other Liabilities	307	390	713	550	584	660	803
Net Worth	1,653	1,668	1,741	1,781	1,677	1,767	1,626
Total Liabilities and Net Worth	$19,838	$21,167	$22,331	$23,520	$24,896	$26,229	$27,299

EXHIBIT 2:

Warren Federal Savings and Loan Association
Operating Statements (31 December of Each Year)
(in $ thousands)

	1970	1971	1972	1973	1974	1975	1976
Total Operating Income	$1,329	$1,435	$1,570	$1,637	$1,720	$2,136	$2,052
Operating Expense	235	283	302	379	412	464	508
Net Operating Income	$1,094	$1,152	$1,268	$1,258	$1,308	$1,672	$1,544
Interest on Borrowed Money	147	152	211	225	403	435	535
Nonoperating Income (+) or Expense (−)	+18	−18	−12	+6	−10	+12	−9
Income Taxes	35	61	79	82	76	69	73
Net Income After Taxes	$ 930	$ 925	$ 966	$ 957	$ 819	$1,180	$ 932
Dividends Paid Savers	$ 901	$ 910	$ 893	$ 917	$ 923	$1,090	$1,073
Addition to Net Worth	$ 29	$ 15	$ 73	$ 40	$ (104)	$ 90	$ (141)

EXHIBIT 3:

Warren Federal Savings and Loan Association
Analysis of Mortgage Portfolio—31 December 1976
(in $ thousands)

Type of Loan	Principal Amount	Interest Payments Received	Amortization (Payments on Principal)	Loan Pay-Offs (Additonal Repayments in Full)
Purchased:	$ 2,736	$ 164	$102	$160
Over Four Years Old				
Single Family FHA/VA				
Less than Four Years Old	3,618	272	60	38
Others Less than Four Years Old	2,126	162	85	55
Total Purchased	$ 8,480	$ 598	$247	$160
Generated by Association:				
Over Four Years Old	$ 8,660	$ 604	$476	$190
Less than Four Years Old	5,472	504	116	49
Total Locally Generated	$14,132	$1,108	$592	$239
Total Loans	$22,162	$1,706	$839	$399

Yields (Annual Rates)	Per-Cent of Total	Interest Yield	Amortization Rate	Pay-Off Rate
Purchased:				
Over Four Years Old	12.1%	6.01%	3.71%	2.45%
Single Family FHA/VA				
Less than Four Years Old	16.0%	7.52%	1.67%	1.06%
Others Less than Four Years Old	9.4%	7.63%	4.02%	2.61%
Generated by Association:				
Over Four Years Old	38.3%	6.98%	5.50%	2.20%
Less than Four Years Old	24.2%	9.21%	2.13%	0.90%
Total Loans	100.0%	7.54%	3.71%	1.76%

EXHIBIT 4:

Warren Federal Savings and Loan Association
Savings Transactions 1975 and 1976
(in $ thousands)

	Deposits	Dividends Credited	Withdrawals	Net Savings
1975:				
January	$ 229		$ 530	$ (301)
February	209		346	(137)
March	290		45	245
April	205		130	75
May	196		54	142
June	266	$ 548	162	652
July	280		597	(317)
August	219		406	(187)
September	254		392	(138)
October	288		167	121
November	277		171	106
December	216	542	196	563
1975 Total	$2,929	$1,090	$3,195	$ 824
1976:				
January	$ 158		$ 619	$ (461)
February	212		409	(197)
March	179		78	101
April	206		211	(5)
May	239		76	163
June	330	$ 521	173	678
July	168		599	(431)
August	184		387	(203)
September	277		413	(136)
October	439		181	258
November	207		140	67
December	353	552	276	629
1976 Total	$2,952	$1,073	$3,562	$ 463

EXHIBIT 5:

Warren Federal Savings and Loan Association
Loan Transactions 1975 and 1976
(in $ thousands)

	Loans Closed		Purchased		Total Payments (Principal)
	Number	*Value*	*Number*	*Value*	
1975:					
January	2	43	4	115	103
February	1	31	0	0	92
March	3	97	0	0	74
April	4	160	5	127	91
May	5	213	0	0	100
June	7	280	0	0	118
July	6	243	1	28	80
August	4	86	0	0	130
September	3	91	7	168	105
October	2	38	5	174	85
November	2	56	6	197	97
December	1	39	3	103	103
1975 Total	40	$1,377	31	$912	$1,178
1976:					
January	1	36	0	0	137
February	2	78	0	0	83
March	4	127	2	73	92
April	3	91	1	15	108
May	5	163	1	18	113
June	8	251	0	0	170
July	9	376	0	0	94
August	3	98	5	162	73
September	2	47	4	149	81
October	2	54	3	82	95
November	1	38	2	44	83
December	1	43	1	29	109
1976 Total	41	$1,402	19	$572	$1,238

EXHIBIT 6:

Warren Federal Savings and Loan Association
Projected Cash Flow January–June 1971
(in $ thousands)

	January Estimated	January Actual	February	March	April	May	June
Beginning Cash Balance	$773	$630	$541	$516	$1,104	$1,007	$1,087
Receipts:							
Mortgage Loans-Interest and Principal	$250	$238	$250	$250	$250	$250	$250
Loans on Savings-Interest and Principal	2	3	2	2	2	2	2
Other Loans	1	2	1	1	1	1	1
Escrow Account	30	21	30	30	30	30	30
Borrowed Money	100	75	—	250	—	150	—
Other Receipts	5	2	5	5	5	5	5
Net Savings	(300)	(400)	(150)	275	100	150	700
Total Receipts	$ 88	$ (59)	$138	$813	$388	$588	$990
Total Cash Available	$861	$571	$679	$1,332	$1,492	$1,595	$2,077
Disbursements:							
Mortgage Loans	$190	$300	$ 40	$100	$350	$375	$400
Loans on Savings	12	16	12	12	12	12	12
Other Loans	6	8	6	6	6	6	6
Interest on Borrowed Money	60	64	55	60	65	65	60
Escrow Payments	—	9	—	—	—	—	—
Taxes	—	—	—	—	—	60	—
Expenses	50	57	50	50	50	50	50
Other Disbursements	2	3	—	—	2	—	—
Dividends on Deposits	—	—	—	—	—	—	600
Total Disbursements	$320	$457	$163	$228	$485	$508	$1,128
Ending Cash Balance	$541	$114	$516	$1,104	$1,007	$1,087	$949

EXHIBIT 7:

Savings and Loan Association: Selected Assets and Liabilities
(in $ millions, end of period)

	1970	1971	1972	1973	1974	1975	1976
Assets							
Mortgages	$150,331	$174,250	$206,182	$232,104	$249,301	$278,590	$323,130
Cash and Investment Securities	16,526	21,042	24,355	21,027	23,251	30,853	35,660
Other	9,326	10,731	12,590	19,227	22,993	28,790	33,209
Total Assets	$176,183	$206,023	$243,127	$272,358	$295,545	$338,233	$391,999
Liabilities and Net Worth							
Savings Capital	$146,404	$174,197	$206,764	$227,254	$242,974	$285,743	$336,030
Borrowed Money (FHLBB and Other)	10,911	8,992	9,782	17,100	24,780	20,634	19,087
Loans in Process	3,078	5,029	6,029	5,132	3,244	5,128	6,836
Other	3,389	4,213	5,132	6,220	6,105	6,949	8,015
Net Worth	12,401	13,592	15,240	17,108	18,442	19,779	22,031
Total Liabilities and Net Worth	$176,183	$206,023	$243,127	$272,358	$295,545	$338,233	$391,999

(Source: Federal Reserve Bulletin)

EXHIBIT 8:

Operating Statements of All Savings and Loan Associations 1970–75*
(in $ millions)

	1970	1971	1972	1973	1974	1975
Operating Income	$11,039	$13,073	$15,572	$18,692	$21,477	$24,354
Operating Expense	1,967	2,180	2,524	3,026	3,490	4,112
Net Operating Income	$ 9,072	$10,893	$13,048	$15,666	$17,987	$20,242
Interest on Savings Deposits	7,187	8,604	10,266	12,012	14,015	16,460
Interest on Borrowed Money	785	623	493	942	1,731	1,569
Net Income Before Taxes	$ 1,152	$ 1,739	$ 2,378	$ 2,729	$ 2,213	$ 2,145
Taxes	248	448	649	779	681	634
Net Income After Taxes	$ 904	$ 1,291	$ 1,729	$ 1,950	$ 1,532	$ 1,511

Source: Savings and Loan Fact Book, 1976 (Chicago: U.S. League of Savings Associations, 1976).

*Items do not add to totals because of the omission of minor nonoperating income and expense items.

EXHIBIT 9:

**Savings and Loan Associations Maximum Interest Rates
Payable on Time and Savings Deposits—December 1976**

	December 1976		Previous Maximum	
Type and Maturity of Deposit	*%*	*Effective Date*	*%*	*Effective Date*
Savings	5¼	7/6/73	5	1/21/70
Negotiable Order of Withdrawal	5	1/1/74	—	—
90 Days to 1 Year	5¾	7/6/73	5¼	1/21/70
1 to 2 Years	6½	7/6/73	5¾	1/21/70
2 to 2½ Years	6½	7/6/73	6	1/21/70
2½ to 4 Years	6¾	7/6/73	6	1/21/70
4 to 6 Years	7½	11/1/73	None	—
6 Years or More	7¾	12/23/74	7½	11/1/73

(Source: Federal Reserve Bulletin)

EXHIBIT 10:

**Selected Interest Rates—Money and Capital Markets
(Averages, Percent per Annum)**

	1970	*1971*	*1972*	*1973*	*1974*	*1975*	*1976*
Prime Commercial Paper (4 to 6 Months)	7.72	5.11	4.69	8.15	9.87	6.33	5.35
Treasury Bills (3 Months)	6.39	4.33	4.07	7.03	7.84	5.80	4.98
U.S. Treasury Bond (Long-Term)	6.59	5.74	5.63	6.30	6.99	6.98	6.78
State and Local Bonds (Mixed Issues)	6.42	5.62	5.30	5.22	6.17	7.05	6.64
Corporate Bonds (All Industries)	8.51	7.94	7.63	7.80	9.03	9.57	9.01
Conventional Mortgages (FHLB Series)	8.44	7.74	7.60	7.95	8.92	9.01	8.99

(Source: Federal Reserve Bulletin)

Case 15

D.C. Neighborhood Reinvestment Commission

BACKGROUND INFORMATION

The American city has been the hub of industry, commerce, and government, and the center of major cultural activity. The variety of ethnic and racial neighborhoods gave the city its vitality. The city has had a deep and lasting influence over the life of the rest of our country.

Today, many large cities are in deep trouble. They are plagued with high unemployment, a diminishing tax base, increasing crime, greatly reduced commercial activity, high concentration of low- and moderate-income families, middle-class flight to the suburbs, and neighborhood deterioration.

This case was prepared by Edwin L. Carey, Professor of Finance, and Cecil Howard, Associate Professor of Marketing, in the School of Business and Public Administration, Howard University, as a basis for class discussion rather than to illustrate either effective or ineffective handling of an administrative situation.

Copyright 1977 by Professors Edwin Carey and Cecil Howard.

Presented at a Case Workshop and distributed by the Intercollegiate Case Clearing House, Soldiers Field, Boston, Mass. 02163. All rights reserved to the contributors.

One of the major causes of urban decline is private and public disinvestment, popularly known as "redlining." Redlining is a process used by lending institutions to draw imaginary boundaries around neighborhoods considered to be "bad risks" or "bad investment areas." The immediate result is that families and businesses are unable to obtain loans, because of their geographic location. The nonloan decision is based solely on location and is not due to the credit rating of the applicant or the structural soundness of the property.

As disinvestment continues, mortgage and loan funds flow to the suburbs and more affluent city areas; businesses and middle-class residents leave; and, in the inner city, only low- and moderate-income families—particularly minorities and the aged—remain.

Community groups, city administrations, and civil rights groups have organized to fight the pattern of disinvestment. The U.S. Congress passed a Mortgage Disclosure Act which became effective 30 September 1976. The Act requires annual disclosure by federally insured commercial banks, savings and loan associations, and credit unions of all first-mortgages, home-improvement loans, federally insured loans, and home loans to owner-occupants.

WASHINGTON, D.C.

In the 1940s, and especially after World War II, Washington, D.C.'s surrounding suburbs became the target of development activities and subsequently experienced tremendous growth. The city began to experience disinvestment as housing loans became unavailable to "changing" neighborhoods. Without financing, these neighborhoods began to deteriorate; they changed from racially integrated to predominantly black.

During the 1960s, speculators began purchasing homes in areas where federal housing programs were being initiated. The homes were then sold to unsuspecting home-buyers at artificially high prices. Major repairs were often needed and the homeowners, unable to afford both the cost of repairs and the mortgage payments, often were forced to default on the mortgage. Many abandoned and boarded-up homes followed in their wake.

Similar conditions in several cities led to an investigation by a special "Ad Hoc Sub-committee on Home Financing Practices and Procedures." The main target of the sub-committee's inquiry was Washington, D.C. In 1970, one of the recommendations of the subcommittee was directed toward financial institutions.

> The housing needs of this nation will never be met by financing from the private sector so long as the commercial banks of the District and the nation consider that their first and perhaps only responsibility is to make as much money as possible in the shortest amount of time with the least amount of risk, and so long as the savings and loan associations of the District and the nation conclude they have fulfilled their responsibility to promote thrift and home-ownership by placing most of their energy and assets at the service of middle- and higher-income families.[1]

By the early 1970s, a new wave of speculation surfaced in the District of Columbia. Many younger, middle-income families and individuals were returning to the city and willing to pay high prices for older townhouses in low- and moderate-income neighborhoods. The higher cost of transportation, combined with disillusionment with suburban living, motivated many of these families to find more conveniently located housing close to the center of the city.

As revitalization of disinvestment neighborhoods continues, many of the existing low- and moderate-income families are forced to move to less desirable areas.

THE D.C. NEIGHBORHOOD REINVESTMENT COMMISSION

In 1974, the D.C. City Council decided to develop a workable housing reinvestment program to assist moderate-income families. Therefore, the Council created what is now the D.C. Neighborhood Reinvestment Commission (NRC). The Commission is composed of seventeen members:

> The chairpersons of the Council Committees on Employment and Economic Development, Housing and Community Development, and Finance Revenue; two members of the executive branch of the D.C. government; two representatives of the local savings and loan associations (including one minority representative); one local credit union representative; one member of the mortgage banking industry; one representative of the local real estate industry; one representative of the minority business community; two representatives of disinvested neighborhoods; and two public members.

Much of the work activities of the NRC is carried out by the executive director and his staff of three people plus consultants.

In July 1976, the D.C. City Council gave the following mandate to the NRC:

> 1. Develop and implement a survey of the past and current mortgage, rehabilitation, and commercial investment performance of all local commercial banks, savings and loan

---

[1]U.S. Congress, House, Committee on Banking and Currency, *Report and Recommendations of the Ad Hoc Subcommittee on Home Financing Practices and Procedures,* 91st Congress, 2nd session, 1970, p. 1.

associations, mortgage banking firms, credit unions, and life insurance companies.

2.   Survey the past and present employment patterns of local lenders.

3.   Develop an affirmative marketing and employment program.

4.   Help lenders, city and federal goverment agencies, and community groups to develop reinvestment mechanisms and programs.

5.   Work with the D.C. City Council for the enactment of legislation supporting the revitalization of city neighborhoods.

The Commission did a base line survey of all commercial banks and savings and loans (S&Ls) based in the city from 1971 to mid 1975; and a pilot neighborhood study of the total mortgage-lending activity and the relative housing finance demand for 1973 and 1975 in each of the city's 36 neighborhoods.[2]

In this case study it is not possible to present all the findings. Some of the more significant findings and conclusions were:

1.   The banks and S&Ls did a disproportionately high number and dollar amount of loans in those areas of the city with high incomes and low percentage of black population.

2.   Some areas with relatively high affordability of home ownership (affordability was determined by comparing the average 1974 family income with the average mortgage amount reported by banks and S&Ls) plus a high percentage of blacks had lower number and dollar amount of loans than lower affordability areas with low percentage of blacks.

3.   It was possible to rank banks and S&Ls as institutional groups (i.e., total banks compared to total S&Ls), and as individual lenders using a rating system which included such items as average mortgage amounts, average interest rates, average monthly payments, number and dollar amount of loans made to

areas with a high percentage of black population, proportion of mortgage loans made on 1- to 4-unit housing, and other factors available in the data.

4.   There is a large, untapped demand for mortgage loans in areas populated with moderate income earners who meet basic affordability criteria for home-ownership in their area of residence.

THE HOUSING FINANCE PLAN

The NRC proposed a positive-action plan to increase the availability of housing for moderate-income families. The major features of this Housing Finance Plan were:

1.   Local lenders who join the housing finance plan would, in conjunction with the NRC, review, discuss, and where appropriate, revise all housing-loan policies and procedures to conform with actual neighborhood lending "risk."

2.   A new joint lending mechanism would be established through which the local banks and S&Ls would provide home loans to homebuyers traditionally unable to obtain financing from conventional sources. For example, a "mortgage pool" is an aggregation of funds allotted by two or more lenders, and available to borrowers of a specific geographic area of socio-economic level.

3.   A loan review committee, composed of lender representatives and selected commission members, would be established to review complaints from loan applicants and, where a loan rejection is unjustified, to assure placement of the loan.

4.   Local lenders would be asked to participate in neighborhood-based home ownership counseling programs designed to provide a wide range of home-purchase and maintenance services.

5.   Participating lenders would be required to develop and implement a uniform affirmative marketing program to meet the existing

---

[2] *Strategy for Change: Housing Finance in Washington, D.C.*, Commission on Residential Mortgage Investment, Government of the District of Columbia, (January 1977).

and potential home loan demand in the minority community.

6. Local lenders would be required to make mortgage, refinancing, and rehabilitation loans to all qualified homebuyers in every area of the District.

7. Special consideration would be given to all moderate-income home loan applicants, and particularly to those families that have been, or soon will be, displaced because of private or public housing redevelopment.

8. Every prospective homebuyer in the District would have the right to complete a home loan application.

9. Every loan applicant would have the right to receive a copy of the property appraisal report, where the applicant bears the appraisal cost.

10. Local lenders would be required to provide an explanation in writing for the rejection of a home-loan application within thirty days after the lender's receipt of the application, and would guarantee to the applicant the right of appeal to the loan review committee.

A SURVEY OF MORTGAGE LENDING POLICIES AND PRACTICES IN D.C.

Under the mandate from the D.C. City Council, the NRC contracted two consultants to investigate the mortgage lending policies and practices of a representative sample of financial institutions. Interviews were conducted with officers in selected commercial banks, mortgage banks, and savings and loan associations. A by-product of the study was an assessment of the availability of socio-economic and demographic characteristics of loan applicants. The summarized results of that survey are as follows:

Loan Policies Of the three types of financial institutions surveyed, the commercial banks have the most conservative mortgage loan policies. They require the largest down payments

(25 percent) in relation to the property value and lend for shorter periods (twenty–twenty-five years). They seem to experience few delinquency problems and defaults (foreclosures) are rare. These policies and experience indicate the commercial banks expose themselves to very little risk in their mortgage lending activities.

Commercial banks have alternative situations in which to invest funds (commercial loans, bonds, consumer loans) and they may be content to leave the inner city mortgage loan market to those that specialize in mortgages—savings and loan associations and mortgage bankers.

Savings and loan associations (S&Ls) make loans up to 90 percent of property value for periods up to thirty years. Other available data indicate the S&Ls prefer mortgage loans in the more affluent areas in the District.[3]

However, although three of the four surveyed mortgage bankers are not located in the District of Columbia, they seem to provide more mortgage loans in the District than do comparably sized commercial banks or S&Ls located in D.C.

Mortgage bank management aggressively seeks out customers for mortgage loans and seems to be more willing to make inner city loans to higher risk neighborhoods and/or borrowers. The mortgage bank's customers tend to be middle and low-middle income earners and thus the average value of the residential unit tends to be lower than for banks or S&Ls.

Mortgage banks are willing to make larger loans in relation to property value (90 to 95 percent), and lend for longer terms (up to 30 years) than either commercial banks or S&Ls. Thus, the interest yield charged borrowers tends to be higher in the mortgage banks.

All institutions used some ratio of loan to property value to set the limit of the mortgage, and used a ratio of monthly income to monthly payment in determining the basic capability of the borrower. A large flow of mortgage financing to moderate income families would call for more relaxed loan-to-value ratios, and income-to-payment ratios, than are now required by the more conservative financial institutions. Greater

---

[3]Ibid., p. 33.

effort could be made to relate supplementary information about marginal applicants to the risk involved in the specific loan. It may be that an addition of extra charges could compensate for the extra risk. This higher interest rate might be subsidized by government, if it would help produce an increased availability of credit.

Processing of Loan Applications The processing of loan applications in the main office is basically the same in all the surveyed financial institutions. That is, the application information is verified and a credit check is made. If the applicant meets the basic income and credit requirements, a fee-appraisal is made of the property. The final decision on the loan is usually made by two or more officers and the decision is communicated to the applicant in writing.

However, the mortgage banks have branch managers who actively seek borrowers and maintain close contacts with real estate agents. The potential borrower can go through preliminary screening and fill out a loan application in a less formal and institutionalized setting than in the home office. Providing a more relaxed and informal setting for the loan applicant may be a step in meeting (or increasing) the housing finance demands of moderate income families. Also, applications that are initially given an adverse reaction can be more easily reviewed with the loan applicant in an informal setting.

Delinquency and Defaults In comparing the financial institutions, mortgage banks require lower down payments, loan for longer periods, and in general, make loans to those with lower incomes. The mortgage banks also experience higher delinquency rates and more foreclosures. As a consequence, they also stress efficiency in following up on delinquent loans and the provision of financial counseling to borrowers who are experiencing problems.

A housing finance program which aims at increasing loans to moderate-income families must also provide for financial counseling services and efficient handling of delinquency and foreclosure situations—and the cost of providing these services must be covered.

In general, the surveyed financial officers re-

ported marital problems as the number one cause of delinquent loans and defaults.

Data Availability The formal loan applications (both approved and disapproved) are kept by all lending institutions. However, little of the socio-economic and demographic information contained in the applications is available in a form that can be processed by a machine. A study in which sampling techniques are used could set forth a profile of the socio-economic and demographic characteristics of borrowers and rejected applicants. However, it would be a time consuming and costly study to undertake.

Rehabilitation Loans In general, the surveyed financial institutions make rehabilitation loans, primarily to professional rehabers. Servicing these loans and inspecting improvements as rehabilitation progresses adds to the cost and risk involved in these loans.

Institutions which do not make rehabilitation loans may be reluctant to incur the expenses necessary to employ a staff of inspectors and rehab loan specialists. If these institutions could be encouraged to use a pool of qualified, reliable inspectors, more financing of rehab projects could be forthcoming.

Home improvement loans, which are loans to an owner-occupier rather than to a professional rehaber of a whole building, are handled as consumer loans by some financial institutions with monthly payments extending up to seven years. The lender relies on the reputation and creditworthiness of the borrower to see that the work is done and the loan repaid. Thus, lender personnel are not involved in inspection of the premises as work progresses.

Conclusion The risks of inner city lending are greater than the risks of suburban lending. However, many District financial institutions are assuming little or no share of this risk, even though they have both social and legal responsibilities to their community. It should be possible to cooperatively increase the availability of housing financing in the inner city and, at the same time, provide benefits to both the community and to the financial institutions involved.

THE SOCIAL RESPONSIBILITY ISSUE

The managers of D.C. banks and S&Ls subscribe to the general aims of the Housing Finance Plan. However, the Plan's provisions would require significant changes in the mortgage lending policies and procedures within the banks and S&Ls. What alternative courses of action are open for the managers, and what do you recommend?

QUESTIONS

1. How is the term "redlining" defined within the case? How would you define the term?

2. Private financial institutions are obligated to meet the "convenience and needs of the community." Is this obligation consistent with the profit maximization objective?

3. Evaluate the findings and conclusions of the D.C. Neighborhood Reinvestment Commission (NRC) with regard to the commission's base-line survey of lending institutions and the relative housing finance demand.

4. From the point of view of a D.C. lending institution, evaluate the Housing Finance Plan as proposed by the NRC and recommend appropriate responses toward each of the major features of the proposed Housing Finance Plan.

5. What additional steps might the NRC, the city council, and/or the lending community consider in order to achieve the goal of increased financing for housing on behalf of moderate income families?

Case 16

Listerhill Credit Union

Credit unions are state or federally chartered nonprofit cooperative institutions designed primarily to provide credit to members. These financial institutions also provide a place for members to save. Members must have a common bond of some type—they must be employees of a given firm, members of a given profession, or somehow joined by a common activity. Credit unions compete with commercial banks, sales finance companies, personal finance companies, and retailers in making loans to finance purchases. In addition, credit unions compete with banks, savings and loan associations, and other financial organizations in providing a place to save.

The Listerhill Credit Union is located in Sheffield, Alabama and was chartered to serve employees of Reynolds Metals Company. It started in 1953 with assets of $83,407, and a

Copyright © 1978 by Professor Gerald Crawford and Professor William Stewart of the University of North Alabama.

Presented at a Case Workshop and distributed by the Intercollegiate Case Clearing House, Soldiers Field, Boston, Mass. 02163. All rights reserved to the contributors.

membership of 864. Before the credit union was founded, there were several loan companies in the immediate area and it was known that "loan sharking" was taking place. Also, it was not uncommon for Reynolds to receive as many as 100 wage garnishments each week, a problem for employees and for the company. In the early days, Reynolds provided some support of the credit union, usually in the form of personnel and office space. Listerhill soon became self-supporting, but chose to continue serving only the employees of the Reynolds Metals Company.

Steady growth characterized the first eighteen years of operation. A real problem came in 1972 when three local business firms defaulted on a $1.3 million loan from Listerhill. The credit union was forced to borrow $1.5 million to survive. The publicity from this was not favorable. In the following months members withdrew $3.9 million in shares. The credit union did survive, but failed to show new growth in assets and membership until 1975.

At the present time (mid 1976) Listerhill has almost 9000 employee accounts and an additional 2000 family accounts. The principal membership represents 85 to 90 percent of the local Reynolds Metals workforce. In terms of deposit balances, or shares, Listerhill has almost $11 million in various accounts. Of course, some share accounts are more active than others (exhibit 1).

In addition to deposit balances, Listerhill has almost 3500 loans outstanding among members. The average loan balance is approximately $3300. Most loans are made for automobiles (48 percent), real estate (10 percent), furniture and appliances (2.6 percent), signature loans (8.7 percent), and two party "cosigner" loans. Following the financial crisis in 1972, loan policies were revised and strengthened to minimize losses from default.

Listerhill communicates directly with its members in a quarterly newsletter. In addition, a small advertising budget is used to promote the credit union. These funds are traditionally spent on radio advertising, matchbooks, and small birthday gifts for members. The advertising messages used have varied, but usually center on making nonmembers aware of the credit union. There is a general feeling that the best way to recruit members is through present members at the plant level. This seems to have been effective in the past, based on the 85 to 90 percent participation rate among Reynolds employees.

The credit union is considered a nonprofit organization. Net earnings are paid to members in the form of dividends or reinvestment in the business. The two main services offered by the credit union are thought to be a) a place to save, and b) a place to borrow. Other services offered include safety deposit boxes, free travel checks, free notary service, payroll deduction plans, drive-up windows, insurance services, financial counseling, meeting rooms for various groups, and vacation information.

Al Williams has been the manager of Listerhill Credit Union since 1972. Prior to becoming manager, he served as assistant manager for five years. He is presently thirty-eight years old, holds a college degree in business, and is considered to be an excellent administrator. His acknowledged strengths are in the general management and computer applications area. Williams reports directly to a nine-member board of directors. Each director is a member of the credit

union and is elected by the general membership at an annual meeting. The directors represent a reasonably wide range of backgrounds and skills. Most of them, however, work as hourly or salaried employees at the Reynolds plant. The manager has developed good rapport with the directors and with his twenty-seven-member staff.

There are eight banks, each with several branches, three savings and loan associations, several finance companies, and other credit unions located in the quad-cities area of North Alabama. The metropolitan area comprised of Florence, Sheffield, Tuscumbia, and Muscle Shoals has a population of 117,000. There are a large number of plants in the area, most are heavy industry—aluminum, chemicals, paper, and textiles. Most of the plants in the area are unionized and there is generally a prounion attitude among employees.

Listerhill has managed to grow and prosper over the years. While the credit union does not compete directly with many other types of financial institutions, it has managed to carve out a loyal and supportive market segment. It is felt that several factors have provided the basis for this stability and growth: the "common bond" among credit union members, the payroll deduction plans, convenient location, reasonable dividends on deposits, and reasonable interest rates paid on savings. Listerhill has usually paid around 5 percent based on the dividends declared by the board of directors. Recently, banks and savings and loan associations have begun offering a wide array of savings plans and certificates of deposit bearing different rates of interest. These various savings plans pay from 4 to 7.5 percent interest depending on variable dates of maturity. The board of directors at Listerhill has not favored the use of variable interest plans because this seems to conflict with basic union philosophy—"equal treatment for all."

Williams is now starting to develop plans for 1977. He is a progressive individual and feels that Listerhill needs to develop new and better programs to better serve the membership. But change comes slowly and sometimes Williams becomes a little discouraged when he recognizes that the credit union is a nonprofit organization. Success is not measured in profits. Also, he recognizes that the membership is very large—85 to 90 percent of the Reynolds workforce—that does not leave much room for growth.

After some thought, Williams decided that Listerhill could benefit from the development of a better marketing program. Since he does not have the time and experience needed to handle the total marketing area, he has decided that an additional staff member with a marketing background could be a valuable addition. Several candidates for this position were subsequently interviewed. If *you* were the one selected to fill the new marketing position, what action would you take?

QUESTIONS

1. Identify the major problems faced by Williams in his role as manager of Listerhill Credit Union.

2. Develop a list of performance measures by which the credit union management could be evaluated.

3. Outline a management strategy that you believe would be appropriate for the Listerhill Credit Union.

EXHIBIT 1:

Share Account Activity

Share Account Balances ($)	Number of Accounts	Percent of Total Accounts	Percent of Total Shares
*Not prime accounts	1,015	9.22	.66
0 to 10.	1,262	11.45	.05
11. to 25.	1,086	9.85	.08
26. to 100.	1,129	10.25	.54
101. to 250.	1,533	13.91	2.56
251. to 500.	1,133	10.28	4.12
501. to 1000.	1,134	10.30	8.20
1001. to 2000.	1,117	10.14	16.05
2001. to 5000.	1,253	11.38	36.60
5001. to 10,000.	268	2.44	17.95
10,001. and up	85	.78	13.19
Totals	11,015	100.00	100.00

*Secondary accounts that show little activity and generally have small balances.

Case 17

Benneteil Life Insurance Company

Chief financial officer of Benneteil Life Insurance Company, Fred Lawrence had recently learned of the relaxation of regulations barring the insurance industry from the financial futures market. Consequently, he called a meeting of his associates to evaluate the implications of this new development for his company.

Treasurer Neil Rauch indicated during the meeting that he anticipated a sharp increase in interest rates within the next six months. He felt that he could prevent a major loss in the value of the company bond portfolio by selling government bond futures to be delivered in six months. This arrangement is called a short hedge, hedging a cash position with a short futures position. As a result, no matter what happens to interest rates, the losses in one market will be offset with gains in the other market.

Finance committee member David Bauer, who had been with the legal department for the last twenty-five years, raised some questions about the appropriateness of financial futures for an insurance company:

Bauer: The insurance industry enjoys the confidence and trust of the public because of a

This case was prepared by Shahriar Khaksari, Department of Finance, Cleveland State University

long history of cautious and conservative investment management. This reputation should not be lost to the dangerous practice of betting on future interest rates. Furthermore, there are some other hedging techniques that might be used to eliminate interest rate risk, such as repo financing. If the treasurer wants to insure certain rates of return on a $1 million premium to be received three months from now, it is a simple matter to buy six-month T-bills and immediately sell them to a buyer with an agreement to buy them back three months later at a specific price which provides a fixed rate of return.

Laura Smyth, who recently finished her M.B.A. program and had just completed a three-day seminar about futures, was a strong advocate of financial futures:

Smyth: For us, financial futures are not a form of speculation. Failure to take advantage of the financial futures market to hedge would be a form of speculation because financial futures eliminate bets on future interest rates. We are talking about using the futures market to do things like reduce price fluctuation risk associated with bonds. Many of our trades will be with speculators. They will be assuming our risk. On the topic of repo financing, the repo market is simply no substitute for financial futures. The futures market, with its quarterly intervals, provides speculating and hedging opportunities for a period of up to two and a half years. This period is longer than repo financing. Moreover, the futures market provides convenience, flexibility, and liquidity along with readily available price quotations and lower transactions costs.

Noble: (an M.B.A. who had served on the investment committee for the last two years) The reduction of risk through financial futures might be more valuable to insurance companies than to other financial institutions. First, the ability of insurance companies to fully diversify away the unsystematic risk in their portfolios is retarded by a very restrictive set of regulations. Second, their operation is very sensitive to systematic sources of risk such as inflation and interest rates that are viewed as a principal element behind most types of loss bearing by insurance companies (e.g., excessive claim losses, sales declines, losses in investment portfolio value, policy loans, and cancellations).

Lawrence thought that financial futures could be a useful tool. However, he was also aware of banks that had experienced considerable difficulties when traders got out of hand in the currency futures markets. He wanted to be sure that a sound policy and careful controls preceded an entry into the financial futures market. For purposes of further study, he asked Smyth to prepare examples of several possible hedging strategies for the next meeting.

After talking with Rauch and with the chief economist, Ms. Smyth concluded that interest rates would go up significantly during the next six months and then level off. On the basis of this prediction, she considered three major components of the company's portfolio.

GMNA Portfolio

Benneteil had $100 million face value of GMNA CDRs, half with 14 percent coupon rates and half with 12 percent coupon rates. The 12 percent certificates were selling at par while the 14 percent certificates were selling 111 percent of face value.

Corporate Bonds

Corporate bonds contained in the company's portfolio consisted of a well diversified mixture of high-grade bonds with a face value of $4.2 billion and a book value of $4 billion. Since futures contracts in corporate bonds did not exist, a cross hedge would be required. Smyth had estimated that the price sensitivity of six-month future delivery treasury bonds (as a percent of their face value) was 0.9 of that of corporate bonds.

Policy Loans

Historically, policy owners exercise their right to low-interest policy loans as interest rates rise, and pay off these loans as interest rates fall. In light of the predicted increase in interest rates, not only the market value of the present outstanding amount of loans would decline, but there also would be an increase in the total amount of policy loans. To meet increased policy loan demand, it would be necessary to sell securities earning a high rate of interest and then loan out these funds at the 5 percent loan interest rate specified in the policies.

On the basis of past experience, policy loans were expected to increase $108 million over the next six months. Since this increase would take place gradually, Smyth decided to sell the following Treasury bill contracts.

Time	Estimated Cumulative Increase in Policy Loans	Futures Contract to Be Purchased Today
Next 3 months	$54 million	
3–6 months	$108 million	108 3 month contracts
6–9 months	$108 million	108 6 month contracts
9–12 months	$54 million	54 9 month contracts

QUESTIONS

1. Design an appropriate hedge contract for the GNMA portfolio.

2. Design an appropriate cross hedge for the corporate bond portfolio.

3. Evaluate the proposed hedge contracts for policy loans. Would these contracts provide a good hedge? Can you suggest a better hedge?

4. If Benneteil enters the financial futures market, what policy guidelines would you recommend?

5. Would you recommend financial futures trading for Benneteil?

Case 18

Old Reliable Life Assurance Society

In July 1974, Hayden Roberts, an actuarial trainee for the Old Reliable Life Assurance Society, became keenly interested in the effect that increasing short-term interest rates might have on the company's near and intermediate-term asset structure, earnings rate, and underwriting portfolio. With the prime rate hovering in the 8.5 to 11.75 percent range for the two preceding months, and averaging about 9 percent over the period May 1973, to May 1974, Roberts felt confident that many policy holders were exercising their legal right to borrow against their cash value life insurance policies. The interest rate charged (i.e., earned) by the company on such policy loans was contractually fixed at the time the policy was issued. The overwhelming majority of policies in the Old Reliable's underwriting portfolio were issued between 1939 and 1967, and these policies carried a 5 percent loan rate. The borrowing rate associated with policies written after 1967 was, in most state jurisdictions served by the company, increased to 6 percent. For the most part, though, these policies had not

This case was prepared by D. Stuart Bancroft of Pacific Lutheran University, Tacoma, Washington, as a basis for classroom discussion and not to illustrate either effective or ineffective administrative action.

yet developed sizable loan values as of 1974, and Roberts believed it would be many years before the company's return on policy loans would average 6 percent.

The potential for intense arbitrage activity by policyholders—encouraged by the differential between commercial bank loan rates and policy loan borrowing rates—was, Roberts believed, heightened by abnormally high money market rates (see exhibit 1).

Given these concerns, Roberts arranged an appointment with Van Ackerman, Old Reliable's chief actuary. Van Ackerman suggested that John Pershing, a new actuarial trainee, be included in the session. During his conversation with Van Ackerman, Roberts was astounded to learn that the company had taken no steps to clarify either the nature or the consequences of policy loan activity.

"At no time since 1960," he observed, "have we committed less than 9 percent of our total assets to policy loans, and for the last five years, that figure has been closer to 12 percent. So what you are saying, Mr. Van Ackerman, is that the company has a policy of ignoring an increasingly significant proportion of its total assets!"

"Well, that's a pretty harsh way of phrasing the matter," Van Ackerman replied. "After all,

EXHIBIT 1:

Money Market Rates (Percentage per annum)

Period	Prime banker's acceptance 90 days	Federal funds rate	U.S. Government Securities			
			3-month bills		6-month bills	
			Rate on new issue	Market yield	Rate on new issue	Market yield
1967	4.75	4.22	4.321	4.29	4.630	4.61
1968	5.75	5.66	5.339	5.34	5.470	5.47
1969	7.61	8.21	6.677	6.67	6.853	6.86
1970	7.31	7.17	6.458	6.39	6.562	6.51
1971	4.85	4.66	4.348	4.33	4.511	4.52
1972	4.47	4.44	4.071	4.07	4.466	4.49
1973	8.08	8.74	7.041	7.03	7.178	7.20
1973-May	7.15	7.84	6.348	6.36	6.615	6.62
-Jun	7.98	8.49	7.188	7.19	7.234	7.23
-Jul	9.19	10.40	8.015	8.01	8.081	8.12
-Aug	10.18	10.50	8.672	8.67	8.700	8.65
-Sep	10.19	10.78	8.478	8.29	8.537	8.45
-Oct	9.07	10.01	7.155	7.22	7.259	7.32
-Nov	8.73	10.03	7.866	7.83	7.823	7.96
-Dec	8.94	9.95	7.364	7.45	7.444	7.56
1974-Jan	8.72	9.65	7.755	7.77	7.627	7.65
-Feb	7.83	8.97	7.060	7.12	6.874	6.96
-Mar	8.43	9.35	7.986	7.96	7.829	7.83
-Apr	9.61	10.51	8.229	8.33	8.171	8.32
-May	10.68	11.31	8.430	8.23	8.496	8.40

Source: *Federal Reserve Bulletin* (June, 1974), p. A29

you know as well as I do that we are legally obligated to honor a policyholder's legitimate loan request.''

"That's true. We can't exercise any discretion when it comes to adding these loans to our investment portfolio," Roberts observed. "But, on the other hand, we are not restrained from attempting to actively manage the policy loan account, just as we do our other asset accounts."

"What do you mean by that?" Van Ackerman asked.

"Well, it seems to me as if the process of managing any investment account consists, essentially, of two things: 1) forecasting the future status of that account, and 2) taking corrective action where the need for it is indicated. For example, we hold a tremendous volume of marketable bonds. Now, for the most part, we don't just sit on these bonds until they've run their course (i.e., matured). Rather, we scrutinize the market, forecast interest rate movements, and on the basis of such predictions, we decide whether a particular bond is a good or a bad investment. Then, we act accordingly. So why shouldn't we scrutinize our policy loans in the same way?"

"Why should we?" Van Ackerman inquired. "There's obvious merit to attempts to discriminate between bonds that constitute 'good' investments and those that are 'bad' investments, because we can sell the bad ones. But in the case of policy loans, we don't hold the initiative—that always rests with the borrowing policyholder. Besides, when market rates exceed the contractual loan rate, *all* policy loans are 'bad' investments and, if we could, we ought to liquidate the entire policy loan portfolio—something which, of course, we have no way of accomplishing!''

Roberts agreed that everything Van Ackerman had said was true, as far as it went. He continued, ''Yes, given current money market conditions, all of the policy loans on our books are bad investments, but irrespective of money market conditions, some policy loans are always going to be worse investments than others and if we could correctly categorize them as such in advance. . . .''

''Hayden, let me make sure that you understand the rudiments of the life insurance business before we go any further,'' Van Ackerman interrupted. ''A loan against the cash value of a life insurance policy is completely secured, with respect to both principal and interest, by the policy's reserve value. . . .''

''I'm quite familiar with these facts,'' Roberts quickly asserted. ''If the borrowing policyholder neglects or refuses to pay the interest due on his loan, we just add it to the loan balance, by, in effect, apportioning it from the policy's cash value. And, if the insured dies or surrenders the policy, we deduct the principal sum of the loan, including capitalized interest, from the face value due the beneficiary or from the cash value due the insured, whichever the case might be.

''So you see,'' he continued, ''I'm not advocating that we attempt to differentiate between 'good' and 'bad' policy loans on the basis of the degree of risk surrounding the principal and/or interest—that risk is always zero. Irrespective of whether the policyholder lives or dies, persists or terminates, we'll never lose those sums. However, the policy loan is a source of risk and potential loss to the company in another respect.''

''If you're referring to the inducement which policy loans allegedly give to surrender of the policy,'' Van Ackerman interjected, ''I think I'm finally beginning to follow you, Hayden.''

''Precisely,'' Hayden Roberts replied. ''But it's more than an 'alleged' relationship; it's actually fairly well documented. I pulled a few figures together the other day which indicate that, of a systematically selected sample of policies which developed loan balances in 1966, nearly 20 percent were surrendered within one year of the time the loan was initiated! That figure is quite a bit higher than the average surrender rate on our overall book of business (underwriting portfolio).''

At this point, John Pershing inquired as to the way in which surrender caused the company to suffer a loss. Van Ackerman explained that surrender values are normally made available to a policyholder before he has contributed through premiums an amount sufficient to cover the acquisition expenses incurred by the company in the process of getting his business on the books. Such expenses (primarily sales commissions) are generally quite large relative to other expenses associated with the policy and it is not feasible to recoup them by means of the first-year expense loading. Therefore, life companies are allowed to charge the excess of first-year expenses over first-year expense loading against the policy's surrender value and then amortize this ''loan'' against the surrender value out of the expense loading contained in the remaining premiums. If a policyholder surrenders his policy before the acquisition expenses are fully amortized (and this may be twenty years, or more), the company must make up the difference out of surplus and eventually the persisting policyholders must replenish the surplus out of either gross premiums, dividends, or both.

Van Ackerman now sought to bring the entire discussion into focus by summarizing the critical points that had been raised. ''Clearly'' he began, ''the rise in policy loan activity—which seems to have been arbitrage induced—does not bode well for the company, for two reasons: 1) our rate of return on policy loans is considerably below what we could expect on alternative, riskless investments; and 2) loan-supporting policies stand a better than average chance to result in premature surrender of the policy, thereby leaving the company and its persisting policyholders to absorb the unamortized acquisition expenses. In either case," he continued, "the end result is to increase the net cost of insurance."

The policy loan issue, first posed by Hayden Roberts, constituted, in Van Ackerman's words, "an interesting dilemma for the company." Life companies are legally obligated to honor a policyholder's legitimate loan request. They are also charged with the responsibility of protecting the financial interests of all policyholders insofar as the insurance contract is concerned. However, borrowing policyholders may, and quite frequently do, interpret their financial interest in the contract in a manner that conflicts with the nonborrowing policyholder's financial interest in the contract. This situation, occasioned by a loan request, is manifested first in the requirement that the company invest a portion of its assets at suboptimal rates and second, by the transference to persisting policyholders of the financial burden associated with premature termination of the insurance contract. Van Ackerman added that in either instance the company's responsibility to protect the insurance, rather than the financial arbitrage interests of all policyholders should be accorded the greater priority in resolving the conflict.

"Given this line of reasoning," Van Ackerman concluded, "the desirability of managing the policy loan account is irrefutable." He then proceeded to clarify his use of the term, "management."

"If we're going to avoid getting the proverbial cart before the horse, we'd better draw a distinction, at the outset, between what I call 'active' management and 'passive' management. In a passive sense, I would see management of the policy loan account as consisting of developing an *understanding* of the profile of the account and of those factors which influence the time-state disposition of the individual components of the account."

"In a second, 'active' sense, the term, 'management' connotes the taking of action designed to *influence* the time-state disposition of particular policy loan accounts."

"Clearly, we can't expect to be successful in actively managing these accounts until we thoroughly understand what they look like and why they behave as they do. Now, this is a very complex task, so we'd better tackle it one piece at a time. Therefore, Hayden, I would like you to ascertain whether it is possible to differentiate, in a multivariate context, between those policy loans that result in surrender of the policy and those that do not. If we can't accomplish this, then I don't see that there's much hope for our ever successfully influencing what happens to individual policy loan accounts, and we would be well advised to abandon the whole project. If you are successful, though . . . well, then we'll just take it from there and try to see if we can't prevent loan-supporting policies that have a high probability of prematurely terminating from actually doing so."

After the discussion session had ended, Roberts felt elated at the success he had had in convincing Van Ackerman to try to come to grips with the policy loan problem. However, as he began assembling data, he became concerned about the unavailability of information relative to most of the variables he intuitively felt would be the best "discriminators" between loan-supporting policies that terminated and those that persisted. In general, he thought that the time-state disposition (i.e., surrender versus persist) of the policy depended upon two things: 1) the utility the policyholder derived from the policy and 2) the financial outlay required to repay the loan. For example, he thought that the time-state disposition of the borrowed-on policy would be a function of the purpose for which the loan was requested, as well as of the financial, professional, educational, and family profile characteristics of the borrowing policyholder. The company did not maintain—in accessible form at least—information on any of these variables. Moreover, Roberts had serious doubts as to the feasibility of ever aggregating such data, let alone keeping it current. Therefore, he admitted the necessity for working under a major constraint; specifically, he would have to use proxy variables.

To identify the most appropriate proxy variables, Roberts first addressed himself to the following query: What considerations exerted the major influence on the policyholder's initial decision to purchase and, subsequently, to maintain a cash value policy? He concluded that the answer to this question was implicit in the nature of the cash value life insurance product. It provided, essentially, two "commodities": 1) economic protection against premature death, and 2) an investment, or savings element. Thus, he reasoned, the *utility* which the policyholder derived from the policy might be inferred from proxies which tangibly reflect upon either or both of these focal points. After scrutinizing the available data, he selected the following proxies for utility:

1. annual premium

2. face value of the policy

3. policy anniversary (i.e., number of years since its inception)

4. loan value (approximately the same as the policy's cash value)

5. billing status of the policy (i.e., whether it was paid-up or not)

6. existence of automatic premium loans.

In similar fashion, he decided to use the following proxy variables for the purpose of providing insight into the *financial sacrifice* required to repay the policy loan:

1. loan balance

2. loan balance-to-loan value ratio

3. loan balance-to-face value ratio

He felt that these latter three variables reflected, respectively, the absolute outlay required to repay the loan, en toto, and the relative significance of this outlay.

Roberts shared with Van Ackerman his concern over the credibility of these proxy variables. Van Ackerman replied that he appreciated Roberts' concern but added that "if the company were to aggregate and maintain the missing data, the costs incurred in conjunction with the policy loan account would be increased. Then, we would have to ascertain whether these incremental costs could reasonably be expected to be offset by the benefits derived in terms of improved cash planning, reduction of policy terminations, and a reduction in the proportion of assets committed to low-yielding policy loans. At this point, we're not even sure that a workable model is within the realm of reason. Therefore, it's worth a try to see if we can accomplish our objectives with existing data—i.e., at minimum cost. If the results are encouraging, we can make various modifications later."

After several days of steady effort, Roberts had brought together the data displayed in exhibit 2. The three-pronged question that now occupied his time was which of several possible analytical techniques to employ, how to organize the data so as to facilitate the analysis, and finally, how to interpret the results of the analysis, once it had been completed.

QUESTIONS

1. Using appropriate quantitative or qualitative tools, analyze the data presented in this case.

2. As the result of your analysis, develop appropriate management policies on behalf of Old Reliable Life Assurance Society.

EXHIBIT 2:

Summary of Policy and Loan Value Information for a Systematically Selected Sample of Seventy Policies Which Developed Positive Loan Balances during 1966

Policy Number	Int. Rate	Face Value (000)	Periodic Premium	Billing Period	Billing Status	APL*	Policy Anniversary	Initial Loan Value	Initial Loan Balance	LB**/LV	LB***/FV	Policy Surrendered within 1 year of loan
3283	06	5.0	0	—	Paid-up	No	54	1582.86	570.00	.36	.29	Yes
10341	06	3.0	0	—	Paid-up	No	48	2402.86	2402.33	1.00	.80	No
25257	05	2.5	72.28	Annual	Paying	Yes	34	1535.38	39.50	.03	.02	No
33805	05	1.0	22.52	Annual	Paying	Yes	37	419.81	22.52	.05	.02	Yes
43113	05	1.0	24.88	Annual	Paying	No	34	760.38	759.70	1.00	.77	No
51121	05	1.5	34.74	Annual	Paying	Yes	32	660.85	19.22	.03	.01	No
58370	05	1.0	20.76	Annual	Paying	No	30	343.40	343.40	1.00	.35	Yes
60735	05	1.0	30.86	Annual	Paying	No	29	963.21	500.00	.52	.50	No
65017	05	10.0	134.80	Semian.	Paying	No	27	3907.77	3890.00	1.00	.39	No
80012	05	3.0	21.15	Quart.	Paying	No	25	1251.11	1242.68	.99	.41	No
83872	05	2.5	32.61	Semian.	Paying	Yes	21	787.80	32.61	.04	.01	No
85377	05	5.0	123.45	Annual	Paying	Yes	23	1338.10	123.45	.09	.02	No
87441	05	1.0	0	—	Paid-up	No	23	769.52	200.00	.26	.20	No
88707	05	6.0	15.72	Month.	Paying	Yes	22	2229.21	15.72	.01	.00	No
100075	05	2.0	46.36	Annual	Paying	No	22	590.48	565.42	.96	.28	Yes
102763	05	10.0	268.40	Annual	Paying	Yes	21	3352.38	161.60	.05	.02	No
108045	05	1.5	10.14	Quart.	Paying	Yes	20	602.96	10.14	.02	.01	No
111685	05	4.0	265.00	Annual	Paying	No	19	5447.62	2000.00	.37	.50	No
111755	05	2.5	102.90	Annual	Paying	No	19	1757.00	1700.00	1.00	.70	Yes
112222	05	3.0	62.07	Annual	Paying	Yes	19	840.00	62.07	.07	.02	No
113804	05	3.0	18.27	Quart.	Paying	No	16	681.48	260.00	.38	.09	No
115573	05	50.0	1273.50	Annual	Paying	No	16	14952.38	739.50	.05	.01	No
118402	05	25.0	596.75	Annual	Paying	Yes	15	6523.81	3500.00	.54	.14	No
118413	05	2.0	13.66	Quart.	Paying	Yes	15	507.65	28.93	.06	.01	No
120041	05	5.0	17.40	Month.	Paying	Yes	15	1073.03	17.40	.02	.00	No

(Continued)

*Automatic Premium Loan
**Loan Balance-to-Loan Value ratio
***Loan Balance-to-Face Value ratio

EXHIBIT 2: *(Continued)*

Summary of Policy and Loan Value Information for a Systematically Selected Sample of Seventy Policies Which Developed Positive Loan Balances during 1966

Policy Number	Int. Rate	Face Value (000)	Periodic Premium	Billing Period	Billing Status	APL*	Policy Anniversary	Initial Loan Value	Initial Loan Balance	LB**/LV	LB***/FV	Policy Surrendered within 1 year of loan
121135	05	10.0	358.70	Annual	Paying	No	15	3314.29	1812.25	.55	.18	No
124775	05	10.0	47.54	Quart.	Paying	Yes	13	1856.79	47.54	.03	.00	No
127807	05	5.0	28.75	Month.	Paying	No	13	3384.23	500.00	.15	.10	No
128067	05	3.0	26.15	Quart.	Paying	No	13	894.81	876.10	.98	.29	No
139171	05	1.0	14.11	Semian.	Paying	Yes	13	214.15	14.11	.07	.01	No
139856	05	10.0	358.50	Annual	Paying	Yes	12	2819.05	241.80	.09	.02	No
142548	05	5.0	16.10	Month.	Paying	No	12	697.10	504.24	.72	.10	No
145440	05	1.0	23.72	Semian.	Paying	No	11	380.49	94.00	.25	.09	No
146331	05	4.0	19.05	Month.	Paying	No	11	767.47	581.91	.76	.15	No
149443	05	15.0	213.30	Annual	Paying	No	10	1657.14	500.00	.30	.03	No
150757	05	10.0	336.70	Annual	Paying	No	10	2219.05	1800.00	.81	.18	No
152162	05	20.0	295.26	Semian.	Paying	Yes	10	4019.51	295.26	.07	.01	Yes
156302	05	3.0	0	—	Paid-up	No	9	235.00	230.41	1.00	.08	No
157282	05	10.0	42.67	Month.	Paying	No	9	1787.55	600.00	.34	.06	Yes
157303	05	2.0	35.19	Quart.	Paying	Yes	7	459.85	285.57	.63	.14	No
158051	05	1.5	24.40	Quart.	Paying	Yes	9	585.93	24.40	.04	.02	No
159040	05	2.5	10.28	Month.	Paying	No	9	433.20	294.70	.68	.12	Yes
159630	05	10.0	17.00	Month.	Paying	No	9	1249.79	1124.00	.90	.11	No
161184	05	10.0	306.90	Annual	Paying	Yes	8	1714.29	306.90	.18	.03	No
162147	05	10.0	298.00	Annual	Paying	Yes	8	2228.57	1214.94	.55	.12	No
163842	05	5.0	13.85	Month.	Paying	No	8	672.20	105.00	.16	.02	No
164616	05	12.0	25.81	Month.	Paying	No	8	1573.44	343.79	.22	.03	No
165340	05	15.0	379.80	Annual	Paying	Yes	8	2257.14	379.80	.17	.03	No
168121	05	10.0	194.20	Annual	Paying	Yes	7	1009.52	194.20	.19	.02	No

(Continued)

*Automatic Premium Loan
**Loan Balance-to-Loan Value ratio
***Loan Balance-to-Face Value ratio

EXHIBIT 2: (Continued)

Summary of Policy and Loan Value Information for a Systematically Selected Sample of Seventy Policies Which Developed Positive Loan Balances during 1966

Policy Number	Int. Rate	Face Value (000)	Periodic Premium	Billing Period	Billing Status	APL*	Policy Anniversary	Initial Loan Value	Initial Loan Balance	LB**/LV	LB***/FV	Policy Surrendered within 1 year of loan
169811	05	10.0	20.21	Month.	Paying	No	7	1148.55	500.00	.44	.05	No
170467	05	10.0	398.80	Annual	Paying	Yes	7	1571.43	1124.05	.72	.11	No
171225	05	15.0	57.12	Month.	Paying	Yes	5	448.13	381.80	.85	.03	Yes
171683	05	25.0	95.50	Month.	Paying	No	5	5261.41	2000.00	.38	.08	No
172174	05	3.0	21.72	Quart.	Paying	Yes	5	248.00	245.93	1.00	.08	Yes
173658	05	6.0	9.96	Month.	Paying	Yes	5	261.79	9.96	.04	.00	No
175441	05	5.0	14.47	Month.	Paying	Yes	5	299.59	8.71	.03	.00	No
176003	05	10.0	294.40	Annual	Paying	No	5	323.81	251.00	.78	.05	Yes
176463	05	10.0	19.86	Month.	Paying	Yes	4	640.66	19.86	.03	.00	No
179622	05	50.0	2062.00	Annual	Paying	No	4	6190.48	5182.00	.84	.10	Yes
180123	05	10.0	14.16	Month.	Paying	Yes	4	298.76	84.96	.28	.01	No
180614	05	10.0	13.33	Month.	Paying	Yes	4	438.17	132.32	.30	.01	No
180979	05	5.0	14.79	Month.	Paying	Yes	4	345.23	104.39	.30	.02	No
183810	05	10.0	15.56	Month.	Paying	Yes	3	188.38	15.56	.08	.00	No
184504	05	10.0	18.60	Month.	Paying	No	3	314.52	202.00	.64	.02	Yes
185618	05	5.0	28.08	Quart.	Paying	Yes	3	148.15	51.39	.35	.01	No
187568	05	5.0	10.60	Month.	Paying	Yes	3	165.97	8.36	.05	.00	No
188336	05	2.5	12.63	Month.	Paying	No	3	181.33	104.00	.57	.04	No
190865	05	10.0	15.50	Month.	Paying	No	2	486.31	435.70	.90	.04	Yes
191361	05	3.0	11.73	Month.	Paying	No	2	296.51	95.67	.32	.03	No
191770	05	4.0	39.80	Month.	Paying	No	2	1042.99	194.99	.19	.05	No

*Automatic Premium Loan
**Loan Balance-to-Loan Value ratio
***Loan Balance-to-Face Value ratio

Case 19

The Computech Pension Plan

In May 1979, Alecia Snyder was having lunch with Bryan Kemp, president of Computech, the computer software company with which she had been employed since completing her bachelor's degree in mathematics and computer systems four years before. Kemp asked Snyder how she was doing in the evening M.B.A. program at Springfield State, and she mentioned that they were presently studying pension funds in the financial institutions course. Kemp asked her what she thought of Computech's pension plan. She replied that she had not really given it a lot of thought but intended to look at the plan over the week-end. She thought this would be good reinforcement for her classroom exercises.

Kempt had been meaning to sit down and give some thought to the pension plan himself, but did not feel very knowledgeable in this area. He asked Snyder to prepare a written analysis of the plan with any recommendations for changes. He told her he would instruct his secretary to allow her access to all of the files relating to the pension plan. While this was outside Snyder's nor-

mal area of responsibility as a systems programmer, she was pleased with the opportunity to use her newly acquired knowledge and to make a favorable impression on Kemp.

THE COMPANY

Computech was one of the many small software companies spawned by the rapid growth in computer usage. Much of this growth was stimulated by a key antitrust ruling requiring large manufacturers such as IBM to price their software services separately from their computer hardware. This allowed companies such as Computech to enter the business of designing information systems and writing computer programs to meet the needs of individual computer users. This was entirely a service industry, with the software companies offering little more than skilled systems analysts and programmers.

Computech had been organized in 1970, when Kemp and three other employees of a large computer manufacturer resigned to form their own software company. They believed that a small software firm with reduced overhead could serve smaller businesses more effectively.

This case was prepared by Neil E. Seitz with assistance from Fred C. Yeager and William B. Gillespie, Dept. of Finance, Saint Louis University.

Therefore, Computech specialized in providing programs and systems designs for small- to medium-sized businesses.

Because Computech's overhead costs were minimal, and because its concentration on the Springfield market virtually eliminated travel expense, Computech was able to offer its services at lower prices than those offered by the large manufacturers. However, Computech was not alone in this. There were approximately fifteen independent software firms operating in the Springfield area and competing directly with Computech. To succeed in this environment, it was necessary to attract high-quality programmers and analysts, and to offer programming and systems analysis services at the lowest possible prices.

Computech had indeed been able to compete successfully in this environment. From the original group of four people. Computech had grown to a total of twenty-four employees in eight years. Mr. Kemp attributed his success to three factors. First, all four of the original organizers had outstanding "human skills" as well as experience and ability in software creation. Thus, they were able to interact effectively with employees and customers. Computech had continued this pattern by always giving consideration to human skills as well as computer skills when hiring employees. Second, Computech had always offered its employees a good working environment and employee benefit package. This was believed to be important for attracting employees and for developing loyalty in an industry known for high employee turnover. Third, Kemp used the same services he sold to his customers. Very soon after the company began operations, Mr. Kemp implemented a management information system which provided excellent cost accounting data. This system contributed to appropriate pricing policies and provided excellent controls so that costs were kept in line. Thus Computech was competitive in price while providing excellent employee benefits.

Kemp felt that the company was now at a point where greater attention to long-term planning was required. In addition, he felt that there were areas in which increased efficiency could be achieved if he only had the time to do the analysis. If Snyder's study of the pension plan worked out, he hoped to assign her several other studies relating to financial planning.

THE PENSION PLAN

Shortly after the company was formed, Kemp realized the importance of developing inducements to attract and keep employees. A company needed to be cost-effective with employee benefits if it was to attract high-quality employees. While most software firms offered almost no fringe benefits at that time, Kempt believed that the addition of fringe benefits would increase the likelihood of attracting and retaining competent personnel. The first benefit which Computech provided was a term life insurance program. This benefit was obtainable at a low cost since most of the employees were relatively young. This benefit seemed to be helpful in recruiting and more benefits were soon added. These included medical insurance and a pension program.

The pension program, which was begun in 1972, was serviced by an insurance company. Like most smaller companies, Computech could not afford to provide portfolio and administrative management for a pension fund covering a relatively small number of people. Each month, Computech forwarded to the insurance company a sum equal to 10 percent of the gross income of each eligible employee. Half of this was contributed by Computech and the other half was deducted from the employee's salary. While no employee was required to participate, all eligible employees had elected to participate.

Pension fund contributions were used to purchase "units" in the insurance company's portfolio: a bond portfolio and a common stock portfolio. When the employee reached retirement age, the accumulated value of his units could be taken as a lump sum payment or could be used to purchase a fixed or variable annuity, at the employee's option. The variable annuity would provide fluctuating pension payments dependent on financial market returns, while the fixed annuity would simply pay a fixed return based on the number of units owned, the value of these units, and certain actuarial assumptions.

Computech had chosen to have half of the funds used to purchase stock portfolio units and half used to purchase bond portfolio units. The bond portfolio units remained at a constant price of $10. Each year, the beneficiary's bond account was credited with an amount equal to the yield on the pension fund bond portfolio times the value of his account at the beginning of the year, minus an administrative charge of 0.5 percent of asset value. The value of a unit in the stock portfolio changed each month with the values of the stocks in the portfolio. Dividend or interest income was reinvested on behalf of the beneficiary in additional units. Return earned on the stock portfolio each year was computed as

$$\text{Return} = \frac{P_t - P_{t-1} + D_t}{P_{t-1}}$$

where:

P_t = price of a unit at the end of the year,

P_{t-1} = price of the unit at the beginning of the year, and

D_t = dividends per unit during the year.

Annual return on the stock portfolio, as well as average yield on the bond portfolio and relevant market information covering a twenty-year period, appears in exhibit 1. Both sets of returns are before the 0.5 percent per year service charge.

While Computech did not have enough employees to consider managing its own pension fund portfolio, certain options to the existing arrangements were available:

1. Change the bond and stock portfolio mix.

2. Change to a different insurance company.

3. Cancel the pension fund and give each

employee a 5 percent pay raise. Employees who wanted pension protection could make private arrangements to purchase mutual fund shares or make other investments with tax treatments similar to those for the pension fund contributions.

4. Replace the pension program with a profit sharing program in which employees would be given shares of Computech with a book value equal to some fraction of net profit for the year. For the last three years, this would have resulted in an average cost approximately the same as the pension plan, but it would not have represented as great a drain on cash flows. The four founders presently held all of Computech's stock.

In addition to a possible change in the plan format, Kemp wondered if certain plan participant eligibility requirements should be changed. Under present rules, an employee became eligible for participation after three years of full-time employment. One fourth of total wages paid by Computech were paid to employees who worked twenty hours a week or less and one third of the full-time employees left Computech during their first three years of employment. A recent study of the software industry, conducted by an industry trade association, concluded that half of the employees of a typical software firm changed employers before completing three years of service and only one fifth of the employees tended to stay with the same company ten years or more. Kemp wondered whether the present eligibility rules were optimal with regard to cost and with the objective of attracting and maintaining a stable, talented workforce.

Kemp did not give Snyder the impression that he was considering any particular change in policy with regard to the pension plan. As near as she could determine, his only interest was in a complete review to determine if the pension plan was the best available for achieving the objectives desired in a cost-efficient manner. Snyder collected information on the performance of the insurance company's fund in the years since Computech had been involved and for earlier years. She also collected the information on general stock market performance and interest rates that appears in exhibit 1. She took this material home with her for the weekend to begin examining the problem.

QUESTIONS

1.   Analyze the performance of the pension plan as compared to overall market perfor-

mance. Has the insurance company fund outperformed the general market with regard to equity? debt?

2.   In what ways would a stock distribution plan as an alternative to the pension plan for Computech be more desirable? be less desirable?

3.   What changes, if any, should Snyder recommend to Kemp?

EXHIBIT 1:

	Equity Portfolio Return	Bond Portfolio Return	S&P 500 Return	Inflation Rate	10 Year U.S. Gov. Bond Rate	6 Month T-Bill Rate
1959	13.89%	4.14%	27.32%	1.5%	4.33%	3.83%
1960	3.36	4.35	.80	1.5	4.12	3.25
1961	18.60	4.52	21.85	.7	3.88	2.61
1962	−14.36	4.68	−2.50	1.2	3.95	2.91
1963	18.34	4.79	15.18	1.6	4.00	3.25
1964	12.66	4.88	19.47	1.2	4.19	3.69
1965	17.75	4.99	11.36	1.9	4.28	4.06
1966	−4.66	5.11	.10	3.4	4.92	5.08
1967	23.42	5.24	11.02	3.0	5.07	4.63
1968	6.12	5.45	10.43	4.7	5.65	5.47
1969	−5.51	5.72	2.37	6.1	6.67	6.85
1970	−3.22	5.95	−11.11	5.5	7.35	6.56
1971	20.25	6.28	21.25	3.4	6.16	4.51
1972	17.07	6.58	13.94	3.4	6.21	4.47
1973	−18.14	7.16	1.44	8.8	6.84	7.18
1974	−30.96	7.59	−18.41	12.2	7.56	7.93
1975	32.06	7.82	8.31	7.0	7.99	6.12
1976	21.19	8.13	22.17	4.8	7.61	5.27
1977	−6.44	8.39	.89	6.8	7.42	5.51
1978	8.68	8.71	3.06	7.8	8.41	7.57

Case 20

Nello L. Teer Company

It was 6:30 P.M. and Robb Teer, assistant treasurer of Nello L. Teer Company, had just called his wife to tell her that he would be home late for dinner. The next day, 15 December 1976, was the submission date for bids on the Dantokpa-Akpakpa Bridge project in Benin (formerly the Republic of Dahomey), and he had still not decided whether to take out an Overseas Private Investment Corporation (OPIC) Construction Insurance Policy. Once the decision on the amount and timing of the coverage was made, Teer would have to cable Howard Frederich, the head of Nello Teer's African office so that the premium could be factored into the company's bid.

COMPANY BACKGROUND

Nello L. Teer Company of Durham, North Carolina, is a full-service construction firm, actively involved in projects throughout the world.

Founded in 1909 by Nello L. Teer, Sr., the firm remains privately held with two generations of the founder's descendants active in the management of the enterprise.

Among Teer's more prominent jobs have been sections of the Massachusetts and Pennsylvania turnpikes; Broken Bow Dam in Oklahoma; the North Carolina Blue Cross & Blue Shield headquarters building, Chapel Hill, North Carolina; and primary highways of Tanzania, Panama, Nicaragua, Honduras, and Guatemala. Approximately 20 percent of Teer's business is conducted outside of the United States. The company has an average worldwide payroll of 2,500 employees.

THE DANTOKPA-AKPAKPA BRIDGE PROJECT

The Dantokpa-Akpakpa (D-A) Bridge Project was part of a larger effort by the country of Benin to upgrade its primary transportation system. In order to finance the project, Benin had successfully enlisted the assistance of the Agency for International Development in providing the majority of the funding. Local sources would

This case was prepared by Professor Mark R. Eaker of Southern Methodist University. This case is designed to be used as a basis for class discussion rather than to illustrate either effective or ineffective handling of an administrative situation.

provide the rest, but the AID participation, and the terms of payment outlined in the project's bid specifications meant that exchange risk and default need not be considered by the bidders. However, the possibility of expropriation of materials or loss due to war, civil insurrection, or natural disaster was still a consideration; and it was this type of OPIC coverage (see appendix 1) that Robb Teer was trying to evaluate.

Robb was aware that he had to consider a number of factors. First, he had to evaluate the political climate in Benin. In order to accomplish that, he spent some time researching Benin at the library as well as soliciting information from various government agencies (appendix 2). Second, it was necessary to measure the extent of Teer Company's exposure. This information was essential in arriving at the quantity of coverage. In order to assess Teer's vulnerability, Robb had had the project manager provide a materials flow-chart related to the project.

To this he added his own projections of the outstanding pay estimates and the average bank balance required in country (schedule below).

1 April 1977–30 September 1977	$1,600,000
1 October 1977–31 March 1978	1,500,000
1 April 1977–30 September 1978	1,500,000
1 October 1978–31 March 1979	1,500,000
1 April 1979–30 September 1979	800,000
1 October 1979–31 March 1980	200,000

Although it could only be an estimate based upon the bid specifications and engineering plans, Teer was reasonably confident of the numbers and dates (exhibit 1).

Although the Teer Company had operated overseas for a number of years, their experience with African countries was not extensive. Company policy had been not to utilize this type of insurance for any of the Latin American projects. Within Latin America where the company has had a long-standing presence, the feeling was that the company could accurately assess the climate, and provide sufficient guarantees in the process of negotiating a contract. With regard to Africa, that same confidence was not felt and as a result, Robb was carefully weighing the situation.

EXHIBIT 1:

TO:	Robb Teer
FROM:	Howard Frederich
SUBJECT:	Materials Flow and Cost Estimates Related to the Dantokpa-Akpakpa Bridge Bid

Equipment and Materials

A.	General construction equipment with six-year life and no salvage value. Arrive in Benin on 1 April 1977.	$1,651,000
B.	Specialized equipment to be written off during the thirty-three months of construction.	75,513
C.	Materials for site preparation and initial construction. Arrive in Benin on 1 April 1977.	422,622
D.	Miscellaneous support services and materials to be used during first twenty-four months of construction.	569,416
E.	Miscellaneous expendable equipment to be used at a rate of $20,000 per year beginning 1 April 1977.	100,000
F.	Materials incorporated in the job to be used at the rate of $167,000 per year. $100,000 to arrive 1 April 1977, and $400,000 on 1 October 1977.	

Teer was certain that there were other companies interested in the project, so the bidding was expected to be highly competitive. As a result, every effort had to be made in order to minimize the cost of erecting the bridge. A success on this project could pave the way for other work on the Benin highway system. Yet, at the same time Teer Company expected a profit on every undertaking. Therefore, Robb was being particularly careful in assessing the risk to Teer, and the cost of insuring against loss. Too much caution could lead to not getting the job, but too little might eventually lead to significant losses.

Robb sat down to go through the background material one more time, not wanting to miss dinner entirely, and knowing that the decision had to be made that night.

QUESTIONS

1. Using data provided in the case and assuming straight-line depreciation, calculate Teer's Financial Exposure for each of the six time periods identified in the schedule contained within the case.

2. What factors might cause a divergence from the projected exposure?

3. To what extent does Teer face exchange rate risk?

Nello L. Teer Company

Appendix 1: The Overseas Private Investment Corporation (OPIC)

The Overseas Private Investment Corporation was created by the Foreign Assistance Act of 1969 and formally established 19 January 1971. OPIC was organized in order to foster two primary goals: to assist in development projects in less developed countries, and to make U.S. firms more competitive in participating in development related projects worldwide. The mechanism for attaining those goals is the provision of insurance services that allow U.S. firms to protect themselves against a variety of risks related to overseas business activity. Since similar insurance was not available through private channels, yet was in many cases provided to foreign firms by their governments, it was believed that U.S. firms operated at a competitive disadvantage. Furthermore, it was believed that the inability of U.S. firms to acquire insurance reduced the overall flow of funds into development related projects.

OPIC provides insurance for qualified projects in approximately ninety less developed countries. Specifically, OPIC is authorized to provide coverage against the following types of risk:

1. Inability to convert local currency into dollars. This applies to profits or earnings, as well as the return of the original investment.

2. Loss of investment due to expropriation, nationalization, or confiscation by a foreign government.

3. Loss due to revolution, war, or insurrection.

OPIC offers a variety of insurance programs of which the Special Incentive Program for U.S. Construction and Services Overseas is specifically designed for contractors engaged in overseas projects. The package provides insurance against all three of the risks outlined above, and coverage can be extended to 90 percent of the amount expected to be at risk during a policy year.

At the time an OPIC policy is applied for, the firm must indicate the maximum amount of coverage that might be required. This is usually done when a $100 registration fee is paid to OPIC. The insuree can then allocate that maximum amount between two types of coverage, current and standby. Current coverage refers to the amount of active insurance in force during a half of a contract period (six months). Any claims against OPIC can not exceed the current coverage. Standby coverage is the difference between the maximum and the current amounts. It represents the additional amount of current coverage available to the insuree during the life of the policy. Prior to the first day of a half of a contract period, the policy holder elects the amount of current and standby coverage for that period. The total coverage during a period sets the maximum coverage during all subsequent periods.

The premiums are determined by the amount of current and standby coverage. The rate for current coverage is 1.5 percent per annum. Standby coverage carries a premium of 0.75 percent per annum. Premiums accrue from the first day the policy is in force, which also marks the beginning of the first contract period.

In order to qualify for OPIC Construction and Services coverage, a project must be development related and have host country approval. The host country must agree to arbitrate any claims and there must not be any illegal boycott or other restrictions as conditions for doing business.

Nello L. Teer Company

Appendix 2: Benin

Benin (43,483 sq. miles, pop. 3,191,628) is situated along the western African coast between Togo and Nigeria. Formerly a part of French West Africa, the country achieved full independence on 1 August 1960, as the Independent Republic of Dahomey. Initially a constitutional democracy, Dahomey experienced a succession of military governments brought into power through six coups between 1960 and 1972. Currently, the country is governed by a military council headed by Lt. Col. Mathier Kerekou, who assumed power by coup d'etat on 26 October 1972.

On 3 December 1974, President Kerekou declared Dahomey to be a ''Marxist-Leninist state.'' Two days later, the nation's banks, insurance companies, and oil distribution facilities were nationalized. Additional control of business activity has since been mandated in order to

''protect the revolution from sabotage.'' On 30 November 1975, the country was renamed the People's Republic of Benin. Despite several attempted coups, President Kerekou has retained power.

Benin's economy is mainly agricultural. The gross domestic product was estimated to be $80 per capita in 1970. The country has had severe balance of payments problems and has experienced an inability to balance its local budget. Deficits have largely been met by virtue of bilateral aid, primarily from France.

Benin does have one of the more highly educated populaces among African countries. However, economic problems resulting in severe unemployment have led to unrest among the educated citizens and is probably a major factor explaining the political instability.

Appendix A

Time Value of Money
Tables

TABLE A-1:

Compound Value of a Dollar (Annual Compounding)
$$(1 + i)^n$$

Year	1.00	2.00	3.00	4.00	5.00	6.00	6.25	6.50	6.75	7.00
1	1.0100	1.0200	1.0300	1.0400	1.0500	1.0600	1.0625	1.0650	1.0675	1.0700
2	1.0201	1.0404	1.0609	1.0816	1.1025	1.1236	1.1289	1.1342	1.1396	1.1449
3	1.0303	1.0612	1.0927	1.1249	1.1576	1.1910	1.1995	1.2079	1.2165	1.2250
4	1.0406	1.0824	1.1255	1.1699	1.2155	1.2625	1.2744	1.2865	1.2986	1.3108
5	1.0510	1.1041	1.1593	1.2167	1.2763	1.3382	1.3541	1.3701	1.3862	1.4026
6	1.0615	1.1262	1.1941	1.2653	1.3401	1.4185	1.4387	1.4591	1.4798	1.5007
7	1.0721	1.1487	1.2299	1.3159	1.4071	1.5036	1.5286	1.5540	1.5797	1.6058
8	1.0829	1.1717	1.2668	1.3686	1.4775	1.5938	1.6242	1.6550	1.6863	1.7182
9	1.0937	1.1951	1.3048	1.4233	1.5513	1.6895	1.7257	1.7626	1.8002	1.8385
10	1.1046	1.2190	1.3439	1.4802	1.6289	1.7908	1.8335	1.8771	1.9217	1.9672
11	1.1157	1.2434	1.3842	1.5395	1.7103	1.8983	1.9481	1.9992	2.0514	2.1049
12	1.1268	1.2682	1.4258	1.6010	1.7959	2.0122	2.0699	2.1291	2.1899	2.2522
13	1.1381	1.2936	1.4685	1.6651	1.8856	2.1329	2.1993	2.2675	2.3377	2.4098
14	1.1495	1.3195	1.5126	1.7317	1.9799	2.2609	2.3367	2.4149	2.4955	2.5785
15	1.1610	1.3459	1.5580	1.8009	2.0789	2.3966	2.4828	2.5718	2.6639	2.7590
16	1.1726	1.3728	1.6047	1.8730	2.1829	2.5404	2.6379	2.7390	2.8437	2.9522
17	1.1843	1.4002	1.6528	1.9479	2.2920	2.6928	2.8028	2.9170	3.0357	3.1588
18	1.1961	1.4282	1.7024	2.0258	2.4066	2.8543	2.9780	3.1067	3.2406	3.3799
19	1.2081	1.4568	1.7535	2.1068	2.5270	3.0256	3.1641	3.3086	3.4593	3.6165
20	1.2202	1.4859	1.8061	2.1911	2.6533	3.2071	3.3619	3.5236	3.6928	3.8697
25	1.2824	1.6406	2.0938	2.6658	3.3864	4.2919	4.5522	4.8277	5.1191	5.4274
30	1.3478	1.8114	2.4273	3.2434	4.3219	5.7435	6.1641	6.6144	7.0964	7.6123
35	1.4166	1.9999	2.8139	3.9461	5.5160	7.6861	8.3467	9.0623	9.8373	10.6766
40	1.4889	2.2080	3.2620	4.8010	7.0400	10.2857	11.3021	12.4161	13.6369	14.9745
50	1.6446	2.6916	4.3839	7.1067	11.4674	18.4202	20.7227	23.3067	26.2056	29.4570

TABLE A-1:

(Continued)

Year	7.25	7.50	7.75	8.00	8.25	8.50	8.75	9.00	9.25	9.50
1	1.0725	1.0750	1.0775	1.0800	1.0825	1.0850	1.0875	1.0900	1.0925	1.0950
2	1.1503	1.1556	1.1610	1.1664	1.1718	1.1772	1.1827	1.1881	1.1936	1.1990
3	1.2336	1.2423	1.2510	1.2597	1.2685	1.2773	1.2861	1.2950	1.3040	1.3129
4	1.3231	1.3355	1.3479	1.3605	1.3731	1.3859	1.3987	1.4116	1.4246	1.4377
5	1.4190	1.4356	1.4524	1.4693	1.4864	1.5037	1.5211	1.5386	1.5563	1.5742
6	1.5219	1.5433	1.5650	1.5869	1.6090	1.6315	1.6542	1.6771	1.7003	1.7238
7	1.6322	1.6590	1.6862	1.7138	1.7418	1.7701	1.7989	1.8280	1.8576	1.8876
8	1.7506	1.7835	1.8169	1.8509	1.8855	1.9206	1.9563	1.9926	2.0294	2.0669
9	1.8775	1.9172	1.9577	1.9990	2.0410	2.0839	2.1275	2.1719	2.2171	2.2632
10	2.0136	2.0610	2.1095	2.1589	2.2094	2.2610	2.3136	2.3674	2.4222	2.4782
11	2.1596	2.2156	2.2730	2.3316	2.3917	2.4532	2.5161	2.5804	2.6463	2.7137
12	2.3162	2.3818	2.4491	2.5182	2.5890	2.6617	2.7362	2.8127	2.8911	2.9715
13	2.4841	2.5604	2.6389	2.7196	2.8026	2.8879	2.9756	3.0658	3.1585	3.2537
14	2.6642	2.7524	2.8434	2.9372	3.0338	3.1334	3.2360	3.3417	3.4506	3.5629
15	2.8573	2.9589	3.0638	3.1722	3.2841	3.3997	3.5192	3.6425	3.7698	3.9013
16	3.0645	3.1808	3.3012	3.4259	3.5551	3.6887	3.8271	3.9703	4.1185	4.2719
17	3.2867	3.4194	3.5571	3.7000	3.8483	4.0023	4.1620	4.3276	4.4995	4.6778
18	3.5249	3.6758	3.8328	3.9960	4.1658	4.3425	4.5261	4.7171	4.9157	5.1222
19	3.7805	3.9515	4.1298	4.3157	4.5095	4.7116	4.9222	5.1417	5.3704	5.6088
20	4.0546	4.2479	4.4499	4.6610	4.8816	5.1120	5.3529	5.6044	5.8672	6.1416
25	5.7535	6.0983	6.4630	6.8485	7.2560	7.6868	8.1420	8.6231	9.1314	9.6684
30	8.1643	8.7550	9.3868	10.0627	10.7854	11.5582	12.3845	13.2677	14.2116	15.2203
35	11.5853	12.5689	13.6334	14.7853	16.0316	17.3796	18.8375	20.4140	22.1182	23.9604
40	16.4396	18.0442	19.8012	21.7245	23.8296	26.1330	28.6530	31.4094	34.4237	37.7194
50	33.1028	37.1898	41.7699	46.9016	52.6496	59.0863	66.2923	74.3575	83.3820	93.4773

TABLE A-1:

(Continued)

Year	9.75	10.00	10.50	11.00	11.50	12.00	13.00	14.00	15.00	20.00
1	1.0975	1.1000	1.1050	1.1100	1.1150	1.1200	1.1300	1.1400	1.1500	1.2000
2	1.2045	1.2100	1.2210	1.2321	1.2432	1.2544	1.2769	1.2996	1.3225	1.4400
3	1.3219	1.3310	1.3492	1.3676	1.3862	1.4049	1.4429	1.4815	1.5209	1.7280
4	1.4508	1.4641	1.4909	1.5181	1.5456	1.5735	1.6305	1.6890	1.7490	2.0736
5	1.5923	1.6105	1.6474	1.6851	1.7234	1.7623	1.8424	1.9254	2.0114	2.4883
6	1.7475	1.7716	1.8204	1.8704	1.9215	1.9738	2.0820	2.1950	2.3131	2.9860
7	1.9179	1.9487	2.0116	2.0762	2.1425	2.2107	2.3526	2.5023	2.6600	3.5832
8	2.1049	2.1436	2.2228	2.3045	2.3889	2.4760	2.6584	2.8526	3.0590	4.2998
9	2.3102	2.3579	2.4562	2.5580	2.6636	2.7731	3.0040	3.2519	3.5179	5.1598
10	2.5354	2.5937	2.7141	2.8394	2.9699	3.1058	3.3946	3.7072	4.0456	6.1917
11	2.7826	2.8531	2.9991	3.1518	3.3115	3.4786	3.8359	4.2262	4.6524	7.4301
12	3.0539	3.1384	3.3140	3.4985	3.6923	3.8960	4.3345	4.8179	5.3503	8.9161
13	3.3517	3.4523	3.6619	3.8833	4.1169	4.3635	4.8980	5.4924	6.1528	10.6993
14	3.6784	3.7975	4.0464	4.3104	4.5904	4.8871	5.5348	6.2613	7.0757	12.8392
15	4.0371	4.1772	4.4713	4.7846	5.1183	5.4736	6.2543	7.1379	8.1371	15.4070
16	4.4307	4.5950	4.9408	5.3109	5.7069	6.1304	7.0673	8.1372	9.3576	18.4884
17	4.8627	5.0545	5.4596	5.8951	6.3632	6.8660	7.9861	9.2765	10.7613	22.1861
18	5.3368	5.5599	6.0328	6.5436	7.0949	7.6900	9.0243	10.5752	12.3755	26.6233
19	5.8571	6.1159	6.6663	7.2633	7.9108	8.6128	10.1974	12.0557	14.2318	31.9480
20	6.4282	6.7275	7.3662	8.0623	8.8206	9.6463	11.5231	13.7435	16.3665	38.3376
25	10.2356	10.8347	12.1355	13.5855	15.2010	17.0001	21.2305	26.4619	32.9190	95.3962
30	16.2981	17.4494	19.9926	22.8923	26.1967	29.9599	39.1159	50.9502	66.2118	237.376
35	25.9513	28.1024	32.9367	38.5749	45.1461	52.7996	72.0685	98.1002	133.176	590.668
40	41.3220	45.2592	54.2614	65.0009	77.8027	93.0510	132.782	188.884	267.864	1469.77
50	104.767	177.391	147.270	184.565	231.070	289.002	450.736	700.233	1083.66	9100.44

416

TABLE A-2:
Compound Value of a Dollar (Monthly Compounding)

$$\left(1 + \frac{i}{12}\right)^{12n}$$

Year	1.00	2.00	3.00	4.00	5.00	6.00	6.25	6.50	6.75	7.00
1	1.0100	1.0202	1.0304	1.0407	1.0512	1.0617	1.0643	1.0670	1.0696	1.0723
2	1.0202	1.0408	1.0618	1.0831	1.1049	1.1272	1.1328	1.1384	1.1441	1.1498
3	1.0304	1.0618	1.0941	1.1273	1.1615	1.1967	1.2056	1.2147	1.2238	1.2329
4	1.0408	1.0832	1.1273	1.1732	1.2209	1.2705	1.2832	1.2960	1.3090	1.3221
5	1.0512	1.1051	1.1616	1.2210	1.2834	1.3488	1.3657	1.3828	1.4001	1.4176
6	1.0618	1.1274	1.1969	1.2707	1.3490	1.4320	1.4536	1.4754	1.4976	1.5201
7	1.0725	1.1501	1.2334	1.3225	1.4180	1.5204	1.5471	1.5742	1.6019	1.6300
8	1.0833	1.1734	1.2709	1.3764	1.4906	1.6141	1.6466	1.6797	1.7134	1.7478
9	1.0941	1.1970	1.3095	1.4325	1.5668	1.7137	1.7525	1.7922	1.8327	1.8742
10	1.1051	1.2212	1.3494	1.4908	1.6470	1.8194	1.8652	1.9122	1.9603	2.0097
11	1.1162	1.2458	1.3904	1.5516	1.7313	1.9316	1.9852	2.0402	2.0968	2.1549
12	1.1274	1.2710	1.4327	1.6148	1.8198	2.0507	2.1129	2.1769	2.2428	2.3107
13	1.1388	1.2966	1.4763	1.6806	1.9130	2.1772	2.2488	2.3227	2.3990	2.4778
14	1.1502	1.3228	1.5212	1.7490	2.0108	2.3115	2.3934	2.4782	2.5660	2.6569
15	1.1618	1.3495	1.5674	1.8203	2.1137	2.4541	2.5474	2.6442	2.7447	2.8489
16	1.1734	1.3768	1.6151	1.8945	2.2218	2.6055	2.7112	2.8213	2.9358	3.0549
17	1.1852	1.4045	1.6642	1.9716	2.3355	2.7662	2.8856	3.0102	3.1402	3.2757
18	1.1971	1.4329	1.7148	2.0520	2.4550	2.9368	3.0712	3.2118	3.3588	3.5125
19	1.2092	1.4618	1.7670	2.1356	2.5806	3.1179	3.2688	3.4269	3.5927	3.7665
20	1.2213	1.4913	1.8208	2.2226	2.7126	3.3102	3.4790	3.6564	3.8429	4.0387
25	1.2839	1.6480	2.1150	2.7138	3.4813	4.4650	4.7514	5.0562	5.3804	5.7254
30	1.3497	1.8212	2.4568	3.3135	4.4677	6.0226	6.4892	6.9918	7.5332	8.1165
35	1.4189	2.0126	2.8539	4.0458	5.7337	8.1235	8.8624	9.6684	10.5474	11.5061
40	1.4916	2.2241	3.3151	4.9399	7.3584	10.9574	12.1037	13.3696	14.7675	16.3114
50	1.6484	2.7160	4.4733	7.3645	12.1194	19.9359	22.5760	25.5651	28.9491	32.7803

TABLE A-2:
(Continued)

Year	7.25	7.50	7.75	8.00	8.25	8.50	8.75	9.00	9.25	9.50
1	1.0750	1.0776	1.0803	1.0830	1.0857	1.0884	1.0911	1.0938	1.0965	1.0992
2	1.1555	1.1613	1.1671	1.1729	1.1787	1.1846	1.1905	1.1964	1.2024	1.2083
3	1.2422	1.2514	1.2608	1.2702	1.2797	1.2893	1.2989	1.3086	1.3184	1.3283
4	1.3353	1.3486	1.3621	1.3757	1.3894	1.4033	1.4173	1.4314	1.4457	1.4601
5	1.4354	1.4533	1.4715	1.4898	1.5085	1.5273	1.5464	1.5657	1.5852	1.6050
6	1.5429	1.5661	1.5896	1.6135	1.6377	1.6623	1.6872	1.7126	1.7382	1.7643
7	1.6586	1.6877	1.7173	1.7474	1.7781	1.8092	1.8409	1.8732	1.9060	1.9394
8	1.7829	1.8187	1.8552	1.8925	1.9304	1.9692	2.0086	2.0489	2.0900	2.1319
9	1.9166	1.9599	2.0042	2.0495	2.0958	2.1432	2.1916	2.2411	2.2917	2.3435
10	2.0602	2.1121	2.1652	2.2196	2.2754	2.3326	2.3913	2.4514	2.5129	2.5761
11	2.2147	2.2760	2.3391	2.4039	2.4704	2.5388	2.6091	2.6813	2.7555	2.8317
12	2.3807	2.4527	2.5269	2.6034	2.6821	2.7632	2.8468	2.9328	3.0215	3.1128
13	2.5591	2.6431	2.7299	2.8195	2.9120	3.0075	3.1061	3.2080	3.3131	3.4217
14	2.7509	2.8483	2.9491	3.0535	3.1615	3.2733	3.3891	3.5089	3.6329	3.7613
15	2.9572	3.0694	3.1860	3.3069	3.4324	3.5626	3.6978	3.8380	3.9836	4.1346
16	3.1788	3.3077	3.4419	3.5814	3.7265	3.8776	4.0346	4.1981	4.3681	4.5449
17	3.4171	3.5645	3.7183	3.8786	4.0459	4.2203	4.4022	4.5919	4.7897	4.9960
18	3.6732	3.8412	4.0169	4.2006	4.3926	4.5933	4.8032	5.0226	5.2520	5.4919
19	3.9486	4.1395	4.3395	4.5492	4.7690	4.9993	5.2408	5.4938	5.7590	6.0369
20	4.2446	4.4608	4.6880	4.9268	5.1777	5.4412	5.7182	6.0091	6.3149	6.6361
25	6.0924	6.4829	6.8983	7.3402	7.8103	8.3104	8.8424	9.4084	10.0105	10.6510
30	8.7448	9.4215	10.1505	10.9357	11.7815	12.6925	13.6737	14.7305	15.8688	17.0949
35	12.5518	13.6922	14.9360	16.2925	17.7719	19.3852	21.1446	23.0633	25.1557	27.4375
40	18.0162	19.8988	21.9777	24.2733	26.8081	29.6070	32.6975	36.1098	39.8774	44.0375
50	37.1176	42.0276	47.5859	53.8780	61.0004	69.0627	78.1885	88.5179	100.209	113.443

TABLE A-2:

(Continued)

Year	9.75	10.00	10.50	11.00	11.50	12.00	13.00	14.00	15.00	20.00
1	1.1020	1.1047	1.1102	1.1157	1.1213	1.1268	1.1380	1.1493	1.1608	1.2194
2	1.2144	1.2204	1.2326	1.2448	1.2572	1.2697	1.2951	1.3210	1.3474	1.4869
3	1.3382	1.3482	1.3684	1.3889	1.4097	1.4308	1.4739	1.5183	1.5639	1.8131
4	1.4747	1.4894	1.5192	1.5496	1.5806	1.6122	1.6773	1.7450	1.8154	2.2109
5	1.6250	1.6453	1.6866	1.7289	1.7723	1.8167	1.9089	2.0056	2.1072	2.6960
6	1.7908	1.8176	1.8725	1.9290	1.9872	2.0471	2.1723	2.3051	2.4459	3.2874
7	1.9734	2.0079	2.0788	2.1522	2.2281	2.3067	2.4722	2.6494	2.8391	4.0087
8	2.1746	2.2182	2.3079	2.4013	2.4983	2.5993	2.8134	3.0451	3.2955	4.8881
9	2.3964	2.4504	2.5623	2.6791	2.8013	2.9289	3.2018	3.4998	3.8253	5.9606
10	2.6407	2.7070	2.8446	2.9892	3.1409	3.3004	3.6437	4.0225	4.4402	7.2683
11	2.9100	2.9905	3.1581	3.3351	3.5218	3.7190	4.1467	4.6232	5.1540	8.8628
12	3.2068	3.3037	3.5062	3.7210	3.9489	4.1906	4.7191	5.3136	5.9825	10.8073
13	3.5338	3.6496	3.8925	4.1516	4.4277	4.7221	5.3705	6.1072	6.9442	13.1783
14	3.8942	4.0317	4.3215	4.6320	4.9646	5.3210	6.1117	7.0192	8.0606	16.0695
15	4.2913	4.4539	4.7978	5.1680	5.5666	5.9958	6.9554	8.0675	9.3563	19.5950
16	4.7289	4.9203	5.3265	5.7660	6.2416	6.7562	7.9154	9.2723	10.8604	23.8940
17	5.2112	5.4355	5.9135	6.4333	6.9985	7.6131	9.0080	10.6571	12.6063	29.1361
18	5.7426	6.0047	6.5652	7.1777	7.8471	8.5786	10.2514	12.2486	14.6328	35.5283
19	6.3282	6.6335	7.2887	8.0083	8.7986	9.6666	11.6665	14.0779	16.9851	43.3229
20	6.9735	7.3281	8.0919	8.9350	9.8656	10.8926	13.2768	16.1803	19.7155	52.8275
25	11.3323	12.0570	13.6479	15.4479	17.4845	19.7885	25.3435	32.4513	41.5442	142.421
30	18.4153	19.8374	23.0186	26.7082	30.9872	35.9497	48.3772	65.0847	87.5411	383.964
35	29.9256	32.6387	38.8232	46.1762	54.9178	65.3097	92.3451	130.535	184.465	1035.15
40	48.6302	53.7008	65.4793	79.8347	97.3294	118.648	176.274	261.802	388.701	2790.75
50	128.420	145.371	186.265	238.638	305.707	391.585	642.294	1053.09	1725.92	20283.9

TABLE A-3:

Compound Value of an Annuity of \$1 (Annual Payments, Annual Compounding)

$$1 + (1 + i) + (1 + i)^2 + (1 + i)^3 + \ldots + (1 + i)^{n-i}$$

Year	1.00	2.00	3.00	4.00	5.00	6.00	6.25	6.50	6.75	7.00
1	1.0000	1.0000	1.0000	1.0000	1.0000	1.0000	1.0000	1.0000	1.0000	1.0000
2	2.0100	2.0200	2.0300	2.0400	2.0500	2.0600	2.0625	2.0650	2.0675	2.0700
3	3.0301	3.0604	3.0909	3.126	3.1525	3.1836	3.1914	3.1992	3.2071	3.2149
4	4.0604	4.1216	4.1836	4.2465	4.3101	4.3746	4.3909	4.4072	4.4235	4.4399
5	5.1010	5.2040	5.3091	5.4163	5.5256	5.6371	5.6653	5.6936	5.7221	5.7507
6	6.1520	6.3081	6.4684	6.6330	6.8019	6.9753	7.0194	7.0637	7.1084	7.1533
7	7.2135	7.4343	7.6625	7.8983	8.1420	8.3938	8.4581	8.5229	8.5882	8.6540
8	8.2857	8.5830	8.8923	9.2142	9.5491	9.8975	9.9867	10.077	10.168	10.260
9	9.369	9.755	10.159	10.583	11.027	11.491	11.611	11.732	11.854	11.978
10	10.462	10.950	11.464	12.006	12.578	13.181	13.337	13.494	13.654	13.816
11	11.567	12.169	12.808	13.486	14.207	14.972	15.170	15.372	15.576	15.784
12	12.683	13.412	14.192	15.026	15.917	16.870	17.118	17.731	17.627	17.888
13	13.809	14.680	15.618	16.627	17.713	18.882	19.188	19.500	19.817	20.141
14	14.947	15.974	17.086	18.292	19.599	21.015	21.387	21.767	22.155	22.550
15	16.097	17.293	18.599	20.024	21.579	23.276	23.724	24.182	24.650	25.129
16	17.258	18.639	20.157	21.825	23.657	25.673	26.207	26.754	27.314	27.888
17	18.430	20.012	21.762	23.698	25.840	28.213	28.845	29.493	30.158	30.840
18	19.615	21.41	23.414	25.645	28.132	30.906	31.648	32.410	33.194	33.999
19	20.811	22.841	25.117	27.671	30.539	33.760	34.626	35.517	36.434	37.379
20	22.019	24.297	26.870	29.778	33.066	36.786	37.790	38.825	39.894	40.995
25	28.243	32.030	36.459	41.646	47.727	54.865	56.836	58.888	61.024	63.249
30	34.785	40.568	47.575	56.085	66.439	79.058	82.625	86.375	90.317	94.461
35	41.660	49.994	60.462	73.652	90.320	111.435	117.547	124.035	130.923	138.237
40	48.886	60.402	75.401	95.026	120.800	154.762	164.833	175.632	187.213	199.635
50	64.463	84.579	112.797	152.667	209.348	290.336	315.564	343.180	373.416	406.529

TABLE A-3:

(Continued)

Year	7.25	7.50	7.75	8.00	8.25	8.50	8.75	9.00	9.25	9.50
1	1.0000	1.0000	1.0000	1.0000	1.0000	1.0000	1.0000	1.0000	1.0000	1.0000
2	2.0725	2.0750	2.0775	2.0800	2.0825	2.0850	2.0875	2.0900	2.0925	2.0950
3	3.2228	3.2306	3.2385	3.2464	3.2543	3.2622	3.2702	3.2781	3.2861	3.2940
4	4.4564	4.4729	4.4895	4.5061	4.5228	4.5395	4.5563	4.5731	4.5900	4.6070
5	5.7795	5.8084	5.8374	5.8666	5.8959	5.9254	5.9550	5.9847	6.0146	6.0446
6	7.1985	7.2440	7.2898	7.3359	7.3823	7.4290	7.4760	7.5233	7.5709	7.6189
7	8.7204	8.7873	8.8548	8.9228	8.9914	9.0605	9.1302	9.2004	9.2713	9.3426
8	10.353	10.446	10.541	10.637	10.733	10.831	10.929	11.028	11.129	11.230
9	12.103	12.230	12.358	12.488	12.619	12.751	12.885	13.021	13.158	13.297
10	13.981	14.147	14.316	14.487	14.660	14.835	15.013	15.193	15.375	15.560
11	15.994	16.208	16.425	16.645	16.869	17.096	17.326	17.560	17.798	18.039
12	18.154	18.424	18.698	18.977	19.261	19.549	19.843	20.141	20.444	20.752
13	20.470	20.806	21.147	21.495	21.850	22.211	22.579	22.953	23.335	23.724
14	22.954	23.366	23.786	24.215	24.652	25.099	25.554	26.019	26.493	26.977
15	25.618	26.118	26.630	27.152	27.686	28.232	28.790	29.361	29.944	30.540
16	28.476	29.077	29.693	30.324	30.970	31.632	32.310	33.003	33.714	34.442
17	31.540	32.258	32.995	33.750	34.525	35.321	36.137	36.974	37.832	38.713
18	34.827	35.677	36.552	37.450	38.374	39.323	40.299	41.301	42.332	43.391
19	38.352	39.353	40.384	41.446	42.540	43.665	44.825	46.018	47.248	48.513
20	42.132	43.305	44.514	45.762	47.049	48.377	49.747	51.160	52.618	54.122
25	65.566	67.978	70.490	73.106	75.830	78.668	81.623	84.701	87.907	91.246
30	98.818	103.399	108.217	113.283	118.611	124.215	130.108	136.308	142.828	149.687
35	146.004	154.252	163.012	172.317	182.201	192.702	203.858	215.711	228.305	241.688
40	212.960	227.257	242.596	259.057	276.722	295.682	316.035	337.882	361.338	386.520
50	442.798	482.530	526.064	573.770	626.056	683.368	746.198	815.084	890.616	973.445

TABLE A-3:

(Continued)

Year	9.75	10.00	10.50	11.00	11.50	12.00	13.00	14.00	15.00	20.00
1	1.0000	1.0000	1.0000	1.0000	1.0000	1.0000	1.0000	1.0000	1.0000	1.0000
2	2.0975	2.1000	2.1050	2.1100	2.1150	2.1200	2.1300	2.1400	2.1500	2.2000
3	3.3020	3.3100	3.3260	3.3421	3.3582	3.3744	3.4069	3.4396	3.4725	3.6400
4	4.6240	4.6410	4.6753	4.7097	4.7444	4.7793	4.8498	4.9211	4.9934	5.3680
5	6.0748	6.1051	6.1662	6.2278	6.2900	6.3528	6.4803	6.6101	6.7424	7.4416
6	7.6671	7.7156	7.8136	7.9129	8.0134	8.1152	8.3227	8.5355	8.7537	9.9299
7	9.4146	9.4872	9.6340	9.7833	9.9349	10.089	10.405	10.730	11.067	12.916
8	11.333	11.436	11.646	11.856	12.077	12.300	12.757	13.233	13.727	16.499
9	13.437	13.579	13.868	14.164	14.466	14.776	15.416	16.085	16.786	20.799
10	15.748	15.937	16.325	16.722	17.130	17.549	18.420	19.337	20.304	25.959
11	18.283	18.531	19.039	19.561	20.100	20.655	21.814	23.045	24.349	32.150
12	21.066	21.384	22.038	22.713	23.411	24.133	25.650	27.271	29.002	39.581
13	24.120	24.523	25.352	26.212	27.104	28.029	29.985	32.089	34.352	48.497
14	27.471	27.975	29.014	30.095	31.221	32.393	34.883	37.581	40.505	59.196
15	31.150	31.772	33.060	34.405	35.811	37.280	40.417	43.842	47.580	72.035
16	35.187	35.950	37.531	39.190	40.929	42.753	46.672	50.980	55.717	87.442
17	39.617	40.545	42.472	44.501	46.636	48.884	53.739	59.118	65.075	105.931
18	44.480	45.599	47.932	50.396	52.999	55.750	61.725	68.394	75.836	128.117
19	49.817	51.159	53.965	56.939	60.094	63.440	70.749	78.969	88.212	154.740
20	55.674	57.275	60.631	64.203	68.005	72.052	80.947	91.025	102.444	186.688
25	94.724	98.347	106.052	114.413	123.487	133.334	155.620	181.871	212.793	471.981
30	156.903	164.494	180.882	199.021	219.101	241.333	293.199	356.787	434.745	1181.88
35	255.910	271.024	304.159	341.590	383.879	431.664	546.681	693.573	881.170	2948.34
40	413.559	442.592	507.252	581.826	667.850	767.092	1013.70	1342.03	1779.09	7343.86
50	1064.28	1163.91	1393.05	1668.77	2000.61	2400.02	3459.51	4994.52	7217.72	45497.2

TABLE A-4:

Compound Value of an Annuity of $1 (Monthly Payments, Monthly Compounding)

$$1 + \left(1 + \frac{i}{12}\right) + \left(1 + \frac{i}{12}\right)^2 + \left(1 + \frac{i}{12}\right)^3 + \ldots + \left(1 + \frac{i}{12}\right)^3 + \ldots + \left(1 + \frac{i}{12}\right)^{12n-1}$$

Year	1.00	2.00	3.00	4.00	5.00	6.00	6.25	6.50
1	12.0552	12.1106	12.1664	12.2225	12.2789	12.3356	12.3498	12.3640
2	24.2314	24.4657	24.7028	24.9429	25.1859	25.4320	25.4939	25.5561
3	36.5300	37.0701	37.6206	38.1816	38.7533	39.3361	39.4835	39.6317
4	48.9521	49.9290	50.9312	51.9596	53.0149	54.0978	54.3730	54.6499
5	61.4990	63.0474	64.6467	66.2990	68.0061	69.7700	70.2201	70.6740
6	74.1720	76.4305	78.7794	81.2226	83.7642	86.4088	87.0866	87.7712
7	86.9723	90.0838	93.3419	96.7541	100.329	104.074	105.038	106.013
8	99.9012	104.013	108.347	112.919	117.740	122.829	124.144	125.477
9	112.960	118.223	123.809	129.741	136.043	142.740	144.479	146.245
10	126.150	132.720	139.741	147.250	155.282	163.879	166.122	168.403
11	139.472	147.509	156.158	165.471	175.506	186.323	189.157	192.045
12	152.929	162.597	173.074	184.435	196.764	210.150	213.674	217.271
13	166.520	177.990	190.505	204.172	219.109	235.447	239.767	244.186
14	180.248	193.693	208.466	224.713	242.598	262.305	267.539	272.904
15	194.114	209.713	226.973	246.090	267.289	290.819	297.098	303.545
16	208.119	226.057	246.043	268.339	293.243	321.091	328.557	336.238
17	222.265	242.730	265.693	291.494	320.524	353.231	362.040	371.120
18	236.553	259.740	285.940	315.592	349.202	387.353	397.677	408.339
19	250.985	277.093	306.804	340.673	379.347	423.580	435.606	448.050
20	265.561	294.797	328.302	366.774	411.033	462.041	475.975	490.421
25	340.670	388.821	446.008	514.129	595.509	692.993	720.273	748.836
30	419.628	492.725	582.737	694.049	832.258	1004.51	1053.92	1106.18
35	502.633	607.548	741.563	913.730	1136.09	1424.71	1509.59	1600.31
40	589.891	734.435	926.059	1181.96	1526.02	1991.49	2131.91	2283.62
50	778.053	1029.61	1389.32	1909.35	2668.65	3787.18	4142.59	4535.09

TABLE A-4:
(Continued)

Year	6.75	7.00	7.25	7.50	7.75	8.00	8.25	8.50
1	12.3783	12.3926	12.4069	12.4212	12.4356	12.4499	12.4643	12.4787
2	25.6185	25.6810	25.7438	25.8067	25.8699	25.9332	25.9967	26.0604
3	39.7805	39.9301	40.0804	40.2314	40.3831	40.5356	40.6887	40.8427
4	54.9287	55.2092	55.4916	55.7759	56.0619	56.3499	56.6397	56.9315
5	71.1315	71.5929	72.0581	72.5271	73.0000	73.4768	73.9576	74.4424
6	88.4626	89.1609	89.8663	90.5788	91.2984	92.0253	92.7595	93.5012
7	107.000	107.999	109.009	110.032	111.066	112.113	113.173	114.245
8	126.829	128.199	129.587	130.995	132.422	133.869	135.335	136.821
9	148.038	149.859	151.708	153.586	155.493	157.429	159.396	161.394
10	170.724	173.085	175.487	177.930	180.416	180.946	185.520	188.138
11	194.989	197.990	201.048	204.165	207.342	210.580	213.882	217.247
12	220.944	224.695	228.525	232.436	236.430	240.508	244.674	248.928
13	248.706	253.331	258.061	262.901	267.853	272.920	278.105	283.410
14	278.402	284.037	289.812	295.732	301.801	308.022	314.400	320.939
15	310.164	316.962	323.943	331.112	338.475	346.038	353.806	361.786
16	344.139	352.268	360.632	369.238	378.095	387.209	396.589	406.243
17	380.479	390.126	400.071	410.324	420.896	431.797	443.038	454.630
18	419.349	430.721	442.467	454.600	467.135	480.086	493.467	507.294
19	460.926	474.250	488.040	502.313	517.088	532.382	548.217	564.613
20	505.397	520.926	537.030	553.730	571.052	589.020	607.660	626.998
25	778.746	810.071	842.884	877.260	913.279	951.025	990.587	1032.06
30	1161.46	1219.97	1281.89	1347.44	1416.85	1490.36	1568.22	1650.70
35	1697.31	1801.05	1912.02	2030.76	2157.84	2293.88	2439.55	2595.56
40	2447.57	2624.81	2816.48	3023.82	3248.17	3491.00	3753.91	4038.64
50	4968.74	5448.06	5978.08	6564.42	7213.31	7931.70	8727.34	9608.86

TABLE A-4:

(Continued)

Year	8.75	9.00	9.25	9.50	9.75	10.00	10.50	11.00
1	12.4931	12.5076	12.5221	12.5365	12.5510	12.5656	12.5947	12.6239
2	26.1244	26.1885	26.2528	26.3173	26.3820	26.4469	26.5773	26.7086
3	40.9973	41.1527	41.3089	41.4658	41.6234	41.7818	42.1009	42.4231
4	57.2251	57.5207	57.8182	58.1177	58.4191	58.7225	59.3353	59.9562
5	74.9312	75.4241	75.9211	76.4223	76.9276	77.4371	78.4689	79.5181
6	94.2503	95.0070	95.7714	96.5435	97.3235	98.1113	99.7112	101.344
7	115.329	116.427	117.538	118.662	119.799	120.950	123.294	125.695
8	138.328	139.856	141.405	142.975	144.567	146.181	149.477	152.864
9	163.423	165.483	167.576	169.702	171.861	174.054	178.544	183.177
10	190.803	193.514	196.273	199.081	201.938	204.845	210.815	216.998
11	220.677	224.175	227.740	231.376	235.082	238.861	246.642	254.733
12	253.273	257.711	262.245	266.876	271.606	276.438	286.418	296.834
13	288.839	294.394	300.080	305.899	311.855	317.950	330.577	343.807
14	327.644	334.518	341.567	348.795	356.208	363.809	379.602	396.216
15	369.984	378.405	387.058	395.949	405.084	414.471	434.030	454.690
16	416.181	426.410	436.941	447.782	458.944	470.437	494.456	519.930
17	466.586	478.918	491.638	504.760	518.297	532.263	561.542	592.720
18	521.583	536.351	551.615	567.393	583.703	600.564	636.021	673.932
19	581.591	599.172	617.381	636.242	655.778	676.016	718.707	764.543
20	647.064	667.886	689.495	711.924	735.204	759.370	810.506	865.639
25	1075.53	1121.12	1168.93	1219.07	1271.66	1326.84	1445.47	1576.14
30	1738.11	1830.74	1928.93	2033.04	2143.42	2260.49	2516.41	2804.52
35	2762.69	2941.78	3133.71	3339.47	3560.07	3796.65	4322.65	4928.31
40	4347.09	4681.31	5043.56	5436.31	5862.17	6324.10	7369.06	8600.15
50	10585.9	11669.1	12870.4	14203.3	15682.4	17324.4	21173.1	25924.1

Year	11.50	12.00	13.00	14.00	15.00	20.00
1	12.6531	12.6825	12.7415	12.8007	12.8604	13.1635
2	26.8406	26.9735	27.2417	27.5132	27.7881	29.2149
3	42.7484	43.0769	43.7434	44.4228	45.1155	48.7878
4	60.5852	61.2226	62.5228	63.8577	65.2284	72.6549
5	80.5849	81.6697	83.8945	86.1951	88.5745	101.758
6	103.010	104.710	108.216	111.868	115.674	137.247
7	128.154	130.672	135.895	141.376	147.129	180.521
8	156.347	159.927	167.394	175.290	183.641	233.289
9	187.958	192.893	203.242	214.269	226.023	297.634
10	223.403	230.039	244.037	259.069	275.217	376.095
11	263.146	271.896	290.464	310.560	332.320	471.771
12	307.708	319.062	343.298	369.740	398.602	588.436
13	357.674	372.209	403.426	437.758	475.540	730.698
14	413.698	432.097	471.854	515.935	564.845	904.170
15	476.516	499.581	549.726	605.787	668.507	1115.70
16	546.952	575.622	638.348	709.057	788.833	1373.64
17	625.928	661.308	739.202	827.749	928.502	1688.17
18	714.481	757.861	853.977	964.168	1090.62	2071.70
19	813.771	866.660	984.596	1120.96	1278.81	2539.37
20	925.102	989.256	1133.24	1301.17	1497.24	3109.65
25	1720.12	1878.85	2247.09	2695.83	3243.53	8485.28
30	3129.10	3494.97	4373.28	5492.98	6923.29	22977.8
35	5626.21	6430.97	8431.85	11103.0	14677.2	62049.3
40	10051.8	11764.8	16179.1	22354.4	31016.1	167385.
50	31795.5	39058.4	59196.4	90179.1	137993.	1216971.

TABLE A-5:

Present Value of a Dollar (Annual Compounding)

$$\frac{1}{(1 + i)^n}$$

Year	1.00	2.00	3.00	4.00	5.00	6.00	6.25	6.50	6.75	7.00
1	0.9901	0.9804	0.9709	0.9615	0.9524	0.9434	0.9412	0.9390	0.9368	0.9346
2	0.9803	0.9612	0.9426	0.9246	0.9070	0.8900	0.8858	0.8817	0.8775	0.8734
3	0.9706	0.9423	0.9151	0.8890	0.8638	0.8396	0.8337	0.8278	0.8220	0.8163
4	0.9610	0.9238	0.8885	0.8548	0.8227	0.7921	0.7847	0.7773	0.7701	0.7629
5	0.9515	0.9057	0.8626	0.8219	0.7835	0.7473	0.7385	0.7299	0.7214	0.7130
6	0.9420	0.8880	0.8375	0.7903	0.7462	0.7050	0.6951	0.6853	0.6758	0.6663
7	0.9327	0.8706	0.8131	0.7599	0.7107	0.6651	0.6542	0.6435	0.6330	0.6227
8	0.9235	0.8535	0.7894	0.7307	0.6768	0.6274	0.6157	0.6042	0.5930	0.5820
9	0.9143	0.8368	0.7664	0.7026	0.6446	0.5919	0.5795	0.5674	0.5555	0.5439
10	0.9053	0.8203	0.7441	0.6756	0.6139	0.5584	0.5454	0.5327	0.5204	0.5083
11	0.8963	0.8043	0.7224	0.6496	0.5847	0.5268	0.5133	0.5002	0.4875	0.4751
12	0.8874	0.7885	0.7014	0.6246	0.5568	0.4970	0.4831	0.4697	0.4567	0.4440
13	0.8787	0.7730	0.6810	0.6006	0.5303	0.4688	0.4547	0.4410	0.4278	0.4150
14	0.8700	0.7579	0.6611	0.5775	0.5051	0.4423	0.4280	0.4141	0.4007	0.3878
15	0.8613	0.7430	0.6419	0.5553	0.4810	0.4173	0.4028	0.3888	0.3754	0.3624
16	0.8528	0.7284	0.6232	0.5339	0.4581	0.3936	0.3791	0.3651	0.3517	0.3387
17	0.8444	0.7142	0.6050	0.5134	0.4363	0.3714	0.3568	0.3428	0.3294	0.3166
18	0.8360	0.7002	0.5874	0.4936	0.4155	0.3503	0.3358	0.3219	0.3086	0.2959
19	0.8277	0.6864	0.5703	0.4746	0.3957	0.3305	0.3160	0.3022	0.2891	0.2765
20	0.8195	0.6730	0.5537	0.4564	0.3769	0.3118	0.2975	0.2838	0.2708	0.2584
25	0.7798	0.6095	0.4776	0.3751	0.2953	0.2330	0.2197	0.2071	0.1953	0.1842
30	0.7419	0.5521	0.4120	0.3083	0.2314	0.1741	0.1622	0.1512	0.1409	0.1314
35	0.7059	0.5000	0.3554	0.2534	0.1813	0.1301	0.1198	0.1103	0.1017	0.0937
40	0.6717	0.4529	0.3066	0.2083	0.1420	0.0972	0.0885	0.0805	0.0733	0.0668
50	0.6080	0.3715	0.2281	0.1407	0.0872	0.0543	0.0483	0.0429	0.0382	0.0339

TABLE A-5:

(Continued)

Year	7.25	7.50	7.75	8.00	8.25	8.50	8.75	9.00	9.25	9.50
1	0.9324	0.9302	0.9281	0.9259	0.9238	0.9217	0.9195	0.9174	0.9153	0.9132
2	0.8694	0.8653	0.8613	0.8573	0.8534	0.8495	0.8456	0.8417	0.8378	0.8340
3	0.8106	0.8050	0.7994	0.7938	0.7883	0.7829	0.7775	0.7722	0.7669	0.7617
4	0.7558	0.7488	0.7419	0.7350	0.7283	0.7216	0.7150	0.7084	0.7020	0.6956
5	0.7047	0.6966	0.6885	0.6806	0.6728	0.6650	0.6574	0.6499	0.6425	0.6352
6	0.6571	0.6480	0.6390	0.6302	0.6215	0.6129	0.6045	0.5963	0.5881	0.5801
7	0.6127	0.6028	0.5930	0.5835	0.5741	0.5649	0.5559	0.5470	0.5383	0.5298
8	0.5712	0.5607	0.5504	0.5403	0.5304	0.5207	0.5112	0.5019	0.4928	0.4838
9	0.5326	0.5216	0.5108	0.5002	0.4899	0.4799	0.4700	0.4604	0.4510	0.4418
10	0.4966	0.4852	0.4741	0.4632	0.4526	0.4423	0.4322	0.4224	0.4128	0.4035
11	0.4631	0.4513	0.4400	0.4289	0.4181	0.4076	0.3974	0.3875	0.3779	0.3685
12	0.4318	0.4199	0.4083	0.3971	0.3862	0.3757	0.3655	0.3555	0.3459	0.3365
13	0.4026	0.3906	0.3789	0.3677	0.3568	0.3463	0.3361	0.3262	0.3166	0.3073
14	0.3754	0.3633	0.3517	0.3405	0.3296	0.3191	0.3090	0.2992	0.2898	0.2807
15	0.3500	0.3380	0.3264	0.3152	0.3045	0.2941	0.2842	0.2745	0.2653	0.2563
16	0.3263	0.3144	0.3029	0.2919	0.2813	0.2711	0.2613	0.2519	0.2428	0.2341
17	0.3043	0.2925	0.2811	0.2703	0.2599	0.2499	0.2403	0.2311	0.2222	0.2138
18	0.2837	0.2720	0.2609	0.2502	0.2400	0.2303	0.2209	0.2120	0.2034	0.1952
19	0.2645	0.2531	0.2421	0.2317	0.2218	0.2122	0.2032	0.1945	0.1862	0.1783
20	0.2466	0.2354	0.2247	0.2145	0.2049	0.1956	0.1868	0.1784	0.1704	0.1628
25	0.1738	0.1640	0.1547	0.1460	0.1378	0.1301	0.1228	0.1160	0.1095	0.1034
30	0.1225	0.1142	0.1065	0.0994	0.0927	0.0865	0.0807	0.0754	0.0704	0.0657
35	0.0863	0.0796	0.0733	0.0676	0.0624	0.0575	0.0531	0.0490	0.0452	0.0417
40	0.0608	0.0554	0.0505	0.0460	0.0420	0.0383	0.0349	0.0318	0.0290	0.0265
50	0.0302	0.0269	0.0239	0.0213	0.0190	0.0169	0.0151	0.0134	0.0120	0.0107

TABLE A-5:

(Continued)

Year	9.75	10.00	10.50	11.00	11.50	12.00	13.00	14.00	15.00	20.00
1	0.9112	0.9091	0.9050	0.9009	0.8969	0.8929	0.8850	0.8772	0.8696	0.8333
2	0.8302	0.8264	0.8190	0.8116	0.8044	0.7972	0.7831	0.7695	0.7561	0.6944
3	0.7565	0.7513	0.7412	0.7312	0.7214	0.7118	0.6931	0.6750	0.6575	0.5787
4	0.6893	0.6830	0.6707	0.6587	0.6470	0.6355	0.6133	0.5921	0.5718	0.4823
5	0.6280	0.6209	0.6070	0.5935	0.5803	0.5674	0.5428	0.5194	0.4972	0.4019
6	0.5722	0.5645	0.5493	0.5346	0.5204	0.5066	0.4803	0.4556	0.4323	0.3349
7	0.5214	0.5132	0.4971	0.4817	0.4667	0.4523	0.4251	0.3996	0.3759	0.2791
8	0.4751	0.4665	0.4499	0.4339	0.4186	0.4039	0.3762	0.3506	0.3269	0.2326
9	0.4329	0.4241	0.4071	0.3909	0.3754	0.3606	0.3329	0.3075	0.2843	0.1938
10	0.3944	0.3855	0.3684	0.3522	0.3367	0.3220	0.2946	0.2697	0.2472	0.1615
11	0.3594	0.3505	0.3334	0.3173	0.3020	0.2875	0.2607	0.2366	0.2149	0.1346
12	0.3275	0.3186	0.3018	0.2858	0.2708	0.2567	0.2307	0.2076	0.1869	0.1122
13	0.2984	0.2897	0.2731	0.2575	0.2429	0.2292	0.2042	0.1821	0.1625	0.0935
14	0.2719	0.2633	0.2471	0.2320	0.2178	0.2046	0.1807	0.1597	0.1413	0.0779
15	0.2477	0.2394	0.2236	0.2090	0.1954	0.1827	0.1599	0.1401	0.1229	0.0649
16	0.2257	0.2176	0.2024	0.1883	0.1752	0.1631	0.1415	0.1229	0.1069	0.0541
17	0.2056	0.1978	0.1832	0.1696	0.1572	0.1456	0.1252	0.1078	0.0929	0.0451
18	0.1874	0.1799	0.1658	0.1528	0.1409	0.1300	0.1108	0.0946	0.0808	0.0376
19	0.1707	0.1635	0.1500	0.1377	0.1264	0.1161	0.0981	0.0829	0.0703	0.0313
20	0.1556	0.1486	0.1358	0.1240	0.1134	0.1037	0.0868	0.0728	0.0611	0.0261
25	0.0977	0.0923	0.0824	0.0736	0.0658	0.0588	0.0471	0.0378	0.0304	0.0105
30	0.0614	0.0573	0.0500	0.0437	0.0382	0.0334	0.0256	0.0196	0.0151	0.0042
35	0.0385	0.0356	0.0304	0.0259	0.0222	0.0189	0.0139	0.0102	0.0075	0.0017
40	0.0242	0.0221	0.0184	0.0154	0.0129	0.0107	0.0075	0.0053	0.0037	0.0007
50	0.0095	0.0085	0.0068	0.0054	0.0043	0.0035	0.0022	0.0014	0.0009	0.0001

TABLE A-6:

Present Value of a Dollar (Monthly Compounding)

$$\frac{1}{\left(1 + \dfrac{i}{12}\right)^{12n}}$$

Year	1.00	2.00	3.00	4.00	5.00	6.00	6.25	6.50	6.75	7.00
1	0.9901	0.9802	0.9705	0.9609	0.9513	0.9419	0.9396	0.9372	0.9349	0.9326
2	0.9802	0.9608	0.9418	0.9232	0.9050	0.8872	0.8828	0.8784	0.8740	0.8697
3	0.9705	0.9418	0.9140	0.8871	0.8610	0.8356	0.8294	0.8233	0.8172	0.8111
4	0.9608	0.9232	0.8871	0.8524	0.8191	0.7871	0.7793	0.7716	0.7640	0.7564
5	0.9512	0.9049	0.8609	0.8190	0.7792	0.7414	0.7322	0.7232	0.7142	0.7054
6	0.9418	0.8870	0.8355	0.7869	0.7413	0.6983	0.6880	0.6778	0.6677	0.6578
7	0.9324	0.8695	0.8108	0.7561	0.7052	0.6577	0.6464	0.6352	0.6243	0.6135
8	0.9231	0.8523	0.7869	0.7265	0.6709	0.6195	0.6073	0.5954	0.5836	0.5721
9	0.9140	0.8354	0.7636	0.6981	0.6382	0.5835	0.5706	0.5580	0.5456	0.5336
10	0.9049	0.8189	0.7411	0.6708	0.6072	0.5496	0.5361	0.5230	0.5101	0.4976
11	0.8959	0.8027	0.7192	0.6445	0.5776	0.5177	0.5037	0.4901	0.4769	0.4641
12	0.8870	0.7868	0.6980	0.6193	0.5495	0.4876	0.4733	0.4594	0.4459	0.4328
13	0.8781	0.7712	0.6774	0.5950	0.5228	0.4593	0.4447	0.4305	0.4168	0.4036
14	0.8694	0.7560	0.6574	0.5717	0.4973	0.4326	0.4178	0.4035	0.3897	0.3764
15	0.8608	0.7410	0.6380	0.5494	0.4731	0.4075	0.3926	0.3782	0.3643	0.3510
16	0.8522	0.7263	0.6192	0.5279	0.4501	0.3838	0.3688	0.3544	0.3406	0.3273
17	0.8437	0.7120	0.6009	0.5072	0.4282	0.3615	0.3465	0.3322	0.3185	0.3053
18	0.8353	0.6979	0.5831	0.4873	0.4073	0.3405	0.3256	0.3113	0.2977	0.2847
19	0.8270	0.6841	0.5659	0.4683	0.3875	0.3207	0.3059	0.2918	0.2783	0.2655
20	0.8188	0.6705	0.5492	0.4499	0.3686	0.3021	0.2874	0.2735	0.2602	0.2476
25	0.7789	0.6068	0.4728	0.3685	0.2873	0.2240	0.2105	0.1978	0.1859	0.1747
30	0.7409	0.5491	0.4070	0.3018	0.2238	0.1660	0.1541	0.1430	0.1327	0.1232
35	0.7048	0.4969	0.3504	0.2472	0.1744	0.1231	0.1128	0.1034	0.0948	0.0869
40	0.6704	0.4496	0.3016	0.2024	0.1359	0.0913	0.0826	0.0748	0.0677	0.0613
50	0.6067	0.3682	0.2235	0.1358	0.0825	0.0502	0.0443	0.0391	0.0345	0.0305

TABLE A-6:

(Continued)

Year	7.25	7.50	7.75	8.00	8.25	8.50	8.75	9.00	9.25	9.50
1	0.9303	0.9280	0.9257	0.9234	0.9211	0.9188	0.9165	0.9142	0.9120	0.9097
2	0.8654	0.8611	0.8568	0.8526	0.8484	0.8442	0.8400	0.8358	0.8317	0.8276
3	0.8051	0.7991	0.7931	0.7873	0.7814	0.7756	0.7699	0.7641	0.7585	0.7529
4	0.7489	0.7415	0.7342	0.7269	0.7197	0.7126	0.7056	0.6986	0.6917	0.6849
5	0.6967	0.6881	0.6796	0.6712	0.6629	0.6548	0.6467	0.6387	0.6308	0.6230
6	0.6481	0.6385	0.6291	0.6198	0.6106	0.6016	0.5927	0.5839	0.5753	0.5668
7	0.6029	0.5925	0.5823	0.5723	0.5624	0.5527	0.5432	0.5338	0.5247	0.5156
8	0.5609	0.5498	0.5390	0.5284	0.5180	0.5078	0.4978	0.4881	0.4785	0.4691
9	0.5218	0.5102	0.4989	0.4879	0.4771	0.4666	0.4563	0.4462	0.4364	0.4267
10	0.4854	0.4735	0.4619	0.4505	0.4395	0.4287	0.4182	0.4079	0.3979	0.3882
11	0.4515	0.4394	0.4275	0.4160	0.4048	0.3939	0.3833	0.3730	0.3629	0.3531
12	0.4200	0.4077	0.3957	0.3841	0.3728	0.3619	0.3513	0.3410	0.3310	0.3213
13	0.3908	0.3783	0.3663	0.3547	0.3434	0.3325	0.3219	0.3117	0.3018	0.2923
14	0.3635	0.3511	0.3391	0.3275	0.3163	0.3055	0.2951	0.2850	0.2753	0.2659
15	0.3382	0.3258	0.3139	0.3024	0.2913	0.2807	0.2704	0.2605	0.2510	0.2419
16	0.3146	0.3023	0.2905	0.2792	0.2683	0.2579	0.2479	0.2382	0.2289	0.2200
17	0.2926	0.2805	0.2689	0.2578	0.2472	0.2370	0.2272	0.2178	0.2088	0.2002
18	0.2722	0.2603	0.2489	0.2381	0.2277	0.2177	0.2082	0.1991	0.1904	0.1821
19	0.2533	0.2416	0.2304	0.2198	0.2097	0.2000	0.1908	0.1820	0.1736	0.1656
20	0.2356	0.2242	0.2133	0.2030	0.1931	0.1838	0.1749	0.1664	0.1584	0.1507
25	0.1641	0.1543	0.1450	0.1362	0.1280	0.1203	0.1131	0.1063	0.0999	0.0939
30	0.1144	0.1061	0.0985	0.0914	0.0849	0.0788	0.0731	0.0679	0.0630	0.0585
35	0.0797	0.0730	0.0670	0.0614	0.0563	0.0516	0.0473	0.0434	0.0398	0.0364
40	0.0555	0.0503	0.0455	0.0412	0.0373	0.0338	0.0306	0.0277	0.0251	0.0227
50	0.0269	0.0238	0.0210	0.0186	0.0164	0.0145	0.0128	0.0113	0.0100	0.0088

TABLE A-6:

(Continued)

Year	9.75	10.00	10.50	11.00	11.50	12.00	13.00	14.00	15.00	20.00
1	0.9075	0.9052	0.9007	0.8963	0.8919	0.8874	0.8787	0.8701	0.8615	0.8201
2	0.8235	0.8194	0.8113	0.8033	0.7954	0.7876	0.7721	0.7570	0.7422	0.6725
3	0.7473	0.7417	0.7308	0.7200	0.7094	0.6989	0.6785	0.6586	0.6394	0.5515
4	0.6781	0.6714	0.6582	0.6453	0.6327	0.6203	0.5962	0.5731	0.5509	0.4523
5	0.6154	0.6078	0.5929	0.5784	0.5642	0.5504	0.5239	0.4986	0.4746	0.3709
6	0.5584	0.5502	0.5341	0.5184	0.5032	0.4885	0.4603	0.4338	0.4088	0.3042
7	0.5067	0.4980	0.4810	0.4646	0.4488	0.4335	0.4045	0.3774	0.3522	0.2495
8	0.4599	0.4508	0.4333	0.4164	0.4003	0.3847	0.3554	0.3284	0.3034	0.2046
9	0.4173	0.4081	0.3903	0.3733	0.3570	0.3414	0.3123	0.2857	0.2614	0.1678
10	0.3787	0.3694	0.3515	0.3345	0.3184	0.3030	0.2744	0.2486	0.2252	0.1376
11	0.3436	0.3344	0.3166	0.2998	0.2839	0.2689	0.2412	0.2163	0.1940	0.1128
12	0.3118	0.3027	0.2852	0.2687	0.2532	0.2386	0.2119	0.1882	0.1672	0.0925
13	0.2830	0.2740	0.2569	0.2409	0.2259	0.2118	0.1862	0.1637	0.1440	0.0759
14	0.2568	0.2480	0.2314	0.2159	0.2014	0.1879	0.1636	0.1425	0.1241	0.0622
15	0.2330	0.2245	0.2084	0.1935	0.1796	0.1668	0.1438	0.1240	0.1069	0.0510
16	0.2115	0.2032	0.1877	0.1734	0.1602	0.1480	0.1263	0.1078	0.0921	0.0419
17	0.1919	0.1840	0.1691	0.1554	0.1429	0.1314	0.1110	0.0938	0.0793	0.0343
18	0.1741	0.1665	0.1523	0.1393	0.1274	0.1166	0.0975	0.0816	0.0683	0.0281
19	0.1580	0.1508	0.1372	0.1249	0.1137	0.1034	0.0857	0.0710	0.0589	0.0231
20	0.1434	0.1365	0.1236	0.1119	0.1014	0.0918	0.0753	0.0618	0.0507	0.0189
25	0.0882	0.0829	0.0733	0.0647	0.0572	0.0505	0.0395	0.0308	0.0241	0.0070
30	0.0543	0.0504	0.0434	0.0374	0.0323	0.0278	0.0207	0.0154	0.0114	0.0026
35	0.0334	0.0306	0.0258	0.0217	0.0182	0.0153	0.0108	0.0077	0.0054	0.0010
40	0.0206	0.0186	0.0153	0.0125	0.0103	0.0084	0.0057	0.0038	0.0026	0.0004
50	0.0078	0.0069	0.0054	0.0042	0.0033	0.0026	0.0016	0.0009	0.0006	0.0000

TABLE A-7:

Present Value of an Annuity of $1 (Annual Payments, Annual Compounding)

$$\frac{1}{(1+i)} + \frac{1}{(1+i)^2} + \frac{1}{(1+i)^3} + \ldots + \frac{1}{(1+i)^n}$$

Year	1.00	2.00	3.00	4.00	5.00	6.00	6.25	6.50	6.75	7.00
1	0.9901	0.9804	0.9709	0.9615	0.9524	0.9434	0.9412	0.9390	0.9368	0.9346
2	1.9704	1.9416	1.9135	1.8861	1.8594	1.8334	1.8270	1.8206	1.8143	1.8080
3	2.9410	2.8839	2.8286	2.7751	2.7232	2.6730	2.6607	2.6485	2.6363	2.6243
4	3.9020	3.8077	3.7171	3.6299	3.5460	3.4651	3.4454	3.4258	3.4064	3.3872
5	4.8534	4.7135	4.5797	4.4518	4.3295	4.2124	4.1839	4.1557	4.1278	4.1002
6	5.7955	5.6014	5.4172	5.2421	5.0757	4.9173	4.8789	4.8410	4.8036	4.7665
7	6.7282	6.4720	6.2303	6.0021	5.7864	5.5824	5.5331	5.4845	5.4366	5.3893
8	7.6517	7.3255	7.0197	6.7327	6.4632	6.2098	6.1488	6.0888	6.0296	5.9713
9	8.5660	8.1622	7.7861	7.4353	7.1078	6.8017	6.7283	6.6561	6.5851	6.5152
10	9.4713	8.9826	8.5302	8.1109	7.7217	7.3601	7.2737	7.1888	7.1055	7.0236
11	10.3676	9.7868	9.2526	8.7605	8.3064	7.8869	7.7870	7.6890	7.5929	7.4987
12	11.2551	10.5753	9.9540	9.3851	8.8633	8.3838	8.2701	8.1587	8.0496	7.9427
13	12.1337	11.3484	10.6350	9.9856	9.3936	8.8527	8.7248	8.5997	8.4774	8.3577
14	13.0037	12.1062	11.2961	10.5631	9.8986	9.2950	9.1528	9.0138	8.8781	8.7455
15	13.8651	12.8493	11.9379	11.1184	10.3797	9.7122	9.5555	9.4027	9.2535	9.1079
16	14.7179	13.5777	12.5611	11.6523	10.8378	10.1059	9.9346	9.7678	9.6051	9.4466
17	15.5623	14.2919	13.1661	12.1657	11.2741	10.4773	10.2914	10.1106	9.9346	9.7632
18	16.3983	14.9920	13.7535	12.6593	11.6896	10.8276	10.6272	10.4325	10.2432	10.0591
19	17.2260	15.6785	14.3238	13.1339	12.0853	11.1581	10.9433	10.7347	10.5322	10.3356
20	18.0456	16.3514	14.8775	13.5903	12.4622	11.4699	11.2407	11.0185	10.8030	10.5940
25	22.0232	19.5235	17.4131	15.6221	14.0939	12.7834	12.4852	12.1979	11.9208	11.6536
30	25.8077	22.3965	19.6004	17.2920	15.3725	13.7648	13.4043	13.0587	12.7272	12.4090
35	29.4086	24.9986	21.4872	18.6646	16.3742	14.4982	14.0831	13.6870	13.3088	12.9477
40	32.8347	27.3555	23.1148	19.7928	17.1591	15.0463	14.5843	14.1455	13.7284	13.3317
50	39.1961	31.4236	25.7298	21.4822	18.2559	15.7619	15.2279	14.7245	14.2495	13.8007

TABLE A-7:
(Continued)

Year	7.25	7.50	7.75	8.00	8.25	8.50	8.75	9.00	9.25	9.50
1	0.9324	0.9302	0.9281	0.9259	0.9238	0.9217	0.9195	0.9174	0.9153	0.9132
2	1.8018	1.7956	1.7894	1.7833	1.7772	1.7711	1.7651	1.7591	1.7532	1.7473
3	2.6124	2.6005	2.5888	2.5771	2.5655	2.5540	2.5426	2.5313	2.5201	2.5089
4	3.3682	3.3493	3.3306	3.3121	3.2938	3.2756	3.2576	3.2397	3.2220	3.2045
5	4.0729	4.0459	4.0192	3.9927	3.9665	3.9406	3.9150	3.8897	3.8646	3.8397
6	4.7300	4.6938	4.6582	4.6229	4.5880	4.5536	4.5196	4.4859	4.4527	4.4198
7	5.3426	5.2966	5.2512	5.2064	5.1622	5.1185	5.0755	5.0330	4.9910	4.9496
8	5.9139	5.8573	5.8016	5.7466	5.6925	5.6392	5.5866	5.5348	5.4838	5.4334
9	6.4465	6.3789	6.3124	6.2469	6.1825	6.1191	6.0567	5.9952	5.9348	5.8753
10	6.9431	6.8641	6.7864	6.7101	6.6351	6.5613	6.4889	6.4177	6.3476	6.2788
11	7.4062	7.3154	7.2264	7.1390	7.0532	6.9690	6.8863	6.8052	6.7255	6.6473
12	7.8379	7.7353	7.6347	7.5361	7.4394	7.3447	7.2518	7.1607	7.0714	6.9838
13	8.2405	8.1258	8.0136	7.9038	7.7962	7.6910	7.5879	7.4869	7.3880	7.2912
14	8.6158	8.4892	8.3653	8.2442	8.1259	8.0101	7.8969	7.7862	7.6778	7.5719
15	8.9658	8.8271	8.6917	8.5595	8.4304	8.3042	8.1810	8.0607	7.9431	7.8282
16	9.2921	9.1415	8.9946	8.8514	8.7116	8.5753	8.4423	8.3126	8.1859	8.0623
17	9.5964	9.4340	9.2757	9.1216	8.9715	8.8252	8.6826	8.5436	8.4081	8.2760
18	9.8801	9.7060	9.5367	9.3719	9.2115	9.0555	8.9035	8.7556	8.6116	8.4713
19	10.1446	9.9591	9.7788	9.6036	9.4333	9.2677	9.1067	8.9501	8.7978	8.6496
20	10.3912	10.1945	10.0035	9.8181	9.6381	9.4633	9.2935	9.1285	8.9682	8.8124
25	11.3958	11.1469	10.9067	10.6748	10.4507	10.2342	10.0249	9.8226	9.6269	9.4376
30	12.1037	11.8104	11.5286	11.2578	10.9974	10.7468	10.5058	10.2737	10.0501	9.8347
35	12.6025	12.2725	11.9568	11.6546	11.3651	11.0878	10.8219	10.5668	10.3220	10.0870
40	12.9541	12.5944	12.2516	11.9246	11.6125	11.3145	11.0297	10.7574	10.4968	10.2472
50	13.3764	12.9748	12.5943	12.2335	11.8910	11.5656	11.2562	10.9617	10.6812	10.4137

TABLE A-7:
(Continued)

Year	9.75	10.00	10.50	11.00	11.50	12.00	13.00	14.00	15.00	20.00
1	0.9112	0.9091	0.9050	0.9009	0.8969	0.8929	0.8850	0.8772	0.8696	0.8333
2	1.7414	1.7355	1.7240	1.7125	1.7012	1.6901	1.6681	1.6467	1.6257	1.5278
3	2.4978	2.4869	2.4651	2.4437	2.4226	2.4018	2.3612	2.3216	2.2832	2.1065
4	3.1871	3.1699	3.1359	3.1024	3.0696	3.0373	2.9745	2.9137	2.8550	2.5887
5	3.8151	3.7908	3.7429	3.6959	3.6499	3.6048	3.5172	3.4331	3.3522	2.9906
6	4.3874	4.3553	4.2922	4.2305	4.1703	4.1114	3.9975	3.8887	3.7845	3.3255
7	4.9088	4.8684	4.7893	4.7122	4.6370	4.5638	4.4226	4.2883	4.1604	3.6046
8	5.3838	5.3349	5.2392	5.1461	5.0556	4.9676	4.7988	4.6389	4.4873	3.8372
9	5.8167	5.7590	5.6463	5.5370	5.4311	5.3282	5.1317	4.9464	4.7716	4.0310
10	6.2111	6.1446	6.0148	5.8892	5.7678	5.6502	5.4262	5.2161	5.0188	4.1925
11	6.5705	6.4951	6.3482	6.2065	6.0697	5.9377	5.6869	5.4527	5.2337	4.3271
12	6.8979	6.8137	6.6500	6.4924	6.3406	6.1944	5.9176	5.6603	5.4206	4.4392
13	7.1963	7.1034	6.9230	6.7499	6.5835	6.4235	6.1218	5.8424	5.5831	4.5327
14	7.4682	7.3667	7.1702	6.9819	6.8013	6.6282	6.3025	6.0021	5.7245	4.6106
15	7.7159	7.6061	7.3938	7.1909	6.9967	6.8109	6.4624	6.1422	5.8474	4.6755
16	7.9416	7.8237	7.5962	7.3792	7.1719	6.9740	6.6039	6.2651	5.9542	4.7296
17	8.1472	8.0216	7.7794	7.5488	7.3291	7.1196	6.7291	6.3729	6.0472	4.7746
18	8.3346	8.2014	7.9451	7.7016	7.4700	7.2497	6.8399	6.4674	6.1280	4.8122
19	8.5053	8.3649	8.0952	7.8393	7.5964	7.3658	6.9380	6.5504	6.1982	4.8435
20	8.6609	8.5136	8.2309	7.9633	7.7098	7.4694	7.0248	6.6231	6.2593	4.8696
25	9.2544	9.0770	8.7390	8.4217	8.1236	7.8431	7.3300	6.8729	6.4641	4.9476
30	9.6271	9.4269	9.0474	8.6938	8.3637	8.0552	7.4957	7.0027	6.5660	4.9789
35	9.8612	9.6442	9.2347	8.8552	8.5030	8.1755	7.5856	7.0700	6.6166	4.9915
40	10.0082	9.7791	9.3483	8.9511	8.5839	8.2438	7.6344	7.1050	6.6418	4.9966
50	10.1585	9.9148	9.4591	9.0417	8.6580	8.3045	7.6752	7.1327	6.6605	4.9995

TABLE A-8:

Present Value of an Annuity of $1 (Monthly Payments, Monthly Compounding)

$$1/\left(1+\frac{i}{12}\right) + 1/\left(1+\frac{i}{12}\right)^2 + 1/\left(1+\frac{i}{12}\right)^3 + \ldots + 1/\left(1+\frac{i}{12}\right)^{12n}$$

Year	1.00	2.00	3.00	4.00	5.00	6.00	6.25	6.50	6.75	7.00
1	11.9353	11.8710	11.8073	11.7440	11.6812	11.6189	11.6034	11.5880	11.5725	11.5571
2	23.7518	23.5071	23.2660	23.0283	22.7939	22.5629	22.5056	22.4486	22.3917	22.3351
3	35.4508	34.9131	34.3865	33.8708	33.3657	32.8710	32.7489	32.6275	32.5067	32.3865
4	47.0335	46.0933	45.1787	44.2888	43.4230	42.5803	42.3732	42.1675	41.9632	41.7602
5	58.5009	57.0524	55.6524	54.2991	52.9907	51.7256	51.4158	51.1087	50.8041	50.5020
6	69.8543	67.7946	65.8169	63.9174	62.0928	60.3395	59.9120	59.4887	59.0695	58.6545
7	81.0948	78.3243	75.6813	73.1593	70.7518	68.4531	67.8947	67.3426	66.7969	66.2573
8	92.2235	88.6456	85.2546	82.0393	78.9895	76.0952	75.3949	74.7036	74.0212	73.3476
9	103.241	98.7628	94.5453	90.5718	86.8261	83.2934	82.4419	81.6026	80.7753	79.9599
10	114.150	108.680	103.562	98.7702	94.2814	90.0735	89.0630	88.0685	87.0897	86.1264
11	124.950	118.401	112.312	106.648	101.374	96.4596	95.2840	94.1286	92.9931	91.8772
12	135.642	127.929	120.804	114.217	108.121	102.475	101.129	99.8083	98.5122	97.2402
13	146.228	137.269	129.045	121.490	114.540	108.140	106.621	105.131	103.672	102.242
14	156.709	146.424	137.044	128.478	120.646	113.477	111.781	110.121	108.496	106.906
15	167.086	155.398	144.806	135.192	126.455	118.504	116.629	114.796	113.006	111.256
16	177.359	164.195	152.338	141.644	131.982	123.238	121.184	119.179	117.222	115.313
17	187.531	172.817	159.649	147.843	137.239	127.698	125.463	123.286	121.164	119.096
18	197.601	181.269	166.744	153.799	142.241	131.898	129.485	127.136	124.850	122.624
19	207.571	189.553	173.629	159.523	146.999	135.854	133.263	130.744	128.295	125.914
20	217.441	197.674	180.311	165.022	151.525	139.581	136.812	134.125	131.516	128.983
25	265.342	235.930	210.877	189.453	171.060	155.207	151.591	148.103	144.736	141.487
30	310.907	270.549	237.189	209.461	186.282	166.792	162.412	158.211	154.179	150.308
35	354.251	301.875	259.841	225.849	198.142	175.380	170.336	165.521	160.923	156.530
40	395.482	330.223	279.342	239.270	207.384	181.748	176.137	170.807	165.740	160.919
50	472.012	379.089	310.581	259.264	220.197	189.968	183.496	177.394	171.637	166.199

TABLE A-8:
(Continued)

Year	7.25	7.50	7.75	8.00	8.25	8.50	8.75	9.00	9.25	9.50
1	11.5417	11.5264	11.5111	11.4958	11.4805	11.4653	11.4501	11.4349	11.4198	11.4047
2	22.2787	22.2224	22.1664	22.1105	22.0549	21.9995	21.9442	21.8891	21.8343	21.7796
3	32.2669	32.1479	32.0296	31.9118	31.7947	31.6781	31.5622	31.4468	31.3320	31.2179
4	41.5586	41.3584	41.1595	40.9619	40.7657	40.5708	40.3771	40.1848	39.9937	39.8039
5	50.2024	49.9053	49.6107	49.3184	49.0286	48.7412	48.4561	48.1734	47.8930	47.6148
6	58.2435	57.8365	57.4336	57.0345	56.6394	56.2481	55.8606	55.4769	55.0968	54.7205
7	65.7238	65.1964	64.6749	64.1593	63.6494	63.1453	62.6469	62.1540	61.6666	61.1846
8	72.6826	72.0260	71.3779	70.7380	70.1062	69.4824	68.8666	68.2585	67.6580	67.0651
9	79.1561	78.3637	77.5826	76.8125	76.0534	75.3049	74.5670	73.8394	73.1220	72.4146
10	85.1781	84.2448	83.3260	82.4215	81.5311	80.6545	79.7915	78.9417	78.1051	77.2812
11	90.7803	89.7022	88.6424	87.6006	86.5765	85.5696	84.5797	83.6065	82.6495	81.7084
12	95.9918	94.7664	93.5636	92.3828	91.2237	90.0856	88.9683	87.8711	86.7938	85.7358
13	100.840	99.4659	98.1189	96.7985	95.5040	94.2348	92.9904	91.7701	90.5734	89.3996
14	105.350	103.827	102.336	100.876	99.4466	98.0471	96.6767	95.3 6	94.0202	92.7327
15	109.546	107.873	106.239	104.641	103.078	101.550	100.055	98.5955	97.1636	95.7648
16	113.449	111.629	109.852	108.117	106.423	104.768	103.152	101.573	100.030	98.5231
17	117.079	115.113	113.196	111.327	109.503	107.725	105.990	104.297	102.645	101.032
18	120.457	118.347	116.292	114.291	112.341	110.441	108.591	106.787	105.029	103.315
19	123.599	121.348	119.158	117.027	114.955	112.938	110.974	109.064	107.203	105.392
20	126.522	124.132	121.810	119.554	117.362	115.231	113.159	111.145	109.186	107.281
25	138.350	135.320	132.393	129.565	126.831	124.189	121.633	119.162	116.770	114.456
30	146.590	143.018	139.585	136.284	133.109	130.054	127.113	124.282	121.555	118.927
35	152.331	148.315	144.472	140.793	137.270	133.894	130.657	127.552	124.573	121.712
40	156.330	151.959	147.794	143.821	140.029	136.408	132.949	129.641	126.477	123.447
50	161.058	156.193	151.585	147.216	143.070	139.132	135.389	131.827	128.435	125.202

TABLE A-8:

(Continued)

Year	9.75	10.00	10.50	11.00	11.50	12.00	13.00	14.00	15.00	20.00
1	11.3896	11.3745	11.3445	11.3146	11.2848	11.2551	11.1960	11.1375	11.0793	10.7951
2	21.7251	21.6709	21.5629	21.4556	21.3491	21.2434	21.0341	20.8277	20.6242	19.6480
3	31.1043	30.9912	30.7669	30.5449	30.3251	30.1075	29.6789	29.2589	28.8473	26.9081
4	39.6154	39.4282	39.0573	38.6914	38.3303	37.9740	37.2752	36.5945	35.9315	32.8619
5	47.3390	47.0654	46.5248	45.9930	45.4698	44.9550	43.9501	42.9770	42.0346	37.7446
6	54.3478	53.9787	53.2510	52.5373	51.8372	51.1504	49.8154	48.5302	47.2925	41.7487
7	60.7080	60.2367	59.3096	58.4029	57.5160	56.6484	54.9693	53.3618	51.8222	45.0325
8	66.4796	65.9015	64.7668	63.6601	62.5807	61.5277	59.4981	57.5655	55.7246	47.7254
9	71.7171	71.0293	69.6822	68.3720	67.0976	65.8578	63.4776	61.2231	59.0865	49.9338
10	76.4700	75.6711	74.1097	72.5953	71.1260	69.7005	66.9744	64.4054	61.9828	51.7449
11	80.7830	79.8730	78.0978	76.3805	74.7188	73.1107	70.0471	67.1742	64.4781	53.2302
12	84.6969	83.6765	81.6899	79.7731	77.9231	76.1371	72.7471	69.5833	66.6277	54.4482
13	88.2486	87.1195	84.9255	82.8138	80.7808	78.8229	75.1196	71.6793	68.4797	55.4471
14	91.4716	90.2362	87.8399	85.5392	83.3295	81.2064	77.2043	73.5029	70.0751	56.2662
15	94.3963	93.0574	90.4650	87.9819	85.6025	83.3216	79.0362	75.0896	71.4496	56.9380
16	97.0504	95.6112	92.8296	90.1713	87.6297	85.1988	80.6459	76.4702	72.6338	57.4889
17	99.4589	97.9230	94.9594	92.1335	89.4377	86.8647	82.0604	77.6713	73.6539	57.9407
18	101.645	100.016	96.8778	93.8923	91.0502	88.3431	83.3033	78.7164	74.5328	58.3112
19	103.628	101.910	98.6058	95.4686	92.4882	89.6551	84.3954	79.6257	75.2900	58.6151
20	105.428	103.625	100.162	96.8815	93.7708	90.8194	85.3551	80.4168	75.9423	58.8642
25	112.216	110.047	105.912	102.029	98.3797	94.9465	88.6654	83.0729	78.0743	59.5787
30	116.393	113.951	109.321	105.006	100.980	97.2183	90.3996	84.3973	79.0861	59.8437
35	118.964	116.323	111.342	106.728	102.448	98.4688	91.3081	85.0576	79.5663	59.9420
40	120.546	117.765	112.540	107.724	103.276	99.1571	91.7840	85.3869	79.7942	59.9785
50	122.118	119.174	113.672	108.634	104.006	99.7446	92.1639	85.6329	79.9536	59.9970

Appendix B

The Standard Normal Distribution

TABLE B-1:

The Standard Normal Distribution

z	.00	.01	.02	.03	.04	.05	.06	.07	.08	.09
0.0	.0000	.0040	.0080	.0120	.0160	.0199	.0239	.0279	.0319	.0359
0.1	.0398	.0438	.0478	.0517	.0557	.0596	.0636	.0675	.0714	.0753
0.2	.0793	.0832	.0871	.0910	.0948	.0987	.1026	.1064	.1103	.1141
0.3	.1179	.1217	.1255	.1293	.1331	.1368	.1406	.1443	.1480	.1517
0.4	.1554	.1591	.1628	.1664	.1700	.1736	.1772	.1808	.1844	.1879
0.5	.1915	.1950	.1985	.2019	.2054	.2088	.2123	.2157	.2190	.2224
0.6	.2257	.2291	.2324	.2357	.2389	.2422	.2454	.2486	.2517	.2549
0.7	.2580	.2611	.2642	.2673	.2704	.2734	.2764	.2794	.2823	.2852
0.8	.2881	.2910	.2939	.2967	.2995	.3023	.3051	.3078	.3106	.3133
0.9	.3159	.3186	.3212	.3238	.3264	.3289	.3315	.3340	.3365	.3389
1.0	.3413	.3438	.3461	.3485	.3508	.3531	.3554	.3577	.3599	.3621
1.1	.3643	.3665	.3686	.3708	.3729	.3749	.3770	.3790	.3810	.3830
1.2	.3849	.3869	.3888	.3907	.3925	.3944	.3962	.3980	.3997	.4015
1.3	.4032	.4049	.4066	.4082	.4099	.4115	.4131	.4147	.4162	.4177
1.4	.4192	.4207	.4222	.4236	.4251	.4265	.4279	.4292	.4306	.4319
1.5	.4332	.4345	.4357	.4370	.4382	.4394	.4406	.4418	.4429	.4441
1.6	.4452	.4463	.4474	.4484	.4495	.4505	.4515	.4525	.4535	.4545
1.7	.4554	.4564	.4573	.4582	.4591	.4599	.4608	.4616	.4625	.4633
1.8	.4641	.4649	.4656	.4664	.4671	.4678	.4686	.4693	.4699	.4706
1.9	.4713	.4719	.4726	.4732	.4738	.4744	.4750	.4756	.4761	.4767
2.0	.4772	.4778	.4783	.4788	.4793	.4798	.4803	.4808	.4812	.4817
2.1	.4821	.4826	.4830	.4834	.4838	.4842	.4846	.4850	.4854	.4857
2.2	.4861	.4864	.4868	.4871	.4875	.4878	.4881	.4884	.4887	.4890
2.3	.4893	.4896	.4898	.4901	.4904	.4906	.4909	.4911	.4913	.4916
2.4	.4918	.4920	.4922	.4925	.4927	.4929	.4931	.4932	.4934	.4936
2.5	.4938	.4940	.4941	.4943	.4945	.4946	.4948	.4949	.4951	.4952
2.6	.4953	.4955	.4956	.4957	.4959	.4960	.4961	.4962	.4963	.4964
2.7	.4965	.4966	.4967	.4968	.4969	.4970	.4971	.4972	.4973	.4974
2.8	.4974	.4975	.4976	.4977	.4977	.4978	.4979	.4979	.4980	.4981
2.9	.4981	.4982	.4982	.4983	.4984	.4984	.4985	.4985	.4986	.4986
3.0	.4987	.4987	.4987	.4988	.4988	.4989	.4989	.4989	.4990	.4990

Appendix C

Answers to Selected End-of-Chapter Problems

Chapter 2

1. a. no; b. 900; c. $9,000;
   d. $880, $7,333

2. a. $0; b. no; c. yes:
   $8.50; d. $56.67

4. a. $10 million; b. $100 million

Chapter 4

1. 10.8%

2. 11.26%

3. 97.97, 8.76%

4. $11,507

5. Return on treasury bills = 14.93%

Chapter 5

1. corporate after tax yield = 8.77%

2. a. 0%; −100%
   b. 20%; −100%
   c. 40%, 90%

Chapter 6

1. $6770.50

2. The former; new C.D. will grow to
   $6,719.50

3. $54,914.40

4. $589,020

5. $6,209

6. $923.40

7. $1,085.31

8. Simple interest, APR = 8%; add-on,
   APR = 13.69%; discount, APR =
   16.69%

9. 6.60%

10. p = 88.35

11. $250.93, $220.13

12. 8.53%

13. $14,564.10

14. 12.75%

Chapter 7

3. 2.86%

4. $50.00, $33.33, $25.00

5. 3.91 years, 5 years, the second is more
   sensitive

Appendix 7-A

1. 1.47

2. 13.8%

Appendix 7-B

1. $6.14

2. V = $8.22; underpriced

Chapter 8

1. 21.30%, 21.11%
2. 11.78%
3. 9.29%
4. 9.50%
5. a. 7.78%;   b. 9.00%
6. a. 10.31%;   b. 11.81%;   c. 5.81%

Chapter 9

1. a. yes; effective rate earned = 12%
2. Return = 11.33%, thus the purchase is attractive

Chapter 10

1. b. $14.214 million
2. 1.28%

Chapter 11

1. a. profit after operating costs = $7.00
   b. loss after operating costs = $15.00
2. a. $273.95;   b. 14.14%; c. 12.64%

Chapter 12

1. 10.75% (approximately)
2. $42,906, $30,211, 30%

Chapter 13

1. a. yes;   b. no
2. a. $396.22;   b. $521.69;
   c. $235.26, $282.46

Index